HANDS
IN
CLAY

POTTER

This flat plate. This ladle and bowl.
clay whirled on a wheel, raised slowly to the table.
Straight and curved, our primal gestures
take and give — speak out about
the way we stand and breathe.
Every leaf is saucer for the bread,
Every falling drop prepares its cup.
Always we are eating and drinking earth's body,
Making her dishes.
    Potters like sun and stars
    perform their art —
    endowed with myth,
    they make the meal holy.

                               — M. C. RICHARDS

Ross Spangler, U.S.A.

HANDS IN CLAY

An Introduction to Ceramics

THIRD EDITION

CHARLOTTE F. SPEIGHT

JOHN TOKI
California College of Arts and Crafts

MAYFIELD PUBLISHING COMPANY

Mountain View, California
London • Toronto

Library of Congress Cataloging-in-Publication Data

Speight, Charlotte F.
    Hands in clay: an introduction to ceramics / Charlotte
F. Speight, John Toki. — 3rd ed.
        p.   cm.
    Includes bibliographical references and index.
    ISBN 1-55934-312-5
    1. Pottery craft. I. Toki, John. II. Title.
TT920.S685   1994
738—dc20   94-7357
                                              CIP

Manufactured in the United States of America
10 9 8 7 6 5 4 3 2

Mayfield Publishing Company
1280 Villa Street
Mountain View, California 94041

Sponsoring editor, Janet M. Beatty; production editor, Lynn Rabin Bauer; manuscript editor, Margaret Moore; text designer, Anna Post George; cover designer and art editor, Susan Breitbard; illustrators, Robin Mouat and Judith Ogus; manufacturing manager, Martha Branch. The text was set in 9.5/12 Melior by Thompson Type and printed on 60# Chromotone Matte by Banta Company.

All photographs not otherwise credited are by Charlotte F. Speight.

Preface

Hands in Clay can be read in a variety of ways: as a story of humanity, as a glimpse into the wellsprings of creativity, and as a challenge to learn the skills that offer a lifetime of joyous experiment and creative expression in clay.

Ceramics was one of the earliest technologies humans developed, and through the millennia humans have used clay to form innovative objects that range from the first container that revolutionized cooking to the heat-resistant tiles on the space shuttles. Not only has clay been shaped by human hands for thousands of years, but the objects created by those hands also have shaped the daily lives of the people who used them. In addition to objects crafted to fulfill everyday functions, artists have formed clay into works that have communicated each era's deepest beliefs, its strongest communal emotions, its aesthetic concerns, and its most pressing spiritual needs. Expressions and symbols of these human needs, fears, joys, and hopes—permanently preserved in fired clay—give us tantalizing glimpses of lost cultures and insights into their makers' and users' lives.

The story we tell in the first part of the book, "Shaping the Past," takes a winding path through time and geography. Along the way, we lay out many of the basic techniques that must be mastered to work comfortably with clay, and as ceramic developments through history unfold around the world in these early chapters, we include most of the ceramic terms that will be encountered in later technical chapters. In presenting this historical background, we have included short discussions of the shape, form, and decoration of ceramic objects from the past, thereby addressing a number of the formal considerations ceramists face as they begin to work in clay.

Chapter 8, "Worldwide Interaction," the final chapter in the historical overview, gives a short survey of the radical changes the field of ceramics has undergone in the recent past. It also discusses the greatly accelerated exchange of ideas globally, as well as the new technologies used in twentieth-century ceramics.

In the second part of the book, "Shaping the Present," Chapter 9, "The Artist's Vision," explores the aesthetic philosophies of a number of contemporary ceramics artists, disclosing how their creativity stems from their personal, geographic, and ethnic roots. This chapter encourages students of ceramics to explore their own creative roots and to draw on them imaginatively for inspiration.

In "Getting Started" (Chapter 10) and "Handbuilding" (Chapter 11), the emphasis shifts to hands-on, as these chapters explore the possibilities inherent in clay. The text walks through the most basic ceramic processes and provides photographs of contemporary ceramists wedging, coiling, pinching, rolling out and building with slabs, sculpting solid, hollowing out, and reassembling a head and bust. Included is a chart showing basic tools and drawings that explain the workings and use of large studio equipment. These chapters offer a progression of techniques and processes as groundwork for the more technically challenging chapters on throwing on the wheel (Chapter 12), slip casting and mold making (Chapter 13), glaze information and testing (Chapter 14), firing (Chapter 15), and large sculpture and installations (Chapter 16).

Chapter 14 examines the qualities of ceramics materials and compounds and how they interact in the kiln. Chapter 15 provides information about the most modern kilns and firing methods appropriate to pottery and sculpture; it also shows how the ancient techniques of wood firing, sodium vapor firing, and raku can be adapted to contemporary usage. The intricacies of building and firing large sculpture are discussed in Chapter 16; in this chapter readers will also find a glimpse into the world of gallery installations and site-specific works, with a special emphasis on mixed media and commissioned work.

Finally, for those who have become deeply involved with the craft and art of ceramics, Chapter 17 provides a primer in setting up a studio. This chapter offers advice that will help ceramists plan a studio set-up, decide what equipment to buy, and create a safe and healthy studio.

The appendixes provide further help for both beginners and more advanced students: specially formulated clay and glaze recipes for testing; recipes from other ceramists; temperature charts; detailed charts to ensure that ceramics materials are used safely and successfully; material and equipment sources; and book, video, and health and safety information resources. An expanded glossary explains the specialized terms that appear in bold type in the text.

NEW TO THIS EDITION

This third edition has grown and changed in much the same way that a clay sculpture grows and changes in its maker's hands. We worked on it as a sculptor does, figuratively stepping back from it to view it critically, looking at it from all sides as if it were revolving on a sculpture stand. In this way we could see that it needed some ad-

ditional material here, some carving away there, some more detail here. As we reworked it, we strove to maintain the freshness and strength of its form.

In response to the many helpful suggestions from teachers, students, reviewers, artists, and our own muses, we've made the following changes and additions:

- We've added a timeline at the beginning of the book, complete with outline drawings of shapes and styles, to show the development of ceramics and how information and aesthetic influences gradually spread between geographic areas. As a visual link to the body of the text, the drawings are keyed with figure numbers that refer to illustrations within chapters.
- New maps in "Shaping the Past" place the areas discussed in geographic context and display drawings that are keyed to photographs in each chapter.
- A new chapter, "Setting Up Your Studio" (Chapter 17), takes the advanced student beyond the classroom. It contains useful information on preplanning, budgeting, and buying new or used studio equipment, and it discusses the necessary wiring and plumbing to create a safe and healthy studio space.
- In Chapter 9, "The Artist's Vision," we give greater emphasis to contemporary mixed media works and to gallery installations in order to widen students' awareness and inspire their creativity.
- A new tool chart in Chapter 10 illustrates all the basic hand tools students will need in the studio. Because we believe that knowing how things work (instead of simply pushing the "start" button) will help students feel more confident, we have added drawings here that show the interior workings of large equipment such as mixers and pug mills.
- Chapter 11, "Handbuilding," now includes new illustrations of building, cutting, hollowing, and reassembling a head before firing. New drawings explain the process of building on an armature and the workings of a slab roller, and illustrate an extruder with examples of extrusions.
- In "Working on the Wheel" (Chapter 12), the photos and text explaining the steps of throwing from coning to centering to opening and shaping are now linked in a more logical rela-

tionship; we've added illustrations of thrown vessels to inspire both the beginner and more advanced student.

- Through additional sculptural examples, "Working with Molds" (Chapter 13) reflects the wider contemporary use of molds and slip casting as it teaches the basic steps of making a simple mold.

- In Chapter 14, "Texture, Color, and Glaze," new photos introduce students to various methods of producing texture in clay, to the use of a slip trailer, and to the decorative effects possible with a variety of brushes; a new drawing explains how a spray booth functions. A convenient chart illustrates basic glaze equipment, and we've added instruction in line blending and fusion testing. The test tiles that display the *Hands in Clay* glazes are now reproduced in color plates so that students may look at the tiles, choose a glaze to test, and then find its recipe in the appendixes.

- Chapter 15 contains a chart that emphasizes the continuity of ceramics by tracing the advances in firing from the open fires to computerized kilns. New photos illustrate raku, wood firing, and vapor firing in greater depth. An even stronger emphasis is placed on safety, health, and environmental concerns (keyed in the margin with this symbol: ▲).

- Chapter 16 and related color plates give greater emphasis to gallery installations, site-specific works, and architectural commissions; working drawings introduce students to the processes involved in building and firing large sculptures.

- Increased cross-references between "Shaping the Past" and "Shaping the Present" emphasize the continuity of ceramics and give students a sense of tradition, inspiring them to turn to their own ethnic roots for inspiration.

- In addition to numerous new black-and-white illustrations of recent works by ceramists from a number of countries, eight additional pages of color offer new images chosen to illustrate the forming methods, color-developing processes, and firing techniques described in the text.

NOTE TO THE READER

 Health and safety in the ceramics studio figure prominently in this book, and this visual sign in the margin alerts readers to the need for precautions. In addition, the materials list in the appendixes rates ceramics materials according to their toxicity. The most up-to-date research in the field of ceramics forms the foundation of this book, and every effort has been made to provide appropriate warning where potentially hazardous substances or procedures are involved. Anyone following these procedures should use his or her best judgment and common sense. The author and publisher shall not be liable in any event for incidental or consequential damages in connection with, or arising out of, the furnishing, performance, or use of the theories, procedures, and techniques herein.

ACKNOWLEDGMENTS

People in the ceramics field are a friendly group, and those who we approached for help graciously took the time and energy to pose for photos, to explain their forming methods, to share glaze and firing information, and to encourage our efforts. We could never have done it without their help. There are a few people we would like to mention whose assistance was especially lengthy and intense. David Vallilee and Melissa McRaney did a noble job of gathering the permissions. David also obtained some hard-to-find illustrations. Our friend in London, Tom Cook, brought a number of ceramists to our attention and obligingly gathered material for us there. Yvette Lardinois at the European Ceramics Work Centre in Holland was also extremely helpful in providing us with information and photos. We are grateful to all of you.

We would also like to thank those reviewers and instructors who made suggestions to make the book more useful for ceramics courses: Linda J. Arbuckle, University of Florida; Carolyn Broadwell, Napa Valley College; Richard Buncamper, Kean College of New Jersey; Aurore Chabot, University of Arizona; Margaret C. Clark, Boston University; Larry Dell'olio, Camden County College; John Ground, Millersville University; Don Herron, University of Texas, Austin; Jeff Johnson, Los Medanos College; Kevin A. Hluch, Montgomery College, Rockport campus; Don D. Jennings, Orange Coast College; David W. Jones, Kean College of New Jersey; Kathryn McCleery, University of North Dakota; Marion Munk, Middlesex County College; Eleanor Rappe, City College of San Francisco; Don Santos, City College of San Francisco; and John Whitney, City College of San Francisco.

When it came to turning the manuscript into a book, many more people became essential to the process, and we were in good hands with Mayfield's editors, designers, and production team. We consider ourselves fortunate to have had the support of two sponsoring editors — first Lansing Hays, then Jan Beatty — who gave us the benefit of their years of insight and experience in book development. Copyeditor Margaret Moore's sharp eyes and discriminating judgment improved the manuscript immeasurably, and designer Anna George created an elegant design that enhanced the appearance and improved the clarity of the book. Susan Breitbard oversaw the production of a number of new lucid drawings and designed the colorful cover. Last, but far from least, production editor Lynn Rabin Bauer magically pulled the mass of detail together. We were linked to her for several months by telecommunication, and even at the most intense times she was always competent, cheerful, and supportive. A sincere thank you to all.

Contents

10,000 B.C.	5000 B.C.	4000 B.C.	3000 B.C.	2000 B.C.	1000 B.C.

The movement of ceramics history reflects continuity and constant interchange between peoples.

WESTERN ASIA

Turntables to wheels

1-27

1-29

1-15

Anatolia

1-9

Sumer
Clay tablets

1-3

1-22

Covered updraft kilns

1-32

Babylon
Glazed tiles

3-33

Painted pottery throughout western Asia

Persia

1-2

EGYPT

Mythical inventor of the wheel

1-28

Figurines

1-1

1-23
Painted pottery

Egyptian paste

Color Plate 51

Egypt develops glaze

MEDITERRANEAN

Cyprus

1-16

GREECE
Crete

Minoan painted ware

2-8

Geometric

2-12

EUROPE

Painted pottery spreads from Asia through the Balkans

Incised ware

6-2

ICE AGE EUROPE

Fired figurines c. 37,000–12,000 years ago

JAPAN

Handbuilding

3-21
Incipient Jōmon

Cord pattern

3-22

Mid-to-Late Jōmon

Figurines

3-23

Handbuilding until wheel brought from China

CHINA

Hillside kilns

3-4

Incised ware

3-3

Painted ware

3-2

Pit kilns

3-5

AMERICAS

c. 12,000 to 14,000 years ago

Hunters cross from Asia to North America to Mesoamerica and South America

MESOAMERICA

Tlatilco

5-3

Olmec

5-2

500 B.C.	100 A.D.	1000 A.D.	1100 A.D.	1200 A.D.	1300 A.D.

ISLAM

Glazed bricks in architecture

Luster decoration on tiles

Luster and underglaze on pottery

Glazed tiles in architecture

3-37

Color Plate 6

Tin glaze and luster spread through North Africa to Spain

AFRICA

Nok

Life-sized figures

4-2

Islamic influences in North Africa

Handbuilding and open firing of domestic ware

4-10

Greek potters work throughout Mediterranean

Athens

Black and red figure vases

2-17

Tanagra figurines

2-22

Byzantium
Lead glazes

EUROPE

Wheel and kiln technology return to northern Europe

Lead glaze

6-14

Spain

Hispano-Moresque tiles influenced by Islamic art

6-4

ETRUSCAN

2-25   2-24a

ROME

Ceramic factories: Terra sigillata kilns

2-27

Roman Empire falls, ceramics technology lost in northern Europe

KOREA

Old Silla pottery

Figure vessels

Chambered kilns

JAPAN

Wheel comes to **Japan** from **China** through **Korea**

Chinese-style kilns
High-firing ash glaze

3-29

3-28

3-27

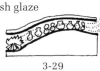

3-26

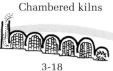

3-24

3-18

CHINA

Bronze shapes

3-6

Life-sized figures

3-7

High-firing kilns

3-9

Ash glaze on stoneware

3-10

Tang figurines

3-14

Lead glazes

3-13

Porcelain

3-15

Celadon glaze

Color Plate 1

Chūn glaze

Color Plate 2

Imperial kilns at Cheng-te-chen

Export ware

Tea ceramics

MESOAMERICA

Maya painted vases

Color Plate 5

Maya figurines

5-4

SOUTH AMERICA

Early pottery in Ecuador

5-10

Moche

5-11

Western Mexico

Figurines

5-7

NORTH AMERICA

Mimbres

5-13

1400	1500	1600	1700	1800	1900

AFRICA

Ife sculpture

Handbuilt, open-fired ceramics for ritual use and domestic ware

Ashanti funerary sculpture

Ghana

Sudan

4-9
pipe bowls

Ethiopia

Clay sculpture in Benin for bronze casting

4-3

4-4

4-5

4-7
figurines

EUROPE

Wheel and kiln technology return

Italy

Tin glazes from Spain via Majorca

6-6

"Maiolica" tin glazes spread throughout Europe

Color Plate 4

Austria
Stoves

6-12

Holland

Blue and white tin-glazed "Delftware"

6-18

Great Britain

Pew groups

Staffordshire potteries
6-19

Wedgwood factory

6-20

Arts and crafts movement: tiles

6-25

France

Studio pottery

6-22

Chinese glazes popular
Color Plates 2, 3

Wheels and kilns improved

Clay sculpture

6-9

6-7

6-8

Germany

Salt-fired stoneware

6-15

England

Slip-decorated ware

6-16

Germany

Secret of porcelain discovered, kaolin found in Europe

Factories established

Scandinavia

Factories established

Art pottery

6-24

JAPAN

Bizen ware

3-31

Tea ceramics

Raku tea bowls

3-30

Art pottery: Kenzan

3-32

Japanese factories fill European demand for decorative wares

CHINA

White porcelain, blue underglaze

3-19

Imperial kilns at Cheng-te-chen produce court porcelain

Chinese porcelain reaches Europe

Chinese glazes influence West
Color Plate 3

UNITED STATES

Techniques and styles from Europe

Slip-decorated ware

7-2

Sgraffito

7-3

Lead glazes

7-6

Stoneware

7-5

Architectural ceramic decoration

7-9
Louis Sullivan

African-American potters make face pots

7-4

AMERICAS

Mound builders
5-21

Mississippi and eastern peoples

Northern indigenous cultures

Mississippi Valley

5-20

5-22

Handbuilding, pitfiring, burnished blackware

Painted ware

5-14

1910	1920	1930	1940	1950	1960	1970	1980	1990

AFRICA

Traditional forming
and firing techniques

Naa Jato

4-8

Ladi Kwali

4-13

Ethnic traditions inspire
contemporary artists

Oyekan
11-12

MacDonald
11-61

EUROPE

Gas-fired kilns, electric kilns,
and wheels aid potters

15-5

8-2

Bernard Leach
goes to Japan;
works with
Shōji Hamada

8-1

Traditional methods
adapted by potters
everywhere

Traditional forms

Casson
12-58

12-55

Mansfield
12-10

Figurative sculpture worldwide

Viková
Color Plate 16

Frey
Color Plate 49

De Staebler
9-2

Duckers
11-1

The vessel as art

Notkin
9-8

Bayle
12-1

15-16; *Color Plates
8, 10, 13, 15, 20*

European artists
emigrate to U.S.A.

Grotell
7-13

Natzlers
7-14

Coper
8-7

Sculptors and painters
work with potters

Fontana
8-8

Matisse
8-6

JAPAN

Rosanjin
8-3

Japanese tea ceramics
and rural pottery
influence west

Slip-cast
sculpture

Shaw
8-14

U.S. West Coast

New approach
to clay

Pots to sculpture
Zauli
8-10

Voulkos
8-9

Mason
8-11

De Staebler
8-30

Color comes
to sculpture:
low-fire glazes,
china paint,
luster, decals,
postfiring paint

Price
8-12

Nagle
*Color Plate
23*

Gilhooley
8-16

Funk and Nut art

Bailey
8-15

Arneson
8-24

New uses for clay

Mixed media
11-60
11-64
11-66

Installations
9-1, 9-6, 9-16
Color Plate 43

Site-specific works
16-1, 16-12, 16-14

Traditional firing techniques
adapted for contemporary use

Salt firing: Law *Color Plate 36*

Wood firing: Japanese kilns

Chaleff
8-32

Callas
15-17

Soldner
popularizes
raku and
post-firing
smoking
15-34

Raku firing

15-29
15-30

U.S.A.

Art pottery

George Ohr:
humor and
experiment

7-8

Robineau
7-7

Art deco designs
in architecture

7-11

U.S. artists
developing
American style

Poor
7-12

WORLDWIDE INTERACTIONS

U.S. Southwest

Painted ware

Handbuilding, pitfiring,
burnished blackware

5-16

Historic meeting
between Martinez,
Leach, and Hamada

Ethnic traditions
inspire contemporary
artists

Kent 15-30
Suarez 16-18

Pit firing

15-35

SHAPING
THE
PAST

Overleaf:
A Hopi woman in Arizona at the turn of the century, seated outside her home, worked with local materials and simple tools. A lump of clay to form the pot, a basket for support, a container of water, and a half circle of dried gourd for smoothing the clay were all she needed to create beauty from the earth. Arizona, c. 1900. *Courtesy Field Museum of Natural History (Neg. #A133).*

1

An Introduction to Clay

Clay feels soft and pliable in your hands. Pick up a lump of it, let your fingers respond to its **plasticity,** and as you pinch and poke, the **clay** seems to have a life of its own, to which your fingers respond. Perhaps you will find yourself forming a human figure, an animal, or a small pot.

By responding to the clay's plastic quality with these pinching gestures, you are repeating the actions of untold numbers of humans who have worked with clay even as far back in time as the Ice Age, thirty-seven thousand to twelve thousand years ago. The earliest known examples of clay objects formed by human hands are unfired representations of animals modeled on a clay bank in a cave in France and some fired clay animal and female human figures found at an Ice Age site in eastern Europe.

This very early use of fire to harden clay, though it predated the oldest **pottery** yet found, was apparently localized. Some pottery, like the proto-Jōmon (3-21) in Japan, has been dated as early as 11,000 to 10,000 B.C., but not until around 6000–4000 B.C. did the knowledge of how to fire clay become widespread and the craft of **ceramics** develop in a number of areas. Among the simple pots found in excavations of early sites around the world, archaeologists have frequently dug up small fired clay figures of women. While their exact purpose is unknown, the clay figures

Figure 1-2
Female figure from excavations at Tureng Tepe, Persia, shows the scratched and applied details that so often decorated these figures wherever they are found (5-3). *Courtesy the University Museum, University of Pennsylvania (Neg. #21863).*

Figure 1-1
Female figures made of clay have been found in quantity in many areas of the world. This one, formed from the mud of the Nile River about six thousand years ago in Egypt, is believed to be a bird deity. Fired at a very low temperature, these early Egyptian figures are usually grey in color. Ht. 11½ in. (29.3 cm). *Courtesy the Brooklyn Museum, Museum Collection Fund, Fund Acc. #07.447.505.*

are believed to have had a magical or religious purpose that was probably linked to fertility worship (1-1, 1-2).

The new craft of ceramics depended on the exploitation of several intrinsic qualities of clay—its plasticity, its ability to hold the shape into which it is formed as it dries, and the fact that heating it to **maturity** transforms it into a new, permanently hard substance. Learning to control fire and using it to create this new material was one of humanity's first great technical achievements. In many cultures, ceramics developed along with the craft of metallurgy, with the discoveries in each technology aiding the other.

The knowledge and technique necessary to transform damp clay into a ceramic material developed at various times in different cultures, but no matter where the craft evolved, it influenced the development of that culture. For example, the knowledge of ceramics allowed villagers to make vermin-proof storage jars, which meant they could store grain against future crop failures and accumulate surpluses with which to trade with neighboring communities.

A RECORD OF HUMANITY IN CLAY

The close relationship between human hands and clay, along with the fact that a ceramic object is indestructible unless it has been crushed into such minute fragments that it cannot be repaired, has made it easier for archaeologists and historians to reconstruct how people lived in cultures that have long since disappeared (1-3). Even if a clay pot or sculpture has been broken, its **shards** can often be put together again; or, if the fragments are too scattered, the archaeologist can still study the type of clay in the remaining shards, the nature of the decoration on the fragments, or the original shape of a pot or sculpture as suggested by the preserved sections. From these ceramic remains, it is possible to learn a considerable amount about a society — its degree of technical development, the extent of its trade, and its exposure to migrations of other peoples that may have introduced new ceramic techniques. For example, pottery from six thousand years ago found in Sian, China, reveals techniques and painted designs similar to those on older pottery found in Russian Turkistan in western Asia, showing that interchanges occurred among the potters of these areas.

Ceramics aids archaeology in another important way. Since most archaeological sites are rich in pot shards, through modern dating methods the excavator can often establish a pottery sequence that allows the dating of other materials found in the same stratum. But an archaeologist may spend years establishing such a sequence and rarely have the luck to stumble on a dramatic discovery.

Figure 1-3
The Sumerians used slabs of damp clay as writing surfaces, and the impression of the marking tool that a clerk pressed into a tablet around 2100 B.C. is still legible. This tablet records the prescription of a local doctor: "Pulverize the seed of the 'carpenter plant,' the gum resin of the markasi-plant, and thyme; dissolve it in beer; let the man drink." *Courtesy the University Museum, University of Pennsylvania (Neg. #55887).*

Masada: An Early Drama Revealed

In the 1960s, however, Dr. Yigael Yadin, then professor of archaeology at Hebrew University in Jerusalem, Israel, unearthed a clay artifact that evoked a moment of great human drama. Dr. Yadin was directing the excavation of a large fortress and palace built by Herod the Great on top of the Rock of Masada, a massive outcrop that towers 1,300 feet above the Dead Sea plain. In A.D. 73, this rock had been the site of an heroic last-ditch stand made by a thousand Jewish rebels against their Roman rulers. These Zealots of Masada, as they are called, withstood three years of siege, but finally realizing that a Roman breakthrough was imminent, they decided to die by their own hands rather than surrender. Each man first killed his wife and children; the survivors chose ten men by lot to be their executioners. According to the historian Josephus, the men "offered their necks to the stroke of those who by lot executed that melancholy office." The last ten then drew lots among themselves to decide who would kill the other nine, and this last man finally killed himself.

Almost two thousand years later, members of the Masada expedition found eleven pottery *ostraca,* or lots, lettered with the names of men

Figure 1-4
Found by the Masada Expedition in Israel, this *ostraca,* or lot, may be one of those used to determine the order of death of the Zealots of Masada, patriots who chose to die by their own hands rather than surrender to the Romans. Their bravery inspired the modern Israeli cry, "Masada shall not fall again." Masada, A.D. 73. *Courtesy Israel Exploration Society. Photo: Y. Yadin.*

(1-4). One of them bore the name of the Zealots' leader, Eleazar ben Ya'hir'. Were these pieces of clay the tragic lots described by Josephus?

Clay Artifacts in Burials

Since ceramic containers do not disintegrate as do those made of wood, it is not surprising that ancient peoples frequently buried their dead in fired clay vessels. They also buried with them small ceramic containers of oils and perfumes and clay reproductions of servants and objects they believed the deceased might need in the afterlife. Through study of these burial finds, archaeologists are able to theorize about a culture's religious beliefs and attempt to reconstruct its daily life. Looking at these records of life preserved in clay, we can identify with the human feelings, needs, and beliefs of people who lived in widely separated places and in times far removed from our own. Anthropologists can even learn much about the physical makeup of a people from fingerprints preserved in clay (1-5, 1-6).

For example, the artifacts discovered in digs can help us visualize the Sumerian doctor dictating his pleasant-sounding remedy to a scribe

Figure 1-5
A potter who lived on Crete about fourteen hundred years ago left the enduring mark of his thumb in the damp clay of a large *pithos,* or storage jar. Mallia, Crete. *Photo: James McGann.*

Figure 1-6
With the same gesture, a Cretan village potter today pressed his thumb in the damp clay to attach the handle to a smaller version of the ancient jar. These two prints, spanning thousands of years, symbolize the long-continuing tradition of human hands working in clay.

Figure 1-7
Grinding corn on a metate, unaware of her child trying to steal a tortilla from her lap, this figure shows us an aspect of family life in the Colima area of Mexico around A.D. 300–900. To an expert, a realistic clay figure like this also tells much about the culture's agriculture, cooking and eating habits, clothing and jewelry, as well as its custom of binding the heads of babies in order to achieve an elongated skull. *Courtesy Museo National de Antropologiá, Mexico.*

(1-3), or feel the joyous excitement of two children swinging in ancient Veracruz (5-5). Talented early sculptors captured in clay the gestures of women performing household chores (1-7), the trappings of a war horse (3-24), and the exploits of heroes (2-20).

THE ORIGINS OF CLAY

Just what *is* this substance called clay, which tells us so much about the past? What is there in the makeup of this material that is responsible for its unique qualities? And where does clay come from?

The fertile areas of the earth are covered with a layer of topsoil that is rich in rotted organic matter. Under this soil, or sometimes under a layer of rock, lie deposits of various types of clay. You can see these clay beds in highway cuts or at construction sites where they have been exposed by earth-moving machines, and as rivers erode and cut into their banks, they also reveal beds of clay.

The earth's surface was formed from melted rock that cooled and solidified. Over millions of years, the weathering action of alternating freezing and thawing, along with the grinding of glaciers, the pounding of rain, the flow of rushing streams, and the probing of tree roots, slowly breaks down the earth's crust into boulders, then into stones, then pebbles, and finally into the small particles that make up different types of clay (1-8). At the same time, chemical changes take place as oxygen combines with minerals to form **oxides.**

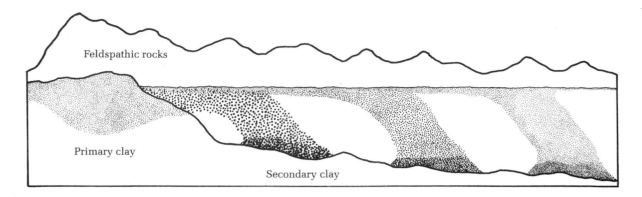

Figure 1-8
Rain, snow, wind, and water wear down the earth's feldspathic rock, causing it to decompose in place to become **primary clay.** Particles are also moved by the action of water to be deposited elsewhere, forming beds of **secondary clay.** Different types of clay such as **stoneware, earthenware,** or **ball clay** are dug from these deposits to be transformed by human hands into vessels or sculptures. *Drawing by John M. Casey.*

Feldspar, the most abundant mineral on the earth's surface, is an essential component of granite rocks and is the basis of clay. Made up for the most part of the oxides **silica** and **alumina** combined with such **alkalies** as **potassium** and some so-called impurities such as **iron,** it is this feldspathic origin of clay that makes it possible to fire it to a dense and permanent hardness. Just as the intense heat of a volcano can fuse the elements in certain rocks into the glassy substance obsidian, so can the heat of the fire fuse and transform the mineral components of clay into ceramic. To be capable of producing ceramic, a clay must contain, along with other components, a **flux** and a heat-resistant material, or **refractory.** The amount of flux a clay contains in relation to the refractory material is one factor that controls the point at which a clay reaches its optimum density, or maturity.

TYPES OF CLAY

Potters refer to the particular types of clay they use as **clay bodies.** The clay a potter uses may consist of clay as it was found in its natural state, but the term *clay body* usually refers to a combination of materials that the potter, sculptor, or supplier has formulated for a specific purpose. To fuse and mature, each type of clay requires a different heat level and duration in the fire. Some,

like low-fired **earthenware** clay, never do become as dense and **vitreous** (glassy) as high-fired clays like **stoneware** and **porcelain.** The variations in size of the clay particles and the varying temperatures at which clays reach maturity account for the differences in texture and appearance between, say, a white porcelain vase and a reddish flowerpot. Color variations are produced by the presence or lack of coloring oxides such as iron or manganese.

Later chapters contain more detailed information about the composition of clays and the appropriateness of each type to a particular type of work, but in the first part of this book we are primarily concerned with understanding how the characteristics of the material affected ceramic technology as it developed in various areas of the world.

The Plasticity of Clay

If you stop to think about the difference between fired and unfired clay, you will realize what an amazing material it is. Dampened with water, it is easy to form, holding together as you shape it. Air-dried, it is fragile, crumbling easily. But when fired to its correct maturing temperature in a fire or a **kiln,** it becomes hard and permanent, capable of keeping its form for thousands of years.

Clay's plasticity when damp is mainly due to the fineness of its particles (or **platelets**), to their flat shape, and to the action of the water between them. In addition, the organic materials that have become mixed with the clay in its journey from rock to riverbed play their part in making it malleable.

When water is absorbed by dry clay, the film it forms between the platelets lubricates them so that they slip against each other, but also makes them cling together, just as smooth pieces of glass both cling to and slide against each other when they are wet.

Clays differ greatly in their degree of plasticity. Some are so sticky they are almost impossible to shape; other clays, which might work well when used in a semiliquid **slip** state for **casting,** would never hold together if used damp for **throwing** on a potter's wheel. And a clay that is a joy to shape on the wheel may not be successfully modeled into a large sculpture. Thus, the clay worker must take into account the properties of each clay in relation to the desired results. These variations in clay as well as the local availability of specific clays had an important effect on how the craft of ceramics developed in different areas of the world.

EARLY USES OF CLAY

When people found that they could domesticate animals and store wild seeds for food, they began to exchange their nomadic lives for life in more permanent communities; the campfire now became a homefire. Traces of the changes that took place during such transitional periods have been found recorded in clay.

There is always the possibility that archaeologists will discover other sites that will fill in some of the gaps in our knowledge of the history of ceramics, but we will probably never be able to set an exact date for when a human first discovered that clay would become hard when exposed to fire and that this newly found material could be used to make receptacles for holding water and cooking or storing food. Perhaps pottery making was discovered when a hut burned down and the clay floor was accidentally fired. Or perhaps someone built a fire in a clay-lined pit, thus unintentionally firing it. In Jarmo, in northern Mesopotamia, excavators discovered that by the seventh millennium B.C., clay-lined pits in the floors were used as hearths. Some of these excavated pits contained stones, suggesting that hot stones may have been placed in them for cooking. One theory that has been widely accepted but is now questioned by some experts is that a woman in a prehistoric community lined a basket with clay to keep out mice, set it too near

a fire, and found that the clay had hardened when the basket burned. For example, around 9000 B.C. in a village that was located at a spring near what would later become Jericho, the simple houses contained clay-lined pits in which wild grains were stored, a fact that indicates that the people who lived there were developing an agricultural society. The presence of unbaked clay figures in Jericho indicates that the deliberate firing of clay to harden images or pots was as yet unknown in this area. On the other side of the world, however, deliberately fired pottery, examples of which have been found at sites in Japan, Taiwan, and China, is believed to have appeared between 11,000 and 10,000 B.C.

In whatever manner the discovery was made that fire changed clay into a solid substance, and whether it was made in one place then spread or, as is more likely, in several different areas independently, the finding initiated the long exploration of ceramics technology — an exploration that still continues in both the potter's workshop and the scientific laboratory.

The development of ceramics changed the domestic lives of women wherever it occurred, and it eventually led to changes in the fabric of society as a whole. For example, after they learned to fire clay to hardness, women could make pots to contain liquids or to protect grain from rodents, and now, instead of having to heat the water in a basket by dropping hot stones into it, they made pots that allowed them to cook grains, roots, and meats in liquid directly over a fire (1-9). Devel-

Figure 1-9
When people learned to make pottery, this technological advance changed cooking methods. Foods no longer had to be roasted over an open fire; they could be boiled in liquids directly over the fire (2-18). Various ceramic vessels and stands made this possible: **(a)** In ancient China, a pot on three legs held liquids; in prehistoric Anatolia **(b)** the cooks placed casseroles on another form of three-legged stand; while in ancient Greece **(c)**, a stand with a built-in shield protected the fire from breezes and the cook from smoke.

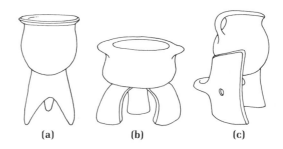

(a)   (b)   (c)

Figure 1-10

The photo shows Julian Martinez digging clay from an exposed bed on a mesa in New Mexico in the 1940s. Maria Martinez recalled that in her grandmother's day the digger always scattered corn as an offering before removing the clay — a custom that many potters still practice in the Southwest. New Mexico, c. 1940. *Wyatt Davis, Courtesy Museum of New Mexico, neg. no. 723. Detail.*

opments like these encouraged people to settle into more permanent living situations and to cultivate foodstuffs instead of depending on gathering.

As time went on, permanent settlements in various parts of the world grew larger and life became more complex. Simultaneously, surpluses of food and other necessities accumulated. As a result, trade based on these surplus commodities developed, leading to the exchange of ideas and technologies. Scholars suggest that it was at this point in the development of a society that the craft of pottery became specialized and that the men rather than the women became the potters, producing wares for trade as well as for local use. Even today in some traditional cultures, however, the potters are women and the men are forbidden to make pottery.

In most early cultures, clay was so much a part of everyday life that we might say these early communities existed in a Clay Age, just as later eras have been classified as Iron and Bronze Ages because of their wide use of those metals. At any rate, these historical periods did not follow each other in a direct line. Rather, overlapping technologies and time lags in the technological developments meant that ceramics appeared at different times in different areas of the world.

EARLY CERAMIC TECHNOLOGY

Any reconstruction of history involves educated guesses, so we cannot say for certain how the earliest potters actually made their pots. However, experts can learn a good deal about their methods through the microscopic examination of the ceramics found in excavations and the study of methods of potters whose techniques are believed to be similar to those of the earliest cultures. By watching a village potter in Africa or the American Southwest, we can hope to learn something of the problems encountered and the processes worked out by our earliest potting ancestors. For this reason, ceramic historians and archaeologists are making every effort to record these methods before metal and plastic utensils become universal and pottery for regular domestic use is no longer made by hand.

Gathering the Clay

For the early potter, the first step in making a pot would naturally have been the gathering of the necessary material (1-10). A village potter who had no cart or pack animal would have tried to find a clay source near enough to the village so that she could carry the clay back in baskets or leather bags. Sometimes a particular clay would have to be brought from quite a distance, but pottery was apparently important enough to the village to make even a difficult trip worthwhile. For

Figure 1-11
After digging and transporting the clay to the village, the early potter sometimes used it as it came from the earth, but this often required cleaning or aging. Chunks of clay, stored outside a workshop in Greece, are drying before being broken up and soaked in water. Once thoroughly wet again, they will be spread in the sun and wedged until the clay reaches throwing consistency.

example, in the Hebrides Islands, off the Scottish coast, in the second millennium B.C., clay and the wood for firing it were scarce, and both had to be fetched from across the open water by dugout canoe.

Early potters, like all agricultural peoples, felt their dependence on the earth. To them the earth was a sacred mother on whom they depended for life and health, and in many cultures the potters would not dig the clay without proper religious observances. In the American Southwest, for example, potters asked the earth's permission to remove the clay before digging it out with a stick. Mothers taught their daughters the required rituals, calling the earth Mother Clay, and to this day, many potters in New Mexico scatter corn on the ground as an offering before digging their clay.

Adding Temper to Clay

When people first started making pottery, they probably used the clay just as it came from the riverbank or hillside (1-11), merely picking out the larger impurities. At some point, they must have discovered that a pot made of coarse-textured clay was less likely to burst or crack in firing than one made of fine-grained clay. This is because the vapors could escape more readily through the pores. Sand, pounded rock, mica, ground-up seashells, volcanic ash, and similar materials open the pores of clay. Of course, some clays already contain a natural **temper,** so no other addition is

needed, but as potters observed what happened in the firing, they learned to add these and similar materials to the clay if it lacked enough tempering material.

If one potter changed and altered a local clay by adding a particular temper and her pottery became the best in the village, her knowledge about where to go for clay and what materials to add might be copied by others, and from then on the other potters in the village would use the same mixture. This fact has helped archaeologists, who can often tell the origin of a piece of pottery by noting what tempering material was used. For example, around 6000 B.C. in some areas of the Middle East, potters mixed straw in their clay to open the pores, while in certain parts of the American Southwest traditional potters still use volcanic rock or sand as temper.

Early Forming Methods

After carrying the clay home, mixing it with temper, and working it to the right consistency, the potter was ready to shape a pot. Local clays, local tempering materials, local firing methods, and even local climate would all have their effect on how a potter worked.

Nowadays we can control humidity and drying by artificial means, but the early potter was at the mercy of the climate. In hot, dry Mesopotamia, for example, the work of building up a pot would have had to be done quickly, before the evaporation of moisture made the clay unmanageable, but that difficulty would not have existed for the Bronze Age potter in misty Scotland (6-2). There, getting the pots dry enough to fire safely would have been the problem, and the potter probably would have had to dry them beside a fire for a long time before the moisture in their walls was completely driven out.

PINCHING   If you pick up a lump of clay, let your thumb sink into it, turning it while pinching and pulling up the sides, squeezing and compressing the walls as they grow between your fingers and thumb, you will find it easy to shape the clay into a rough, thick-walled but serviceable pot. The earliest containers probably were made this way by women pinching the clay into shape. However, it takes considerably more skill to shape a thin-walled, aesthetically pleasing pot using the pinching method. If the clay is stretched too much during this process, it tends to crack, or the walls may collapse. It is also difficult when pinching to control the shape of the pot—for example, narrowing in a neck from a swelling body or opening it out into a flaring bowl. For this rea-

Figure 1-13
Resting their pots on bases of grasses and leaves, potters in the Fiji Islands form them with flat slabs of clay, which they will later shape through paddling. The paddling will also help to meld the slabs together. *Courtesy Fiji Museum, Suva, Fiji.*

Figure 1-12
As we look at this woman in New Guinea building a pot on her lap using thick, damp coils, it is easy to imagine how the world's earliest potters pressed chunks and coils of clay together to make roughly constructed pots. Lokanu, New Guinea. *Courtesy Field Museum of Natural History, Chicago (Neg. #32000).*

son, some potters found it easier to build up the walls of a pot using rolls of clay that they spiraled up in a method called **coiling** (1-12).

COILING   In the coiling method, the coils had to be attached to some type of a clay base to form the bottom of the pot before the walls could be built. It is possible to make a flat-bottomed pot by coiling clay into a spiral, but to form a pot with a rounded bottom, the potter would have been more likely to pat some clay out over a smooth rock or press it into half a dried gourd, a basket, a broken pot, or even a hollow tree stump. In order to keep the damp clay from sticking to this simple **press mold,** the potter might have placed leaves or ashes under the clay (1-13). Special baked clay molds were also sometimes used in which to form the base. In the Tewa culture of the American Southwest, these molds were called *puki,* a word that has been adopted into our ceramics vocabulary.

Once a base was formed, the potter rolled out coils between her hands or on a flat surface and then attached them to the base to build up the walls. This is the most common pottery-building method still used in traditional cultures, and it was widely used by the earliest potters. We can imagine a woman sitting on the ground in some early settlement as she formed a pot for cooking. Turning the pot constantly as the coils were added, she would push the coils together to make them stick to each other, smoothing them on the inside and outside as she went along. By doing this, the potter not only could shape the pot, but also could make the walls thinner and stronger by forcing the clay particles together. Whether the pot was built up of coils or slabs, paddling was sometimes used to force the clay particles together (1-14). Methods of coiling undoubtedly varied in different areas of the world just as they do today. In parts of Southeast Asia, for instance, instead of turning the pot itself, several people in

a line hold a long coil of clay and walk around a pot placed on a stand, building the coil up into a spiral that is then pounded into shape. Alternatively, in one area of Africa, a potter starts the pot in a hollow tree stump and then walks around it backwards adding the coils.

Sometimes, in the process of making a large pot through coiling, a potter might find that so much clay has been built up on the base that the walls have collapsed under its weight. As a solution, she might build up her next pot only part way and set it aside to harden somewhat before adding more damp clay. Whatever the method of applying the coils, the process of coiling has played an important role in the history of ceramics and is still used by potters everywhere (11-12).

Figure 1-14
The potter pounds the pot into shape with a wooden paddle while holding a round stone against the inside. Sometimes the paddles are carved or wrapped with matting to produce a textured surface on the damp clay. *Courtesy Fiji Museum, Suva, Fiji.*

SHAPE

Once potters had learned to make basic vessels, they let their imaginations range, drawing ideas from the world around them to create an infinite variety of shapes. The early potters who lived close to the earth, planting, reaping, sorting, and grinding their food, had responsive fingers, and their pottery reflected this sensitivity. Living in a world where nature was part of everyday life, they were also alert to the stances and movements of the animals that shared their lives, so they sometimes shaped their pots into simplified, exaggerated, or distorted images of those furred and feathered creatures (1-17, 1-18, 1-19). Some of the forms they developed were based on containers made from other materials (1-15), while others were humorous adaptations to specific functions (1-16). Still others resulted from the potter's sensitive attention to the relationship between the rim and base of a pot and the manner in which

they both were related to the body of the pot. Animal vessels like these were often buried with the dead or used to hold liquid offerings at a grave. Even if the early potter was making a vessel to hold a ritual libation, his work could still be lively and inventive within the limits set by tradition, showing keen observation and even humor.

1-18
Bird-shaped pottery vessel from Africa. The neck of the lifelike bird forms the spout, and its head becomes the vessel's stopper. Ht. 10 in. (25.4 cm). Suto, Lesotho. *Copyright British Museum.*

1-16
The shape of this earthenware feeding vessel is emphasized by the painted face with its pointed nose. Cyprus, tenth or eleventh century B.C. *By courtesy of the Board of Trustees of the Victoria & Albert Museum.*

1-15
A Bronze Age jar from Yortan, Anatolia, is shaped for safe carrying and the easy pouring of liquids. Ht. 9¾ in. (24.8 cm). Third millennium B.C. *Copyright British Museum.*

1-19
Potters of the Old Silla dynasty in Korea frequently modeled vessels in the shape of animals or people. Fifth or sixth century A.D. *Courtesy National Museum of Korea, Seoul.*

1-17
The Amlash potter's depiction of a domesticated animal on this bull-shaped vessel is lifelike. Ht. 6⅞ in. (17.4 cm). First millennium B.C. *Copyright British Museum.*

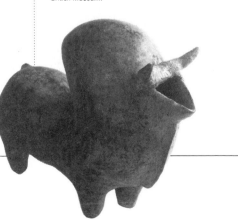

FINISHING   As the coiled walls rose up under the potter's hands, she would thin the walls and scrape and smooth the inside and outside with a tool made from a natural material—perhaps a piece of dried gourd or a shell. Sometimes this was all the finishing that she would do to a pot before it was fired. But if she wanted an even smoother surface, she could **burnish** the clay when it had stiffened to a consistency called **leather hard.** To burnish, the potter took a smooth pebble, a piece of bone, or a shell, and with rhythmic gestures stroked the surface of the pot, polishing the surface to a glossy finish. This works well on natural clay that does not contain large grains of temper, but to burnish the surface of a pot made of coarse clay, the potter might first paint the pot with a coating of fine clay soaked in water—called slip—and then burnish this to a smooth surface (1-20).

Burnishing forces the particles of clay on the surface closer together, and coating the pot with a finer slip before burnishing fills more of the pores. However, this treatment did not make low-fired earthenware watertight, because earthenware clay was not fired high enough to become impervious. So early potters used various methods to try to close the pores of the clay to make it hold water or to give it a smooth surface on which to paint decoration. Sometimes, in an attempt to solve the problem of porosity, potters treated their fired pots with a mixture made by boiling certain plants; alternatively, they coated the still-hot pots with pitch from native trees. Cooking in earthenware over a period of time also helps to make it less porous, as does soaking it for a long time in water. The porosity of earthenware can, however, be an advantage in hot climates, where water is usually stored in unglazed earthenware jars so

Figure 1-20
Burnishing with a smooth stone while the clay is stiff but still damp gives the pot an attractive glossy surface. It also serves to press the clay particles together, making the earthenware less porous. Smooth stones, like the one this potter in Ndola, Zambia, is using, were treasured possessions, often handed down through several generations. Ndola Rural. Chipulukusu Compound. *Courtesy Zambia Information Services Department, Lusaka, Zambia.*

that evaporation through the pores of the clay cools it.

DECORATING THE DAMP CLAY Some pots were left plain or burnished, but others were decorated with awareness, imagination, and restraint. The simplest decoration consisted of incised lines the potter scratched into the clay while it was still damp using natural tools chosen to achieve texture and pattern. Even just a fingernail repeatedly pushed into the clay can form a design, while holes poked into it with a stick, lumps or coils of clay pressed onto it, or the serrated edge of a shell combed across it could all create patterns and texture. Sometimes this decorative texture served a function, as on a water vessel that would otherwise be slippery and difficult to carry when wet (1-21). Early potters had a keen sense of the relationship between a pot's decoration and its shape, often solving a basic design problem with discernment and obvious pleasure. For example, a potter in ancient Japan might decorate his pot with a combination of texture and carving (3-22), while a Bronze Age potter in Scotland might combine simple cross-hatching and horizontal lines into effective decoration (6-2), or a woman in Africa might roughen the surface of a water pot for a functional reason, but add to its attractiveness as well (1-21).

The scratched or applied decoration was enriched by the color of the clay body, which could range from buff to reddish, from light to dark brown, or from gray to black, depending on its mineral composition or the firing methods used. Some pots, owing to uneven firing, came out of the fire with dark and light red and black splotches on the outside, a decorative effect still sought by many potters.

Figure 1-21
The rough texture on the lower pot was probably added to make it less slippery to lift when it was wet. Woman, probably Fulani, in Sanga Region, Mali. *Courtesy National Museum of African Art, Eliot Elisofon Archives, Smithsonian Institution. Photo: Eliot Elisofon, 1970.*

1-22
Mesopotamian potters formed their urns and jars in a variety of shapes, many of them decorated with earth colors applied in bold linear patterns that accentuated the curves of the vessels. Ht. 4½ in. (11.5 cm). Nineveh, Mesopotamia, third millennium B.C. *Copyright British Museum.*

Once a pot was finished, the potter often took the time to decorate it, especially if it was to be used for ritual or burial. In early cultures, making art was not seen as an activity separate from daily life, and the impulse that led early humans to decorate their tools, their clothing, and even their bodies reached into every facet of life. When clay crafters discovered that certain pigments could make colored decorations on their fired ware, they often washed their pottery over with mineral color or painted it with simple designs using various minerals (1-22). These early painted decorations ranged from stylized human figures, fishes, or birds to intricate abstract patterns. Many of the early painted pots from widely separated cultures carry similar designs, leading some scholars to speculate about a possible

common decorative ancestry. Perhaps these symbols did have common origins, but more likely the shapes of the pots themselves suggested the motifs. For example, there is a strong similarity among the spiral designs seen on pots around the world. Scratched on a pot in ancient Japan (3-22) or painted on an early Egyptian (1-23) or Chinese vessel before 3000 B.C. (1-24), or on a Cretan jar (1-25), the spirals could have had a religious significance, but it is also possible that the potters used these swirls and spirals because their rhythms were particularly appropriate to the curving profiles of the vessels.

1-23
Spirals of purple painted on its surface relate to the bulbous shape of a pot made in Egypt sometime before 3000 B.C. Ht. 7½ in. (19 cm). *Copyright British Museum.*

1-24
Elegantly decorated with spirals painted in red and black, this earthenware vessel was found in a cemetery in Hanzu, China. Ht. 13 in. (33 cm). Pan Shan culture, 2500–1500 B.C. *Courtesy Collection Haags Gemeentemuseum, The Hague.*

1-25
The spiraling, wavelike design on a large urn from the palace at Phaistos carries our eyes around the jar's form. Crete 2000–1700 B.C. *Courtesy Archaeological Museum, Herakleion, Crete, Greece.*

Turntables to Wheels

We have seen how early potters built up their pots with coils, shaping them as they turned them in their hands or on a base mold. To understand how turntables evolved and eventually became true potter's wheels, picture yourself kneeling or squatting in the sun outside a mud-daubed hut sometime around 6000 B.C., coiling a pot in your lap. Perhaps you have started the base in an old broken pot, and as you smooth the coils you turn it to keep the walls even as you build them up. Tiring of holding it, you might set the pot and base down on a stone, finding that you can turn it more easily there.

Eventually, someone had the idea of using two stones, the top stone revolving on the lower. Then it probably took several generations before someone thought of shaping the stones to make a socket that would hold and pivot a flat disk. Made from a smooth stone like basalt, such shaped pivots could revolve quite quickly and smoothly, making it much easier to coil, smooth, and polish a pot evenly (1-27). Other early turntables were made of stone, wood, or clay disks that revolved on wooden shafts fitted into a stone (1-26, 1-29).

Figure 1-26
The diagram shows various types of turntables from a variety of cultures.
(a) A broken bowl resting on a stone helps the potter turn the pot as it is built.
(b) A specially shaped, fired-clay base swivels on its rounded protrusion. **(c)** A turntable with two stones shaped to fit together made it easier for the potter or an assistant to turn it. **(d)** Some village potters still use this type of turntable, which pivots on a wooden axle turned in a socket (2-4a). *Drawing by John M. Casey.*

Figure 1-27
This stone pottery-wheel bearing would have turned a disk—probably made of clay or wood—on which a pot was placed, making the forming of the pot easier and quicker. Beth Shean, Israel, c. B.C. 500. *Courtesy Israel Antiquities Authority.*

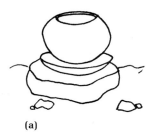

(a)

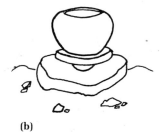

(b)

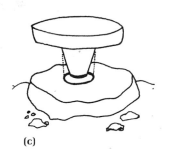

(c)

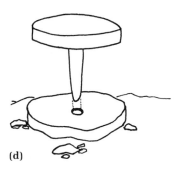

(d)

The Potter's Wheel

At some point—we don't know exactly where or when—the simple turntable evolved into a true potter's wheel. Neither do we know exactly what type of wheel it was or exactly when or where someone added a lower disk that could be kicked by the potter's foot to start it whirling. Perhaps a potter put an assistant to work spinning the turntable (2-13) and found that the work of shaping a pot became easier as the wheel revolved faster. This would have led to the development of the potter's wheel. A true wheel must turn quickly enough—at least one hundred revolutions per minute—to give the necessary centrifugal force to the lump of clay so that only a comparatively light pressure of the hands is needed to make the walls rise. The main energy comes from the wheel rather than from the potter's hands.

The development of the potter's wheel was a technological advance of great importance, marking the beginning of thrown as opposed to hand-built pottery. The invention was considered so important, the Egyptians believed that the god Khum invented the wheel (1-28). Archaeologists have studied the characteristic finger marks on pots thrown on true wheels and have set probable dates for the first known use of a kick wheel at around 3500 B.C. in Mesopotamia, 2300 B.C. in Sumer, and after 2750 B.C. in Egypt and China (1-29). Even with the introduction of this more efficient way to produce uniform pots, many potters continued to use turntables, and in some areas the kick wheel was never used and turntables are still common. Contemporary potters also often use modern adaptations of them in handbuilding.

Figure 1-28
Based on an Egyptian carving of the god Khum, this drawing shows him using an early kick wheel. Myths from many cultures tell of gods or goddesses forming humans from clay, while others recount the discovery of pottery making in legendary terms. *Drawing by John M. Casey.*

Figure 1-29
One of the earliest pottery-turning devices yet found. Used by a potter in Ur around 3500 B.C., it may have pivoted on an axle in a stone socket similar to those still used in Crete. Diameter 29½ in. (75 cm). *Copyright British Museum.*

Figure 1-30
Potters in Ogbomosho, Nigeria, warm their pots by burning straw in them before subjecting them to the heat of the fire. *Courtesy Field Museum of Natural History, Chicago (Neg. #70026).*

Firing

Whatever method was used to shape the vessel or sculpture, the piece eventually had to be fired before it would be changed permanently into ceramic. It was the clay's natural mineral content that made it possible for early potters to develop their firing technology, because the clay used in ancient workshops could be fired at a comparatively low temperature, reaching maturity in a relatively short time. This was due to the large amounts of iron in it that acted as a flux, making it possible for the refractory components to melt at a low temperature. Used throughout the world in most periods of history for making domestic ware, this low-fired clay body still supplies the bulk of cooking and storage containers in areas where industrial products have not taken over the potter's market.

OPEN FIRING   The first earthenware was undoubtedly fired in **open firing,** or in pits, much as it is still done in some villages in Africa, Fiji, and parts of the Middle East and the American Southwest (5-18). Before firing, the potter would have air-dried the pots and perhaps, to speed the drying process and drive out all the water from the clay, would have burned dried grass or dung inside the containers (1-30). This process would also have heated the pots slowly, minimizing the **thermal shock** that could have caused them to crack in the fire.

Once the pots were thoroughly dry, they were stacked along with the fuel. This might be wood, dung, sugar cane, peat, rice straw, palm fronds, or any combustible material that could be gathered locally in the necessary quantity (1-31).

How to stack the pots, how much straw or wood to use, how long to burn the fire, when to cool the pots were all technical decisions that potters worked out slowly through experimentation. A potter may have found that in her area the best time for firing was in the evening when the wind dropped. This might become a habit and then a tradition unquestioned by potters of later generations. Similar empirically learned techniques have been the basis of the potter's craft throughout history, passed on within potting families and through the apprentice system.

EARLY KILNS Where the firing was done in pits instead of on top of the ground, the potters realized that they had more control over the fire and found that wind was less of a problem. By 4000 B.C. in a Neolithic village in Panpo, China, the potters constructed perforated floors in their firing pits, which meant that the pots could be separated from the fire. The next step was to build clay walls up around the pits to shelter the fire more fully. This increased control of the fire and cut down on breakage owing to erratic winds that caused abrupt temperature changes. By around 2900 B.C., in what is now Israel, potters were building enclosed kilns. By the same date in China, a more efficient type of kiln was developed with a tunnel that led to a beehive-shaped chamber, creating a forced draft and resulting in an improved use of fuel. In Mesopotamia, kilns were built with domed roofs and perforated floors that gave potters still more control over the firing (1-32).

The earthenware fired in these early kilns was fired for varying periods of time, depending on fuel and kiln type and the number of pieces being fired. After the pots matured and the fire was allowed to die down, the pots were taken out and set aside to cool.

EVOLVING TECHNIQUES

Because we must depend on excavations to supply information about early forming and firing methods, there are gaps in the story of the development of ceramics. Much of the story is built on conjecture based on studies of traditional methods still in use today, but one thing is certain — later generations of potters built directly on the discoveries made by their potting forebears. In this overview of the beginnings of ceramics, we have compressed thousands of years and the ex-

Figure 1-31
The earliest potters undoubtedly fired their pots in open fires, just as many village potters do today, using a local source of fuel. In Fiji the pots are stacked together with palm fronds and grasses piled over them. Pots undergoing this type of firing can be damaged by gusts of wind that suddenly cause the fire to burn hotter. *Courtesy Fiji Museum, Suva, Fiji.*

Figure 1-32
Potters in Mesopotamia around 4000 B.C. built vertical kilns that gave greater control over the fire. Similar kilns, in which the heat rises from a firing chamber under a perforated floor, are still used in Crete today (2-7). *Drawing by John M. Casey.*

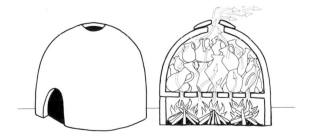

periments of untold numbers of individual potters in isolated villages around the world.

The techniques described evolved at different times and in different places. At times, the migrations of peoples or the capture of slaves would bring new potters into an area. They would then teach the local potters new techniques. New ideas were generally absorbed slowly, however, and it took hundreds of years for modifications and refinements in ceramic methods to be developed. In some cultures, pottery techniques were so well adapted to the local needs and ecology that the processes stayed the same almost indefinitely.

Our contemporary ceramics technology, which makes use of modern chemistry, space-age kiln insulation, and computer-controlled kilns, gives the modern potter a wider range of techniques and methods from which to choose than that open to our early potting ancestors. No matter how complex modern ceramics has become, a handmade pot is still made of decomposed rock and is still formed by human fingers responding with sensitivity to the plasticity of clay.

2

The Mediterranean World

As early agricultural societies evolved into more complex ones, new skills and crafts emerged alongside the older crafts of weaving and pottery. In many cultures, metal working and ceramics developed around the same time, each borrowing techniques from the other. In fact, it has been suggested that the idea of using heat to produce workable metal may have occurred to an observant fire tender who saw how the impurities in clay fused when the clay was fired. These technical developments in metallurgy and ceramics occurred at different times around the world. Clay techniques in the Orient, for example, quite often predated or paralleled those in the Mediterranean world, so we could equally well continue our survey of ceramic history there as in the Mediterranean area. However, since in the Western Hemisphere we have been accustomed to taking a Western-oriented approach to art history, it seems logical to start this historical survey with the Mediterranean cultures.

Once settled village life was well established around the shores of the Mediterranean Sea and on its many islands, trade routes developed, towns appeared along the trade routes, and kingdoms and empires grew, flourished, declined, and disappeared (2-1). On the mainland of western Asia, in the Fertile Crescent between the Tigris and Euphrates rivers, a succession of cultures built elaborate cities based on the irrigation of

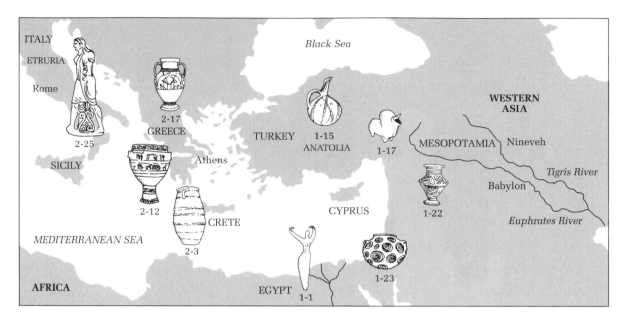

Figure 2-1
Potters and sculptors of the Mediterranean area and western Asia used clay to form tiny figurines and to make vessels. The drawings on the map show the geographic areas where some of the pots and sculptures illustrated in Chapters 1 and 2 were made.

crops and on trade with neighboring communities, while along the Nile River, the Egyptians constructed temples and tombs using the labor of thousands of slaves.

In some of these areas where there was little good building stone, only sun-dried clay bricks were used for construction of temples and palaces, but in others fired and glazed clay tiles were applied to the surface to cover the sun-dried bricks. And throughout the Mediterranean area, potters continued to produce earthenware vessels for both ritual and domestic use. The surface of the pots was left plain on utilitarian ware and painted with earth colors when the vessels were made for ritual or aristocratic use.

EGYPT

In Egypt, pottery making was carried on in workshops under the supervision of master potters who formed the ware while their assistants mixed the clay, loaded the kilns, and stacked the fired ware. Since the pharaohs and priests used vessels of expensive alabaster or even gold rather than earthenware for their oils and perfumes, the bulk

of the ceramic production was low-fired domestic ware for everyday use and vessels for storing the inventory of merchants and the wealth of the ruling class. Some small luxury items, however, were made of a clay body that, when fired, glistened with a blue-green **glaze.**

Egyptian Paste

The discovery that clay could assume such brilliance was Egypt's most important contribution to the story of ceramics. The potters there had, apparently accidentally, discovered the first ceramic glaze. Glazes are compounds of glass-forming minerals that fuse in the heat of the kiln and adhere to the clay body, coating it with what is essentially a thin layer of glass. Glazes, like clay, are of geological origin. They consist essentially of the refractories (heat-resistant materials) silica and alumina and a flux to make the ingredients fuse. Sand and flint (or quartz) are almost pure silica, and if they are heated to 3270°F/1798.8°C, they will fuse and form glass. At that temperature, however, the clay under them would also melt, so a flux is necessary to make lower firing feasible.

The first Egyptian-glazed ceramics, known as **Egyptian paste** (or sometimes, incorrectly, as *faience*), were not coated with an applied glaze. Rather, the glaze was actually formed by ingredients in the clay body itself that were carried to the surface with the water as it evaporated, creating a shiny blue-green coating. This integral glaze probably was discovered by accident when desert sand containing soda ash and potash happened to be mixed into the clay as temper. When such a piece was fired, the **soluble** sodium would have fused with the glass-forming minerals in the sand, and particles of copper contained in the clay body would have given its characteristic color. Once this glaze-forming clay body was discovered and potters realized what caused the color to appear, the Egyptians learned to add alkaline salts deliberately to the clay body to produce the colored, glassy surface. Obtained in the lakes formed by the alkaline springs in the Nile Valley, the salts became an article of commerce whose revenues went to the pharaohs. The glaze-producing clay body was used mostly for small sculptures, ceremonial vessels, and jewelry, but given the number of these objects found in tombs, the revenues the pharaohs realized from the mining operations must have been considerable. The Egyptian method of making small objects with integral glazes became known through trade to the potters in Crete, who also made small statuettes and luxury items of the same type of clay body containing glass-forming minerals.

Applied Glazes

The Egyptians were expert at glass making, and it is possible that their first applied glazes were discovered when glass workers saw how the melted glass coated the pottery crucibles in which it was heated. By the middle of the second millennium B.C., the Egyptians had learned to apply an **alkaline glaze** that fired blue-green owing to the copper it contained, but since this applied alkaline glaze did not adhere well to the surface of fired clay or to the soapstone on which they also applied it, they used it only for small sculptures and other nonutilitarian objects. The Egyptian use of applied glaze probably became known through trade between Egypt and western Asia, where the exploration of this technique was carried further.

THE MINOANS

Situated as it is in the Mediterranean between Egypt and western Asia, the island of Crete naturally developed a seagoing society. With a well-disciplined navy, the island was safe from invasion, so it enjoyed the peace that made it possible for its inhabitants to develop an elaborate and sophisticated culture based on commercial relations with its mainland neighbors. Influenced by artistic and religious ideas from both Egypt and western Asia, this culture, called Minoan after Minos, one of its kings, lasted from around 2500 to 1100 B.C.

The early Cretans worshipped a goddess, made images of her in clay, left offerings to her on decorated ceramic platters, and sculpted clay figurines of her priestesses dancing a sacred dance (2-2). Cretan women, at least those of the upper classes, apparently enjoyed more freedom than women in other Mediterranean cultures and took part in ritual sports as well as dances. It is possible that they were also artists, making or at least decorating some of the ritual vessels.

The nobility lived luxurious lives in large palaces whose rooms, arranged in a complex layout, were decorated with colorful murals. They also enjoyed such comforts as baths, which were hooked up to **terra-cotta** drainage systems, some of whose pipes can still be seen under the palace of Knossus. Also under the floors of the palace lay a vast subterranean storage area, where grain, oil, and other foodstuffs for the palace were stored in large jars, or *pithoi* (2-3). Many of these *pithoi* are still in place, testifying to the permanence of clay, for they survived the fire that destroyed the palace around 1450 B.C. The maze of storerooms that held these *pithoi* may have been the basis of the Greek belief in a labyrinth where the half-bull, half-human Minotaur roamed and roared, demanding human sacrifice. According to this legend, the monstrous creature demanded a yearly tribute of young men and women from mainland Greece. Finally, the Greek hero Theseus killed the Minotaur and rescued the captives by unwinding a ball of string as he penetrated the maze and then following the string back out to lead them to safety. In a folk dance still popular in Greece, a line of dancers winds in and out, supposedly representing Theseus leading the young men and women of Athens out of the Minotaur's labyrinth.

Figure 2-2
Homer described a circular dance, comparing the velocity of the whirling men and women to the motion of the potter's wheel. These Minoan dancers — noblewomen or perhaps priestesses — may also portray the revolutions of the turntables that potters used to form Minoan pottery. Palaikastro, Crete, 1400–1100 B.C.

Figure 2-3
Storage jars, called *pithoi,* still in place in the storerooms of the royal palace at Knossos, Crete, once held grain, oil, or honey. According to legend, the young son of King Minos died by falling into a similar jar of honey; he was found with only his legs sticking out. The *pithoi* were built up with coils in six bands with applied coils pressed on with the potter's thumb to mark and strengthen the joints. Knossos, Crete, c. 1400 B.C.

Not only can one see the ancient *pithoi* that survived the fire still in place in the storerooms at Knossus, but not far away in the hills is a monastery that keeps the olive oil it produces in similar, more recently made *pithoi*. These jars, taller than people, were made more than fifty years ago in the nearby village of Thrapsanon, where some potters still use techniques that are the same as or similar to those in use on Crete around 1400 B.C.

Cretan Pottery-Building Techniques

Thrapsanon has been a potter's village for generations. One of the older monks in the monastery remembers that fifty years ago more than one hundred potters were building the *pithoi* there. Nowadays only a few potters still build these jars on turntables and fire them in vertical kilns similar to the ancient ones. During the cool months of the year, the potters work indoors making thrown domestic ware, but in June they move out into the fields near the kiln to make smaller versions of the thick-walled ancient storage jars.

Revolved by an assistant who sits in a trench at the potter's feet, the turntable on which a modern jar is built consists of a disk of moisture-resistant plane tree wood that rotates on an axle of olive wood. Wrapped in leather and held by an ingeniously knotted rope, it becomes smooth from the friction and revolves quite easily (2-4a). These contemporary wheels may well be modeled on

the ancient ones. A Cretan potter's wheel in the Heraclion Museum dating from 1700–1450 B.C. consists of a clay disk with a socket in the underside into which a wooden axle would have been fitted, probably revolving in a stone socket just as the Thrapsanon ones do today (2-4b).

Continuing Traditions

Thrapsanon potters work in teams. After a row of the pots has been started, an assistant moves along from one turntable to another, adding new coils to each pot as the first section hardens somewhat. Then the master potter progresses along the row, working on the jars in succession, sitting on the edge of the trench while another assistant turns the wheel (2-4b). These wheels do not revolve fast enough to allow the clay to be **centered** and the walls to be raised by **centrifugal force,** so the master must pull up and smooth out the coils, form one section on a jar, then move along the trench to another wheel. When he has completed a section on all the jars, the first ones are usually stiff enough for him to start over again to add another section. Just as the ancient *pithoi* were built in six sections, so are the present-day versions, with an extra coil added at each seam to strengthen the wall at that vulnerable point (2-3, 2-5).

When a row of jars is completed, handles are added and designs may be scratched into the walls. The pots are then left to harden, and by the

Figure 2-4
(a) Detail of the wheel and axle of a turntable used today on Crete. Braced by a crosspiece of wood resting on the sides of the trench, the axle passes through a notch in the plank. **(b)** The assistant, sitting at the bottom of the trench, turns the wheel. As the jar rises, the master potter sits higher, finally standing to shape the last band. *Based on observation and on the article "The Potters of Thrapsano," by Maria Voyatzoglou, in* Ceramic Review *(November-December 1973). Drawings by John M. Casey.*

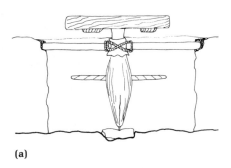

(a)

(b)

Figure 2-5
A few potters still make large storage jars on Crete, working outdoors on turntables set in trenches. Like the earlier ones, these jars are built up in sections by an assistant, followed by the master potter who shapes and completes the pot.

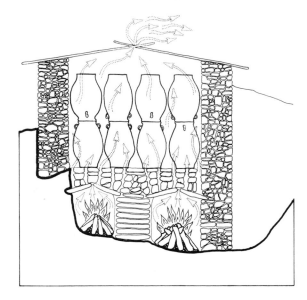

Figure 2-6
A schematic diagram of a kiln in use today on the island of Crete. It shows the cylindrical form typical of the kilns of the Mediterranean area that were derived from those in ancient Mesopotamia. Minoan potters who made the *pithoi* in the Palace at Knossos probably fired their jars in kilns like this, using shards of pottery instead of sheet metal to close the top. *Based on observation and on information in the article "The Potters of Thrapsano," by Maria Voyatzoglou, in* Ceramic Review *(November-December 1973). Drawing by John M. Casey.*

next day they are usually stiff enough to be removed from the turntables. Placed in the hot sun, they are left until they are thoroughly dry, ready for firing in the kiln.

Cretan Firing Methods

As soon as enough jars have been made to fill a kiln, they are fired in a vertical kiln that is basically the same as those used in most ancient Mediterranean cultures (2-6). Made of rocks smeared with heavily tempered refractory clay, the modern kiln is sunk into the ground with a perforated clay floor above the **firebox.** Access to the firebox is down a sloping trench at the back, giving the stoker access to feed dry brushwood through an opening in the wall. The fire is started in the early afternoon and is tended carefully until the firing is completed around sunset (2-7).

This method of building and firing the large jars is the result of empirical knowledge built up over generations, possibly going back as far as 2000 B.C. The young boys helping in the workshops today are learning the craft through experience just as potters have always learned their craft. Hopefully, some of them will keep the tradition alive, leaving their own thumbprints in the clay to be found by future archaeologists.

Minoan Decorated Pottery

The potters in ancient Crete not only made tall storage jars, but also created elegant utensils and containers in startling variety, forming clay into objects for purposes that ranged from "teapots" with strainers for preparing infusions of herbs, to low tables on which offerings were left for the sacred snake who protected the household, to graceful vases decorated with paintings of plant forms or sea creatures (2-8, 2-9).

The nature-loving Minoans drew inspiration from living forms, translating them into decorations that they applied to their vessels after firing. Freely drawn and painted with black, white, and earth pigments, the palm trees, octopuses, flowers, leaves, dolphins, and shells accentuate the curves of the vases and jars. Although at times the decoration becomes so overwhelming that it distracts the eye from the shape of the vessel, at its best it is flowing and harmonious, expressing the Minoan love of bright colors, luxury, and the rhythms of the dance.

Around 1450 B.C., the sophisticated Minoan civilization either fell to invaders or was destroyed by a natural disaster. Knossus was destroyed by fire, and the huge *pithoi* in the palace were buried until they were unearthed again in the 1920s. After the disaster, Crete lost its powerful position, and Mycenae became the dominant

Figure 2-7
Built of stones covered with clay, this Cretan kiln is basically a vertical cylinder sunk into the ground. The opening in front that allows loading of the jars will be closed with stones and clay after the kiln is full. The heat rises from the fire pit through holes in the floor. A stoker adds wood through a hole at the back during the firing. The duration of the firing depends upon the size and number of jars. Thrapsanon, Crete.

◀ **Figure 2-8**
The palm trees decorating this Minoan *pithos* from the palace at Knossos are outlined with red against a solid background. With their curving fronds emphasizing the swell of its body, the vessel exhibits the love of nature and the vitality so typical of Minoan pottery. Made in one of the potters' workshops at Knossos between 2000 and 1700 B.C. *Courtesy Archaeological Museum, Herakleion, Crete, Greece.*

Figure 2-9
Octopuses encircle and emphasize the curving form of a vessel possibly made in Crete and exported to Mycenae or made by local Mycenaean potters influenced by Cretan styles. 1450–1400 B.C.
Courtesy the National Archeological Museum, Athens.

Figure 2-10
The Mycenaean *Warrior Vase* shows soldiers marching in full war gear with shields, spears, and plumed helmets, while the female figure on the left stands with her hands over her head in the traditional Greek pose of grief. Compared with the Minoan urns, this vessel's decoration illustrates the profound contrast between the peaceful Minoan culture and the aggressive Mycenaean society. 1300–1200 B.C. *Courtesy the National Archeological Museum, Athens.*

state in the Aegean for the next two hundred or more years.

MYCENAE

The Mycenaeans, named for one of their massive palace-citadels on the Greek Peloponnesus, were influenced by the art of the Minoans, but the essence of their aggressive military society is probably best illustrated by the lines of marching soldiers on the *Warrior Vase* (2-10).

The king, or overlord, of the commercial town of Mycenae lived in the fortress-palace on the top of a hill. In the workshops surrounding the palace, potters, goldsmiths, and armorers produced decorated vases, rich golden cups, and beautifully inlaid bronze weapons for royal use or for burials. But, along with these luxury goods, Mycenae also depended on the potters to supply storage jars and their accompanying inscribed tablets for the palace storerooms or for the warehouses containing the commodities of the wealthy merchants. Since the powerful Mycenaeans held territorial and trading rights throughout what later became Greece, and even on the mainland of western Asia, it may well be that the Trojan War was really fought for strategic and commercial reasons rather than, as Homer tells it, to rescue Helen, the abducted wife of Menelaus.

In about 1200 B.C., the great Mycenaean citadels fell in their turn to Doric invaders, and the area that later became Greece entered a period of disruption characterized by waves of migrations. The armored men painted on the *Warrior Vase* vividly portray the type of soldiers who tried with little success to hold back these invasions. Life became unsettled, and the only record we have of this period is in its pottery. From the chaos a new civilization emerged, one that was to have a profound effect on the history of the Western world.

GREECE

It is apparent from Greek legends and mythology that clay held an important place in early Greek life. According to legend, the first ceramic wine cup was molded over the breast of the beautiful Helen of Troy. Mythology also tells us that the goddess Athena was the inventor of many useful articles, including the earthenware pot, and that she became the patroness of Greek potters. Clearly, the early Greeks recognized clay's special qualities, and Athenian potters lived up to the reputation of their goddess, for under her patronage they created some of the world's most admired pottery.

The type of vertical kiln in which early Greek ceramists fired their wares probably was brought there by potters from western Asia, an area with which Greece had strong ties and whose decorative motifs Athenian potters adapted to their work. Later, the Greeks refined the kilns by adding a side tunnel to hold the fire so that the heat, but not the flames, would reach the pottery. We do not know when the true wheel was introduced into Greece, but turntables were efficient enough by 800 B.C. for the potters to build huge vases.

Geometric Style

More than four feet tall, the Geometric-period urns are a testament to the shaping and firing skill of the early potters (2-11, 2-12). Called Geometric because of their stylized painted decoration, these vessels represent a remarkable technical achievement.

2-11
Detail of painting on Geometric style urn depicts warriors and chariots in a funeral procession. Such tall urns were placed on graves in the Athenian Diplyon Cemetery, where they served as memorials as well as vessels used during funeral rites. The decorator's brushstrokes are clearly visible, filling in the solid black, detailing the manes of the horses, and creating bands of abstract decoration. *Courtesy the National Archeological Museum, Athens.*

The decoration used on the Geometric urns was totally different from the flowing forms painted on Minoan ceramics. Deceptively simple and abstracted, it showed a new sense of discipline and an intellectual approach to design. It is clear that the person who painted these alternating bands of abstract decoration and human figures approached the design rationally, carefully choosing the placement that would best emphasize the impressive shape and size of the vessel. No decoration could have accomplished this better than the simple patterns and rows of severe figures that encircle them. Although the paintings of funeral processions in the areas between the bands of meanders, zigzags, and diamond patterns project a strong emotional quality, its expression is subordinated to the structure of the vessel and does not destroy the successful relationship between shape and ornament. In this rational, carefully thought out Geometric pottery (2-11, 2-12), we can see the developing characteristics of later Greek art.

2-12
On this huge Geometric *krater,* the figure of a dead warrior is shown lying in state, surrounded by followers in the characteristic mourning pose. These vessels, which are more than four feet tall, illustrate a long tradition of forming and firing. Eighth century B.C. *All rights reserved, The Metropolitan Museum of Art, Rogers Fund, 1914 (14.130.14).*

Figure 2-13
A Greek potter works on a wheel rotated by an assistant in about 600 B.C. According to legend, Talos, nephew and apprentice of the Greek craftsman Daedalus, invented the potter's wheel, whereupon Daedalus became so jealous that he pushed Talos off the rock of the Acropolis in Athens. *Drawing by John M. Casey.*

It is clear that the potters now had the technical knowledge and skill to produce magnificently shaped pottery, so when Greece began to recover from the effects of the disruptions, the pottery industry expanded rapidly (2-13). Corinth, which was located near beds of white and cream-colored clay, was the first big ceramic center in early Greece, but by around 550 B.C., the potters of Athens had surpassed those of Corinth, and Athens became the main Greek ceramics center. From that time on, through the classic period of Greek art to the last days of the Roman Empire, the greatest vase makers in the Mediterranean world were the Greeks, and their wares were transported throughout the Eastern world and into Europe.

Greek **amphorae,** containing wine, have been found in sunken ships off Southern France, while the greatest amount of Greek pottery ever found has actually been unearthed at various sites on the mainland of Italy, where many of the most beautiful Athenian vases were sent as export items.

Athenian Pottery

Athenian potters worked in a quarter of Athens called the Kerameiskos, located near large deposits of clay, or **keramos,** from which our word *ceramics* is derived. Most of the master potters who worked there were foreigners, drawn to Athens

Figure 2-14
In this portrait of the potter at work in his shop, painted on the interior of a black-figure cup, he is shown sitting on a low stool, apparently adding handles to the wine cup on his turntable. Fifth century B.C. *Copyright British Museum.*

from all parts of the Mediterranean. As the ceramics center of their world, Athens offered these potters the opportunity to make a good living. Working alongside each other and exchanging knowledge and techniques, these potters who came from many cultures melded ideas and styles from many sources, thereby enriching the craft of pottery in Greece as well as influencing the art of painting there. Here, in the Kerameiskos, pottery production was organized into a factorylike situation—in some of the potters' shops, as many as seventy assistants worked under the master potter who owned the business. Working on a wheel propelled by an assistant, the master potter probably filled the most important orders for nonutilitarian vases himself (2-14). If they were to be especially large, he would make them in sections and then attach the parts with slip—a process called **luting.**

The celebrities of the day—political, sports, and theater figures—would visit the most famous potters' shops to order vases celebrating a ritual dance (2-15), commemorating a victory or the death of an important person, or honoring the winner of an Olympic contest (2-16). Now, for the first time, individual artists signed their pottery, and because many vessels bear inscriptions such as "Exekias made and painted this" (2-17), we know that some of the accomplished painters were also master potters, who often became as famous as the star athletes. It is also known that although the commemorative vases and cups were made by men, some of the painters who decorated them were women.

The inscriptions on vases contained challenges to other potters, or sometimes the painters named the mythical characters depicted on the vases with their own names or with those of other painters. The master potters and painters who created these vessels became well known and were highly respected, and some even apparently became wealthy.

Figure 2-15
Dionysus was the Greek god of wine, so the festival of Dionysus was a popular theme of decorations on drinking cups such as this black-figure *kylix*. Originally religious rituals, Dionysian festivals were later performed in theaters with actors portraying the god, his attendant satyrs, and maenads; from them developed the classic Greek theater. *Photo: Hannibal, Athens.*

The master potters of Greece in the classical period refined the traditional Geometric shapes and developed new vessel forms. These included flasks to contain the oil that athletes rubbed into their skin; flaring bowls, or *kylix,* used for drinking wine mixed with water; and *oinochoe,* jugs used for pouring. As time went on, the shapes of the new vessels in turn became traditional, and the thousands of vessels produced by Greek potters rarely varied from these basic forms. This meant that the skill of the potter was concentrated on refining the vessels to their ultimate elegance (2-16). The potter even followed a prescribed shape when making utilitarian pots like the *amphorae* that carried oil and wine to the colonies, forming pots that were not only well adapted to their use but also graceful and attractive. So successfully did the potter form the traditional shapes that only rarely did he produce an awkward vessel or one whose form seems inappropriate to its use. Actually, most of the Athenian decorated pottery was intended not for its original utilitarian use, but for memorial, display, or commemorative purposes. These display vases were avidly collected by the well-to-do in both Italy and Greece and were prized for their elegant forms as well as for the paintings on them. The paintings themselves, at least those by the best artists, respected the shapes of the vessels, enhancing rather than disrupting their forms (2-17).

These traditional vase shapes first formed by potters near the clay pits of Athens have become part of our Western heritage (6-20), and to this day some of the basic Greek pottery shapes are reinterpreted successfully by contemporary potters.

2-17
Famous black-figure amphora by potter-painter Exekias shows Achilles and Ajax playing a game during a lull in the siege of Troy. Exekias drew the detail on their flowered cloaks and the curls of their hair, by scratching through the slip with a fine point, skillfully subordinating it to the dignified figures of the heroes and to the curving form of the vase. 540–530 B.C. *Courtesy the Vatican Museum.*

2-16
Some of the many shapes so skillfully formed by the potters of classic Greece. **(a)** The *amphora,* generally oval-shaped, with a narrow mouth and a small lid, was used for carrying liquids as well as for prizes for winners of athletic and drama contests. **(b)** The *kylix,* a drinking cup, was used for serving wine mixed with water. **(c)** The *krater,* whose shape and handle position varied, was used for mixing wine and water. Its wide mouth made blending easy. **(d)** The *cantharus* was a drinking globlet with high, curved, exaggerated handles.
Drawing by John M. Casey.

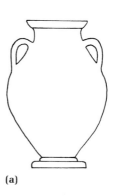

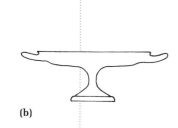

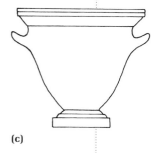

(a)   (b)   (c)   (d)

Figure 2-18
Woman Cooking with Young Girl Looking On, which shows a
kitchen pot on a stand over a fire, illustrates that cooking methods had not changed that much from the earlier Anatolian pot and
stand shown in Figure 1-9. Tanagra. Fifth century B.C. *Purchased by
contribution, courtesy Museum of Fine Arts, Boston.*

On the other hand, throughout the history of
Greece, hundreds of unknown potters created
utilitarian ware, forming and firing everything
from wine-coolers to portable ovens and useful
cooking pots made to heat on stands over a fire
(2-18).

Black-Figure Pottery

Developed originally in Corinth, the decorative
style called **black figure** became popular by the
end of the seventh century B.C. In this style, the
figures were painted on the light-colored clay
body with a specially formulated slip. The artist
drew in details of clothing and features by scratching lines through the slip with a sharp instrument,
revealing the lighter color of the clay beneath.
The new style was soon taken over by Athenian
potters, who refined it and quickly captured the
export market for this type of pottery (2-14 to 2-17).

FIRING PROCESS The firing process used to achieve
the contrast between the black figures and the
buff or reddish background was a complex one.
The fine, purified slip with which the figures
were painted contained iron oxide that turned
black when fired in a reduction atmosphere (2-19,
2-20). **Reduction** occurs when a fire is smothered
and the flame does not get enough oxygen to burn
freely. Put simply, in an attempt to get more oxygen, the flame will draw oxygen from the metal
oxides in the clay, and in so doing will release the
metal and change its color. The black and red colors
were the result of a single firing in which reduction and oxidation atmospheres were produced
alternately in the kiln. To achieve black-figure
decoration, the Greek potter first fired the pottery
in an oxidizing atmosphere in which the flame
burned freely, firing the clay to its natural reddish
color. **Oxidation** occurs when adequate oxygen
reaches the fire, allowing it to burn cleanly. The
artist then smothered the kiln chamber to create
a reduction atmosphere, which turned the painted-

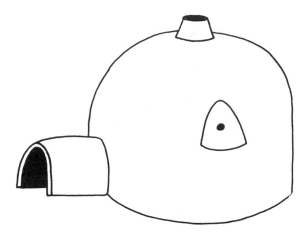

Figure 2-19
Greek kilns were built in a beehive shape with a tunnel at the side for the fire and a vent on the top to control the draft that was covered with a potsherd to dampen down the fire and create a reduction atmosphere. Paintings on pottery show potters opening or closing the vent to change the kiln atmosphere in order to create the black and red decoration on the pottery. They could watch the progress of the firing through the spy hole in the side of the kiln. *Drawing by John M. Casey.*

Figure 2-20
When painting the red-figured pottery, the decorators painted around the figures, leaving them the natural red of the fired clay, and painted the lines with a fine brush. On this *stamnos,* probably a presentation piece, Odysseus is shown resisting the song of the Sirens. He first stuffed his crew's ears with wax and then bid them tie him to the mast so that he would not be lured onto the rocks by the Sirens flying above the ship. Ht. 13⅞ in. (35.2 cm). Vulci, c. 490–489 B.C. *Copyright British Museum.*

on slip black. If the slip had been correctly formulated and the firing not too high, the slip-covered areas remained black when the kiln was returned to an oxidizing atmosphere. The areas that are not covered with slip came from the kiln the natural reddish or buff tone of fired earthenware clay. The glossy brilliance of the black that is such a feature of these Greek vessels resulted from the beginnings of vitrification in the fine slip under the action of an alkali such as wood **ash,** while the purple-red used for hair or clothing was achieved by mixing red iron oxide with the black slip. This firing method requires great care and control of the kiln atmosphere and temperature, since the pot can turn completely black if the kiln is not oxidized at the right time. The Agora Museum in Athens displays a series of fired test tiles excavated from a potter's shop. These show how he tested the slip in the kiln, and it is clear that he continued to draw out tests from the kiln during firing in order to control the complex process. A spy hole in the kiln wall allowed the potter to peer in and observe how the color on the pot was developing during firing (2-19).

Red-Figure Pottery

Around 525 B.C., vessels painted in a new style appeared in Athens. These were created with what is called a **reserve** (not reverse) process. In it, the black-firing slip was painted *around* the figures, thus reserving the color of the red clay for the figures themselves (2-20). When the vessel was fired and the background slip became a lus-

trous black, the red figures stood out in contrast. To intensify the skin tone of the figures, the artist sometimes first coated the vase with a wash of iron oxide or a thin iron-laden slip that fired a rich orange-red. Within the red figures, the details of faces, bodies, clothing, and armor were painted with thin black lines, for which the painter used a single-haired brush. Once it was painted, the pottery was fired in alternating reduction and oxidation atmospheres, the same technique as that used for black figure pottery.

Architectural Ceramics

Greek ceramicists did not limit themselves to producing elegant presentation vessels; they also used clay for more practical purposes. One of these was the protection of the wooden structure of early temples. The early builders sheathed the ends of the wooden roof beams with terra-cotta tiles vertically grooved to allow rainwater to run down off them. Between the beams, and alternating with the grooved tiles, ungrooved terra-cotta tablets displayed painted designs. Both of these features were later copied in marble in the sculptured details on the classic temples. The gable fronts of the early temples were also decorated with sculptures modeled in clay—forerunners of later marble sculptures—and the cult images inside the temples representing the gods or goddesses to whom the temples were dedicated were also made of clay. Built up with coils and wads, these sculptures were fired, then painted in realistic colors. Not many examples of sculptured decorations from the early temples have been uncovered in Greece, but a number have been found in excavations in the Greek colonies in Sicily and southern Italy. The painted terra-cotta sculptures at the apex of the roof, called *acroteria,* and the brilliantly painted figures in the gable ends would later be copied and exaggerated by Etruscan sculptors.

Terra-cotta reliefs that were mass-produced in molds apparently played the same role for the Greeks as inexpensive art reproductions do in modern life, for they were used in homes as decoration, as well as in temples as votive offerings. They, too, show us how the Greeks lived—a cook in her kitchen, a housewife putting folded garments away in a chest, and heroes and athletes achieving feats of bravery and skill.

Terra-Cotta Figurines

For centuries Greek potters created a profusion of small terra-cotta figurines from which we can envision a vivid picture of life in Greece (2-21). At first handformed, the Tanagra figures were later produced in quantity through the use of **press molds.** These were negative molds made by stamping an impression into damp clay using the fired original. The resulting negative was then fired to harden the mold. Next, a slab of damp clay was pressed into the mold to create a positive reproduction of the image. Sometimes as many as fourteen molds were used to make one figurine, and parts of figurines were often interchanged to vary the pose. All the figures were brightly painted after firing, and some still show traces of color—white, blue, and bright pink. From the fourth century B.C. on, quantities of these figures made in the mainland pottery centers of Boetia were sent to the Greek colonies in Italy and Sicily and to western Asia, where there was a large market for them. In fact, the molds themselves were sent abroad, where the ones made by well-known mainland potters and sculptors were sold for extremely high prices. In this way, a potter in Sicily using molds sent from Athens could produce figurines of popular actors playing in an Athens theater in the latest comedy by Aristophanes (2-21). However, although a potter might make a figure that looked exactly like a Tanagra product, experts can determine a figure's origin by analyzing the makeup of the clay or the type of temper used.

In addition to comedy figures, graceful figurines of women dancing (2-22), arranging their hair, gossiping, and caring for children were also in demand. These give us a glimpse into the sheltered life of Greek women. Even in these small sculptures, we can see the grace, elegance, and dignity so characteristic of Greek classic art.

Greek Influences Abroad

As we have seen, Greece extended her colonies and trading networks throughout the Mediterranean, sending Athenian pottery, soldiers, traders, and colonists to distant ports. Contact with Italy had begun early—Mycenae traded with southern Italy as early as 1400 B.C.—and Greek traders were attracted to central Italy by the metal ore of

Figure 2-21
Characters from the theater were extremely popular subjects in Greece, where comedies were broad and earthy. Actors' figures were often distorted with padded tights and jerkins. Here two actors portray drunken old men. Terracotta. Middle of the fourth century B.C.
Courtesy Bildarchiv Preussischer Kulturbesitz, Berlin.

Figure 2-22
The freedom of action typical of later Greek sculpture is shown in this figure of a dancing woman. Called Tanagra figurines for the town in Greece where they were made, small figures like this one were also copied in the colonies, using molds bought from master Tanagra potters. Arms and heads were often interchanged to vary the gestures or poses, and sometimes as many as fourteen molds were used. All were painted in lifelike colors after firing. Ht. 10½ in. (26.7 cm). Second century B.C. *Copyright British Museum.*

the region's mines as well as by the timber of its forests. The Greek ships carried in them the best productions of the Corinthian and Athenian potteries, and prominent local officials in far-flung colonies proudly added these works to their collections. Greek potters also sailed aboard the ships, carrying with them their knowledge of clay techniques. In southern Italy, these potters developed a flourishing industry, and the vases and sculpture they produced were traded throughout the Italian peninsula. In this way, Greek ceramics were brought in quantity to the Etruscan inhabitants of central Italy, and greatly influenced potters and artists there.

THE ETRUSCANS

The origin of the Etruscans has long remained a mystery. Some scholars believe they emigrated from western Asia; some say they came from Egypt. Others suggest that the Etruscans were

Indo-Europeans who came down from the north, and still others that they were indigenous to Italy. Whatever their origin may finally prove to have been, the Etruscans adopted and profited from ideas and techniques from many different sources, including the local farming peoples of Italy who may actually have been their ancestors. These farmers—called Villanovans, for the name of the town where objects from their culture were first excavated—used clay molds to produce metal tools and agricultural implements, buried the ashes of their dead in clay pots with helmetlike covers, and also used earthenware clay for domestic vessels. Like the Villanovans, the vigorous, commercially oriented Etruscans also made use of Italy's rich natural resources, developing a metal industry whose smelting furnaces polluted the air around their industrial towns. Drawing inspiration from Greek religion and mythology, they also absorbed Greek ceramics technology. Adapting the imaginary animals, sphinxes, winged bulls, and griffons of western Asia to their own uses (2-23) and merging these influences with their own inventive and artistic vitality, they created a characteristic art that reached its peak between 700 and 400 B.C.

Etruscan Clay Sculpture

The local clay from the fertile earth of Etruria was regarded by the Etruscans as a noble material. Perhaps because clay is a medium that encourages spontaneity and immediacy, it was particularly well suited to the exuberant Etruscan temperament. When their sculptors used it for the life-sized figures that decorated hilltop temples, they manipulated the clay vigorously (2-24, 2-25). Etruscan art expressed an unrestrained love of life and its pleasures along with a cheerful attitude toward death and the afterlife. Because fired clay was an excellent material on which to paint, the Etruscans could exhibit their love of color and surface decoration on it. Always brightly painted, their sculpture was sometimes heroic, sometimes comic, sometimes tender (2-26), and at other times demonic.

Etruscan architectural sculpture, like the early Greek sculpture from which it developed, was used to cover the wooden structure of temples and other buildings. At the excavations of the Etruscan town of Misa, outside present-day Bologna, excavators unearthed the terra-cotta fac-

Figure 2-23
The animal-head pouring spout of this thick-walled, highly polished jug exhibits the characteristic Etruscan taste for fantasy. The jug's decoration also shows the influence of Greek myths on the potters of Etruria: Hercules is shown capturing the Cretan bull that the god Poseiden had given to Minos. Sixth to fifth century B.C. Archaeological Museum, Florence. *Courtesy Superintendent of Antiquities, Florence.*

ings of the building that had enclosed the sacred spring. These architectural components probably were made in the potter's shop that was also excavated there. The well-organized shop contained storage bins for clay and piping that brought water into the shop from a distance, indicating its importance to the community.

One suspects that the Etruscans continued to use clay long after the Greeks had begun building with stone because they felt particularly at home with the material. In fact, when the Etruscans

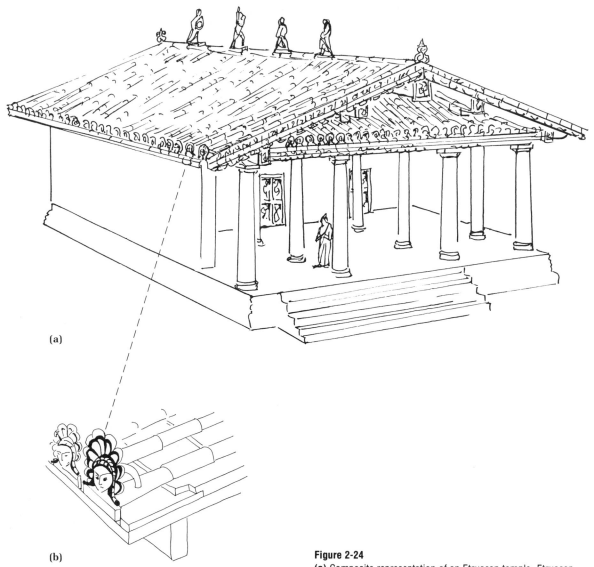

(a)

(b)

Figure 2-24
(a) Composite representation of an Etruscan temple. Etruscan temples were built on stone platforms, but their structure was wooden. To protect the wood, the builders covered much of the structure with terra-cotta tiles and decorative elements. They also masked the ends of the roof tiles with terra-cotta antefixes and the gable ends with reliefs, and they topped the roof with free-standing sculptures like the Apollo from Veii (2-25). This terra-cotta decoration was brightly painted with earth pigments.
(b) Schematic sketch (detail) showing how antefixes were used on the roofs of Etruscan temples. To make the joints between the slab roof tiles watertight, the builders placed half-round tiles over them; antefixes covered the ends of these and added decorative elements. Made in quantity in press molds, antefixes usually de-picted mythological beings.

Figure 2-25
Vulca, a famous Etruscan sculptor, made this free-standing, brightly painted figure of Apollo. Fired in one piece, with an opening in back to allow vapors to escape, it was part of a life-sized group that once stood on the roof of the Temple of Apollo at Veii depicting the conflict between Hercules and Apollo. The decorated shape between the legs was necessary to support the striding figure. Ht. 68½ in. (175 cm). Veii, 510 B.C. Museo Nazionale di Villa Giulia, Rome. *Alinari/Art Resource, N.Y.*

Figure 2-26
The Sarcophagus of the Married Couple is an illustration of the permanence of fired clay and the durability of emotion expressed in it. The ability of clay to withstand centuries of neglect and damage allows us to sense the affection of the couple on their ritual banquet couch and to appreciate the technical knowledge of the Etruscan sculptor whose sensitivity and creativity made this work of art possible. *Photo taken with permission, Museo Nazionale di Villa Giulia, Rome.*

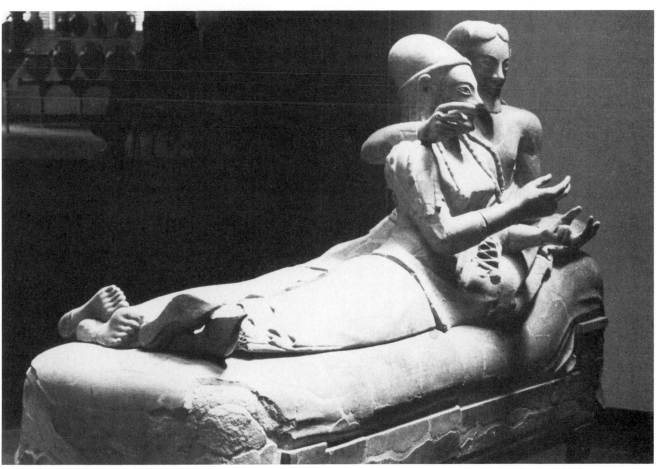

occasionally built stone temples, they sometimes attached terra-cotta decorations to them.

A typical Etruscan temple would be decorated with rows of standing figures along its roofline (2-25), a figure on horseback or in a chariot behind four horses at the gable peak, human or demon faces on **antefixes** at the ends of the roof tiles (2-24), and a sculptured group in the pediment, all of them painted with blue, purplish black, and liberal amounts of red.

In addition to the temple figures, the sculptors also modeled life-sized terra-cotta figures of the dead for the coffins of the rich (2-26). These figures on the sarcophagi were painted realistically, while the side panels frequently carried mold-formed reliefs of battles and heroic deeds. Some of the figures on the sarcophagi are obviously mass-produced in molds, personalized only by an added portrait head, but many are individually sculpted, portraying the deceased on a banquet couch.

For an Etruscan who could afford to have an individually made sarcophagus, the sculptor Vulca from Veii made one of the great works of Etruscan art, now called the *Sarcophagus of the Married Couple* (2-26). On it a man and his wife recline together on their banquet bench in an affectionate pose that suggests not only their close relationship but also the equal position of men and women in Etruscan society. In contrast, in Greece and Rome wives never attended banquets.

Later Etruscan sculptors, influenced by Hellenistic Greek art, became increasingly interested in portraiture, and lifelike representations of bald, obese individuals occur frequently on the coffins. Etruscan sculptures, dug up later, during the Renaissance search for antiquities, influenced such Italian sculptors as Donatello (6-9).

ROME

The Etruscans, who settled before the Latins in what is now Rome, were the first rulers of that area, and just as the Etruscans drew on Greek technology, so the Romans drew on the Etruscan knowledge of art, engineering, and ceramics. In fact, they hired a famous Etruscan sculptor, Vulca (2-25), to create the sculpture for Rome's most important temple, the Temple of Jove. The Romans also continued to use clay for portrait sculptures, frequently casting them in bronze from the clay models.

Pottery

The Romans adapted much of their ceramic technique from the Etruscans or the Hellenistic Greeks, and with their characteristic organizational skill, they transformed their pottery workshops into factories. Although the most characteristic Roman ceramics—domestic red earthenware with decoration in relief—was of a type originally produced by the Hellenistic Greeks, it was the Romans who developed ways of producing it in great quantities, using **parallel-flue kilns** (2-27). This **ware** was made in stamped or carved negative molds that were revolved on potter's wheels. When damp clay was pressed into the revolving mold, it produced a positive impression of the design (2-28). Production soared, and the ceramics factories were highly successful, shipping their ware throughout the northern colonies.

This Roman pottery ware was coated with the same type of extremely fine slip as that was used in Greece for the red and black pottery, but in Rome it was known as **terra sigillata** (literally, "sealed earth"). Although some potteries were noted for their all-black ware, fired in a reducing

Figure 2-27
Roman terra-sigillata kiln. Originally developed in Greece, the process of using fine terra-sigillata slip to coat the surface of pottery was adapted by Roman potters, who used it to make their relief-decorated red ware (2-28). This ware required oxidation firing to achieve its characteristic color, so the potters fired it in special kilns with built-in flues to protect it from the smoke and ash of the fire.

Figure 2-28
To make this relief-decorated ware, the Roman potter pressed damp clay into a fired mold, smoothing it against the walls as the mold turned on the wheel. When the formed vessel was removed from the mold, the impression appeared in relief on its exterior. **(a)** A fired pottery stamp used to impress the decoration into a mold. **(b)** This terra-cotta mold was used to form a bowl depicting the mysteries of Dionysus. **(c)** A fragment of a relief-decorated bowl made in a mold shows a satyr playing a flute. Late first century B.C. to early first century A.D. *(a) All rights reserved, The Metropolitan Museum of Art, Purchase, Funds from Various Donors, 1926 (26.81.2) (b) All rights reserved, The Metropolitan Museum of Art, Rogers Fund, 1923 (23.108) (c) All rights reserved, The Metropolitan Museum of Art, Gift of J. Pierpont Morgan, 1917 (17.194.1931).*

(a)

(b)

(c)

atmosphere, the most famous of the Roman ware was fired in an oxidizing atmosphere so that it came out a rich red, whose glossy finish is largely the result of a micalike material in the clay that made up the slip (2-28). This red ware, with or without its molded reliefs, was produced in Italy but was copied in other areas of the Roman Empire—Switzerland, Gaul, and England also produced typical terra sigillata–finished pottery.

Like the Greek potteries, the Roman factories made tiles and ceramic plaques to decorate their elaborate public buildings and luxurious homes. Particularly in the early days of Rome, buildings were frequently made of brick and faced with stone, but at the height of the Roman Empire, brick and terra-cotta were no longer in fashion, and Emperor Augustus could boast, "I found Rome of brick, I leave it of marble." In the less highly developed areas of the Roman Empire, however, it was the use of clay building materials—bricks, roof tiles, ceramic floor coverings, and ornamentation—that often differentiated the homes of the well-to-do Roman conquerors from the simpler wooden houses of the local inhabitants. The Roman colonists also built such luxuries as public bath houses, whose rooms were heated by hot air sent from wood-burning furnaces through terra-cotta pipes in the floors or walls.

With a large population at home to feed and far-flung armies to supply, the Romans also perfected the transport of grain, oil, and wine, carrying it in terra-cotta amphorae designed to be stacked in the holds of ships (2-29). So many of these amphorae were brought to Rome filled with foodstuffs from the colonies that there still is a hill in Rome, *Il Testaccio*, that was gradually built up of the broken amphorae thrown away after their contents had been transferred to the warehouses along the Tiber River.

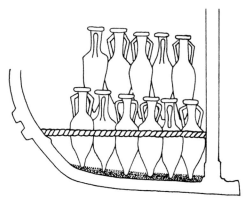

Figure 2-29
The Greeks, Etruscans, and Romans shipped millions of *amphorae* filled with wine, oil, and grain throughout the Mediterranean area. Fitted into the holds of merchant ships, these containers became the unit of measure by which the capacity of a vessel was calculated. The drawing shows how they were stacked. *Drawing by John M. Casey.*

Wherever they settled, the Romans introduced the use of the pottery wheel and the expertise of firing in vertical kilns, both techniques that had been unknown in Northern Europe before the Roman Legions arrived. When the Roman Empire crumbled and Europe settled into the Dark Ages, the knowledge of the potter's wheel and the Roman kiln were lost. In England, their use was only reintroduced around the ninth to the twelfth centuries A.D. Chapter 6 will pick up the story with the return to Northern Europe of advanced ceramic technology that made it possible for ceramics to regain its importance there in the Middle Ages. Now, however, we will turn to other areas of the world where rich clay traditions also developed, some of which profoundly affected the history of ceramics in the Western world.

3

Asia

Until quite recently, the West has known much more about art in early Mediterranean societies than about the artistic developments in other parts of the world, and Westerners have tended to believe that all civilization started in the Mediterranean. This was largely due to the fact that when archaeology began as a science in the 1800s, it centered on that area because it was familiar ground, made so by the Bible and by Greek and Roman mythology, literature, and history. This attitude also reflected a cultural egocentricity that caused us to favor the Western cultural heritage.

Now, however, archaeological exploration has extended our knowledge of early ceramics beyond Europe and the Mediterranean to Africa, to the Russian steppes, to eastern Asia, to the Americas, and to Asia (3-1). We now know more about the uses of fire and tools and the development of pottery making in many areas of the world, and excavations in Japan, Taiwan, and China have unearthed extremely early pottery, of which the Japanese is at present considered to be the oldest. Fashioned by human hands between twelve thousand and nine thousand years ago, this is the oldest example yet known of fired vessels. (Small fired sculptures found in eastern Europe that date from around 26,000 B.C. are so far the oldest fired-clay artifacts found.) As excavations in various parts of the world continue to unearth sites of early human habitation, our knowledge of crafts

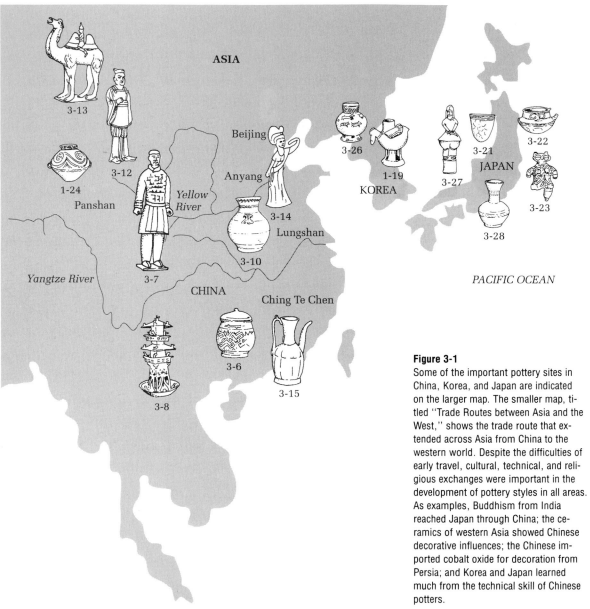

Figure 3-1
Some of the important pottery sites in China, Korea, and Japan are indicated on the larger map. The smaller map, titled "Trade Routes between Asia and the West," shows the trade route that extended across Asia from China to the western world. Despite the difficulties of early travel, cultural, technical, and religious exchanges were important in the development of pottery styles in all areas. As examples, Buddhism from India reached Japan through China; the ceramics of western Asia showed Chinese decorative influences; the Chinese imported cobalt oxide for decoration from Persia; and Korea and Japan learned much from the technical skill of Chinese potters.

Trade Routes between Asia and the West

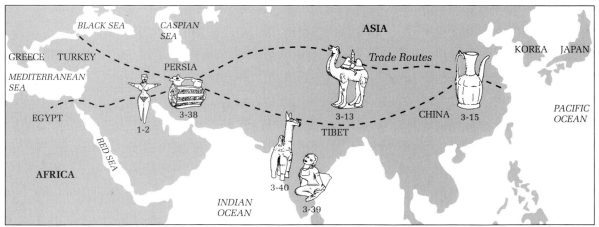

Figure 3-2
Neolithic potters in China made urns, low
bowls, and jars of red earthenware clay
on turntables, burnishing them before
firing. After firing, they painted the vessels with mineral oxides in geometric
patterns and flowing spiral designs
in red, purple, and black. Ht. 13 in.
(33 cm). Found in a grave. Panshan,
China, 2500–1500 B.C. *Courtesy Collection
Haags Gemeentemuseum, The Hague.*

Figure 3-3
Called a *li,* this early tripod shape may
have developed from three pots joined
together. The potter paddled the outside
of the walls, thinning and texturing them.
Gray pottery. Ht. 6 in. (15.2 cm). China,
c. 2000 B.C. *Courtesy Asian Art Museum of San
Francisco, The Avery Brundage Collection, B60 P2074.*

developed by early humans widens. Perhaps by
the time you read this paragraph, experts will
have dated an even earlier example of the use of
fire to harden vessels made of clay.

CHINA

The term *Neolithic,* once used to denote a settled
community that farmed and made pottery, is now
also used for earlier cultures that farmed and
made stone implements of an advanced type, but
did not make pottery. These cultures are also
called *pre-ceramic.* When we use the term *Neolithic* here it refers to the ceramic period.

An important site that has given us a considerable amount of information on early ceramics
technology was discovered at the village of Panpo,
on the Yellow River in central China. Excavations
there have shown that between six and four thousand years ago hunters settling there created a
farming civilization, founding villages in which
people lived in permanent houses, maintained a
cemetery, and fired pottery.

Skilled in the crafts, these Neolithic villagers
made tools from stone and pottery from *huang*

tu, a local yellow clay rich in alumina that they
tempered with sand. They ornamented their pots
with fingernail and tool-impressed textures and
painted them with decorations, consisting mainly
of geometric shapes and lines composed with
great sensitivity to the form of each pot (3-2).

Then, by about 2,000 B.C., in Kansu province,
potters were shaping clay into thin-walled pottery, which they usually painted with **hematite**
powder (red iron oxide) and manganese oxide in a
variety of line designs—bands of circles, crosses,
dots, and triangles. They painted other vessels
with elegant spiral patterns or fluid lines that
suggest waves or the currents of a river.

At various places in central and eastern China,
potters around four thousand years ago also made
vessels in a tripod shape with three hollow legs,
their form probably based on three pots joined
together (3-3). Called a *li,* this shape may have
had fertility significance or may have been derived from pots originally designed to boil liquids on an open fire. The example shown is
decorated only with striations, its form rather
squat, but some of these pitchers are well propor-
tioned, with graceful long spouts and swelling
legs tapering down to pointed feet. Other vessels

are decorated with applied coils and pellets of clay in designs similar to the bronze urns of the Shang period.

At about the same time (2000 B.C.), another clay culture called Lungshan, on the lower Yellow River, was making extremely thin-walled black pottery fired in reduction. From marks on the vessel walls, archaeologists have deduced that this pottery was made with a relatively advanced wheel— apparently a true potter's wheel that turned at least a hundred revolutions per minute.

The kilns in which the early Chinese potters fired their ware were built into the ground with a side tunnel in which a wood fire burned so that the heat flowed up into the chamber where the pots were placed (3-4). These kilns were small— only able to fire three or four large pots and about ten smaller ones up to a temperature of around 1470°F/800°C.

Shang Dynasty (c. 1500–1100 B.C.)

As the Neolithic villages in China grew in size and complexity, class lines developed. Local chiefs became overlords, ruling a society in which serfs and slaves farmed the land for the landlords, while artisans produced luxuries for the upper classes.

Eventually the first true Chinese dynasty, the Shang, placed a central ruler above the local landed lords, and from then on dynasty succeeded dynasty. There is no need for us to remember the intricacies of China's political history, but since certain dynasties were more significant in the history of ceramics or contributed particular innovations to its technique, we emphasize their contributions to China's long history and skim over other dynasties.

By now cities were built with large religious centers and palaces where the rulers and nobles lived. When they died, these kings and nobles were buried, along with the bodies of their sacrificed slaves and horses, in elaborate tombs that contained ritual bronze urns and pottery.

Living on the edges of this stratified society were the herd-tending nomadic tribes of central Asia who moved constantly through the mountains, steppes, and deserts of that vast area. Periodically they appeared on their swift horses to raid the more settled Chinese communities, sometimes destroying them, sometimes becoming assimilated and passing on new artistic styles they

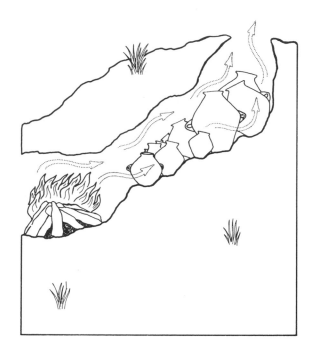

Figure 3-4
The earliest Chinese pottery was fired in kilns dug almost horizontally into the earth with side tunnels for the fires. Another type had small heat vents in the projecting floor to distribute the heat more evenly around the pots. *Drawing by John M. Casey.*

had absorbed in their nomadic wanderings. Often, the reason for these raids was to force the farming villagers to trade the products of their crafts, such as pottery, in return for the horses the nomads bred.

The Shang were influenced by the peoples who lived around them in Asia, copying elaborate burial rituals from the northern tribes, as well as the designs of stylized dragons on the stamped pottery of their crocodile-worshipping southern neighbors. They melded all of these influences into a characteristic style that was reflected in both their pottery and their bronze vessels.

SHANG KILNS   As a thriving pottery industry developed, kiln design changed somewhat. We know what the Shang kilns looked like because at Chengchow, a Shang city, excavators discovered fourteen kilns in the potters' quarter. These kilns were vertical, about four feet in diameter, and had a central pillar or wall that supported a perforated clay floor on which the pots were placed (3-5). As kiln technology improved, potters learned to fire at temperatures of up to 2190°F/1200°C, and by around 1400 B.C., the Chinese had made

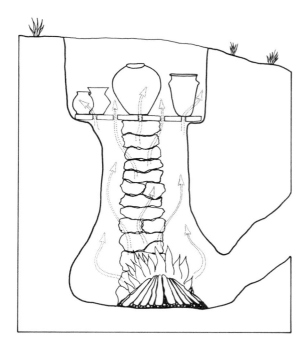

Figure 3-5
By the end of the Shang dynasty, the firing chamber was larger, the ware was placed above the fire on a permanent grate supported on a pillar, and the kilns may have had domed roofs built up over the top opening each time they were fired. *Drawing by John M. Casey.*

the first high-fired pottery, known as **proto-porcelain** (a form of what we call stoneware), made with **kaolin,** a white primary clay found in large deposits in China.

SHANG GLAZES Along with the technical advances they made in kiln building and firing, the Shang potters also discovered how to cover their pots with glaze. This knowledge probably developed as they observed the accidental ash glaze that formed when ashes from the wood fire fell on the shoulders of vessels in the kiln. Wood ashes contain alkalies, such as potash and soda, as well as silica and alumina, and the high kiln temperature caused the minerals in the ash to fuse with the silica in the clay, forming a glaze. Noticing how the ashes formed a shiny coating on the shoulders of their pots, the potters undoubtedly began to experiment with different materials, eventually succeeding in creating a deliberately applied high-fire feldspathic glaze that fused with the proto-porcelain clay body to make a coating that became an integral part of the fired pottery. One can imagine the amount of glaze testing that went on in Shang potters' shops before the first successful deliberately applied glaze was formulated. This

yellowish-brown or greenish glaze marked the first step in the long search for refinement in glazes, a search that occupied potters in China for many centuries (Color Plates 1 and 2).

In the later days of the Shang dynasty, some very fine white vessels were made of almost pure kaolin in shapes very similar to the bronzes (3-6). Decorated with designs that show probable influences from Southeast Asia and the cultures in western Asia that used animal decorations, these rare, fragile vessels were made from a clay body that was the direct predecessor of the true porcelain of the Sung period.

Chou Dynasty (c. 1100–722 B.C.)

The ceramics of the Chou dynasty continued along the lines established in the Shang dynasty, with Chou potters creating earthenware copies of the more expensive bronze vessels. These potters

Figure 3-6
Made of almost pure kaolin, this fine white urn was fired to around 1832°F/1000°C. Too fragile for ordinary use, it probably was kept for ceremonial use. Excavated potter's tools include stamps with dragons and squared spirals like the decorations on this jar. Ht. 8 in. (20.3 cm). Anyang, Honan, China, late Shang dynasty, 1300–1028 B.C. *Courtesy Asian Art Museum of San Francisco, The Avery Brundage Collection, B60 P538.*

were also kept busy making proto-porcelain into wine vessels, bells, and footed basins. Building on Shang technical knowledge, they improved the stoneware body and learned to cover it with a smoother, more translucent, and more resistant glaze. These developments resulted partly from a more advanced kiln design that now distributed the heat around the firing chamber through complex duct systems. This achieved a more uniform firing temperature throughout the kiln.

Clay and Bronze Casting

As so often happened in early cultures, metallurgy and ceramics were interrelated in China. During several later dynasties and into the Warring States period (c. 480–21 B.C.), the bronze industry flourished. Clay played an important part in the production of the impressive bronze objects made by artisans using highly developed casting techniques. For example, excavation of fifth-century B.C. bronze workshops have revealed more than thirty thousand clay models and fired-clay molds used for casting bronze vessels.

Confucianism and Taoism

After the decline of the Chou dynasty and the Warring States period, China entered a time of chaos, but one of great intellectual ferment. At this time, two scholars propounded two quite different philosophies, initiating a moral and intellectual conflict that was reflected in China's later social, political, and artistic history. Confucius (or Kung Fu-tse, 551–479 B.C.) taught that one could be fulfilled only by following one's appointed role in a rigid social order. This idea was in direct opposition to the teaching of Lao-tze (604?–531 B.C.), who believed that discipline and authoritarianism wrongly repressed the natural instincts that would lead to harmony with the universe. Both the scholarly orderliness of Confucianism and the mysticism of Taoism were reflected in the art of China, and Taoism also would become an important influence on certain segments of Japanese society and their ceramics.

Qin Dynasty (c. 221–202 B.C.)

The totalitarian Qin emperors conquered all of China, unifying it under a powerful central government and ruling their people through fear. Until recently, they were seen as ruthless tyrants who made little contribution to Chinese culture. Certainly they were ruthless—their philosophy was that it should be worse for the people to fall into the hands of the regime's police than to fight an enemy state. The First Emperor Qin Shih Huang Ti used seven hundred thousand laborers to create the imperial tomb, and the Qins' greatest contributions to art in general were for their own

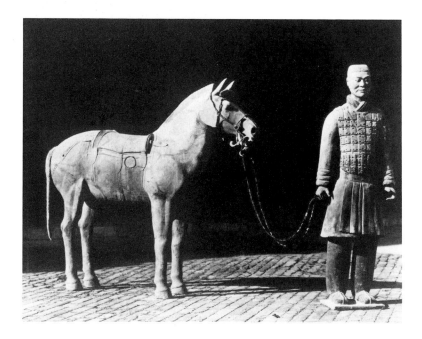

Figure 3-7
Part of a seven-thousand-strong terra-cotta army, this horse and groom were placed in the tomb of the first Emperor Qin. The hollow-built soldiers and horses were supported on solid legs and held real weapons, and each one was sculpted as an individual portrait. China, 246–210 B.C. From the exhibition The Great Bronze Age of China: An Exhibition from the People's Republic of China. *All rights reserved, The Metropolitan Museum of Art, Asian Art Department (cat. #101, 102).*

glorification. One of these is the army of terra-cotta soldiers and horses that was buried with the First Emperor Qin Shih Huang Ti. It is arranged in battle formation, facing eastward toward his enemies in the lower Yellow River valley (3-7). The elaborate tomb included models of the Yellow River and automatic crossbows fixed to kill any grave robbers attempting to enter it. Started when Emperor Qin came to the throne at the age of thirteen in 246 B.C., seven thousand of these life-sized figures were made in clay to represent the army that protected him from his enemies. When this remarkable army was excavated, it was discovered that although the soldiers' bodies were somewhat standardized, their faces were individual portraits—no two faces were alike. These are the earliest realistic Chinese clay sculptures yet found, revealing a highly developed ceramic sculpture tradition and mastery of firing technique. Made of the heavy clay found in the vicinity of Mount Li, their bodies are solid from the abdomen down.

Han Dynasty (c. 206 B.C.–A.D. 220)

Under the Han, China again enjoyed a period of comparative peace; however, the Han took from the Qin the concept of a powerful central government, so the life of the ordinary people probably changed very little. Much of what we know of their lives comes from the countless ceramic grave models made for the nobles, the landed farmers, and the warriors (3-8). These grave models, called *ming-chi,* were buried with the dead instead of live slaves and horses for their use in the afterlife.

HAN LEAD GLAZE   Made of earthenware, most of the grave models were unglazed and painted with unfired pigments that have largely worn off, but some were coated with a newly developed lead glaze. How mysterious the action of the fire on clay and glaze appeared to the potters themselves is illustrated by a legend that tells of a hard-working potter whose firing of a large and precious pot had failed. Distraught because his work was destroyed, the potter jumped into the kiln to die in the flames. After that sacrifice, miraculously all the pots fired perfectly, so from then on potters worshipped him as the god Tung, "Genius of Fire and Blast" (3-9).

Lead glazes had been in use in Mesopotamia since the sixth century B.C., leading to speculation about whether knowledge of these glazes had

Figure 3-8
Peasant rebellions were frequent in the Han period, so landlords and their families took refuge in watchtowers such as this one guarded by archers and sentries. Grave model, green lead glaze. Ht. 33¼ in. (84.4 cm). Han dynasty, second century A.D. *Courtesy of the Freer Gallery of Art, Smithsonian Institution, Washington, D.C. (acc. no. 07.68a).*

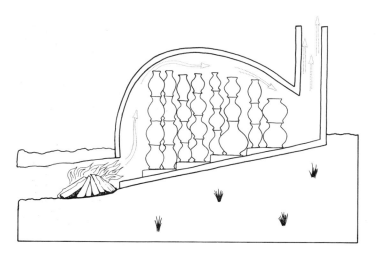

Figure 3-9
Later kilns were built with permanent domes designed to direct the heat up over the stacked ware and then downward before it went up the chimney. This type of kiln—called downdraft—could reach a temperature of 2192°F/1200°C. Because the chamber was open to the smoke and ashes of the fire, the combination of ash, silica in the clay, and high temperature usually caused an ash glaze to form on the ware. *Drawing by John M. Casey.*

Figure 3-10
During firing, wood ashes fell on the shoulder of this Han stoneware jar, fused with the silica in the clay, and formed an accidental glaze. Stoneware. Han dynasty, 200 B.C.—A.D. 221. *Courtesy of the Royal Ontario Museum, Toronto, Canada.*

been brought to China by traders following the Silk Route. Established in the second century B.C., this caravan route led from China through Afghanistan to western Asia and on to Rome, carrying China's fine silks and lacquer ware to the West. In about 550 B.C., the Persians had conquered large areas of western Asia, extending their empire as far as the Indus River in India. These Sassanid Persians, as they are called, traded with the Chinese silk merchants, selling them Persian gold and silver vessels that were transported back with the caravans to China. When the potters saw them, they adapted their Western motifs and shapes to their own ceramics. For example, Chinese pottery flasks modeled on Persian forms show Sassanian figures in relief under a brownish glaze. We do not know whether some Sassanid potters actually came to China with the returning caravans and taught the Han potters their glaze techniques or whether Han potters traveled to western Asia and brought back the knowledge. It is true, however, that lead glazes appeared in China at this time and that Chinese pottery was traded across large areas of Asia. Clearly, each culture absorbed artistic influences from the other, and international trade came to be vitally important to the Han potter.

HAN TECHNICAL IMPROVEMENTS   Firing and glazing techniques continued to improve during these centuries and on into the following periods as potters continued to experiment with high-fire glazes (3-10). By the end of the Han dynasty, potters in southern China were making a type of high-fired-glazed stoneware called Yuëh ware, whose greenish glazes came close to the famous green **celadon** glaze of the later Sung period (Color Plate 1). In fact, so many kilns were being fired with wood in the ancient kingdom of Yuëh that a ninth-century poet, Lu Kuimeng, wrote:

> In autumn, in the wind and dew, rises the
>   smoke of the kilns of Yue
> It robs the thousand peaks of their kingfisher
>   blue.

Toba Wei (A.D. 386–617)

After the fall of the Han dynasty, northern China was overrun with waves of nomadic horsemen until the Toba Wei, a Turkish tribe, took control in A.D. 386. These invaders ruled through mili-

Figure 3-11
In this northern Wei period tomb model we can see how architectural roof tiles and ornaments were used on palaces and temples. China's ceramics industry turned out quantities of molded or stamped bricks and glazed tiles decorated with scenes of farm life, craft shops, hunters, and processions of notables. Northern Wei, A.D. 386–534. *By courtesy of the Board of Trustees of the Victoria & Albert Museum.*

Figure 3-12
The Toba Wei, a Turkish tribe, conquered northern China in A.D. 386, ruling through military officials who were realistically depicted in painted earthenware. Ht. 35 in. (88.9 cm). *Courtesy Asian Art Museum of San Francisco, The Avery Brundage Collection, B60 S498.*

tary officials who had become part of the Chinese bureaucracy, abandoning their nomadic lives and adopting Chinese language, building styles (3-11), and dress along with the Buddhist faith. We can see their Western faces reflected in the ceramic sculpture of the time (3-12). Various groups of Wei and other succeeding dynasties ruled China until the beginning of the Tang dynasty.

Architectural Ceramics

From at least the Warring States period on, the making of roof tiles had been part of the ceramics industry in China (3-11). The decoration was made by stamping with fired-clay stamps into the clay, or the tiles were made in carved molds lined with cloth to keep the clay from sticking. Decorated bricks, tiles, and architectural ornaments were an integral part of the decoration on wooden buildings, even before the knowledge of glazes made brightly colored clay tiles possible. Once the knowledge of lead glazes reached China in the Han period, the greenish lead glaze that covered the grave models (3-8) was adapted to cover earthenware tiles as well. From then on, as more and more colors became available to the potter, ceramic tiles and roof ornaments also became more brilliantly colored.

◄ **Figure 3-13**
Chinese potters made many models of the western Asian camels and their drivers who traveled the Silk Route. First they modeled the camels; then they made their humps and packs and drivers, attaching them before glazing the pieces with yellow, green, and brown glazes that were allowed to run down the sides. Buff earthenware, brown and green glazes. China, Tang dynasty, A.D. 618–907. *By courtesy of the Board of Trustees of the Victoria & Albert Museum.*

Figure 3-14
A slender dancer from the Tang court was modeled in earthenware and then painted. Traces of pigments can still be seen on her clothing. Tang dynasty, A.D. 618–907. *By courtesy of the Board of Trustees of the Victoria & Albert Museum.*

Tang Dynasty (A.D. 617–906)

Tang ceramics reflect the cosmopolitan aspect of this period in China's history. Outside influences arrived with the caravans, following the trade routes that reached across central Asia, down into India, and through the Roman colonies into western Asia. Foreign ships brought people of all races and creeds to the ports of Canton and Yangchow, while noble Turks arrived with their retinues whose clothing and faces fascinated the Chinese. Along with the camels and their drivers from the silk caravans, these foreigners appear in the clay figurines that were made in quantity and glazed with polychrome lead glazes (3-13). Made by mixing copper, iron, or cobalt with lead silicate, these blue, green, brown, and yellow glazes were often applied over a white slip. They were apt to be runny because of the action of the lead flux, and the potters applied them freely so that they ran down the side of the figures, color over color. The Tang potteries also produced many unglazed sculptures of female musicians, dancers (3-14), and court ladies, reminding us that during this dynasty China was governed for fourteen years by the Empress Wu. During her reign, upper-class women were educated, wrote poetry,

rode horseback, and played polo. It was a tolerant society; foreign religious groups were allowed to build their temples and churches in the capital, among them the Buddhists, whose religion eventually became dominant in China.

Western shapes continued to be popular in Chinese ceramics. These ranged from pilgrim bottles from Sassanid Persia, to pottery copies of metal ewers (3-15) to Hellenistic *amphorae*. All were absorbed into the Tang potter's repertoire but, as is usually the case in the exchanges of art styles, they were adapted to local taste and materials.

THE FIRST TRUE PORCELAIN Under the Tang, the fine ware from the Yüeh kilns became more refined, until finally a true porcelain was attained and perfected in the Tang dynasty. Porcelain is a clay body composed of kaolin, feldspar, and silica, and when fired to a temperature of 2370°–2440°F/ 1300°–1450°C or more, it becomes vitrified and translucent. China's fine porcelain was described by a Moslem merchant as so thin one could see the sparkle of water through it; it was this translucence that caused it to be treasured by Chinese connoisseurs and poets. They called it white as snow or silver, preferring it for cups from which to drink tea. Only the finest porcelain was considered good enough to be used at court, and eventually the court established the official Imperial Kilns in order to control the quality of the ware. These kilns were established in the ceramic center of Ching te chen because of the rich deposits of kaolin nearby. The ware was shipped by river and lake to Nanking, then on by the Grand Canal to the Imperial Palace in Peking.

Chinese potters were able to develop this fine porcelain because of their discovery of China's large deposits of both the white primary clay, kaolin, and **petuntze,** or *pai-t'un-tzu,* a white feldspathic rock essential to the making of porcelain. During high firing, the petunze (our **Cornish stone,** or **Cornwall stone**) melts and surrounds the particles of kaolin so that they can fuse.

Sung Dynasty (A.D. 960–1270)

The ceramics of the Sung dynasty, like those of the Tang, reflected the taste of the court, where every educated person studied painting and calligraphy and even the emperors were painters and poets. In this atmosphere of culture and artistic accomplishment, the ceramics were elegant, formal, and exquisitely crafted (3-15). Produced in several pottery centers, some of which had as many as two hundred kilns, much of Sung porcelain was formed with carved molds that transferred their designs onto the damp clay.

SUNG GLAZES When Westerners think of Sung ceramics, a soft green glaze usually comes to mind. Called *ch'ing t'zu* in China, in Europe it was named celadon for a character in French theater who was dressed in that shade of green (Color Plate 1). The soft green was the result of centuries of experimentation in an attempt to achieve the color and surface of sacred jade. In fact, celadon glaze comes in many shades because the iron oxide in the glaze, when fired in reduction, can create a wide range of tones from leafy green to watery bluish-green, depending on the oxides present in the clay body and in other glaze materials. At the time of the Sung dynasty, potters were limited to local materials, so the results varied greatly from area to area and period to period. Two types of celadon ware illustrate how these local factors influenced the color of the glaze: The celadon from northern China was formed of a gray porcelaneous body on which the glaze was

first fired in reduction at a high temperature, then in an oxidizing atmosphere as it cooled. The glaze emerged from the kiln a greenish-brown. On the other hand, at the Lungchuan potteries, the glaze was used on a grayish-white stoneware body, and it fired in reduction to a pale olive green.

Ashes were also an important part of the Sung glazes, and rice-straw ash was a popular ingredient. Rice straw is high in silica, and its ashes contributed to the stability and hardness of the glazes. The minerals in rice-straw ashes could vary from place to place according to the soil in which the rice was grown, so another factor made for variations in the quality of local glazes.

Figure 3-15
Pure white, hard, translucent, and resonant when struck, Sung porcelain became the standard against which all later porcelain was measured. Chinese potters had the necessary firing technology, and China had the kaolin and *petuntze* (feldspar) needed to achieve its purity of body. Ht. 7¾ in. (19.7 cm). White porcelain ewer, Sung dynasty, eleventh to twelfth century A.D. *By courtesy of the Board of Trustees of the Victoria & Albert Museum.*

Figure 3-16
Often mottled or streaked with "oil spots" or "hare's fur," the *tienmu* glaze developed by the Sung potters, became popular in Japan, where it was known as *tenmoku*. Bowl, Chien ware, *tenmoku* glaze. Ht. 2¾ in. (7 cm). China, Sung dynasty, tenth to thirteenth century A.D. *Courtesy Asian Art Museum of San Francisco, The Avery Brundage Collection, B60 P1718.*

Chinese ceramics continued in great demand abroad; the Arab countries bought it in great quantities. Thousands of shards of both Yuëh ware and white porcelain were found in the ruins of the summer palace of the caliphs. In western Asia, celadon was also popular, because the uneasy rulers believed that the Chinese celadon ware would crack and change color if exposed to poison, so it was used to detect assassination plots. This idea may have been a result of the **crackle glaze** deliberately exploited for its decorative effect by Chinese potters who found that the glaze would crack if it were not properly formulated to shrink along with the clay body. The porcelain made from the excellent clays of China was envied by the potters in Persia, who used white tin glazes to cover their coarse red clay in an effort to compete with the Chinese imports. This use of white glaze later spread to Europe.

In addition to making the classic white-glazed porcelain and soft green celadon and crackle glazes, the Sung potters produced the brilliant Chun glaze (Color Plate 2), whose purple and red splashes were created when areas of copper and manganese oxidized in the glaze during firing. Another glaze developed in the Sung period was exported to Japan, where it became popular with Japanese potters, and eventually, through them,

with Western potters. This was the blackish-brown *tienmu* glaze, named for a mountain near Hangchow (3-16). This **slip glaze** was called **tenmoku** in Japan, the name by which we still call it. A thick, oily-looking glaze that often collects in rolls and drops at the bottom of a piece, its surface may show "oil spots" or "hare's fur," an effect that was deliberately sought. These glazes perfected during the Sung dynasty represented a developing expertise and aesthetic sensibility in the formulation and use of glazes that would later cause a sensation when they became known in Europe.

SUNG KILNS The kilns that now fired the ware were much more advanced, often built into a hill in a series of stepped levels, sometimes as long as 165 feet (50 meters). The firing kilns were vividly portrayed by Chinese writers as giant dragons spitting fire. Most were fired with wood, although some smaller ones used coal, and the potters had to solve the problem of the free ashes spoiling the celadon glaze. Their solution was to fire each separate piece in a fire-resistant container, a **sagger** (3-17), that would protect it from the wood ash. The Lungchuan kilns could fire as many as twenty thousand saggers at one time (3-18).

Figure 3-17
In multichamber kilns (3-18), different types of saggers were used to protect the porcelain from the flame and ash during firing. **(a)** This type held a single piece of pottery upright. **(b)** Other saggers could hold several nested bowls of different sizes resting on their rims one inside the others. *Drawing by John M. Casey.*

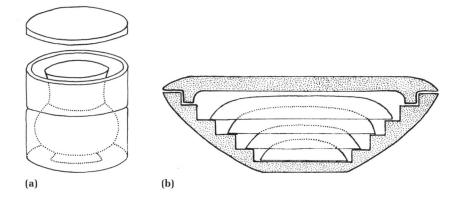

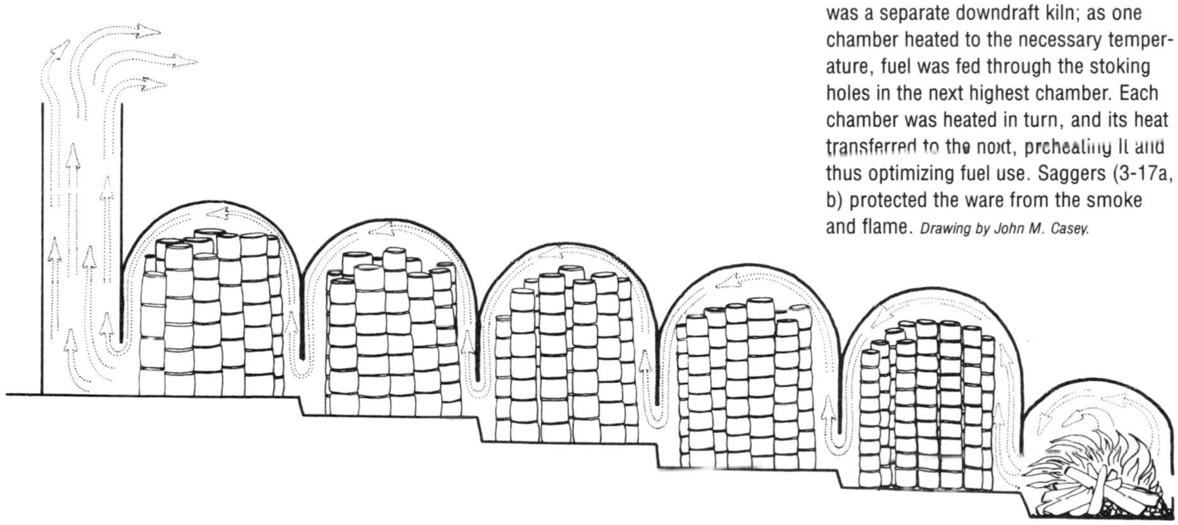

(a)   (b)

Figure 3-18
Kilns built on sloping ground were now divided into chambers. Each chamber was a separate downdraft kiln; as one chamber heated to the necessary temperature, fuel was fed through the stoking holes in the next highest chamber. Each chamber was heated in turn, and its heat transferred to the next, preheating it and thus optimizing fuel use. Saggers (3-17a, b) protected the ware from the smoke and flame. *Drawing by John M. Casey.*

UNDERGLAZE We have seen how Persia and China carried on trade across Asia. One result of this trade was that Sassanian designs were copied first by silk weavers in China and then by Chinese potters. Toward the end of the Sung dynasty, the potters had become increasingly interested in colorful, high-fire glazes and other methods of surface decoration, and had also experimented with painting floral designs in black under a transparent glaze. This type of painting, called **underglaze,** had been used in western Asia since the ninth century (3-34), and now Chinese potters tried their hands at it, entering a new phase of pictorial decoration that would have a great effect on later Japanese and European ceramics. In the fourteenth century, they experimented with using copper oxide to paint red underglazes on their porcelain, but the red was difficult to control, bleeding into the white or losing its color when fired. Giving up on the copper, they began to use cobalt for underglaze decoration. To apply underglaze, the artist first allowed the body to dry, then applied the pigment to the unglazed body, and finally covered the vessel with a semi-opaque glaze. After a single firing, the cobalt blue became suspended in the translucent glaze between the outer surface and the body, acquiring luminosity and brilliance (3-19). The Chinese cobalt, however, contained a high proportion of both manganese and iron impurities, so it fired to a dull blue; Persian cobalt, on the other hand, contained no manganese and fired to a clear blue. To satisfy the Chinese demand for brilliant color, the trading caravans brought Persian cobalt to

Figure 3-19
Mythical beasts in a fanciful landscape decorate this white porcelain plate with underglaze decoration made in the reign of Emperor Wan Li. The underglaze was painted with cobalt oxide on the unglazed body, and the plate was then covered with a semi-opaque glaze that, when fired, allowed the blue to show through. Blue and white ware, Ming dynasty, A.D. 1575–1619. Diameter 12¼ in. (31.1 cm). *By courtesy of the Board of Trustees of the Victoria & Albert Museum.*

China, where it was called *hui hui ching,* or Mohammedan blue. Eventually, the Chinese learned to refine the iron out of their own cobalt, but they could never completely eliminate the manganese, so they mixed local cobalt with some of the expensive imported oxide, using this mixture for the bulk of the blue and white ware. Only the court porcelain, made in the official Imperial Kilns, was underglazed with the pure imported cobalt.

BLUE AND WHITE EXPORT WARE Chinese blue and white ware became popular all over Asia. As the demand for it grew, much of this ware was made for export to Persia, and to increase its popularity potters decorated it with Persian inscriptions. Near the turn of the seventeenth century, however, Chinese potteries began to export a thin, rather brittle blue and white porcelain ware to Europe. Because the European potters were unable to produce such a fine, white clay body, its appearance caused a sensation there. Soon the Dutch were importing the ware by the shipload, and to satisfy Western customers, the Chinese factories adapted their shapes and decorations to European taste. They even illustrated European

folk tales on the ware, but showed the episodes occurring in the Chinese manner, in succession, as if painted on a Sung scroll.

Ming Dynasty (A.D. 1368–1644)

The Ming rulers liked to consider themselves the heirs to the refinement of the Sung dynasty, but in reality they preferred elaborate decoration rather than the simplicity of Sung design. At the Ming court, artists were honored and treated with great respect, but only if they followed the rigid rules of court conduct the emperor laid down. For example, they could be disgraced, exiled, or even executed for a slight deviation in their work such as painting an ordinary person wearing a color reserved for high officials.

Lovers of rich, luxurious living, the Ming officials commissioned lacquer ware, embroidered silk, enameled metal objects, and highly decorated ceramics—the "three-color" and "five-color" wares painted with **china paint,** or **overglaze enamel.** These **overglazes** were colored with metallic oxides and contained a great deal of lead so that they would melt at a low tempera-

Figure 3-20
An unusual Chinese kick wheel, rotated by an assistant who provided the power with his foot while hanging on to a rope. Such ingenious methods of speeding production turned the potters' workshops into the seventeenth-century equivalent of assembly lines. *Courtesy John M. Casey.*

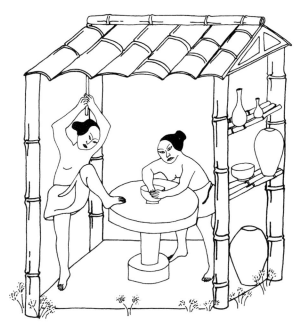

ture, around 1470°F/800°C. The overglaze enamels were painted over the body glaze and, when the pottery was given a final low-temperature firing, the overglaze melted and the lead in the main body glaze also softened it enough so that the overglaze fused into it. This many-colored type of decoration became so popular and the demand for enamel-decorated ware so great that the potter could no longer decorate his own pieces.

The potteries now became factories (3-20). We know a good deal about the Imperial Kilns, where the export porcelain and overglaze-decorated ware were produced, because a European priest who lived in China from 1698 to 1741 visited the kilns and described them in letters sent back to Europe. He wrote how the work in the decoration studios was so specialized that one decorator would paint only one type of leaf, flower, or figure, and as many as seventy potters might work on one piece of porcelain. Obviously, the personal relationship between potter and pot was now broken.

Manchu (Ching) Dynasty (A.D. 1644–1912)

Under the Manchu, Tsang Ying-hsuan, the director of the Imperial Kilns, was responsible for the development of a group of glazes that became extremely popular with connoisseurs of fine porcelain, first in China and later in Europe. Along with such colorful glazes as clear yellow, spotted yellow, turquoise, and rich black, the most famous glazes of this period were the **sang de boeuf,** or ox blood (Color Plate 3), the subtle "peach bloom," and the *claire de lune,* or moonlight, glaze. It was the fashion at this time for affluent scholars in China to collect porcelain objects covered with rich glazes. The porcelain was shaped into boxes to hold the red paste with which the scholars stamped their names on their calligraphic scrolls, as well as pots for washing or holding their brushes. These classic pieces, whose forms revived the dignified simplicity of Sung pottery, were the envy of European collectors, who spent fortunes to buy them. Under Tsang Ying-hsuan's direction overglazes were used subtly, and the *famille verte* and *famille noire* vases and bowls on which sprays of flowing trees, birds, and butterflies were painted were also avidly collected in Europe.

To compete with the Chinese imports, European potters tried for years to copy the thin, translucent porcelain, but it was not until 1710, in Germany, that porcelain was finally produced in Europe.

JAPAN

The fired-clay pottery made in Japan during the prehistoric period, when the islands that now make up Japan were isolated by the surrounding ocean, may be the earliest of its kind so far discovered in the world. This ware was made in a style called Incipient Jōmon and was decorated with bands of appliqued clay (3-21). The characteristic heavy, deeply carved Jōmon sculpture and pottery (3-22, 3-23) was produced from about 10,000 to 300 B.C. Made of a reddish low-firing earthenware, both of these types of pottery show the vigor of the early people who inhabited these islands.

Figure 3-21
Unearthed from Ishigoya cave, Suzuka city in the Nagano prefecture, Japan, this vessel is among the most ancient pottery yet found — about 10,000 B.C. The word *jo* means straw rope or mat, while the word *mon* means design, indicating that the designs were derived from cord patterns. The pottery of this period is also called Incipient Jōmon, because this recently discovered pottery predates earlier finds and displays the beginnings of the characteristic decoration of Jōmon pottery. *Courtesy of the Museum of Archeology, Kokugakuin University, Tokyo, Japan.*

▼ **Figure 3-22**
The name Jōmon, meaning "cord pattern," is applied to a type of Japanese pottery that was decorated, as is this pot, with incised lines and applied clay. The name is now applied to a style that was produced over a long period from about 10,000 B.C. to c. 300 B.C. Ht. 3⅞ in. (10 cm). Japan, late Jōmon period, first millennium B.C. *Copyright British Museum.*

Figure 3-23
Like the Late Jōmon pottery (3-22), Jōmon sculptured figures were carved with swirls and textured areas alternating with highly polished sections. Full of vitality, they may have had a fertility significance. Aomoni Prefecture, Japan, Late Jōmon, first millennium B.C. *The Seattle Art Museum, Floyd A. Naramore Memorial Purchase Fund, 76.35.*

The early inhabitants of the isolated islands of Japan practiced an animistic religion, in which the world was given life by supernatural beings called *kami*. They believed that these all-pervading spirits breathed life into everything that existed — trees, rivers, ocean waves, and plants. Just as all of nature was animated by the *kami,* so too were the skillful hands of a fisher, an archer, or a potter. This vitality, which the hands of the potter passed on to the clay, was a characteristic of native Japanese ceramics, one that manifested itself through the later centuries despite continuing influences from China and Korea.

With mountains and deep valleys separating villages from each other, Japanese society developed intense local rivalries from the very earliest days, and civil war between chieftans and clans was almost constant. During centuries of upheaval, artisans lived quietly in their villages, staying on the same land for generations, digging clay from the same bank, and firing their kilns on the same hillside. As a result, Japanese potters developed an intense personal relationship with clay and kept this characteristic attitude for centuries. Their innate understanding of clay still appears in the most modern work (Color Plate 53).

JŌMON POTTERY AND SCULPTURE As mentioned earlier, the first inhabitants of the Japanese islands are among the earliest known to have learned to fire pottery. Made of a reddish earthenware, their rough handbuilt pottery, produced about 10,000 B.C., was called Incipient Jōmon (3-21), meaning "cord," because the decoration consisted of cord impressions along with carving (3-22). The potters of the Mid to Late Jōmon periods also made vigorously modeled and carved male and female figures (3-23), possibly fertility figures, that probably were used for rituals associated with appeasing the nature spirits. The Jōmon vessels and figures reflect the Japanese response to the earthy quality of their material, and are among the most impressive of humanity's creations in clay. Although there naturally are differences in the ceramics produced within such a long span of time that has been divided by art historians into Incipient, Early, Mid, and Late Jōmon, the overall characteristics of the pottery and sculpture of the entire period are similar: Thick-walled and built by a slab or coil method, probably without a turntable, this pottery was made of a coarse reddish earthenware clay containing a considerable amount of impurities. Like all early ceramics, it was low-fired, either in open fires or in simple pit kilns.

Chinese Influences on Korea and Japan

The Korean peninsula, close as it is to China, was deeply influenced by Chinese thought and art. By the beginning of the third century B.C., a new people, the Yayoi, immigrated into Japan from the north by way of Korea. These Korean immigrants had been much influenced by China, and among other innovations they brought the potter's wheel to Japan. As Japanese potters learned to use the wheel, they quite naturally modified the characteristics of their indigenous pottery; their pots became thin-walled and rather graceful in shape.

KOREA

Although moving back and forth between Japan, Korea, and early China becomes confusing, it is necessary in order to understand how these cultures influenced each other. The original prehistoric people of Korea, the Yemaeks, who settled the peninsula in a time known to historians as the Plain Coarse Pottery period, apparently came from the north. Legend has it that Tan'gun, the founder of the first kingdom, was the son of a female bear and a Yamaek, who himself was a son of the divine creator. His kingdom was said to have been founded in 2333 B.C.

Documented Korean history, however, begins at the end of the second century B.C., when the Han dynasty armies from China invaded and occupied an area of the northern Korean peninsula, holding it until A.D. 313. Buddhism also arrived with the invaders, and although the local inhabitants resisted the new religion for some time, it eventually became the main religion in Korea, whence it was taken to Japan. While the Chinese invaders settled in the north, the native Koreans established a series of states further south — the Three Kingdoms — of which the Silla is the most interesting to us because of its characteristic ceramics. Along with clay figures and objects made to be placed in tombs (3-24, 3-25), the Silla pot-

Figure 3-24
An ash-glazed stoneware tomb model of a Korean warrior wearing leather-plated armor. The funnel on the back of his horse and the spout on the horse's chest suggest it was a ritual vessel for pouring libations. The ring on the spout probably held a "dangler" of clay links, a characteristic decoration on such vessels.
Ht. 9¼ in. (25.5 cm). North Kyongsang province, Korea. Old Silla dynasty, fifth to sixth century A.D. *Courtesy National Museum of Korea, Seoul.*

Figure 3-25
This stoneware chariot model from a tomb of the Old Silla dynasty in Korea reproduces all the details of the carts in use at that time. It is made with movable wheels. North Kyongsang province. Old Silla dynasty, fifth to sixth century A.D. *Courtesy National Museum of Korea, Seoul.*

ters also produced pottery, frequently made in several parts, with the bottom perforated to create a stand (3-26). By the time of the Tang dynasty in China (A.D. 617–906), the Silla rulers had unified the three kingdoms and formed an alliance with the imperial Chinese court. Goods were exchanged actively with China, and Korean scholars and functionaries went there to study the economic and cultural policies of the Tang court. Those at home in Korea founded a university that taught Confucian studies, and throughout the Korean peninsula, Buddhism grew in influence, while Chinese art and ceramics continued to be popular. At this time, the technique of intentional glazing reached Korea and was adopted by the Korean potters and through Korea eventually reached Japan.

Figure 3-26
Fired to stoneware hardness, the gray clay of this jar is covered in places with a natural ash glaze. The openwork pedestal base is typical of Old Silla pottery, and the incised line drawings of deer suggest a relationship with the northern tribes, who used deer horns in shamanistic practices. Uljn-gun, Korea. Old Silla dynasty, fifth to sixth century A.D. *Courtesy National Museum of Korea, Seoul.*

JAPANESE OLD TOMB PERIOD (c. A.D. 300–600)

During this period, named for its many tombs, entire communities of potters came, or were brought, to Japan from Korea. The ware they made—a pottery known as Sue—was fashioned of a high firing, dense gray body into what was undoubtedly a luxury item (3-26). At the same time, proto-porcelain was being brought to Japan from Korea, and with it arrived the technique of applying glazes.

Although the Japanese potters, like the Chinese and Koreans, now became dedicated to refining clay and glaze, some of the vitality of the earlier Jōmon period was maintained in the vigorously modeled *haniwa* sculptures made during the Old Tomb period (3-27). Legend tells us that the *haniwa,* literally "clay circles," were originally made as substitutes for the live personal attendants who had formerly been left to starve to death half-buried in the ground around the tombs of notables. In actuality, the sculptures were derived from the simple cylinders that were embedded in the ground around the mounded earth of the tombs, possibly to keep the earth from sliding. These *haniwa* pictured the everyday life of Japan, portraying warriors, farmers, singers and dancers, houses, horses, and other animals, and some, sculpted as waterbirds, were placed so that they appear to be swimming on the water of the shallow ponds next to the mounds.

Tradition tells us that a thirteenth-century Japanese Buddhist priest, Toshiro Kato Shirozaemon, went to China to learn more about ceramics techniques, and that when he returned in 1227, he carried some Chinese clay with him. When he later discovered good clay in Japan, he was said to have founded the pottery industry of Japan in the Seto area, still the largest pottery-producing area in the country. The ceramics industry in Japan then expanded, and crafts guilds became part of Japan's highly organized class system.

Figure 3-27
The cut-out eyes and mouth of this *haniwa* warrior give his face expression as well as let the vapor and gases escape in the firing. He is fully armed with helmet, sword, and arm protectors. The *haniwa* were originally simple clay cylinders sunk in the ground around the mounded royal tombs, in Japan. Later they were modeled to depict dancers, singers, farmers, warriors, and animals. Earthenware, Fujioka, Japan, Late Tumulus period, c. sixth century A.D. *Courtesy Asian Art Museum of San Francisco, The Avery Brundage Collection, B60 S204.*

Japanese Kilns

Whether or not this Chinese-trained potter was actually the founder of the industry, there is no doubt that much of the technique at that time originally came from China and that the workshops in Japan fired their stoneware (3-28) in kilns. Sometimes known as snake kilns because of their length and form, these kilns were built up a hill in one long tunnel with no interior dividing walls (3-29). Called *anagama,* they were

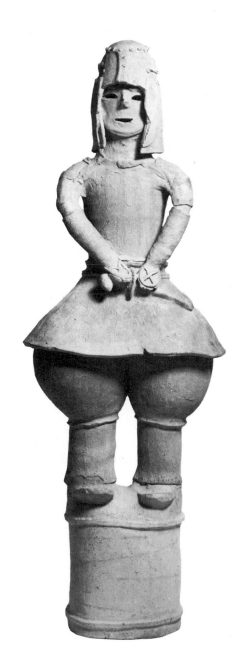

Figure 3-28
Comparing this ash-glazed Japanese stoneware jar with a similar Han jar (3-10), it is clear how much the early stoneware of Japan owed to Chinese influences. However, the lively, almost awkward way in which the narrow neck sits on its swelling body exemplifies the direct and vital Japanese attitude toward clay. Ninth or tenth century A.D. *By courtesy of the Board of Trustees of the Victoria & Albert Museum.*

modeled on the sloping kilns of China and Korea. In them, the Japanese potters fired pottery whose glazes were meant to imitate the celadon and other Chinese glazes of the Sung period. But because the Japanese lacked the centuries of accumulated knowledge of the Sung potters, their ware was coarser and coated with a greenish and sometimes yellow glaze that did not attain the quality of the glazes the Chinese potters had developed by that time.

As Buddhism became the dominant religion in Japan, Japanese sculptors formed sculptures of the Buddha and the heavenly beings associated with Buddhism. These sculptures were similar to the Chinese and Indian images. In the Nara period (A.D. 710–784), the Japanese created temple figures—some made of clay mixed with straw and built over wooden forms—that reflected the restrained spiritual quality of the Buddhist religion. These unfired figures were coated with fine clay and then painted; incredibly, some have survived to our day.

Zen and the Tea Ceremony

The tea ceremonies that had become popular in China during the Tang dynasty were intimately associated with ceramics. Although many Chi-

Figure 3-29
In early Japanese snake kilns like this one, modeled on similar Chinese and Korean kilns, the pots were packed on top of one another on circular stands with slanting bases to keep them level on the sloping floor. Sometimes the ware was placed in saggers to protect it from the flames and ash that roared up through the kiln as the firing reached its height. *Drawing by John M. Casey.*

nese connoisseurs preferred white or celadon tea cups, others felt that the black *tienmu* glazed tea bowls were the most effective background for the foamy green tea that was beaten to a froth before serving. During the Sung dynasty in China, the Chan sect of Buddhism had emerged; like the Taoists they emphasized self-cultivation and meditation. Called Zen in Japan, this sect developed a highly ritualized ceremony, in which the drinking of tea and its attendant rituals became a means of acquiring nobility and purity of thought. Brought to Japan by returning Buddhist monks around A.D. 1200, Zen became an integral part of the search for enlightenment in Japan, where all aspects of the ceremony expressed the Zen ideal of simplicity and refined poverty. Chinese tea bowls were introduced, along with tea houses where the ceremony was performed. The participants in the ceremony walked through a stylized garden, approached the tea house on steppingstones, and crouched to enter through a low door in a symbolic leave-taking of the outside world and a humbling of themselves in preparation for the ceremony.

Figure 3-30

Classic Japanese raku tea bowls were carved in one piece, not thrown or coiled. The shape of the lip, the "tea pool" in the bottom, and the interior spiral that leads the tea to the drinker's mouth were all regulated by strict rules. Raku, earthenware with black-brown glaze. Japan, seventeenth century A.D.

By courtesy of the Board of Trustees of the Victoria & Albert Museum.

Tea Ceramics

An influential Japanese tea master, Sen no Rikyu (1521–1591) preferred to use the simple rice bowls of Korea and the brown and black iron glaze (called *tienmu* in China and in Japan called *tenmoku*) for his tea bowls. Others followed his lead, and soon there was a demand for these *chato,* or tea ceramics, which included tea caddies, bowls, jars, and flowerpots along with the tea bowls (3-30). First made in Kyoto in the sixteenth century by a Korean who had married a Japanese woman, these roughly shaped tea bowls were made on his death by his widow. Her son Chojiro (1515–1592) carried on the tradition, as did a grandson, who was given the right to mark the character *raku* ("pleasure") on the bottom of his bowls. From then on, successive generations of the family made **raku** tea bowls in Kyoto into the twentieth century.

These Japanese *chawan* (tea bowls) were pinched from a solid lump of clay, then carved into their final shape. This method produced a bowl with no joints and was done for practical as well as aesthetic reasons, because the bowls were subjected to damaging temperature changes when they were placed in and removed from the red-hot raku kiln. This firing, done in a special small kiln, generally created cracks, pits, and other variations in the glaze, individualizing each bowl. The coarse clay body from which the tea bowls were made did not conduct heat quickly, and part of the enjoyment of the ceremony was the gentle, slow warming of the hands by the hot tea served in them. The experience included an appreciation of the rough surface of the bowls as they were held in the hands. Each piece of *chato* expressed the character of the master potter who made it; some famous bowls were given names and are now classified as National Treasures of Japan. Also among the treasured tea ceramics are the *cha-ire,* or tea containers, in which the finely powdered tea was kept.

Bizen Kilns

Among the most famous of the tea ceramics were those that came from the **Bizen** kilns, where a rustic type of pottery greatly valued by tea masters was fired in a deliberate effort to achieve accidental fire markings (3-31). To create a wide range of surface effects on one pot—rosy red,

Figure 3-31
Bizen ware was made of coarse, low-fire clay fired over a long period of time. In order to achieve the dark fire splashes and varied surface effects that appealed to the Zen masters, potters introduced straw into the kiln, causing local reduction. This jar exemplifies the rough surfaces and asymmetrical shapes of the Bizen tea ware. Earthenware. Japan, seventeenth century A.D. *By courtesy of the Board of Trustees of the Victoria & Albert Museum.*

matt black, greenish glaze, with areas of opalescence—the potters packed the *cha-ire* inside other pots lined with straw, or placed bags of straw next to them in the climbing *anagama* kilns. As the straw burned, it produced areas of local reduction that were responsible for the variations on the surface.

Both the raku method of placing tea bowls in the hot fire and the Bizen use of local reduction firings have had an influence on contemporary Western pottery, especially since the resurgence of interest in Zen. Potters all over the world now use tenmoku glazes, fire in wood kilns of Japanese-derived style, and practice variations of the raku firing process, some of which the early tea masters might have difficulty recognizing (15-31). They probably would, however, feel in accord with the aesthetic attitudes of contemporary potters who use raku methods and appreciate the expressive qualities of their work.

Japanese Porcelain

Japanese potters did not limit themselves to these deliberately rough wares produced in the Tamba,

Tokoname, Bizen, and Shigaraki kilns. At the beginning of the sixteenth century, a Japanese potter visited China to study the porcelain industry there, hoping, without success, to find the necessary ingredients for porcelain in Japan. Finally, in around 1605, an immigrant Korean potter, Ri Sampei, did find kaolin in the Arita district of Japan, and the porcelain industry founded there grew so rapidly that by 1664, forty-five thousand pieces of porcelain were being shipped to Holland each year. Japan quickly outpaced China in the export trade, and so many trees were cut down to fuel the kilns that the government restricted the building of new ones. By this time, the Japanese kilns, like those of China, were divided into chambers, and potters had also learned from China the techniques of underglazing with cobalt blue and using brightly colored overglazes. With a natural sense of design and skill with the brush, Japanese potters created some enameled ware of great beauty, but like Chinese potters, they often had to satisfy the Western taste for garish colors and overelaborate forms. To speed production, many people worked on each piece, which meant that much of the ware exported to Europe did not meet the high aesthetic standard demanded by knowledgeable collectors in Japan.

Edo Period (1615–1868)

Despite the emphasis on mass production of export ware, there were potters in Japan who maintained a close personal relationship with clay, forming their pottery themselves with restraint and decorating it with graceful underglaze brush paintings. In the seventeenth century, the capital of Japan moved from Kyoto to Edo, from which city the period takes its name. Two brothers, potter Ogata Kenzan (1663–1743) and painter Ogata Kōrin (1658–1716), remained in Kyoto, however, and applied their highly developed taste and visual awareness to ceramics (3-32). Inspired by nature, they often worked together, and both signed the pieces on which they collaborated. The decoration was brushed on simple shapes with masterly strokes in brown or black on a white clay body, or on a colored clay covered with a white slip (3-32). Other Edo period potters who remained in a close relationship with clay greatly admired the Kenzan heritage, and throughout the years that name has been bestowed to honor potters considered worthy of it. In the twentieth century, one Western potter, Bernard Leach of

Figure 3-32
Ogata Kenzan, the potter, signed this square tray on the base, and the painter, Ogata Kōrin, his brother, signed it above his brush painting of irises. Stoneware tray by Ogata Kenzan, decorated by Ogata Kōrin, Kyoto ware. 8⅝ in. square (21.7 cm). Edo period, 1615–1868. *Courtesy of the Freer Gallery of Art, Smithsonian Institution, Washington, D.C. (acc. no. 02.220).*

England (8-2), was honored with the name Kenzan VII.

Today, Japanese ceramics encompasses an active industry, a vigorous, honored traditional craft, and it also includes many artists working with a contemporary approach to sculpture (Color Plate 53).

ANCIENT WESTERN ASIA

We must backtrack now to the sun-baked areas of western Asia where first farming communities, then urban centers, developed on the fertile land beside the rivers. That the early inhabitants there recognized and honored the malleable qualities of clay is made clear in the *Poem of Creation* from about 1500 B.C. In that epic, the creation of the deities, kings, ordinary people, mountains—in fact, the whole universe—was ascribed to the god Ea, who was believed to have pinched the first people out of clay.

The early societies of western Asia used clay for innumerable objects, from the slabs of clay on which records were stamped (1-3) to a wide va-

riety of domestic wares. Several theories exist as to how potters first developed the firing of clay in western Asia, but one possible explanation is that the experience of drying and hardening clay bricks in the sun, along with the domestic activity of mixing, forming, and baking grains into bread in ovens, may have provided the needed background for developing a ceramics technology. In whatever way the potters there first acquired this knowledge, archaeology tells us that by at least 6500 B.C. they had begun to fire pottery and by around 4000 B.C. had learned how to use some form of wheel. Eventually, they developed the true potter's wheel, which may have been the factor that transformed pottery from a homemade product for domestic use into an important trade commodity. With the growth of large religious centers, the demand for votive figures also grew, so these images were no longer individually made, but were mass-produced in molds of fired clay.

By the middle of the second millennium B.C., when the development of glass-making techniques led to the use of applied glazes on pottery, western Asia had become an important center of ceramics production. Although the original discovery of glazes was probably an accident, their refinement was certainly a conscious effort, proved by the glaze formulas and instructions for applying them to greenware that were stamped into damp clay tablets—the first potters' glaze notebooks. Pottery was now carried by the trade caravans that crisscrossed the deserts and mountains of Asia, and through this trade the ornamental motifs and shapes of one area influenced the work of potters in distant areas. In fact, scholars can now trace trade routes and the migrations of ancient Asians by studying the varying shapes and decorations of excavated pottery.

Early Architectural Ceramics

As early as 2600 B.C., before glazes were developed, the urge to decorate buildings was strong, and in Sumeria and Babylonia, pegs of fired clay painted with red, black, and white earth pig-

ments were pushed into the mud walls of important buildings to form geometric mosaic patterns. Later, the sun-dried brick walls of Assyrian, Babylonian, and Persian buildings were covered with fired glazed tiles that protected them from the weather and added colorful decoration. These tiles were first made—probably in press molds—in relief, with images of humans, lions, bulls, and mythical animals (3-33). They were then coated with colorful opaque **tin glazes** that covered the reddish color of the earthenware clay.

Once the tile-makers had learned to add opacity and color to glazes, they began to experiment with ways to use several colors on a tile. One of these methods separated the areas of the design with raised lines of slip that kept the glazes from running into each other. Their techniques of glazing tiles were handed down through generations of potters, and in later centuries tiles became extremely important in the rich ornamentation of mosques and palaces built throughout the Islamic world, while the glazes and underglazes

Figure 3-33
The Ishtar Gate, built in the sixth century B.C. in Babylon, was decorated with tile reliefs of bulls. Tin-lead glazes. Babylon, c. 580 B.C. *Courtesy Bildarchiv Preussischer Kulturbesitz, Berlin.*

were refined to achieve elegant decoration on plates and bowls (3-34).

Around 550 B.C. the Persians had conquered large areas in western Asia, Egypt, India, and Greece, absorbing cultural and artistic influences from the past as well as from all parts of their empire, and combining these influences with their own taste for the ornate and luxurious to create a new art style called Sassanid. Persian cities became the meeting place of two worlds — central Asia, India, and China to the east, and Syria and Rome to the west. Then, in the seventh century A.D., when the Moslems conquered Persia and other eastern territories, the taste of the Sassanid Persians began to influence Islamic ceramics and the Persians' knowledge of lead-tin glazes was passed on to wherever Islamic styles spread.

ISLAMIC CERAMICS

At the beginning of the fourteenth century, Abu'l Qasim, who lived in Kashan, wrote a ceramic "how-to" book that gave, among many recipes, one for a clay body that became a popular substitute for Chinese porcelain. It consisted of a glass **frit,** quartz, and white clay, and was formed on the wheel. Because the clay was not very plastic, vessels had to be made in small sections. Later sections would be either thrown onto the already leather-hard first section or made separately and luted to it when it too became leather hard. Then, when the entire vessel was leather hard, the potter would thin it by gradually scraping away clay from the walls as the vessel turned on the wheel. Vessels made of this clay body, if thinned enough, could become translucent like the Chinese porcelains but were never as hard. Abu'l Qasim also gave directions for heating quartz and soda ash for many hours, constantly stirring it and then throwing it into a pit full of water to form the frit, which was eventually ground into powder. He described the terrifying, thunderous roar that was produced when the water and molten glass met, saying that if anyone had not seen and heard it he would fall trembling on his knees.

Ceramic tiles became important elements in Moslem architecture. One factor of great importance in the development of Islamic art was the prohibition in the Koran, the Moslem religious text, against the portrayal of human figures in the mosques or on pottery used for religious pur-

Figure 3-34
The inscription in Kufic script on this Iranian plate creates an abstract design but also preaches a lesson: "Deliberation before work protects you from regret." The potter decorated the plate with underglaze on white slip-covered earthenware in an attempt to copy the underglaze-decorated porcelain of Sung China. Diameter 14⅝ in. (37.2 cm). Persia (Iran), Samanid period, tenth century A.D. *Courtesy The Saint Louis Art Museum, purchase.*

poses. These same strictures limited much of the ceramic decoration to abstract patterns, floral motifs, and stylized calligraphic proverbs or quotations from the Koran, although human images did appear on some of the pottery made for secular use. Far from limiting the creativity of potters, however, the regulations forced them to develop a rich style of floral decoration, called *arabesque* (3-35, 3-36).

Tile Decoration

The tile-makers of the Moslem world used their artistry to apply these motifs to ceramic decoration on mosques, minarets, prayer niches, and palaces (3-35). Their brilliantly colored tiles were used on buildings throughout the Islamic world from Persia to Anatolia, Turkestan, Afghanistan, and Spain, encompassing a wide variety of styles that flowered during an equally wide span of time — from about the ninth to the eighteenth centuries A.D. A few very early tiles survive from

Figure 3-35
Earthenware tiles glazed with opaque tin glazes decorated palaces, mosques, and tombs in Persia and later throughout the Moslem world. Brilliantly colored in blues, greens, and yellows, the tiles were often cut in the shape of stars, leaves, and flowers. Vines and flowers twine in interlaced decorations called *arabesque,* while Arabic script is used as decoration. From a tomb. 21 in. square (53.4 cm). Persia, thirteenth century A.D.
By courtesy of the Board of Trustees of the Victoria & Albert Museum.

the ninth century, decorated with **luster glaze** painted over the base glaze and refired in a reduction atmosphere. In the thirteenth century, the tiles were often cut into small shapes that were carefully fitted together to create mosaics. Over the centuries, the tile-makers produced tile decorations ranging from simple turquoise and cobalt designs (Color Plate 6) on tombs or mosques to elaborate multicolor panels that created a garden-like atmosphere in the palaces and harems of the Ottoman Turks. In the sixteenth century, the tile-makers in Turkey discovered that an iron-rich clay (called Armenian bole) would give a brilliant red underglaze, and they applied it thickly.

Luster Ware

It was also against the teaching of Islam to use precious metals on earth, for the Koran taught that the faithful would be rewarded in paradise with vessels of gold and silver. In addition, in Sassanid Persia there was a shortage of silver, so silver vessels became even more expensive and difficult to obtain. Potters, therefore, looked for a substitute material that would give the appearance of metal but would still allow its owners to remain good Moslems. This led them to develop a form of overglaze called luster. This iridescent decoration was made with metallic salts—copper or silver, for example—mixed with a paste of gum or clay and painted on top of the glaze. The piece was then given a low firing at 1112°F/600°C, in a reducing atmosphere, after which the kiln was sealed and allowed to cool. Although the Egyptians had used luster earlier, it was the Islamic potters who had perfected it, using it with rich effect). As the religious climate of Islam grew less strict, potters did begin to portray the human figure (3-37) along with animals and

Figure 3-36
Persian potters often used black, white, and blue glazes on pottery or tiles. The inscriptions on such bowls might read "Sovereignty is God's" or "Blessings and beneficence." Kashan, Persia, thirteenth century A.D.

Figure 3-37
Opaque white tin glaze makes an excellent background for colored glazes and iridescent yellow luster overglaze decoration on a bowl from Kahr, near Teheran, Persia (Iran). Diameter 7½ in. (19.1 cm). Late twelfth to early thirteenth century A.D.

birds, sometimes combining them into fantasy
creatures or using animal shapes for ceramic jugs
or other objects (3-38). But the human figures did
not appear in the tiles that enhanced the walls of
the prayer niches. These continued to display
pious inscriptions and arabesques of plant forms.

As the Islamic styles in art spread west through
the Mediterranean and along the northern coasts
of Africa, pottery techniques and designs from
the East changed the native art wherever local
inhabitants were converted to Islam. Then, when
the Moors crossed to Spain around A.D. 700, the
influence of Islamic art reached the European
continent.

INDIA

Despite the oceans and mountains that ring the
vast territory of India, the land has received numerous waves of migrating peoples. These in-
fluxes have ranged from the invasions of the
Aryans in about 1500 B.C. through those of the
Iranians, Greeks, Arabs, and finally the British,
in 1815. As a result, there has always been great
diversity in the peoples of India, and the three
main religions—Hinduism, Jainism, and Buddhism—have offered the artist a rich heritage of

images upon which to draw. Clay had been an
essential part of Indian life for thousands of
years. Not only was the earth of the river valleys
essential to the Indian people for their livelihood,
but it was also a source of the material they
needed for making essential vessels, buildings,
toys, and religious images.

The artist in India was a member of a guild
and worked closely with representatives of the
different religions who instructed him in the
complex symbolism of the cults so that he might
depict the deities with their proper attributes and
in the proper attitudes. To the Indian viewer, the
sensual and erotic images are always religious,
expressing spirituality through the beauty of the
human form and its sexuality.

Although the artists who created the sculptures decorating the temples were anonymous,
their gestures have been preserved for centuries
in the fired clay of the terra-cotta reliefs that remain from temples and monasteries (3-39). The
best-known temples in India were built of stone,
but in areas where stone was rare, itinerant bands
of terra-cotta craftsmen made and decorated brick
temples well into the nineteenth century. A symbol of the fertility of the earth, the clay they used
on these temples was in itself sacred. Working
under a master, the guild members made the

Figure 3-39
Sensuously modeled figures of nature spirits and fertility deities covered the facades of the temples in India. Whether modeled in clay or carved in stone, they exemplified a sculptural tradition in which the forms of the human body imply the bounty of the earth. Fragment of a relief from a temple or monastery near Allahabad, India. c. A.D. 700. *By courtesy of the Board of Trustees of the Victoria & Albert Museum.*

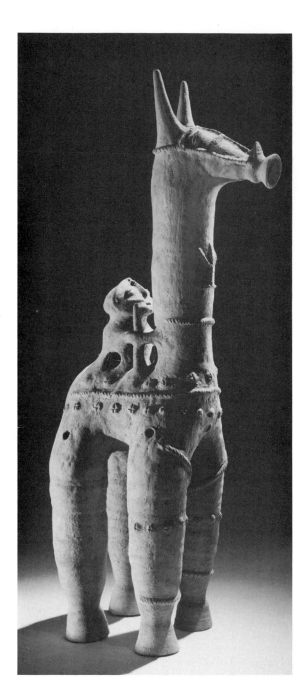

bricks and built the temples, while the modelers made the sculptures of fertility deities and mythological personages that decorated the facades. Generally, the sculpture was made in molds and then worked over when leather hard. The clay was frequently burnished and the decorative details were incised with pointed instruments made of bone or bamboo. Looking at the sculpture, we can see how the modeler used each of these processes. Finally, the reliefs were fired in kilns built at the site and were installed on the temples.

Today, the tradition of clay sculpture in India is still alive in rural areas, where village shrines are decorated with deities and protective spirits of fired clay (Color Plate 7). Ranging in size from small votive sculptures up to huge fired-in-place horses, these rural ritual images express the hopes and fears of an agricultural society dependent on the weather for the success of their crops. The Spirit Riders who protected the village fields, riding their boundaries at night, were often depicted in clay (3-40). In addition to the fired-clay figures that remain in place, large unfired-clay figures are made for local religious festivals, and when the ceremonies are over they are placed in the river to disintegrate and return to the earth.

Figure 3-40
The tradition of modeling votive images from the earth is a long one in India, and the horse has been a favorite image there since the remote past, symbolizing hope and protection. It is the steed of the Spirit Riders, who are believed to guard the villages. Votive horse and rider, terracotta. Bhil tribe. Ht. about 3 ft. (91.4 cm). India, twentieth century. *Courtesy Philadelphia Museum of Art: Purchased (67-197-1).*

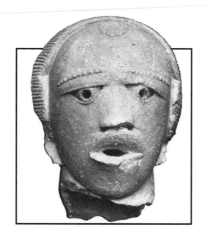

4

Africa

The African continent is vast, encompassing many different natural environments and peoples. Wide-open grassland; hot, dry deserts; deep rainforests, and cool mountain highlands — each is part of Africa's rich natural heritage. Just as the land is infinitely varied, so are the people who have lived on it. Like all major continents, Africa has seen a procession of peoples moving across its land for thousands of years, hunting its wild animals, driving their domestic herds to new grazing lands, moving on in search of a better place to live, resulting in a complex intermingling of peoples and racial strains. The life styles, beliefs, the ceremonies, legends, and arts of the African peoples vary greatly from group to group and place to place, for this reason, we cannot speak of African art or African ceramics as if they were the products of a single culture (4-1).

EARLY AFRICA

At one time, what is now the Sahara Desert was grassland, supporting herds of animals, the home of a pastoral people who covered the walls of caves with paintings and carvings of animals. They also made pottery that has been found along with the cave paintings, dating from between 4000 and 1200 B.C. Then, when years of drought hit the area and vegetation died, the people and

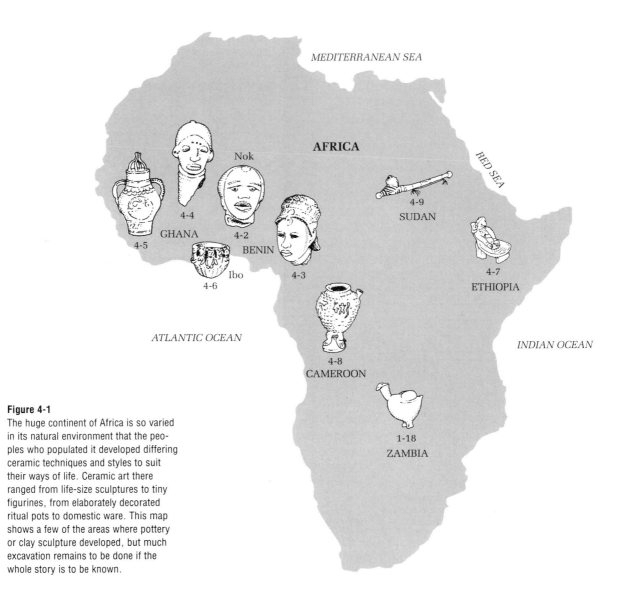

Figure 4-1
The huge continent of Africa is so varied in its natural environment that the peoples who populated it developed differing ceramic techniques and styles to suit their ways of life. Ceramic art there ranged from life-size sculptures to tiny figurines, from elaborately decorated ritual pots to domestic ware. This map shows a few of the areas where pottery or clay sculpture developed, but much excavation remains to be done if the whole story is to be known.

animals moved on, leaving behind them only ceramic shards and the paintings on the walls.

Eventually, groups of people living in different parts of the African continent settled into agricultural ways of life that allowed them to develop crafts. As in most other early cultures, clay and metal working developed here simultaneously—not surprising, since both pursuits are fire-related. In Upper Nigeria, for example, the wives of the iron workers were the potters.

NOK (c. 500 B.C.–A.D. 200)

In northern Nigeria, near the village of Nok and at Taruga, iron-working furnaces, tin mines, and iron tools dating from around the fourth or fifth century B.C. have been found along with frag-

ments of almost life-sized terra-cotta sculptures of humans and animals (4-2). The technical knowledge required to build and safely fire such large sculptures suggests that people must have been working with clay here for some time. The expressive ways in which the sculptors indicated human feelings suggest a rich artistic heritage. The sculptures, made of rough, heavily-tempered clay and exhibiting a sophisticated simplification of form, speak to us across the centuries.

Whether these sculptures represent important persons or ancestor figures we do not know. We do know, however, that Nok was one of the cultures in Africa to develop a royal court art, centering around the king or chief, and that sculptor-potters in these societies were often retained by the king to create ceremonial and status objects in addition to ancestor figures. Ancestors were of

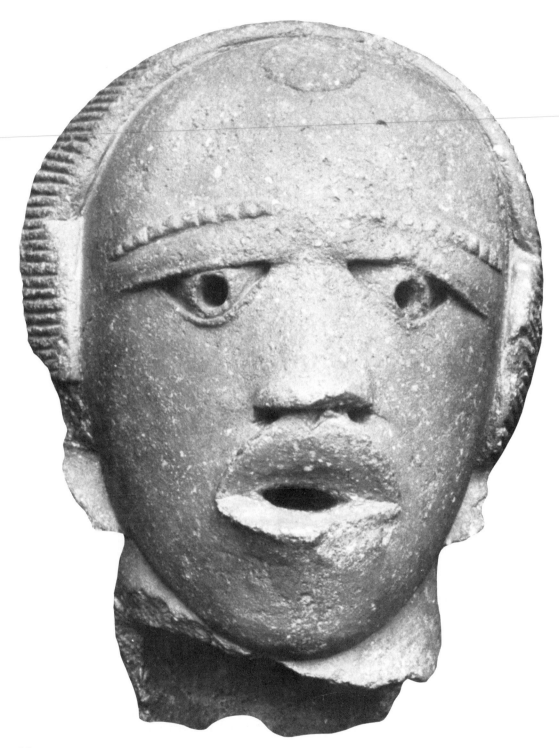

Figure 4-2
Ancient Nok sculptors shaped clay into images that express a sense of urgent life. The faces appear carved, suggesting that their forms may have been based on wood carving. Almost life-size, the figures are a remarkable technical achievement in building and firing clay. Nok culture, second century B.C. *Courtesy Jos Museum, Nigeria.*

the greatest importance among many peoples in Africa, who believed that if the traditions the ancestors handed down were broken, misfortunes would result.

Interestingly, women today in some of the small groups living in this area make pottery similar in shape to ancient Nok pottery and also occasionally make sculptures for grave memorials and ritual use. It is possible that they are the inheritors of the Nok culture, but, like so much in the story of African ceramics, this is only conjecture. Until more archaeological exploration has been done there, our knowledge of the history of clay working in Africa will be far from complete.

IFE (c. A.D. 800–1400)

One of the royal courts of Africa centered in the city of Ile Ife, in southwestern Nigeria, where, from around A.D. 800 to 1400, the Yoruba people produced a rich and lively art. There have been no archaeological finds yet that can fill the gaps in our knowledge about the years between the end of the Nok culture and the flowering of the Ife culture. It is possible that the two cultures were not connected, but some similarities between them suggest that the Nok sculpture may have influenced Ife sculptors (4-3). Both cultures made large, almost life-sized terra-cotta sculptures on which the forms were simplified, and some of the detailing of beaded decorations and hair on the bodies are similar. But the Ife sculptures are more realistic than those of the Nok sculptors, and closer in many ways to Benin sculpture, in which individuals were represented in terracotta portraits that were models for bronze casts.

By the eleventh century A.D., the sculptors of Ife were skilled in bronze casting, a craft that relied on clay for the crucibles in which the metal was melted and the molds in which bronze objects were cast. The original images from which the molds were made were also made of clay.

BENIN (c. A.D. 1250–1897)

In Benin as in the Nok culture, sculpture was a court art focused on the king, who, it is said, brought a talented Ife sculptor, Iqu-igha, to Benin to teach the local sculptors the craft of working

Figure 4-3
Ife sculptures are more realistic than Nok sculptures, but some of the details of clothing and hair are similar. The dates of Ife sculptures are uncertain; some scholars date them at A.D. 600–1200 and others at A.D. 800–1400. Terra-cotta. *Nigerian Museums. Copyright British Museum.*

in bronze. As in other African cultures, preserving the memory of historic happenings and the images of royalty and their ancestors was one of the main assignments of sculptors. Most of the known Benin sculpture consists of portraits cast in bronze, but enough terra-cotta portraits have been found to show that clay was undoubtedly the material in which the original models were created. Although the Benin culture probably dates back to the thirteenth century, its sculpture flourished in the 1500s.

Figure 4-4
Terra-cotta sculptures like this one were apparently used in Ashanti funeral ceremonies or as memorials to the dead. This example was sculpted more than a hundred years ago by a craftsman of the Kwahu, an Ashanti group. Ht. 15 in. (38 cm). Kajebi, Ghana. *Copyright British Museum.*

RITUAL CERAMICS

What we call art has served ceremonial and ritualistic functions in many cultures throughout the world, and the ceremonial and ritual ceramic objects all had functions, albeit not everyday ones, that were just as essential to religious ceremonies or rituals as pieces of domestic pottery were to daily life (4-6).

In earlier days in Africa, the ritual objects were made for use and were associated with the passage from one period of life to another, or with death; in Ashanti graveyards, terra-cotta sculptures of heads were given an honored place, probably as memorials to the deceased (4-4). Many ceremonial objects and ceramic vessels were used by the secret male societies that governed the initiation of youths into manhood, while others were related to the puberty rites of the women. Still other pots were used in ceremonies, festivals, and rituals dedicated to the spirits of crops and fertility or to bringing good fortune (4-5).

Figure 4-6
The Ibo, who lived west of the Niger River, placed sculptured pots on altars dedicated to Ifijiok, the Yam spirit. This pot shows images of the chiefs, their wives and children, and attendant musicians. Ht. 13¾ in. (35 cm). Ibo, Osisa, Nigeria. *Copyright British Museum.*

One outstanding group of sculptured pots from the Ibo village of Osisa, on the west bank of the Niger River, was made to be placed in the village shrines dedicated to Ifijiok, the Yam spirit (4-6).

Other ceremonies, such as the initiation of the leather artisans of the Korhogu region, also required sculpture or pottery. In these ceremonies, unbaked clay figures, realistically modeled, were used to teach initiates about the guild of craftsmen they were joining. Burial rites also required ceramics: In Ghana, the Ashanti placed a type of ornamented pot called the *abusua kuruwa,* along with a cooking pot, utensils, and hearthstones, beside the grave of the recently buried. In it was placed hair that all the blood relatives of the deceased had shaved off their heads. In Africa, as in most other preindustrial societies, art was not separated from everyday life as it has been in Western societies since the Renaissance. The artist in African cultures was never divorced from the people who used his or her creations, and

although some persons may have achieved the highest skill at weaving, pottery making, singing, or dancing, their work was considered to be a reflection of normal human activity. That beauty was part of everyday life is testified to by a Yoruba poet who celebrated equally the beauty of fast-running deer, children, a rainbow, and a well-swept veranda, saying, "Anybody who meets beauty and does not look at it will soon be poor."

FOREIGN INFLUENCES

Just as China and Japan absorbed and modified the Buddhist art that came from India, so Africa has absorbed and modified many artistic ideas that have come to the continent through invasions, migrations, and trade with other peoples. The Cretans, Greeks, and Romans all came to northern Africa, and along with the Coptic Church in

Figure 4-7
Tiny, burnished black pottery figures
from Ethiopia were made by a group
of Jews who settled there long ago. In
scenes from daily life, a woman grinds
corn while a child peers over her shoulder, and another woman carries water
from the spring or river in a clay pot.

Photo: Mogens S. Koch, Denmark.

Egypt and Ethiopia, all had varying effects on
local ceramic styles. In addition, the Moslems
brought to Africa their religious prohibitions
against representing human forms, changing the
styles of ornament in the areas that were converted to Islam, and from the time the Europeans
came to Africa, in the 1600s, local art often
reflected the new teachings of Christianity. In
Ethiopia a small group of Jews made figurines
depicting domestic life (4-7). Unfortunately for
the traditional crafts, however, the exposure to
twentieth-century foreign influences has been
largely a destructive one.

EARLY TECHNIQUES

Our knowledge of early pottery techniques in Africa is scant, and in order to form some sense of
how prehistoric potters made and fired their creations we can only study traditional methods that
remain in use today. Among the African ceramic
treasures in the storerooms of the British Museum is a modest box labeled "African female
potter's tools," collected in the 1880s. This box

contains only a piece of metal for scraping, a
wooden tool for making designs, smooth stones
for polishing, a pointed shell for punching holes,
and a corn cob and smooth seed pods for im-
pressing designs—touching and mute reminders
that potters all over the world have shaped,
smoothed and decorated clay pots in very much
the same fashion for thousands of years (1-20,
5-16). The methods used today may have been
changed by contact with other cultures, so we
cannot take them as "living archaeology," but
rather must see them as only suggestions of some
of the traditional methods that have been handed
down from one generation to another. Although
there are some similarities in technique among artisans across the African continent, there are also
great variations in the traditions of the widely
separated groups who have lived there.

One factor does remain the same throughout
all cultures there. Until recently, pottery in most
of Africa has always been handbuilt; only in
Egypt were turntables on axles, kick wheels, and
permanent kilns known and used. In addition,
with few exceptions, in Africa pots have always
been fired in open firings (4-12).

Until recently, low-fired earthenware pots were
used for all domestic needs—for cooking; for
storing food, beer, or honey; for carrying water
(1-21); and for dyeing fibers. Because there was no
need for a higher fired ware, none was developed;
in fact, earthenware was better adapted to the rural life than high-fired ceramics would have been.
Earthenware is, for example, better for cooking
over an open fire. This is due to the coarse texture
of the clay, which allows the pots to withstand
the shock of the heat and reduces the likelihood
of cracking. Earthenware is excellent for storing
drinking water in a hot climate, because the porosity of the clay body allows the water to cool
by evaporation.

Architecture

Like many other peoples in warm countries, Africans have for centuries built storage buildings,
houses, and mosques with mud and clay. Where
clay was plastered over a frame of wood and
straw to build the walls of houses, it was used
because it was the most plentiful material and
could be built up into thick walls that kept out the
heat. Another traditional use for clay in certain

areas of Africa was the building of storage bins that look like large pots with straw hats. These clay granaries protect the grain from weather and rats. After the beginning of the nineteenth century, the walls of many such buildings were decorated with sculptured clay reliefs, and the mud bricks with which the walls were built were often set in decorative patterns.

Division of Labor

Traditionally, African men and women have had distinct roles, and pottery making is still usually reserved for the women. As in the American Southwest, African mothers teach their daughters, handing down the empirical knowledge of generations. The hands of African women traditionally dig the clay, prepare it for use, and shape it, often according to rules and taboos. For example, the Mongoro potters of the Ivory Coast sacrifice a goat or rooster before digging clay as a way of asking forgiveness from the gods. Until recently, among the Shai people of Ghana, every house had a potter, all of them women. In earlier centuries, the pits where the Shai dug their clay were under the control of priestesses, who presided over the rituals governing its removal—for example, only women who had passed puberty

Figure 4-8
Naa Jato, who was active in the Cameroon in the 1930s, handbuilt this palm wine container, depicting on it scenes of village life. She applied the relief figures while the clay was damp, and once the walls were leather hard, she burnished the area between them with a smooth stone. Earthenware. Ht. 16½ in. (42 cm). Cameroon, Northern Mfunte, Lus group, 1936. *Courtesy Portland Art Museum, Portland, Oregon. The Paul and Clara Gebauer Collection of Cameroon Art.*

Figure 4-9
In the Sudan, tobacco pipe bowls, attached to long hollow stems, were used in male ceremonies, so often the men made them. They rubbed white chalk or ash into the incised crosshatching typical of their decoration to emphasize it. Length of bowl 3⅛ in. (8 cm). Shilluk, Sudan. *Copyright British Museum.*

could dig the clay. Another rule forbids Ashanti women from making pots decorated with human figures. The reason given is that a woman who did this once became sterile because she had made an image of a human instead of bearing a child. In the diversity of these rules and taboos, we can see that ceramics reflect the richness and variety of the many cultures that have flourished in Africa.

Although women have been potters for centuries in Africa, only comparatively recently have the names of women potters become known. One such potter, Naa Jato, lived in a village in the Cameroon, where she made palm wine containers commissioned by the male clubs and local chiefs (4-8). Hers were not domestic pots, and the relief decoration she added to the clay of the handbuilt walls was lively and humorous, giving a vivid portrait of the daily life of the people in her small village.

Where men have been involved in pottery in Africa, they have frequently made only a special type of pottery or have used techniques that differed from those of the women. In Ghana, for instance, taboos forbade men to make domestic ware. On the other hand, among some peoples the men make pottery and the women are forbidden to come near them during certain parts of the process. In some cultures, ceremonial ceramics — objects traditionally associated with the men such as ritual drums, pipes (4-9), and bellows tips for smelting — were made only by the men.

CONTEMPORARY TECHNIQUES

Almost every type of handbuilding technique is used today in Africa. A potter might start by pressing the clay into a base mold, first leaving it to stiffen somewhat and then building the rest with coils. Conversely, sometimes potters start by forming the upper section of a pot first, letting it stiffen, and then when it is firm enough, building coils onto it to form the lower section upside down (4-10). The Ashanti women, however, use no coils at all; they make the whole pot by pulling up the sides from one lump of clay, walking around it backwards as they do so. Elsewhere, a potter may form the base of a pot by hollowing out a lump of clay with her fingers and then building the walls. Still others start the base by pressing clay into a mold lined with leaves or ashes to keep the clay from sticking; as they build the walls, they pound the clay with a wooden beater while holding a stone inside — much as the women in Fiji shape their pots (1-14). The base may be part of a dried gourd or the bottom of an old pot turned with the hands or feet as the pot is built. Sometimes a potter uses the hollowed-out stump of a tree or a large fired pot as a stand on which to build her pot (4-11).

Where coils are used, they are scraped, pressed, or beaten as they are added to meld the walls together. The outside is then smoothed with the fingers, a shell, or a bit of dried gourd or a piece of leather.

Figure 4-10
An Ashanti woman potter, making a series of large pots, builds
the upper section first. When these sections are stiff enough to
support more clay, she turns them over and completes the bottom
section. Ghana. *Photograph by Eliot Elisofon, The National Museum of African Art,
Eliot Elisofon Photographic Archives, Smithsonian Institution.*

Figure 4-11
Some African women today continue to shape pots using methods
that are thousands of years old. From them, we can learn the
traditional methods and hope to preserve that knowledge. Here,
a potter uses both a fired pot and a broken one as a base in
which to form her pot. *Courtesy Field Museum of Natural History, Chicago (Neg.
#70034).*

Finishing

There seem to be as many methods of finishing pots as there are peoples in Africa. Some potters burnish pots with stones or smooth seed pods, rubbing until the leather-hard surface is polished (1-20). Sometimes the clay of the pots has been tempered with mica or covered with a mica-containing slip so that after it is fired the surface of the burnished pot sparkles as bits of glistening mica reflect the light.

In many villages, the potters coat fired pots with resin, palm oil, or mixtures made from boiling certain leaves in order to reduce their porosity. Applying these mixtures may change the color of the red clay body to a dark brown. Because the color of this sealing material appealed to some potters, they now apply this vegetable material for decoration, in patterns of bands, lines, or triangles, or they sometimes splash it over the whole pot while it is hot to achieve a marbled effect.

Decoration

Depending on the local pottery tradition, African potters use a great variety of decorative techniques to enhance the surfaces of their pots. They may scratch their designs into the damp clay with a knife or stick, press patterns into it with twisted or plaited straw or a natural object such as a corn cob, or roll repeat designs onto the clay with a carved wooden wheel, called a **roulette.** Water or milk pots from Botswana are decorated with patterns in which dark-toned graphite triangles contrast with areas of untreated clay body, while the Ibo color only the raised bands of clay that they attach around their large-bellied vases in undulating patterns.

Some of the decorative techniques may have had their origin in function. For example, impressed, carved, or raised designs on a water pot make it easier to lift a heavy, slippery pot full of water (1-21). In Uganda, some potters copy in clay the shapes of calabashes used originally as

Figure 4-12
Ashanti women of Ghana arrange their pots for firing, alternating several layers of pots with fuel. Sometimes they fire as many as three hundred pots at one time; at other times they may fire just one large pot using wood, grass, millet, or straw for fuel. In a few places in western Africa, a low wall is built around the pots to deflect the wind and hold in the heat, making a rudimentary kiln. Ghana. *Photograph by Eliot Elisofon, The National Museum of African Art, Eliot Elisofon Photographic Archives, Smithsonian Institution.*

containers or ladles, while others carve lines on their pots that duplicate the patterns originally made by the fiber or leather thongs that were laced around the gourds as handles. Whatever the method of decoration, each region or group of peoples has stayed within its own tradition, repeating its designs consistently over time.

Firing

Once the pots are finished, they are left to dry. If the weather is too hot, they are placed in a cool spot with fired pots placed over them to keep them from drying too quickly. Before firing, the potters might heat them by burning grass inside them, as in Ogbomosho, Nigeria (1-30).

Almost all pottery firing in Africa is done in an open fire. Living close to the earth, the rural African potters have always adapted their firing techniques to the ecology of the countryside around them, using the most readily available fuel. The length of firing time varies from place to place and according to the size, number, and thickness of the pots. It may last for several hours or only for a few minutes. Indeed, some potters fire their pots for only a short time at a low temperature, leaving it to the housewife who buys them to give them a second firing when she gets home.

Placing pots in an open fire might seem like an easy way to fire, but heating a large number of good-sized pots to maturity in an open fire is actually an intricate process, requiring skill and patience. How to place the pots, how to stack the fuel, what fuel to use, how to keep the fire burning, and even when to fire to avoid gusty winds that might create sudden flare-ups — all of this accumulated knowledge results from generations of experimentation (4-12).

CHANGING CRAFTS IN CHANGING TIMES

Even today, large numbers of pots are produced in Africa using traditional methods, and in some places women potters still carry their fired pots on their heads for ten or fifteen miles to market them. But there, as all over the world, the rich African heritage of ceramics techniques is being eroded as the continent becomes more urbanized. Since plastic and factory-produced domestic ware

now take over much of the market, the future of traditional pottery is uncertain.

A number of African potters, such as Ladi Kwali (4-13) and Daniel Cobblah, are preserving their heritage and developing a respect for the old crafts among the younger potters. Cobblah, who

Figure 4-13
Ladi Kwali, from Nigeria, demonstrates the building and decorating of a water pot. As she narrows the neck, she adds coils to form the rim. She later added decoration by pressing a textured tool into the clay. *Courtesy Field Museum of Natural History, Chicago (Neg. #82515).*

broke his tribe's tradition that only women could make pots, worked with British potters Harry Davis and Michael Cardew in ceramics training programs, and when Ghana became independent he gave his energies to the reemerging crafts traditions there. In an attempt to save some of the older ceramics traditions, several workshops were established where older shapes and decorations are adapted to wheel techniques and glazed stoneware.

At the same time, a modern world calls for new attitudes and methods (4-14), and as these are absorbed, a new type of ceramics — expressive of present-day cultures in African nations — is developing.

Figure 4-14
A potter in a studio in Lusaka, Zambia, uses local stoneware clay on a kick wheel. Similar workshops have been started in several African countries to meet the demand for pottery that is more durable than earthenware. *Courtesy Zambia Information Services Department, Lusaka, Zambia.*

5

Indigenous America

Based on new excavations, some scholars now state that people came to the North American continent as early as 28,000 years ago. Others push the date even further back, while more conservative estimates set the arrival of people at somewhere between 12,000 and 14,000 years ago. Geologists say that thousands of years ago the American and Asian continents were connected by a land bridge (5-1). Before that bridge was flooded by the rising water of melting Ice Age glaciers, groups of Asian hunters followed their prey—mammoths, bison, and other large animals—across it. These hunters stayed on to move slowly down the continent. Some groups, we know, spread out into the North American Great Lakes area, the Plains, the Mississippi Valley, and the East Coast. Others gradually pushed farther south into what is now Mexico, down through the Isthmus of Panama, and on into South America, eventually reaching its very tip. Excavations in Chile unearthed a community of fourteen small attached structures, each with a clay-lined hearth pit. Two large community hearths and stockpiles of clay were found outside the buildings, the clay having been brought from distant bogs and rivers. These finds suggest that people had settled there for at least a season or two, and from radioactive carbon dating of the charcoal and animal bones found around the huts, the excavators concluded that the settlement was between 12,500 and 14,000 years old.

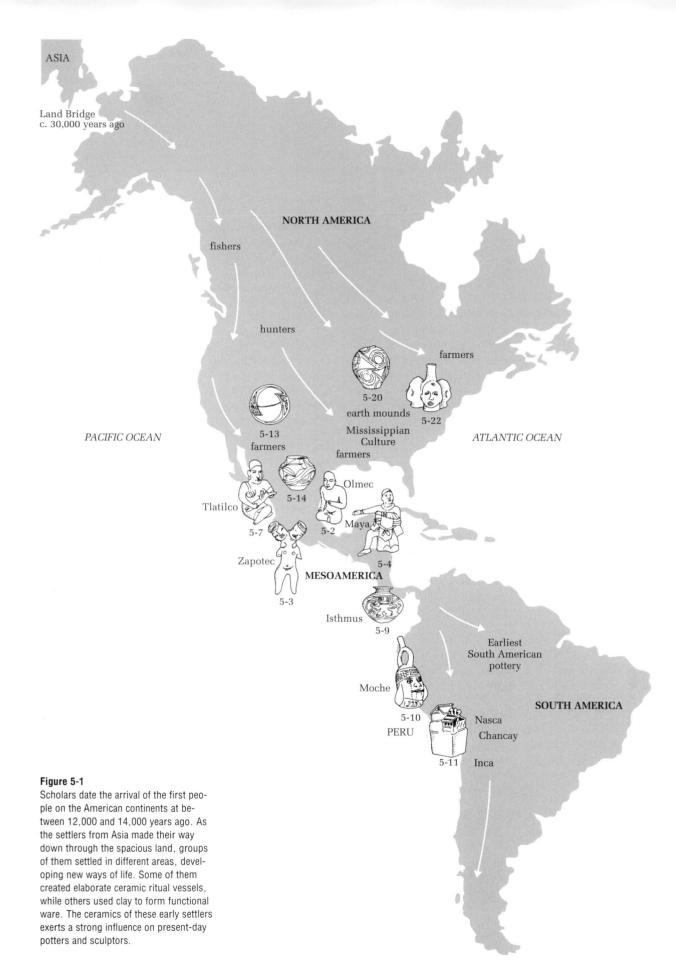

ASIA

Land Bridge
c. 30,000 years ago

NORTH AMERICA

fishers

hunters

farmers

5-20

earth mounds
Mississippian
Culture
farmers

5-22

PACIFIC OCEAN

5-13
farmers

ATLANTIC OCEAN

5-14

Olmec

Tlatilco

Maya

5-7

5-2

Zapotec

5-4

MESOAMERICA

5-3

Isthmus

5-9

Earliest
South American
pottery

Moche

SOUTH AMERICA

5-10
PERU

Nasca
Chancay

5-11   Inca

Figure 5-1
Scholars date the arrival of the first people on the American continents at between 12,000 and 14,000 years ago. As
the settlers from Asia made their way
down through the spacious land, groups
of them settled in different areas, developing new ways of life. Some of them
created elaborate ceramic ritual vessels,
while others used clay to form functional
ware. The ceramics of these early settlers
exerts a strong influence on present-day
potters and sculptors.

At any rate, it is generally accepted that some time between twenty thousand and twelve thousand years ago, small groups of hunters stopped along the way, adapting their lives to differing local environments. They gradually developed varying characteristics, languages, religions, and art styles. The settled descendants of these early hunters became the artisans, potters, and sculptors whose skill and artistic ability created the advanced and sophisticated cultures that later flourished in Mesoamerica and South America (5-2 to 5-11).

MESOAMERICA

Mesoamerica is a name coined by archaeologists to describe central and southern Mexico, Guatemala, El Salvador, and parts of Honduras. Although the cultures that developed in those areas vary, some features are common to all of them: Most cultivated maize, used hieroglyphics, built large stone monuments, created calendars, and understood and used some form of mathematics. In their attempts to control the environment, improve their crops, and ensure the continuance of the race, they developed religions oriented toward fertility and centering on gods that were the personifications of animals or humans.

In the ancient civilizations of both North and South America, the domestication and cultivation of maize preceded the growth of urban civilizations, and the seasonal rebirth of the maize came to have religious significance that was reflected in art. As the young maize plants pushed through the earth each year, were watered by the rain, and ripened in the sun, the promise of food and life was renewed. This yearly event led the farming villagers to express, in rituals and offerings to the fertility gods and goddesses, their hopes for good crops, fears of drought, and gratitude for sunny skies. The fact that they were able to store away the maize ensured them of the necessary leisure to engage in crafts and made it possible for them to develop rituals, art, music, and dance, to build the temples needed for the ceremonies, and to make vessels from clay to use in the rituals.

Along with the large numbers of artisans needed to build, carve, and paint the walls of their temples, potters were needed to shape elaborate burial and offering urns. Most of the ceramics that have survived in Mesoamerica have come from tombs, where they were protected from

Figure 5-2
Olmec terra-cotta figures with the typical pouting mouth were usually coated with white or cream-colored slip. Since the Olmec religion saw the jaguar as the source of all life, some authorities believe the sculptures represent were-jaguars, offspring of the union of a woman with a jaguar. Ht. 3 in. (7.6 cm). Olmec, Las Bocas, state of Puebla, Mexico. *Courtesy of the National Museum of the American Indian, Smithsonian Institution (#33855).*

breakage. This makes it appear that the bulk of ceramic-vessel production was devoted to religious objects, but we know from wall paintings, sculptured reliefs, and a few codices, or illustrated books, that Mesoamerican potters also made simpler vessels for storage, cooking, drinking, and other household uses.

The early potters of the Americas used hand-building techniques and simple turntables; the true potter's wheel did not appear on the continent until the Europeans brought it. The early artisans of the Americas shaped their vessels with coils, smoothed them on some type of turntable, modeled the figurines by hand, or, in some areas, pressed clay into molds to speed up production of sculptured pots and figurines. Firing was done in an open fire or a pit surrounded by a low wall of stones and clay.

Olmec Influences (c. 1200–500 B.C.)

Many of the common features of the Mesoamerican cultures are believed to have come originally from the Olmecs (5-2). Some scholars have suggested that the Olmec artifacts represent an art style rather than a separate culture, but it may be that there actually was a separate Olmec people whose civilization was centered in the eastern coastal regions of what is now Mexico. It is also possible that the Olmecs were the basic group from which each of the subsequent cultures in the surrounding areas of Mesoamerica derived. Whichever is the case, their advanced agriculture and crafts, their astronomical observations, and their irrigated or drained coastal lands indicate that they had developed sophisticated technology. The ceremonial centers, which contained courts for a ritual ball game, and the enormous stone heads that were rafted across sixty miles of water to the island of La Venta also indicate that the people who made them were capable of complex community efforts. They traded jade, kaolin, turquoise, and shells with other groups, and passed along with their trade goods their religious concepts, which included the cult of a jaguar god, whom they believed controlled the rain and fertility.

Some scholars believe that the typical "Olmec mouth" is based on the shape of a jaguar's mouth. The stone sculptures at La Venta display this childlike pouting mouth with down-turned lips that appears in the sculpture of many areas in Mesoamerica.

Tlatilco (c. 1300–900 B.C.)

One culture in which this feature is particularly prevalent is known as Tlatilco, a name that means "the place where things are hidden." The name is appropriate, because high on the Central Plateau, near present-day Mexico City, at the site of a village named Tlatilco, archaeologists have found large numbers of graves in which innumerable clay figurines (5-3) and pottery were buried. This large and wealthy village seems to have been the center of a culture that borrowed technology and artistic ideas from the Olmecs while creating its own characteristic style.

The Tlatilco potters scraped, polished, and stamped their pots, or decorated them with textures made with the edges of shells traded from the coastal areas. They also painted their pottery with red, yellow, and white geometric designs or stylized snakes or jaguar claws, another Olmec influence. One type of jar from Tlatilco had a double-necked spout—the "stirrup" shape that later

Figure 5-3
Clay figures of two-headed or double-faced women with carefully styled hair are frequently found in burials at Tlatilco. Some authorities suggest that the figures represent the duality of nature. This one shows traces of the color that usually decorated them. Tlatilco, Mexico, 1300–800 B.C. *Courtesy Museo Nacional de Antropologia, Mexico.*

appeared in Peru and the North American Southwest, probably carried to those areas through trade or migrations (5-10).

The sculptors who worked the abundant clay of the Tlatilco region modeled it into human figures — the bulk of which portray large-hipped women, the so-called "pretty ladies." Most of these figures are naked but some are wearing short skirts, and they are usually painted with lines suggesting tattoos, clothing, or body paint. All have elaborately styled hair, and the most unusual ones have two heads or two faces that share a third eye.

Male figures — of musicians, acrobats, and dwarfs, along with masked figures that probably represent priests or shamans — have also been found in burials. Among them is the earliest clay representation of a ball player, wearing the characteristic padding used in the ritual ball game that is depicted in paintings and sculptures throughout early Mesoamerica.

The Maya (c. 1000 b.c.–a.d. 900)

The Maya worshipped the four Chacs, or rain gods, along with the gods of wind and sun — all-important elements in a society based on maize. Their advanced civilization also recorded past history in hieroglyphics on stone monuments, developed an accurate calendar, and created impressive stone pyramids and temples in the jungle area of Mexico and Guatemala.

According to the *Popul Vuh,* the sacred book of the Quiche Indians in Guatemala, who still speak Mayan, the first humanlike creatures were modeled out of clay by the gods. The gods are said to have destroyed these clay people, however, because they could not think, and finally, says the sacred manuscript, "only maize was used for the flesh of our first fathers."

The ceremonial pottery of the Maya was simple in shape; the potters seemed more interested in producing a smooth painting ground than elaborate pottery shapes. These cylindrical vases were often covered with plaster to give the painters a better background on which to compose figurative paintings in black, red, and white slips and oxides on an orange background. These stylized paintings often show priests, warriors, and nobles wearing ornate headdresses and engaging in raids on other tribes for prisoners. They also vividly depict the rituals that followed the raids when the prisoners were brought to the temples for sacrifice.

Maintaining the succession of the dynasties was an all-important aspect of Mayan culture, and many rituals involving the kings and their heirs centered around ensuring legitimate inheritance from generation to generation. The kings, and often the queens, were expected to participate in ritual self-bloodletting. In these ceremonies, held on the high temple platforms where the populace could see them, the royalty induced visions through self-bloodletting and ingestion of herbs — visions they believed the Vision Serpent brought to them. Many such acts are represented on pottery, on painted walls, and on carved stone reliefs.

MAYAN TERRA-COTTA FIGURINES   Although a few illustrated books, called codices, survive, one of the best sources of information about Mayan life is the large number of terra-cotta figurines buried with the dead on the island of Jaina, opposite Yucatan. Expressive, lively, and beautifully crafted, these clay sculptures show us kings and notables in huge headdresses, statuesque ladies wearing heavy jewelry, and ball players in ritual costume, intent on the ritual acts in which they perform.

The so-called ball game in which these padded Mayan players contended was played in courts outside the temples, where many spectators watched and bet on the outcome (5-4). Brightly painted Mayan vessels depicted the players, often showing the ball in play between the contestants, who wore heavy padding and elaborate headdresses (Color Plate 5). Recreation was not the purpose of this athletic contest, however; the ball probably symbolized the sun, and the "game" often ended in sacrifice — probably to the gods of sun and rain. The rules varied from culture to culture throughout Mesoamerica, but in all of the games the ball was passed from player to player from one end of the court to the other — at the Mayan center of Chichén Itzá there was a stone ring on each side, and whichever team got the ball through the ring won immediately.

Despite the rituals requiring sacrifice or auto-sacrifice and the slave economy that supported the nobility and the priesthood in luxury, some of the figurines show that a gentler side existed in the Mayan culture. In these small clay sculptures, women weaving, cooking, and caring for children, the old, and the ill all come alive in clay.

Figure 5-4
Maya players in the ritual ball game wore protective belts, helmets, gauntlets, and knee pads; players were usually forbidden to use their hands or feet, so they kept the ball in motion with their bodies. Reliefs on the Toltec ball court at Chichén Itzá show the decapitation of a ball player; it is possible that the losers were sacrificed — although some scholars suggest it was the winners who had the honor of being sacrificed. Shown larger than actual size. Ht. 6 in. (15.2 cm). Jaina, Campeche, Mexico, A.D. 700–800.
Courtesy Museo Nacional de Antropologia, Mexico.

The Mayan civilization eventually lost its vitality; its cities declined and the jungle grew over them, but the influence of the Mayan culture, like that of the Olmec culture, was felt in other parts of Mesoamerica and continues to this day.

Veracruz — Remojadas (c. 500 B.C.–A.D. 900)

On the Gulf Coast, in central Veracruz, a culture that centered in Remojadas and later in El Tajín produced a large number of clay figures, many of them joyful and smiling. Such cheerfulness is rarely represented in Mesoamerican art, and the thousands of figures found there, many of them captured in clay in the middle of a belly laugh, give the impression of a fun-loving people who faced life and death with a smile (5-5).

Some of the figures have emblems of life and movement on their headdresses and other figures depict priests playing musical instruments, so they may have had some connection with ritual dance. The earliest of these lively figures were modeled individually by hand, whereas the later ones were made in molds or built up hollow into nearly life-sized figures.

Teotihuacán (c. 100 B.C.–A.D. 850)

On the Central Plateau north of Mexico City, rising steeply from the flat plain, loom the ruins of the sacred city of Teotihuacán. Its immense pyramids stand as mute reminders of the bustling city that once flourished there. Teotihuacán was not only a religious center—the focus of rituals ded-

Figure 5-5
The Remojadas culture centered in Veracruz was one of the few to depict happy people—many of the figurines show laughing children. This sculpture of two children swinging is also a whistle. Veracruz, c. A.D. 500. *Courtesy of the National Museum of the American Indian, Smithsonian Institution, (#29374).*

icated to the deities associated with water, fertility, and agriculture—it was also a residential
center. During its height, the potters and sculptors lived in a special area given over to the crafts
where they shaped large, three-footed ritual cylinders decorated with jaguars or human heads or
coated with plaster and painted with images of
the gods in brilliant color. The shape and decoration of these vessels have led some scholars to
suggest a link with Chinese Bronze Age urns.

According to an anthropologist who has studied the fingerprints of the potters of Teotihuacán,
the prints on the earliest clay artifacts—mostly
simple domestic pottery—are women's. Later vessels, made at a time when pottery was no longer
made solely for domestic use, show male prints,
and in the final period, when the culture was
declining, the prints are female again, suggesting

that the craft was once more directed toward sup-
plying the needs of the home.

The Zapotecs (c. A.D. 300–900)

Twelve hundred feet up the mountain at Monte
Albán, near present-day Oaxaca, the Zapotecs
built a great ceremonial center. Some dispute
exists about earlier settlements there—some scholars argue that the Zapotecs were strongly influenced by the Olmec culture, others that the Olmec civilization itself actually began in the valley
below and radiated outward from there.

The most characteristic ceramics created by
the Zapotecs are large sculptured urns representing human or jaguar figures (5-6). The humans in
turn often hold small containers with offerings of

fire, incense, food, or water destined for the gods that appear on their masks or headdresses. These figures may represent priests or possibly individuals bringing votive offerings. The urns were originally handmodeled, but toward the end of the Zapotec period many were formed in molds, and by then the standard of craftsmanship was in general lower. Eventually the Zapotec culture itself declined, and Monte Albán was taken over by the Mixtecs, who were noted more for their gold work than their ceramics.

The Aztecs (c. A.D. 1325–1520)

The Aztecs, whose city at Tenochtitlán astounded the Spaniards when they arrived in 1520, built their great ceremonial center on an island where Mexico City now stands. Known for their engineering skill in building aqueducts, draining marshes, and creating a network of canals, the Aztecs dominated their neighbors, demanding tribute from them. They also raided them to procure the constant stream of victims they needed for their human-sacrificial religious rites. The Aztecs believed that the sun god had to be fed blood every day in order to be strong enough to win his nightly battle with the jealous gods of the stars and moon, who wanted to keep him from returning to light the sky.

Aztec art owed much to the surrounding cultures, especially the Mixtecs of Oaxaca from whom the Aztecs learned the craft of painted pottery — a delicate orange ware decorated with gray, yellow, or white. Aztec trade was extensive, as was the tribute they extracted from other people. Paintings in codices show the arrival of the tributes: feathers for ritual costumes, skins, and fabrics, often carried to the city in pottery vessels. Other paintings show babies being baptized in pottery tubs, tripod urns with food in them, and elderly people drinking their daily allotted ration of *pulque,* the Aztec liquor, out of wide, shallow pottery cups. All the usual domestic pots appear, giving us a clear idea of the importance of clay in the daily life of early Mesoamerica.

Western Cultures

In the western areas now covered by the states of Michoacán, Guanajuato, Jalisco, Colima, and Nayarit, the villages were isolated from other Meso-

Figure 5-7
The flat heads seen on figurines from Jalisco were not a distortion but the result of the custom of binding infants' heads to a board at birth. The clothing of this mother nursing her child shows typical designs applied after firing. Ht. 17½ in. (44.5 cm). Magdalena, Jalisco, Mexico, A.D. 300–900. *Courtesy of the National Museum of the American Indian, Smithsonian Institution (#29629).*

american cultures and show only a few traces of Olmec and Teotihuacán influences. Nor did they develop as powerful or wealthy a priesthood — no monumental religious centers were built here — for the inhabitants were apparently not as deeply involved with ritualized religion as in other areas of Mesoamerica.

What has remained of early cultures here is a wealth of small clay figurines that suggest the artists were more concerned with portraying life on earth than with pleasing the gods (5-7, 5-8). From around A.D. 300 to 900, sculptors in western Mexico modeled clay into figures that depicted nursing mothers, musicians, dancers, priests or shamans, children at play, rabbits, armadillos, mice, and parrots, along with houses, temples, and ball courts. In comparison with, say, the stylized, elaborated figure on a Zapotec funerary urn

Figure 5-8
A group of figures from Jalisco, about 7 inches (18 cm) tall, recreates a scene in which a man wearing a snake and feather headdress, possibly a priest or a shaman, beats time with paddles as he accompanies the dancers. Since we can only guess at their original grouping, it may suggest relationships that never actually existed. Jalisco, Mexico, A.D. 300–900. *Courtesy of the National Museum of the American Indian, Smithsonian Institution (#31198).*

(5-6), the sculpture from this area is lively and human.

Although there is great similarity among these small sculptures from various parts of western Mexico, regional differences tell us about local customs. For instance, we learn that the women of Nayarit usually went naked or sometimes wore short skirts but always dressed their hair carefully and wore large earplugs and, usually, necklaces. The men are often shown wearing light armor woven from fibers, carrying clubs and throwing spears. Many of the Nayarit figurines are almost caricatures, with the ill or deformed represented in an exaggerated manner. In Jalisco, on the other hand, despite some exaggeration of the deliberately deformed heads (5-7), people are shown more realistically—a woman nursing her child, a young man looking into a mirror, an old

man carried in a litter—which brings us close to life as it was lived in this part of the central plateau of Mexico.

THE ISTHMUS AREA

In the narrow neck of land between the two Americas, in what is now Panama, Costa Rica, and parts of Colombia, rich gold mines yielded quantities of the shining metal. Although clay was used to make simple pottery here as early as 2000 B.C., gold was the most important art medium in this area. But clay had a functional purpose in the fabrication of gold artifacts; the goldsmiths used two-part ceramic molds to cast their solid-gold ornaments.

Figure 5-9
There is such a remarkable resemblance between the decoration and shape of this vessel and those of vessels made in ancient China (3-2), some writers suggest there may have been communication between China and Mesoamerica. The stylized painting of the crocodile god is in black and red on a cream slip. Ht. 9¾ in. (24.8 cm). Veraguas, Panama, A.D. 1000–1500. *Courtesy of the National Museum of the American Indian, Smithsonian Institution (#31240).*

Later, in the province of Veraguas in Panama, potters working during the centuries just before the arrival of the Europeans created elegantly shaped bowls, jars (5-9), and pedestaled urns. They decorated these pieces with forceful and stylized figures of animals and gods painted in red, black, and purple in a rhythmic style unlike other Mesoamerican or Peruvian pottery. Some historians have suggested a link between the decoration of these pots and Chinese Neolithic pottery (3-2).

After the Europeans arrived, this sophisticated ceramic craft was lost, and today in Panamanian villages the women who still make their own domestic pots form them with coils in a few simple shapes. Only a handful of the traditional potters there still make the type of three-legged pot that might be an echo of earlier days.

SOUTH AMERICA

Thousands of years ago, as bands of hunters made their way along the western coast of the southern American continent, some of them found hospitable surroundings that led them to settle in the low, fertile valleys that break up the long coastline. Others hunted wild animals into the high mountain plains and valleys; still others made their way into the dense jungles on the eastern side of the towering Andes. These early peoples did not make pottery, but they formed fertility figures and representations of birds and animals out of clay, leaving them unbaked.

It is not known for certain just where in South America fired pottery was first made, although finds in Ecuador suggest that farming cultures producing pottery developed there at least as early as in western Asia. Since there are still large areas in this vast continent where there has been little excavation, the picture that has emerged is somewhat uneven. Nevertheless, we do know that sometime between 1800 and 900 B.C., people in the north and south coastal areas of South America settled into villages and that they made improvements in agriculture, weaving, pottery, and architecture. The pottery of this period was well made but simple, with only a little decoration, usually geometric.

By around 900 to 600 B.C., in the southern Paracas area of what is now Peru the potters were already forming clay into the whistling jars and stirrup-spouted pots whose basic forms would be used for centuries by the potters of the Andes region.

Chavin (c. 900–200 B.C.)

Contemporary with the Paracas culture, the Chavin, inspired by a new religious cult that may have spread from the eastern rainforests, conquered a large area and built a huge stone religious center in a high valley at Chavin de Huantar. Sculptors there carved, among other god images, a monumental stone image of a human with a smiling fanged mouth, influencing much of the pottery that was to develop in the central Andes.

Moche (c. 200 B.C.–A.D. 600)

Whether or not it was a result of Chavin influence, the Mochica ceramics showed a strong sculptural sense. In around A.D. 400, at their most productive and creative, the talented sculptor-potters working in and around Moche modeled stirrup-spouted drinking vessels into realistic portrait heads (5-10, 5-11), made models of houses and temples, and modeled amusing figurines por-

Figure 5-10
A stirrup-spouted jar from Peru is also a portrait, possibly of the person with whom it was buried; the paint or tattooing on the face may indicate his rank. Most Mochica jars were made with a combination of handbuilding and molds. Ht. 12 in. (30.5 cm). Mochica culture, Trujillo, Peru, A.D. 200–600. *Courtesy of the National Museum of the American Indian, Smithsonian Institution (#34205).*

Figure 5-11
An earthenware model of a house from Peru shows how the Moche people built their homes around A.D. 400. From clay pots, figurines, and representations of habitations like this, archaeologists can reconstruct almost every aspect of a society, from its religious rituals to how its people waged war and made love. Ht. 5¾ in. (14.8 cm). North Coast, Peru.
Courtesy Linden-Museum, Stuttgart, Germany. Photo: Didoni.

traying daily life for grave offerings and also for ceremonial use.

The potters formed the vessels by hand modeling, or by building with coils, by pressing clay into two-part molds, or using a combination of these methods. The pots are often so well finished that it is difficult to tell where each technique was used on a vessel. The process of making and using molds first required that the sculptor shape a model in solid clay and then make a mold by pressing two slabs of damp clay onto the front and back of the original. After allowing the clay to stiffen somewhat, the sculptor removed it and low-fired the resulting two-part impression. The sculptor then pressed damp clay into the two halves of the fired mold to form the two parts of the pot. Finally, he would join these two parts when they were leather hard. To make the spouts,

the potter-sculptor wrapped strips of clay around wooden rods; when the clay stiffened enough to allow removal of the rods but was still pliable, he bent the spout to shape and attached it to the pot. Once the spouts and handles were attached, he would add the details of face or body by carving into the clay or by adding additional clay forms by hand. The pots would then be slip-painted, burnished, and usually fired in an oxidizing atmosphere, although occasionally they were deliberately reduced in order to turn them gray or black. Some had details drawn on them with applications of an organic black pigment. There is no doubt that many of the pots were individual portraits, and it is possible, by studying large numbers of these pots, to recognize the work of individual artists. We may even see what the artists looked like themselves, for sculptured pots depicting potters have been found. Most of them carry bags over their shoulders. Similar bags, containing burnishing pebbles, pointed sticks, molds, and stamps, have been found buried with their owners.

The liveliness and skill with which the Moche potters modeled their sculptured vessels were outstanding, and it is small wonder that later artists, from Paul Gauguin to contemporary ones, have been influenced by the creations of these skillful and sensitive potters.

Nazca (200 B.C.–A.D. 600)

Another local culture that developed after the decline of the Chavin empire was that centering on the Nazca valleys along the southern coast. The people who lived there built shrines, adobe pyramids, plazas, and cemeteries; they wove intricate textiles and slip-painted their pottery with symbolic decorations. Less interested in realism than the Moche, they outlined their flat, stylized painting with black lines around each area of colored slip; potters sometimes used as many as nine colors on their pots. Mythological creatures, masklike faces, and catlike images appear on their bridge-handled pots.

At this point, the story of the groups who lived in what is now Peru becomes confusing. Between A.D. 600 and 1000, centers of power shifted frequently. Cities gained and then lost dominance, and new regional cultures developed.

Chancay (c. A.D. 1000)

One of many regional cultures—that of the Chancay Valley on the central coast—produced pottery with decorative geometric and stylized animal designs, sometimes painted on a layer of plaster, in black or brown and white. At times, decorations were combined with three-dimensional modeling, and the painted animals were reduced to squares, rectangles, and triangles.

Chimu (Mid-1300s)

The Chimu rulers, on the north coast, conquered territory far beyond the boundaries of the Moche sphere of influence, placing their court in the city of Chan Chan. The ruins of this city, laid out in an urban plan, cover more than eight square miles and are surrounded by enormous walls of sun-dried bricks plastered with clay and carved with stylized animals and geometric designs. The Chimu were fine metal workers, creating intricate jewelry by casting it in one-part or two-part ceramic molds, and they also made highly burnished vessels. Although they tried to rival the earlier Mochica pottery, their black ware did not achieve the high level of Mochica ceramics.

Inca (c. A.D. 1400–1533)

The Inca empire developed in one century from a small, unimportant group of people fighting with its neighbors to an awesome power that maintained military and administrative control over a huge area from Chile to Ecuador. Rich, with treasuries full of gold, the Inca nobility generally used bronze and silver vessels, while the poor and the large army that policed them used clay pots. Much of the pottery that survives was apparently government issue for military posts, and it is rather standardized.

The Inca splendor and military dominance over other cultures in South America abruptly ended in 1533, when the Spaniard Pizarro entered Cuzco and looted its famous treasuries in order to send gold back to the rulers of Spain.

Folk Traditions Today

The cultural disruption that occurred with the arrival of the Spaniards broke the tradition of making decorative and ritual clay vessels in which the indigenous Mesoamerican and South American cultures had excelled. New technology—the true wheel and more advanced firing methods—modified the native clay traditions, while changes in religion, life style, and eating and cooking habits brought new shapes to the pottery. In some villages, pottery somewhat reminiscent of the earlier cultures has persisted, and in some of the more isolated mountain villages, where transportation is still difficult, families continue to make pottery for their own use. But in general the traditional potters make their ware only when they can sell it locally more cheaply than metal or plastic containers or when they are able to sell decorative pottery or small sculptures to collectors or tourists.

The techniques used by village potters today are variations of those we have seen elsewhere in

Figure 5-12
In many parts of Mexico, potters use a pine pole to remove pots from the fire — the larger the pot, the more leverage is required to move it. The pot this Mexican potter is removing from the fire has been fired to maturity at about 700°F/371.1°C. Once removed, the pots are placed on three stones to cool evenly. *Photo: Jens Morrison.*

mother, father, and children do all the forming, firing, and finishing, each family developing an individual decorative style that collectors recognize.

Since the arrival of the Spaniards, the ceramic arts of Mexico have been greatly influenced by the Hispano-Moresque styles brought by the invaders. Tiles and wheel-thrown pots and bowls are colorfully decorated with motifs very similar to those the Arabs brought to Spain. But despite these outside influences and the spread of plastic and metal for domestic use, in some areas of Mexico the local traditions persist: Porous earthenware jars are still used for drinking water, and shallow earthenware casseroles are utilized for cooking on charcoal fires. Much of the "folk art" may now be made more for the tourist market than for local use, but potters continue to make the beautiful polished black pottery, to sculpt the small group scenes called *chiangos,* and to shape clay into figurative vessels and toy whistles — all evidence that today's descendants of the early inhabitants still see life with artists' eyes and use the ancient techniques of their ancestors (5-12).

NORTH AMERICA

Some of the groups of nomad hunters who came down into the North American continent from Asia settled in the areas of present-day New Mexico, southern Colorado, and Arizona. Known to us as the Basketmakers, they probably received stimulus for their pottery making from Mexico. Contact with Mexico's more northerly cultures was close enough for their influences to be felt. For example, the adobe clay houses built under overhanging cliffs in New Mexico and Colorado had their exact counterparts in northern Mexico, and the decoration on certain early pottery from Arizona shows many resemblances to motifs used on Mexican pottery.

How Pottery Came to the Southwest

Legend gives us a more colorful story of the beginnings of pottery in the American Southwest. According to Cochita legend, pottery making was learned from Clay Old Woman, who was sent to the village from *Shipap,* the underworld, the place of origin of all people. Her mission was to teach the villagers how to make pots, so Clay Old Woman mixed the clay with sand, softened it

the world. Most of the pottery is handbuilt in bases formed of old bowls or other convex objects and revolved on a flat stone, sometimes with the help of a clay disk with a protruding pivot on which it turns (1-26). In one area, the potters drape slabs over the bottom of old pots covered with burlap, much as some contemporary potters form their pots over plaster hump molds. Firing techniques vary from open firing with grass, straw, and dung (5-12) to updraft, Mediterranean-style kilns modeled on those brought by the Spaniards.

Recently, in parts of Peru, a revived interest in ancient cultures has led some potters to make imitations of Nazca ware, and in other areas of South America potters are handforming or using molds to make sculptural groups of human figurines, birds, and animals for tourist and export trade. Often these are made in family workshops, where with water, and then began to coil a pot. While she was busy demonstrating her skill, her husband, Clay Old Man, danced and sang. The village people watched her carefully, but when the pot was about a foot and a half high, Clay Old Man broke it with his foot and ran off with it. Clay Old Woman chased him around the village, retrieved it, made it into a ball of clay again, and built another pot. Each person of the pueblo then took a piece of clay from this pot and started to make pottery.

Whether you prefer the archaeological or mythical version of the beginnings of pottery in the American Southwest, there is no doubt that the craft of pottery making has played a large part in both the sacred and domestic life of the peoples who live in this land of mesas and spacious skies.

Southwestern Ceramics

In the region where present-day New Mexico, Colorado, Utah, and Arizona meet, the descendants of the Basketmakers merged with new peoples from the South and, between A.D. 700 and 1100, began to build clusters of permanent homes, some of whose ruins still stand. These were the first *pueblos,* the name the Spanish later gave to the villages. The same name, capitalized, has also been used by outsiders as a name for the inhabitants, but nowadays most village dwellers there prefer to be known by their native names, such as Tewa or Cochita. At various times, in different villages or groups of villages, pottery production reached a peak of creativity, declined, and was then renewed. The art of the Native Americans who lived in the many pueblos in this part of the country was a living art, developed to meet the needs of daily or ceremonial life, and as those needs varied from place to place, so did the pottery.

Mimbres (c. A.D. 700–1100)

One outstanding ceramic tradition that developed in the Southwest was that of the people the Spanish called Mimbres (meaning "willows"), who settled in the southwestern area of New Mexico near what are now the Arizona and Mexican borders. Originally, they built their homes on the heights above the valley, perhaps for defense, but after about A.D. 550, when they became dependent on agriculture, the group moved down to the Mimbres River plain, founding small villages near their crops. It was after this move that they began the custom of burying pottery bowls along with the dead under the floors of their houses. By about A.D. 1000, the inhabitants carefully placed the bowls over the heads of the dead, with a small hole broken through the bottom of the bowl. Interpretations of this custom differ—some say it was to release the spirit of the bowl.

Coil-made, scraped smooth, and thin-walled, the Mimbres pottery in the earlier years was coated with a layer of iron-rich slip, burnished, and fired to a rich red. By around A.D. 750, the pottery was fired in reduction, and the bowls, small jars, and large jars showed the characteristic black and white decoration (5-13). By about A.D. 1150, the Mimbres culture had collapsed, and by A.D. 1400, large areas of the Southwest had been abandoned by the indigenous groups of peoples, possibly owing to years of drought. At that time, the population became more concentrated in the Hopi, Zuñi, and Rio Grande areas.

Old and New Influences

From around A.D. 1600—when the Spaniards first arrived—until the present, so many new ways of life, new power structures, and new religious influences came to the area that the native peoples had to struggle to maintain their traditions. But whether these influences came from Mesoamerica, from the Spaniards, from contact with other native peoples, or from the tourists who began arriving when the railroad came in 1880, the potters in the pueblos usually took the new ideas and adapted them to fit their own way of life. The local potters continued to use ancient forms and create designs that were well adapted to the forms of each pot and to their own traditions (5-14).

Some of the potters active in the Southwest today make a special double-spouted wedding vessel with a bridged handle reminiscent of early South American spouted jars (5-10). Drinking jars such as these are known to have been used at wedding celebrations as recently as forty years ago; the bride and groom drank from opposite sides of the jar, and then it was handed around so that the men could drink from the groom's side and the women from the bride's. It is not known if the shape was devised at that time or if it is traditional.

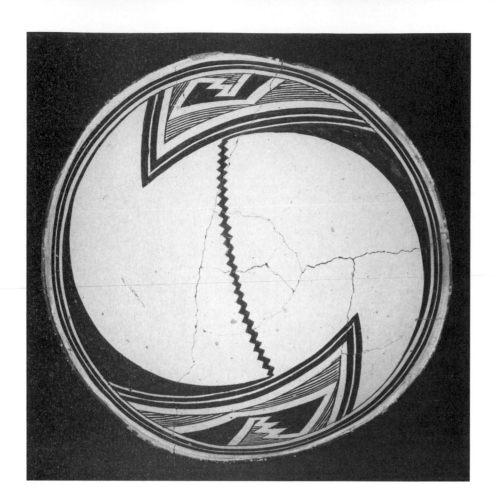

Figure 5-13
Responding to the "contemporary" appearance of such bowls from the classic Mimbres period, we tend to forget that the artists who painted them had different cultural and artistic motivations. This bowl, although broken and mended, has no "kill hole"—the hole usually made in the bottom of bowls to be buried in graves. Found on the Pruitt Ranch, Mimbres Valley, New Mexico. *Courtesy Arizona State Museum, University of Arizona.*

Figure 5-14
Water jar made in an Acoma village in the nineteenth century. The flowing bands that swing around the swelling shape are painted in two shades of orange. Ht. 9¾ in. (25 cm). McCartys, New Mexico, c. 1890. *Photo: Arthur Taylor, Courtesy Museum of New Mexico.*

Figure 5-15
A Hopi potter in Arizona around the beginning of the twentieth century shaped her pot with coils, using a basket as a base. She spread her wet clay in the sun to stiffen it slightly before using it. *Courtesy of the National Museum of the American Indian, Smithsonian Institution (#35277).*

The men sometimes made, or at least decorated, the ceremonial vessels needed for the religious life of the village. These were shaped in forms that were dictated by their use in the sacred rituals. Since many of these ceremonies have remained secret, the use of certain types of vessels or the meaning of their symbolic decoration is not known. Pitchers, rectangular bowls, footed bowls (some with handles), low bowls (some with sculptured figures of frogs)—all of these were used ceremonially.

Traditional Southwest Techniques

Potters in different villages varied in the ways they dug, prepared, and finally shaped the clay. Generally, however, the women, who were the potters, dug the clay out with sticks, speaking to the earth and asking its permission, for they felt that the clay had life and feelings deserving of respect. Sometimes they had to travel quite a distance to find the right clay (1-10). In Santa Clara, for example, the clay—*Na p*—was gathered at a place called *NA Pii we,* about a mile west of the pueblo, while the tempering material, *Shunya,* was found about seven miles away. Once dug, all materials had to be carried in a basket or a hide container back to the village, where a great deal of work went into its preparation. The dry lumps had to be pounded out, the stones and other impurities removed, and often the clay was ground on a stone until it was fine-grained.

TEMPERING MATERIALS Next, the gritty material, the temper, was mixed in. The villagers based the amount they added on experience—so many handfuls of temper to so much clay. This temper coarsened the texture of the clay, allowing the air to escape so that the pot would not crack while drying or burst in firing. Each village or area had its own kind of temper. The Zuñi, for example, have always added ground-up broken pottery to the new clay, thereby each generation incorporating a bit of its history into its pots. On the other hand, the potters of Taos and Picuris needed no temper, for there was abundant mica already in the local clay. Other pueblos have used volcanic sand or laboriously ground lava-rock into a powder, mixing it with their hands or sometimes their feet. Once the potters mixed it, they wrapped the clay in a damp cloth or sometimes buried it in the ground to keep it out of the sun until they were ready to use it.

BUILDING WITH COILS Coiling was the traditional method of pot building. The bottom of a pot was first formed in some sort of base mold—a basket, a broken pot, or a *puki,* a specially made shallow bowl (5-15). Potters kept a set of base molds shaped to suit different types of pots; they started water jars, for instance, in molds that had convex bottoms so that the base of the water jar would be concave to fit the bearer's head for carrying (5-14).

The coiled walls were built up straight, carefully pushed outward to the desired shape, and

Figure 5-16
Tewa potter Maria Martinez of San Ildefonso, in a photo taken around 1940, shapes and thins the walls of a pot by scraping with a piece of dried gourd. The base of the pot rests in a *puki*. She carefully presses the clay outward with her left hand. San Ildefonso, New Mexico, c. 1940. *Courtesy Museum of New Mexico, neg. no. 3801.*

scraped while being shaped (5-16). Using this method, potters could form pots of many shapes: flaring or narrow-necked storage jars to hold maize; open dough bowls that would hold a week's supply of bread dough; narrow-necked water jars; shallow, flat bowls; canteens; many types of swelling, globular vessels; and some special shapes.

FINISHING THE POTS   After a pot had been shaped, it was dried away from the sun and watched by the potter for cracks. Little cracks were mended with damp clay, but pots with large ones were discarded. The exterior was then smoothed again with a pottery fragment or a piece of dried gourd and coated with slip to cover the rough, coarse texture of the clay body and provide a smoother base for painted decorations. The slip was usually red, white, or off-white and made of fine clay that could only be found in certain places. Those villages without adequate slip clay near them traded with others for it. The white slip was basically kaolin, the cream slip was largely bentonite, and the red was iron-bearing clay. After the slip was applied, the pot was burnished with smooth, rounded stones or pieces of leather or rags (5-17). Collections of rubbing stones in var-

ious shapes and sizes were handed down through generations of potters, and it was considered bad luck to lose one. Less often, the damp clay body was left uncoated and was puddled, a method of stroking the clay body with a stone to float the finer clay particles to the surface to smooth it.

DECORATION   After the slip had been burnished, the artist applied the design. Various types of pigment such as fine mineral-colored slips and vegetable pigments were used. The mineral slips usually fired to shades of dark brown, black, and sometimes red. The matt black decoration, which contrasts so handsomely with the glossy finish of contemporary Santa Clara and San Ildefonso pots, is produced by painting designs with fine slip on top of the polished surface, then firing in a reduction atmosphere, which turns the pot black. The slip paint comes out of the fire with a matt surface, while the burnished part of the pot stays shiny. Some potters used a vegetable paint that burned black during firing. Called *guaco,* this paint was made by boiling new shoots and leaves of the Rocky Mountain bee plant into a syrup. Hardened and formed into a block, the paint could be kept for years and mixed with water when needed. Traditionally, the artist applied the paint with a brush made from yucca leaf or other vegetation.

Decorative motifs have varied throughout the years and in different areas from geometric and symbolic designs painted in black on white (5-13), to flowing polychrome decorations, to stylized images. Some of the images painted on early pots portrayed bird, animal, and plant forms; the sacred twin clowns; symbols of clouds, rain, and lightning; plumed serpents; and feathers. Others are decorated with what appear to be totally abstract patterns. Some of the early pottery is circled by bands of color or black lines, and these encircling lines, sometimes called the spirit path, almost always have a break in them somewhere. Some authorities say the break was put there to keep the soul of the pot from being imprisoned, whereas other scholars believe that its true meaning is lost.

FIRING   After a pot was decorated, it was ready for firing. The traditional methods of firing have remained very much the same to the present day, except that today's pottery—most of which is made for decorative purposes and is not intended for domestic use—is fired at a cooler temperature

Figure 5-17
Maria Martinez burnishes a slip-painted pot with a smooth stone to give it a rich, glossy finish; there are no glazes on her pots. San Ildefonso, New Mexico, c. 1940. *Photo by Wyatt Davis, courtesy Museum of New Mexico, neg. no. 68353.*

than in earlier times. Like the potters of Fiji, Africa (1-31, 4-12), and other traditional cultures, potters in pueblos such as San Ildefonso and Santa Clara still fire in open fires, using available local fuels—cow or sheep dung, wood, or even, in the Hopi areas, soft coal. Nowadays the pottery is placed on sheet metal or a metal grill and is covered by sheet metal, but the method is still basically the same open-firing method as that used by potters in the Southwest for centuries (5-18). Usually the firing is done in the evening or early morning to avoid any wind that could cause the fire to burn unevenly, possibly causing breakage. The firing nowadays generally takes from around thirty minutes to an hour and a half, after which some potters leave the pottery to cool in the fire, while others rake away the coals and remove the fired pots with long sticks.

Clay sculpture was not common in the early pueblos, although a few pots were made in the shape of birds or had sculptured animals on them. But by 1890, when the tourists began to come to buy curios, some potters, like Helen Cordero of Cochita (5-19), began to make human figurines. Today this sculptural tradition continues in the Cochita pueblo, while some of the younger potters in San Ildefonso make black and polychrome animal figurines. Today a number of artists are known for the black and polychrome animal and human figures they make. Increasing numbers of Native American artists in the Southwest and elsewhere are working in clay in individual styles that express their people's traditional myths, beliefs, and values while at the same time using contemporary methods and images (11-64, 11-65, 15-30).

Figure 5-18
Julian Martinez removes a burnished double-spouted wedding jar from the open firing, whose reducing atmosphere turned the pots black. Maria Martinez and her husband, Julian, worked together — Maria shaping and Julian decorating — to develop their famous black pottery. Later, their son, Popovi Da, was the decorator. San Ildefonso, New Mexico, c. 1940. *Photo by Wyatt Davis, courtesy Museum of New Mexico, neg. no. 30932.*

Figure 5-19
Helen Cordero, of the Cochita pueblo, continued a tradition of sculpted figures that started there in the 1880s. Her brightly painted *Storyteller* sits with eyes closed, chanting, while delighted children climb over him. *Courtesy U. S. Department of Interior, Indian Arts and Crafts Board, Washington, D.C.*

NORTHERN INDIGENOUS CULTURES

Some of the migrants who crossed the land bridge to North America spread out over the Great Plains to the Southeast, the Mississippi Valley, and the East Coast. These people did not develop a pottery tradition as complex as that of the Southwest cultures, largely because their life styles were less settled, since many remained hunters living nomadic lives for some time, often until pressure from the United States government forced them onto reservations.

The Mound Builders

In the Mississippi Valley, one group, possibly influenced by weak group memories of Meso-american pyramids, built large images as earth mounds—our first works of earth art (5-21). Once collectively called the Mound Builders, these people also made the most skilled pottery of the more northerly regions of the continent (5-20). Other tribes, including some as widely separated as the Iroquois and the Florida Cherokee, also made black or gray pottery and modeled animal figures as bowls for pipes they used in ceremonies.

The ancestors of other northern Native Americans who also lived more settled lives made utilitarian pots and ritual vessels in human shapes (5-22). Although the ceramics of these peoples is not as widely known to us as that of the Native American artists of the Southwest, a Crow myth

Figure 5-20
Dark, burnished pottery, usually with incised decoration, was typical of the Mississippi Valley culture. Its swirl design is remarkably like designs on pottery from Egypt (1-23), China, (3-2), and Panama (5-9). *Courtesy of the National Museum of the American Indian, Smithsonian Institution (#22191).*

Figure 5-21
The Serpent Mound, in Adams County, Ohio, represents a giant snake that curves nearly a quarter of a mile along the bank of a creek. Its makers, possibly the Adena people or the Fort Ancient people, carefully planned the effigy, outlining it with stones and clay mixed with ashes, then constructed the mound with count-less basketsful of earth. We know that the snake had sacred meanings in several indigenous cultures in early America, but what motivation led to the building of one of America's more fa-mous earth installations is still a mystery. Nearby mounds built by the Adenas are dated between 800 B.C. and A.D. 1. The Serpent Mound may have been built at that time. *Courtesy Ohio Historical Society.*

illustrates that vessels and sculpture made of clay were definitely part of their cultures. The myth states that Old Coyote Man made the earth, hu-mankind, horses, and buffalo as well as a wife for himself from mud. This, the Native American version of an early human belief in the impor-tance of malleable clay, is just one of many such myths surrounding clay as the source of life.

Figure 5-22
A triple-headed vessel, known as the *Triune Vessel,* found before 1883 near Caney Fork Cumberland River, is an example of the skill of the indigenous potters in eastern North America. Ht. 17 in. (43 cm). Chestnut Mound, Smith County, Tennessee. *Photograph courtesy of the National Museum of the American Indian, Smithsonian Institution (#33747).*

6

Europe

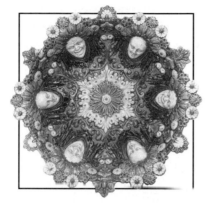

Neolithic and Bronze Age potters in the northern areas of Europe (6-1), had made urns and vessels by hand, decorating them with patterns of incised lines and textures. Handbuilt black vessels with incised lines often emphasized by white chalk, funerary urns painted with swirls, rough pots with fingernail textures — all of these had been made in early periods from Scotland (6-2) to Denmark, from Switzerland to Hungary. Many of them, especially the pots of the La Tène and Halstatt cultures, were shaped with a fine sense of form and decorated with sensitivity to the relationship between form and decoration. But a continuing and developing tradition of pottery making had not blossomed in northern Europe into anything approaching Greek or Roman ceramics, probably because urban centers such as those in the Mediterranean had not developed there.

As the unifying force of the Roman Empire waned in Europe, new ideas and influences appeared and were spread throughout Europe. The Christian religion, brought to Rome by missionaries from Judea, had created an art that incorporated styles and motifs from classic Greece and Rome. At the same time, influences from Byzantine art, which had in turn been influenced by art from India, Egypt, Persia, and the ancient Mesopotamian cultures, merged with the art of medieval Europe. The influence of Islamic art was also spreading as the Arabs thrust westward (6-3).

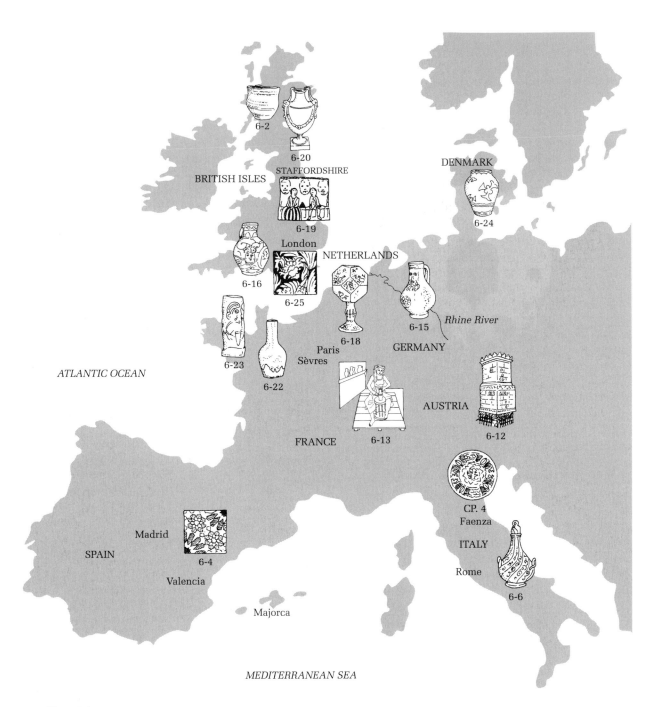

Figure 6-1

The early peoples living in what later became the countries of Europe made simple pots with incised lines. Then came
waves of migrants who often brought
new techniques and new aesthetic attitudes. The ceramics of each succeeding
age reflected these attitudes, and separate traditions developed as national
identities became differentiated. Today,
however, ceramic art is bursting through
the boundaries of national identity, and
the exchange of ideas is worldwide.

Figure 6-2
Prehistoric pottery in Europe, like this Bronze Age urn from Scotland, was made of local clays fired to a low temperature and was decorated with scratched lines. Similar linear decoration, scratched on the walls while the clay was still damp, appeared on early pots around the world. Ht. 5¾ in. (14.6 cm). Terradale, Scotland, Bronze Age (1700–1300 B.C.). *By courtesy of the Board of Trustees of the Victoria & Albert Museum.*

Figure 6-3
The dark green, yellow, and grey-blue glazes on a Hispano-Moresque tin-glazed plate are separated by lines painted with a mixture of manganese and grease in a technique called *cuerda seca*, used to keep the glazes from running into each other. Tin-glazed earthenware. Diameter about 9 in. (22.9 cm). Spain, fifteenth century. *All rights reserved, The Metropolitan Museum of Art, Rogers Fund, 1930 (30.53.1).*

SPAIN

The Islamic Moors invaded Spain from North Africa around A.D. 700, and potters came with them, bringing their knowledge of glazes and lusters as well as the characteristic Moslem style of decoration.

The Moors occupied a large part of Spain for nearly eight hundred years, developing there an art style that combined the native and imported styles into a new one, known as **Hispano-Moresque** (6-3). This style made use of decorative ideas and ceramics techniques that eventually spread far beyond Spain and profoundly influenced European pottery as well as pottery in Hispanic America.

In Spain, the potters found ample supplies of tin to use in their lead-tin glaze. They added cobalt, copper, manganese, and iron, creating blue, green, purple, yellow, and brown glazes. In addition, to give the ware a rich metallic sheen, they often fired lusters onto the glazed surfaces using a reducing atmosphere in the kiln. When they removed these bowls or tiles from the kiln, in the words of a fourteenth-century Islamic writer on ceramics, "Everything which has had a fire of this kind glistens like red gold and shines like the light of the sun."

The region of Valencia, on the Mediterranean coast, was—and still is—one of the most important Spanish pottery centers, and even after the Moors were expelled from Spain, the potters there continued to decorate their pottery with Islamic glazes and lusters, using Moorish-influenced designs.

Tiles

The characteristic Islamic use of tile first appeared in Spain on the walls of Moorish palaces and mosques around A.D. 1300. The tiles were made with two techniques, called *cuerda seca* and *cuenca*, whose purpose was to keep the multicolored glazes from running into each other when they were fired. In the *cuerda seca* technique, the potter drew lines around the areas of the design using a mixture of manganese and grease, and then filled in each area with a different color of glaze. This method was also used on pottery, where it gave dark outlines to the designs (6-3). Later, the *cuenca* method became more popular for use on tiles. In this technique, the

Figure 6-4
Hispano-Moresque tiles like this one glazed in black, yellow, and green were decorated using the *cuenca* technique, in which designs were first impressed into the damp clay and then filled with glaze: The indentations kept the colors separate in the firing. Glazed earthenware. Spain, seventeenth century. *Gift of Sarah and Eleanor Hewitt, 1929-17-20. Courtesy Cooper-Hewitt National Museum of Design, Smithsonian Institution/Art Resource, N.Y.*

Figure 6-5
In Deruta, in northern Italy, techniques learned from Spain were used to create pottery known as *maiolica* (Color Plate 4). This dish is decorated with mother-of-pearl luster outlined in blue. Diameter about 10 in. (25.4 cm). Deruta, 1530. *All rights reserved, The Metropolitan Museum of Art, gift of Henry G. Marquand, 1894 (94.4.330).*

potter used stamps to impress designs into the damp clay, forming indentations and ridges that kept each color of glaze from spilling over onto the neighboring areas (6-4).

Even though travel on sea and land was dangerous and difficult, people and goods nevertheless moved constantly across the Mediterranean and overland throughout Europe. Italian potters, for instance, are known to have worked in Spain in the late medieval period. Conversely, much of the tin-glazed decorated pottery made in the Valencia area was exported to other parts of Europe via Mallorca in the Balearic Islands. The term **maiolica,** which is the Italian name for decorated tin-glazed pottery, is believed by some to come from a corruption of the place name Mallorca, whereas others say it derived from the phrase *obra de mélica,* a term used as early as 1454 to describe the pottery made at Manises, near Valencia. Whatever its derivation, the term *maiolica* (or *majolica*) is still used for this type of pottery (6-5).

ITALY

Lead glazes had been used in Italy since at least the ninth century A.D., and tin-glazed ware had been made in Sicily and southern Italy by the eleventh or twelfth century A.D., but the brilliant color and luster of the maiolica that came from Spain had a greater appeal. In addition, it arrived in northern Italy at an opportune time, when a rich ruling and mercantile class that could afford the luxury of this imported ware was growing in the Italian city-states. Popes, bankers, and princes bought the imported glazed and decorated bowls and plates to display on their walls, and Italian potters soon began to copy this ware, hoping to get a share of the luxury market for themselves.

By the thirteenth century, decorated pottery from Spain was being traded to Italy, and it, along with glazed and decorated Byzantine pottery, which was imported through the port of Venice, exerted a strong influence on Italian ceramics. That the Italians treasured glazed and lustered pottery bowls from Spain and the Byzantine Empire is clear from the place of honor they gave to those bowls by setting them into the brickwork of the towers and facades of their Romanesque churches. These lustered bowls, still to be seen in towers in Italy, were placed there, it is said, to glorify God as they reflected the first rays of the sun in the morning and the last in the evening.

Figure 6-6
Called a pilgrim bottle because its shape was based on the flasks tied to the harnesses of travelers' horses, this maiolica bottle was made in Faenza, the leading Italian ceramic center in the sixteenth century. On it, Gothic and Renaissance motifs merged to create a characteristic design of dolphins entwined in tendrils of vines. Height 13⅝ in. (34.6 cm). Faenza, c. 1540. *Courtesy the Cleveland Museum of Art, gift from J. H. Wade, 23.914.*

Maiolica

By the turn of the fifteenth century, as their knowledge of glazing techniques was being perfected, the potters in numerous ceramics towns in Italy were producing white and colored maiolica and learning how to apply luster as well.

The Italian cities of Faenza, Deruta, Vicenza, Siena, and Perugia all developed pottery industries that embodied the new aesthetic ideas of the Renaissance. Potters in those cities now made glazed pottery that was both colorful and practical (6-6, Color Plate 4). Because it could be easily washed, the tin-glazed ware was at first especially popular in pharmacies for jars containing herbs, medicines, oils, and ointments. The earliest Italian maiolica had been decorated with geometric designs—crosshatching, circles, and dots—but soon other types of ornament came into use. Asian motifs, traceable back to Persia, and designs and motifs from medieval illuminated manuscripts from northern Europe appeared along with classical and Renaissance ones. Now the maiolica was considered elegant enough to be given as a gift to the Medici ruler, Lorenzo the Magnificent. Acknowledging a gift of the ware, he wrote in 1490, "They please me by their perfection and rarity, being quite novelties in these parts, and are valued more than if of silver. . . ."

IMPROVED TECHNIQUES By the time the maiolica had reached that degree of elegance, the methods of forming and firing it had improved and pottery workshops had been organized around the apprentice system, with assistants working under the supervision of the master potter. One of these master potters, a sixteenth-century Italian named Cipriano Piccolpasso, wrote *The Three Books of the Potter's Art,* describing his methods and those of other potters. By reading this early ceramics manual, potters could learn how to work more efficiently. For example, Piccolpasso tells them to make the pivot of the wheel axle from steel, to set it to revolve on a flint socket or steel plate, and to wrap the bearing near the top of the axle with oiled leather to make it turn more easily. He also describes how to mix clay, how to form pots on the wheel (6-7), how to finish them, and how to build a kiln and fire it (6-8). According to Piccolpasso, vases and jugs were sometimes made in two parts, with the neck attached with slip while damp, or even sometimes stuck on with glaze after the first (**bisque**) firing. Bowls, Piccolpasso said, were often finished upside down on the wheel, with their walls thinned and smoothed by a template held against the side walls while the piece was turned on the wheel. In the same way, he stated, the wheel could be used while decorating pots.

Figure 6-7
Kick wheels are shown in an Italian potter's shop of the sixteenth century. Piccolpasso states that the diligent artisan must work as carefully on the outside surface as on the inside, smoothing out the ridges of clay that appear on the walls of the vase. Cipriano Piccolpasso, *The Three Books of the Potter's Art,* Italy, c. 1556. *By courtesy of the Board of Trustees of the Victoria & Albert Museum.*

DECORATION   Toward the end of the fifteenth century, presentation pieces—*piatti di pompi*—became an important part of the output of Italian potters. These consisted of souvenirs and gifts, wedding bowls displaying portraits of the betrothed, and dishes painted with portrayals of women and children, intended to be filled with appetizing food as gifts for new mothers.

The earlier maiolica has often been classified as "austere style" or "severe style," owing partly

Figure 6-8
Piccolpasso captures the tension of firing as the master potter urges assistants to load in wood to keep the fire going, while he times its duration with an hourglass. This sixteenth-century kiln was built of brick with flues in the floor that allowed the heat to rise through the stacked pottery; after the arched door had been bricked in, the smoke and heat escaped from vents in the roof. Cipriano Piccolpasso, *The Three Books of the Potter's Art,* Italy, c. 1556. *By courtesy of the Board of Trustees of the Victoria & Albert Museum.*

to the simplicity of its forms and partly to the style of the painted decoration that used flat areas of color, often outlined with dark lines or with the details of faces and clothing drawn in with a brush. No attempt was made to show perspective, and as a result, the figures remained on the flat plane of the plate. As time went on and the techniques of painting with glazes improved, the decorators used the white-glaze surface of the maiolica merely as a ground on which to display their knowledge of the new Renaissance method of depicting space. Now, the pottery decorators copied engravings of paintings by famous artists such as Raphael and used perspective and shading to create illusionary space and three-dimensional

form, and the biblical and mythological figures in landscapes and architectural settings appeared to be three-dimensional, with little relation to the shape of the vase or the flat plane of the plate.

Renaissance Clay Sculpture

While Renaissance painters were producing the illusion of space on the walls and ceilings of palaces and religious buildings, and ceramic painters were following their lead in their own medium, sculptors were modeling the human figure in the round, instead of in **bas relief.** Clay, as we saw in Chapter 2, had been used by the ancient Etruscans to model large free-standing figures for their temples (2-25) and tombs (2-26), and this tradition of using clay for sculpture had continued in some areas of Italy. For example, in the late fifteenth century in northern Italy, sculptors in Ferrara, Modena, and Bologna created religious groups out of the abundant local earthenware clay, painting them with realistic colors after firing.

During the height of the Renaissance, however, most sculptors used clay (as well as wax) to make the originals from which bronze statues were cast. But some, such as Donatello (6-9) and Verrocchio, used terra-cotta clay to create portraits that were apparently intended not for casting but as works of art in themselves. Indeed, Verrocchio had some of his sculpture glazed in the workshop of the Della Robbia family so that its surface would be more durable than the paint normally applied to terra-cotta sculpture after firing.

Architectural Ceramics

Like the Islamic countries, Italy traditionally used ceramics in architecture. In some areas of northern Italy, where there was little good local stone for building, decorative unglazed bricks were molded for use around windows, doorways, and sometimes even the whole facades of buildings. With the development of maiolica, the tiles used on the floors of churches and palaces could be glazed with blue, orange, green, and purple.

In the mid-fifteenth century, Luca Della Robbia (1399–1482), impressed with the colors that could be obtained with opaque tin glazes, saw the possibility of applying them to sculpture. After much experimentation, he succeeded in developing richly

Figure 6-9
This terra-cotta bust attributed to Renaissance sculptor Donatello (1385–1466) probably represents Niccolo da Uzzano, leader of a group of merchants who tried to resist the rising power of the Medici in Florence. Portrait sculptures like this one, which may have been made from a death mask, continued the portrait tradition of the Etruscans and represented a break with medieval religious sculpture. *Courtesy Alinari/Art Resource, N.Y.*

Figure 6-10

The Virgin Worshipping the Child by Luca Della Robbia (1399–1482). He was the first to apply brightly colored tin glazes to large terra-cotta reliefs, and three generations of his family carried on the tradition into the sixteenth century. His nephew, Andrea Della Robbia (1455–1525), made the frame, decorating it with fruit and flowers in the typical family style. Luca Della Robbia, fifteenth century. *Courtesy the Philadelphia Museum of Art, purchased by the W. P. Wilstach Collection (#30.1.1).*

colored glazes, which he used on terra-cotta panels and medallions modeled in relief, many of which can still be seen on buildings throughout northern Italy (6-10). His depictions of the Madonna are usually surrounded by wreaths of flowers and fruit that display the colorful glazes to great advantage. The composition of the glazes remained a secret that was handed on to three generations of the family but was eventually lost. Some historians say it was hidden in the head of one of the sculptures. More than one Della Robbia figure, the story goes, was smashed in the attempt to find the composition of the glazes.

NORTHERN EUROPE

The wealthy city-states of Italy and the mercantile cities of northern Europe alternately traded with and periodically waged war against each other. Considering the barrier imposed by the Alps, travelers and armies moved between the areas with remarkable ease. Northern artists came to Italy to study the classical remains being unearthed there, and Italian artisans went north to work. For example, potters from the Italian ceramics town of Faenza went to France, and it was from the French spelling of the name of their town that the word **faience** came to be applied to tin-glazed earthenware.

The Romans had brought their ceramics techniques to northern Europe, where the local potters learned from them to use the true wheel and to build more advanced kilns such as the parallel-flue kiln. But after the Romans left, most of northern Europe forgot these techniques, and it was not until sometime between the mid-ninth and the twelfth centuries that potters there again learned to use the kick wheel and to fire in more efficient kilns.

Some medieval kilns were basically the same as the simple Mediterranean **updraft** types—circular, vertical, having some sort of perforated floor resting on a central pillar, the fire underneath, and a vent at the top. However, by the thirteenth century, double-flue kilns were used in which the pots were stacked on the floor of the firing chamber and a temporary vault of turf or of clay smeared on a wicker support was built over them. Eventually, in the fifteenth and sixteenth centuries, potters fired their ware in circular, multiflue updraft kilns with fires built in each of five or six radiating flues, and simple versions of the Roman parallel-flue kilns were also reintroduced. The kiln designs varied in detail from area to area, however, and potters still fired in pits in rural areas. In pit or open firing, they placed their ware in saggers and covered it with shards.

Northern Architectural Ceramics

By the time the Roman Empire had declined and the legions had returned home, the large-scale production of bricks and roof tiles that the Romans had developed to build their military posts and urban centers had died out. Later, when the parallel-flue kiln reappeared, potters in northern

Figure 6-11
For the castle museum in Lenzburg, Switzerland, Ernst Häusermann and Peter Schmid researched and built a reconstruction of an early medieval heating stove. They built the firebox of brick, coated it with layers of local low-fire clay mixed with straw, sand, and weed seeds, and then painted the unfired exterior with whitewash. They set wood-fired pots into the rounded top to radiate the heat, and with even a small fire, the pots send out a remarkable amount of warmth. Steps at the side provide a cozy sitting space. Lenzburg, Switzerland, 1986. Ht. 71 in. (180 cm). *Courtesy Ernst Häusermann. Photo: Hans Weber.*

Europe began to make bricks again along with tiles, chimney pots, drains, water pipes, and decorations to be placed atop gabled roofs.

A characteristic use of clay for architecture during the medieval period in England was for tiles for the floors of churches and large homes. These tiles were made by *tyghlers,* men who traveled around making tiles near the site at which they were to be installed. The tiles were made of earthenware, with white clay lines inlaid in the red clay depicting floral motifs, animals, saints, bishops, and nobles.

Another use of clay at this time was for stoves to heat the cold homes of northern Europe. Early medieval stoves were built of ordinary bricks and then coated with layer upon layer of coarse, wet clay mixed with straw and sand as temper (6-11). In many of the early stoves, earthenware pots

Figure 6-12
By the sixteenth century, heating stoves in Europe were covered with tin-glazed tiles molded in relief that served to radiate heat from the wood fire and provide a decorative surface. The repeat-pattern tiles are green, while the middle border of figures and the top decorations are multicolored. Austria, 1589. *Courtesy Philadelphia Museum of Art: given by Henry Dolfinger (#29.56.1).*

were set into the sides or top to conduct the heat outward. Later, the stoves were constructed with hollow glazed tiles that radiated the heat while serving as colorful decoration (6-12).

Jugs

Probably the largest part of the European potter's output took the form of jugs. Ordinary people at this time ate off wooden plates and drank from horn or wooden cups, and the nobility used metal plates, goblets, and bowls. Everyone, however, needed jugs for carrying water, wine, or beer, and jugs remained part of the potter's staple output for at least two hundred years (6-13).

The earliest medieval jugs were rough and crude but strong and bold in shape, with varied decoration—stamped and combed designs (6-14), trailed slip decoration, and human and animal figures and faces in relief were all used. Others were coated with a lead glaze that fired a yellowish-brown. The main glaze used in northern Europe at this time was made from a lead powder called **galena;** it was dusted onto the ware, where it adhered to the surface to create a yellowish transparent glaze. This lead glaze could be colored with oxides—copper to make it green and iron to make it reddish—but the addition of these oxides did not make the glaze opaque, so it did not cover the body color completely.

By the end of the thirteenth century, pottery as tableware had become widespread in northern Europe, and the ware was produced in great quantity. Now the domestic objects made of ceramics included the ever-present jugs along with cook-

Figure 6-13
A medieval potter makes a characteristic cylindrical jug using a kick wheel. Rotating the wheel with her foot, she uses a notched tool to decorate the jug as the wheel turns. The wheel head was supported and attached to the base with several wooden posts. Redrawn from a fifteenth-century playing card. *Drawing: John M. Casey.*

German Stoneware

While the potters of Britain and France were making lead-glazed jugs from local earthenware, the potters working along the Rhine Valley in Germany were discovering that the abundant local clay could be fired to a high temperature (2218°F/1250°C), making it dense, impervious to liquid, and resistant to acids. The Rhine Valley was a logical area for the development of high-fire pottery in Europe, for in addition to the large supplies of stoneware clay, the forests of northern Europe provided ample wood for the kilns and the river served as a waterway for shipping the pottery easily. The first stoneware was made near Bonn in the middle of the twelfth century, and from then on the potters along the Rhine made jugs (6-15). The basic form of these jugs remained the same for several centuries, but the styles of decoration changed as new fashions and techniques developed. From about A.D. 1300 on, the use of stamped, applied decoration was particularly characteristic of the Rhenish jugs. Many of the jugs were decorated with medallions in bas relief. To create these medallions, the potter first carved an original in stone. Apparently, carving the original in stone allowed more precise details. The stone carving was pressed into clay to create a positive that was fired at a low temperature. From this clay positive, any number of negative clay molds could be made, and it was from these that the relief medallions were created. The low-fired clay molds were porous so that the medallions could be removed easily when the mold had absorbed water from the damp clay. Once the medallions were made, they were **luted** to the jug. The clay body of the stoneware jugs fired to a dull gray color, so the jugs were often coated with an iron wash to give them more color.

Salt Glazing

The potters found that the lead glaze they used on earthenware was unsatisfactory for glazing stoneware, for it would melt and run off at the high temperature needed to fire that heat-resistant ware. We do not know if they deliberately attempted to discover a glaze that could be fired at the high temperature stoneware required or if the discovery of salt glazing was accidental. At any rate, at some point the potters found that if salt were introduced into the kiln, it would vaporize

Figure 6-14
The jugs made in medieval England were glazed with a lead powder (galena) that was sprinkled onto the surface of the clay. During firing the lead combined with the silica in the clay, forming a glaze. The incised lines on this jug, made with a notched tool, were typical decorations, as were designs made with stamps and small wheels called roulettes. Ht. 14⅝ in. (37 cm). Lead glazed, England, c. 1300. *Reproduction by permission of the Syndics of the Fitzwilliam Museum, Cambridge.*

ing pots, bowls, skillets, lamps, cups, weights for spinning wool, mortars—the list is a long one. Potters settled near available clay sources, digging their clay from pits near their cottages. As they dug them deeper and rains filled them with water, the pits became so dangerous to travelers that in England in the fifteenth and sixteenth centuries the courts ordered potters not to dig clay within eight yards of the highway.

in the heat, and as the sodium in the vapor settled on the stoneware, it would combine with the silica in the clay body to create a shiny, transparent coating on the pottery (6-15).

Salt-glazed ware became extremely popular, and the Rhine Valley potteries were organized to produce it in large quantities. Large quantities of jugs were exported down the river to the Netherlands, France, the whole of western Europe, and on to England, even reaching the early American colonies. Because the industry was important economically, the stoneware potters kept their techniques secret, creating ill feeling and envy among the earthenware potters. As a result, the

Figure 6-15
Salt-glazed Bellarmine stoneware jug with face. The potters along the Rhine River in Germany found that their local clay became vitreous and impervious to liquid when fired to high temperatures. This gave them an advantage over potters who had to depend on porous earthenware clay for their pots, and the further development of salt glazing gave them an even greater superiority. The faces on these jugs were generally press-formed in molds and then applied to the jugs. *Courtesy the Smithsonian Institution.*

Figure 6-16
Brown earthenware "Harvest" jug. To decorate such jugs, the artists trailed white slip over the surface and then scratched lines into it revealing the fired clay below, thus creating the detail. This one includes the royal coat of arms, the lion and unicorn, and an inscribed motto. White slip over earthenware, sgrafitto decoration, England, 1775. *Courtesy Royal Albert Memorial Museum, Exeter City Museums, England.*

stoneware potters were expelled from one city, ostensibly because of the danger of fire posed by the kilns, but probably because political pressure was exerted by the earthenware potters.

The potters in Germany continued to guard the secret of the salt glazing zealously, and it was not until the mid-sixteenth century that French potters began to make salt-glazed stoneware, and not until 1671 was a patent taken out in England for the manufacture of this product. Even then, country potters continued to make slip-decorated earthenware jugs (6-16) into the nineteenth century, and today ceramists still reinterpret the jug shape (12-58).

The Spread of Tin Glazing

In the fourteenth century, potters from Spain had brought the technique of opaque tin glazing to France, but it was not until the sixteenth century, when Italian potters came to work in France, that the French potters learned their methods of glazing, painting, and firing. Eventually they created their own style of multicolored ware, decorating it with the Renaissance motifs that were popular all over Europe. With this colorful tin-glazed ware, the French took over a large part of the European market.

One individualistic artist in France whose work was quite different from the usual decorated tin-glazed pottery was Bernard Palissy (1510–1590). Originally a glass painter whose work led him to an interest in glazes, Palissy created sculptural work—figurines colored with lead glazes—and a distinctive series of sculptural display plates modeled in brightly colored relief with faces, fish, eels, and fruit (6-17), which became popular with the aristocracy. Palissy was so fascinated by glaze experimentation and so determined to develop new glazes, that at one time he sat up for six days and six nights tending his kiln. Palissy wrote that after ten years of this intensive work, "I became so thin that my legs had no roundness of shape left about them. . . . as soon as I began to walk, the garters with which I fastened my stockings used to slip down." Palissy used molds for his forms, often making them from life, and when he died his followers continued to use his molds to produce copies of his work.

European Blue and White Ware

When the first shipments of blue and white Chinese porcelain arrived in Europe around 1600, Europeans were accustomed to the Italian maiolica, French faience, and Dutch delftware (all of these terms mean essentially the same thing—that is, earthenware covered with an opaque

Figure 6-17
Relief-decorated plate by Bernard Palissy (or in his style). Palissy (1510–1590), a French glass painter, became interested in pottery glazes and used them in rich colors to enhance the realism of the modeled objects on his plates. France, sixteenth century.

Figure 6-18
Made in Holland in the town of Delft, this wig stand of white-glazed earthenware decorated with cobalt blue shows the influence of Chinese exported ceramics in its painted flowers and birds. Delft, Holland, seventeenth century. *By courtesy of the Board of Trustees of the Victoria & Albert Museum.*

white tin glaze and decorated with a variety of colors). Such pottery was thick, not translucent like porcelain, and despite the glaze coating not totally impervious to liquids or resistant to acid. The new fine porcelain caused a sensation; people had seen nothing like it before. In order to compete with the imported porcelain, the potteries in Italy and elsewhere, especially in the Low Countries, immediately began to imitate it. Since they did not know the secret of making porcelain, they made their imitations in earthenware. The opaque white glaze on earthenware did provide a good background for cobalt blue decoration, so the European potters were able to produce a relatively inexpensive copy of the Chinese porcelain that had the general appearance of the fine white Oriental ware even if it lacked its delicacy and translucence.

DELFTWARE Although blue and white ware was produced throughout Europe, the town of Delft in Holland became especially noted for it, and as with Faenza, its name became synonymous with its product. This Dutch town became a major pottery center as a result of events that had little to do with ceramics: The breweries of Delft at this time were having economic difficulties, and it was decided to turn them into potteries and teach the unemployed brewers to be potters. A great variety of tin-glazed earthenware objects was made there; apothecary jars, tiles, mugs, barber's dishes, bowls for the bleedings so popular in medical practice, and wig stands were all decorated with cobalt blue, reflecting the rage for Chinese-inspired decoration called **Chinoiserie** (6-18). The Dutch became expert in making tiles, and the blue and white glazing became especially popular in Holland, where it was used for shining tiled walls in kitchens, dairies, and hallways, reflecting the Dutch housewives' industrious housecleaning.

Different factors affected the way the expanding ceramics industry developed in each country. In France, for example, two quite different motives gave impetus to the industry: royal pride and French taste in food. In 1709 King Louis XIV was in need of money, so he had the royal gold and silver bowls, cups, and plates melted down, leaving himself with no appropriately elegant tableware. He then commissioned the potters of Limoges to make faience of the Italian type to replace it, thereby giving royal patronage to the industry. Meanwhile, expanded mustard manufacturing in Dijon kept the potters there busy making the faience jars in which the mustard was shipped.

The Ceramics Industry

PORCELAIN   Although the use of stoneware had become widespread throughout Europe and it was made in great quantities, potters there continued to search for the secret of porcelain. As early as the late sixteenth century, Italian potters had made what is known as **soft-paste** porcelain; unlike true porcelain, soft-paste porcelain can be scratched with a sharp steel instrument. Finally, around 1710, Johann Friedrich Böttger, a chemist and alchemist in Germany, discovered how to make the true high-fired, translucent material known as **hard paste.** On the order of the king of Saxony, Böttger had been trying to make gold from less expensive materials to fill the depleted royal treasuries. It was during his research that he experimented with clays, and in the process of his experiments he discovered how to make a fine stoneware that was so hard it could be cut on a lathe. His discovery led to the founding of the Meissen ceramics factory. Then, when he discovered kaolin in Saxony, he succeeded in making true porcelain. Thus, Böttger's unsuccessful attempts to make gold led to a discovery that turned out to be a commercial goldmine.

After production of porcelain began in Germany, intense competition developed among other countries, and a race was on to discover its secret so that they could compete with the flood of imports from China and the output of the German factories. Eventually, other European countries did learn how to make porcelain, and many of them found the kaolin supplies needed to make the fine, translucent ware.

In Denmark the ceramics industry was at first supervised by French and German technicians who brought their techniques and even their clay with them because the local clay did not fire well. In 1779 a factory was established that became the Royal Copenhagen Porcelain Factory, and a French potter who had come to work for the Danish king was ordered to teach two of the local technicians his porcelain-making secrets before he was allowed to return to France. This was typical of the competitiveness of the ceramics industry in Europe after the arrival of Chinese porcelain.

BRITAIN

It was partly as a result of a political event that the production of blue and white ware spread to Britain. In 1689 William of Orange became king of England as well as king of the Low Countries, and at this time potters from Delft went to England, taking their knowledge and techniques with them.

Along with the blue and white porcelain, tea was also being imported from China, and Chinese tea and Arabian coffee became the fashionable drinks in English drawing rooms and coffee houses. Like the Japanese potters who had had to adapt their products to the imported tea ceremony (3-30), the English potters were affected by this new social habit and had to develop new shapes for pouring out the popular new beverages, so teapots and coffeepots now constituted a large part of the potter's output.

Slip-Decorated Earthenware

While the blue and white tin-glazed ware gained popularity among the wealthy and fashionable, simple earthenware vessels were still used in most rural areas. In Britain, for example, potters continued to make large quantities of lead-glazed earthenware decorated with slip, and traveling pot sellers marketed the ware from village to village, selling it directly from their carts. The slip-decorated pottery was made with techniques that remained very much the same in country areas well into the eighteenth and nineteenth centuries — and these techniques are still used by some studio potters there today. In one technique, the decorative slip was **trailed** onto wet slip of a contrasting color, and then a comb or another tool was dragged across it in a technique called **feathering,** which created a marbled effect (7-2). In another technique, **sgraffito,** the ware was covered with a coating of light-colored slip; then, when the slip was dry, the lines were drawn through it with a sharp instrument, revealing the darker body clay below it (6-16).

Earthenware plates, often formed by draping a slab of clay over a hump mold, were now in use on the tables of most homes. The potters also made plates for display or as wedding and christening gifts, decorating them with impressed designs filled with black and brown slips.

Kilns remained basically the same, except that now the ware to be fired was often stacked on thin slabs of stone used for shelves, and in order to keep the pots from sticking to the saggers when the glaze melted — a problem that had resulted in many ruined pots and saggers in the past — small pellets of heat-resistant clay were placed under each pot. Although the potteries were still basically small, family-run workshops, the basis for a much expanded ceramics industry was gradually being built up.

English Stoneware

In the seventeenth century, some English potters had learned to make high-fired, nonporous, acid-resisting stoneware — a big improvement over earthenware pottery. Potters experimented with different types of stoneware bodies — dark red and dark brown were usually used for teapots, coffeepots, and jugs. In 1671 a Fulham potter, John Dwight, applied for a patent to make porcelain and stoneware. Actually, his efforts to make porcelain had not quite succeeded, but he had developed a fine, white stoneware body that was especially successful for small figure sculptures, on which he used salt glaze. The salt glaze fitted

the clay body well and did not obscure sculptural details by filling up indented areas. By the eighteenth century, in Staffordshire, where large numbers of potters had settled because good clay was available there, white stoneware was used in a combination of mold and handbuilding techniques to make small sculptures (6-19). These were built with thin rolls of clay that acted rather like the skeletons of the figures; over these, thin slabs of clay were draped to form the clothing.

The English Ceramics Industry

England took longer to learn to make true porcelain, but in the process of experimenting with clay bodies, the potters there developed a type of soft paste that fused at a lower temperature than porcelain because it contained **bone ash** that acted as a flux. Still in use in England for making **bone china,** this soft-paste clay body was to have a profound effect on the world's tableware.

One potter, Josiah Wedgwood (1730–1795), probably had more responsibility than any other person for transforming the English potteries from small family workshops into a mass-production industry that used steam power and large-scale distribution methods. This transformation made

Figure 6-19
In the early eighteenth century, potteries in Staffordshire, England, adapted German salt-glazing techniques to small sculptured groups made of a dense, white stoneware body. The details of faces and clothing were accentuated with dark brown clay slip. Ht. 6 in. (15.2 cm). Pew group, Staffordshire, c. 1730. *Reproduction by permission of the Syndics of the Fitzwilliam Museum, Cambridge.*

it possible for ordinary people to afford attractive, easily washed tableware. In addition, Wedgwood experimented with a variety of clay bodies and developed a speciality called **Basalt ware,** which was formed into classically inspired vase shapes (6-20).

Some of the social changes occurring in England during the eighteenth and nineteenth centuries had a bearing on the ceramics industry there. The development of transportation, for example, played an important role in the industry, and by 1777 a new canal was bringing cheap water transport to the door of Wedgwood's newest factory. Wedgwood also urged other pottery owners to join him in improving roads so that wagons could carry their ware easily. On the negative side, in the process of manufacturing large

amounts of tableware, the pottery-producing areas of England became polluted with the fumes and smoke that poured from the kilns; one pottery alone might have had two dozen bottle kilns in operation at a time. Bottle kilns were the type most widely used in the industrialized pottery towns during the eighteenth and nineteenth centuries. Basically these kilns were of an updraft design; the bottle-shaped outer structure both increased the draft to the inner kiln and protected the men as they loaded the saggers into the kiln from inclement weather.

As Europe moved into the Industrial Revolution, the goal in the potteries was to make more and sell it cheaper. Steam power was harnessed to turn the mixing machinery, improved potter's wheels were sped by mechanical means, molds were used in order to form the ware faster, and workers were organized into assembly lines. Although expert potters were absorbed into the factory system, individuals no longer could participate in all aspects of the ceramic process. Thus, a separation developed between the individual potter and the product.

Before this separation, the artisan potter had been part of the mainstream of village life; the men and women who worked with clay had filled basic needs of the community, whether for vessels to be placed on religious altars, simple cooking pots, or even rabbit hutches or cricket cages (6-21). The potters were not concerned with the place of the artisan in society, for their place in it was secure. But in an industry that was rapidly becoming machine-oriented, there seemed to be little place for the clay worker who took pride in his or her own work—who was an artist as well as an artisan.

STUDIO POTTERY

In some situations, however, an individual artist or potter could still exercise direct control over at least part of the process—either in the forming of the work or in its design or decoration. For example, in rural areas, where village crafts-people continued to work in small shops, pottery making remained very much the same as in earlier centuries. These potters supplied the local needs for a variety of domestic objects made from earthenware—and still do so in parts of Europe, although now the tourist and export trade is becoming more lucrative.

By the 1880s, a new category of potter appeared—the studio potter. The term *studio potter*

can cover a variety of situations. For example, Ernest Chaplet (1835–1909) in France worked for two large pottery companies, but he also maintained his own workshop, in which he worked in both stoneware and porcelain, covering his creations with glazes that rivaled those from China (6-22). It was in this shop that painter Paul Gauguin (1848–1903) first made ceramics—coil-built pots and sculptures that he considered to be an

◀ **Figure 6-22**
French potter Ernest Chaplet developed an interest in Oriental glazes, which he used on simple shapes reminiscent of those of Chinese porcelain (Color Plate 3). His glazes influenced many other European potters to experiment with colorful glazes. Ernest Chaplet, France, porcelain, 1906. *Courtesy the Museum of Decorative Art, Copenhagen.*

Figure 6-23
In the 1880s, painter Paul Gauguin worked in Ernest Chaplet's studio hand-building sculptural vases and figures, glazing them with Chaplet's brilliant glazes. This one, however, was made of coarse, low-fire clay, probably in a rural potter's shop in Brittany. It depicts Tahitian gods and goddesses. Stoneware. France, c. 1893–1895. *Courtesy the Museum of Decorative Art, Copenhagen.*

important part of his artistic output (6-23). Gauguin glazed his work with some of Chaplet's glazes, but he applied them in his own distinctive, painterly manner, creating pieces that were expressive of his own sense of form and surface. On the other hand, some artists both in Europe and in the United States at this time did not form the ware themselves, but created paintings or decorations on pieces made by professional potters (6-24). They saw a piece of pottery almost as a dimensional canvas on which to paint rather than as an expressive composition.

The Arts and Crafts Movement

In the 1880s, a number of artists and art critics, in rebellion against the spread of machine-made objects and the pompous ugliness of Victorian taste, preached a return to the handcrafts. Led in England by William Morris (1834–1896) and John Ruskin (1819–1900), this group urged craftspeople to respect the materials in which they worked, and join in a revival of handcrafts that would beautify the surroundings and help the human spirit survive in a materialistic world. Morris and his followers rejected the factory situation and became influential in leading many craftspeople back to the small workshop situation of preindustrial days.

The Romantic movement in literature and art influenced many of these artists to take their inspiration from the Middle Ages, Persia, and the art of the early Italian Renaissance. William Morris and other artists of his circle, such as William Frend De Morgan (1839–1917), designed wallpapers, tiles, stained glass, fabrics, and panels of maiolica tiles (6-25), using flowing floral forms and the greens and blues of Persian pottery.

Figure 6-24
Danish artist Thorvald Bindesbøll stimulated an interest in painting on ceramics among European artists. Using professionally thrown earthenware as a ground, he painted strong abstract designs in black and white glazes, outlining them with sgraffito lines. Ht. 22¾ in. (58 cm). Copenhagen Earthenware Factory, Valby, Denmark, 1893. *Courtesy the Museum of Decorative Art, Copenhagen. Photo: Ole Woldbye.*

Figure 6-25
William Frend De Morgan, a member of the Arts and Crafts Movement in England, started his own ceramic factory in London to produce vessels and tiles designed by himself and other artists. His tiles, their designs frequently based on plant forms, were generally glazed in blue and green, sometimes with luster overglazes. Blue, green, and turquoise-glazed earthenware tile. Sand's End Pottery, 1898–1907. *Purchase in memory of Georgiana L. McClellan, 1953-104-4. Courtesy Cooper-Hewitt, National Museum of Design, Smithsonian Institution/Art Resource, N.Y.*

In Spain another believer in the medieval craft guild system was the Catalonian architect Antoni Gaudí (1852–1926). His work is of particular interest to ceramists because of his manner of using glazed pottery shards to surface many of his buildings. Gaudí's plans called for mosaics that, by the very nature of their collage process, had to be designed as they were created, so he entrusted the execution of the mosaics to a young architect, Josep Maria Jujol (1879–1949). Jujol was responsible for supervising the tile setters at the sites as they covered the facades of buildings, roofs, fountains, benches, and ceilings with pottery rejects, broken tiles, and other found objects.

Although the members of the Arts and Crafts Movement might yearn for lost craft traditions and attempt to restore the past by returning to earlier styles of art, it was clearly impossible for an art-school-graduate studio-potter to return to the role of unsophisticated village potter. Too much had happened to change the world, and the studio potter was now faced with questions that would never have occurred to a Minoan, Islamic, Japanese, or early African village potter: how to resolve the conflict between the machine and human hands, and how to choose between the desire to form clay with honesty and integrity and the need to compete with cheap, machine-produced goods. Some potters resolved the conflict successfully by designing handsome ceramics for industrial production while creating their own individual pieces in their studios, and a number of Scandinavian factories gave ceramic artists the opportunity to work in this way. The manner in which others resolved or avoided some of these questions is part of the story of the more recent past and is covered in Chapter 8.

7

The United States

At the time Europeans "discovered" the Americas, there were already many ceramic-making cultures on both the northern and southern continents; these are discussed in Chapter 5. But the arrival of the Europeans brought totally different ceramics traditions to the continents. Historical records show that potters were aboard the ships that brought settlers to the North American wilderness (7-1). Many of them were coming as free settlers searching for a better life in a "new" land, some were coming as indentured servants, while others came as slaves. Written records indicate that in New England and parts of the South, potters were at work in the colonies by the mid-seventeenth century, and once settlements had been established, all the villages and many plantations had potters who made their domestic ware. These potters, who came from many different backgrounds, brought with them the national or local ceramics designs, styles, and techniques of their homelands, and very soon after their arrival in the New World they began to make pottery from the local clay to supply the new colonies with functional ware.

COLONIAL CERAMICS

In the seventeenth century, when the settlers embarked for the New World, low-fire earthenware covered with opaque tin glazes had been popular

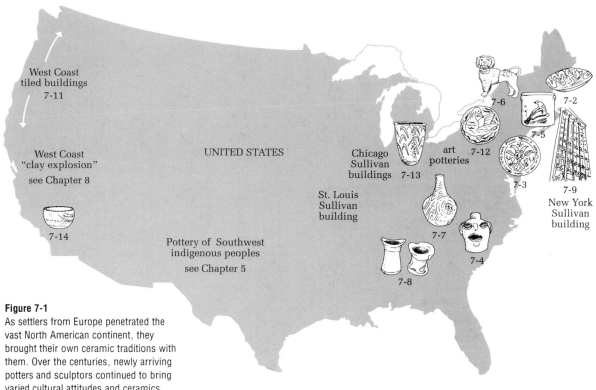

Figure 7-1
As settlers from Europe penetrated the vast North American continent, they brought their own ceramic traditions with them. Over the centuries, newly arriving potters and sculptors continued to bring varied cultural attitudes and ceramics techniques, and as a result, no single American tradition has ever existed. Now, with growing appreciation of the continent's indigenous cultures, combined with influences from every part of the world, American ceramics exhibits a vigorous energy but no one identifiable style.

Figure 7-2
This slip-decorated platter is an example of how the potters who came to New England from old England reflected the types of ceramics they had made at home. Their pottery was made for everyday use. Earthenware, slip-decorated.
Courtesy the Shelburne Museum, Shelburne, Vermont.

throughout Europe as dinnerware for the more affluent and as display and gift ware. Since most of the early potters who first settled in New England came from old England, the pottery they made reflected that background, and since their ware was produced for utilitarian use, they made it as they had made earthenware at home — slip-decorated and lead-glazed (7-2).

New England

Although little of the earliest New England–made pottery has survived, enough shards have been found at excavated kiln sites and enough town records have been found referring to potters' activities for us to know that potters were well established there very early. The wealthier colonists could afford to import their tin-glazed tableware and other ceramics from Europe, so the local potters concentrated on making simple earthenware utensils. For this reason, colonial ceramics in North America was not greatly influenced by European maiolica wares, and it was some time before any decorative ceramics that could compete with more sophisticated European wares were produced in the colonies.

The colonial potter in New England was usually a farmer or fisherman who dug his clay in the fall, dried it in the winter, reconstituted it in the spring, and made pottery whenever he could spare the time. The master potter — the father of the potting family — would usually do the throwing, and a couple of his assistants — often his sons — would do the rest of the work.

The earthenware was thrown on a kick wheel and then glazed with red lead, which was ground with sand and water in a glaze mill consisting of two millstones. To the transparent glazes, the potter added cobalt, manganese, or iron, depending on which oxides were locally available, and he frequently applied the glaze in spots, streaks, or splatters. Slip decoration was popular; the jars, tubs, wash basins, pie plates, crocks, and porringers were trailed or painted. None of the decoration was elaborate, probably because of the Puritan attitude that condemned frivolity. But despite the strictures of the Pilgrim Fathers, the potters in New England tried to make their products as attractive as the material and the social and religious mores allowed.

Although pottery making was generally a male occupation, women did a good deal of the deco-

Figure 7-3
Another type of European decoration — from Germany — was used in Pennsylvania. First covered with a white, overall slip, this earthenware plate was then decorated with slip-trailed tulips and Hapsburg eagles. George Hübner, Pennsylvania, 1786. *Courtesy Philadelphia Museum of Art: given by John T. Morris (#00-21).*

rating and glazing, and apparently some women were potters as well. In 1716, for example, an advertisement offered the services of women potters who had arrived as indentured servants and who were available for hire, and there are records of widows who ran potteries after their husbands died.

Pennsylvania

The distinctive pottery made by the Germans who settled to farm in Pennsylvania reflected the decorative traditions of German country pottery. In the mid-seventeenth century in northern Europe, decorated plates commemorating important events were placed on shelves or hung on walls. The more prosperous colonial farmers also wanted to preserve the memories of births, weddings, or other events on plates, so dates, names, proverbs, and other inscriptions circled the edges of display plates (7-3). The plates were made of earthenware covered with slip or a glaze, with many of the design motifs — such as the Hapsburg double-headed eagle — taken directly from the decorative motifs used in Germany. These designs were trailed, painted, or scratched on in the style of northern European peasant art.

Figure 7-4
Face Vessel from Bath, South Carolina. When Africans came to the New World, they brought with them the ceramic traditions of their homelands, which they integrated with the European techniques to which they were exposed. Along with utilitarian ware, the plantation potters created these lively, expressive face pots. Red earthenware with ash glaze. Early nineteenth century. Ht. 8 in. (20 cm). *Photographs and prints division, Schomburg Center for Research in Black Culture, The New York Public Library, Astor, Lenox and Tilden Foundations.*

African-American Pottery

Recent discoveries and reevaluations have shown that in the earliest colonial days in Virginia and Maryland the few African Americans worked as indentured servants and craftspeople rather than as slaves. Not until later — at the end of the seventeenth century as slavery became widespread — did they become primarily field workers.

Some of the decorated clay tobacco pipes, once believed to be Native American, have recently been recognized by anthropologists as having been made by these African-American craftspeople. Apparently the pipes — made between 1650 and the end of the century — were made on European molds, but the incised and applied designs were African. The designs on hundreds of these pipes bear a striking resemblance to those on the pottery and pipes of West

Africa. For example, one such design included tiny circlets of applied clay that can be seen on Ife sculpture (4-3), while others were scratched into the clay and then emphasized with white clay rubbed into the lines (4-9). Later, a number of slaves used their pottery skills to make pots that sometimes combined European vessel forms with African imagery, including sculptured three-dimensional "face pots" (7-4). A few of these slave potters were well known, and they sold their functional work at nearby market towns, earning income for their masters.

Stoneware

The perfecting of stoneware was the most important development in eighteenth-century European functional ceramics because containers made of this clay body were impervious to liquids and acids (see Chapter 6). When, as early as 1730, English and European potters who knew the technique of firing stoneware arrived as settlers in the mid-Atlantic states, they searched for and found local stoneware clay, and began to use it to make a wide variety of utilitarian ware. By the end of the eighteenth century, stoneware had for the most part replaced earthenware in domestic ceramics in the new country. Because the English potteries shipped the fine products of their **china** factories to the colonies to grace the tables of the wealthier colonists, and the clipper ships brought the treasured blue and white ware from China, American potteries concentrated primarily on producing utilitarian stoneware to satisfy the needs of simpler households. These needs were many and various: In the days before home canning or refrigeration, housewives required large numbers of containers in which to store pickled vegetables, salted pork, vinegar, and homemade beer. Stoneware was perfect for these uses, as it was impervious to acid as well as water and its salt glaze contained no lead (7-5).

Stoneware clay did not exist in New England and upper New York, and the potters who made the ware in lower New York, New Jersey, Pennsylvania, and Virginia guarded the secret of its manufacture jealously and exported the finished ware to the northern areas. As the market grew larger, however, and potters in other parts of the colonies finally learned how to salt-glaze stoneware, raw stoneware clay from New Jersey was shipped via waterways to northern potteries so that they

Figure 7-5
New York and Vermont potters specialized in simple jugs, stoneware crocks, and pots decorated with chickens, eagles, and shorebirds as well as patriotic images. Sometimes stacked 6 feet (1.82 m) high in the kilns, the cylindrical crocks were thick-walled enough to support the weight of those placed on them. Firing and salt-glazing the utilitarian stoneware in wood kilns required from six to eight days. Ht. 11½ in. (29.2 cm). *Courtesy New York State Historical Association, Cooperstown, N.Y.*

could make their own stoneware. After 1820, when the Erie Canal and a network of waterways made raw materials and markets even more accessible to these potteries, a flourishing ceramics industry developed in Vermont and upstate New York.

These early stoneware potteries began as simple workshops, but they turned out a remarkable amount of ware. For example, one pottery mentioned in the 1850 census was described as making a hundred thousand pieces of earthenware a year with a staff of only three men, a woman, and a horse. The horse was undoubtedly used to turn the **pug mill** that mixed the clay and to carry the ware to market. This mixing mill usually consisted of a wooden tank with iron spikes set on its inside walls. The tank was filled with dry or damp clay, sand, and water, and a central shaft with spikes was turned by horse or water power, agitating and mixing the clay and water slurry. After the ingredients were thoroughly mixed, the semiliquid clay was screened to remove impurities and larger particles, then set aside to stiffen and age.

As time went on, the workshops actually did become small factories, and the work of the potter became more specialized. The master potter, using a kick wheel, would throw the basic shapes, making tall, wide-mouthed cylinders for meat tubs; low tubs for butter pots; tall, narrow cylinders for butter churns; medium-sized cylinders as water dispensers for poultry; and smaller cylinders with an added neck and spout as jugs. Next, a finisher carefully smoothed the inside and outside and sometimes impressed decorations in the damp clay using a carved or textured wheel, called a **roulette.** A third person would add the handles, and yet another worker would decorate the crock with slip of a contrasting color. The inside of the stoneware was generally coated with **Albany slip,** made from a fine clay mined near Albany, New York, that fired to a dark brown or black slip glaze. The stoneware was lined with this slip glaze because it was stacked in the kiln rim to rim and base to base, so the vaporized salt did not penetrate to glaze the interiors of the crocks and pots.

Decoration

Much of the decoration was done with slip, and some decorators developed great facility in wielding the slip cup, using it to draw designs directly on the damp clay. This type of **slip trailer** was a small pottery flask with a thin neck into which a quill was inserted; the slip ran out the hollow quill onto the unfired ware. Laid down in separate lines and dots, the slip flowed together in some places to form solid areas and formed lines that stood out in relief in others. The same type of slip trailer was used to flow on oxides such as the cobalt that produced the characteristic blue decoration on many country crocks. The designs drawn on the stoneware—patriotic themes such as the American eagle or flower designs, birds, or grazing deer—reflected the interests of the people for whom the pottery was intended.

Salt Glazing

The technique of salt glazing used in the colonies was basically the same as that used in Europe. The ware was fired in a single firing; the usual low-temperature preliminary (bisque) firing that would have driven the moisture out of the clay was eliminated. For this reason, the kiln operator had to regulate the wood fire carefully, increasing the temperature slowly to be sure that the pots would not burst as the water left the clay. When the kiln was firing at 2300°F/1260°C, the worker shoveled ordinary rock salt down into the kiln and closed the opening again. The salt vaporized almost instantly, and the sodium vapor covered the ware (as well as the kiln interior), forming a glaze as it combined with the silica in the clay body. In the words of a local potter's instruction manual, "When fit to glaze, have your salt dry. Scatter it well in every part of your kiln, during this act you must keep a full and clear blaze so as to accelerate the glazing and give the ware a bright gloss. Stop it perfectly tight and in six days you may draw a good kiln of ware."

After the introduction of the salt, the kiln would be kept at high heat for about three days, and then the temperature would be reduced so that the kiln would cool slowly to avoid damaging the ware. Finally, after about six or eight days, the door would be unbricked and, with luck, a kiln full of perfectly glazed ware would be revealed. But mishaps did occur, and many wasters—pieces of pottery that had buckled or cracked in the kiln—have been found at the pottery sites. Wastage was not the only problem facing the potters. When salt vaporizes it gives off a dangerous chlorine gas, and some citizens living near the salt kilns complained about gases released as the salt vaporized.

Potters followed the westward movement as the settlers moved into Ohio and beyond, setting up potteries in the new territories to provide the utensils needed in the farming communities. Eventually, as in Europe, the potteries in the colonies became industrialized in order to supply the growing market, and small workshops could not compete with the low prices of the factory-produced goods. After the middle of the nineteenth century, many factories used molds and other industrial techniques to increase production, making it even more difficult for the small workshops to compete.

Figurines

Once the colonists settled into small-town or urban life, a market developed for small figurines that could be displayed in middle-class parlors or placed on the kitchen dressers of humbler homes. Many of these small sculptures, like the Rockingham-glazed animals, were lively and humorous (7-6).

For the wealthier, there were more self-consciously elegant figures, made of a white material called Parian Marble—actually porcelain. This material was modeled or cast into sentimental statues of children or miniature sculptures of draped ladies in classical poses that imitated in small scale the work of noted nineteenth-century sculptors.

CONTINUING TRADITIONS

It was only in isolated rural areas or in mountain areas such as Appalachia, where factory-made products were hard to come by, that the tradition of the small, family-run pottery continued into the nineteenth century—and even to the present day in some places. In the Carolinas, Kentucky, the Virginias, and other southern states, a few family potteries using local clays have continued

Figure 7-6
Stoneware figure of a poodle. The deep brown glaze colored with manganese that was used on pottery figurines like this poodle originated at the Rockingham China Works in Swinton, England. When nineteenth-century American pottery and animal figurines were coated with a similar glaze in America, it was usually deliberately mottled and runny. Stoneware, 1849–1858. Ht. 8¼ in. (21 cm). *Courtesy the Brooklyn Museum, H. Randolph Lever Fund. Acc. #74.19.3.*

an almost unbroken tradition, producing the functional ware needed in a rural community—milk pans, bread pans, jugs, butter churns, and the usual storage crocks. At first, as in New England, such potteries produced earthenware, but by the nineteenth century most of the ware they made was salt-glazed stoneware like that made in New York (7-5). The potters in these potteries always used kick wheels, but here the potter stood, rather than sat, at the wheel to throw the pots. Kilns were built of bricks made of the local earthenware clay and were partially dug into the ground with the earth piled up around the sides of the arch to brace it. These kilns were called groundhog kilns, and kilns of this type are still used today by some country potters in that area.

Other traditional methods survive today in small potteries in isolated rural and mountain areas although the potter's wheels may be mechanized with jury-rigged motors made from old car parts, and the mixing mills may now be run by electricity rather than turned by the family mule. However, the jugs, churns, and crocks the potters make are now more likely to be bought by collectors or tourists than by local farmers. Despite these changes, the potters there are carrying on some of the traditions of earlier American ceramics.

Art Pottery

By the end of the nineteenth century, life had become more urban in the New World, and a growing leisure class had become interested in the arts. With increasing urbanization and the competition from large pottery factories, it no longer made economic sense for the small potteries to make utilitarian ware. These factors led many potteries to hire artists to design vases, lamps, and decorative tiles to beautify the homes of the newly wealthy. Many of the old pottery companies that were scattered across the country from Ohio to California, Colorado to New York, began to produce "art pottery" in styles influenced by contemporary art movements in both the United States and France. The owner or artist often went to the international or national expositions, where large exhibitions of art pottery were shown, and returned with new design ideas.

The Grueby Faience and Tile Company of Boston and the Rookwood Pottery in Cincinnati were in many ways representative of these art pottery companies, each of which produced distinctive wares for which they quickly became famous. These companies tended to follow the art styles of Europe and appealed to middle-class housewives who wanted their homes to reflect the newest styles.

GRUEBY FAIENCE AND TILE COMPANY Inspired by the French pottery shown at the Columbian Exposition of 1893, the Boston pottery run by William Grueby (1867–1925) made handmade semiporcelain decorated with reliefs and coated with distinctive **matt glazes.** Like most of the art potteries, Grueby's depended on young women to do the decorating, in this case graduates of art schools in the Boston area. The designs were usually based on natural forms—flowers and leaves. These were formed separately, applied to the ware, and then hand-detailed.

ROOKWOOD POTTERY Started by Mrs. Maria Longworth Nichols Storer "as," she said, "an expensive luxury, for which I, luckily, could afford to pay," the Rookwood Pottery grew out of its owner's interest in china painting—a popular activity considered acceptable for the well-bred woman. The earliest Rookwood output was largely the work of Mrs. Storer and her "lady amateurs," but once the company was put on a business basis, artists, some of whom came from Japan, were hired to design its ware. The Rookwood artists never worked from imposed designs but were allowed to choose their glazes or develop their own. The Standard Ware of Rookwood, frequently decorated by women students from the Art Academy of Cincinnati, was painted with colored slips and then coated with glazes. The use of colored slip under the glazes created a depth and richness that made the ware famous.

ADELAIDE ALSOP ROBINEAU Like numerous other women art potters in this period, Adelaide Alsop Robineau (1865–1929) came to pottery through china painting. Frustrated with decorating other people's work, however, she began to cast her own ware and then learned to throw her forms on the wheel. With the help of her husband, who did the firing, and greatly influenced by the glazes of Taxile Doat of the Sèvres Porcelain Factory in France, Robineau began to experiment with high-fire glazes, many of them **crystalline glazes.** But Robineau herself was particularly proud of her carved pieces, on which she often worked for

Figure 7-7
Vase, by Adelaide Alsop Robineau, 1913. Carving, characteristic of her work and often more elaborate than the swirling lines on this vase, was accomplished before firing when the piece was dry. Ht. 14½ in. (36.8 cm). *Copyright © The Detroit Institute of Arts, gift of George G. Booth, acc. no. 19.101.*

hundreds of hours. These were either incised (7-7) or excised—in the latter method she cut out the background, leaving raised patterns and, in at least one case, a lacy openwork.

GEORGE E. OHR In contrast to the pottery studios dedicated to creating beautifully decorated vases and bowls, George E. Ohr (1857–1918), an unusual but widely known figure in the ceramics scene, made vases and pots that expressed his unique personality. He produced his ware at his Biloxi Art Pottery in Mississippi and advertised himself on signs outside as "the greatest potter on earth." George Ohr, who saw himself as a genius and emphasized his similarity to Bernard Palissy, (6-17), was certainly the most innovative potter of his time, anticipating in his work an attitude toward clay that would not surface again until the 1950s (7-8).

ARCHITECTURAL CERAMICS

In the mid-nineteenth century, builders in the rapidly expanding American cities began to decorate their buildings with details made from terra-cotta. This material was easier and cheaper to model than stone and was appropriate when used along with the brick of which so many U.S. buildings were constructed. Although terra-cotta was often made to resemble the more expensive

Figure 7-8
Six O'Clock in the Evening and *Three O'Clock in the Morning,* by George Ohr, U.S.A. Much of Ohr's work was outside the decorative studio-pottery tradition of turn-of-the-century America, almost foretelling the attitudes of some convention-breaking potters of the 1950s and 1960s. Glazed earthenware. c. 1900. *Courtesy the Smithsonian Institution, photo no. 78–2604.*

stone facing, it was also used for construction details—for example, as fireproof tiles for ceilings. The use of terra-cotta in architecture did not become widespread until after the devastating Chicago fire of 1871, which destroyed many iron and stone buildings. After that disaster, builders realized that these materials were not as fireproof as was once believed. Many of these buildings, presumed to be fireproof, had actually collapsed in the heat of the Chicago fire, while older ones with terra-cotta or brick exterior facing survived. To avoid a repetition of the Chicago fire's destruction, builders now faced many of the new metal-frame buildings in Chicago and across the nation with ceramic. The walls of these buildings became "curtain walls" rather than load-bearing walls, and the use of malleable clay for the components made it easy to apply ornamental areas to their facades.

Louis Sullivan

The innovative American architect Louis Sullivan (1856–1924) exploited the aesthetic possibilities of this new structural system by using terra-cotta to face the metal frames of his buildings (7-9). He successfully used richly detailed terra-cotta decoration to contrast with the thin piers and columns. This ornamentation combined natural forms with a mixture of Gothic and Renaissance decorative motifs, and the whole was marked with Sullivan's highly individualistic style. For many years, designer George G. Emslie and sculptor Kristian Schneider worked with Sullivan, designing and modeling the plaster originals from which the molds for the distinctive terra-cotta decoration were made. On the facade of the Bayard Building, in New York, erected in 1897–1898, Sullivan used a combination of plain terra-cotta sheathing and columns along with cast ceramic ornament in such a way that the decoration at the top of the building seems to grow almost like foliage out of the upward-thrusting verticals.

Tiles

Many of the art potteries—the Grueby Company and Rookwood among them—made decorative tiles. A tile factory particularly famous at the turn of the century that is still producing tiles today,

Figure 7-9
The Bayard Building in New York was designed by architect Louis Sullivan and built in 1897—1898. Sullivan often used ceramics to clad his metal-framed buildings, working with his designers to create the ornamentation that became characteristic of his architecture.

the Moravian Pottery and Tile Works of Doylestown, Pennsylvania, was founded by an archaeologist, Henry Chapman Mercer. Many of his tile designs were influenced by the Arts and Crafts Movement in England (6-25), while additional inspiration came from Persia (7-10), from Moravian iron stove decorations, from Pennsylvania earthenware pottery, and from the decorations on French, Italian, and English pottery and tiles.

Figure 7-10
Tile, entitled *Persian Antelope,* made at the Moravian Pottery and Tiles Works in Pennsylvania in 1937. Founded by Henry Chapman Mercer in 1898, this tile factory reflected its founder's interest in historical ceramics, using designs such as this one, influenced by Persian as well as medieval and early Pennsylvania-German pottery. Glazed earthenware. *The Sarah and Eleanor Hewitt Fund, 1937-62-3. Courtesy Cooper-Hewitt, National Museum of Design, Smithsonian Institution/Art Resource, N.Y.*

Figure 7-11
The Art Deco period was a busy one for American ceramics factories, for architects often specified panels and tiles to clad many of their metal-framed buildings, taking advantage of the colored surfaces that glazed ceramics created. This Oakland, California, building for a local furniture company still displays pale green curtain walls decorated with typical Art Deco designs.

Art Deco

Just as art styles of the nineteenth century influenced the potteries of that time, so did new styles in the twentieth-century decorative arts have an impact on the architects who commissioned ornamental details from tile manufacturers. As a result, in the late teens and early twenties of the new century, an interest in color in architecture developed. At first, color was used only on small areas, contrasting with the solid beige or white of the building, but as time went on, ceramic was used on larger areas until eventually the entire front of the building was faced with glazed terracotta (7-11). Cast or extruded ceramics lent itself well to the low-relief decoration characteristic of Art Deco ornament, and designers soon realized its color potential. Some of the most colorful and fantastic decoration was applied to the "movie palaces" built throughout the country, many of which showed the influence of Hispano-Moresque in their architecture and tile decoration (6-4).

POTTERY

There never had been one national style of ceramics in the United States, and now that production of everyday dinnerware and other utility ceramics was industrialized, many art-oriented ceramists chose to work in a workshop/factory such as the Cowan Pottery in Ohio, where they

created art pottery and figurines. At the same time, in some rural areas, such as Appalachia, the tradition of utilitarian wheel-thrown pottery was still alive—although on the verge of dying out. It took the Depression of the 1930s and the cottage-industry relief programs—including a pet project of Eleanor Roosevelt's—to turn regional crafts into viable commercial ventures with markets outside the local areas.

Painter-potter Henry Varnum Poor (1888–1971), (7-12), on the other hand, approached the rural earthenware tradition from a sophisticated viewpoint, searching for an alternative to what he despised about the American ceramics tradition—he called it "sanitary hotel china." Asking himself how he could find a new tradition, he decided the answer was to develop a warm relation to the material, and by living close to the natural forms from which one's images evolved. Still maintaining his art orientation, from 1920 on, Poor made his living for many years as a potter in rural Rockland County, New York, decorating much of his utilitarian earthenware with images based on the animals and birds that lived near him.

Potters also came from Europe to the United States, bringing with them new perspectives and technical expertise. Among them were Marguerite Wildenhain, from Germany; Maija Grotell, from Finland (7-13); and Gertrude Natzler and her husband, Otto Natzler, from Vienna (7-14). Maija Grotell, who came to the United States in 1927, became head of the ceramics department at Cranbrook Academy of Art, a school that was ahead of the times in teaching the crafts on an equal footing with painting, sculpture, and architecture. At Cranbrook, Grotell's dedication to ceramics as an art, her disciplined craft, and her years of research into glazes that resulted in rugged surfaces and brilliant color inspired several generations of students.

Considering how widespread ceramics instruction is today, it is hard to believe that in 1938 nobody knew how to use the one potter's wheel at the University of California in Los Angeles, where Laura Andreson taught coil building and casting. Andreson had to wait until Gertrude and Otto Natzler arrived from Vienna a year later and taught her how to use it.

Figure 7-12
Painter-potter Henry Varnum Poor, U.S.A. (1888–1971), began to make pottery in 1920, building his own wheel, digging clay from his land, and learning to make pots and glazes by experimentation and persistence. He believed that *a good design is a living thing. . . . it is evolved out of a way of life (A Book of Pottery, From Mud Into Immortality,* Henry Varnum Poor, 1958). This plate with a duck design is made of earthenware, with yellow, brown, and green decoration under a transparent glaze. Diam. 11 in. (28 cm).

Figure 7-13
Maija Grotell was noted for her imaginative use of glazes and textures. A gifted potter, Grotell emigrated from Finland in the 1920s to become an important influence, through her own work and her teaching, in the development of ceramics in the United States. Stoneware, superimposed and inlaid glaze in turquoise and blue-grey. 1949. Ht. 12⅝ in. (32 cm).
Courtesy the Everson Museum of Art. Photo: Courtney Frisse.

Figure 7-14
Earth Crater Bowl. Gertrude and Otto Natzler, U.S.A., came to this country from Austria in 1938. They worked together, Gertrude throwing the pots and Otto formulating the glazes for use on her simple forms. The Natzlers were also influential teachers, passing on their aesthetic philosophy as well as their interest in glazes. Earthenware, green-grey glaze. 1956. Ht. 8¾ in. (22 cm), diam. 12¼ in. (31 cm). *Courtesy the Everson Museum of Art. Photo: Courtney Frisse.*

SCULPTURE

In the late twenties and early thirties, a number of artists from Europe emigrated to England or to the United States to work and teach. Among those who came to the United States were the Viennese Vally Wieselthier, who brought a sophisticated style and interest in color to American ceramics. A number of Americans became interested in ceramic sculpture through the influence of these Europeans, and some of them went to Europe to study. One of these was Viktor Schreckengost, who had been raised in an American pottery-making family and worked at the Cowan Pottery in Ohio—a center of small ceramic sculpture making. Schreckengost was impressed with the Austrians' respect for clay and felt more at home with this attitude than with that usually accepted by American artists who were more likely to use the ceramic process to make the fired clay look like another material. Schreckengost created sculpture that frankly displayed the material from which it was made, using images that were often humorous and sometimes bitingly so (7-15). Speaking of his 1940 work, *The Dictator,* he says,

> *The Dictator was an attempt to comment on what I saw in Europe, about which few people seemed to be aware. . . . I did receive some criticism at the time for mixing politics with art.*

A number of other ceramic artists active in the United States in the 1930s and 1940s also believed that clay was a material deserving respect. Among them were Weylande Gregory, who also worked at Cowan (his large-scale ceramic figures on the *Fountain of the Atoms* were a feature of the 1940 World's Fair); Carl Walters, noted for his sculptures of animals; and Thelma Winter Frazier, who expressed the feeling among these artists that they should try to make clay sculpture take its place as a fine art. Also during this time, other artists—painters and sculptors such as Elie Nadelman, Reuben Nakian, Isamu Noguchi, and

Figure 7-15
The Dictator, by Viktor Schreckengost. Of this 1940 piece the artist says, *Hitler, Mussolini, Stalin and Hirohito seemed to be following the old pattern of Nero, who fiddled while Rome burned. They are represented by little cupids trying to crawl up into the throne while the British Lion lies sound asleep at his feet.* Red clay, black **engobe,** white, turquoise, yellow, and black glazes. In the permanent collection of the Everson Museum, Syracuse, 1940. *Courtesy the artist and the Everson Museum. Photo: the Cleveland Museum.*

Louise Nevelson—used clay on occasion, in the same way that they might use any other medium to express their concepts. It is interesting to speculate what course American ceramic sculpture might have taken if World War II had not disrupted what was promising to develop into a vigorous American use of clay. But the war did disrupt it, and although some artists continued to work in the material after the war, clay did not reemerge as a widely used sculpture medium until the 1950s.

As has happened so often throughout history in other countries, the arrival of foreign potters and sculptors enriched American ceramics, but the war years had interrupted the process by which new influences were melded into an American style. It was not until the postwar years, with the added influence of potters such as Bernard Leach (8-2), Shōji Hamada (8-1), and Maria Martinez (5-17) that the stage was set for the "clay explosion" of the 1950s.

Color Plate 1
Ceremonial jar, China. Porcelaneous stoneware, celadon glaze. Late Northern Sung dynasty, 11th century A.D.
9.5 x 5 in. (24 x 12.7 cm). *Courtesy Asian Art Museum of San Francisco, The Avery Brundage Collection, B60 P147.*

Color Plate 2
Chūn ware bowl, China. Sung dynasty, A.D. 960–1279. Stoneware, lavender glaze splashed with purple. Diameter 7.5 in. (19 cm).
By courtesy of the Board of Trustees of the Victoria & Albert Museum.

Color Plate 3
Vase with red copper glaze, China. K'ang-hsi period, A.D. 1662–1722. *By courtesy of the Board of Trustees of the Victoria & Albert Museum.*

Color Plate 4
Lead-tin-glazed plate from Deruta, Italy, c. A.D. 1530. Diameter 8 in. (20.6 cm).
Courtesy Indiana University Art Museum. Photo by Michael Cavanaugh, Kevin Montague.

Color Plate 5
Cylinder vase from the central lowlands of the Maya area, Mesoamerica. The painted scene depicts the ritual ball game. Found at the Ik Emblem Glyph site. A.D. 650–800. Ceramic, with slip. 8 1/16 in. x 6 1/4 in. (20.3 x 15.9 cm). *Courtesy Dallas Museum of Art, gift of Mr. and Mrs. Raymond D. Nasher. 1983.148. Photographic materials copyright 1994, Dallas Museum of Art. All rights reserved. Reproduction forbidden without permission.*

Color Plate 6
Glazed tile mosaic decoration in the former Karatay Medrese (Talmudic law school), Konya,
Turkey, now a museum. Seljuk Period, c. A.D. 1251.

Color Plate 7
Figures in a village shrine, India. Painted terra-cotta.
Photo: Alain-M. Tremblay.

Color Plate 8
Paul Chaleff, U.S.A. Wood-fired jar.
Stoneware, with stone inclusions. 1993.
16 x 18 in. (41 x 46 cm). *Courtesy Frederick H. Schultz,*
Jr. Collection, New York, and the artist. Photo: Bernard Vidal.

Color Plate 9
Pierre Bayle, France. Terra-sigillata coated vessel, burnished.
Courtesy the artist.

Color Plate 10
Shore. Robert Turner, U.S.A. Porcelaneous.
11 x 9 in. (28 x 23 cm). 1985. *Courtesy the artist.*
Photo: Brian Oglesbee.

Color Plate 11
Jack Troy, U.S.A. Stoneware paddled bottle. Anagama fired.
Reducing atmosphere, cone 6–8. Height 8 in. (20 cm).
Courtesy the artist. Photo: Me Sun Lee.

Color Plate 12
Strong Support. Tony Hepburn, U.S.A. Stoneware, wood.
37 x 35 x 15 in. (94 x 89 x 38 cm). *Courtesy the artist.*
Photo: Brian Oglesbee.

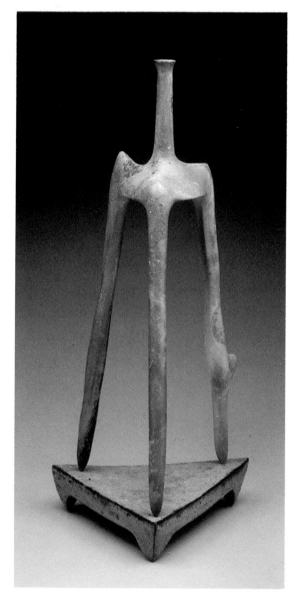

Color Plate 13
Vessel and Stand #15. Coper-Metti Series. Richard Hirsch, U.S.A.
Terra sigillata, low-fire glazes, raku. 22.5 x 10.5 x 10.5 in.
(57 x 27 x 27 cm). *Collection of Contemporary Ceramics, Ghent, Belgium.*
Courtesy the artist. Photo: Dean Powell.

Color Plate 14
Stephen DeStaebler, U.S.A. The courtyard of his studio. *Standing Figure with Tilting Head* (left). 91.5 x 15 x 21 in.
(232 x 38 x 53 cm). *Standing Figure with Yellow Aura* (right). 92.5 x 21 x 19 in. (235 x 54 x 48 cm).
Courtesy the artist. Photo: Scott McCue.

Color Plate 15
Arnold Zimmerman, U.S.A. Installation, sculptural vessels, at the Everson Museum, Syracuse, NY. Stoneware. 1987.
Courtesy the artist.

Color Plate 16
Attempt of Definition of One Moment. Jindra Viková, Czech Republic. Porcelain, metal tubing. 43 x 26 in. (110 x 65 cm). 1987.
Courtesy the artist.

Color Plate 17
Facing It. Anthony Natsoulas, U.S.A. Ceramic, glaze, canvas. Painting by Martin Camarata.
70 x 32 x 40 in. (178 x 81 x 101 cm). *Courtesy the artist.*

Color Plate 18
Tornado Teapot and Creamer. Belinda Gabryl, U.S.A. White
earthenware, low-fire glaze. 13 x 8.5 x 9 in. (33 x 21.5 x 23 cm).
*Collection of Everson Museum of Art, Syracuse, NY. Purchase Prize, 27th Ceramic
National Exhibition, Robert and Dorothy Riester Fund. Photo: James Beards.*

Color Plate 19
Harris Deller, U.S.A. Soup tureen.
Porcelain. Celadon and copper red glazes.
Height 11 in. (28 cm). *Courtesy the artist.*

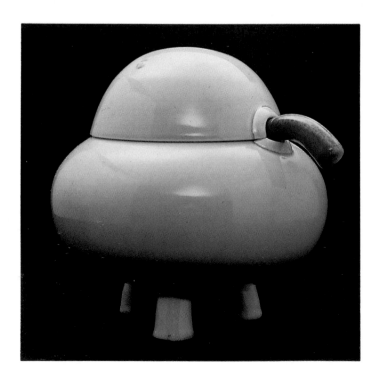

Color Plate 20
Tunnel Vision. Aurore Chabot, U.S.A. Carved, inlaid earthenware, underglazes, glazes. 22.5 x 15 x 15 in. (58 x 38 x 38 cm). 1993. *Courtesy the artist.*

Color Plate 21
Construction #3. Benet Ferrer, Spain. Glazed terra-cotta. 23 x 12.5 x 12.5 in. (59 x 32 x 32 cm). 1986.
Courtesy the artist.

Color Plate 22
Tall Dangos. Jun Kaneko, U.S.A. Stoneware. 70 x 22 x 30 in. (178 x 56 x 76 cm). *Courtesy Dorothy Weiss Gallery.*

Color Plate 23
Ron Nagle, U.S.A. Untitled. Earthenware, glaze, and acrylic enamel. 20 x 14 x 18.5 in. (51 x 36 x 47 cm).
Courtesy Rena Bransten Gallery.

Color Plate 24
Drop Coin, Fight Satan. Clayton Bailey, U.S.A. Low-fire clay, imitation fire, light, sound. 30 x 24 x 12 in. (76 x 61 x 30 cm). 1987.
Courtesy the artist.

Color Plate 25
Patrick Loughran, U.S.A. Plate and detail.
Glazed terra-cotta. Diameter, 24 in. (61 cm).
1987. *Courtesy the artist.*

Color Plate 26

Bad Manners. Marilyn Lysohir, U.S.A. Detail, installation. Low-fire clay, wood, underglaze, transparent glaze. 1983–1984.

Courtesy the artist. Photo: Rick Semple.

Color Plate 27

Reverb. Dan Gunderson, U.S.A. Low-fire clay, underglaze, transparent glaze. 24 x 16 in. (61 x 40.6 cm). 1987. *Courtesy the artist.*

Color Plate 28
John Glick, U.S.A. Stoneware tray. Multiple slips, glazes.
6.5 x 15 x 1.5 in. (16.5 x 38 x 3.81 cm). 1987.
Courtesy the artist. Photo: Robert Vigiletti.

Color Plate 29
Musselshell Vessel. Rudy Autio, U.S.A. Stoneware.
35.5 x 28 x 24.5 in. (90 x 71 x 62 cm). 1987.
Courtesy Dorothy Weiss Gallery. Photo: Gerald Kling.

Color Plate 30
Arnold Zahner, Switzerland. Vase. Crystalline glaze. Electric kiln, propane reduction. 1986. *Courtesy the artist.*

Color Plate 31
Oriole. M. C. Richards, U.S.A. High-fired clay painted with acrylic. 4.5 x 5.5 in. (11 x 14 cm). 1993. *Courtesy the artist.*

Color Plate 32
Autumn Louise. Susan and Steven Kemenyffy, U.S.A.
Raku-fired wall piece. Approx. 2.5 ft. x 4 ft. x 8 in.
(76 cm x 121 cm x 20 cm). 1987. *Courtesy the artists.*

Color Plate 33
Jim Gremel, U.S.A. Slip-cast raku vase. Copper matt glaze. 4 x 9 in. (10 x 23 cm). 1991.
Courtesy the artist. Photo: Richard Sargent.

Color Plate 34
Maria Bofill, Spain. Group of vessels. Porcelain, engobes. Heights 4 to 6 in. (10 to 15 cm). 1986. *Courtesy the artist.*

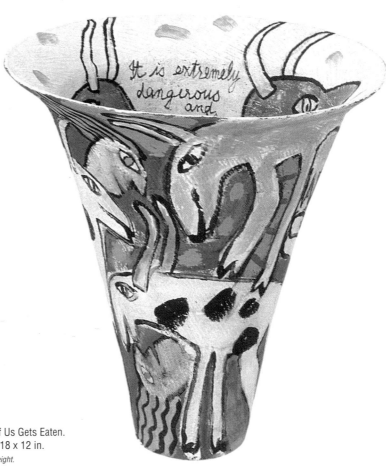

Color Plate 35
It Is Extremely Dangerous, and Generally One of Us Gets Eaten.
Sandra Taylor, Australia. Multi-fired terra-cotta. 18 x 12 in.
(46 x 30 cm). 1992. *Courtesy the artist. Photo: Greg Weight.*

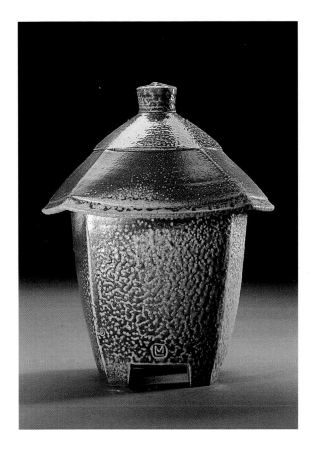

Color Plate 36
House Pot. Mary Law, U.S.A. Sodium-vapor-fired stoneware
with high-kaolin slip. Cone 11. 9 x 7 in. (23 x 18 cm). 1993.
Courtesy the artist. Photo: Richard Sargent.

Color Plate 37
Moon. Hedi Ernst, Switzerland. Sculptural plate.
Low-fire clay and glazes, Egyptian paste.
Diameter 23 in. (58 cm). 1993. *Courtesy the artist.*
Photo: Cathrin Marchetti.

Color Plate 38
Construction. Elena Colmeiro, Spain. Mixed media; high-fire clay containing silicon carbide with iron frame. Oxide colors. 50 x 69 x 8 in. (127 x 175 x 20 cm). 1993. *Courtesy the artist.*

Color Plate 39
Paint Swirler. Patti Warashina, U.S.A.
Low-fire clay, underglaze, glaze, wood.
43.5 x 26.5 x 25 in. (110 x 66 x 64 cm). 1993.
Courtesy the artist and Bentley Tomlenson Gallery, Scottsdale, AZ.
Private collection. Photo: Paul Macapia.

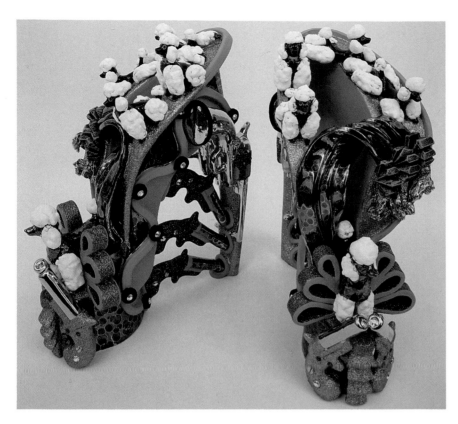

Color Plate 40
Poodle Puff Gun Shoes.
Toby Buonagurio, U.S.A. Low-fire
clay and glazes, lusters, acrylic
paint, flocking, glitter, glaco gomo.
17.5 x 11.5 x 7.5 in. (44 x 29 x
19 cm). 1993. *Courtesy the artist.*
Photo: Edgar Buonagurio.

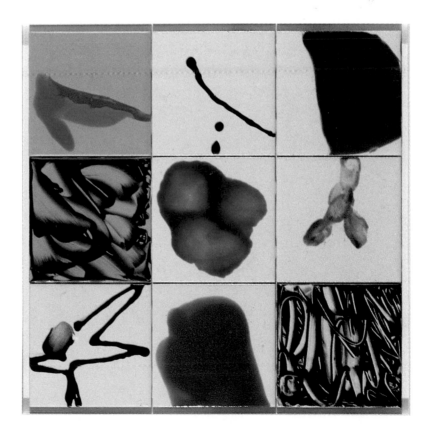

Color Plate 41
Night Sounds in Camoglie. James
Melchert, U.S.A. Ceramic tile, china paint.
14 x 14 in. (35 x 35 cm). 1986.
Courtesy the artist.

Color Plate 42
Field. Antony Gormley, England.
Installation in Salvatore Ala Gallery,
New York. Low-fire clay. Figures made
in Cholula, Mexico. 1993. *Courtesy the
artist and the Salvatore Ala Gallery. Photo:
Joseph Coscia.*

Color Plate 43
Detail of *Field*. Antony Gormley, England. Installation in Salvatore Ala Gallery, New York.
Courtesy the artist and the Salvatore Ala Gallery. Photo: Joseph Coscia.

Color Plate 44
Rise and Shine Magic Fish.
Kate Malone, England. Glazed
fish, permanent installation in
a pond, Lea Valley Parks,
England. *Courtesy the artist.*

Color Plate 45
Underground Room. Deirdre Daw, U.S.A. Installation at Rena Bransten Gallery, San Francisco, California. Low-fire clays, maiolica glazes,
multi-fired. 1992. *Courtesy the artist. Photo: John Wilson White.*

Color Plate 46
Bernard De Jonghe, France. Mountaintop installation. Wood fired, cobalt glaze. 1986. *Courtesy the artist.*

Color Plate 47
Form Echoes Series. Alexander Lichtveld, Netherlands. Installation exhibited in Amsterdam and Japan. Stoneware, metal, handmade paper.
63 x 22 x 10 in. (160 x 56 x 25 cm). 1993. *Courtesy the artist; the Foundation for Visual Arts, Amsterdam; and the Nishida Gallery, Nara, Japan. Photo: Cherry Kamp.*

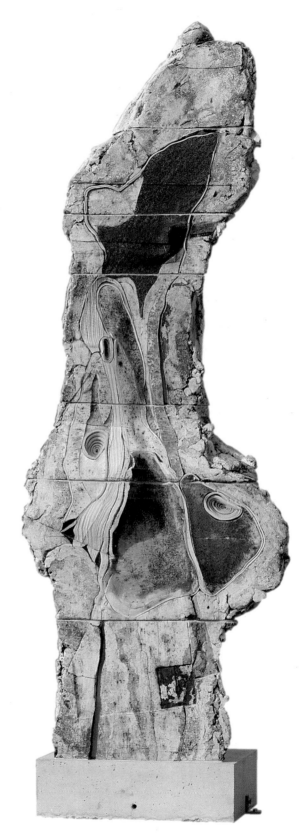

Color Plate 48
's-Hertogenbosch. John Toki, U.S.A. Stoneware with porcelain inserts.
29 x 46 x 144 in. (.73 x 1.7 x 3.66 m). 1992. *Courtesy the artist. Photo:*
Scott McCue.

Color Plate 49
Viola Frey, U.S.A. in the courtyard of her studio with several of her tall figures.
Low-fire clay, low-fire glazes. Figure approximately 8 ft. tall (2.4 m). 1983.
Courtesy the artist.

Color Plate 50

Architectural installation by Madola, Spain. Fountain in Plaza de la Font, Ayuntamiento de Barcelona, Spain. Overall view and detail. Glazed clay pavers, concrete, water. 1992. *Courtesy the artist.*

Color Plate 51 *Hands in Clay* clay test tiles.

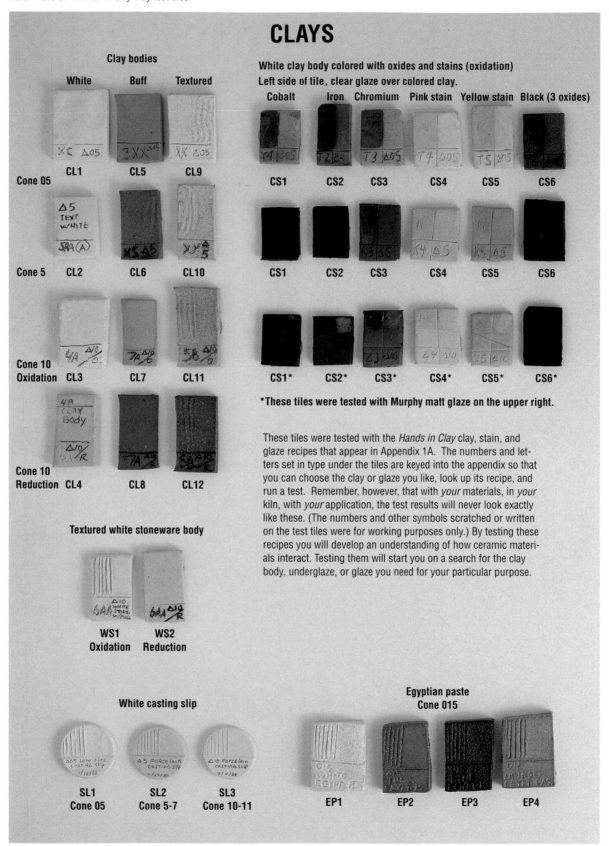

CLAYS

Clay bodies

	White	Buff	Textured
Cone 05	CL1	CL5	CL9
Cone 5	CL2	CL6	CL10
Cone 10 Oxidation	CL3	CL7	CL11
Cone 10 Reduction	CL4	CL8	CL12

White clay body colored with oxides and stains (oxidation)
Left side of tile, clear glaze over colored clay.

	Cobalt	Iron	Chromium	Pink stain	Yellow stain	Black (3 oxides)
	CS1	CS2	CS3	CS4	CS5	CS6
	CS1	CS2	CS3	CS4	CS5	CS6
	CS1*	CS2*	CS3*	CS4*	CS5*	CS6*

*These tiles were tested with Murphy matt glaze on the upper right.

These tiles were tested with the *Hands in Clay* clay, stain, and glaze recipes that appear in Appendix 1A. The numbers and letters set in type under the tiles are keyed into the appendix so that you can choose the clay or glaze you like, look up its recipe, and run a test. Remember, however, that with *your* materials, in *your* kiln, with *your* application, the test results will never look exactly like these. (The numbers and other symbols scratched or written on the test tiles were for working purposes only.) By testing these recipes you will develop an understanding of how ceramic materials interact. Testing them will start you on a search for the clay body, underglaze, or glaze you need for your particular purpose.

Textured white stoneware body

WS1	WS2
Oxidation	Reduction

White casting slip

SL1	SL2	SL3
Cone 05	Cone 5-7	Cone 10-11

Egyptian paste
Cone 015

EP1	EP2	EP3	EP4

Color Plate 52 *Hands in Clay* surface color and glaze test tiles.

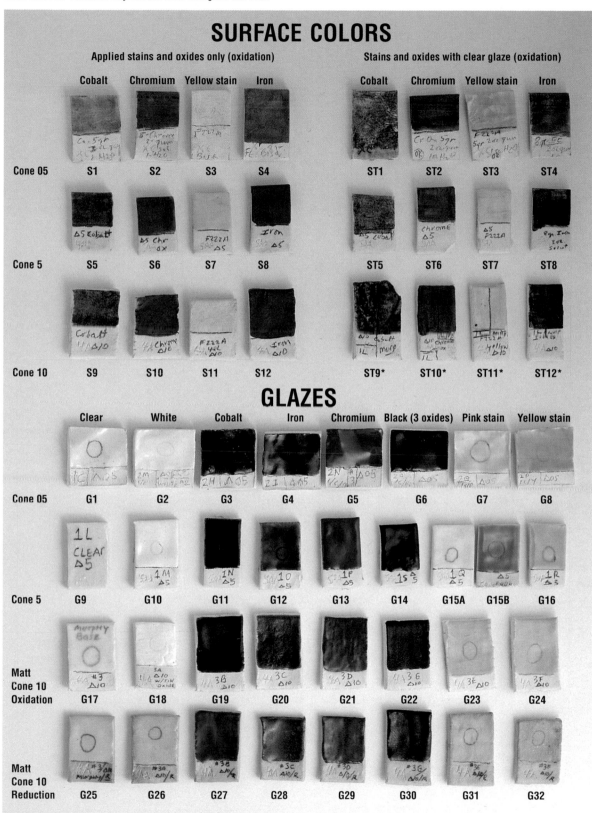

SURFACE COLORS

Applied stains and oxides only (oxidation)   Stains and oxides with clear glaze (oxidation)

	Cobalt	Chromium	Yellow stain	Iron		Cobalt	Chromium	Yellow stain	Iron
Cone 05	S1	S2	S3	S4		ST1	ST2	ST3	ST4
Cone 5	S5	S6	S7	S8		ST5	ST6	ST7	ST8
Cone 10	S9	S10	S11	S12		ST9*	ST10*	ST11*	ST12*

GLAZES

	Clear	White	Cobalt	Iron	Chromium	Black (3 oxides)	Pink stain	Yellow stain
Cone 05	G1	G2	G3	G4	G5	G6	G7	G8
Cone 5	G9	G10	G11	G12	G13	G14	G15A	G15B	G16
Matt Cone 10 Oxidation	G17	G18	G19	G20	G21	G22	G23	G24
Matt Cone 10 Reduction	G25	G26	G27	G28	G29	G30	G31	G32

*These tiles were tested with clear glaze on the left and Murphy matt glaze on the right.

Color Plate 53
Outdoor installation in Shigaraki, Japan, by Kimpei Nakamura. High-fired tiles; photo decal decoration, overglaze brushwork.
Individual tiles about 22 x 22 x 5/16 in. (57 x 57 x 0.8 cm). Mold-made sculptural forms; glazes, photo decals, overglazes, lusters. 1993.
In collaboration with Otsuka Ohmi Ceramic Co. Ltd, Shigaraki. Courtesy the artist. Photo: Takashi Hatakeyama.

8

Worldwide Interaction

There is nothing new about potters exchanging ideas and techniques; throughout history potters traveled from one part of the world to another, bringing with them their own ways of working in clay and trading their techniques and styles with the local potters wherever they settled. In the past, new ideas traveled slowly, but since the beginning of the twentieth century, exchange has been speeded by accelerated communications, and with increased air travel, personal contacts between ceramists have become more common. Thus, everyone active in the field has been exposed to a greater diversity of influences than ever before. For this reason, any overview of twentieth-century ceramics must encompass the entire globe.

EAST MEETS WEST

One important interchange of ideas that came about in the early part of the century was largely due to the friendship of two potters. In 1909 art-school-trained Bernard Leach (1887–1979) left England to live in Japan, where he studied with the sixth Kenzan, Miura Kenya (see Chapter 3). He said that what led him to ceramics was participating in a raku party at which each artist and poet present decorated and fired a plate. Seeing the pots put into a red-hot raku kiln and watching

as one was plunged into water on its withdrawal, Leach decided on the spot to be a potter. He stayed in Japan until 1920 and came to know Shōji Hamada (1894–1978), who worked in the pottery town of Mashiko. Hamada formed his pots with local clay and glazed them with ash from nearby woods, creating pottery that reflected Japan's rich rural ceramic tradition (8-1).

When Leach returned to England in the 1920s to start a pottery in Cornwall, Hamada helped him set up his kiln and stayed as his partner for three years. Later, the two traveled widely, lecturing around the world and meeting with potters and students. On a trip in 1952, during which they visited the United States, they met two people who also became influential — Maria Martinez of San Iledefonso (5-17) and Peter Voulkos (8-9). Like Hamada, who worked within the traditions of *mingei*, or Japanese folk art, Leach drew on the background of English folk pottery, combining its traditions with those he absorbed during his stay in the Orient (8-2). Leach's writing in *A Potter's Book*, first published in 1940, inspired potters around the globe, and his Cornwall workshop became a place of pilgrimage and training for young potters. His ceramics were also greatly admired in Japan, where he was honored as the seventh Kenzan, while Hamada was designated a National Living Treasure by the Japanese government.

Figure 8-1
Shōji Hamada, of Japan, dedicated himself to the production of useful, folk-inspired pottery. Along with the English potter Bernard Leach, Hamada was influential in creating a bridge between Eastern and Western ceramics. Stoneware, wax-resist decoration. c. 1931. *By courtesy of the Board of Trustees of the Victoria & Albert Museum. Crown Copyright.*

Figure 8-2
English potter Bernard Leach's work reflected aspects of Japanese folk pottery as well as the slip-decorated earthenware made by English country potters. Leach said that through working with clay and kiln he wanted to share that "primitive energy that created the world." Stoneware, gray-green glaze. St. Ives Cornwall, c. 1931. *By courtesy of the Board of Trustees of the Victoria & Albert Museum.*

Figure 8-3

Chop Dish with Moon and Grasses, by Kitaoji Rosanjin of Japan, was made from a slab and fired in the Bizen method, in which straw or other organic material is introduced into the kiln to produce local reduction in order to create surface markings. Bizen was only one of the many types of work made by painter-calligrapher-potter Rosanjin (1883–1959). *Gift of Miss Margaret O. Gentles, 1969.697. Photograph © 1994, The Art Institute of Chicago. All rights reserved.*

One of Leach's assistants in Cornwall for a time was Michael Cardew (1901–1983), who was influential in the 1960s and 1970s. Cardew spent several years in Ghana and Nigeria, where he set up pottery training centers to teach local potters to make stoneware. When he lectured, African potters sometimes traveled with him to demonstrate their traditional methods (4-13).

Another potter active in the global interchange in the 1950s was Kitaoji Rosanjin (1883–1959), of Japan (8-3), who lectured and gave workshops in the United States demonstrating Oriental ceramic techniques.

Originally, Rosanjin made his name as a calligrapher, painter, and gourmet restaurateur. He said he took up pottery in order to replace the restaurant's antique tableware that was destroyed in an earthquake in 1923, because he felt that good food required beautiful plates. To replace the lost ware, he became a master of diverse styles of ceramics—Bizen (8-3), Oribe, Shino, Seto, and porcelain decorated with his famous calligraphy in blue—but he always infused his work with his personal transforming touch. Rosanjin thus came to pottery from a different orientation than Hamada, and it is revealing that when he made *his* trip around the world he visited Picasso and Chagall.

TWENTIETH-CENTURY ART INFLUENCES

In fact, an important influence on twentieth-century ceramics came from a number of European painters and sculptors who on occasion turned to the medium of clay, sometimes forming their own pieces, sometimes working in close collaboration with trained potters. Among these artists were Joan Miró (1893–1983; 8-4), Pablo Picasso (1881–1973; 8-5), and Henri Matisse (1869–1954; 8-6), each one responding to the innate quality of the material in his individual style. These artists themselves had been influenced by art from around the world such as the African sculpture and Oceanic artifacts they had seen in the Musée de l'Homme in Paris.

Picasso showed a true Mediterranean understanding of clay, working closely with French potters Georges and Susan Ramié to construct animals and figurines made up of combined and imaginatively altered vessel forms (8-5). Matisse, on the other hand, viewed pottery as a painting ground and decorated professionally thrown plates with characteristic images and brushwork (8-6).

Of these artists, Miró was perhaps the most finely attuned to the clay medium. He usually executed his sculptures with his own hands and made use of accident and chance in his clay work just as he had in his nonceramic sculpture, combining disparate forms, enlarging the scale of other forms, and reusing ideas from his earlier sculptures. For example, his 1963 sculpture *La Déesse,* made for the Labyrinth at Foundation Maeght in the south of France (8-4), reflects elements of some of his earlier ceramic vessel-like figures, and it also incorporates a tortoise-shell form that he later used as the whole body in a bronze figurative work.

Miró frequently participated in the firing of his sculptures with his collaborator and Catalan friend, master potter Josep Llorens Artigas (1892–1980), delighting in the excitement of their transformation in the wood-fired kiln, commenting that in ceramics *fire is the master.*

Figure 8-4
Déesse was created in 1963 by Joan Miró of Spain, working with his friend, Josep Llorens Artigas, using an assemblage of forms, including that of a tortoise shell. Miró and Artigas collaborated over a number of years, creating ceramics that included plates, large and small sculptures, and a number of murals. This large sculpture is part of the Labyrinth at Foundation Maeght, France. Ht. about 60 in. (1.50 m). © 1994 ARS, New York/ADAGP, Paris.

Figure 8-5
Picasso, who worked for several years with Georges and Susan Ramié at their pottery in Vallauris, designed *Cavalier* by imaginatively combining thrown forms. Earthenware, c. 1951. Ht. 15½ in. (39.4 cm). *By courtesy of the Board of Trustees of the Victoria & Albert Museum;* © 1994 ARS, New York.

Figure 8-6
Henri Matisse painted this portrait plate at the Ramié pottery in Vallauris. The drawing is black with some sgraffito, and the face is reserved in the clay body color against blue. *Courtesy Museo Internazionale delle Ceramiche, Faenza;* © 1994 ARS, New York.

Figure 8-7
Composite pots made in two parts from altered wheel shapes by
German born English potter Hans Coper. The flattened upper sections are attached to cylindrical bases; the pots are colored with
manganese and white slip. Stoneware. *Courtesy Alphabet and Image.*

Another influence came from the Bauhaus
School, founded in Germany in 1919 and influential there and worldwide until it closed during
the Hitler regime. The school taught the doctrine
of "form follows function," stating that applied
decoration had no place on any contemporary
product. Bauhaus ideas influenced the design of
many factory-produced objects in the late 1920s
and 1930s, and individual potters as well as such
factories as Arabia in Finland and Wedgwood in
England reflected these changing attitudes with
simple, cleanly designed functional tableware.

During the 1930s, a number of potters left their
native lands due to political or artistic repression.
Among them were Ruth Duckworth, Maija Grotell (7-13), and Gertrude and Otto Natzler (7-14),
who emigrated to England and the United States
from Austria, Germany, and Scandinavia.

Lucie Rie had studied and maintained a studio
in Vienna in the 1920s before she went to England, where she set up a studio in 1939. Hans
Coper (1920–1981) came to ceramics through an
assistantship with Lucie Rie in postwar London
(8-7). His work exhibited an intense interest in
the formal, as opposed to the decorative, aspects
of ceramics, and he created pottery that combined the classic and the innovative.

In Italy in the 1930s, the painter Lucio Fontana
(1889–1973) had made three-dimensional still
lifes in clay, compositions that prefigured the ges-
tural quality of Abstract Expressionist paintings.
Later, Fontana began to slash and puncture his
paintings on paper and canvas, calling the results
Spatial Concepts. He then returned to clay, making what he called *Spatial Ceramics,* punching
holes and creating craters in the flat surface of his
plates (8-8). Given Italy's ceramic tradition, it is
not surprising that others there — among them
Leoncillo Leonardi — brought twentieth-century
painting and sculpture influences to clay, modeling the plastic material freely and using bright,
low-fire glazes to create works influenced by Cub-
ist and Futurist painting.

Factory Studios

Some ceramics factories encouraged innovation
and interchange through a variety of programs.
For example, after World War II, European ceramic factories, such as De Porcelyne Fles in Holland, Bing and Grøndahl in Denmark, and Arabia
in Finland, set up experimental studios where
artists have a working relationship with the fac-

Figure 8-8
Italian painter-sculptor Lucio Fontana, after experimenting with punctured and slashed paper and canvas, did the same with clay. Fontana's innovative ceramics influenced other Europeans to approach clay with greater freedom. Maiolica fired at 1650°F/900°C. Black background with blue and gold metallic luster, fired in reduction. Diameter 16½ in. (42 cm). *Collection Carlo Zauli.*

Figure 8-9
In the United States, Peter Voulkos led the "clay movement" of the 1950s and 1960s, slashing, puncturing, and altering his plates, initiating a new approach to working in clay. Stoneware and porcelain. 1973. Diam. 18 in. (46 cm). *Courtesy Toki Collection.*

tory and at the same time are given the freedom to create their own work. There is no doubt that the establishment of these programs was of great assistance to studio ceramics during the difficult postwar recuperative period in Europe, and they have continued to play a supportive role to the present. Since then others, among them the Kohler Company in the United States and the Sèvres factory in France, as well as a number of brick and pipe factories in various countries, have welcomed artists into their workshops to use their facilities and technical expertise.

Interest in what was happening in ceramics outside their own countries now led some students and potters to travel and study or work with well-known potters around the world. In ancient times, potters had been part of the migrations of tribes that slowly made their way across continents, but now air travel brought groups of ceramists together frequently to exchange ideas.

CONVERGING INFLUENCES

In the 1950s and 1960s, many influences came together: Leach's, Hamada's, and Rosanjin's writing and lecturing; the growing interest in Zen Buddhism; awareness of the indigenous cultures of the Americas, Africa, and other less-well-known areas; the painting and ceramics of artists

such as Picasso (8-5), Miró (8-4), and Fontana (8-8); and New York's Abstract Expressionist painting and constructive sculpture. Collaborations and friendly associations between sculptors and ceramists led at this time to an exchange of ideas, and many experimented with each other's materials. For example, the renewed interest in color in sculpture among nonceramic artists led artists who were working in clay to expand their own color pallettes by using postfiring paint and enamels on their work. Conversely, nonceramic sculptors began to experiment with clay, coloring their works with the brilliant glazes characteristic of the ceramic process, often turning to ceramists for assistance in the technical aspects of firing.

The Clay Revolution

These currents in the art world affected the work of a number of potters and sculptors in the United States (8-9) and Europe. Italian sculptor Carlo Zauli (8-10), who started as a potter in the ancient ceramic town of Faenza, collected pottery shards and slumped, overfired **wasters** (discards) from the fifteenth-century kilns that made the town's famous maiolica (6-6). With these twisted wasters in mind, and impressed with the innovative work of Leoncillo and Fontana, Zauli began to alter his vessels, crushing them or allowing the soft clay to take on its own form as it tilted and collapsed. By the 1970s, Zauli was creating large sculptures and murals (8-10), although he still continued to make vessels.

Just as the work of Fontana, and later Zauli, influenced potters and ceramists in Europe to work in a freer manner, the iconoclastic approach of Peter Voulkos, who set up the ceramics department at the Otis Art Institute in Los Angeles in 1954, led to a new approach to clay in the United States (8-9). Originally a painter who followed the contemporary art movements of Europe and New York, Voulkos was already known for his skill in throwing when he began to attack his vessel forms. He combined, altered, paddled, and slashed them as the clay responded to his gestures, and he began to use bright, low-fire glazes on his stoneware forms, finally supplementing these with nonceramic paint, saying that by painting on his sculpture he was using color not to enhance the form, but rather to violate it in order to add to the excitement of the piece. Voulkos's vital personality gathered other artists and students around him at Otis. Among these were John Mason, Paul Soldner (15-34), Jerry Rothman, Kenneth Price, and Billy Al Bengston, all of whom went on to become influential in the 1960s and 1970s.

John Mason had been a potter, but while at Otis he began to alter his vessels, and by 1957 he was building sculptures and walls of clay with chunks and strips, using the medium to record his spontaneous gestures. By the 1960s, Mason's work became simplified into large forms, many of them variations of the cross, almost monochromatic, and at times seeming closer to Color Field painting than to sculpture (8-11). In the 1980s he returned to the vessel form, creating sharp-edged geometric vessels with striped glazed surfaces.

Kenneth Price, another of the group centered at Otis, created brilliantly glazed, egglike forms with erotic overtones (8-12). These forms showed

Figure 8-10

In *Crollo di Cercope*, Italian sculptor Carlo Zauli, perhaps inspired by the landslides that occur on the clay soil of the Apennine foothills, allowed the clay to collapse as it responded to gravity. He then carefully reworked the surface of the forms. Black stoneware with touches of black glaze. 1980. 33 × 17 in. (85 × 45 cm).

Courtesy the artist. Photo: Antonio Masotti.

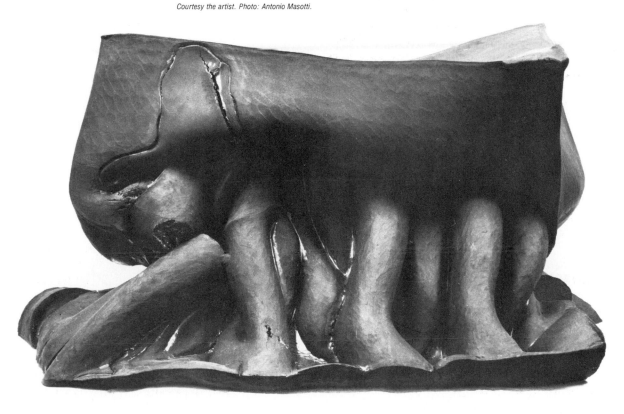

Figure 8-11
Red X, by John Mason, U.S.A. In the 1960s, Mason coated his cross forms with monochromatic glazes that created fields of color. Stoneware. 1966. 58½ × 59½ × 17 in. (148.5 × 151.1 × 43.2 cm). *Courtesy Los Angeles County Museum of Art. Gift of the Burt Kleiner Foundation.*

more affinity with the work of Miró than with that of Voulkos and Mason. By 1970 Price was working with the cup form, first in association with biological references, then with geometrical abstractions. After Price settled in New Mexico, he created installations containing curios inspired by Mexican folk pottery.

Another influence in mid-century ceramics centered in Northern California during the 1950s and 1960s. The term *Funk* has been applied loosely to the work of several artists whose only real similarity was their irreverence toward established art concepts. One such artist, Robert Arneson, worked in the vessel form for some time, using processes that were closer to those of conventional ceramics. But the vessels Arneson made in the 1960s depicted toilets and sexual organs, images that were startling, even shocking, when

seen in the context of the glazed ceramic vessel. When Arneson switched from using high-fired stoneware to low-fired earthenware in the 1970s, he began a series of self-portraits, utilizing low-fire glazes in the manner of a realistic painter. From that time on, Arneson used both his own and others' portraits to express his satirical ideas—political, artistic, and psychological. Some of his works of the 1970s, such as the installation *Fragments of Western Civilization* (8-13), point toward his later work, in which he commented on the nuclear arms threat and militarism in general (8-24).

Other artists on the West Coast also expressed their irreverence in sculpture that tended to startle, frequently using popular material in highly personal ways. Richard Shaw used everyday objects—playing cards, letters, books, soup cans—from which to cast components. When he combined these in *Stack of Cards on Brown Book* (8-14). Shaw created an image that was static but, given its insecure balance, was apparently captured just as it was about to collapse. Other Shaw pieces made use of unlikely objects to create new realities, such as humans made up of sticks, cans, and baseballs. Clayton Bailey, who with Chris Unterseher and other artists called their work Nut Art, juxtaposed clay images with everyday

Figure 8-12
S. L. Green, by Kenneth Price, U.S.A. One of the transformers of ceramics in the 1960s, Price focused on contained organic forms, touched with eroticism. The surfaces, frequently painted with car enamel, are brash and startling but the overall effect is elegant. Clay and paint. 1963. 9⅝ × 10½ in. (24.45 × 26.67 cm). *Collection of Whitney Museum of American Art, N.Y. Gift of the Howard and Jean Lipman Foundation, Inc., 66.35.*

Figure 8-13
In his installation *Fragments of Western Civilization,* American Robert Arneson combined bricks and a crumbling self-portrait. He said, "I try not to take myself too seriously, and when I think I might be, it is time to knock over a big piece." Terra-cotta. 60 × 260 in. (152.4 × 660.4 cm). *Collection: National Gallery of Australia, Canberra. Photo: Bayens Photo Co. Quotation courtesy John Michael Kohler Arts Center.*

Figure 8-14
Stack of Cards on Brown Book, by Richard Shaw, U.S.A. Shaw used molds to form the decal-decorated porcelain components of his sculptures and then assembled them into constructions that create a new reality. Ht. 14 in. (35.6 cm). *Courtesy Braunstein/Quay Gallery.*

Figure 8-15
Clayton Bailey's *Nose Lamp* combined
a functioning electric lamp with glazed
ceramic noses. Earthenware, low-fire
glazes. 1968. Ht. 11½ in. (29.2 cm).
*Courtesy M. H. de Young Museum Art School. Photo:
Robert Hsiang.*

objects in an amusing way, as when he surrounded a banal electric lamp with cast ceramic
noses (8-15), but sometimes his work was disturbing or downright gory.

Fantasy and Narrative

As more and more potters and sculptors began to
use clay as an expressive medium, some turned
to narrative while others turned to fantasy or the
creation of personal mythologies. West Coast artist David Gilhooly (8-16) brought to life an imaginary world in which frogs worshipped a frog
god and goddess of fertility, producing a glut of
food to whose color and texture low-fire glazes
were ideally suited. The multitude of shiny green
frogs that emerged from Gilhooly's hands served,
under the guise of humor, as a serious commentary on human society. Another Californian,

Figure 8-16
American David Gilhooly created a mythological Frog Land, in which the shiny
green inhabitants engaged in behavior
just as outrageous as that of humans.
The base of this portrait of *Mao Tse Toad*
displays biographical drawings of the
Chinese dictator. 1976. 31 × 19 in.
(78.7 × 48.3 cm). *Private collection. Courtesy
the artist.*

Figure 8-17
In *Summit Conference* by American sculptor Louise McGinley, the artist joins her sinister group of traders as they bargain for spoils over a campfire. McGinley fires her work at a very low temperature and paints the surface with acrylics after firing. Life size.
Courtesy the artist.

Louise McGinley, also used fantasy to comment on the human condition; her half-human, half-bird figures often warned of lurking dangers waiting to destroy us (8-17).

Fantasy was not confined to California or the United States. In Holland, Nicholas Van Os and Jan Snoeck (16-9) also expressed their personal fantasies in clay. Inhabiting a world that appears far removed from the tidy landscape of Holland, Van Os's life-sized creatures are part human, part animal, part pure Van Os. Other ceramists were intrigued with images of human habita-

tion — for example, Bryan Newman in England, Jacques Bucholtz in France, and American sculptor Charles Simonds, who built miniature unfired villages in unexpected places around the world (8-18a). Simonds's *Dwellings* are the abandoned homes of a race of Little People who migrated frequently, leaving mysterious evocations of their lives behind. On occasion, as in the Museum of Contemporary Art in Chicago, Simonds built permanent archaeological ruins with crumbling altars, pottery shards, and other relics of the world of the Little People (8-18b).

(a)

(b)

Figure 8-18

(a) Charles Simonds, U.S.A., works on one of his *Dwellings*. In the 1970s, Simonds traveled the world, creating groups of buildings in unusual sites, using miniature unfired bricks, leaving them to disintegrate in weather or traffic. In the Passage St. Julien La Croix, Paris, 1978. **(b)** Simonds also constructed a few of his *Dwellings* in sheltered museum or gallery settings. Sections of this one continue along a wall eight by forty-four feet (2.4 × 13.4m). 1981. *(a) Courtesy the artist. Photo: Jacques Faujour. (b) Collection of the Museum of Contemporary Art, Chicago, gift of Douglas and Carol Cohen.*

Figurative Sculpture

In the 1920s and 1930s, in both the United States and Europe, figurative ceramics had for some time been largely confined to colorfully glazed figurines. Some of these were modeled by sculptors or ceramists for factory reproduction, such as those done for porcelain or low-fire clay by Marguerite Friedlander Wildenhein and Ernst Barlach in Germany or by American artists working in factories like the Cowan Pottery Studios in Ohio. These works reflected the art styles of each era — from European 1920s figurines to international Art Deco decoration. In the United States, during the 1940s, a number of artists used clay to create individual works of sculpture that included political pieces by Viktor Schreckengost (7-15), who had studied in Vienna; the animals of Carl Walters; and Weyland Gregory's large figures for a fountain at the 1939 World's Fair. Clay was also used occasionally for semiabstract figurative work by abstract sculptors like Louise Nevelson and Isamu Noguchi, both of whom were better known for their sculpture in other media. By and large, under the influence of constructive nonceramic sculpture and the then-current abstract painting, artists working in clay during this period reflected a general lack of interest in the figure. It was not until the late 1960s and early 1970s that figurative images reappeared in any quantity, often in narrative, fantasy, or Funk sculpture.

By the late 1970s, however, the figure as a subject in clay sculpture was reestablished in the United States, where Stephen De Staebler continued to push his landscape forms toward the figurative; eventually he developed these into monumental standing figures (8-19, Color Plate 14), and later he detached them from the plinths on which they had grown, almost liberating them from their earthy material (9-2). At the same time, Mary Frank was folding and shaping slabs into lyrical figures (11–56), and Karen Breschi and Robert Brady were also using the figure expressively, while in Europe, Carmen Dionyse was encrusting her expressive human images with rich multilayers of glaze.

In the United States, as interest in polychrome sculpture grew, Viola Frey (Color Plate 49) used glazes in a painterly manner that broke up the forms of her large figures, while Richard Shaw applied underglazes and china paint to color figures that stood and gestured like humans but were constructed of baseballs, sticks of wood, tin cans, and other super-real cast components.

Figure 8-20
In the 1970s, Jill Crowley, England, coiled, pinched and handmodeled the portrait of *Tom* from clay mixed with crushed red brick. Stoneware. *Courtesy the artist.*

Figure 8-19
Standing Man and Woman, by Stephen De Staebler, U.S.A. In the 1970s, De Staebler created massive plinths of clay from which fragments of male and female figures seemed to grow — or into which they seemed to recede. *Courtesy the artist. Photo: Susan Felter.*

Through the 1980s into the early 1990s, figurative sculpture grew in popularity everywhere. In England, Jill Crowley explored the features and forms of men and women whose faces showed the wear and tear of their lives (8-20), and in the United States Jack Earl cast his down-home images at the Kohler Company in clay normally used for bathroom fixtures (8-21). In Italy, Guido Mariani modeled clay into full-sized figures or made installations of human clothing that evoked its owners; Beverly Mayeri, in the United States, painted her realistic figures (8-22); Marilyn Levine, also in the United States, described people through the old shoes and handbags they left behind them; Pip Warwick, in England, used slip-cast components to assemble life-sized interpretations of Pop stars; while in eastern Europe Jindra Viková (Color Plate 16) and Gertraud Möhwold used human faces to send messages from behind the Wall.

Figure 8-21

Ohio Boy, by Jack Earl, U.S.A., was formed in molds from the clay used for bathroom fixtures. In 1976 Earl was part of an innovative program at the Kohler Company, which, along with the John Michael Kohler Arts Center and the National Endowment for the Arts, made it possible for a number of artists to work with industrial materials and techniques. Slip cast and handbuilt, glazes and underglaze pencil. 1976. 15⅞ × 17¾ × 11⅞ in. (40.3 × 45.1 × 30.2 cm). *Courtesy the collection of the John Michael Kohler Arts Center. Photo: Bayens Photo Co.*

Figure 8-22

In *Checkered Woman,* Beverly Mayeri, U.S.A., created a compelling figurative sculpture at a time when she was one of a few artists heralding the return to the figure. Clay painted with acrylics. 1978.

Courtesy the artist. Photo: Colin C. McRae.

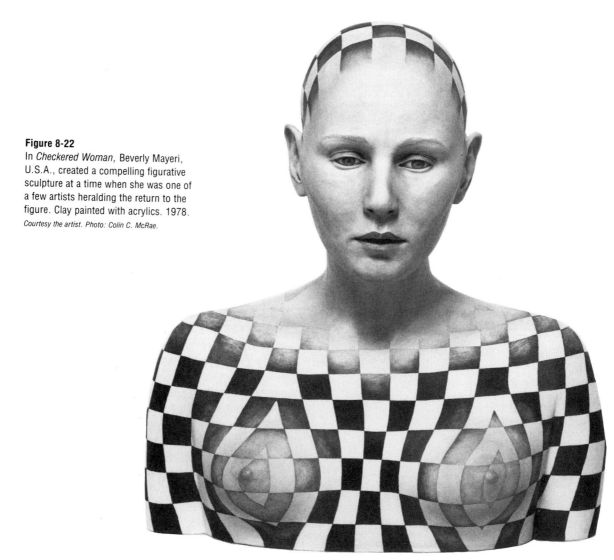

Figure 8-23
You Captured My Heart, by Patti Warashina, U.S.A., combined two-dimensional painting and sculptured forms. The figure is painted on a flat background, with nose, arms, and hands in relief. Low-fire clay, wooden arrows, oxidation firing. Height 30 in. (76.2 cm), width 18 in. (45.7 cm), depth 15 in. (38.1 cm). *Courtesy the artist.*

Figure 8-24
Global D and D, by Robert Arneson, U.S.A. Many of Arneson's works addressed his concern about increasing militarism and the possibility of nuclear war. 1982–83. 75 × 26 × 25 in. (190 × 66 × 64 cm). *Courtesy Private Collection.*

By the mid 1990s, figurative sculpture was once more widespread, and clay sculpture came full circle, responding in contemporary terms to the concerns of humans just as Greek (2-21), Etruscan (2-26), and Renaissance artists (6-10) had responded to the human needs, hopes, or fears of earlier worlds. To name only a few of the many other artists working figuratively, Judy Moonelis (9-14), Anthony Natsoulas (Color Plate 17), Patti Warashina (8-23, Color Plate 39), Deborah Horrell (8-26), and Marilyn Lysohir (14-23) used the figure to explore aspects of the human condition—love, loss, and the effect of society on individuals—while Robert Arneson questioned whether humanity would survive (8-24).

CERAMICS AND THE ART WORLD

During the 1970s and 1980s, critics were concerned with the place of ceramics in relation to the " fine arts," debating whether an object made with the ceramic process was art or craft. For many years, the West, unlike Japan, which has always honored fine pottery, has tended to place anything ceramic in the "decorative art" category. Ceramists who had begun to explore the sculptural possibilities of clay found they were not warmly welcomed in commercial galleries or in museums, and they responded in various ways which brought them more fully into the art scene.

Performance and Installations

One way in which the ceramic artist entered the current art scene was by becoming involved in happenings or performance, exploring the innate characteristics of clay. For a while, such events as dancers wallowing in slithery slip, or sculptures formed by shooting bullets into ceramic forms, were welcomed for their new and exciting approach. James Melchert, who was influential in developing polychrome ceramic sculpture, was also involved with performance. In *Changes,* a production he staged in Holland, he and other participants dipped their heads in slip, allowing it to drip down over their bodies; then they sat in a room that was hot at one end and cool at the other while a camera recorded the clay drying unevenly on their bodies. Another artist, Marek Cecula, excavated clay from a roadside bank, shaped and fired it, then returned to insert the sculpture carefully into the bank from which it had come.

An alternate route by which ceramists entered the art scene in the 1970s and 1980s was through installations: Arneson's crumbling bricks and self-portrait *Fragments of Western Civilization* commented on nuclear disaster (8-13); George Geyer installed panels of unfired clay in the Southern California surf; John Mason arranged fire bricks in geometric patterns in a piece called the *Hudson River Series;* Bernard De Jonghe carried his blue-glazed columns to the top of a Provençal mountain and video-taped the installation (Color Plate 46); Valerie Otani, Andrée Thompson, and Elizabeth Stanek registered the effect of weather on clay slip (8-25); Deborah Horrell drew on autobiographical experience in *Flesh and Bones* (8-26); Marilyn Lysohir sculptured groups of women Marines and a headless dinner party, in *Bad Manners* (14-23); and Judy Chicago rallied

Figure 8-25
Clay in Change, an environmental installation by Valerie Otani, Elizabeth Stanek, and Andrée Thompson, U.S.A. Sand, stabilized adobe, and fired clay blocks were surrounded by slip poured from a mixer. Allowed to dry in the sun and to become liquefied again in the rain, the installation exhibited many aspects of clay. The artists said they were *fascinated with this material and the powerful metaphor of time and change it implies.* 1984. Installation at the Walnut Creek Civic Arts Center Gallery, California. Photo taken after one week. *Courtesy the artists.*

Figure 8-26
Pappa Can You Hear Me? Deborah Horrell, U.S.A. Horrell says this installation *is particularly poignant for me. . . . Simultaneously it addresses the human/ archetypal desire for transcendence, loss of body concurrent with the awareness of spirit.* Porcelain, wood, etched glass, paper, acrylic, graphite; fired at cone 10. 10 × 15 × 20 ft (3 × 5 × 6 m). *Courtesy the Wida Gardiner Gallery and the artist. Photo: Stephen Sartori.*

feminists and shocked other viewers with her work, *The Dinner Party*. Throughout the 1980s and into the 1990s, installations have continued to intrigue ceramic artists, and a number of them have combined mixed media with ceramics both indoors and out. Kate Malone responded to ecological concerns by placing brightly glazed fish in a former water-purification pond outside London, Paul Astbury covered secondhand clothing with clay (9-6) and carefully resurrected a chopped-down street tree to form the basis of another installation, while Frans Duckers placed a figure at a bar in Holland (9-11). Thus, ceramics entered the art world through a number of doors and the argument over art or craft seemed at least to be in abeyance.

Given the fact that ceramics is material- and object-oriented, it is not surprising that Minimalism and Conceptualism have had less effect on it than other art movements have had. Of course, every work of art is based on a concept, but since the "pure" Conceptual artist does not create an object (beyond a written statement or plan), few ceramists could be said to have created truly Conceptual works of art. Nevertheless, in Conceptualism there are various levels of "purity," and to a certain degree a number of ceramists have been influenced by both movements. Sculptors like Johannes Gebhardt (11-57) show the influence of Minimalism, whereas Rita Pagony's plan for a fountain (16-5) was indeed Conceptual. Others, like Ellen Driscoll (16-3) and Pjotr Müller (9-10), could be said to have been primarily concerned with the concept behind their work, yet they consider the object they create from the material to be equally important.

ARCHITECTURE AND CERAMICS

Another avenue for the ceramic artist who wished to move outside pottery opened up in the architectural field. The use of ceramics in architecture has had a long past, but in the post–World War II period, the ascendancy and dominance of

the starkly functional International Style of architecture left little opportunity for the ceramist to work in architectural settings. In the 1930s, a few ceramists had been employed to design public projects such as the tile-decorated stations of Stockholm's subway system, but the use of ceramic components and sculpture in architecture was rare during this period. However, by the early 1960s, as some sectors of the public and a few architects became concerned with the dehumanizing aspects of much contemporary building, the use of ceramics to bring color and human scale to architecture began to reappear.

By 1968 there was enough such large-scale work in Europe for two young men in Holland to open Strucktuur 68, a workshop dedicated to helping artists fabricate large ceramic works — the work of Jan Snoeck, whose colorful sculpture brightens shopping plazas, parks, and hospital

Figure 8-27
Italian sculptor Carlo Zauli contrasted sharp-edged slab forms with rough areas of clay, developing a series of visual and tactile relationships that carry the viewer's eyes along the wall. Stoneware with "Zauli white" glaze. 1974. Ht. 59 in. (1.5 m), length 29½ ft. (9 m). *Courtesy of the artist. Photo: Antonio Masotti.*

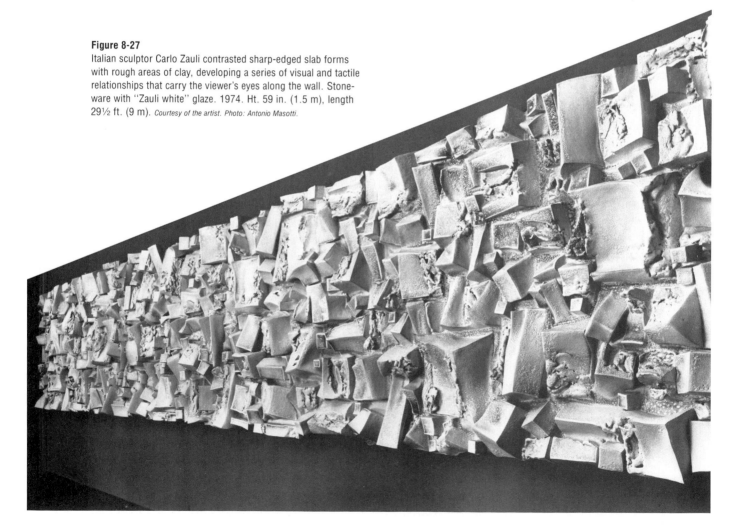

courts (16-9), is built and fired there. Italy also returned to its ancient tradition of ceramics in architecture with Carlo Zauli's massive walls (8-27), and Japan was active in this revival, with Kimpei Nakamura (Color Plate 53) as only one of many artists creating ceramic works for public and private buildings.

The United States, despite its tradition of architectural ceramics through the Art Deco period (see Chapter 7), was slower to accept ceramics in contemporary architecture, but Ruth Duckworth, who emigrated from England, was commissioned early-on for mural works, and Stephen De Staebler created site-specific works for a number of different architectural settings—from college chapel to government buildings (16-13). Marylyn Dintenfass, who left pottery to concentrate on commissioned work (16-14 to 16-17), competed with artists from other media for government and private commissions, as did Robert Sperry, whose black, white, and gray wall (16-10) made dramatic use of his method of applying slip. Although at first a good deal of the work tended to be monochromatic, eventually brightly colored tile works brought pattern and image to interior and exterior. Ceramic artists now tackled ever-larger projects, such as the traffic circle installation that Madola created in Barcelona, Spain, in which she combined water with glazed ceramics to provide a visual and physical buffer between the roaring traffic and pedestrians (Color Plate 50), while Jaime Suárez's towering ceramic-clad column (16-18) carried references to Puerto Rico's Hispanic heritage.

THE VESSEL

But what had been happening to pottery during these years of change and innovation? Artists like Voulkos (8-9) and Zauli (8-10) turned their pots into sculptural objects, then went on to create large sculptural works with no references to pottery. Faced with this challenge and with the realization that factories could produce and market well-designed ware more cheaply than they could by hand, potters began to question their current role. Some returned to creating one-of-a-kind pots, and what in the nineteenth century had been called "studio pottery" evolved into "the vessel." Numerous potters made pots more for viewing than for using, and among the many examples of aesthetically pleasing work created by

these skillful potters are vases or bowls by Hans Coper (8-7), Edouard Chapallaz (14-33), Pierre Bayle (12-1, Color Plate 9), Frank Boyden (9-18), Robert Turner (Color Plate 10), Maria Bofill (Color Plate 34), Ursula and Karl Scheid (12-5, 14-6), and Eileen Lewenstein (14-37), to name only a few.

Production Pottery

While exploration and innovation continued to attract attention, and many vessels were made with art gallery exhibition in mind, potters around the world like Karen Karnes (8-29), Janet Mansfield (12-9, 12-10), Ross Spangler (12-59), and Mick Casson (12-58) continued to supply satisfying and beautiful pieces for widespread use as utilitarian ware, along with their own versions of the studio pot. Influenced by the past in their perfection of form and glaze or by their interest in decoration, their work has ranged from the precisely crafted vases of Catherine Hiersoux (14-36) through John Glick's slip and glaze-decorated trays and plates (Color Plate 28) and Suzanne Ashmore's teapots (14-34), to Patrick Loughran's domestic ware decorated with contemporary images (9-19). It is clear that potters everywhere are still determined that the thousands-of-years-old functional pottery tradition will not be lost.

Sculptural Vessels

Once galleries and museums began to accept ceramic sculpture for display, many potters felt their work was being ignored in favor of sculptural work. This led ceramists to a reevaluation of the vessel form and to a new category, that of the "sculptural vessel." This was not a new concept— ancient Anatolian figurative pots and African-American face pots (7-4), Gauguin's sculptural pots (6-23), and the forward-looking work of the eccentric George Ohr (7-8) were forerunners of this approach. In the 1970s, a number of works fell between the categories of container and ceramic sculpture. For example, Jill Crowley's nonfunctional teacup made with a pitted and lumpy clay poked fun at conventional British bone china (8-28). Toshiko Takaezu, on the other hand, made enclosed, noncontaining pots with painterly glazed surfaces and later carried the same color sensibility to her large sculptural forms. On

Figure 8-28
To create the rough texture of *Cabbage Cup with Soil Saucer,* Jill Crowley, England, used clay heavily tempered with crushed brick, then raku-fired it. *Courtesy Crafts Advisory Committee, London, and the artist.*

Figure 8-29
Karen Karnes, U.S.A., referring to her slit-footed vessel says, *The cut slit adds a mystery to the piece. When you remove the cover you see that the bottom of the piece is above the slit, and that only reveals itself from a particular view.* Stoneware, wood fired. Ht. 10½ in. (27 cm). *Courtesy the artist.*

occasion, scale alone seemed to move the vessel into the sculptural category. Voulkos sometimes continued to work within the pot format, throwing massive vessels that would never contain anything, but which became sculptures; Arnold Zimmerman's towering carved vessels hold their sculptural presence against the strong planes of a museum building (Color Plate 15); Stephen De Staebler's urns with walls as thick as an Etruscan sarcophagus became mythical sculptures that at the same time could contain (8-30); Ron Nagle's cups grew ever larger (Color Plate 23); while Robert Turner (Color Plate 10) and William Daley (8-31) invested their pots with meaning far beyond the usual confines of functional pottery.

Figurative Vessels

The growing interest in figurative sculpture and the sense of continuity with the past that ceramists feel through their material led a number of potters in the 1980s and 1990s to reexplore history and mythology and to create vessels that refer to or were influenced by ancient cultures. Jack Thompson (15-33), Richard Notkin (9-8), Frank Boyden (9-18), David MacDonald (11-61), Richard Hirsch (Color Plate 13), and Clayton Bailey (14-58), among others, have made reference to the vessels made by early potters as far apart in time and place as prehistoric Asia, ancient Italy, the Moche cultures in Peru, and plantations of the American South. Others, like Rudy Autio (Color Plate 29), treated the figurative vessel more realistically or more colorfully.

Environmental Interests

A renewed interest in our natural resources led ceramists to explore the material in which they work in relation to its origins: Ernst Haüsermann and his students went to a clay pit to experiment with the material in its natural state (10-1), while other ceramists dug and pushed the soil into earthworks reminiscent of those made by Native Americans (5-21). Kate Malone placed brightly glazed ceramic fish in a former purification pond (16-1) to bring attention to ecological problems (Color Plate 44), and in *Clay in Change,* Andrée Thompson, Valerie Otani, and Elizabeth Stanek poured out slip and left it to erode in response to the action of sun, rain, and wind (8-25).

Materials and Process

Another area of experimentation and exploration involved the material itself. The frustration of spending days on a piece only to have the fire alter or destroy it led a few sculptors—Joyce Kohl and Robert Lyon, among them—to experiment with additives that would stabilize the clay so that unfired sculptures could at least endure for a time. Nobody has come up with an acceptable way to replace the fire's ability to make clay permanent, although Alain Tremblay has developed a mixture of clay and cement that makes his work more durable in the Canadian climate.

FIRING METHODS On the other hand, many ceramists find the firing process itself particularly intriguing, so there has been a growing interest in firing methods with artists around the globe adapting ancient techniques to modern use. Many have found that wood-burning kilns can produce a pleasing variety of surface, so they fire their ware in kilns that are reinterpretations of the traditional Japanese *anagama* kiln (8-32, 15-15, 15-17, Color Plates 8 and 11). Contemporary potters have also discovered not only that raku firing is useful for the effects it can achieve, but also that the process itself has its own fascination (15-30, Color Plate 33). Other potters have developed modern adaptations of traditional vapor firing (15-1, 15-20), open firing, or pit firing (15-36).

John Roloff, on the other hand, explored the firing process from a different angle, building impermanent sculptural kilns in unexpected places and firing and photographing them at night.

INTERNATIONAL INTERCHANGE

With the proliferation of ceramics magazines, books, and videos, and the ease of travel, along with the numerous workshops, conferences, competitions, and tours offered throughout the world, a student from Japan can watch a Turkish potter working in a cave in Anatolia, German potters can learn from a rural Spanish potter, Australians may participate in a wood firing in a Japanese village, or Russians can work in a ceramics workshop in Holland. Ideas and technical information can travel by fax at a speed that would have been the envy of the ancient Chinese potter waiting for Persian cobalt to arrive by caravan across the desert. Although such exchanges of methods and

Figure 8-30
Although this massive urn by Stephen De Staebler, U.S.A., is functional, its ritualistic presence takes it beyond the utilitarian. Formed of four slabs joined at the legs. 1977.

Figure 8-31
In *Pentagonal Destination,* William Daley, U.S.A., created a sculptural vessel that refers back to the Shang bronze-vessel makers and the Anasazi Native Americans, whom he sees as his masters. Unglazed stoneware. Ht. 15¼ in. (39 cm).
Courtesy Helen Drutt Gallery.

techniques have been characteristic of potters through the ages, today, due to developments in communication, friendly contacts between ceramists have deepened, creating a truly international ceramics community. In fact, we might call the decade of the 1990s the era of internationalism in ceramics.

Figure 8-32
Paul Chaleff, U.S.A., says that ancient Japanese methods of wood firing are now being adapted to so many ways of working that he prefers the term *kiln-glazed* or *naturally ash glazed* for his work. Using these methods, he says, has allowed him to *learn a new language of forms and surfaces* (Color Plate 8). *Courtesy the artist. In the collection of the Everson Museum.*

SHAPING
THE
PRESENT

9

The Artist's Vision

Just what is the "artist's vision"? Is it different from everyone else's? Isn't the urge to make an object or an image innate in us all? What makes it possible for one particular person to bring an image to life? Questions like these probably can never be answered satisfactorily, and certainly not in one short chapter, but listening to what artists have to say about their ways of working may give us some insight into our own creativity.

THE CREATIVE PROCESS

Psychologists and neurologists have often puzzled over creativity, over the reason why one person and not another may have the vision, the need to express it, and the ability to do so.

Perceptions, the basic components from which we form our concepts, can refer to any insight, intuition, or knowledge gained through any of the senses. What the brain makes of visual or tactile perceptions depends on each person's accumulated experiences and background, and since each perceives objects and experiences somewhat differently, what each one makes of those perceptions will, of course, be different. Creativity and the individuality that fosters it seem to develop in part from an acute sensitivity to one's perceptions and an honest effort to express the concepts or feelings that those perceptions generate. Just

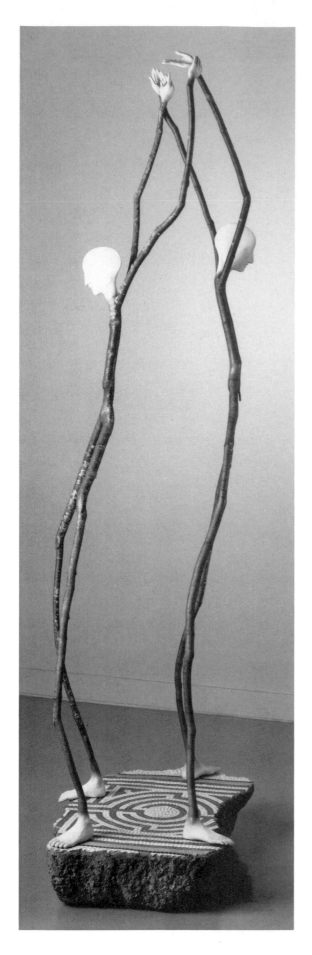

why a person is motivated to express these visually is another matter, which science does not explain.

A number of artists refer to the importance of reveries, dreams, and daydreams in the creative process. For Margaret Ford (9-1), dreams or daydreams are not only a source of material but also are subject matter, whereas William Daley, who makes vessels that are aesthetically pleasing to our eyes and appealing to our tactile and kinetic sense, says that he dreams them in a state of reverie (8-31, 9-17).

Usually near dawn, he says, *I often make great pots. I usually can't remember them clearly, but I know how they feel. They are large, mysterious, yet familiar.*

Our dreamlike reveries so easily unite our physical perceptions, intuitions, and intellectual concepts, allowing the creation of mysterious pots, moving poetry, or wondrous paintings. Carl Jung called these dreams "the almost invisible roots of our conscious thoughts."

Dreams may not only provide a source of material for art, but their persistence may itself provide some of the content. Margaret Ford says that she

has always dealt with the persistence of memory. I am intrigued with the connection of memory to daydreams. That is, the relationship between the ongoing vitality of the past with the images one uses to bring the future into being.

Although the enigmatic quality of Ford's *The Bower* (9-1), leaves the viewer the latitude to see and interpret it, Ford is specific about the sources of the imagery. Her sculpture is a good example of how an artist can cull references from a variety of sources, then combine them in a totally new context. Let's follow her through the process.

The image of *The Bower,* Ford says, refers to the Bower Bird, which is so named for the elabo-

Figure 9-1
The imagery of *The Bower,* by Margaret Ford, U.S.A., grew from a number of sources—visual, autobiographical, and psychological. It took the artist's vision to bring these concepts together and to present viewers with a work of art which they may interpret as they wish. Clay, wood, mosaic. Ht. approx. 7 ft (2.1 m).
Courtesy the artist.

rate structure the male bird builds to court the female:

The complexity of this construction is fascinating; the bird spares no effort assembling plant material into two columns, wide at the base, then narrowing and arching to join at the top. Under the archway he places shells and bright objects. All this solely for the purpose of attracting and winning the female.

In Ford's sculpture the arch is implied in the branches and in the pose of the figures, which stand on a mosaic maze. This maze also has a direct reference to an event in the artist's life:

Prior to the making of the piece, she says, my partner and I had been remodeling my house. The complexity of combining a personal relationship with the construction of one's home was far more like the twisting and turning of a maze than a clear-cut architectural plan.

Ford had also recently read about a hedge maze in England called "The Bower" that the lord of the manor was supposed to have built as a sheltered, secret place to meet his mistress. To Ford, this bower image added its own symbolic meaning to the sculpture:

In my mind these two images, the maze and the arch of the Bower Bird, give form to the complexity of male/female relationships.

In the sculpture, we can see how Ford's imagination gathered together a collection of visual, symbolic, zoological, botanical, and personal references. Then, rather like the Bower Bird, she used them to create a special environment: With her creative vision, she saw an image that she believed would embody all of these references, and, using her visual, critical and technical skills, she developed that image into a piece of sculpture—a sculpture which, despite the particular meaning it has to her, is open enough to allow us to experience and interpret it as we wish.

In retracing the creative journey that brings William Daley to the final form of his vessels (8-31, 9-17), Daley says that one type, the bowl, suggests to him habitation, place, and location. He asks himself,

How does the volume want to invite the mind to enter? Is the opening expansive or constricted? At what rate do I move when I come in? Is it slow or rapid? How do I move inside, all around lazily or more tightly as I go down?

Alexander Lichtveld (Color Plate 47), asked how he observes, answered,

Actually in two ways. The first is the everyday way of looking at things just to be able to function and the second is seeing the same things, but then disconnected from their meaning and function, like an autonomous form with its own emotional charge: the feeling I get by looking at that form. I store away the things I see and experience in this second manner and later draw on them for my work.[1]

Many artists refer to the importance of intuition, improvisation, and dreams that lead them toward their creative solutions. Often the images that appear will surprise the artist. Reuben Kent says of his sculptures, which he refers to as *Night Dancers* (11-64, 11-65), that they are

representational of entities which probably do not exist in anyone else's imagination but mine.
Startled me.
Was quite relieved when other individuals began to recognize them as being a necessary part of their reality.

Other artists speak of the importance of learning about themselves as they create. For example, Beverly Mayeri (9-13) says that *when the images leap ahead of the expected, the art feels like a celebration in self-discovery.* Ann Roberts (9-7), whose sculpture frequently deals with personal experience in mythical terms, is aware that

through the action of sculpting, ideas become concrete images, or pieces of my life become enmeshed in the fabric of each sculpture. . . . Making is a discovery just as thinking is.

In the same vein, Stephen De Staebler (9-2) said,

A life without making things that tell you who you are and what you feel is not enough. So I make things.

Christina Bertoni (9-3) says that art for her has become the means of working out her deepest musing on the nature of existence and nonexistence.

---

[1]From an interview by Friso Broeksma in *Form and Echoes* (the artist's catalog).

SOURCES OF IMAGERY

Some artists are reluctant to discuss the sources of their imagery in too much detail because they fear that if they do, this may hinder viewers from bringing their own imaginations into play as they observe the work.

The statements by artists quoted here are not intended to limit you as you look at their work. You will bring to the act of viewing your own perceptions and your own experiences, which inevitably will influence what you see and how you respond to a particular work.

Mary Frank, whose creative works include clay sculptures, drawings, paintings, and prints, sometimes explores the same image in all of these media (9-4, 9-5, 11-56). Speaking of how a childhood experience is related to the images that appear in her *Chimera* drawings and sculptures, she says,

> *What happens to experience? Many images and ideas are fugitive. Others, over the years, slowly make their way toward me. Imagine! I first saw the chimera when I was a child. It appeared in a book of Etruscan art which belonged to my mother. I took the book to bed with me even though the image frightened me. Forty years later, in Florence, I saw the bronze chimera. It was more terrifying but it was even more amazing.*

A work may start with a specific image that comes from the artist's immediate environment, and sometimes an artist's visual perceptions of his or her surroundings will lead to a deeper understanding of that environment and the lives of people who live in it. In *Rural Sculptural Allegory,* Tony Hepburn created a series of sculptures about the lives of the people who lived near his home in rural New York that included one he titled *Strong Support* (Color Plate 12). Hepburn says he came to understand that

> *working the land is an unpredictable battle which forges the body and the soul. Gnarled trees and frost-turned rocks reflect the faces of those who accept the difficulties of maintaining lives and plants through a 100 degree difference in temperature. . . . One talks of artistic integrity, which has something to do with honesty of intent and execution. In these pieces I have to contend with the integrity of the people I am working from. The work has to maintain their integrity and,*

Figure 9-3

For It Is Begun in This Life, Christina Bertoni, U.S.A. Bertoni says that her recent work is *drawn almost entirely from instinct/intuition. . . . After I make pieces I often find the piece confirmed by someone's writing about similar philosophic ideas.* Earthenware bisque fired, then painted with acrylic. 24 × 24 in. (61 × 61 cm). *Courtesy Victoria Munroe Gallery and the artist.*

hopefully, live up to their stature as good, hard-working people. This aspect has, on occasion, required some adjustments to my formal instincts.

Frank Boyden creates vessels on which he incises with sure, strong gestures images selected from his environment in the Pacific Northwest — images that are also important in the mythology of the earliest inhabitants of the region (9-18, 12-3). Speaking of traveling in Peru, where he immersed himself in the work of pre-Columbian Mochica and Nazca potters (5-10), Boyden says of the pots he saw there,

These are things that are so exquisite and so mysterious and so powerful that they literally changed my life and the way I think about my environment and the way I felt about myself. . . . These things are really about the people's lives, where they live, a total reflec-

tion of their environment. Really nothing was passed up. Every aspect of their culture was dealt with, somehow or other, and it's all right here. I really felt akin to that in many ways because of the microcosm of the material that I deal with in my own backyard.

Paul Astbury (9-6, 11-63), who lives in London, finds both inspiration and components for his sculpture nearby in the types of shops artists love: building supply stores, ironmongers, secondhand shops. He also checks out rubbish bins for discarded bicycles or other such treasures, bringing them back to his studio where they become part of his imaginative storehouse, waiting for the moment when he will transform them with additions of clay. When he found a cherry tree knocked over by a truck, he chopped and sawed up its trunk and branches, carefully numbering each piece, then put them in a corner until

Figure 9-4
Chimera, Mary Frank, U.S.A. As a child, Frank saw a photo of the famous Etruscan bronze *chimera*, and years later she returned to its image as inspiration for sculptures and drawings. This a a clay version of a sculpture that she originally created in wire and papier-mâché, using some of her own monoprints for its outer skin. Terra-cotta. 18½ × 30 × 13 in. (47 × 76 × 33 cm). *Courtesy Zabriskie Gallery and the artist.*

Figure 9-5
Drawing of *Chimera*, Mary Frank, U.S.A. *After I had finished the sculpture,* Frank says, *I made many drawings of it. I saw that I had made a creature destroying itself. Had the chimera now become a metaphor for our destruction of the earth?* Charcoal on paper. 29 × 42 in. (74 × 107 cm). *Courtesy Zabriskie Gallery and the artist.*

he could reassemble them and give them new life as part of a ceramic/wood sculpture.

Before creating *Garden I* and *Garden II* (9-6 a, b), Astbury became interested in the contours and textures of old skirts and dresses. They were the seed of an idea that took shape as *Garden I.* In this, he used their faded fabrics as backgrounds for flower beds of clay, between whose cracks the patterns and colors are barely visible. A whole range of possible interpretations are evoked by this unfamiliar combination of clay and cloth spread out like patterns on a cutting table—obsolescence and usefulness, age and rebirth, or simply memories of childhood play in muddy clothes. After *Garden I* was well along, a secondhand man's suit caught Astbury's eye, and he created the companion piece with male clothing. This juxtaposition of male and female clothing confronts gender interrelationships, adding another dimension to the work.

(a)

(b)

Figure 9-6
(a) *Garden I* by Paul Astbury, England. Astbury saw the patterned
material of discarded feminine clothing as an appropriate background for cracked clay slabs that allow the fabric color to show
between them, suggesting a parched flower bed. Clay, cloth,
wood, felt. Size variable, but in this installation approximately 12
ft (3.6 m) across and 2½ in. (6.4 cm) thick. 1992. **(b)** *Garden II*
followed naturally, the more rugged contours of the male clothing
contrasting with the dresses and skirts—the two gardens together now offer a considerably wider range of interpretations.
Clay, wood, metal, clothing, vinyl. 10 ft × 10 ft × 2½ in.
(305 × 305 × 6.4 cm). 1993. *From the traveling exhibition "On the Edge,
Art Meets Craft," organized by Kettles Yard Gallery, Cambridge, and Aberystwyth Art
Centre, Aberystwyth, Wales. Photo: Michael Harvey.*

Visual perceptions of the landscape, seascape, or cityscape in which an artist lives are frequent sources of imagery for those who work with clay. Eileen Lewenstein (14-37), speaking of the sea just outside the door of her studio, says,

Since setting up my studio on the beach . . . I have more and more drawn inspiration from the sea. It is there, constant, but continually changing. There are also concrete and wooden groynes and breakwaters — worn away by the sea, but built up with encrustations of barnacles, mussels, and seaweeds — changing shape slowly but inevitably.

The influence of a particular landscape on an artist's work may not always be direct; it may also be revealed symbolically. To Ann Roberts (9-7), who lives on the banks of the Grand River in Canada, the river's flowing waters and their alternation between flood and ebb — a fluctuation that can bring fertility or destruction, life or death — became in her work the *River Goddess*, symbol of that duality. The river also appears in her work in a series of sculptures, *The River Riders*, in which oddly assorted boatmates, such as a woman and a rabbit, a woman and a fish, float together down life's river.

Historical Sources

There are those to whom the long tradition of pottery is in itself a source. Janet Mansfield of Australia, for example, sets herself the challenge of creating new and fresh pots within the craft's ancient traditions (12-9, 12-10). Speaking of her sources she says,

Looking at Cypriot pottery in museums, the forms, the mellowness of the decoration, the aptness of the decoration to the form, the purpose for which the pot was made, the mystery of the unknown people that needed those wares, one can only hope for similar relevance for the pot we make today.

Paul Chaleff (8-32, Color Plate 8) says he feels that one of the reasons

wood firing has such allure for potters besides the obvious excitement of the firing process is that the finished work imparts a sense of history, a continuum of human emotion. Indeed, I try to preserve that respect for history throughout my work in concept, process and in form.

Figure 9-7
Spirit Stone: Sheela-Na-Gig, by Ann Roberts, Canada. Sheela-na-gig was the Celtic goddess of both fertility and destruction. Horrifying images of her duality appeared on the columns of Romanesque churches — here she shows her vulnerable side. Roberts says, *My work often uses women to portray the interaction of life forces. I view contemporary women as wishing to be in control of their lives and destiny, yet tied to the deeper forces of nature of which they are a pivotal part. (Idea and Image,* Ann Roberts, in *Ceramic Review 133,* pages 20–22.) White earthenware with zinc matt glaze and overglaze stains. 24 × 14 in. (60.6 × 35.5 cm). 1992. *Courtesy the artist. Photo: Robert McNair.*

There are those whose interest in history comes from childhood experiences of unearthing shards of pottery. Carlo Zauli, for example, speaks of finding slumped and deformed kiln rejects in the earth of his native Faenza. Their distorted forms directly influenced his later altered pots and sculpture (8-10). Walter Keeler (15-26), says that many of his forms

> spring from a boyhood obsession with collecting fragments of ancient pots on the shores of the Thames in London.

Michael Casson also says,

> History is for me the great teacher, but I hope to interpret the forms for today's function.

Casson has taken a traditional form — the jug (6-14 to 6-16) — and, like Mansfield and Keeler, sees the form's long history not as a limiting restriction, but as a source from which to draw inspiration (12-58).

> My sources? Well, mainly European, from Cretan (great jugs), Cypriot (even better), and Medieval (best?) times.

Of his *Totem Telurico* (16-18), erected to honor the people of the Americas on the occasion of Puerto Rico's 500th-year celebration, Jaime Suárez says of his work,

> In many ways it is archaeology — part of our history is buried and in many ways what I have done is to rescue it in order to create symbols.

Mythology

Whether or not they are responding to the fact that ceramics is an ancient media, and that any study of its history leads one back to the beginnings of humanity, many clay artists sense deep roots in the past and are drawn to the myths and legends by which humankind has attempted to understand and explain the world. Mythology is an important source for Ann Roberts, who takes personages from myths and turns them into new symbols which she uses for comments on human relationships and especially those between women and men. Of her sculpture *Spirit Stone: Sheela-Na-Gig* (9-7), Roberts says,

> the Sheela-na-gig is a devouring female in my lexicon of creatures! I think she was on

Figure 9-8
Cube Skull Teapot (Variation #6) — Yixing Series, Richard T. Notkin, U.S.A. Notkin's teapots borrow certain aspects — miniature size, color, tightly finished surface — from the Yixing teapots, but they are completely contemporary in imagery, commenting tellingly on our society. Stoneware, fired in electric kiln in oxidation, cone 5 to 6, Ht. 5¼ in. (13 cm). *Courtesy Esther Saks Gallery. Photo: Richard Notkin.*

> the church columns to scare away evil and remind men of the terrors of fornication. In my Spirit Stone she is exposing her weaker side and more vulnerable self (the "Woman Experienced" rather than the "Used Woman").

Social Concerns

Although political action and social concern are not among the most frequent sources of imagery in contemporary ceramics, there are those, like Richard Notkin, who use clay to comment on pressing social or political issues. Notkin believes that humanity has a choice between using its abilities for destruction or toward the betterment of our world. It is the artists, he believes, who

> provide and nurture the warm spark of our creative human spirit that keeps hope alive.

Notkin's own work often addresses vital contemporary issues — as in his *Cube Skull Teapot (Variation #6),* from his *Yixing Series* (9-8). Notkin feels strongly, however, that his works should reflect contemporary imagery and express our society's situation as it enters the twenty-first century. He says that by defending the artist who

Figure 9-9
Tipsy Tansu, by Chris Unterseher, U.S.A. A tottering Japanese house, glazed in rich browns and greens, displays interior images that allude to the traditional spirits associated with Japanese dwellings. Stoneware. 8 × 11 × 6 in. (20 × 28 × 15 cm). 1990. *Courtesy the artist.*

chooses social criticism and commentary, he does not

> *intend to understate the role of the abstract sculptor, or dedicated potter. Every act of creativity is a positive statement in itself, benefiting the creator and those around him. The ripple effect of many creative acts — our collective creativity — eventually reaches, touches and benefits the whole of humanity. In this lies our power as artists.*

Chris Unterseher's recent work, responding to visits to Japan, comments on the clashes of culture in present-day Japanese society, using ancient rural architecture with its handcrafted wooden structure and its associated useful objects to contrast with the barren inhuman scale of the new urban architecture (9-9). He comments,

> *While visiting Japan I was impressed by the stark cold appearing post-war architecture intruding on the landscape. . . . The more successful building almost became a kind of techno-fantasy in concrete and steel, while the less successful ones appeared awkward and out of scale with their surroundings.*

Marilyn Lysohir says that the

initial impetus for my work always comes out of personal experiences and feelings. The end result however is an accumulation of fact and fancy and form and function, never a simple historical account. To explain the complete creative process is difficult and I feel most comfortable when my work can be enjoyed on several levels and especially when those levels can be experienced simultaneously.

Her installation *Bad Manners* (14-23, Color Plate 26) can indeed be experienced on several levels, from the purely sensual one of color and texture to that of biting comment on our social mores. Of this work she says,

> *Bad Manners is about confusing luxuries*
> *with necessities.*
> *Bad Manners is about conspicuous*
> *consumption.*
> *Bad Manners is also about greed.*
> *Bad Manners is about revenge and the accu-*
> *mulation of securities for the insecure.*
> *Bad Manners is about world hunger being ig-*
> *nored while world armaments aren't.*
> *Bad Manners are often never honestly recog-*
> *nized or understood for what they are.*

Commenting on his piece *Schaalcorrectie* (Correction of Scale) (9-10), Pjotr Müller, gives a short history of the project:

> *The making of a sculpture is a compilation of previous and new issues. During this very process so many things are involved. Before making the object [Schaalcorrectie], I was making a large drawing commenting on the events in China at that time (the student revolution in Peking at the famous "Square of Heavenly Peace"). I was then working out an idea of whenever a war would start somewhere on this world, I would add a drawing to it. Without realising that nearly every day some new war is beginning (how naive). "Happily" enough, somebody bought that drawing before it turned all black (maybe bought by an "artless" person who wanted to stop all the wars by buying this particular drawing).*
>
> *In 1991 I wanted to use that idea again for making a work in terra cotta, but then without commenting upon an actual war event. This is the reason why I used a difference in scale. The cannon in real scale, and the city in a reduced one. Just playing with scale to express the fact that the actual scenery of a war-zone might change, but war itself will always be present.*

Frans Duckers (9-11), who lives in the southern part of The Netherlands, says,

> I've got a good bit of the Burgundian (French)
> culture in me. Cafés are a part of life here,
> the extension of the living-room, a place to
> socialize, to meet people. In the café you can
> see both pleasure and loneliness at the same

time. The sculpture is placed so that if the café is crowded it's just one of them. The moment there are only a few people, it just sits there by itself, isolated. "Hump" embodies both aspects. The sculpture makes it clear that it's your frame of mind that gives him his meaning.

Autobiographical Sources

One could say that all art is in some manner autobiographical, but the work of certain artists seems to deal more directly with personal experiences than that of others. For example, Deborah

Figure 9-12
Flesh and Bones, Deborah Horrell, U.S.A. Horrell combined bones cast in Kohler porcelain, with images drawn with graphite, and acrylic, to create her personal "nest." 72 × 53 × 60 in. (183 × 135 × 152 cm). *Courtesy the Kohler Collection, Wila Gardiner Gallery, and the artist. Photo: P. Richard Eells.*

Horrell, bemused by the magic of art that allows the artist to create an object or entity that speaks of his or her interior world, wonders if there is any other realm of human activity in which an individual can express such personal feelings. Horrell's work is often based directly on her life experiences as in her installation *Pappa Can You Hear Me?* (8-26). Of *Flesh and Bones* (9-12), Horrell says it was

conceived in a much more self-conscious context—struggle with "I" and desire for a home from which to evolve, transcend.

Beverly Mayeri (9-13) is deeply interested in the world of the human psyche and finds clay an excellent medium for exploring it.

In my art, she says, I like to explore the emotional texture of the inner life especially during times of transition when one is searching for meaning, strength, and new ways of being.
During moments of introspection I'll reflect on aspects of my life such as the struggle between independence and connection, love of nature and alienation from our environment, vulnerability and personal armor, social constraints and personal growth. The images that unfold in this process become the start of a sculpture. When the images leap ahead of the expected, the art feels like a celebration in self-discovery.

Of *Second Growth* (9-13), Mayeri says,

Some pieces begin very simply. I'll see a garden and want to do something that captures the rich colors, fertility and forms. . . . The plant forms also suggest another meaning as a metaphor for internal growth which I pursued further in the torso, "Second Growth." In this piece I asked myself what is growing in my garden, in my backyard? Surprisingly, rather than flowers, a strange assortment of characters popped into my head. Whoever they may be, they became the creatures hiding out among the plants.

Judy Moonelis (9-14) prefers to let her work stand for itself rather than comment on it in words. Although it is up to each viewer to interpret any art work or to see in it whatever he or she wishes to see, Moonelis's powerful visual statements appear, to this viewer at least, to be deeply concerned with autobiographical events or emotions—with the relationships of one human to another, of the individual to her inner world, and with the shared human experiences of love and hate, birth and death.

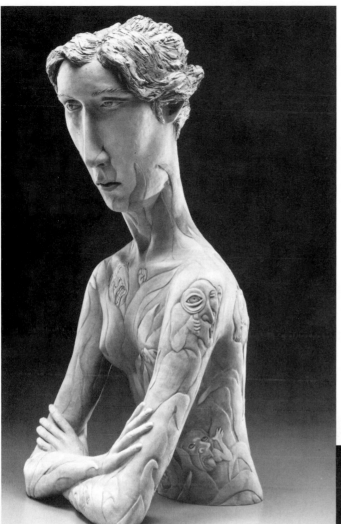

Figure 9-13
Second Growth, by Beverly Mayeri, U.S.A. Mayeri says of this piece that she simply started with her garden as the image but that she was surprised when she found the creatures hiding in the plants, and that she does not know who they are. An artist finding images occurring unexpectedly is far from rare. Clay and acrylic paint. 25 × 11 × 11 in. (64 × 28 × 28 cm). 1991. *Courtesy the artist and Dorothy Weiss Gallery. Photo: © Mel Schockner.*

Figure 9-14
By presenting two totally disparate compositions on the front and back of her sculptures, Judy Moonelis, U.S.A., shows the facade that an individual presents to the world and the frightening figures that lurk behind us all. A difficult assignment to carry out successfully, nevertheless it can create powerful images of duality: life and death, love and hate. Earthenware, terra sigillata, low-fired. 55 × 33 × 30 in. (140 × 84 × 76 cm). *Made possible by support from Cranbrook Academy of Art. Courtesy the artist. Photo: Doug Long.*

Travel can take artists out of their day-to-day lives, sharpening their awareness. Through travel, Ann Roberts says, she observes cultures different from her own, yet recognizes the universality of their images in art. Memories gathered in travel—the colors of a landscape, a fleeting glimpse of a face in a train, architectural forms that are new and exciting—may implant an image or idea in your mind. Such memories are sometimes transformed into new works immediately, but often, like the underground vault that Johannes Gebhardt saw in Kurdistan (11-57), they can stay alive, waiting for years before they are transformed into sculpture, painting, or the written word.

After making sculptures involving other parts of the body, Rosa Verhoeve (9-15) started making forms of her forehead, pressing it into the clay. From these, she says,

> the work evolved into a "library of thought" and I decided to honor this thought by giving them their own space: by putting each and every one of the clay forms in a wooden box. . . . I decided to place the column [of boxes] right where it belonged: in my study right in the middle of my book-case.
>
> I felt something was missing in the column—I only emphasized the cerebral side of the head. I then decided to add the spiritual part as well.

For this spiritual aspect, Verhoeve drew with her fingers in wax on a copper plate, then etched it with acid and installed the plate itself over a fireplace on the facing wall. The etched plate serves to show how sculptors not only may draw to plan the visual aspects of their pieces (9-17), or to plan their construction or firing (15-10b), but also may incorporate drawing in their work, or like Verhoeve, Mary Frank (9-5), and Tony Hepburn (9-16) make drawings based on or suggested by completed pieces.

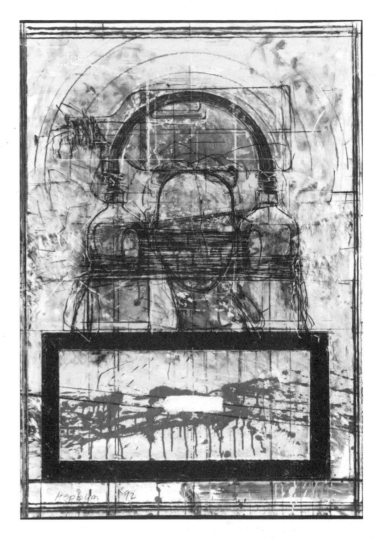

Figure 9-16
Tony Hepburn, U.S.A., who draws both before and while working on a piece, made this drawing to explore his work *after* it was completed. A recent Hepburn installation included drawings and the artist himself making large pots—images that are echoed in the drawing. Used for the poster of the Hepburn exhibition at the Cranbrook Museum of Art. Charcoal, conté crayon, acrylic on Stonehenge paper. 42 × 29 in. (107 × 74 cm). 1992.
Courtesy the artist. Photo: Robert Hensleigh.

◀ **Figure 9-15**
eerste druk (first impression), by Rosa Verhoeve, Holland. Combining fired clay and an etching on a copper plate (not shown), this installation in Verhoeve's study incorporates both the cerebral and spiritual aspects of the human mind, symbolized by clay impressions of the artist's forehead. Verhoeve says, *It was not my intention to work from a concept while making the forms of clay. I just wanted to mold the clay with specific parts of my body from which a sculpture might evolve.* Terra-cotta, wood, copper. 94 × 39 in. (2.40 × 1 m). 1991. *Courtesy the artist.*

DRAWING

Drawing plays an important role in the work of many clay artists (see also Chapter 10). They may make quick notes of ideas or images to use later in their work like William Daley (9-17), who makes many sketches, then continues by making more detailed drawings:

> When something merits further play it is drawn on my studio walls in full scale, most often in plan and elevation. When this works, I make forms and build.

Daley uses these large-scale plans and elevations as working drawings from which to make the supports on which he builds his forms, and they also allow him to explore the way in which the clay form will develop without having to contend with gravity.

Pierre Bayle also uses drawing to make decisions before touching the clay (12-1, Color Plate 9). He says,

Figure 9-17
William Daley, U.S.A., says that sketches like this one represent a continuous flow of possibilities. If he feels one might work for a vessel, he redraws it full scale on the wall of his studio and uses it as a working drawing from which to construct the form. *Courtesy the artist.*

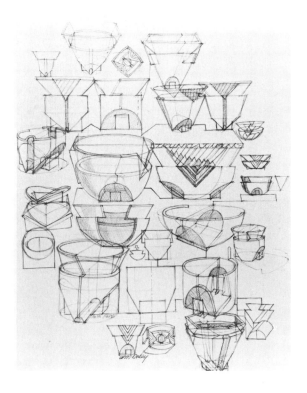

> It is not the clay which decides the forms I make. When I settle down at my wheel, I already have a form in my head which I have drawn hours, days, weeks ago.

Tony Hepburn (9-16) comments,

> I draw in three ways. Before making, to sort ideas without thinking about quality. During, to restructure ideas. And after the sculpture is finished. This drawing is the latter. It makes one examine one's work in a very special way that just looking does not do.

Alexander Lichtveld (Color Plate 47) combines drawing with his ceramic forms and even makes the special handmade paper on which he draws them.

Drawing *on* Ceramic Forms

Drawing has another function in relation to ceramics: The potter has used skillful drawing throughout history, from the spiraling decorations on early Egyptian or Chinese urns (1-23, 1-24, 3-2), to the funeral scene on an early Greek vase (2-11), through the brush-decorated platters by Japanese potter-painters (3-32), to the images on Michelle Gregor's St. Crow Plate (14-14).

Potter-painter Henry Varnum Poor, who decorated many of his pots with brush drawings of animals and birds (7-12), commented,

> To decorate beautifully you should above all draw beautifully; but beautiful drawing lies in decision and clarity in expressiveness rather than accuracy; in sensitive judgment of scale and placing in relation to the object. . . .[2]

Drawing, says Frank Boyden,

> is a joyous way of exploring my world.

Originally a painter, accustomed to drawing on flat surfaces, Boyden says that when he started to make pots he quite naturally drew on them, and that this opened up an entirely new graphic world, a world that involved three dimensions as well as movement and time (9-18). Since his drawings often move around the vessel, they

[2]Henry Varnum Poor, *A Book of Pottery, From Mud Into Immortality* (Englewood Cliffs, N.J.: Prentice-Hall, 1958).

Figure 9-18

Dead Salmon and Raven Plate, Frank Boyden, U.S.A. Boyden prefers to use incised rather than applied lines because they are direct and interact with the light, catching it on their edges and losing it in their hollows. Stoneware, cone 5. Diameter 25 in. (63 cm). *Courtesy the artist. Photo: Jim Piper.*

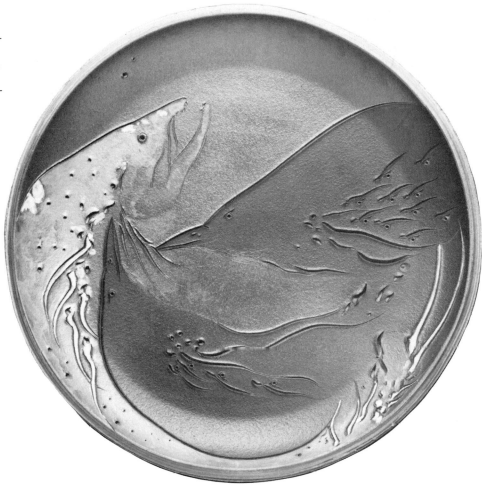

force *him* to move in order to make them, and they also force the viewer to move around to see the whole.

The recording of a perceived image by the artist may not be the only way in which he or she develops a drawn image. Patrick Loughran (9-19, Color Plate 25) says that his images come directly from the way he works on the surface. He says,

> The way I work has to do with responding. . . . You put a mark down and respond to it. You make another one and respond to that. . . .[3]

Loughran sees his work as having antecedents in the long tradition of decorated ceramics that in-

clude Italian maiolica (6-6, Color Plate 4) and the work of Palissy (6-17).

The act of drawing or painting on three-dimensional forms naturally leads the artist to consider how to relate the drawn image to the three-dimensional form of the pottery or, alternatively, how to plan the shape of the vessel to fit the drawing that will become part of its surface.

In some cases, expression is best served if the vessel is formed to show the drawn or painted image in a close compositional relationship with it. On the other hand, the tensions that are set up when there is a strong contrast between the drawn or painted image and its shape may better express the artist's concept. As an example, the contrast between the surface spirals and angular forms of James Caswell's vase, *The Arcade,* exploits this tension to bring vitality to the vessel (14-30).

Clearly, drawing can perform a number of important functions in relation to the ceramic pro-

[3]*Functional Glamour,* catalog, Museum for Contemporary Art Het Kruithuis, 's-Hertogenbosch, The Netherlands, 1987.

Figure 9-19
Patrick Loughran, U.S.A. Loughran considers his limited edition domestic ware to be in the long tradition of decorated pottery — maiolica, Japanese and Mexican folk pottery, and Mimbres earthenware. His decoration, however, is contemporary in both its style and its cooling tower imagery. Glazed earthenware. Cup ht. 3 in. (8 cm). (See also Color Plate 25.) *In Collections of Museum Het Kruithuis, 's-Hertogenbosch, The Netherlands and Provinciaal Museum voor Moderne Kunst, Ostende, Belgium. Photo: the artist.*

cess, and an aspiring potter or sculptor would do well to foster the skill, continually using and perfecting it.

AESTHETICS AND TECHNIQUE

The manner in which creative people turn perceptions around to generate pottery or sculpture varies from person to person, but in all true creation, there was originally a vision, an idea, or a concept, which, through skillful use of technique, has been translated into an actual object that we can perceive in space, can look at, touch, or use.

As you read the following chapters on ceramics techniques, it is important to keep in mind your own inner visions, whether they originate in visual or tactile perceptions, intuitions, or your emotions. As an art material, clay is quite forgiving, allowing you to change and add to it within reason. However, since fired clay will permanently preserve not only the imprint of your fingers but also the imprint of your ideas, the clarity or confusion of those ideas will also become apparent in your creations, forever recorded in the clay.

10

Getting Started

Hands—pinching, pulling, poking, and patting clay—have formed useful and beautiful objects for thousands of years and are still leaving their imprints on clay today.

Today's ceramic artist is exposed to a flood of information and stimuli from history, from other cultures, and from other craftspeople—no clay worker in the past ever had access to so much information. Museums, galleries, and books show us a multitude of techniques, and every month the ceramics magazines publish the new work of contemporary potters and sculptors almost as soon as they open their kilns. Such a great deal of information can be confusing, but as you look at illustrations of pottery and sculpture and of people working in clay, remember that others can do only just so much to help you find your way of working. What you decide to do with this malleable, marvelous, and sometimes aggravating material depends on what feels right for *you*.

EXPLORING CLAY

There are many ways to explore clay. Swiss potter-sculptor-teacher Ernst Häusermann, for example, sometimes has taken his students camping for a few days near a clay pit to live with clay and build caves, houses, and slides in it (10-1). Some potters, sculptors, and dancers have cov-

Figure 10-1
Potters have dug clay from the earth throughout history. Now we tend to think of it as coming from a plastic bag. To familiarize his students with clay at its source, Ernst Häusermann, Switzerland, took his students camping near a clay deposit for a few days. There, they got to know the material by living with it, digging in it, building with it, and learning what they could do with it. *Courtesy the artist.*

ered themselves with clay, dipped their heads into it, or danced in creamy colored slips to celebrate the earth material, while other artists have poured slip out to let it dry and crack in the sun (8-25). You may not care to explore clay in such an intense or engulfing manner, but you can squeeze lumps of it in your hands and feel how it responds, see what it does when you add more water to it, learn how far you can push it before it collapses, and discover what you can make of it when it does collapse.

The technical information offered in the remainder of the book is intended to help you discover your own way of working, not to dictate absolute rules. *For an artist,* says U.S. sculptor Stephen De Staebler, *the most valuable motto would be "No rules."*

THE WORK SPACE

You may be starting your work in a school studio, a potter's workshop, or even on your back steps. In the chapters that follow, you will see that considerable equipment is available that will make things easier for you, but you can also choose to work in the way that potters have for centuries — using whatever clay is available, forming it by the simplest methods with nothing more than the ground as your work space. Maria Martinez, for example, needed little equipment and only a few homemade tools to make her beautiful pots (10-2). In contrast, a potter may work in a studio that he or she has designed for production and teaching (10-3). Californian Eric Norstad, on the other

Figure 10-2
To create beautiful pottery, Maria Martinez needed nothing more than a level spot in the sun. In this photograph taken around 1940, she showed how she moistened her clay, kneaded tempering material into it, and worked it until she had eliminated the lumps. *Photo by Wyatt Davis, courtesy Museum of New Mexico (neg. no. 50085).*

Figure 10-3 ▶
The Potter's Shop, run by Steven Branfman and Carol Temkin. Both are production potters, but, like many such workshops, their studio is also a teaching studio, where students, hobby ceramists, and children can learn about working in clay. *Courtesy The Potter's Shop.*

hand, employs several people in an operation that makes use of mechanical aids, yet also relies on the handwork of experienced potters and on the careful attention he himself gives the process (12-60). A sculptor may have to deal with completely different problems and of necessity be ready to adapt any available space to his or her needs (10-4). If you are lucky, you may be able to set up your own work space, even if only in your backyard (10-5, 11-22a). If so, there are some aspects of ceramics that you should take into consideration when you arrange your space (see Chapter 17). But even if you are a student working in a studio over whose arrangements you have no control, you should become aware of health and safety considerations as well as the ecological impact of your work.

Figure 10-4
An artist's work space reflects the type of work done there, the personality of the artist, and the methods he or she uses to create that work. Here, Marilyn Lysohir works on *Bad Manners* surrounded by partially finished figures for the installation (Color Plate 26). *Courtesy the artist. Photo: Arthur Okazaki.*

◀ **Figure 10-5**
You don't have to have an elaborate studio to work in clay. If you live in a temperate zone you can set up a work space outside, at least in the summer. Ptah, who lives in California, mixes his clay in buckets and bins, wearing gloves and respirator. Once the clay is ready, he climbs a ladder and applies it to his sculpture. (See also opening photo for "Shaping the Present" and 11-22.)

Figure 10-6 ▶
You can avoid using the most obviously toxic ceramic materials, but exposure to others is unavoidable. This chart shows you some of the devices that will protect you against hazards while working in ceramics. Many variations of these are available commercially, or frequently you may make your own systems. Precautions that you should take include careful monitoring of studio cleanliness, the use of exhaust fans and hoods close to the source of contamination (with strong enough suction to remove the contaminants before you become exposed), protection against injury and eye damage, and care in handling the kiln. These are discussed in greater detail in the appropriate process sections, and throughout the book the alert symbol will warn you when safety or health hazards exist.

Take care!

Symbol will alert you to take precautions

Exhaust systems

Fans and hoods for venting toxic fumes, mists, heat, and fumes from kiln.

Air purification

Room-sized air cleaner collects fine airborne dust particles.

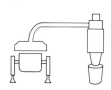

Dust collector

Collector close to source picks up heavy dust particles; for mixing, grinding, sanding, carving clay, and sandblasting.

Spray booths

Vented booth with exhaust fan for spraying glazes, lusters, china paint, or booth with water curtain.

Supplied air

Mixing large amounts of clay, toxic materials, chemical powders, grinding clay, sandblasting requires filtered supplied air.

Respirators

Use correct filters rated for dusts, mists, and toxic vapors. Use when no adequate local exhaust venting present, and for salt firing.

Special vacuum

Vacuum with special filters for microscopic particles for dust pick-up. Or wet mop.

Goggles/Shields

Shaded goggles or hand-held welding shield for looking into kiln. Clear goggles for grinding clay and keeping dust from eyes and contact lenses.

Face shields

Clear for grinding, hazardous liquids, clay mixing. Shaded for looking into kiln.

Heat-resistant gloves

Aramid fiber gloves for unloading kiln, and protecting hands and arms from heat of raku kiln.

Protective gloves

For handling glaze chemicals, rubber molding compounds, and toxic adhesives.

Ear protection

Ear muffs and ear plugs for use when grinding or using noisy machinery.

Fire extinguisher

Keep near all fire and heat sources and combustibles.

First aid kit

Complete kit with eye wash, burn treatment, and first aid instruction.

Ecological Concerns

Ceramists are more and more aware of the necessity of eliminating hazardous waste and of finding ways to reprocess ceramic materials. For example, Bill Roan and Clayton Bailey developed a method of reprocessing ceramic materials in a nonpolluting manner (see Appendix 1C), and some artists use a salt substitute compound (see Appendix 1C) for vapor firing instead of salt, which gives off hydrochloric acid into the atmosphere. In Holland, at the European Ceramic Work Centre, the entire new studio was set up to handle all toxic wastes. Every bit of material is recycled and disposed of in an ecologically responsible manner.

For some time, Kimpei Nakamura in Japan has been incorporating industrial ceramic objects into his sculptural works. Recently, as part of an installation at the Ishikawa Prefectural Museum of Art in Kanazawa, he covered the floor with hundreds of waste parts reclaimed from a renovated transformer substation. In a noteworthy example of the reuse of ceramic materials, Nakamura tells us, *After the exhibition they are further broken down and then ground. The powder is mixed with clay and reused.*

You may not be able to grind down porcelain insulators to mix with your clay, but recycle as much ceramic material as you can, and dispose of toxic materials in as ecologically proper a way as possible. It is important that ceramists everywhere stay up to date on current recycling and disposal methods of the toxic materials they use in their studio. The time has come when the air we breathe, the land on which we live, and the water we drink must be treated with respect in order for us all to live healthy and productive lives, now and in the future. (See Appendix 5A or contact local recycling agencies.)

Figure 10-7
After digging, drying, pulverizing, and soaking the local clay, potters in Thrapsanon, Greece, spread it in the sun to stiffen. When it reaches working consistency, they will wedge and store it. This same system can be used to recycle clay.

HEALTH AND SAFETY

Before you start to work in ceramics, it is important that you realize that many ceramic materials are toxic in varying degrees and that they present hazards to those who work with them. In the past, when the hazards of ingesting or inhaling clay and glaze materials were unknown, many workers fell ill with silicosis or chemical poisoning because of their continuous exposure to dangerous substances when they worked without proper ventilation or in unsafe working conditions. Nowadays, however, basic safety and health precautions have been developed in order to minimize the dangers of working with ceramic materials. There are steps that you should always take to protect yourself.

It goes without saying that the work space should be efficient and safe. For example, all electric equipment should be properly wired and grounded to prevent possible electrical shock. Heavy materials should be placed so that you can reach and lift them without straining your muscles. If you have to lift heavy sacks of clay, bend your knees and lift with your entire body so that the weight is distributed and the force comes from your knees, not your back. Proper seating should be available for those working on the wheel to avoid strain on the back as much as possible.

In addition to using common sense in setting up the work space, you can now find many safety aids and considerable information that will help you avoid problems (Appendix 5A and Chapter 17). It is important, for instance, that you inform yourself about the materials with which you work and that you do not use any of whose composition and degree of toxicity you are not aware. Appendix 1E lists the ceramic materials you are likely to use along with their toxicity. Become familiar with this list, and whenever possible, substitute less hazardous materials. For example, you can eliminate a lot of clay dust by using damp, premixed clay, but if you do wish to mix dry clay, try to choose clays that contain only small amounts of free silica and use an asbestos-free talc.

Not only should you be aware of the need for protection against immediate toxic substance exposure, but you should also take into account the fact that nowadays we are all exposed to many other pollutants in our daily lives, so we must also consider the total burden of toxic substances to which our bodies are exposed. That burden is increased substantially if you smoke.

Schools and public art centers can call on various government agencies and private organizations that will make health-hazard surveys of studios or offer short courses for teachers and professionals in safe studio design and management. As an individual, you can call on the same agencies for advice or information, and you can subscribe to newsletters that will keep you up to date. Some of these agencies are listed in Appendix 5A, and some books that deal with safety and health are listed in Further Reading at the end of the book. However, since new research is constantly being done, do not rely completely on these; keep up with the available *current* material. Also be sure that your protective equipment meets government standards.

Precautions and Safety Equipment

The composite safety chart (10-6) has drawings of the safety and health equipment that can be used at different times to protect you as you work with ceramic materials or equipment. Throughout the book, you will see a symbol in the margin that will alert you to the fact that a hazard exists. To learn which protective equipment you can use, refer to Figure 10-6.

Right now, at the very beginning of your experience in the ceramics studio, learn and follow these basic precautions:

- Do not smoke, eat, or drink in the ceramics studio. Keep your hands away from your mouth.
- Before starting to work, and periodically thereafter, make sure the ventilation systems are working properly and that the filters within the systems are clean. Be sure that they are cleaned or changed on a regular basis.
- Use all required and recommended protective equipment.
- When respirators are not in use, store them in a plastic bag in a clean area. Do not hang them in the open where dust and pollutants can collect inside the face piece.
- Respirators will not function properly without a good seal between the face and the face piece. Beards and sideburns interfere with the seal.

- Clean up tables and floors with special vacuums that filter out the microscopic ceramic material particles, or if not available use a damp mop and damp sponges for cleanup. Sweeping with brooms and brushes merely sends the particles into the air. Wear a respirator while cleaning.
- When you have finished working, clean off dusty or dirty clothing while still wearing the respirator. Following any extensive use of clay or glaze materials, it is wise to shower and shampoo dust particles from your hair.

In addition, proper precautions are discussed throughout "Shaping the Present" in relation to specific processes, to ensure that your experience with clay will be both healthful and satisfying.

TOOLS

Whether you are throwing on the wheel or handbuilding, you can begin with no more equipment than your hands. In fact, limiting yourself at first to exploring the clay with your hands and fingers can be satisfying and can teach you a considerable amount about the material. Then, once you have the feel of the clay you will be ready to use some tools (10-8). Although a wide variety of useful tools are commercially available, only your imagination will limit you in finding or making others. Most people who work in clay adapt a variety of objects to their work—ordinary odds and ends they have found in nature, in the house, or on the scrap heap. These may include a smooth stone or the back of a spoon for burnishing, a hand-shaped piece of wood or metal, or scraps of leather, twigs, shells—all of these and many more can be adapted as useful tools, and frequently will become among your favorites. You should also know about the specialized tools that have been developed for working in clay, and recognize them and their purposes when you encounter them in the studio. The chart in Figure 10-8 will help to identify these tools for you.

WORKING WITH CLAY

This chapter introduces you to different types of clays and explains how to mix and test clay bodies for your own use. If you are a beginner, we

Figure 10-8 ▶
These are the basic tools you will use for shaping and trimming pottery and sculpture or for finishing your work.

suggest that you study this material in conjunction with later chapters so that you will be doing the clay tests at the same time you start to work with handbuilding methods or on the wheel. You will also find additional information on testing clays in Appendix 1A.

TYPES OF CLAY

You learned in Chapter 1 how clay was formed through the action of geological forces and the weathering of the rocks that make up a large part of the earth's crust. Figure 1-8 shows how some clays remain in place as the feldspathic rocks of which they are largely formed decompose and how other clay components are moved by the action of rain, streams, and rivers and deposited in beds of different types of clay. Some clays can be dug up and used as they come from the ground, because they are naturally plastic and can be worked without additional chemicals. However, contemporary ceramists who mine their own clays often find it necessary to add other ingredients to the body. For example, they may add **fire clay,** a refractory material that increases the clay body's resistance to heat and, depending on the type of fire clay, may also add plasticity to the body. A ceramist may also modify the natural clay by adding **grog,** made from fired clay that has been ground, for body strength. Oxides such as iron, chrome, or cobalt may also be added for color (10-9).

Primary Clays

Clays that remain at their original site of decomposition are known as **primary clays.** These deposits supply the white china clay or kaolin that is used in porcelain, bone china, and glazes. The chemical formula of kaolin is the closest to "theoretical clay"—a completely unadulterated clay never actually found in nature. Kaolin's formula includes mineral oxides in the following proportion:

$$Al_2O_3 \cdot 2SiO_2 \cdot 2H_2O$$

Fettling knife

General-purpose tapered knife for cutting soft and leather-hard clay.

Sculpture tool

Wooden diagonal blade with rounded thumb end for cutting, trimming, and sculpting soft clay.

Pin tool

Needle for cutting thin slabs and for trimming and piercing air bubbles in soft clay.

Cutting wire

Wire for cutting soft and leather-hard clay and removing ware from the wheel.

Pear pitter

Versatile tool for trimming and hollowing moist and leather-hard clay.

Ribbon tool

Tool with square and looped metal ribbon ends for trimming and hollowing soft and leather-hard clay.

Wire loop tool

Tool has looped metal wire ends for hollowing and sculpting soft clay.

Fork

Kitchen fork for scoring and texturing soft and leather-hard clay.

Rib

Wood, metal, or plastic rib, with straight edge and curve for shaping soft clay.

Sponges

Synthetic sponge for cleanup. Natural sponge for wheel work or smooth finishing of soft, leather-hard, or dry clay.

Chamois

Soft leather strip for smoothing rims during wheel throwing.

Sponge tool

For absorption of excess water in hard-to-reach areas such as the interior of bottle shapes.

Throwing tool

For shaping bottle forms from the inside.

Caliper

For measuring and transferring measurements from one object to another.

Sgraffito tool

Arrow point and thin double-point fork for carving leather-hard and dry clay.

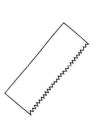

Serrated rib

Flexible metal rib for scraping, scoring, and texturing soft, leather-hard, and dry clay.

Figure 10-9
Jens Morrison, U.S.A., searched for and dug local clay that he found by roadsides or streams, dried it in the sun, crushed it with a rolling pin, then used it for texture and color on his sculptures. *Courtesy the artist.*

Secondary Clays

Secondary clays are clays that have washed away from the feldspathic rocks and deposited in beds that may be far from their origin. Over millions of years, as the rocks of the earth's crust broke down, the particles were weathered into increasingly smaller sizes and were continually moved down the mountains by rain and streams. As the movement continued, larger particles were dropped first, and increasingly smaller particles were carried on farther by the water to become mixed with other minerals and organic matter. These particles were finally deposited in river bottoms, on plains, or below the ocean. Similar-sized particles were deposited together; each deposit had a particular mineral and physical composition that determined the type of clay and its individual properties. Among the secondary clays are the fire clays — made up of coarse and heavy fragments that were usually dropped ahead of the smaller particles — and the common earthenware clays and the stoneware clays.

LOW-FIRE CLAY Earthenware clay is a low-firing secondary clay commonly found in deposits around the world. It was the first type of clay to be widely used by humans to create ceramic objects through hardening in fire, because the considerable amount of iron this natural clay contains meant that it could reach maturity at the comparatively low temperatures achievable with early firing methods. Made up of decomposed rocks along with organic material and iron, earthenware clays remain porous when they are fired to mature temperatures that range from cone 010 to cone 1 (1641°–2109°F/900°–1080°C). (**Pyrometric cones,** explained more fully in Chapter 15, are devices that indicate when a particular clay is reaching maturity. Here, and throughout the book, when cones are referred to, the temperature reference is to large Orton cones. The small cones used in **kiln sitters** fire to maturity at a different rate. You will find a chart of cone temperatures of both American Orton cones and English Seger cones in Appendix 2A).

Natural low-fire earthenware varies in color from reddish to yellowish, depending on the amount of iron or lime it contains. The most likely place you will see it used is in the reddish-brown flowerpot that holds your philodendron or fern. Some earthenware clays can be dug up and used just as they come from the ground, with very little more preparation than cleaning out large impurities. Such clays were used by our Neolithic ancestors to make pots and ritual objects and are still used by traditional village potters today, but nowadays many specialized low-fire earthenwares have been developed. These include white earthenware containing only small quantities of iron.

HIGH-FIRE CLAYS The natural high-fire clays were first used in China (3-6, 3-9); then, after boat loads of Chinese stoneware and porcelain objects arrived in Europe, potters there searched for and eventually found the necessary materials with which to make their own high-fired ceramics (6-20). Used for domestic ware as well as sculpture, these clays are still popular with many contemporary potters and sculptors.

FIRE CLAYS Because fire clays are heat resistant, they are used to make bricks for lining furnaces or fireplaces, or to build kilns. They are also used as ingredients in stoneware clay bodies. Fire clays can be used pretty much as they come from the ground.

STONEWARE CLAYS Stoneware clay is a secondary clay made up of finer particles than those of fire clay. This clay is formed when the rock particles became mixed with small particles of iron and with decayed plants containing potassium, a mineral that acts as a flux. Large deposits of stoneware along the Rhine Valley made it possible for German potters to develop the salt-glazing techniques that gave them a competitive edge over potters in other areas (6-15). When stoneware clay is fired to maturity — depending on its composition, anywhere from cone 1 to cone 10 (2109°–2381°F/1154°–1305°C) — it becomes dense, vitreous, and resistant to water and acid. It generally fires to a buff or brown color, although it is possible to mix white stoneware. Your coffee mug or the plate from which you eat your dinner is probably made of stoneware.

BALL CLAY Ball clay is a secondary clay that contains little iron. Fired, it turns a light gray or buff color. This clay is used in both low-fire and high-fire clay bodies that require plasticity.

FORMULATED CLAY BODIES

A clay that is mixed for a particular use is known as a clay body. This mixture may be made up at a factory and packaged either in dry bulk or damp in plastic bags, or mixed from dry ingredients at the studio or workshop (10-9 to 10-12). In either case, it will contain a variety of components that have specific functions in the clay body. An example of a clay body might be a white earthenware mixed without iron in order to produce a low-fire body that can take color well. Another example, porcelain, is a mixed body made up of high-firing components that will fire to the pure white, translucent ware so esteemed in China and envied in Europe. When fired to maturity at a range of from cone 8 to cone 13 (2305°–2455°F/1263°–1346°C), porcelain is impervious to liquids. Because of its density and imperviousness, porcelain is also used for sinks, toilets, and electrical insulators. For additional information on blended clay bodies, mixing, and testing, see Appendix 1A.

Figure 10-10
Carlo Zauli, Italy, jokingly demonstrates a spectacular way of mixing clay. Normally, he uses a mechanical mixer. *Courtesy the artist. Photo: Antonio Masotti.*

CHOOSING A CLAY BODY

As a beginner, digging your own clay or mixing your own clay body from dry ingredients may seem rather overwhelming, so it is likely that you will start working with a premixed clay body that has been developed commercially or by your school for a particular use and labeled as to its firing range. But even if you use a premixed body, you will have to choose *which* clay body to buy for your purpose. For example, if you were planning to make coiled pots and to fire them at a low temperature, you probably would use a somewhat porous earthenware, not a high-fire porcelain

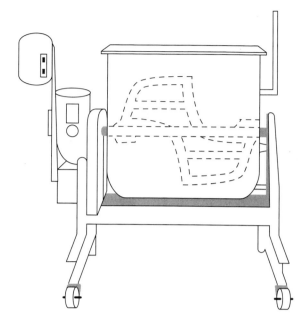

Figure 10-11
Mechanical clay mixers have revolving blades or paddles, indicated by the dotted lines, that mix large quantities of clay in a tilting container. The clay is dryblended first; then the water is added.

Figure 10-12
A pug mill has an auger blade inside and will mix, homogenize, and recycle clay. The clay is extruded in a solid mass. Some mills will also de-air the clay.

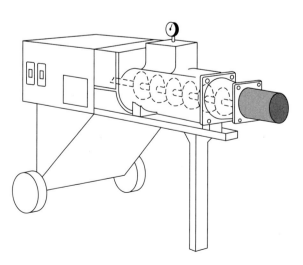

clay, whereas if you were planning to throw on the wheel, you would prefer a plastic clay. Very fine clays shrink more when they dry than those that are coarser or contain more temper or filler, so you probably would not use a fine body such as porcelain for building large, thick sculptural forms. (This does not mean this cannot be or has not been done, however. There are always exceptions). If you wanted to fire a large piece of sculpture to a higher temperature than earthenware will stand, you would be likely to use a stoneware body containing a lot of temper (grog, or **chamotte**), which would make it less likely to crack. Clays to be thrown on the wheel, however, must be more plastic than sculpture clays, so they are made with as little nonplastic material — flint or feldspar — as possible, and with additional plastic materials such as ball clay or small quantities (1 to 3%) of bentonite or macaloid.

You can see from these examples that there is usually a trade-off to be made in choosing a clay body. On the other hand, it is possible to push the limits of a particular clay in a remarkable way. For example, one would not expect to use porcelain for a large sculpture, yet Carlo Zauli used it to create a thick wall relief about thirty feet long. Asked why he used porcelain for such a large piece, he replied that it was partly to see if he could do it and partly because he wanted the porcelain's whiteness on which to use color. This is not the first time porcelain has been used for interior architectural components — in the 1750s, the walls of an entire room in a royal villa were covered with nearly three thousand relief-decorated porcelain panels, made at the Capodimonte factory in Naples, Italy.

Despite the fact that clay can sometimes be pushed beyond the limits one would expect, there are certain considerations to bear in mind in choosing a clay for specific applications. For example, for sculpture placed outdoors in a severe climate, clay type is critical because of weather fluctuations. In such conditions, moisture collecting in the open pores of low-fired clay will alternately contract and expand as it freezes and thaws, and this will eventually crack the piece. Therefore, water must not collect in open cavities or pockets and must drain off the ceramic. For that reason a coarse heavily grogged clay such as stoneware, fired to vitrification, is essential in exterior applications where there is a danger of subfreezing weather.

A low-fire clay body, although not as strong as stoneware, can accept outdoor conditions in areas where freezing does not take place. You could safely use it in a mild climate in a spot where it would not be easily broken.

Low-fire, stoneware, and porcelain clays can all be used in the production of utilitarian ware. Each, however, possesses unique characteristics that will affect how it is used. For example, low-fire clay tends to be either reddish or buff (although white is also available) in color, and because it is not watertight, it usually requires glaze to form a waterproof surface. To make a piece watertight, the ceramist will often glaze the whole piece, including the **foot,** so it is necessary to place the ware on **stilts** during firing (15-9). Low-fire dinnerware does not take stove-top or oven temperatures well, because the ware may crack and the glaze can **craze.**

Stoneware clay is usually chosen by potters for dinnerware because it is strong, durable, and takes handling well. It is also water- and acid-proof. Depending on the composition of the body, some stoneware clays can accept oven temperatures or even low stove-top temperatures. Stoneware colors range from white to brown.

Porcelain is also especially popular for dinnerware because of its smooth white surface. On it, glaze colors can achieve brilliance and depth, and when it is fired to maturity (in a range from cone 8 to cone 13, or 2305°–2455°F/1263°–1346°C), porcelain is waterproof without glaze. Cherished by the aristocracy of China, where the most precious creations of the official potteries were reserved for the emperor's household, porcelain has always had an aura of elegance surrounding it.

Firing each clay to its maturity is especially critical in the production of dinnerware. Equally critical is the proper **fit** of the glaze to the clay body. As we will see in Chapter 14, each glaze must be carefully chosen to match the shrinkage rate of the particular clay body on which it is used, or the glaze may craze, or crawl and separate from the ware. Crazing is not acceptable in cooking or tableware, because food can be difficult to remove from the cracks, creating health hazards.

SUITING THE CLAY BODY TO YOUR NEEDS

When it comes to deciding what clay body is best for your purposes, the choices may sound confusing at first, but as you become familiar with the material, it will gradually make sense.

Sometimes finding the right clay body can take considerable effort. The potters on Crete gather their clay, crush it, saturate it with water, and leave it in the sun to let the water evaporate (10-7). In the days when the early potters in the American Southwest dug their clay, they sometimes had to walk miles to find it. Today, Etsuko Tashima, who uses some of the best clay in Japan, from Shigaraki, reports, *When I go over there in a truck, I buy two tons!*

Why Mix Clay Bodies?

Since a natural clay body, or a commercially mixed body, may not always meet an individual's need, many potters and sculptors prefer to mix their own bodies or have them mixed to their recipes.

For example, American sculptor Richard Notkin (9-8) says,

> *Although porcelain is one of my favorite clays, as it accepts the greatest amount of detail, I believe in using whatever materials and techniques are the most appropriate to achieve the intended results of each new series of work. . . . For the Yixing Series, I have developed a range of fine-particled cone 5–6 stoneware bodies from a combination of ingredients available commercially: stoneware and earthenware casting slips, various dry clays, Mason stains, etc.*

On the other hand, Janet Mansfield (12-9, 12-10), who has a studio in an area of Australia rich in clays and other minerals useful to a potter, says,

> *In my pots I use all these materials, hoping to discover the qualities in them that will direct my work and give it distinctiveness. Wanting to work in this way means that I need to do much experimenting with the clay bodies, and also with how the clay will serve the forms.*

American Patrick Siler likes the process of blending his clay body:

> *One of the things I enjoy most about starting a group of pieces is the process of making my batch of clay. Although really I haven't varied the kind of clay I use for years, I enjoy the initiation rites of the process.*

Jill Crowley, in England, prepares her own clay in order to be able to mix crushed bricks into it to give the lumpy texture she wants for the surface of her sculpture (8-20), while American potter Eileen Murphy (15-27) had to develop a clay body that would be strong in the green state (dried, but not fired), because her method of drawing and painting on the **greenware** means it must stand up to a lot of handling.

One reason for learning to mix at least a few basic clay bodies is to become familiar with the ingredients and how they act in the clay. Even if you do not plan to make your own clay bodies in bulk, some knowledge of formulating, mixing, and testing clay bodies will add to your understanding of how the different ingredients affect the body and how a particular clay will respond to your hands, to drying, or to firing. By learning to blend clay bodies, you can learn to develop superior ones specially formulated for your own sculpting or wheel throwing. You can make a body with the particular color or texture you want, formulate it to fit the nuances of your own kiln's firing, and perhaps mix a casting slip with an especially fluid property to fit the intricacies of your plaster mold. By learning to mix your own clay, you gain control over its water content, its consistency, and its quality. You also learn how to make subtle changes in a body, and—a vitally important consideration when glazing your work—your knowledge of clay body formulas can directly affect the quality of the results you get from glazes.

Early potters had no knowledge of the chemical components of clay, of *why* different clays responded to the heat or atmosphere of the kiln in different ways, or *what* made one clay more plastic than another. They simply saw what happened when they used certain materials. But even without knowledge of the chemical structure of clay, the early potters experimented with different types of clay, and throughout history, it was this experimentation that led to the successful development of new ceramics techniques or materials—or to disasters in the kiln! By learning to mix and test clay bodies, you will be approaching ceramics with the same attitude, applying the try-it-and-see approach. This attitude, combined with some knowledge of the chemical properties of various ceramic materials, will help you carry out controlled experiments that can greatly expand your experience in ceramics.

For these reasons, we suggest that you try mixing and testing at least some of the clay bodies that have been formulated for you using only a few components; as you test them you will not

have to deal with too many variables. These recipes are part of a complete section devoted to clay and glaze testing in Appendix 1. In the same appendix, you will also find other recipes for somewhat more complex clay bodies shared by some potters and sculptors, and as you gain experience in mixing and testing clays you can try some of these.

MIXING CLAY BODIES

Throughout history, people have used a variety of methods for mixing dry clay ingredients, using their feet or hands (10-2), water power, or mule power to blend the components. In the past, the hazards of breathing clay dust were not recognized, so potters who were constantly exposed to the dust, those who mined dry clay ingredients, and those who worked in dusty pottery factories, often developed silicosis, a lethal disease of the lungs.

It is not the particles you can see floating in the air that are most dangerous; rather, it is the microscopic particles that can penetrate an ordinary paper mask that do the damage. Clay dust can also be spread through a studio from the bits and pieces of clay that dry on tables or on wheels, and on the floor; sponging these off at the end of work is important.

Protection Against Clay Dust

Breathing clay dust is harmful to your respiratory system, so proper protection is essential. One way you can protect yourself against breathing clay dust is to keep the studio as clean as possible. Cleaning with the proper type of vacuum cleaner or damp-mopping or hosing the work space at the end of work will help to keep clay from being tracked around the studio and its dust from entering the air (10-6).

Active Local Ventilation

In addition to keeping the studio clean, you should provide yourself with proper ventilation. Do not rely only on general studio ventilation. It is recommended that a studio be provided with local exhaust systems that capture the dust at its source—that is, where dry clay is mixed, carving is done, or dry clay objects are sanded. Although most studios are now provided with such active local ventilation systems that vent the dust from near to the source, if you find that you have to mix clay in a situation where such a system has not been installed, wear a respirator rated by the Occupational Health and Safety Administration (OSHA) to protect yourself against the microscopic clay particles. Wear protective goggles as well. If you are going to be mixing large quantities of dry clay materials, the ultimate protection is a supplied-air system in which your head is completely enclosed and filtered air is supplied through a hose (10-6).

Once you are properly protected against the clay dust, short of harnessing a mule to a mixer or contriving a water wheel, you have several choices of how to mix your clay (10-2, 10-9 to 10-12). Your first experience with mixing clay bodies probably will be through mixing relatively small batches in order to make test tiles which you will then fire at varying temperatures and in different atmospheres.

HOW TO MIX CLAY

Mechanical Mixers

Commercial clay mixers are basically the same as dough mixers, but are larger and are made specifically for clay. This is the type of mechanical mixer you are most likely to find in a school studio (10-11). Recommended mixers have blade guards and safety electrical shut-off switches. Never put your hands in a functioning mixer, but if an accident should occur, reach first for the switch to turn it off.

Used in the same way as a dough mixer, a clay mixer is probably the most useful piece of equipment in a studio, because in addition to mixing clay it can also be used to recycle clay that has been discarded in the process of making pots or sculpture. Putting dry scraps directly into the mixer is not recommended, because hard chunks usually find their way into the processed clay. Rather, the dry scraps should be moistened first in a bucket; then fresh, dry clay ingredients and additional water should be added and the mixture blended. The recycled clay can then be wedged to eliminate air bubbles and make it more homogeneous.

Commercial mixers have tops that totally close up the mixing area. They eliminate the danger of any dust escaping into the air. They also have an opening for a hose or a valve to allow you to add water without lifting the lid.

Dough mixers can be used to mix clay—in fact, many aspects of clay or glaze mixing remind one of kitchen procedures. To use a dough mixer, simply weigh out the dry materials, usually just over half the capacity of the dough mixer; then turn the mixer on, blend the ingredients dry, and slowly add the water.

Pug Mills

Pug mills are machines that are used for mixing and sometimes for de-airing clay (10-12). The process of pugging (putting the clay through a pug mill) can eliminate the need for **wedging**, although many potters and sculptors still prefer to wedge the clay even after it goes through a pug mill. Since pug mills will also accept and process dry scraps, they can be used for recycling clay as well. However, if you use a pug mill to reprocess clay scraps, make sure the scraps are not so large that they bind in the blades, possibly damaging the machine. Producing a high-quality recycled clay from dry chunks usually requires that the clay be pugged two or three times. As a rule it is better to dampen any scraps before reprocessing them; this is easier on the machine and cuts down on processing time.

Some pug mills are equipped with a de-airing system that produces a clay body that is free of air, is well compacted, and has the particles pressed close together. The clays that you can buy premixed in plastic bags in ceramic supply stores have been processed in this way.

To blend porcelain clay, you should use a pug mill with stainless steel blades and stainless steel or aluminum barrel hopper (mixing container). With such a pug mill there is no rust which might contaminate the pure white porcelain body, and it is also much easier to clean.

Commercially Mixed Clay

Many ceramists use commercially mixed clay with great success, including prize-winning Canadian potter Susanne Ashmore (14-34), who makes her teapots from a premixed porcelain,

P-300, used by many Canadian potters. American sculptor Richard Notkin (9-8) says,

> I generally use a good commercial cone 6 vit-rified porcelain (which porcelain "purists" may scoff at), but it works quite well for my purposes, in compatible plastic clay and slip-casting batches.

Mixing for Tests

Learning to mix and test—whether clay bodies or glazes—is one of the most important skills a beginner in ceramics can learn. Not only will testing show you how to vary a clay body (and, later, a glaze), but it will introduce you to the many variables in the materials you buy and to the varying conditions that can exist in a kiln. Testing can also teach you how to use coloring materials.

CLAY RECIPES TO MIX AND TEST   The simple clay body recipes given in Appendix 1A will start you out in the testing process. Since a clay body affects the glaze you put over it, we suggest you use these clay bodies, formulated for *Hands in Clay*, to make the tiles on which you will test the glazes that were also specially formulated for your experiments. You might want to make and fire extra tiles to set aside for later use.

Even those who know a good deal about what clay ingredients do are not able to visualize exactly what will happen when the clay goes through the fire. And when glazes are formulated to fit a particular clay body, you can expect even more variables. Sculptor John Toki says,

> Ceramics is all variables. In dealing with clay and glazes one can be specific only to a point. The sooner you recognize and accept this, the sooner you will feel at home with the process.

Each time you change the type of work you are doing, you may have to do more clay body tests. In fact, in some cases you may have to continue testing for many months to get the clay body that suits your particular needs exactly.

Color in Clay Bodies

You will want to consider the color of the clay body in relation to whatever you are planning to make with it. If you were using stoneware or earthenware for unglazed sculpture, for instance, or if you wanted to leave sections of a pot un-glazed, you probably would want to use a clay body with a rich color. If you wanted to make a dark brown or black clay to use unglazed in a sculpture, as do Carlo Zauli in Italy and John Toki in the United States, you would add iron and manganese and possibly other **oxides** or **stains** to the clay body. It is the amount of iron and/or other coloring oxides in natural earthenware and stoneware that gives them their earthy tones. Because the iron acts as a flux, earthenware con-taining a lot of iron can be fired at the low tem-peratures commonly achieved with an open or a pit firing. This is what made it possible for early cultures to develop pottery. Since the clay con-tains a lot of iron, it will fire to buff, brown, or reddish brown. We saw how potters, first in the Middle East and then in Spain, Italy, and the rest of Europe, used opaque tin glazes to cover the reddish-brown tones of earthenware because they wanted to provide a white background on which they could paint with cobalt blue.

Once the technology of firing clay to a high temperature was developed in China (Chapter 3), the clay bodies high in feldspar could be brought to maturity, and feldspar became a valuable flux. Feldspar, such as Cornwall stone (*petuntze*, in China), or a medium-firing flux such as nepheline syenite, has a higher maturing range than iron and can be used as fluxes in porcelain, avoiding the color imparted by the iron.

Because maturity is related to the type and amount of fluxes in the clay body and since some coloring oxides also act as fluxes, when you mix colored clay bodies you should be aware of the temperature and time needed in the kiln to bring the clay to maturity. Maturity, or immaturity, will also affect the color and surface of the fired clay (sheen or matt), as well as the body texture (po-rous or vitrified).

Suppose that you wanted to fire a white, high-firing stoneware clay at a slightly lower tempera-ture than usual; you could add some extra flux to fuse it at the lower temperature. But if you wanted to lower the maturing temperature a great deal, you would use not stoneware but a low-fire body such as earthenware. However, if you wanted to keep the clay body white, you could not use a color-imparting flux, so you would need to know how the different fluxes affected the color of the clay. You can see from this that the maturing temperature of the clay can also affect its fired color and that a change in just one of a clay body's components can alter your clay body considerably. (See Color Plate 51 and Appendix 1A).

Variations in Materials

Clay materials themselves can vary a good deal, thus affecting the results you may get with different batches of the same clay body. When the availability of materials changes or a specific vein of material is exhausted, a supplier might substitute a similar material but one that produces somewhat different effects. For example, when miners of Kingman feldspar hit a new vein that had considerably more iron in it, stoneware potters all over the country had to adjust their firing and glazes. Eventually, when Kingman was mined out, they shifted to Custer feldspar, similar in chemical composition yet differing subtly in color and texture.

American potter Eileen Murphy (15-27) says that she uses her own mixture of clay, because after years of trying different prepared clay bodies, she became tired of finding

some dunted some with too little silica, some very dry, some with too much iron, some too brown, some with too much shrinkage and on and on.

But even now, using her own recipe, she says,

the clay still varies year to year due to changes in the natural materials. The clay I just had mixed according to my recipe has more iron in it than two years previous. This strongly affects my work, because in salt firing the body is exposed, not glazed over. So, with too much iron, I have a kiln load of darker-than-hoped-for pieces, which also affects the slips I use: some rutile slips actually matched the clay body, so the detail was lost.

Using Local Clays

Instead of using commercially produced dry ingredients to mix your clay body, you can search for local clays, dig them, clean them, and test them for color and other qualities. Sometimes you can use such a clay just as it comes from the earth, or with twigs or large pebbles removed by hand and some form of temper (probably grog) added, but if there are too many large impurities in it, you will have to screen them out. In a village in Greece, the local clay is dried into lumps, pulverized, and soaked in water until it can be poured through a screen. Then it is spread in troughs to dry to working consistency in the sun. Using another method, Maria Martinez of San Ildefonso, New Mexico, mixed her pulverized local clay and temper together by hand, added water to it, and continued kneading it by hand to proper working consistency (10-2).

The Availability of Materials

Because clay is such a common material in our earth, we tend to think of ceramic materials as inexhaustible. This is not true; certain feldspars—such as Kingman feldspar—have already been mined out and substitutions made. Natural Albany slip is no longer being mined in upstate New York, and substitutes are now used. As time goes on, there probably will have to be other substitutes made for depleted materials.

People who live close to the earth have a reverence for it and do not waste the bounty it provides. Some of the materials we may need for ceramics are finite, so our attitude should be one of respect for those that the earth now provides us.

Aging Clay

Once you have mixed a batch of clay, you can set it aside like bread dough, not to rise but to age. Clay, like bread, is improved by the action of bacteria. These bacteria develop acids and gels and secrete enzymes that help break down the clay into smaller particles, increasing its plasticity. Some potters add organic materials such as vinegar, red wine, or stale beer to their clay to help in this process. Two weeks is considered by some potters and sculptors to be adequate time to ripen the clay, but other potters say the longer the clay ages, the better it becomes. Legends say that ancient Chinese potters prepared clay to be put aside for use by their grandsons. In this same vein, Michael Cardew told of some clay he buried in a hole because it did not throw well. He left it there while he traveled for ten years, tried it again without success, and then forgot it for another ten or fifteen years. An apprentice found it, and, Cardew said, used it to make fabulous unglazed terra-cotta garden pots.

Wedging

To carry the kitchen parallel further, the action of wedging is like the kneading of bread. It eliminates the lumps and drives out air that may be trapped in pockets or bubbles in the clay. But most important, wedging homogenizes the clay. You *can* eliminate small air bubbles on the wheel or slab by puncturing them with a pin, but if you are trying to throw a pot and find a moist area on one side and a stiff, hard lump in the clay on the other you have encountered an insurmountable difficulty. Even if a commercial body has been premixed, it may not be thoroughly homogenized; perhaps the bag it came in had been sitting on a shelf for a long time, there may have been a small, undetectable puncture in the bag, or the clay may have been left exposed to the air for a while so that, although the interior is moist enough, the exterior has stiffened. Therefore, it is wise to wedge any clay prior to use, especially for throwing on the wheel.

You can see if there are air bubbles in a chunk of clay by cutting through it with a wire and looking at the exposed areas, but that will not tell you about the clay's consistency. One way to understand how wedging blends clay is to wedge chunks of two different colors of clay until they are completely blended.

Like most of the processes you will use when working with clay, wedging does not have to be complex or mysterious. Any method is satisfactory as long as it accomplishes the objective (10-13). For some handbuilding methods, it is enough to cut the clay in half and slam one section down on a solid surface and the other on top of it, but since this separates rather than tightens the clay particles, it does not make the clay cohesive enough for wheel throwing.

SPIRAL AND RAM'S HEAD WEDGING Two traditional wedging methods are shown in Figures 10-14 and 10-15. They should be done on as low a surface as is comfortable. Keep your body higher than the table for maximum leverage, and use your torso and legs as well as your wrists and forearms. Involve your body in the rolling action, or you will tire yourself at the wedging board before you even sit down to throw.

The wedging board should be firm and well anchored to keep it from moving too much as you push down and out on the clay. The surface can be plaster, which will soak up a lot of moisture from the clay. Some potters, however, cover the plaster with a light cloth or use a canvas-covered board as a surface to avoid the possibility of picking up bits of plaster from the table and mixing

Figure 10-13
Wedging the Clay, a wall panel by Patrick Siler, U.S.A., part of a series of panels entitled *Clayworks.* 22 × 26 × 2½ in. (56 × 66 × 6 cm). *Courtesy the artist.*

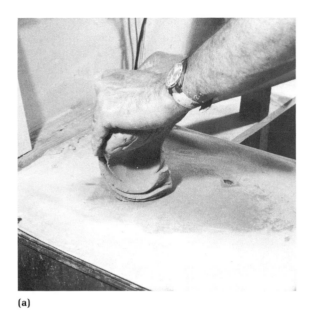

(a)

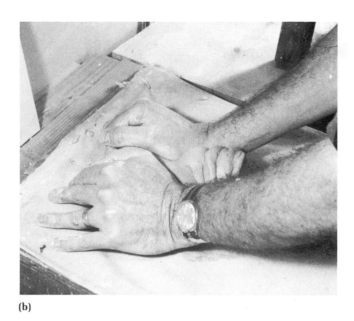

(b)

Figure 10-14
(a) Larry Murphy, U.S.A., pushing and lifting the clay on a canvas-covered wedging table using the "ram's head" method. **(b)** Pushing the clay down and out releases trapped air, eliminates lumps, and makes the clay homogeneous.

Figure 10-15
(a) Ron Judd, U.S.A., demonstrates wedging clay in the spiral method, using a slight twist of the hands. This opens up all parts of the clay ball, allowing any air bubbles to escape. **(b)** Spiral wedging also lines up the clay particles in the direction in which the pot will be thrown on the wheel.

(a)

(b)

them into the clay. Tiny bits of plaster in the clay will expand as they moisten and will eventually pop the fired glaze from the surface.

Either of these two frequently taught methods of wedging, the "ram's head" and "spiral" methods, will prepare the clay for throwing. Some potters feel that the spiral method does a better job, because it lines up all the particles of clay in one direction. Both methods not only de-air the clay and take out lumps and bubbles, but also tighten the clay into a firm, compact ball ready to throw.

Whatever method you use, wedging serves another purpose. It brings you into contact with the clay you are going to use, and to some potters and sculptors this is a very important part of the process. They feel that the rhythmic action of the body and the time spent wedging the clay give them a chance to think about how they will work the clay. They also feel that the intimate contact that this process sets up between their hands and the clay establishes the mood for working. Stephen De Staebler, who once tried having someone assist with wedging and preparing his slabs, said,

I discovered that it was helping me in terms of time, but hindering me in terms of thinking.

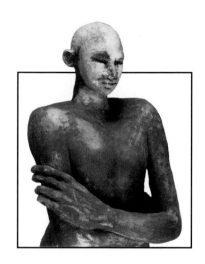

11

Handbuilding

Our hands are remarkable tools; strong yet sensitive, they can pitch out a thin, delicate pot or build a massive sculpture. Every day of our lives we touch things, but how often do we really *feel* them? Our hands — holding the smooth, mechanical surface of a steering wheel; feeling the pitted texture of an orange; lifting a mass of wet laundry; holding a baby — touch and experience so many surfaces, masses, and forms in a day, yet how often do we differentiate between them and remember what our fingertips felt? To bring vitality to clay forms, it is important to rediscover our tactile imagination and memory in order to make full use of the sensations we experience throughout our lives.

Perhaps much of the appeal of clay is the intimate and direct relationship the potter or sculptor can develop with it. Unlike stone or metal, clay can be modeled with few tools or intermediate processes to separate you from your work. You can use only your hands to pinch, to coil, or to make slabs into a pot or sculpture of almost any size (11-1, 11-2, 11-3). Sculptor Stephen De Staebler sees his whole body as a tool, and he uses it to press the clay into the forms of his figures. Speaking of clay's malleability, he says,

I can't think of another sculptural medium that has such a vulnerability to force.

Before you start to handbuild a pot or a sculpture, press your thumb and fingers together and

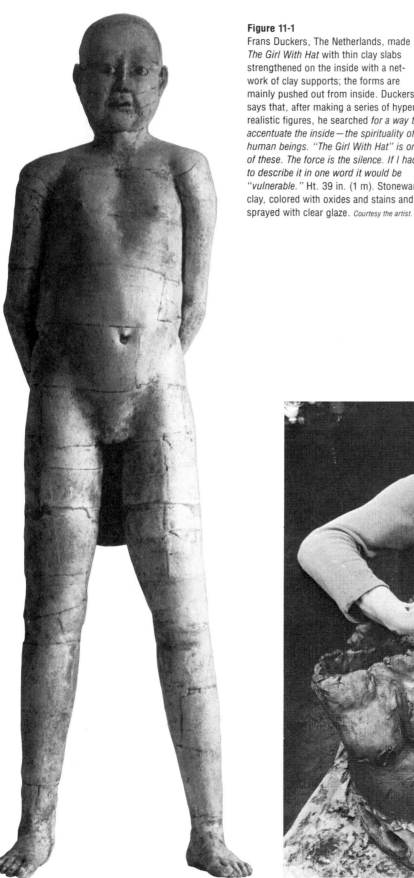

Figure 11-1
Frans Duckers, The Netherlands, made *The Girl With Hat* with thin clay slabs strengthened on the inside with a network of clay supports; the forms are mainly pushed out from inside. Duckers says that, after making a series of hyperrealistic figures, he searched *for a way to accentuate the inside — the spirituality of human beings. "The Girl With Hat" is one of these. The force is the silence. If I had to describe it in one word it would be "vulnerable."* Ht. 39 in. (1 m). Stoneware clay, colored with oxides and stains and sprayed with clear glaze. *Courtesy the artist.*

Figure 11-2
Nicholas Van Os, The Netherlands, handbuilding a large stoneware fantasy figure, adding coils and wads of clay to construct the walls. He incorporates an interior network of clay supports to help keep the damp clay from collapsing. *Courtesy the artist. Photo: Frits Van Os.*

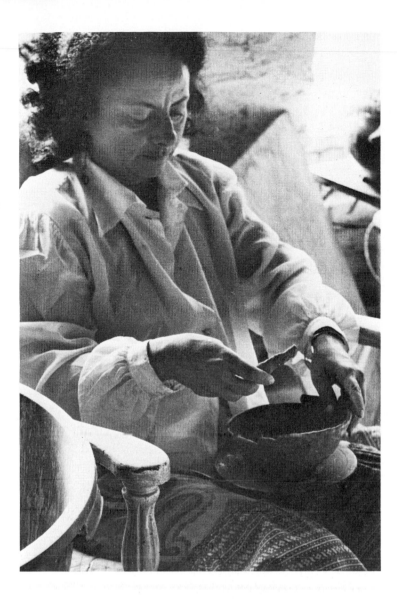

Figure 11-3
Pinching can be done almost anywhere with little equipment. In a quiet spot, the process can be a contemplative activity. Magdalena Suarez Frimkess, U.S.A. *Courtesy the artist.*

see how much force you can exert on the clay. Visualize what you can do to the clay by pressing it with your open or cupped palm. Then, with your hands flat, push down on a table with your upper body and feel the strength you could use from your arms and shoulders. Your hands are an extension not only of your arms, but of your whole body—indeed, of your entire being. It is that being, that individuality, that will give *your* pot or *your* sculpture its expressive quality, for clay captures and holds not only the imprint of your fingers, but also the imprint of your creativity.

WORKING IN THREE DIMENSIONS

Whatever method you use to work in clay, you have to think in three dimensions. As you make your first pot or piece of sculpture, you may have the exasperating but challenging experience of working happily on one part, feeling quite pleased at expressing your ideas so clearly, only to discover when you turn the sculpture or pot or see it from a different angle that the forms and their relationships are unresolved. Most of us tend to see space as framed in two dimensions, perhaps because we are used to looking at photos, paintings, or television screens. When you make even the simplest pot or sculpture, however, you are creating an actual form in real space rather than depicting it in illusionistic space. Most people have to make a conscious effort at first to consider their work from all angles. It helps to place your work on a **banding wheel** or a revolving sculpture stand so that you can turn it constantly, but if the work is too large for these aids, walking around it will ensure that what you do to one part will not totally change all the relationships. Also, be sure you have adequate light; proper lighting is as important while you are working on a three-dimensional piece of sculpture as it is to a painter working on a two-dimensional surface.

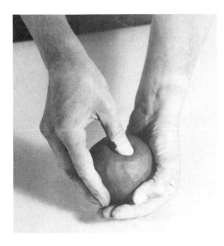

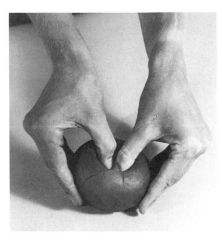

Figure 11-4
To start a pinch pot, pat a lump of clay into a ball. The consistency of the clay is important—too moist and the pot will collapse, too dry and it will crack. Next, press your thumb into the center of the ball to open it.

Figure 11-5
Begin to pinch, rotating the ball as you continue to open it. Be sure to leave enough clay at the bottom for shaping.

Figure 11-6
Resting the ball on a flat surface, rotate it as you begin to pinch up the walls between thumb and finger. Keep the walls consistent in thickness.

As you proceed, you will want to consider how the forms of a pot or sculpture relate to each other and to the space around them, as well as how to treat the surface of the clay itself in relation to these forms. It may help to start out with a few exercises in which you shape the clay into cubes, spheres, and cylinders and combine them into simple compositions. This will force you to think about the relationships of masses in space. Doing some pencil sketches of three-dimensional objects will also help you learn to observe forms in space. Notice, for example, how tensions develop between flat and curved shapes, how jagged forms suggest one type of emotion while swelling soft ones project an entirely different feeling. Be alert as well to what the negative space between the forms contributes to the expression of your idea or emotion. To develop a knowledgeable eye, go to galleries and museums to look at a variety of sculpture and pots, study them, and decide whether you feel they express the artist's concept successfully.

Drawing

At first, it may seem that skill in drawing is not essential for making pottery or even sculpture. But being able to note down your observations, to study forms through drawing them, or to plan your work on paper is extremely useful for *anyone* in the visual arts. In addition, your eye will be sharpened as a result of constant sketching, and your sketchbook can become a source of ideas for your pottery forms or sculptures.

Through drawing, it is possible to capture and distill a perception, to see it more clearly, and to fix it in your mind. And through drawing, you can explore the world around you, using a pencil as if it were an extension of your eyes, probing to see how one form relates to another, how the profile of an object delineates its complexity, and how light and shade define the contours of a figure, sharpening or diffusing them.

Drawing objects at the same scale at which you perceive them is an exercise that can sharpen your vision, and sometimes making a drawing of your sculpture at the same scale will help you plan how to proceed. In doing so, you will learn a considerable amount about the work itself.

HANDBUILDING

Handbuilding methods include pinching, modeling, coiling, and slab building. This chapter demonstrates several of these methods. Remember,

Figure 11-7
Add wads or coils of clay to build up the walls, constantly turning the pot to keep it symmetrical. As the walls grow, check them for thickness, and shape the pot as you go along.

Figure 11-8
Using a flexible metal rib, scrape the walls smooth while stretching and forming the pot, supporting the clay on the inside with your hand.

Figure 11-9
As the pot grows, you may have to let the clay stiffen in order to support additional clay on the top. If you want to narrow the neck, add smaller and smaller coils. Later, you can add a foot to the base.

however, that the particular methods shown here represent only a few of the many ways of working; there is no one "right" way to work in clay. You will develop your own way as you gain experience, and it may vary considerably from these. Clay requires a give and take, and eventually you will come to terms with the material, discovering what it can do and what you can do with it (11-1 to 11-3).

Figure 11-10
Harvest Moon, by Paulus Berensohn, U.S.A. After Berensohn pinched the clay into this thin-walled pot, he bisque-fired it, then sanded it, creating a soft, unglazed surface. White earthenware. *Courtesy the artist. Photo: True Kelly.*

Pinching

Pinching a ball of clay into a simple pot is a good way to start, because it is such a direct way to work, allowing you to see how the clay responds to your hands. By working in this way, you will discover just how stiff the clay needs to be to hold its shape as you pinch it, how the walls feel as they develop between your fingers, how moist the edge of a pot must be to keep it from cracking, and at what point the clay will collapse as you push it beyond its limits. You will also learn to judge the thickness of the walls as you pinch them between your thumbs and fingers. Figures 11-4 to 11-9 show one method of pinching a pot, and Figures 11-10 to 11-18 show pinching and other handbuilding methods.

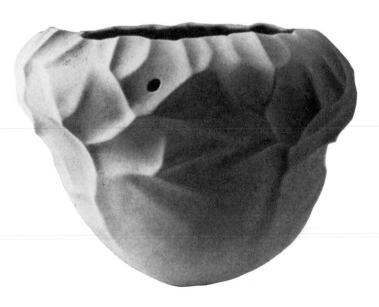

Figure 11-11
Sculptor Robert Brady, U.S.A., building a
large pinched vessel. His fingerprints will
add texture to the painterly quality that
he will achieve on the surface using multiple glaze firings.

SCULPTING SOLID

By definition, a vessel must be hollow in order to
be capable of containing something. Generally a
clay sculpture is also built hollow, not to contain,
but to make it structurally sound and to ensure
greater firing success. Small sculptures, such as the
sketches an artist may do as maquettes (sketches
or models) for a larger work, can be fired solid if
they are not too thick. They can also be sliced
into sections when they are leather hard, hollowed out, and put together again with scoring
and slip (11-14 to 11-18).

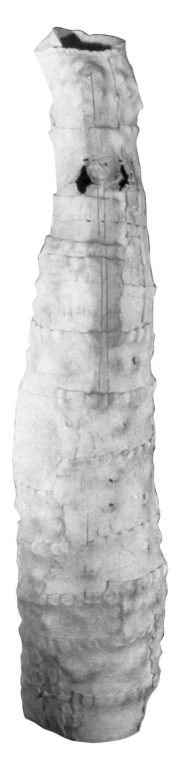

Figure 11-12
Trail with light III t, by Lawson Oyekan,
England. Oyekan says that he is *continually exploring the forms and colour from
both West African and European cultures,
while being drawn to particular themes of
movement and light as derived from each.*
1992. Wrapped terra-cotta. 31 × 8 in.
(80 × 20 cm). *Courtesy the artist.*

Figure 11-13

Tight-Rope Visions, by Lisa Clague, U.S.A. The clay figure was built with the pinch method with added metal to give a linear quality. Clague says, *My work is made up of objects held in a state of tension that is more psychological than physical, suggesting the spontaneity of an unexpected journey.* 1993. Clay, colored with copper oxide, stains, metal. 30 × 24 in. (76 × 61 cm). *Courtesy the artist. Photo: Scott McCue.*

Modeling a Head

To model a head solid, use a groggy sculpture clay and if possible work from a live model. If none is available, an anatomy book can help you work with knowledge of the bone structure and the muscles that give form to the features (11-14). Work as freely as you can, preserving the freshness of the surface.

It is possible, using great care and long, slow firing, to fire solid or thick-walled sculptures or parts of sculptures. But in general, it is better to hollow out a solid sculpture before firing. This technique can lend itself to the building of almost any not-too-large form, but it is especially useful for making a head or bust and preparing it for firing. One advantage of working solid is that it is often easier and more spontaneous to create a mass in space than to build up walls around space. Also, the dense foundation of clay you will have allows for experimentation and gesture without as much danger of the structure collapsing. If you wish to give added support to the clay, you can use a simple armature made with a wooden dowel nailed or fitted into a drilled hole in a board, or a piece of PVC pipe screwed into a metal flange wrapped in plastic, newspaper, or other material that will allow the clay to shrink. This can be twisted out easily before firing.

Cutting, Hollowing, and Rejoining

Once the sculpture is leather hard you can proceed with the cutting (11-15). Plan the cut carefully, placing it where it will be easy to rejoin the sections. Use a strong wire for cutting because a solid chunk of leather-hard clay of this size can take considerable strength to slice through. Proceed with the hollowing, using a ribbon tool (11-16).

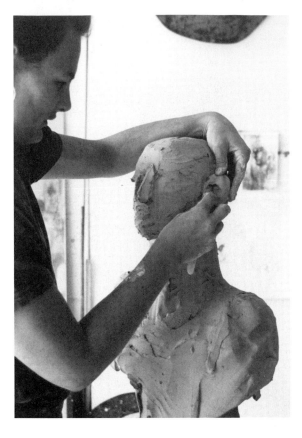

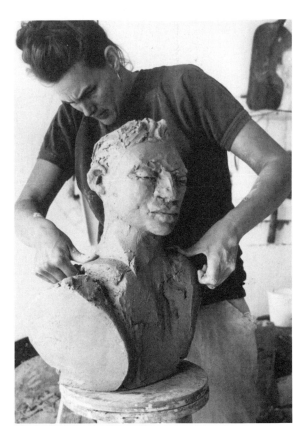

Figure 11-14
Michelle Gregor, U.S.A., builds her portrait heads solid, working quickly and surely as she defines the forms. If a live model is not available, she takes photos of the subject from every angle to use for reference.

Figure 11-15
Gregor slices the sculpture with a strong wire when it is leather hard, choosing the least conspicuous area for the cut—often along the hairline. She has two pieces of foam ready on which to rest the sections to protect the freshness of the sculpted surface while she hollows them.

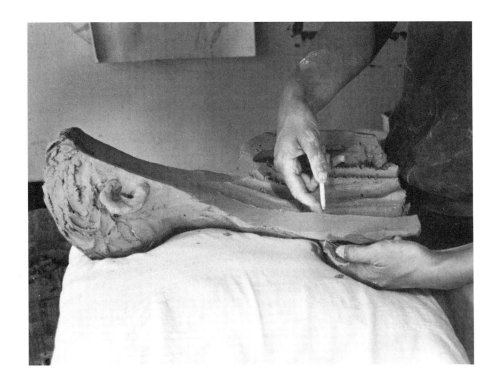

Figure 11-16
She rests each section on the foam and starts to hollow, using a ribbon tool, scooping out the excess clay until the walls are between ¼ inch (6.35 mm) and ½ inch (12.70 mm) thick. To be sure she is not getting the walls too thin, she uses a needle tool to test their thickness.

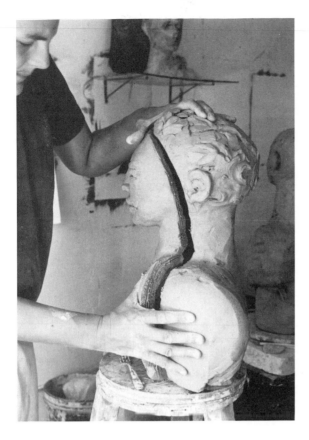

Figure 11-17
Finally, she reassembles the hollowed-out piece, pressing the sections together well after scoring the edges and painting them with slip. During joining she is careful not to damage the surface, and reworks the joint to eliminate the joining line and to bring back any lost detail. Gregor uses slips to color her sculpture, or sometimes a wash of acrylic paint.

Figure 11-18
Crow Boy (detail). Michelle Gregor built this full-size figure using coils and slabs for the body, but she made the head using the solid/hollowed-out technique that she demonstrates in illustrations 11-14 to 11-17. 1992. Sculpture mix body, colored slips. 52 × 26 × 13 in. (132 × 66 × 33 cm). *Courtesy the artist. Photo: Amy Franceschini.*

When you have hollowed out all sections and made sure that the walls are of a consistent thickness, score the edges well and coat them with slip, then press the sections firmly together (11-17). Once they are firmly joined, work over the joint to obliterate any mark and to sharpen smeared detail.

Firing a sculpture built in this way should present no problems if the piece has been hollowed evenly and dried thoroughly. (See Chapter 15.)

BUILDING HOLLOW

Although building solid works well for compact pieces, in general it is easiest to build a sculpture hollow. Building it in this way will help ensure success in drying and firing it (11-18). It is especially important to keep the walls even in thickness as you build; otherwise, the thick and thin sections will dry at different rates, creating tensions that can cause warping or cracking during drying and firing.

Supporting and Strengthening the Clay

It is difficult, especially for a beginner, to build a vertical form of damp clay without some sort of support. When the early Greeks and the Etruscans used clay for large, free-standing figures, they strengthened them by building supports of clay between the legs, either as decorative motifs—as in the Apollo from Veii (2-25)—or as rocks, tree trunks, or other natural supports. To be sure that any large sculpture has sufficient support both as you build it and later during drying and firing, you can include built-in clay supports as part of its construction (11-19). Marilyn Lysohir (11-20) builds in clay reinforcing supports for her figures, and for his large architectural pieces, Stephen De Staebler uses an in-

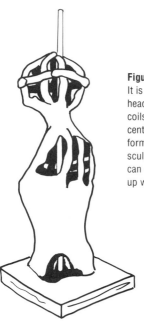

Figure 11-19
It is also possible to build a bust or a head by forming clay over a network of coils. With a dowel or pipe through the center, the interior clay network can be formed to an approximate shape of the sculpture. Allowed to stiffen, the network can support the outer skin, which is built up with slabs or wads of clay.

Figure 11-20
Marilyn Lysohir, U.S.A., builds her figures with interior networks of clay, including holes for inserting supports. Figure from her installation *Bad Manners* (Color Plate 26). *Courtesy the artist and Asher/Faure Gallery, Los Angeles. Photo: Arthur Okazaki.*

terior clay construction that supports the piece as it is built and fired.

Armatures

From the Renaissance period until quite recently, clay was generally used by a sculptor to build a figure up on an **armature**—a support—to provide a model from which to cast metal sculpture. A sectioned mold was made from the model, and the casting of the bronze figure proceeded. The clay that has been pressed onto such an armature must be kept damp, however; otherwise, it will shrink as it dries and, since the armature itself cannot shrink, the clay will crack and fall off the framework. Except in rare exceptions, this type of permanent armature is not used for clay sculpture that will be fired.

Figure 11-21
Sticks and metal pipes that can be pulled out after the clay stiffens enough to hold up by itself, leave hollow passages through which the moisture can escape as the sculpture dries and is fired. Penelope Jenks, U.S.A.

Removable Supports

It is possible, however, to use removable or burnable armatures to support the damp clay as you build. Wooden sticks and dowels or metal pipes (11-21) can be removed or pulled out of the clay when it has stiffened enough to hold its shape. If you use a solid support that has little give, such as wood, you may need to pad it with something that will compress as the clay shrinks as it dries; newspaper, cellulose sponges, and cotton batting are all possibilities. Ptah plans to make a mold from his tall figure, so he keeps the clay damp on the wooden supports (11-22).

Any kind of removable support you can think of that will help you defeat your enemy—gravity—is worth a try. The support may consist simply of wads of clay that hold up an extended form while it stiffens enough to support itself. Or it may be made of crumpled newspapers, cardboard boxes, towel rolls, a brick or a stone, straw, tin cans, sticks of wood, a pillow, pieces of wire, bundles of cloth, foam—anything that works and that can be removed as the clay stiffens. Wadded or rolled paper tied with string to hold the approximate form you wish has the advantage that the paper will compress somewhat, allowing the clay to shrink as it stiffens, thus avoiding cracking. The paper can be pulled out before firing or, if it is impossible to pull it out without damaging the piece, it can be left in to burn out in the fire in a gas kiln.

(a)

Figure 11-22

(a) Ptah, U.S.A., building a 15-foot (4.6 m) Egyptian figure in his backyard. Between work sessions he wraps it in heavy plastic attached with nails pushed through into the clay. When the figure is finished, he will make numerous plaster press molds from it in order to reproduce it in fireable sections. He will reassemble these after firing, and attach the separately built and fired head. **(b)** Schematic working drawing by John Toki for the wooden armature Ptah built to support the clay as he works. The first attempt, built around a single pipe, collapsed, but now the wooden armature is supporting it well. 1993.

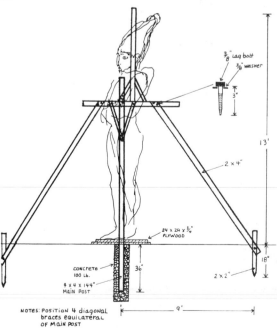

(b)

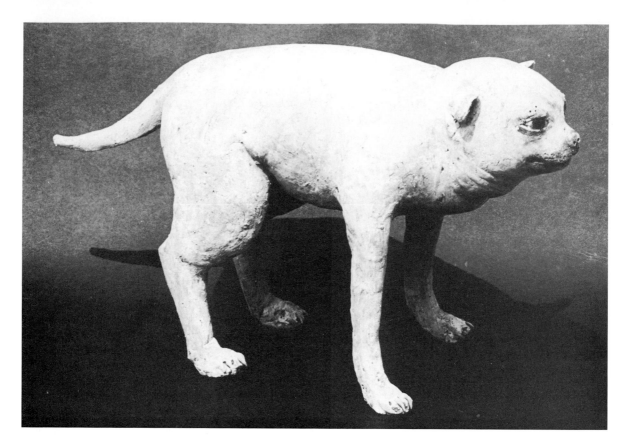

Figure 11-23

Dog, Jose Vermeersch, Belgium. Vermeersch's fat dogs stand, sprawl, or sit in human poses. Their hairless hides are speckled with engobes, and their penetrating eyes are glazed. Low-fire clay. About 19 in. (48 cm) long. *Courtesy the artist.*

You can make another type of removable support by filling a plastic bag with polystyrene beads, vermiculite, or sand. This will give you a rounded support, useful if you want to shape a pot or a sculptured head or similar form. But do not pack the bag too tightly. It should be able to give a little as the clay shrinks. Also, make sure you can get to the opening of the bag easily, because as the clay stiffens, you will want to pour out the contents, leaving the clay to support itself. A balloon will also work as a removable support, because it can be deflated and pulled out when the clay is stiff enough to support itself.

Some sculptors build the clay on a polystyrene armature that has been carved to an approximation of the shape they wish to build. This is convenient, but there are disadvantages in using polystyrene unless it is a simple hump mold from which the clay can be removed *before* firing. This foam releases toxic gases when it is burned out; even if your kiln is well vented to protect you, the gases pollute the general atmosphere, possibly even affecting the ozone layer. Some sculptors have poured solvent through a hole in the clay

to dissolve the polystyrene which then runs out before firing, but solvents are also toxic, polluting, and flammable. Therefore, using this foam as a burnable or soluble support is not recommended. And if you plan to use any other plastic material as a burnable armature, be sure that you keep up to date on its hazards and pollution potential.

Reinforcing Materials

For thousands of years, people have been reinforcing clay by adding natural fibers to it. For example, in many cultures they constructed buildings out of mud applied to a framework of reeds or twigs; others mixed straw into the clay to strengthen the sun-dried bricks they used to build palaces and ziggurats. The straw additive strengthened the clay during both building and drying, but if the brick was fired, the straw burned out in the kiln, and a porous brick was the result.

Although you can still use similar natural materials, there is now a variety of more modern ones — fiber-glass screening, fiber-glass fibers, and woven fiber-glass — that you can add to the clay to strengthen it and which will melt into it on firing. Ptah (11-22) uses nylon fiber in his sculpture clay. This will burn out in the kiln. Nicole Giroud in France and Joan Marmorelis in the United States have both successfully experimented with dipping various fabrics in slip, then drying and firing the draped forms. Marmorelis used fiber glass, while Giroud has tried many types of fabric, from lace to terrycloth. (Use protective measures, including goggles, gloves, and a respirator, when you work with fiber glass, since the floating fibers can be inhaled, irritate the skin, or may damage the eyes). Some sculptors use a fiber mesh developed for concrete to reinforce their sculpture as they build. The mesh burns out in the kiln.

Coiling

Coiling has been used to shape clay into useful and beautiful vessels for thousands of years. From Africa to Greece, from China to New Mexico, potters have used this method in a variety of ways (11-12, 2-5, 5-17). Coiling is still a popular way of making vessels and sculpture, and it is often combined with pinching. With coils, it is possible to build thick-walled vessels that might have come from an earlier age or tall sculptural vessels. On the other hand, it is possible to scrape the walls of a coiled pot quite thin to create a delicate, elegant bowl. Coiling allows you to control the walls as you build them up, and as you carefully place one coil above another you can make the vessel or sculpture slowly bulge outward or narrow inward with less danger of it collapsing.

As you plan how you will use coiling, be aware of its possibilities, and consider using it in combination with pinched or thrown forms or with slabs. You might want to build a pot that reflects quite clearly the coiling process with which it was built (11-39), or you may decide to use the coiling method to build up a large sculpture that, when finished, shows no indication of the method used to form it (Color Plate 22).

PREPARING COIL   As we saw in Chapter 10, the clay and temper you choose depend on the type of work you are going to build, how thick its walls will be, and the temperature at which it will be fired. If your clay has already been put through a pug mill (10-12), wedging will not be as necessary for coiling, but it is still important to make sure the clay contains no lumps or air bubbles. If you will be melding the clay together as you work by pressing the coils together with your fingers, or by smoothing with a rib, or by padding the walls, wedging the clay before use is not as vital as it would be if you were planning to leave your coils unmelded.

MAKING THE COILS   With your idea clearly in mind or with a sketch before you, decide on the thickness of the coils you will use. At this point, it might be a good idea to experiment with making various thicknesses of coils to find the way that is most comfortable for you to work (11-24 to 11-28). If you are rolling out coils on a table, practice making some of different thicknesses. It helps to roll with the base of the hand rather than with the fingers, and to roll the coils from the middle

Figure 11-24
To build his large sculptures, Graham Marks, U.S.A., first forms his coils with an extruder, then rolls them out on a table, readying them for applying over a polystyrene form. *Courtesy the artist and Helen Drutt Gallery.*

Figure 11-25
Marks applies the coils to his sculpture, then scrapes them to smooth and thin the walls. *Courtesy the artist and Helen Drutt Gallery.*

Figure 11-26
Some of Graham Marks's completed sculptures. Note the hoist chain and sling for moving heavy sculpture. The elaborated surfaces are often sandblasted.
Courtesy the artist and Helen Drutt Gallery.

Figure 11-27
Paul Chaleff, U.S.A., attaching a thick coil to one of his tall vessels. Later he will smooth the walls as the vessel revolves on an electric wheel. *Courtesy the artist.*

out. The length of coils to make depends on what you find easiest to handle. Some people prefer to use coils long enough for only one ring at a time, while others build by spiraling a long coil up several times around the diameter of the form.

EXTRUDING COILS   Studio clay **extruders** efficiently produce round coils, squared tubes, and hollow shapes (11-29a). Ceramists find them useful tools for making coils for handbuilt vessels or for adding coils to wheel-thrown vessels. Extruders will also produce handles for pottery, tubes for containers, and forms that can be altered for sculpture. If you plan to work in white clays or porcelain, it is advisable to use an extruder with a stainless steel or aluminum chamber and **dies** to avoid clay contamination (11-29b).

Figure 11-28
When Arnold Zimmerman builds one of his towering coiled works (Color Plate 15), he uses thick, damp coils, melding them well and waiting for the clay below to stiffen enough to carry the added weight of the new coil. *Courtesy the artist.*

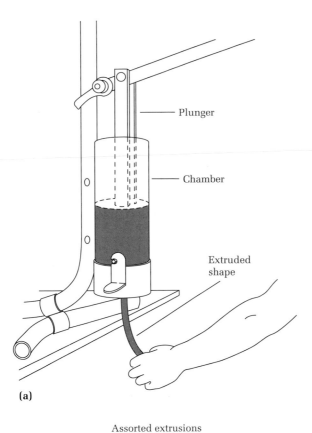

(a)

Assorted extrusions

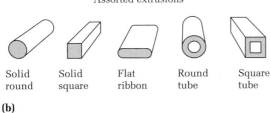

| Solid round | Solid square | Flat ribbon | Round tube | Square tube |

(b)

Figure 11-29
Clay extruders will produce various solid and hollow shapes.
(**a**) The machine contains a steel, plastic, wood, or ceramic die at the end of a hollow steel chamber that holds about 5 to 15 pounds (2.3 to 6.8 kilos) of soft clay. At the top of the chamber is a plunger attached to a lever arm. When the arm is pulled down, the plunger pushes the clay through the die resulting in an extruded shape (**b**). Assorted dies will make solid extrusions, such as coils for coiling pots or for shaping cup handles, and hollow tubes for containers. Others will make wide clay ribbons for forming slab containers, or smaller ribbons for flat loop handles on casserole lids.

Figure 11-30
Jamie Walker, U.S.A., keeps a sketchbook in which he draws notes and plans for future pots. Compare this drawing with the fired and glazed teapot in Figure 11-39 to see its development from concept to finished work.

Graham Marks makes his coils in an extruder and then rolls them out on a flat surface (11-24). If you use extruded coils, dies of different diameters will allow you to control the thickness of the coil (11-29b). Artists use any of these methods to form coils of the appropriate thickness for their work (11-30 to 11-39). Jamie Walker uses the coils straight from the extruder, which forces the clay through plexiglas dies that he cuts himself. With their solid porcelain coils and their large size, his teapots are heavy and largely intended as sculptural vessels, but they are actually functional and pour well.

COILING UP THE WALLS If you are building a pot, it will need a base. You will have to decide whether to make this flat, rounded, or convex. To make a convex base, press lumps of clay into the bottom of an old broken pot, a plastic kitchen bowl lined with cloth or plastic wrap, or into a specially made plaster base mold. On the other hand, to make a flat base, you can pound or roll the clay out on a board or table sprinkled with grog or sand or covered with cloth or plastic, then cut the base to any shape you want (11-31). Another alternative is to shape the base by rolling a coil into a flat spiral and then smoothing it or allowing the coils to show. If you are building a piece of sculpture, however, there is no particular need for a base; in fact, it is generally best to leave the bottom open so that you can reach in later and remove excess clay from the interior if the walls become too thick in places.

Figure 11-31
Walker cautions that lack of care in starting the pot can cause disasters. The base has been rolled out and cut to size and is awaiting the first coil.

Figure 11-32
Scoring the base for the first coil. He prefers to use only water applied with a sponge to prepare the area where the first coil will be placed. Water is faster than slip, he says, and excess slip is difficult to clean off.

Figure 11-33
Walker places the first coil on the scored area. Before joining it, he cuts the end cleanly; then he carefully melds the joint. *When I put the first coil on the slab I usually smooth it in where it joins the slab.*

Figure 11-34
Before building any further, as additional reinforcement, he places a small coil at the crucial joint between the base and the first coil; he then melds it in well.

Figure 11-35
As he begins to coil up the walls, Walker says, *It is mainly in the fingers, in getting the feeling when everything is right and it's going to build up—having the confidence that it is not going to fall down.* As he completes each ring, Walker dampens and scores the coil to ready it to receive the next one.

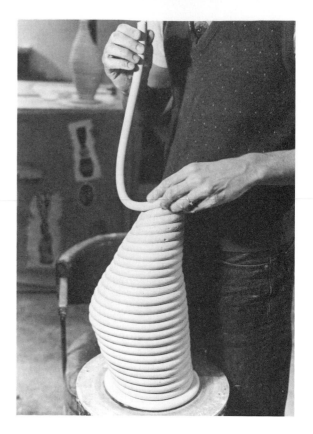

Figure 11-36
As he builds up, adding coils to the asymmetric teapot, Walker continues a rhythm of *water, score and place. When you place it the coil will stick on a little bit. The real adhesion and strength comes from using some pressure when you use the sponge between coils.*

PLACING THE COILS One advantage of coiling is that it gives you considerable control over the shape of the pot or sculpture as you go along. Some potters shape their pots as they place the coils, whereas others build a basic cylinder first, then gently push out the walls to the desired curve. To start a piece of sculpture, you can either lay out the first coils in an approximation of the form of its base and develop it as you build it up, or start with a cylinder that you can push or paddle into shape as you go along. Whether you are building a pot or a sculpture, it is important to revolve your work on a turntable or move around it yourself to see how it is progressing on all sides. You'll need to do this to make a symmetrical pot, but even if you are working asymmetrically, as Jamie Walker does, it is helpful to view your work frequently from all sides as you develop the forms.

JOINING THE COILS Because a coiled pot or coiled sculpture, unlike a pinched one, in which the clay is actually melded together, is made up of

many separate pieces, the joints must be properly made. If they are not, the coils may pull away from each other as they dry, and cracks or breaks may develop at those points when the piece is fired. Whether you add coils while the clay is quite wet or let it stiffen somewhat between rings, you must be sure that each coil is firmly attached to the one below it. If you plan to smooth the coils with a **rib** or to paddle the outside while you hold your hand or a smooth rock inside to support the walls, you may not need to do more than push them together with your thumb, because the smoothing or paddling will also meld them together, constricting the clay and strengthening the walls. Many potters or sculptors meld their coils completely as they go along in order to be sure the joints are strong or to achieve a smooth surface, whereas others may keep the coils distinct in order to create a surface that emphasizes or contrasts with the form of the piece. If you want the coils to retain their separate identity, as in Jamie Walker's work, you will need to score each

Figure 11-37
After dampening and scoring the joint areas, he attaches the spout to his completed teapot.

Figure 11-38
With extruded handle and knob in place on the top, the teapot is completed. The top has short interior legs that fit inside the pot to keep it from falling off. The coils match so well that it is impossible to see where the top rests.

Figure 11-39
Fired and glazed, the completed teapot shows its genesis in the drawings in Walker's sketchbook (11-30), but also displays the changes he made as he built the piece. Walker prefers to use porcelain because its whiteness intensifies the color of the glaze. With added grog, he finds it is stronger than many stoneware clays.

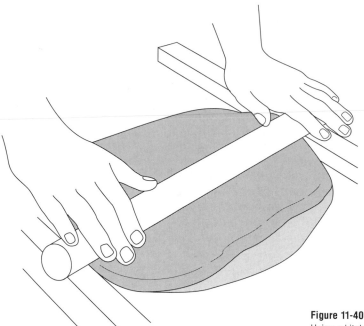

Figure 11-40
Using a kitchen rolling pin or a dowel to roll out the clay between two strips of wood is an easy way to make slabs of even thickness for pots or small sculptures. The wooden strips guide and control the thickness of the slab.

one with a fork or a serrated rib, wet it with water or slip, and press it carefully into place. In Walker's experience, the porcelain clay he uses is wet enough to adhere with scoring, water, and light pressure.

If you are building a small coiled pot or sculpture, you can keep the walls pretty much the same thickness throughout, but if the piece is to be large, with a quantity of clay built on top of the lower coils, it is a good idea to use somewhat thicker coils toward the bottom and then gradually make the coils a bit thinner as you continue. The difference in coil thickness might not be more than a fraction of an inch, but even that can lessen the weight considerably. You will learn by experience just how much you can vary the walls and how thick they need to be at the bottom to support the upper section adequately.

Be patient when you are coiling a pot or sculpture. If the clay starts to sag, it is a sign that too much weight has been applied to too moist clay and the structure is about to collapse. It is often necessary to let the clay stiffen for a few hours or even overnight before proceeding with more building.

Slabs

The constructive method of building pots and sculptures from slabs of clay is a relatively new development in ceramics. It is true that small, flat slabs of clay were used in the past to build pots (1-13, 1-14) or pressed into molds to make figurines, but the method of building up forms from slabs as it is often done today grew out of the changes that took place in twentieth-century sculpture when constructive, as opposed to cast-metal, methods became popular.

MAKING SLABS   You can make the slabs with which to construct, drape, or press-mold pots and sculptures by slamming the clay on alternate sides on a table or floor until it flattens, by rolling it out flat with a rolling pin (11-40), by combining small slabs to make large ones, by putting the clay through a mechanical roller that will give you a slab of even thickness (11-41), or even by casting slabs by pouring slip onto a flat plaster bat or into a two-part mold. You can also extrude a narrow slab or extrude a tube, slice it lengthwise, and flatten it. Slapped, rolled, or pressed slabs gen-

Figure 11-41
A slab roller is useful when even thickness of slabs and well-compressed clay are necessary. Here, Glenda Castain rolls out a thin, dense slab. After removing the soft clay from the roller, she will store it overnight to stiffen before cutting it to shape. *Courtesy the Richmond Art Center Ceramics Studio, Richmond, CA. Photo: Carl Duncan.*

erally provide a structurally strong and dense building material because the pressure exerted on the clay to form them strengthens the slab.

CONSTRUCTING WITH SLABS Whatever method you use to form them, you can use the slabs while the clay is soft, coaxing them to take the desired form and possibly using some of the supports mentioned above. Or you can roll them out, cut them to the desired shape, and then allow them to stiffen to leather-hard consistency and attach them to each other to create hard-edge forms. This method requires advance planning, since you will need to measure and cut the slabs carefully so that they fit cleanly and tightly. Gary Holt (11-42 to 11-52) cuts his slabs with a straight edge that has been shaped to give the correct angle of beveled edge that will allow his slabs to fit tightly. Once cut, the edge of the leather-hard slabs should be scored and painted with water or slip; some people swear by slip, others prefer water alone. The slab edges are then pressed together tightly, and sometimes a small roll of clay is inserted along the joints to make them firmer. This method of building with slabs in a precise manner, cutting out and assembling the leather-hard shapes, allows you to keep a great deal of control over the form as you build it.

There are a number of other ways in which you can manipulate slabs in a more direct manner by allowing them to drape over a hump mold or in a canvas sling while they stiffen. Once you learn just how stiff the clay has to be to stand up, you can build vertical forms or even take advantage of gravity and allow the clay to slump and find its own resting place. Whether you want to make rough-textured and freely shaped pots or sculptures, or to build hard-edged, meticulously finished forms, the range of possibilities available using slabs is almost endless (11-53 to 11-58).

Figure 11-42
After rolling out a slab with a mechanical slab roller, Gary Holt, U.S.A., cuts the leather-hard clay, using one of the beveled straight-edges he has made for cutting different angles.

Figure 11-43
Here he scores the beveled edge of one of the wall sections.

Figure 11-44
Holt applies slip over the scorings along the edge of a wall section.

Figure 11-45
Holt carefully presses together the first two slip-painted beveled edges of a tall slab construction.

228

Figure 11-46
A thin, handformed coil is dipped in
water before it is applied to strengthen
the joint.

Figure 11-47
Holt places the thin coil inside the corner to strengthen the vulnerable joint.

Figure 11-48
He then carefully melds the coil into the joint.

Figure 11-49
To give the corners additional strength, Holt pinches the edges
after joining them.

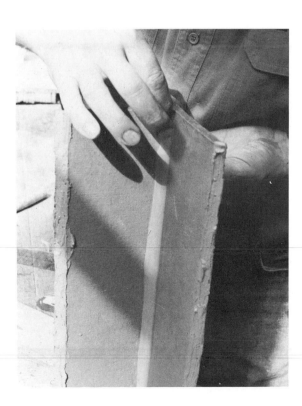

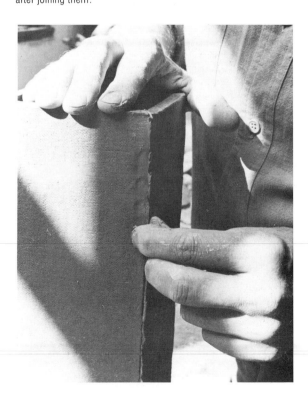

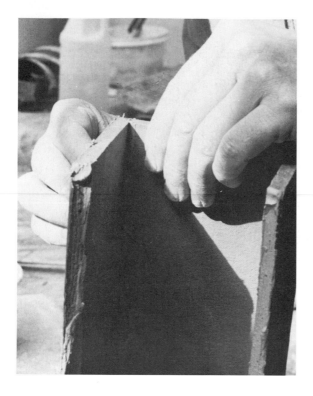

Figure 11-50
The third side goes on neatly, ready for the final section to be attached.

Figure 11-51
Because the clay slabs became quite stiff and the slip rather thick during the photo session, Holt gives the base an extra-heavy application of slip.

Figure 11-52
With the base attached and all walls in place, Holt paints the joints of his form with wax-resist compound to keep them from drying too fast.

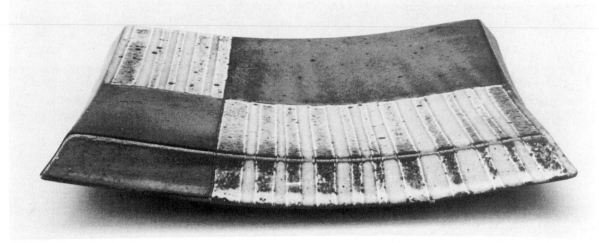

Figure 11-53
Ursula Scheid, Germany, used a slab of clay to create a platter. 1 × 9 × 8 in. (3 × 23 × 20.5 cm). *Courtesy the artist.* *Photo: Jochen Schade.*

Figure 11-54
Folding Box Form, Karl Fulle, Germany, says his forms were inspired by Japanese origami shapes. Built with triangular slabs of clay, Fulle's boxes make the most of the play of light and shade that develops on the fingerpainted engobe surface. *Courtesy the artist.*

Figure 11-55
Rabbit Speaks, by Phillip Cornelius, U.S.A. Cornelius's sculptural containers are made of exceptionally thin porcelain slabs — 1/20 to 1/25 of an inch (1.27 to 1.0 mm) thick. Normally, he fires his work at cone 10 to 12 in a gas kiln to which he adds about 120 pounds (54.5 kilos) of charcoal to produce a wood-fired effect. This one was fired at the factory at cone 15. Porcelain. Made at the Sèvres Porcelain Manufactury, France. *Courtesy Dorothy Weiss Gallery and the artist. Photo: Philip Staratt.*

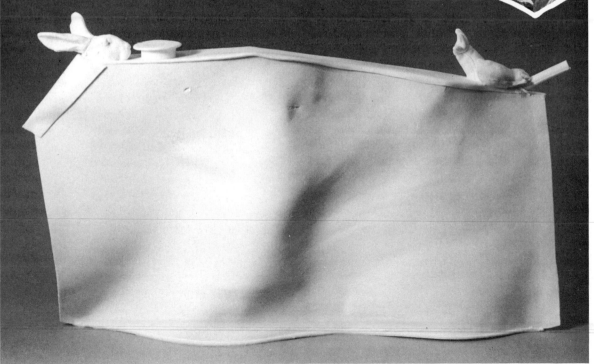

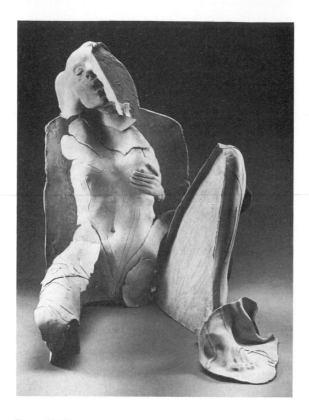

Figure 11-56
Chant, Mary Frank, U.S.A. To create her expressive figure, Frank used damp clay slabs almost as sheets of moistened drawing paper, incising them, then forming sculpture by folding and draping them. Unglazed clay. 44 × 38 × 60 in. (112 × 97 × 152 cm). *Courtesy Zabriskie Gallery and Virginia Museum of Fine Art, Richmond, VA., and the artist.*

Figure 11-57
Hovering Cube, by Johannes Gebhardt, Germany. When Gebhardt visited a subterranean vault in Kurdistan, the impression of light filtering into its gloom stayed with him. The image reappeared later, in a series of sculptures in which the limited space, the encased solid, and the indirect lighting of the vault were transformed through the artist's imagination. 1991. Grogged clay, vitrified white slip. 20 × 12 × 13 in. (51 × 31 × 32 cm). *Courtesy the artist. Photo: Rolf Kiessling, Kiel.*

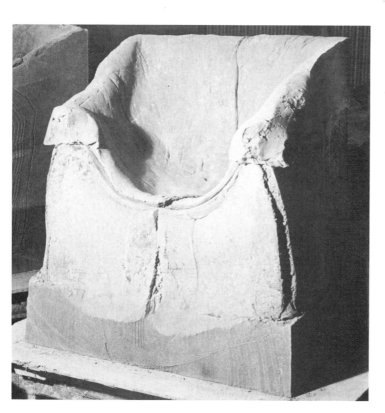

Figure 11-58
Stephen De Staebler's thrones are made from slabs draped over slab-built pedestals and formed by body pressure — by sitting in them.

KEEPING YOUR WORK DAMP

On seeing a room full of mysterious forms shrouded in plastic, a visitor at a school ceramic studio once asked, "Why do the students always hide their work?" The "hidden" forms, of course, were unfinished pieces either being kept damp between work sessions or being dried slowly before firing.

If you do not mind a certain measure of coarse texture, you can add 1 to 5% pearlite to the clay before you start work. This will help keep the work at a consistent moisture level for a longer period of time.

To keep your work damp, first wrap it in cotton rags, blankets, towels, or sheets that have been saturated in water—but that are *not* dripping wet—then cover it completely with plastic.

A misting spray bottle is a useful aid in keeping your work from drying out too fast. Use it to dampen the wrapping cloths to keep them moist but not too wet. Be careful, however, not to over spray a piece or to redampen a too-dry one. Just how damp you will want to keep your work depends partly on how you work. For instance, if you intend to attach new wads of clay to a pinched sculpture, you will need to keep it moist in order to meld in the new parts. Or if you are adding soft clay coils, you will also want to keep your work quite damp. If, however, you are working with stiffer clay, scoring and painting with slip to attach new coils, then you can allow the piece to stiffen until it is firm to the touch. For slabs, leave them to stiffen to leather hardness before proceeding.

Some studios have damp rooms where the humidity is carefully controlled to maintain the dampness of objects or to dry them slowly. If such a facility is not available, you can use a covered canister or tin for small work, an old camping refrigerator or an inexpensive polystyrene cooler for somewhat larger pieces to keep your work damp between sessions. But the best method for large sculptures or thick-walled pots is to wrap them tightly in plastic between sessions.

The thoroughness and care with which you dry your pot or sculpture are as important to the total process as the forming, because hours of work can be destroyed by careless drying. The thicker you make the walls, the more slowly you should dry it before it is safe to expose it to the warm air of a studio. This is because as clay dries and the moisture leaves its pores, the particles move together and shrinkage (generally 5 to 10% and sometimes as much as 20%) occurs. If this happens too fast, it can warp or cause cracks or even breaks in the walls or joints. This is another reason for making sure the walls are reasonably even throughout a piece, for a very thin section will dry much more rapidly than a thick area, causing uneven shrinkage. If this happens, you may face discouragement as the work of hours or days warps or pulls apart. Once your work seems dry to the touch, it can safely be exposed to the air to continue drying, but it must be completely dry before it is fired.

It is best to dry your work slowly and evenly in circulating air. It *is* possible to use a hair dryer or heat lamp to help stiffen the clay, or to place the work near a warm kiln to speed up the stiffening. If you place your work near a heat source, however, don't forget to turn it often to keep one side from drying faster than another. One ceramist sets his work on a slowly revolving electric wheel with a hair dryer directed at it. The key to successful drying is to let the clay dry slowly until the surface changes from a damp to a dry, matte look. When you see that the surface has changed in this way, you will know that it has shrunk about as much as it will until it is fired. Up to this point, any heat to which you subject the work to accelerate the drying must be used only with great care.

One way to judge if a piece is dry enough to place in the kiln is to hold your cheek to the clay. If it feels cool to the touch, the chances are that it still contains moisture and needs additional drying time.

DRYING SCULPTURE BEFORE FIRING

One method of drying clay evenly that is used successfully at the European Ceramics Work Centre in Holland is to construct a newspaper tent. Tape or staple a single layer of newspaper into a shell that conforms loosely to the shape of your work, and place this over it. Unlike plastic sheeting, the newspaper breathes so that the clay dries evenly, and you can slow the drying process further by adding additional layers of paper.

A simple and economical method for accelerating the drying process of pottery or sculpture is to construct a drying tent that gives flexibility, especially for drying oddly shaped work. To do this you will need a small 1000- to 1500-watt electric heater with fan and thin, lightweight clear plastic sheeting, along with a number of bricks or weights.

After your work is leather hard, or appears dry, cover the entire piece with plastic sheeting. Cut the sheeting about 50 percent larger than the area to be covered. Loosely drape it over the work, and place bricks or weights every 1 to 3 feet (.5 to 1 meter) around the perimeter to hold down the plastic. At one end of the tent build up a small brick chamber in which to place the heater, with enough room around it so that it is not touching the plastic. Leave a minimum of 1.5 feet (.46 meter) free of combustible material around the heater.

Now turn the heater on low and let the hot air fill the chamber. Once the plastic tent has expanded, cut three or four hand-sized openings into the top of the sheeting to let out the damp warm air. The heated chamber creates an evenly pressurized drying system that you can adapt to work of any size. It is especially useful in damp climates or during winter when there is a tendency for work to dry too slowly. As the work begins to dry, moisture begins to collect on the interior of the plastic—a clue that the work is drying. When you put your hand in the tent and cease to feel moisture you will know the work is dry.

Once a large piece of sculpture (or sections of a large work) is dry, you can place it in a gas kiln to preheat, leaving one burner on low and the kiln door slightly open (3 to 10 inches) for 24 to 48 hours until you are *sure* that all moisture has been driven out of the clay. For an electric kiln, leave it overnight with the lid propped open 3 to 5 inches, all the spyhole plugs open, and the heat on low. There is no way you can *overdry* your work before firing it, so give it some extra time and slow warmth rather than risk having your piece blow up in the kiln.

Now the pot or sculpture—called greenware at this stage—is ready for firing, an exciting, challenging, and sometimes frustrating process covered in Chapter 15.

REPAIRING DRY WORK

Sometimes, an arm or a finger may break off a totally dry figure or the handle may come off a pitcher. Do you have to throw the whole thing away? No, with care you can dampen the dry sec-tions enough to reassemble them. Wrap the dry sections with moist (not wet) rags overnight. On the next day, remoisten the rag and rewrap, repeating the process until both parts become damp enough to be scored, painted with slip, and reattached. To prevent the sections from crumbling, don't rush the redampening; for a large piece of sculpture, redampening both parts equally may take two or three days.

Sometimes you may have to decide that redampening a broken pot or piece of sculpture would not be worth the effort. In that case, go ahead and fire the main section along with the broken-off part and use an adhesive to glue them together after the final glaze firing. To do this, you can make use of a method employed by industrial ceramic companies: Mix epoxy with ceramic stains to match the glaze. If your clay body is coarse, you may want to mix a little grog into the epoxy to give it texture. (For additional information on repair and adhesives, see Appendix 4C.)

MIXED MEDIA

Mixed media is a modern name for an old way of working. Clay, one of the earliest sculptural media, has always lent itself easily to adding materials—holes poked into the damp clay could hold feathers or grasses after firing or allow objects to be tied onto the fired sculpture. For instance, an ancient Egyptian terra-cotta sculpture of a hippo had holes around the base in which reeds probably were stuck to suggest the rushes along the Nile. In New Guinea, clay, straw, and hair were combined in a fertility object, and in Africa, many materials were commonly used along with clay. There, the artist chose whatever material best suited his or her idea. This attitude toward materials and clay was continued in the work of some African-American artists. It is seen, for example, in the work of the anonymous artists who made the "mixed media" grave markers in nineteenth-century cemeteries in the American South, and in the contemporary *Nyama* vessels of David MacDonald (11-61). At the turn of the century in Europe, influenced by African art, Picasso and the Surrealists began to construct their sculptures out of found objects.

Present-day sculptors combine almost any conceivable material with clay to create sculptures that are not conventional ceramic works but that make use of clay for at least part of the work.

Figure 11-59

Font, by Madola, Spain, is one of a series she calls *Construccions de la Memoria*. Madola explored the relationship of water and ceramics in a large urban installation (Color Plate 50), and in this smaller, mixed-media work she continues to examine the theme, creating the suggestion of a mythical fountain rising between four stele in this mixed-media work. Madola says she likes refractory clay (fire clay) because of its crudeness and texture — here she uses it in roughly surfaced slabs to create an impressive setting for the marble waters. 1992. Refractory clay, porcelain, marble. 53 × 28 × 28 in. (135 × 70 × 70 cm). *Courtesy the artist.*

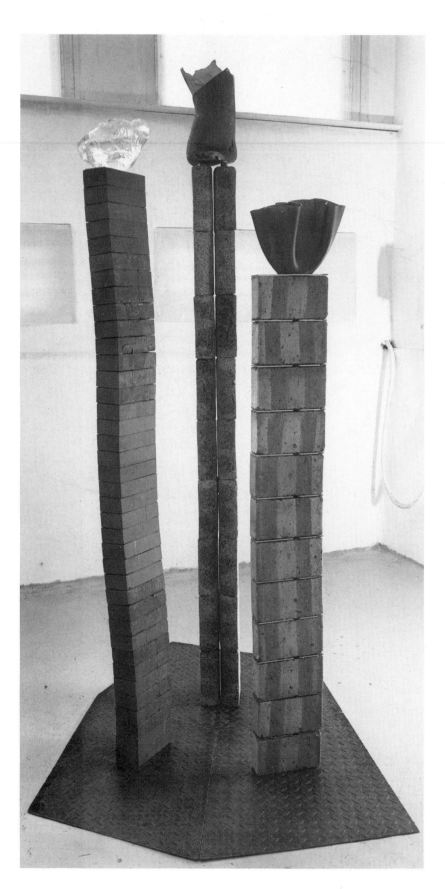

Figure 11-60
Trio Dante, by Helly Oestreicher, The Netherlands. Oestreicher's mixed-media installation includes ceramic forms, fire bricks, steel, glass, and crystal . . . *the glass lifts the bricks*, she says, . . . *the thin patterned steel acts as a fixed sounding-board for the trio, which plays for high stakes*. Mixed media. 1989. 102 × 63 × 50 in. (258 × 160 × 126 cm).
Courtesy the artist. Photo: Tom Haartsen.

Figure 11-61
To enrich his *Nyama Vessel*, David Mac-Donald, U.S.A., draws on African face painting, costumes, jewelry, masks, scarification, and architectural details as sources for his thrown and coiled mixed-media vessels. *Nyama* refers to the "essential force." Earthenware, paint, bone, raffia, and beads. Ht. 23 in. (58 cm).
Courtesy Hanover Gallery, Syracuse, and the artist. Photo: Clifford Oliver.

Eduardo Andaluz fires clay onto lava rock; Helly Oestreicher combines clay, brick, and glass (11-60); David MacDonald combines raffia, beads, and other materials (11-61); Arthur Gonzalez uses a variety of materials such as wood and cowhide (11-62), while Paul Astbury attaches slabs of clay to cardboard (11-63). Reuben Kent's figurines are enhanced with feathers and beads (11-64, 11-65), and Jan Godijns made a mudguard out of clay (11-66). There are other mixed-media sculptures and pots throughout the book. For example, for his mixed-media *Form Echoes* (Color Plate 47), Alexander Lichtveld made his own paper in order to achieve the exact shade of grey he wanted for the drawing that echoes his clay form.

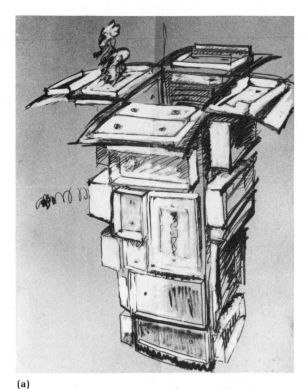

(a)

Figure 11-62

Lifolino: Man with Wishing Well Plant, by Arthur Gonzalez, U.S.A. Vulnerable, puzzled perhaps by the world, he may well need a lifeline to a wishing well. Mixed media. Clay, wood, cowhide. 1991. 75 × 57 × 18 in. (190 × 145 × 46 cm). *Courtesy the artist. Photo: Robert Di Franco, 1991.*

(b)

Figure 11-63

(a) *Study for Evacuated Boxes*, Paul Astbury, England. Astbury is intrigued by the combination of a permanent material—clay—with destructible substances that are vulnerable to time. First, he used ink and gouache to work out the concept of a mixed-media sculpture. **(b)** He then constructed it of fired-clay sections and a cardboard box, and added ink drawings on paper. 27 × 20 × 20 in. (69 × 51 × 51 cm). *Ceramic collection, University of Wales, Aberystwyth. Courtesy the artist. Photo: Keith Morris.*

Figure 11-64
Working on one of his raku-glazed figurines, Reuben Kent, U.S.A., uses a combination of materials such as commercially available feathers, glass, ceramic or metal beads, thread — whatever he feels will give it added expressiveness. *The satisfaction of creating an object is one of the more rewarding pleasures of my existence*, he says. *Courtesy the artist.*

Figure 11-65
Warrior Woman, by Reuben Kent, U.S.A. Kent, who is of Kickapoo/Otoe/Iowa descent, makes use of Native American motifs, although the final image goes beyond the traditional. His figurine is built of a clay body composed of raku clay and sculpture clay with additional fine-sifted grog, and it is raku-fired. Kent says, *the ultimate goal of all this technical knowledge is an object which hopefully speaks to the spirit or soul of the individual viewing the piece*. *Courtesy the artist.*

POSTFIRING CONSTRUCTION

With these expanding concepts of what constitutes ceramic sculpture or vessels, numerous artists have turned to postfiring construction methods. This gives them greater freedom to put together forms that would be unlikely to survive the fire intact, to make larger pieces, or to combine several materials in mixed-media constructions. The sections can be assembled permanently after they have been fired, or they can be designed to be demountable, making a large piece easier to move or ship. These methods depend on the use of modern adhesives that can make the joinings either strong and permanent or capable of being taken apart when needed.

Given the popularity of mixed media and of constructive methods of forming sculpture, it is helpful to become familiar with adhesives (see Appendix 4C). Always follow the manufacturer's instructions when using new products.

Figure 11-66
Jan Godijns, Belgium, made a mold from the mudguard of his motorcycle, then formed and fired a new mudguard for the front of the bike. Godijns believes that objects can act for us as spiritual refueling stops—*they make us dream*, he says. Mixed media. *Courtesy the European Ceramics Work Centre, Holland.*

Silicon

You can use this type of adhesive for the temporary and, in some cases, permanent gluing together of ceramic sections. Its value is that it is flexible and can also fill relatively large gaps between sections. When used in small amounts, the adhesive can be pried loose or cut apart with a knife, so it can also be used for gluing ceramic to concrete, to wood, or even to tile floors for temporary installations. You can also use silicon to glue glazed sections or to repair functional pottery for use in the oven or on top of the stove: It can take some oven heat without disintegrating, but it must not come in direct contact with the flame if used on top of the stove.

Epoxy

Ceramists use two types of epoxy. The five-minute-setting epoxy is valuable for quick repairs that will set while you hold the parts together, but it does not usually hold up when exposed to excessive moisture or direct water contact. Overnight-setting epoxy is generally stronger and more resistant to weather. Neither of these types of epoxy can take direct flame, oven, or kiln heat. Both types of epoxy are compatible with glass fiber for additional strength and can also be thickened with silica (flint) to form a putty-like glue that will not drip. You can color them with ceramic stains, clays, or even tempera paints to match clay or glaze colors for patching or filling cracks. Appendix 4B contains a list of color additives that can be used to color epoxy for repairing fired work along with other information on adhesives.

Polyurethane

This type of adhesive has excellent gripping strength and weather-resistant properties. You can use polyurethane to adhere ceramic to ceramic, ceramic to stainless or galvanized metals, or ceramic to wood (see Appendix 4C).

Acrylic Additives

There are now acrylic emulsion additives for mending and patching cracks in greenware, bisque-fired, and high-fired pieces. To patch or bond a broken piece, you mix the chemical with the same clay body as your ceramic piece and then refire the piece. This ensures accurate compatible color and shrinkage.

POSTFIRING REINFORCEMENT

Frequently, a piece of sculpture or large pot comes through the fire successfully, but the ceramist is concerned about whether it will take the stresses and strains of shipping, hanging, or other installation procedures. In this case, it is wise to reinforce. For example, Marylyn Dintenfass reinforced all the thin porcelain slabs of her work for the Connecticut State Court Building before installing them, and John Toki reinforces his large sculptures with fiber glass (Color Plate 48). In areas where earthquakes are prevalent, strengthening with epoxy and fiber glass and inserting neoprene pads between the sections will help a piece survive a quake. You can also use this epoxy and fiber-glass combination to glue wires or metal brackets to pottery or sculpture for hanging it on a wall.

Anchoring and Hanging

To hang thick and heavy sculptural works, you can set anchor bolts and various metal connectors into predrilled holes in the piece, using quick-setting pourable anchoring cement. This type of cement expands slightly and provides a strong physical bond between the metal anchors and the clay. The hole diameter should be about twice the diameter of the anchor bolt and two to three times as deep as the length of the bolt. Anchor bolt size and type, and hole size for setting connectors, is based on the type and strength of the fired clay, the weight of the piece being hung, and the number of anchors. Consult a structural engineer for specific information about the proper type of connectors and materials to use for hanging large and heavy works.

This chapter on handbuilding has introduced you to a wide variety of working methods, some traditional, but some that you may never have connected with ceramics. By using these methods singly, in combination, or along with wheel-thrown, press-molded, or slip-cast forms, you will greatly expand the number of ways you can work with clay.

12

Throwing on the Wheel

The image of a potter sitting at a whirling wheel, bringing to life a beautifully shaped vessel from a lump of inert clay, has great fascination. Watching the fast-rotating wheel can lead to fantasies of the marvelous pots you would like to make on it. Like any skill, working on the wheel appears easy when experts do it, but when you try it yourself, fantasy, as well as the pot, often collapses in the face of reality.

The potter's wheel developed over centuries from the turntables that potters used to rotate their handbuilt pots so that they could form and smooth them evenly (1-26 to 1-29). The true potter's wheel must spin at a speed of at least 100 rotations per minute; below that speed you would be unable to make use of **centrifugal force** to help you pull up the walls of your pot. The development of this faster wheel made it quicker and easier to make thin-walled pots of a consistent size.

Throwing a successful pot is a skill that takes practice. A book can give you only the basic information. As you work along with the instruction and guidance of an experienced potter, the rest is up to you. Even if it is easier to produce a series of pots quickly once you have learned to throw them on the wheel, only after you have had considerable practice will your body become so trained in the movement of throwing that you can concentrate your attention on the form of the piece you are making.

Figure 12-1
Pierre Bayle, France, stresses that technique is only one aspect of a work of art; the spiritual is equally important, and the two must remain in balance. White earthenware bowl, coated with fine, local red clay slip. Oxidation and reduction firings. *Courtesy the artist. Photo: J. P. LeFevre.*

Figure 12-2
Robert Sperry, U.S.A., says, *As I looked down at this pot spinning on the wheel, suddenly I thought of how everything in the universe is spinning and of how the quality of spinning can't be destroyed* (from a conversation with LaMar Harrington, quoted in *Robert Sperry: A Retrospective*. Bellevue Art Museum, Bellevue, WA, 1986). Stoneware plate, white slip over black glaze. Diameter 28½ in. (72 cm). *Courtesy the artist. Photo: Jim Ball.*

FORM

Before you start learning to use the wheel, give some thought to what you hope to make on it and to the formal aspects of pottery in general. In this chapter, and throughout the book, you will see examples of thrown pottery made by ceramists who use the wheel with such skill that their concern and thought now go into the design of their forms rather than technique. Study their work with a critical eye, not to copy it but rather to see how they used the wheel to bring vitality and strength to a classic form to which handles bring an element of surprise and lightness (12-1) or to suggest the spinning universe (12-2). Look at how they used the wheel to form the profile of a vase (12-3), or to make an assembled form (12-4). Or

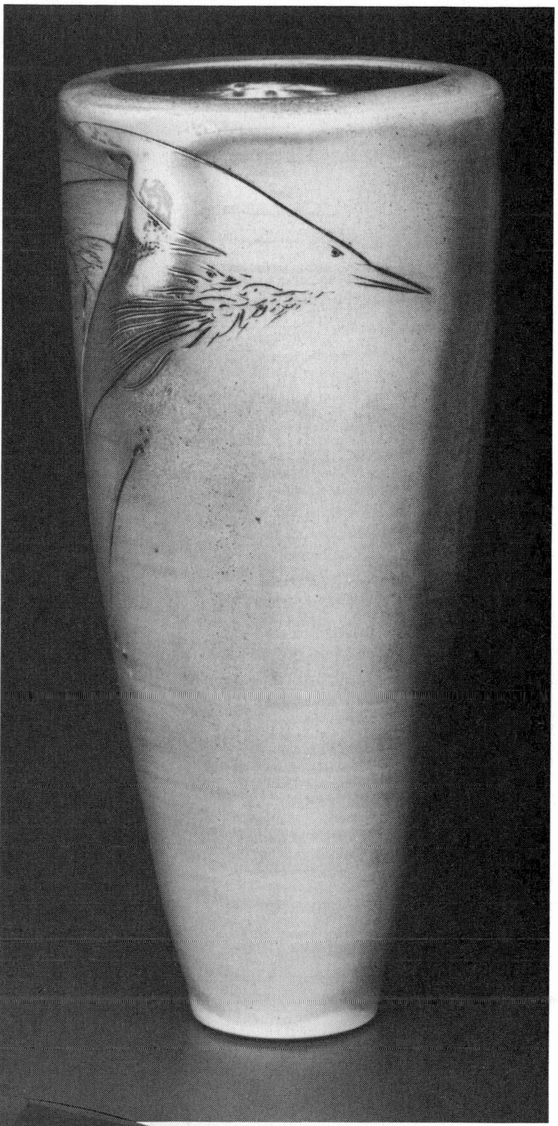

Figure 12-3
Intent on the way a drawing must be distorted to fit the contours of a three-dimensional vessel, Frank Boyden, U.S.A., sees his work as narrative or choreographic, involving movement and time. Wood-fired, Limoges porcelain. Ht. 13½ in. (34 cm). *Courtesy the artist. Photo: Jim Piper.*

Figure 12-4
Olaf Stevens, The Netherlands, wheel-formed this double form in separate sections, then assembled them. The decorations were made by applying adhesive paper stencils and sandblasting the exposed surface. Porcelain, black glaze fired in reduction at 2336°F/1280°C in a gas kiln. *Courtesy the artist.*

Figure 12-5
Ursula Scheid, Germany, adroitly balances form, color, and texture to create a miniature box. Porcelain, reduction firing. Ht. 3 in. (8 cm). *Courtesy the artist. Photo: Bernd P. Göbbels.*

Figure 12-6
Maria Bofill, Spain, combined wheel-thrown porcelain forms and slabs, uniting the entire composition with a black glaze that calls attention to the refinement of the vessel's profile. Porcelain, reduction firing, constructed after firing. Ht. 5 in. (12 cm). *Courtesy the artist.*

see what can be created by refining the basic cylinder form to its ultimate perfection and then glazing it with sensitivity (12-5). Experienced artists like these use the wheel creatively. To them, throwing is not an end in itself, but only a tool they can utilize in order to realize their creations (12-6). They have spent years mastering the skill of throwing, and they continue to practice it with joy. French potter Pierre Bayle, for example, has been working on the wheel since the age of fourteen, when he learned it in a flowerpot factory. He still spends ten days twice a year working in a pottery factory in order to recover and refine his throwing skill. Bayle, master of form, says he knows when one of his pots is beautiful, but that its appearance on his wheel does not come as a free gift—there are years of work behind it (12-1). But, Bayle stresses, technique is only one aspect of a work of art; the spiritual aspect is equally important, and the two must remain in balance (Color Plate 9).

As well as training your hands and fingers to follow your creative impulses, and learning to observe and transfer to the clay the forms you have observed and come to know through your senses,

there is a further dimension to consider in your development: the spiritual one that will give your pots soul.

USING THE WHEEL

Before you can even begin to think in terms of making a pot, you will need to learn to control the wheel, center the clay, and throw a basic cylinder. It may be difficult to curb your enthusiasm and put off trying to make a pot while you practice making basic cylinders, but if you master this part of the process, your persistence will pay off in the end, and the day will come when, with sensitive, skillful fingers you will throw a pot or vase that pleases you (12-7, 12-9, 12-10).

There may be both electric and **kick wheels** in the school or studio where you learn to throw. The electric wheel looks easy, whereas the kick wheel seems difficult to manage. Some beginners do, however, learn more quickly and feel more in control of the wheel's speed by learning on a kick wheel. Others are more comfortable working on an electric wheel. The type you use will be a matter of personal preference or availability.

Figure 12-8
The easiest way to rotate a kick wheel is by kicking outward from near the shaft to take advantage of the favorable gear ratio.

Figure 12-7
Eileen Lewenstein, England, working on the wheel. A potter's hands must be strong and sure in order to wedge and center the clay before starting to throw, but her fingers must also be sensitive in order to feel the thickness of the walls and to give the finishing touches to a simple yet elegant vase.

Figure 12-9
Janet Mansfield, Australia, works at her wheel, creating useful objects that give pleasure to those who hold and use them. Mansfield says, *I wanted to make things and I wanted these objects to be useful and add quality to everyday living.*
Courtesy the artist. Photo: Jutta Malnic.

Figure 12-10
Salt-glazed jar by Janet Mansfield. Mansfield says she was first drawn to clay for practical reasons. *Even more,* she says, *I needed to create a personal expression that had meaning, that I hoped would have integrity and could aspire to some beauty.* Stoneware, salt glazed, cone 10. Ht. 20 in. (50 cm). *Courtesy the artist. Photo: Jutta Malnic.*

Using a Kick Wheel

The photos of the basic wheel processes in this chapter were made of a potter working on a kick wheel (12-8). One advantage of this type of wheel is that it can be used by both right- and left-handed individuals. In general, the methods of working on both types of wheels are the same, but there are a few extra factors to consider in using a kick wheel.

First, put on rubber-soled shoes; then practice getting the wheel in motion. Kick from the inside near the shaft, thrusting out with a rolling motion, making use of the favorable gear ratio close to the shaft. You will find that you can get the wheel moving and keep it going with less effort by working in this way than by trying to keep up with the faster-moving outside rim. The action of kicking the wheel results in the transfer of movements to the rest of your body: notice how your hair falls into your eyes or your sleeves roll down as you kick. These movements transferred through your arms to the clay could cause it to move off center, so don't kick while your hands are on the clay.

A beginner tends to get the wheel up to working speed, let it slow down almost to a stop, kick it back to speed, then let it slow down, over and over. It is better to get a rhythm going, take a breath every couple of seconds, remove your hands from the clay, and give the wheel a couple of kicks to keep the wheel head moving.

Using an Electric Wheel

Electric wheels function the same way as kick wheels with the exception of a variable speed control. They are popular because they are powerful enough to handle any size wheel project, and they are semiportable since they are considerably smaller and weigh less than foot-driven kick wheels. Some people find that throwing on an electric wheel is easier because you can concentrate on the throwing rather than kicking the wheel. Many teachers find that it is also easier to teach using an electric wheel because they can help their students to adjust the speed of the wheel while they learn to judge its speed in relation to the throwing process. Most electric wheels are available with a plastic splashpan that fits around the wheel head and keeps the potter free of flying clay slurry or trimmings, and some have drains built into the tabletop for easy draining of clay slurry into a bucket.

Electric wheels operate on 120 volts (European wire, 230 volts) and can be plugged into any household electrical outlet. Some models have reversing switches that will allow the wheel head to rotate clockwise or counterclockwise—especially useful if you are left handed.

Preparing to Throw

During the first step on the wheel—**centering**—the wheel should be turning rapidly. The centrifugal force created by the speed will help you center the uneven lump of clay. Then, with each succeeding step, you will slow down a little, until at the end of the process of finishing the lip, the wheel will be barely moving. Once you feel you can control the wheel reasonably well, you are ready to learn to center the ball of clay that you have wedged.

Although throwing on the wheel does not expose the worker to the same hazards as mixing clay, it is important to remember to clean up the wheel and the floor daily at the end of the work period, using damp sponges and mop and wearing a mask. This is to avoid spreading dust around the studio. Another consideration when throwing is the physical strain of leaning over the wheel for long hours. Those who will be working for lengthy periods in that position should do exercises that will strengthen the back, and should give thought to the position and type of seat they use. A proper position can eliminate a lot of strain. The traditional potter in our southern states used wheels at which the operator stood; adaptations of these have been developed to lessen back strain. Another physical condition that can cause the full-time potter pain over time is one known as the carpal tunnel syndrome, caused by a pinched nerve in the wrist. This usually develops as a result of repeated actions involving the hands and wrists held in a strained position—for example, while wedging or throwing. If, however, you are aware of these physical problems and learn to minimize them from the beginning you should be able to avoid them even if you do become a full-time potter.

Preparing to Center

One dictionary defines *center* as "the point around which something revolves; an axis," while another gives an alternate definition, "the point toward which any force, feeling or action tends, or from which any force or influence takes its origin." Both definitions have meaning in relation to centering clay. Although centering is a physical process involving placement of your hands, where you press the clay, and how fast the wheel turns, it also has other meanings. We think of a centered person as being steady, in balance. It is this inner steadiness that you will want to draw on as you start to center the clay on the wheel.

The principle behind centering is that if an uneven lump of soft clay turning around the fixed point in the middle of the wheel comes in contact with a steady force pressing against it—your hands—it will become evenly centered and perfectly round. The importance of centering cannot be overemphasized, for if the clay is not perfectly centered, there is no way you can throw an even pot (12-11 to 12-19).

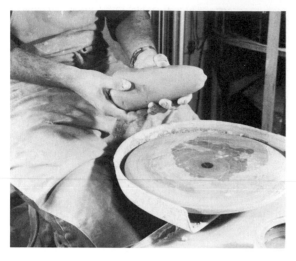

Figure 12-11
Larry Murphy, U.S.A., demonstrates centering. After he has rolled the wedged ball of clay back and forth on the wedging table or wheel head to form a cone, he slams the cone on the wheel.

Figure 12-12
Slamming the cone down drives the cone up into the lump to compress the clay. This gives the base of the pot added strength and helps it resist cracking.

Figure 12-13
He pushes and pats the clay on the wheel into a beehive shape before starting to center it.

Figure 12-14
Before he begins to center, he drips water on the clay, taking care to avoid weakening it by getting it too wet.

Figure 12-15
To center the clay, he links his hands by holding the thumb of one hand with the other, pressing down with the heel of one hand and pressing in with the other.

Figure 12-16
Murphy pulls the clay up, squeezing it back into a cone. He advises against coning up one ball of clay too often, as it can bring too much water into the clay and weaken it.

Figure 12-17
Once the cone has reached full height, he presses it back down with one hand on the side, bending it off center a little as he presses.

Figure 12-18
Experienced potters may cone up only when centering large amounts, but as a beginner you will find it helpful to do it each time you start to center a pot.

Figure 12-19
To see if the clay is centered, hold your hand against the clay as it revolves. If it is not centered properly, you will feel it wobble.

Centering

Centering the clay on a rotating wheel takes steady hands and forearms, so you need to anchor your arms in some way. One way to do this is to press your elbows inward tightly against your body. Or you can press them against your upper legs, your sides, or even the wheel frame — whichever is most comfortable and gives them the best support. Your hands should be joined in some way to keep them steady, functioning together as one tool. Whatever method of joining them you use, be sure that they are not working indepen-

dently. One hint to beginners is to be sure you use soft clay when you practice centering. You don't want to have to fight the clay, and clay that is too hard can exhaust you. Now you are ready to practice centering a not-too-large ball of clay.

Opening

The next step to learn after centering is opening the clay mass (12-20 to 12-25). This is not difficult, but it takes concentrated force. In order to open the centered clay evenly, you will need to

Figure 12-20
Opening the clay mass with his index finger, Murphy presses straight in without letting the hinging motion of his finger pull the clay off center.

Figure 12-21
Cutaway cross-section shows the action of his index finger as it presses straight down into the clay.

Figure 12-22
Opening with the middle finger gives added depth. This is useful when you are throwing a large pot.

Figure 12-23
Whether you use one finger, two fingers, or your thumb, you should make sure the tip presses straight down the clay mass toward the wheel shaft.

Figure 12-24
Move your index finger across the bottom of the opened clay, about ½ inch (12 mm) above the wheel head, to form the base of a cylinder.

Figure 12-25
The cross-section shows the position of the index finger inside the pot as he completes the bottom.

Figure 12-26
Straightening the wall to a 90-degree angle in preparation for pulling it up into a cylinder.

Figure 12-27
Another cross-section shows the position of the finger while straightening the walls.

Figure 12-28
Still another cross-section demonstrates smoothing the bottom with a rib.

continue bracing your arms, keeping your hands working together. As you press your finger or thumb down into the clay, you will be forming a centered lump of clay with a deep indentation in the middle. Beginners often make the mistake of trying to throw from this doughnut-like lump rather than from a fully opened shape. Remember that the clay is not fully opened until you have formed the bottom of a cylinder and straightened the walls. To do this, you will need to move your finger or fingers across the bottom of the clay parallel to the wheel head in accord with the speed of the wheel. Just be sure to leave enough clay on the bottom to form the base of the cylinder. Only now are you ready to pull up the walls.

Pulling Up the Walls

If you have centered and opened the clay properly, this last step is not as difficult as it may appear. However, if you have not performed these steps with care, then pulling up the walls evenly is almost impossible. When you are pulling up the walls, you will find that they rise more easily if you pull them at the same speed as the wheel is revolving—don't try to bring them up faster.

To pull up the walls, place the fingers of both hands opposite each other on the inside and outside walls of the low, opened cylinder. It is the even pressure you exert on the clay between your fingers that makes the walls rise (12-26 to 12-34).

Figure 12-29
Picking up a bead of clay between two fingers is an easy way to learn the proper finger position and spacing for forming the walls.

Figure 12-30
Starting to pull up the walls with the knuckle of one hand on the outside and the fingers of the other hand inside.

Figure 12-31
The clay is forced upward through the space between the fingers, causing the walls to rise as he pulls them up with the outside fingers holding a sponge.

Figure 12-32
This cross-section shows Murphy's finger position as he thins the walls. Some potters use a knuckle on the outside.

Figure 12-33
The weight of a little extra clay left at the top helps to keep the cylinder centered, and the extra clay provides enough material for a rim.

Figure 12-34
A completed cylinder seen in cross-section. *Technical skill takes you this far,* says Murphy, *now the artist in you must take over to shape the cylinder.*

If you place your hands so that they force less clay to pass between them than the thickness of the opened walls, the extra clay will respond by moving, and it has nowhere to go but up.

Remember that the opened clay is revolving on the wheel and that it is being subjected to a centrifugal force that tends to make its walls flare out. To counteract that thrust and make the walls grow straight up, press your hands slightly inward. Visualize a line that goes up the shaft of the wheel and straight up through your clay; then lightly move the walls in toward it.

While you are counteracting the centrifugal force, it is a good idea to counteract any desire you may feel to start making a pot. Continue prac-

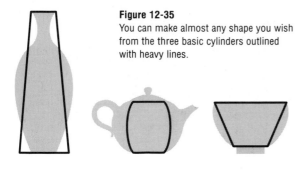

Figure 12-35
You can make almost any shape you wish from the three basic cylinders outlined with heavy lines.

ticing with the cylinder even longer than you think is necessary. If you can throw the three basic types of cylinders (12-35), there is no shape you cannot throw, and as you become more proficient and begin to think about design, you can start with one of the cylinder forms and go on from there (12-36, 12-37). In this way, your pots will be properly engineered before you even start to shape them, and when you come to cut the pot off the wheel you will feel the satisfaction of having created a clean, fresh form.

Shaping

Once you have mastered the basic cylinder shape, you can begin to think about throwing the pot of your dreams. An experienced potter, one who knows what technical problems he or she must contend with, can give attention to both the throwing of the cylinder and the shaping at the same time, but as a beginner you probably will have to separate the two, dealing with them as two distinct processes.

A basic cylinder is rather like a painter's clean, stretched canvas waiting for the first brushstroke. Just as a painter uses a sketchbook to work out ideas or keep notes for possible paintings, so you can use yours to note possible forms as you see them. A rock, a tree trunk, a human figure, parts of machinery, or even smokestacks — almost any form in nature or your daily surroundings may suggest a pot form. Now your creativity comes into play, and just as a painter or sculptor needs to stand back from the easel or sculpture stand occasionally to gain a new perspective, so you should move back from your pot on the wheel occasionally to see how it is progressing.

Keep the clay alive as you work, and do not weaken it by adding too much water or by stretching it. Remember that clay loses its plasticity if it is overworked, so if your desired shape does not appear after a reasonable amount of time, discard that clay and start over with a fresh ball. Do not count on correcting a badly designed or clumsily thrown pot by trimming it later. When you have completed a good cylinder, remove it from the wheel with a wire (12-38) and set it aside until it is leather hard so that you can practice trimming it.

Figure 12-36
Murphy smooths and straightens the walls with a rib. This helps to compress the clay particles that have become separated as you throw.

Figure 12-37
Clean out excess water with a sponge attached to a long stick. Doing this as you throw will keep the water from penetrating and weakening the clay.

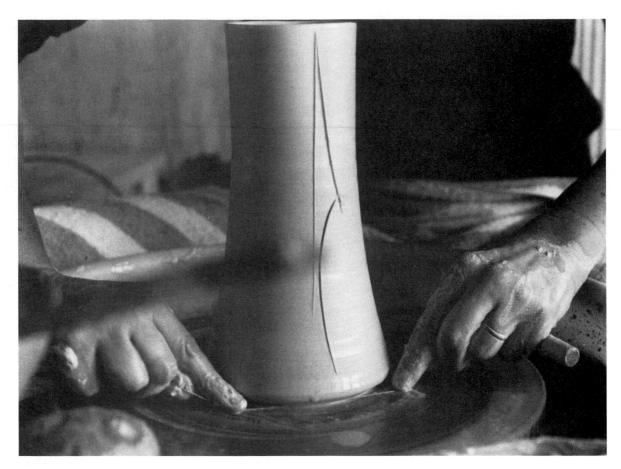

Figure 12-38
Eileen Lewenstein, England, holds a wire taut as she draws it
under the base of her completed vase, cutting it from the wheel.

MAKING A TEAPOT

Although making a teapot is a project beyond the
skill of most beginners, it is shown here because
it illustrates most of the skills a production potter
needs. First, you must be able to develop the basic
cylinder into a shape that will be both pleasing
and functional. You must learn to balance the
handle and the spout; the handle should be large
enough to fit the hand but not so large as to be
out of scale in relation to the spout. You must
design a spout that pours well, attach it so that it
stays bonded to the pot, and learn to make a lid
that fits and doesn't fall in the cup when you
pour. Learning to control the thickness of the
walls is also important, for walls that are too thin
don't have the insulating qualities characteristic
of a ceramic teapot, and walls that are too thick
will make the pot too heavy to lift comfortably.
Finally, you must learn to trim the finished piece.

When you are able to deal with these considerations satisfactorily, you are ready to make just
about anything.

Trimming

The shape of your pot will be fresher if it grows
organically from the action of your hands on the
clay as it spins on the wheel, rather than if you
depend on a great deal of trimming to reshape it.
But trimming is useful to refine your good pieces,
to thin areas that are too thick, and to give sharp
definition to an edge. For these purposes, it is an
important skill to learn. There are two examples
of trimmings in this chapter: Trimming a teapot
and lid are illustrated (12-39 to 12-42), and Catherine Hiersoux demonstrates trimming a plate
(12-70, 12-72).

Figure 12-39
Murphy measures a teapot rim using **calipers** in order to make a lid to fit.

Figure 12-40
Once the teapot and lid are leather hard, he places the lid in the opening of the teapot to keep it in place while trimming it.

Figure 12-41
With a **chuck** holding the teapot steady upside-down on the wheel, he holds a metal jar lid on its base to distribute the pressure of his fingers while he trims excess clay from the base.

Figure 12-42
As he trims, he judges the thickness of the bottom by tapping it. Experience tells him by the sound when the thickness is just right.

Figure 12-43
Here the centered clay is ready for throwing the lid and spout off the hump. Throwing off the hump saves time, and many potters feel it is best to make the whole pot from one clay mass.

Figure 12-44
By opening a small cylinder on the upside-down lid, Murphy makes an extension to hold the lid secure in the teapot while pouring.

Figure 12-45
Checking the measurement with calipers to be sure the lid will fit the teapot.

Figure 12-46
After finishing the lid, he removes it with a wire and sets it aside to stiffen.

Figure 12-47
Collaring in the spout, he shapes it with a metal rib.

Working Off the Hump

Some potters feel that it is best to throw a teapot, spout, and lid from the same piece of wedged clay, and throwing off the hump is a convenient way to do it. Whether or not there is an actual advantage to this method, they find it satisfying to make all the parts from the same cohesive lump of clay.

Although throwing off the hump is not an essential skill, it is a good technique to learn, especially if you want to throw a series of similar pieces quickly. It saves time, because instead of wedging and centering new lumps for each piece, you merely center the top section of the hump, throw the piece, cut it off, and continue throwing (12-43 to 12-47).

Spouts and Handles

The form of a spout or handle can affect the whole appearance of a coffeepot or teapot. A spout can be elegant and formal (3-15), simple and functional (12-56), or perky and cheerful. A handle may be purely decorative (6-20), or it may be both functional and beautiful. It can even be pretentious or suggest parts of the body (8-5, 12-78). Not only does the design of the spout or handle affect the appearance of a pot, but the skill, or lack of it, with which either spout or handle is shaped can make pouring a liquid from a teapot or jug a satisfying or a frustrating experience.

Graceful, pleasing handles that complete the design of a cup, teapot, or pitcher can become important accents. An appropriate handle can carry the eye down toward the base of a pot, completing the composition, and the negative space between the handle and body of the pot is as visually important as the handle itself. It takes thought and care to design a handle that will be both decorative and functional. How the handle fits the user's hand and fingers and whether it helps one tilt the pitcher or teapot to a proper pouring angle are equally important considerations. On the other hand, if function is not important to you, you can treat a handle as part of a sculptural whole, and it may work in contrast to the teapot. Numerous artists use the shape of a teapot or other functional pottery as a springboard to the creation of sculptural vessels (11-39, 14-38, Color Plate 18).

A thrown spout (12-47) or any other part that is thrown separately and attached to another shape, will twist slightly as it is fired. With the spout attached firmly at one end, the free, or pouring end, will make about a 10- to 15-degree turn in the firing. So, if you want your pot to pour tea directly into the cup instead of onto the tablecloth, you must take this into consideration. You will have to learn by trial and error the proper angle at which to cut the lip of a spout in order to counteract the twist.

Of course, it is essential to attach the spout and handle firmly to a teapot (12-48 to 12-51). Nothing could be more embarrassing to a potter than having a handle fall off a pot as the liquid is poured. When you attach a handle with slip, be sure that both leather-hard parts are ready to absorb the moisture of the slip and that the scored clay on both parts blends together into a complete bond.

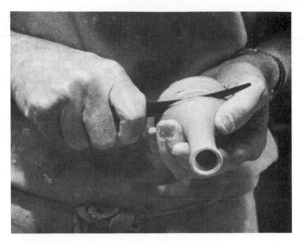

Figure 12-48
Slicing the spout to fit the curve of the teapot, he uses a curved **fettling knife.**

Figure 12-49
He scores the teapot and the end of the spout before painting it with slip and joining it to the pot.

Figure 12-50
An old pen nib makes an excellent tool for cutting strainer holes in the wall of the teapot before fitting on the spout.

Figure 12-51
To compensate for the slight unwinding that will occur on a thrown spout during firing, cut the end of the spout at an angle.

Figure 12-52
To make a handle, attach the moist clay to the scored teapot with a small amount of water.

Figure 12-53
After attaching the handle, he moistens it, then pulls out the clay, using a wiping motion.

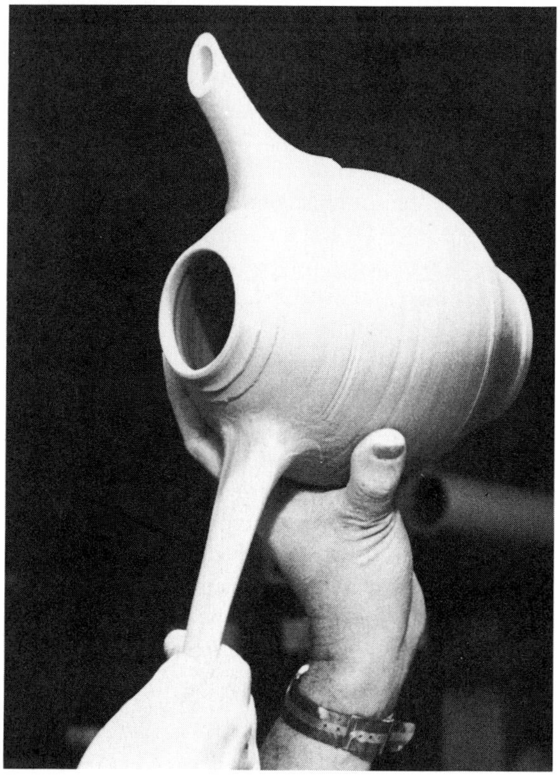

Figure 12-54
Gently stroking the handle, he brings it to the desired length and thickness.

Figure 12-55
Murphy completes the teapot, attaching the handle at the bottom with a final gesture that leaves his fingerprint in the clay.

258

Handles may be made by pulling, as illustrated (12-52 to 12-55), or by using an extruder as Carol Temkin did when she made the arching handle of her teapot (12-56).

Figure 12-56
A 36-ounce (1.06-liter) porcelain teapot by Carol Temkin, U.S.A. Details of spout and handle can totally change the personality of a teapot. A self-assured handle and no-nonsense spout give this one a friendly look. Porcelain; turquoise satin-matt magnesia glaze; oxidation, cone 10. *Courtesy the artist. Photo: Robert Arruda.*

Figure 12-57
With a bold motion of his finger and thumb, Larry Murphy presses the lip into shape to form a functional and attractive pitcher spout.

Pitcher Lips

Making an attractive and functional pouring lip on a pitcher is another skill you must learn if you wish to make a wide range of domestic ware. Once you have shaped the body of the pitcher—whether it is a delicate porcelain creamer or a robust stoneware jug that evokes images of warm milk right from the cow—you will want to make a lip that says "pour me." Most beginners are so delighted when they produce a nice round rim that they cannot bear to change its line with a lip; as a result, they make timid little indentations that would hardly pour satisfying streams of water, wine, or milk. You must learn to be bold about lips and to expect to spoil a good many before you can develop a personal signature that gives character to a pitcher's rim (12-57, 12-58).

Figure 12-58
Michael Casson, England, threw his jug with sensitive fingers, imbuing it with life, carrying on a long tradition of jug making (6-13 to 6-16). He rewords a comment by composer Igor Stravinsky: *Don't despise the fingers; they can release the imagination.* Casson dipped the jug in blue slip and wiped it very quickly, creating a decoration that emphasizes the jug's curves. Stoneware; salt glazed, wood fired, cone 10. Ht. 17 in. (43 cm).
Courtesy the artist. Photo: John Coles.

Figure 12-59
Ross Spangler, U.S.A., uses a mirror in front of his wheel to study the form of his bowl from a different angle as the work progresses. Although Spangler has been a production potter for many years, he still finds that getting a new perspective on his pots in this way—especially vases and taller work—is helpful.

MAKING DOMESTIC WARE

After you have learned to make a basic cylinder, you can begin to think about designing pottery to use in your home—cups, teapots, coffeepots, mugs, casseroles, or any of the other useful objects you can make out of clay. Making domestic ware calls on all your skills, presents you with aesthetic decisions to make, and challenges you to learn about using color, texture, and glazes as well as about firing a kiln. The term *production potter* usually refers to a potter who makes a full range of domestic ware and often what is generally called *studio pottery* as well. This second term covers vases, bowls, and any other pieces that are made more for display than for everyday use. The production potter/studio potter may work alone in a studio, may work with one or two colleagues or helpers, or may set up a large workshop that employs several people (12-59 to 12-61).

(a)

(b)

Figure 12-60
(a) Brian Fallon, assistant in Eric Norstad's production pottery in Richmond, California, measures the thrown, bottomless cylinder from which he will throw a large stoneware sink. In a traditional method called jiggering, he uses a mold in which to shape the sink. He first cuts out a circle from a slab to form the sink bottom then places it in a large plaster mold. He then cuts out a hole for the drain. **(b)** He places a cylinder upside-down in the mold on a wheel and removes the bat using a wire.

Figure 12-61
Fallon opens the cylinder, pressing it against the sides of the mold, shaping and smoothing it as the wheel turns. Here, he finishes the edge. With the use of the mold, he can throw a large sink in about fifteen minutes.

Production potters must deal with numerous problems beyond those the clay, glaze, and fire pose. Of course, they must be capable of making domestic ware of a high standard, but in addition they face the considerations of marketing, building up a clientele, producing items to order, repeating these items to a certain standard, formulating glazes, procuring materials, living on an uncertain income, constructing kilns, maintaining a studio, managing the business, controlling overhead, and paying taxes. At the same time, they must continue to grow as artists, improving their forms and glazes and exploring new ones. If this sounds overwhelming, remember that it *is* a life with compensations. If you are considering becoming a full-time potter, it is a good idea to become aware of all its aspects. Ceramics magazines frequently publish profiles of potters who have made this choice, and from reading these you can form a realistic idea of what might lie ahead. Or you may be able to talk with some production potters in your area to get a firsthand view of their lives.

Jiggering

Making use of a mold on the wheel to form a piece of pottery is an ancient process that is now called **jiggering.** In its simplest form, it consists of placing a bisque-fired or plaster mold on the wheel, pressing clay into it, and proceeding to press the walls against the mold as it turns, often using a curved template — pattern — to shape the inner curve. The Etruscans used this method; and Romans used carved molds in which they produced the red relief-decorated Arrentine ware (2-28) that was exported all over Europe. Using the same basic method, assistants in Eric Norstad's workshop (12-60, 12-61) use molds to create domestic sinks that have a handmade touch. Large factories, however, employ machines that perform the process at great speed and produce identical dinnerware and other objects.

Throwing Plates

It is demanding but rewarding to throw a plate on the wheel (12-62 to 12-72). One of the most important requirements is confidence — something that comes only with practice. It is best to try

Figure 12-62
Catherine Hiersoux, U.S.A., centers a 15-pound (6.81 kilos) lump of clay. As she brings it down, she takes care not to trap air under the extended edge.

Figure 12-63
Using her forearm with a tight fist for added force, she flattens the clay. This also helps her avoid muscle cramps.

Figure 12-64
Once the clay is flat, she starts to open it, using both hands.

Figure 12-65
She begins to pull up the sides, with the clay opened as far out to the edge as possible but still supported by the bat.

Figure 12-66
It is extremely important at this point to compress the clay with a wooden or hard rubber rib for strength and to prevent cracks. Because the flat area can't take a lot of handling, Hiersoux prefers to finish the bottom completely before thinning the walls.

Figure 12-67
Now Hiersoux can begin to work on the walls before extending them to develop the form of the large plate.

Figure 12-68
She gradually decreases the thickness of the walls, paying attention to the visual impact of the curve and maintaining its profile while supporting the rim with one hand as she works.

Figure 12-69
Hiersoux makes sure she maintains the curve as she gives the rim its finishing touches.

Figure 12-70
With a leather-hard plate centered on the wheel, Hiersoux starts to trim the bottom, removing the excess clay and forming the foot.

Figure 12-71
Tapping the bottom to be sure it is not becoming too thin, she completes the double foot needed to support the plate's diameter.

Figure 12-72
Hiersoux finds that old bleach bottles cut into a variety of profiles work well for finishing her porcelain plates.

throwing plates only when you feel you have mastered the other basic skills on the wheel. In throwing plates, keeping the clay alive and fresh is vital, perhaps even more so than with other objects, because the flat bottom of a plate is subject to so many stresses and strains as it is formed, dried, and fired.

Assured and practiced hands are particularly important in throwing plates because you cannot go back and make corrections. For this reason, it is a good idea to have the form of the plate in mind before you start and to think ahead to the motions and actions you will have to perform while throwing. Design considerations include the relationship of the curve of the plate to the base, the design of the rim and foot in relation to the whole, as well as the design of the rim detail. You might, for example, want a rim that has precise tooling on it to create a frame around the plate, or you might prefer to leave it neutral, rather like an unframed canvas. If, while you design the plate, you also keep in mind the type of decoration you intend to use on it, your final product will be better integrated. But, like everything else in ceramics, your plates may not always come out as you planned. Catherine Hiersoux says that sometimes

the elegance I want makes it difficult for the plate to hold up through a firing. Working with clay you have to be flexible, and this applies equally to plates. You may prethink what you are going to do, but along the way if it is starting to take on another look, you have to be ready to change your ideas and go with whatever is happening.

Throwing a plate entails using the basic wheel skills, but there are also special factors to take into account. For example, you must be sure to compress the clay thoroughly in the horizontal area of the plate; otherwise, it may warp or crack on drying or firing. Another area that requires special care is the curve between the base and the sides. It is important to maintain a smooth, concave curve, and as you pull out the walls at the side, you should gradually decrease their thickness. You should, however, take care that they do not become too thin or too extended, or they may crack or collapse (12-67 to 12-69).

Hiersoux throws her plates on a plaster bat that fits the size of her planned plate. She prefers a plaster bat to a wooden bat, because plaster helps the base to dry by absorbing moisture. In addition, the plate will lift right off without the use of a wire: She has found that removing one of her plates with a wire can increase the chances of the porcelain warping or distorting.

Drying and Trimming Plates

Drying a plate can be tricky. It must dry from the inside outward, but in the process the curve and rim must not dry too quickly. For this reason, depending on how humid or dry your studio atmosphere is, you may need to wrap the rim. Hiersoux dries a plate like the one illustrated for about an hour right-side-up until it is stiff; then she removes it from the bat and turns it upside down to continue drying. Once the base is leather hard, she will trim it, turn it right-side-up again, and let it finish drying.

Figure 12-73
Using a mallet made from a four-by-four covered with an old sock, David Mac-Donald, U.S.A., pounds the clay mound flat, then opens the mass using the tip of the mallet. *Courtesy the artist.*

Figure 12-74
He opens the mound wider before starting to flatten out the plate. Until the plate is completely opened, he uses no water. After it is opened, he continues spreading and flattening it to create one of his large carved or slip-decorated plates (14-16). *Courtesy the artist.*

Trimming is especially important in the base area of a plate, because that is where the weight is (12-70 to 12-72). Not only does an excessively thick base make a plate heavy, but also it is visually clumsy. On the other hand, if the base becomes too thin, it will warp. According to Hiersoux,

it is largely a matter of trial and error and feel. . . . You can keep taking it off the wheel to test the thickness, but if you do that, the extra handling makes it more likely to warp. Tapping it to see how it sounds will help you know if it is getting too thin, and if you begin to feel a vibration as you trim, then the next cut may be too much.

The placement of the foot determines the size of the ring of clay Hiersoux will attach. The best size to choose is related to the curve of the sides; the greater the curve, the narrower the foot can be. On a large plate, she uses a double foot, making the middle ring slightly lower than the outer. She does this so that when the plate is turned right-side-up, the base will sink, and the inner ring will be lower. Hiersoux says she used to throw, then bisque-fire her plates, then look at the blank plates and decide on the decoration. Now she has the decoration in mind before she starts to throw. That way, she says, she can make adjustments while throwing that will make the decorating easier.

David MacDonald uses a different method to open his large plates (12-73, 12-74). He first centers the clay, then uses a mallet to hammer out the sides, roughly opening the mass. From this rough opening, he goes on to pull up the sides, level them out, form the curve, compress the bottom, and complete the plate before he decorates it with carving, slip trailing, or glaze (14-16).

ALTERED WHEEL-THROWN FORMS

Basic wheel-thrown shapes **luted** together, altered, or combined with other components made from slabs or coils or with the extruder can bring new and unexpected relationships of volume and profile to thrown vessels. English potter Walter

Keeler, who has moved back and forth between making useful pots and making nonfunctional ones, says,

The idea of assembling components was particularly rewarding, and has led on to many of my current forms. Function, though, has remained a vital catalyst for me in creating new pots. I like my pots to be animated and if possible a little impatient. I am pleased if they make people smile (12-75).

When you stop to think about it, whenever you pinch a lip into a pitcher rim, you are altering a wheel-thrown vessel. Until comparatively recently, most altered vessels stayed within the general category of containers even if, like Palissy's plates (6-17), they were unlikely to be used for anything but display. Hans Coper, for instance (8-7), who altered and recombined wheel-thrown forms, made vessels that *could* contain, although his work is usually treasured for its appearance rather than its usefulness. Many other ceramists continue this tradition of maintaining the basic vessel form while altering it enough to impose on it a new quality or individual style (12-76, 12-77, Color Plates 10 and 18).

Figure 12-75
Walter Keeler, England, threw his *Angular Teapot* upside-down, added a slab base, struck the pot and spout with a metal file to make the score lines, extruded a handle, and assembled the parts when leather hard. Keeler's collection of tinware utensils influenced his choice of forms. Stoneware, cone 10; oxides and stains mixed with engobe, salt glazed. Ht. 8 in. (20 cm). *Courtesy the Aberysthwyth Arts Center and the artist. Photo: Keith Morris.*

(a)

(b)

Figure 12-76
(a) Catherine Hiersoux makes a large jar in sections. She prepares to add the second leather-hard section. Note the flange on the inside, made to fit securely over the scored and slip-painted lower section. (b) She lowers the upper section, still attached to its bat, onto the lower section.

Figure 12-77
After melding the joint with her thumb and cleaning off the excess slip, Hiersoux uses a rib to smooth and shape the tall jar. The third section will provide the neck and lip.

Pablo Picasso, however, working with potter Georges Ramié (8-5), was not interested in making containers, so when he constructed images out of wheel-thrown components, they emerged as sculptures that did not serve the traditional functions of pottery. Starting in the 1950s, such artists as Lucio Fontana (8-8), Peter Voulkos (8-9), and Carlo Zauli (8-10), among many others, altered, deformed, combined, slashed, crushed, and paddled their pots, transforming them from containers into nonfunctional objects. This move toward the sculptural on the part of many ceramists not only altered the appearance of the pots but also altered the directions taken by ceramics in the past two or three decades.

Robert Turner (Color Plate 10) alters his vessels with just a few—but telling—gestures that transform a pot into an expression of our relationship to the universe. This approach, in which the container becomes an expressive object created to be seen, held, or touched rather than to be used for a containing function, led to a continuing debate about whether the resulting creations were pottery or sculpture, art or craft, and where they should "fit" in ceramics. Purists have continued to see the true function of ceramics as providing either useful domestic containers or beautiful ones for display. Probably more has been written

◀ **Figure 12-78**
Composite pot with wheel-thrown and coiled sections by Jamie Walker, U.S.A. Walker says that while traveling in Mediterranean countries he made sketches for pots, but it was not until he was back in his studio working on them that he realized his inspirations were the "earth mother" types he had seen on his travels. Porcelain; slip glaze with glass from Kügler rods. Ht. 26 in. (66 cm).

Figure 12-79
Barbara Reisinger, Austria, made this double vessel from one plate and one bowl, cut and assembled. The parts can be separated or placed together as shown. This one was fired upside-down in a gas kiln in reduction at 2300°F/ 1260°C. Porcelain. Ht. 4 in. (11 cm). Diam. 12 in. (30 cm). *Courtesy the artist.*

about this than about any other subject in contemporary ceramics. Categories aside, there would seem to be room for all—art, craft, sculpture, pottery—on this earth in whatever combination the imagination may place them. If, however, you are interested in seeing just how much emotion this controversy has stirred up, the back copies of ceramics magazines and some of the books listed in Further Reading at the end of the book will provide you with plenty of reading material.

COMPOSITE POTS

What do you do if you want to throw a pot that is taller than your arms? Eileen Murphy, who is not very tall and whose arms are short, has this problem. It is impossible for her to reach in to throw as large a pot as she wants, so she solves the problem by throwing a series of rings on the wheel and then luting the sections together. In this way it is possible to combine several wheel-thrown sections (12-76 to 12-79). Catherine Hiersoux makes all the sections of her tall jars on the wheel and then lutes them together with slip before firing. Other potters alter and combine in a variety of ways, even creating double vessels that can be taken apart and displayed separately.

There is nothing new about combining forms or methods. Traditional potters frequently made pots in sections; many of the jugs that were the mainstay of a medieval European potter's livelihood were made in two parts, and in his "how-to" book published in 1556, Italian potter Piccolpasso explained both how to attach separately thrown forms while they were damp and how to "glue" parts after the bisque firing by using glaze that would melt and fuse the parts together in the second firing. One method of making large pieces, probably used since the days of the Minoan potters on Crete (2-3), has been given a modern touch by Paul Chaleff. He built up and smoothed his six-foot-high jars outside his studio using coils and an electric wheel (12-80, 12-81).

POSTFIRING CONSTRUCTION

The trend toward constructed objects built up of a number of parts has been speeded by the development of modern adhesives. At one time, constructing after firing would have been considered "cheating" in most ceramics circles, but now, whether they want to combine wheel forms into a vase that suggests a human figure (12-78), or attach the components of a wall piece to a ply-

Figure 12-80
Paul Chaleff, U.S.A., uses coils to construct jars that are more than 6 feet (1.83 meters) in height. He works outside his studio, using an electric wheel to turn the jar as he builds. *Courtesy the artist.*

wood base, contemporary ceramists use adhesives freely (see Appendix 4B).

This means that you are freed of many restraints and have available a wider range of methods or combination of methods with which to work than at any time in ceramics. It is still of vital importance, however, to master the basic skills so that you can develop your *own* way of working. In looking at examples of wheel-thrown, altered, or combined forms, try to view them critically to determine which method would be most appropriate to your concept; then adapt and use that one in your own way as honestly as you can.

Figure 12-81
The wheel rotates the jar as Chaleff smooths the walls. Chaleff says that he tries *to preserve that respect for history throughout my work in concept, process and in form.* His wheel and coil method is a modernization of traditional techniques used around the Mediterranean and in Korea and Japan. *Courtesy the artist.*

13

Working with Molds

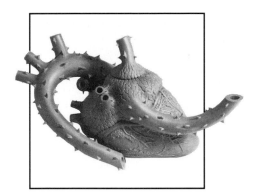

For several thousand years, potters and sculptors have been creating images and useful objects by pressing or pouring clay into **molds.** Archaeologists have found mold-formed clay figures at ancient temple sites—replicas of gods and goddesses made for pilgrims to give as offerings—some of which date from about 2000 B.C. They also have found some of the fired-clay molds in which the figures were made. In addition, molds have been continuously used in ceramics factories to mass-produce a variety of objects such as dinnerware, decorative figurines, plumbing fixtures, and insulators.

Thus, like so many contemporary ceramics processes, the technique of pressing, pounding, or pouring clay into a mold is an ancient one; what *is* new is that using molds to create images is no longer confined to mass production. Contemporary ceramics artists now regularly use molds to make one-of-a-kind vessels or sculptures as well as to make tiles and other types of modules (13-8).

HUMP MOLDS

The first mold may have been a rounded stone over which someone pressed clay to make a simple container. Called a **hump mold,** such a mold can be made of any material over which you can

Figure 13-1
One of a series of hump-molded bowls by Ernst Häusermann, Switzerland. Altered and fired in oxidation in an electric kiln, the bowl is partially coated with a glaze made from beechwood ash from his wood stove. He also adds local earth materials to the clay to give it a rich, roughened surface. Ht. 9½ in. (24 cm). L. 21 in. (53 cm). *Courtesy the artist.*

Figure 13-2
Häusermann shapes a bowl on a porous, bisque-fired hump mold. As the mold absorbs moisture from the clay, the bowl will stiffen enough to be removed. Notice that the mold does not curve inward, for that would cause an undercut that would make it impossible to lift the stiffened bowl off the mold. *Courtesy the artist.*

Figure 13-3
Slapping the stoneware clay, Häusermann thins the walls, at the same time extending them farther down the mold. Once he has thinned the walls, he will attach the foot; then, when the clay has stiffened enough, he will be able to remove the bowl and finish the shaping process. *Courtesy the artist.*

drape or press clay. Many objects—an inflated plastic bag, a balloon, a bag of sand or vermiculite, a polystyrene form, or a specially made plaster or terra-cotta hump mold—will allow you to support the clay as it stiffens and takes on the shape of the mold. Low-fire clay and plaster are, however, particularly useful as mold materials, because their porosity allows them to absorb moisture from the clay, causing it to stiffen quickly.

You can place the clay over a hump mold in the form of slabs, wads, or coils, patting it on with your hand, paddling it, or scraping to compress the particles, or to make it smooth. Whatever method you use to apply the clay, by working on a hump mold you can easily make a wide-mouthed form (13-1), as long as the mold is not shaped to curve inward, causing an **undercut.** If the mold did curve in, the stiffened clay would be tightly held around the inward-curving area, like a clasped fist, and the formed clay would have to be cut in order to be released from the mold.

It is also necessary to watch the clay carefully as it stiffens on a hump mold. You should remove it before it dries too much because as the clay shrinks while on the rigid hump mold, it cannot contract against the mold. The result will be cracks or even breaks in the walls.

You can use hump molds in a variety of ways—for example, to support the wide, flaring form of a bowl that might be difficult to keep from collapsing while being handbuilt right-side-up (13-1 to 13-3). Clay coils can be formed over a large mold and scraped smooth (13-4). There is sometimes little to differentiate hump molds from the type of sculpture supports discussed in Chapter 11.

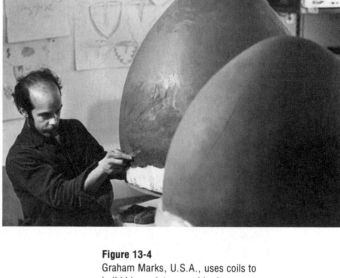

Figure 13-4
Graham Marks, U.S.A., uses coils to build his sculpture upside-down over polystyrene foam hump molds. He melds the coils together by scraping the surface. *Courtesy Helen Drutt Gallery.*

PRESS MOLDS

A **press mold** does not have to be elaborate; you can use a kitchen mixing bowl lined with a piece of plastic wrap or cloth or even a milk carton or cardboard box, and press slabs, wads, or coils of clay into it. Etruscan potters used press molds to make vessels, as their descendants still do; but today, instead of fired terra-cotta, plaster molds are used (13-5).

Figure 13-5
In a hill town in Italy, potters make large decorative urns in simple, two-part press molds, then hand-tool the surface to refine details. They work much as their Etruscan ancestors did, except that the modern molds are plaster. The lower bowl keeps the mold from rocking.

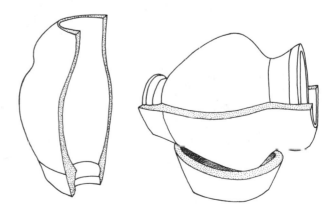

Figure 13-6
Gunhild Aberg, pressing a slab into a plaster mold, uses a smooth, rounded stone to pound the clay gently into the one-part mold. *Photo: Mogens S. Koch, Denmark.*

Figure 13-7
Carlo Zauli, Italy, frequently uses press molds made from plaster to build sections of his sculpture. This small press-molded section shows the network of clay supports that give added support to the section without too much added weight.

Plaster Press Molds

A press mold made from plaster is especially convenient, because it draws the moisture evenly out of the clay, and with proper care the stiffened clay can be removed from it in one piece (13-5). Using a plaster mold also has the advantage of allowing you to reproduce your own work or a section of it, as Carlo Zauli frequently does for sections of his wall reliefs. Christina Bertoni makes a pinched bowl and casts in it plaster, replicating its exterior fingerprinted texture. She then presses clay into the mold with her fingers and in this way creates bowls that carry the impressions of her fingers on both the inside and outside (9-3). Patrick Loughran (Color Plate 25) also uses press molds to form his plates. Another advantage of a plaster or bisque-fired mold is that you can reuse it if you store it in a dry place.

To make a one-part press mold you must choose an object to cast that has no undercutting—for example, the simple mold into which Gunhild Aberg pounds clay with a stone will pose no problem in removing the stiffened clay from the mold (13-6). Pressing clay into this type of mold will result in a simple, open, concave form.

Press molds can be used for more complex projects. Robert Arneson, for example, formed much of his sculpture in plaster molds into which terra-cotta clay was pressed to form one-half of a portrait head; then both parts were joined. Carlo Zauli often uses plaster or wooden molds to make large wall reliefs, pressing clay into them and then firing the sections separately to be assembled later (13-7). A plaster mold used as a press or hump mold can last for hundreds of reproductions, so you can make many copies from the mold, then alter the copies, creating one-of-a-kind pieces from the same mold. By adding clay, by carving or tooling the surface, or by altering the vessel or sculpture's shape, you can use a press-molded form as the basis from which to develop a wholly new work. You can also combine a group of mold-formed sections from your collection of hump or press molds, combining them into new, composite pieces or installations.

Here are just a few examples of creative use of molds. John Toki forms his large sculptures using carefully shaped and placed wood, fiber, and foam as combination hump and press molds laid out on the studio floor; he lets the weight of the added clay press against and into the wood, fiber, and foam to shape the sculpture (Color Plate 48).

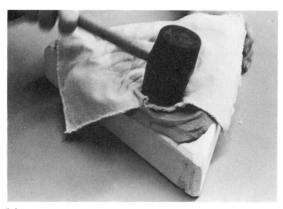

(a)

(b)

Ellen Driscoll used press molds to form the suspended feet for her installation (16-3). To make an unusual mixed-media work, Jan Godijns formed a new clay mudguard in the actual guard he removed from his motorcycle (11-66). Beth Starbuck and Steve Goldner used a press mold to make modules for a wall piece (13-8).

(c)

Figure 13-8
Beth Starbuck and Steven Gardner, U.S.A., made the modules for this dimensional relief, *Wedges,* by **(a)** pounding clay into a plaster press mold, then **(b)** scraping off the excess clay. The shaped module was then removed from the mold **(c).** In this case, the glazed and assembled modules were combined to make a small relief **(d),** but if desired, the modules could be repeated to cover an entire wall. *Courtesy the artists.*

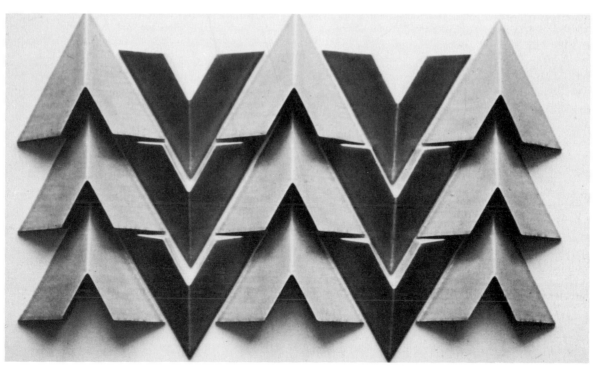

(d)

MAKING PLASTER MOLDS

If you have not used plaster before, you will find it a fascinating and versatile material. The type of plaster used for molds is plaster of Paris, made from one of a group of gypsum cements, essentially calcium sulfate, a white powder that forms a viscous solution when mixed with water and hardens into a solid mass. For the mold used in the demonstration (13-9 to 13-15), John Toki used Pottery Plaster #1. It is best to use a specially formulated plaster; with it your mold will last almost twice as long as one made of ordinary plaster.

There are a few cautions to note before you begin to work with plaster. Although not hazardous, as is clay dust, it can be irritating to your respiratory system if breathed, so be careful when you use it in the dry form. Never pour plaster down a sink! Your plumbing will be totally blocked if you do, because when water is added to it, plaster sets up into a solid mass that cannot be washed out of the pipes.

Store bulk plaster of Paris in the bag in a dry place, preferably on wooden slats that let air circulate around it, for if it becomes damp in the bag the plaster will be useless when you come to use it.

It is possible to smear an object (with no undercutting) very lightly with oil or soap, pour a couple of inches of plaster in a cardboard box, place the original on this layer, pour more plaster around the original up to but not over its top, and end up with a one-part mold that will work reasonably well.

Making a Mold for Slip Casting

If you follow the directions provided by John Toki, who has made molds professionally, you will learn how to make an even-walled mold that can be used for slip casting as well as for press molding. Plaster slip molds do not last as long as press molds, because the sodium silicate and soda ash in the slip are absorbed into the plaster and accelerate its deterioration. In industry, where the highest-quality casting and high-speed production are called for, a plaster slip mold is used only 50 to 150 times owing to the need for perfect replicas and the established production schedule per eight-hour work shift. But a studio potter probably could use such a mold for a cou-

ple of hundred casts. Once you have learned how to make a good one-part plaster mold, you will have mastered the basics of mold making. To go on to make more complex molds, we suggest you study one of the specialized books listed in Further Reading at the end of the book.

To make a demonstration one-part mold, John Toki chose a simple stoneware bowl with no undercutting or details (13-9). Remember that your final clay cast will turn out to be considerably smaller than the original as a result of shrinkage during drying and firing. One refinement to learn in making a mold for slip casting is the **slip reservoir**. The purpose of this reservoir is to form a chamber that will hold extra casting slip which will create pressure on the slip in the mold during casting, thus ensuring that the slip will be pressed against the plaster walls. This in turn will ensure the formation of even clay walls that replicate the mold exactly. This can be especially important in the casting of a thick slab. The reservoir is made by attaching an extra clay mass to the object from which you make the mold, forming it to follow the contour of the object (13-9). The reservoir and object to be cast must have a slope of at least one degree to make it possible to remove the mold.

After the clay for the reservoir has been shaped, the object should be set on a base. Plywood will do. Attach the object to the base with sticky clay or nail cleats to keep it from lifting as the plaster is poured around it. Next, soap the original to keep the plaster from sticking to it (13-10). The clay reservoir mass does not need to be soaped (if the original you are going to cast is made of damp clay, you do not need to soap that either), because you can remove it and wash the damp clay out of the mold. The best thing to use for soaping is a water-base mold soap, diluted two to one with water.

The drawings in Figure 13-9 show the preparations for making a mold. Surround the original and the reservoir with a wall made from linoleum, tar paper, sheet metal, clay, or plastic. For the demonstration, Toki used a strip of floor linoleum bent into a circle and secured with a mold-form clamp, but you can secure yours with duct tape, a metal strip with a turn buckle, a strip of tire inner tube, or a large rubber band to secure the wall. The wall should be placed so that it is about 1 to 1¼ inches (2.5 to 3 cm) away from the original and extends to 1 to 1¼ inches above it. This spacing will create a plaster mold of optimal

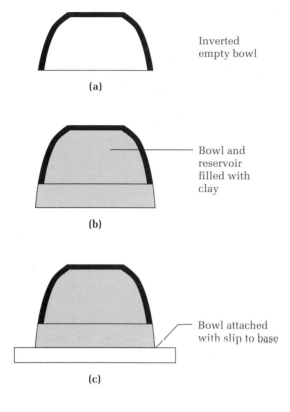

Inverted empty bowl

(a)

Bowl and reservoir filled with clay

(b)

Bowl attached with slip to base

(c)

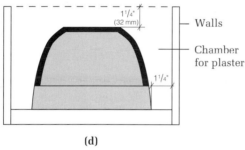

1¼"
(32 mm)

— Walls

— Chamber for plaster

1¼"

(d)

Figure 13-9
Steps in preparation for making a mold. **(a)** The empty bowl from which the mold will be made. **(b)** The bowl filled with clay, with the reservoir mass extending below it. This will make a chamber to hold extra slip that will exert pressure to produce an evenly walled cast. The reservoir must have a minimum slope of 1 degree in order to release the mold easily. **(c)** Soaped bowl and reservoir attached with slip to a plywood base. **(d)** Walls made from flexible linoleum, metal, clay, or plastic should be placed about 1 to 1¼ inches (2.5 to 3.20 cm) away from the original, and they should also extend high enough to allow a solid plaster base of that thickness to form. Seal any cracks where plaster might run out with wads of clay. The dimensions on the drawing are those used for the mold shown in Figures 13-9 to 13-15.

Figure 13-10
Before making a mold from a bowl, soap the original to make it release easily from the plaster mold. Carefully brush out any soap bubbles. The clay reservoir mass already has been formed at the base of the bowl, and both are set on a plywood base.

thickness. Thicker walls would not be any more absorbent, although if the mold is a large one, thicker walls *would* add to its structural strength. On the other hand, too-thin walls will become saturated with moisture too quickly and the casting slip will not set up. To be sure that the wet plaster does not leak out around the walls or at the seam, plug these areas with damp clay pressed firmly into the cracks. Before mixing and pouring the plaster, be sure to soap the walls and the plywood base to keep the plaster from sticking to them, using the same solution of soap you used on the original. Coat the walls first; then sponge the absorbent plywood with water and soap it as well.

Mixing Plaster With a Scale

Although it is possible to measure out and mix plaster by eye, it is more satisfactory to measure the ingredients with a scale. The ratio is based on the water-absorption ability of the plaster. For the mold illustrated in Figure 13-9, Toki used the ratio of:

2¾ lb (1249 gm) plaster to
2 lb (907 gm) water = 81 cu in. (1327 cu cm) of plaster

These measurements yielded a mold weighing 4 pounds 12 ounces (2.15 kilos) wet. If you want to make a larger mold, keep the same ratio of water to plaster when you measure the larger amounts.

Water temperature makes a difference in the setting-up time of plaster; cold water will set up at a slower rate than hot water. This setting-up was based on using water at about 72°F/22.2°C. Learning just how long it will take to pour the plaster and how soon it will set up is a matter of experience. About 20 to 40 minutes is an average time, depending on the type of plaster used, the presence or absence of retardant, and the atmospheric conditions in the work area. It is possible to add **sodate retarder** to the plaster if you feel the mixture will set up too quickly for you to use it comfortably. This chemical slows the setting time; adding ¼ to 2 tablespoons (approximately 1.33–15 gm) of retardant can delay the setting-up time from 10 to 60 minutes. Vinegar also works as a retardant.

Use a pliable plastic bucket or basin for mixing plaster so that when the residue hardens you will be able to squeeze the bucket walls and shatter the plaster into fragments to remove it.

For precise control, measure the mixing time with a timer — a kitchen timer or a photographic lab clock will work. Using a timer will help you avoid overmixing, which can result in a plaster that is too dense, or undermixing, which can result in a mold with walls of unequal density. If different sections of a multipart mold are unequal in density, they will absorb water unequally. This may cause the slip-cast object to crack at the mold seam while it is still in the mold after the slip has been drained. Clearly, for a one-part or a press mold this factor is not as critical as for a multipart mold.

Mixing Plaster Without a Scale

Measuring plaster without a scale and mixing it by hand is not as satisfactory as using a scale to measure the ingredients. It can work for making hump or press molds, but for slip casting it is important to weigh the plaster carefully and mix it with the right amount of water in order to produce consistency in the absorptive properties of the mold. If you have trouble making a satisfactory mold using the hand method, switch to the scale method.

To mix by eye, fill a pliable container about one-half full of water. This amount of water will yield about two-thirds of a bucket of mixed plaster. Instead of weighing the plaster, add it slowly by sifting it in handfuls into the water through your fingers until it mounds above the water line like a steep, mountainous island rising above the ocean. This process, during which the plaster powder becomes chemically combined with the water, is called **slaking.** When the last bit of plaster that shows above the water line becomes moist, let the batch sit *untouched* for two minutes. This will help to eliminate air bubbles and to keep the mixture from setting up too quickly. After two minutes, begin mixing slowly with your hand submerged to avoid creating air bubbles in the plaster. If air bubbles do form, rocking the bucket gently on the floor will help to make them rise to the top. Continue mixing for two minutes; then pour immediately.

To mix the same formula of plaster with an electric mixer, measure as above, add the plaster to the water, and when the last bit of plaster becomes moist, wait two minutes without touching it. Then mix with the mixer for one minute and pour.

Pouring Plaster

Pour the plaster carefully around the reservoir into the space between the original and the walls, always starting at the lowest point (13-11,13-12). Let the plaster rise up and over the original to the top of the walls or to the point at which it is 1¼ inches (3 cm) thick above the bowl. Avoid splashing or dripping plaster on the original as you pour around it, because splashes or drips will cause hard spots in the mold that could create unequal density in the walls. If the walls of the mold are uneven in density, different parts of the mold will absorb water from the slip unequally, creating uneven walls in the final cast. Some casters lightly agitate the plaster with their fingers after pouring it into the mold to make the air bubbles rise to the top and disappear.

Before you try to remove the original from the mold, let the plaster stand for between 20 and 40 minutes, or until the mold begins to get hot (13-13). Removing the original from the mold before the plaster has set properly can damage the mold severely, possibly creating a distorted mold or causing cracks or fractures. Once the plaster starts to get hot, it has expanded to its farthest point and will separate more easily from the original. If the plaster has cooled down, a slight

Figure 13-11
Pour plaster starting at the lowest point around the reservoir. Let plaster rise up and over the original. A metal or plastic pitcher with a tapered, pointed lip gives a controlled plaster flow and any bubbles in the plaster break as they flow over the lip.

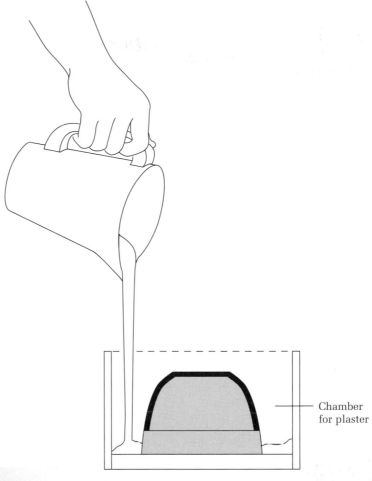

Chamber for plaster

Figure 13-12
Roslyn Myers pours the plaster carefully into the space around the reservoir mass, taking care not to spatter or drip any onto the original.

Figure 13-13
Before removing the original, leave it and the completed mold untouched until the plaster starts to get hot — usually between twenty and forty minutes. With the clay reservoir removed, you can see the space above the rim of the bowl for the extra slip.

amount of moisture may develop between the plaster and the object, causing the plaster to bond to the original through condensation suction. If this happens, the two should be easier to separate if you place the mold and the original in hot water.

Drying the Mold

After you have made the mold and have removed the original, dry the mold slowly in a warm atmosphere or place it near a heat source that will not rise above 120°F/48.8°C, because excessive heat may cause the mold to crack and deteriorate and thus lose its moisture-absorbing properties. Circulating heat is best. The mold must be thoroughly dry before you use it for slip casting, because it must absorb a considerable amount of water.

SLIP CASTING

When you are ready to start casting with slip, you will have to decide whether to mix your own slip from the particular type of clay you wish to use or whether you will use a commercial slip. For clay that will be used for handbuilding, it is important that the clay particles flock together, but for a clay to be used for slip casting, the particles in the water should stay separate and in suspension. For this reason, specially formulated casting slips contain **deflocculants.**

Deflocculants

A deflocculant, such as soda ash, sodium silicate, or Darvan #7, is added to slip to keep the clay particles in suspension and to reduce the amount of water needed to make the slip. It is important to keep the proportion of water as low as you can in casting slip, because if it contains too much water the clay and fluxes will settle in the bottom of the container. But if you add too much deflocculant, you will get settling! Because the proportion of deflocculant added to the clay and water must be exact, and the type of clay used also makes a difference, it is not easy for a beginner to make successful casting slips. Since commercial slips are formulated to avoid most of these problems, we suggest you use them, at least at the start. In this way, you will learn the correct viscosity of slip. However, if you want to try making your own slip, there is a formula for a low-fire slip in Appendix 1A.

Variations in the water quality can also affect the composition of the slip, and water evaporation can cause the slip's consistency to change. You should also remember that some water and deflocculant will have been drawn into the mold during casting, so if you pour the extra slip drained from the mold back into the container, you will change the proportion of water and deflocculant in the remaining slip. To compensate for this loss, you may add very small amounts of water plus a few drops of sodium silicate.

The type of slip you will choose and its firing range depend on what it is that you plan to cast. For your first attempts at slip casting, Toki suggests you use low-fire slip because of its greater flexibility and the fact that warping problems are not as great with this type of slip as they might be with a high-fire slip.

Pouring Slip

Before pouring the slip into the mold, stir it gently for a few minutes until it becomes fluid, then pour it. If you pour it without stirring it, the moisture may not be absorbed evenly into the plaster mold, and the slip may form weak or sagging walls. In addition, the extra slip can become too thick to drain easily from the mold.

Pour the slip into the mold carefully, trying not to spill any on the mold (13-14a). Soon after filling the mold, you will notice that some of the moisture from the slip is being drawn into the mold walls. As this happens, the level of slip in the mold will drop. At that point, top it off with more slip.

As more water is drawn from the slip into the mold, you will see clay walls begin to form around the edge. Wait until the walls reach the thickness appropriate to what you are casting — thin for a small porcelain bowl, thick for a large sculpture. Remember that the walls will become thinner when the water evaporates from them as they dry. Once the walls reach the desired thickness, pour out the extra slip into a bucket or basin (13-14b). Then, up-end the mold over the basin, resting it on two wooden slats, and let the extra slip drain thoroughly out of the mold, usually for 5 to 20 minutes (13-14c).

(a)

(b)

(c)

Figure 13-14
(a) Myers pours colored porcelain slip into the mold, taking care not to splash the rim. When the slip level drops, she will top it off with more. **(b)** Once walls of the desired thickness have formed around the edge of the mold, she pours the extra slip out into a basin. **(c)** She up-ends the mold and places it over a basin to drain out the excess slip.

Wait a few minutes, and then reverse the mold and wait until the clay walls begin to pull away from the mold walls (13-15a). Blowing a little **compressed air** around the edge will speed the process. You can also use a hand-held electric hair dryer and blow warm air into the casting to speed up the drying. Remove the cast from the mold with care and carefully trim off the extra clay from the reservoir (13-15b). Now you have a replica of your original (13-15c). Note, however, that it is slightly smaller than the object from which you made the mold. It will become even smaller as it dries and when it is fired.

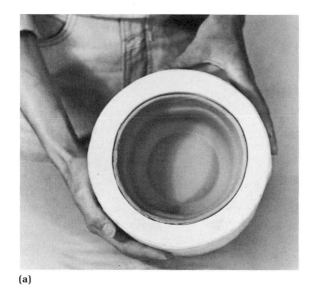

(a)

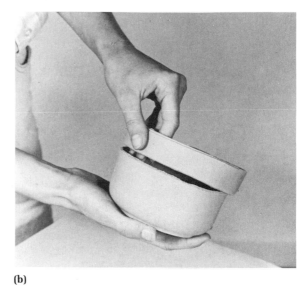

(b)

(c)

Figure 13-15
(a) As the porous plaster absorbs moisture from the clay, the slip-cast walls begin to pull away from the mold. (b) The
porcelain cast bowl is removed from the
mold, and Myers removes the extra clay
of the reservoir mass from the cast.
(c) The cast bowl is finished, with its rim
smoothed, ready for firing. The difference in size between the original and the
cast will become even greater when the
cast bowl shrinks during drying and
firing.

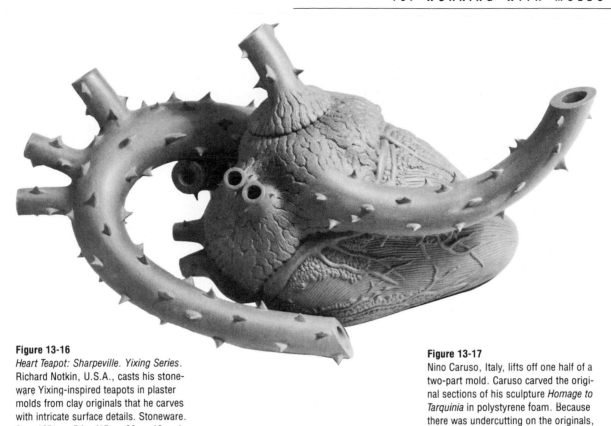

Figure 13-16
Heart Teapot: Sharpeville. Yixing Series.
Richard Notkin, U.S.A., casts his stoneware Yixing-inspired teapots in plaster
molds from clay originals that he carves
with intricate surface details. Stoneware.
6 × 10⅞ × 5 in. (15 × 28 × 13 cm).
Courtesy the artist and Garth Clark Gallery, NY.

Figure 13-17
Nino Caruso, Italy, lifts off one half of a
two-part mold. Caruso carved the original sections of his sculpture *Homage to
Tarquinia* in polystyrene foam. Because
there was undercutting on the originals,
one-part molds would not have released.
Note the registration knobs and sockets
on the mold sections. *Courtesy the artist.*

Using Slip Casting Creatively

As you become more adept at making plaster
molds, you can make two-part or multipart molds
to create more complex works. To make a vessel
or other closed, hollow form, use two concave
press molds, press clay into each, let it stiffen,
then remove it and join the two clay sections
while they are damp. Many of the face pots from
Moche were made in this way (5-10). Slip-casting
techniques can be used to create many different
types of ceramic objects (13-16). In addition to
those in this chapter, look at the assembled sculpture by master mold-maker Richard Shaw (8-14),
the head that Jack Earl made at the Kohler Company (8-21), and Jindra Viková's portrait heads
(14-41, Color Plate 16), which she made from
slip-cast slabs. Nino Caruso (13-17) uses two-
part molds, and John de Fazio used twenty-four
molds to assemble *BlueBoy* (13-18), altering and
interchanging parts of slip-cast figurines much as
did the Greeks who made the Tanagra statuettes
(2-22). Serge Bottagisio and Agnes Decoux developed a unique way to cast multicolored slabs
(13-19).

Clayton Bailey made a multipart mold from an unusual found object—a real shark's head he had kept in his freezer. With this mold, he developed a family of individualized "Landsharks" created by altering the original slip-cast shark head (13-20 to 13-32).

Toby Buonagurio (Color Plate 40) also uses molds to cast images which she then transforms. Of her working methods she says,

I begin by carefully selecting and editing images culled from flea market and dime store objects. My conceptual and technical process of transformation initially involves casting these cliched images in clay and then altering their appearance by addition and deletion. This process physically distances the images from the original context. Unlikely combinations of these images are then constructed anew and given a heavy dose of excessive color and unlikely surface texture.

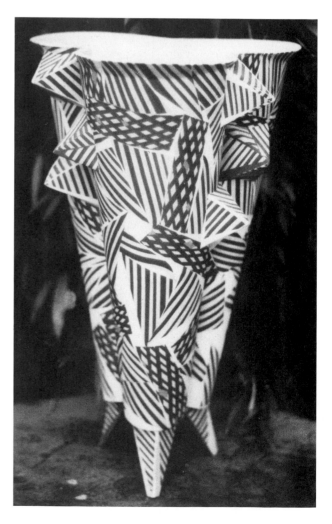

Figure 13-18
John de Fazio, U.S.A., slip-cast *The Assumption of BlueBoy* using twenty-four molds. He made the removable lid by slicing the head off a slip-cast figurine and grafting on a cast eagle head. He then used BlueBoy's face on the hat. Other hybrid figures and birds were made by combining casts of statuettes and attaching them when leather hard. De Fazio handbuilt the cloud. 1992. Earthenware. Glazes and china paint. 26 × 16 × 16 in. (66 × 41 × 41 cm). *Courtesy the artist.*

Figure 13-19
Serge Bottagisio and Agnes Decoux, France, developed a method of slip-casting inlaid colored slabs. They first cast a thin slab of colored clay, cut it in strips, lay the strips out in patterns, and pour white slip over them. This produces white-and-color-patterned slabs with an all-white lining. They then form these slabs into vessels and fire them at 2372°F/1300°C in a gas kiln. 1993. Ht. 24 in. (60 cm). Diam. 14 in. (35 cm). *Courtesy the artists.*

For more advanced projects, such as a complex figure with a great deal of undercutting, you will need to learn to make multipart plaster molds. Consult a book on casting for these.

Learning to make good molds in which to cast what you wish—from plates, cups, and sculptures to architectural details—will widen the range of what you can make with clay, offering you a wealth of new areas to explore.

Figure 13-20
Clayton Bailey, U.S.A., made a mold from a real shark's head his son found on the beach. Using slip-casting techniques, he made multiple images of the shark's head, which he then altered and individualized to create his *Pack of Landsharks* (13-32). Here, Bailey pours slip into the mold through a strainer.

Figure 13-21
Bailey explains the process of casting and altering the sharks' heads: *Lifting and removing the strainer from the mold after it is filled with slip. Strainer came from a flea market.*

Figure 13-22
After coating the edge of the stiffened cast with slip, Bailey reinforces it with a coil, explaining that *the finished piece will hang on a nail from this edge. The metal band and wooden wedged "mold clamp" are from the Kohler Company.*

Figure 13-23
Bailey melds the reinforcing coil well into the cast, then removes the mold.

Figure 13-24
Reaching through a hole in the ware board to change the contours of the casting to individualize each shark.

Figure 13-25
After carving holes for mouth and nostrils with a needle, or knife, the edges of the holes are softened with a wet brush and small sponge.

Figure 13-26
Bailey held the ear in place while he outlined the area he would score for attaching it to the head. He then painted some slip on the hatching before attaching the ear.

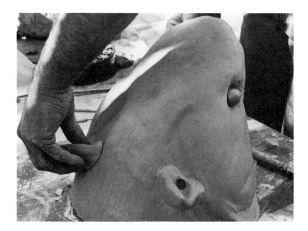

Figure 13-27
This shark with beady eyes and ears becomes a ''Ratfish.'' *Making ears is like pulling handles,* Bailey says. *They have feathered edges so they will easily blend into the head.*

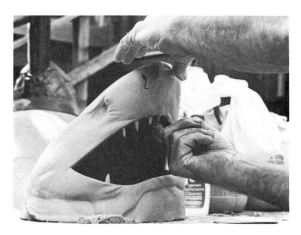

Figure 13-28
Bailey adds *lots of pointed teeth in both upper and lower jaws. They angle inward so it's harder for the victim to get away.*

Figure 13-29
He cast a slab of ''landshark skin'' by pouring a thin coat of slip onto a textured slab. *The texture of the mold was taken from a ''lizard skin'' imprinted plastic purse. A very thin layer of slip is obtained by rocking the bat.*

Figure 13-30
This shark is transformed into a ''land-shark'' by a ''skin graft'' of lizard skin. Bailey painted the head with slip before applying the lizard skin surface, then *patted it down from the center outwards to drive out air bubbles. The teeth and ears have been made and are ''toughening up'' in the air for a few minutes before attaching them.*

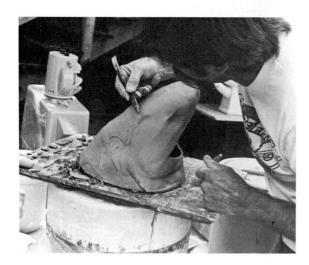

Figure 13-31
Blending edge of ''lizard skin'' into the shark head with a ''pegging tool'' that is used by casters at the Kohler Company for sealing cracks in leather-hard ware.

Figure 13-32
A Pack of Landsharks, Clayton G. Bailey,
U.S.A. Although all were cast from the
same mold, each completed, glazed, and
fired landshark has an individual personality. Slip-cast, low-fire white clay, stain
and glaze. Each shark 12 × 12 in. (30
cm × 30 cm). *Courtesy the artist and Joseph
Chowning Gallery.*

14

Texture, Color, and Glaze

When the word *ceramics* is mentioned, most people tend to think of a bowl or vase with a glossy glaze. But there are many other ways to treat the surface of clay to give it an interesting texture, attractive color, or luscious glossy finish before you fire it to permanence. First of all, your choice of clay body will influence the final appearance of the surface, so you will need to anticipate the type of surface treatment you will be giving the clay *before* you choose the clay body. Fine-grained porcelain, for example, will take detailed carving or delicately colored or translucent glazes, whereas heavily grogged earthenware or stoneware are more appropriate for rougher finishes.

Clay bodies, ceramic coloring materials, slips, and glazes make use of many of the same materials. How you use these materials in relation to each other profoundly affects the final quality and appearance of your work (14-1). Because this relationship is so important, when John Toki formulated some easy-to-make clay bodies for you to mix and test (Chapter 10), he planned them as part of a series that proceeds from mixing the clays, and texturing and coloring them, to, finally, mixing simple glazes to embellish them. These same clay bodies, given in Appendix 1A, are keyed to colorants and the specially formulated glazes in Color Plates 51 and 52. This series of basic clays and glazes was planned for study

Figure 14-1
Doe in Heat, by Michael Gross, U.S.A. The imagery on Gross's deeply carved vessels includes hunting adventures — both human and animal — family scenes, the art and music of many cultures, and deceptively cartoon-like characters suggested by radio talk shows. Looked at closely, however, the faces and forms are agonized, expressing the despair of squalid city environments. Clay, relief carving, glaze. Ht. 49 in. (124 cm). Diam. 25 in. (63 cm). 1990. *Courtesy the Ann Nathan Gallery, Chicago. Anonymous collection.*

purposes to help you understand the materials through testing. Additional information that will prove useful to you as you continue — glaze additives; water percentages; clay and glaze colorants; and frit, feldspar, and **opacifier** composition charts — is located in Appendixes 1A through 1F, along with some clay, slip, and glaze recipes other ceramists have shared. As you progress in testing, you can try those as well (Appendix 1C). Then, if you wish to go further into analyzing glazes, you may read Appendix 3B, "Calculating Glazes Using Chemical Analysis," always remembering that the clay body itself must be in harmony with the glazes you apply to it.

UNGLAZED SURFACES

Many potters and sculptors are interested in exploring the inherent qualities of clay, leaving the surface in its natural state. Others are interested in the effects of the fire on unglazed clay and let

Figure 14-2
Sleeping Mountain, Kyoko Tonegawa, U.S.A., uses a special traditional technique in which she throws from the inside only in order to preserve the natural exterior texture of the clay. Stoneware, reduction firing, cone 10 to 11. Ht. 15 in. (38 cm). *Courtesy the artist.*

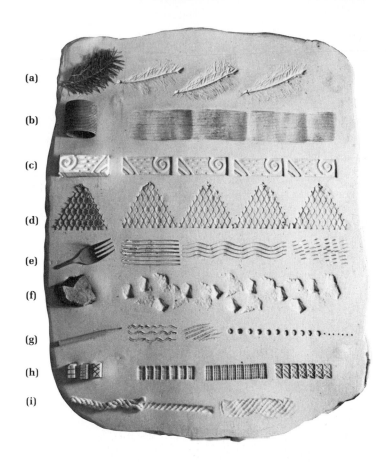

Figure 14-3

Sample textures show how easy it is to decorate soft, damp clay by scratching or pressing into it. In the past, potters used a dried corncob or shells to decorate their pots. To create designs or textures, look for likely objects around your home or outside. You can also make simple stamps from plaster, wood, or fork. **(a)** Pine branch. **(b)** Threaded pipe. **(c)** Carved plaster stamp. **(d)** Metal mesh. **(e)** Fork. **(f)** Rock. **(g)** Pencil. **(h)** Saw-cut wood blocks. **(i)** Rope.

the fire create the surface effects (Color Plates 8 and 11). Still others add texturing material or deliberately develop a texture on the surface.

Of her rough-textured vessels (14-2), Kyoko Tonegawa says,

Based on a special traditional technique of throwing on the wheel, I throw from the inside only, without touching the exterior of the pot. In this way I create untouched surfaces of texture and modify the shape, while allowing natural, earthen textures and colors to express themselves outwardly.

The very earliest potters used no more than their fingers, fingernails, sticks, shells, or other natural objects to scratch, impress, or carve textures onto the surfaces of their pots, frequently showing an innate sensitivity to the relationship of the decoration to the form of the pot (1-22 to 1-24).

You may find equally simple materials or objects you can use to alter the surface of the clay (14-3, 14-4). Look around you, in your home or outdoors, to see what you can discover to stamp, stroke, or stick into the clay to add interest. Almost anything, from beans to bolts, or bits of bark, might give you the surface you want for a particular pot or piece of sculpture.

You can also use carved wooden or plaster stamps to impress designs into the clay, or you can model or carve your own stamps from clay, bisque-fire them, and press them into the damp clay to create positive or negative images. A stamp modeled in relief will make a negative impression in the clay surface, while a concave carving will create a relief when it is impressed on the clay (2-28).

In addition, the method of construction that you use—coils, pellets of clay pressed together, overlapping slabs—can in itself create surface interest.

Figure 14-4

Pompeo Pianezzola, Italy, presses beans and rice into the clay. This organic material will burn out in the firing, leaving the surface pitted. *Courtesy the artist.*

(a)

(b)

Figure 14-5
David R. MacDonald, U.S.A., **(a)** carving one of his large *Nyama* vessels. He bases the designs of his vessels and plates **(b)** on African patterns inspired by fabrics, pottery, and body decoration. Stoneware. Diam. 32 in. (81 cm). *Courtesy the Hanover Gallery and the artist. Photo: Clifford Oliver.*

Carving and Incising

The Jōmon potters of ancient Japan combined impressed patterns with carving, giving a distinctive surface to the unglazed clay, using both methods effectively on their pottery and on their sculpture (3-21 to 3-23).

There is something very satisfying about carving into stiff but still damp clay — it is so easy to put one's mark in it, and even if your marks don't turn out as you wish, you can usually fill the gouge and start over again! But as with all decorative techniques, it is important in carving to consider the relationship of the carved surface to the object's clay body and to its shape and size (14-1, 14-5, 14-6). A taller-than-life-sized vessel, looming over the viewer, calls for deep carving (14-7), whereas the overall patterning of a sculp-

Figure 14-6
Karl Scheid, West Germany, carves his delicate porcelain bowls and boxes with precise patterns that are especially appropriate to their material, size, and shape. Porcelain. Ht. 3½ in. (9 cm). *Courtesy the artist. Photo: Bernd P. Göbbels, Hirzenbain.*

Figure 14-7
Arnold Zimmerman, U.S.A., carving one of his mammoth sculptural vessels, is surrounded by others in various stages of completion. The thick, coil-built walls (11-28) accept—almost demand—the deep carving that becomes an important aspect of their robust surface (Color Plate 15). *Courtesy the artist.*

Figure 14-8
Marilyn Lysohir, U.S.A., carves a flowered pattern into the dress of one of the figures for her installation *Bad Manners* (14-23, Color Plate 26). The clay is leather hard and smooth, allowing her to incise the precise linear designs. *Courtesy the artist. Photo: A. Okazaki.*

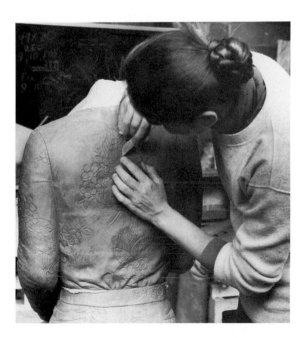

tured figure's dress calls for a more precise incised line (14-8).

Other Surface Treatments

Another technique from the past still sometimes used to create decoration in relief is **sprigging.** By applying pellets, rolls, modeled images, or cutouts of clay to the surface, you can create an overall texture or raised decorations on a pot or sculpture. This sprigged relief can be added to the soft clay as you build, or you can first score and paint a leather-hard surface with slip to be sure the added relief will adhere.

Burnishing the clay object when it is leather hard or dry (1-20, 5-17) also has a long history and is a tried and true way of altering the surface of damp clay. Some ceramists prefer to burnish while the clay is damp, whereas others prefer to work on dry clay. To burnish, stroke the surface with a river-polished stone or any smooth object, such as the back of a kitchen spoon. Some potters and sculptors prefer a piece of cloth or chamois. Burnishing works best when used on a clay body that is not too coarse or that has been coated with a fine-particled slip.

Texturing Dry Clay

You can also achieve surface effects by scratching, carving, drilling, chiseling, filing, or sanding the clay when it is dry rather than leather hard. It is more difficult to texture or carve dry clay than leather-hard clay, but the effect you can achieve by each method is different (14-5 to 14-8). Carving dry clay that is heavily grogged may result in a slightly ragged edge. Care must be taken to avoid chipping edges when carving a smooth body such as porcelain. Lightly dampening the dry clay before carving can make carving easier.

PRECAUTIONS

There is one disadvantage to carving dry clay—clay dust is hazardous to breathe because the microscopic clay particles that carry free silica (silica that has not combined with the clay molecules) can enter and clog your lungs. You can wear a respirator while carving, but since not only you but everyone else in the studio is exposed to the dust, be sure that there is also adequate active ventilation to remove the dust at its source. Adelaide Robineau (7-7) spent more than a thousand hours carving one of her famous pieces of pottery—unaware of the hazards the process entailed. One can say, "Well, lots of potters lived to ripe old ages doing all the unsafe things you warn against," but they were not exposed to the same amount of pollutants and toxic substances in their daily lives as we are now. It is that cumulative effect that is especially dangerous to us, so we must be especially wary of exposure to more.

Since an important purpose of this book is to encourage you to work in clay, we don't want to emphasize the precautions to such a degree that you become fearful of using ceramic materials. If you take the proper precautions, you should be able to work safely and healthily in a ceramics

studio unless you have a health problem that would make you especially vulnerable.

Before starting to use *any* coloring materials—clays, underglazes, glazes, or overglazes—be sure to read the section on good studio procedures and the basic health and safety rules that should be posted in any studio (see page 193). Almost all coloring materials offer some degree of hazard, and if you smoke, have allergies or asthma, are pregnant, or have a heart condition, be aware that your system cannot tolerate much exposure to toxic materials. Children are also more vulnerable to exposure to such materials.

In Appendix 1E, we list the chemicals and ceramic materials that you will use in the studio and rate them according to their degree of toxicity as it was known at the time the book was written. Since such information is always being updated, however, it is important that you stay aware of the new information as it is published. To be sure you know what you are using, read labels and any warnings carefully and ask the dealer from whom you buy supplies to give you the appropriate material safety data sheet (MSDS) that reveals any hazardous ingredients, the effects of exposure, and the necessary protection and precaution information. In Appendix 5A, we also list organizations where you can find out the current information, and in Further Reading there are publications that will keep you up to date on the latest findings. Here, we repeat some of the basic precautions you should take while working with glaze materials. Ultimately, it is *you* who must make the decision to protect yourself from danger and to take responsibility for your own health.

While working with the materials used in ceramic glazes, you must protect yourself from ingesting them by breathing them as dry ingredients or absorbing them through your mouth or skin. Be especially careful if you have any cuts in your skin. Wear protective gloves while throwing or modeling clay if your skin is sensitive, and while mixing glazes. Either use active local ventilation close to the dry materials you are mixing or wear a properly fitting respirator mask with a filter rated for toxic dust. For added protection, mix glaze materials in a plastic-covered mixing box with a hole in the side so that you can reach in and mix the materials.

Spray or **air brush** glazes and overglazes only in a properly vented **spray booth,** and wear a respirator rated for mists, acid mists, and fumes (see page 191). Keep your hands away from your face, mouth, and eyes, and to avoid accidental ingestion, do not eat or smoke when using glaze materials. Never hold a dirty glaze brush in your mouth when your hands are occupied! Wear an impermeable protective apron, keep it clean of glaze materials, and leave it in the glaze room when you are finished. It is also a good idea to shower and shampoo so that you can remove any glaze materials from your body.

Ventilation is as important in the glaze areas as in the clay-mixing areas, so be sure that the proper standards are followed in those areas and that you turn on the fans or dust collectors before working.

The glaze area should be kept clean. Wet-sponge all table surfaces and areas that have been splashed with glaze, and clean the floors with either a wet mop or a wet shop vacuum that has a filter rated to trap the microscopic particles of clay and glaze materials. Glaze materials and glazes should be stored in covered, unbreakable containers and be well labeled.

Although the chemicals and materials list in Appendix 1E identifies certain materials as particularly toxic, remember that *all* materials in a ceramics studio should be used with care. Take all the necessary precautions, and limit your exposure to the toxic materials as much as possible through sensible work habits.

COLOR

The simplest way to achieve a variety of clay colors is by wedging together two different clay bodies, varying the percentages of the clays to obtain the color you want. You can change the earth tones of clay to produce different shades by using this blending process. For example, a low-fire white clay wedged with a red low-fire clay will yield a medium reddish-brown, while a high-fire iron-rich stoneware blended with a white porcelain (also high-fire) will yield a medium brown when fired in an electric kiln (it will be darker if fired in reduction). The important point here is that you should choose two clays that have similar maturing temperatures so that they are compatible in the new clay body.

Coloring Oxides

You can develop a wider palette of clay-body colors by exploring what happens when you blend various oxides in different proportions into the clay. For example, 2 to 5% of red iron added to a clay will give you browns, and .5 to 2% cobalt oxide will create blues when blended into porcelain or very light-colored bodies. Different percentages will give you various shades of each color. You will achieve the truest colors when you blend colorants into light or white clay bodies, but remember that the temperature to which the clay is fired and the atmosphere in the kiln will also affect the colors, so *test!* You did some tests for color changes in clay bodies in Chapter 10, so you know the procedure. You can carry these tests further, creating a wider variety of colors. Information about clay colorants can be found in Appendixes 1A and 1F.

Ceramic Stains

Although the most common oxides provide some of the basic colors, commercial stains offer you the possibility of making a wider range of colored clay bodies. These commercially prepared stains, produced primarily for the ceramics industry, not only provide a wide selection of colors, but within specified firing ranges they are also in general more color-stable than oxides. It is worth it to buy prepared stains; if you wanted to make stains like these in the studio, you would need access to many materials, would need elaborate processing equipment to **calcine** the materials (that is, to heat to the point just below fusing to combine them chemically), and you would also require equipment for washing out the soluble salts, to say nothing of needing a great deal of knowledge and experience. If you want to make it really easy for yourself, buy premixed colored clay bodies — one company even offers a kit that includes small amounts of variously colored clays.

Another advantage of using stains in clay bodies is the fact that the color you see in the dry stain will be similar to the color you will obtain when you blend it into the clay. Oxides, on the other hand — cobalt, for example — do not show their true color until they are fired. Until you are experienced and can predict the colors you will get from oxides, using them can be a bit like painting in the dark, so stains are helpful. As with the oxides, the truest stain colors are achieved when they are blended into light or white clay bodies. The temperature at which the clay is fired can affect a stain just as it does an oxide, so, again, testing is the way to discover what final color you will get.

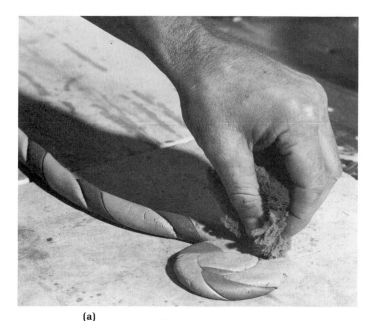

(a)

(b)

Figure 14-9
(a) Using colored clay that he has twined into a rope, Hans Munk Anderson, of Denmark, coils a base for a pot.
(b) Transferring the rope to a mold, he continues to press the colored clay coils together. The trick is to meld the colored clays enough to keep them from cracking apart but not enough to disturb the pattern. *Courtesy the artist. Photo: Mogens S. Koch, Denmark.*

With stains, your color range can extend beyond the basic oxide colors to purples, pinks, yellows, and various shades of blues, grays, greens, maroons, and browns, and in addition the careful processing these stains undergo for industry ensures quality control and color-batch consistency. There is no bright red or orange stain for clay bodies; the brightest red available for coloring clay bodies is maroon. For glazes, cadmium and selenium red and yellow stains are available, but these will not produce color in clay bodies.

To mix stains, you can place the dry stain powder on the **wedging table** and wedge moist clay into the color until it is thoroughly blended, or, for greater control of the color tones, you can add the stains to batches of dry clay, carefully controlling the percentage of stain added. The percentage of color you will need to add to the clay body will be affected by the type of clay body, firing temperature, and atmosphere, so, as always, make tests. Appendix 1A gives percentages of some stains and oxides to add to clay bodies to color and test them, and Color Plates 51 and 52 show fired test tiles.

Egyptian Paste

Egyptian paste is a self-glazing clay, so it is not strictly a clay body, yet it is not only a glaze. Originally discovered — probably by accident — by the ancient Egyptians, it played a role in the development of glazes (see Chapter 2). The clay body used in Egypt was made from local materials that contained a number of natural ingredients which, when fired, combined to form a fragile alkaline glaze on the surface of the clay. This ancient paste usually developed greenish-blue tones due to the copper oxide in the ingredients. Now, however, the commercially available low-firing (cone 015 to 05) paste is colored with glaze stains and oxides that make possible a wide range of colors. (See Appendix 1A for an Egyptian paste formula.) Once mostly used for beads and other small items, it has been used by some sculptors for larger objects, with the clay frequently wrapped around steel wire or steel rods. Sculptor Hedi Ernst (Color Plate 37), however, uses it on some of her sculptured plates in multifiring techniques. First, she bisque-fires the plates at cone 04 and glaze-fires them at cone 06. She then applies Egyptian paste, modeling it into relief, and fires it again at cone 09.

Figure 14-10
Virginia Cartwright, U.S.A., decorates her teapots with a marbled veneering technique. To create the marbled effect, Cartwright cuts thin slices from a loaf of layered clays and rolls each slice onto a thicker slab from which she will build the teapot. As she rolls the two slabs together, the thin veneer becomes bonded tightly to the thicker slab, and its patterns stretch into rhythmic swirls. Porcelain, cone 10. *Courtesy the artist. Photo: Robert Stefl.*

Multicolored Clay

By using more than one color of clay body and combining them using a variety of methods, you can create a range of effects extending from a braid-formed bowl (14-9) to a marbled teapot (14-10). To achieve effects like these, you can simply twist or braid rolls of colored clays together or use a more complex technique in which you combine blocks of colored clays, then cut, layer, and roll them, creating an agate or laminated effect (14-35). It takes a good deal of practice to make agate ware, because you must keep the various colored clay bodies separate while melding them enough to keep cracks from developing at the points where the two colors meet.

Using color in the clay is not, however, simply a matter of picking any color of clay body and combining it with any other clay. Each colorant contributes certain characteristics to the clay, including different shrinkage rates, so when the clay dries or is fired, the colored clays may shrink at different rates and possibly separate. The amount of stain you add to make the colors can

also affect the shrinkage rates; in addition, the maturing temperatures of the different clay bodies used must be similar in order for the piece to come through the fire without cracking. On the other hand, the cracks and crevices that develop in the kiln can become part of the surface interest, as in John Toki's large sculptures (Color Plate 48).

Coloring with Oxides, Slips, and Engobes

OXIDES An oxide is a basic element combined with oxygen. Over a geological period of time, almost all the basic elements on earth have formed a chemical combination with oxygen, and the resulting oxides have proved of great importance in the history of ceramics. They have been used for coloring clay and glaze and to provide fluxes that help to fuse the clay and the glaze in the kiln.

Even if you were limited to using iron oxide alone, you would be able to enhance the surface of your clay with a considerable variety of effects. By adding a second oxide such as cobalt, copper, or manganese to your palette and using the two oxides in combination, you can develop a considerable range of colors.

If you worked through the tests of clay bodies in Appendix 1A, you already have some idea of the action of oxides in clay bodies. In addition to their usefulness in clay bodies, these chemical compounds can also be used for coloring and decorating the surface of damp or bisque-fired clay in a number of ways (14-11 to 14-23). Throughout history, potters applied them with brushes, feathers, twigs, or **slip trailers** (14-15). One popular way to use oxides on bisque is to brush or sponge on the oxide, then wipe it off, emphasizing the texture of the clay. You can also apply it using brushes or by dabbing it on with a sponge to create various textures.

You can paint or wipe the slip or oxide decoration onto a pot after the clay has been through a bisque firing (14-11), although it is also possible to paint it on damp unfired clay (14-12).

There are a number of other ways you can apply an oxide—spraying it on, carefully painting it into incised lines—or you can add depth and color to textures and carved areas by covering the piece with oxide so that it fills the grooves, then sponging it off the raised area. You can also apply oxides with **resist** methods, covering up the

Figure 14-11
A variety of brushes are available for applying slips, engobes, underglazes, stains, oxides, dry powders, and glazes. Each one has a specific use: **(a)** *Liner brush:* fine line decoration with glazes, stains, lusters, underglazes. **(b)** *Sable brush:* smooth application with lusters, metallics, china paint. **(c)** *Sumi brush:* painterly decoration with stains, oxides, general glazing. **(d)** *Camel hair brush:* lusters, underglazes, general glazing. **(e)** *Fan brush, stiff bristle:* design work with dry powders, glazing decoration. **(f)** *Ox hair brush:* general glazing. **(g)** *Hake brush:* general glazing.

Figure 14-12
Oxides can be wiped onto a pot with a sponge and wiped off again, allowing the texture of the clay body to show through. You can also create a dappled surface if you dab two different colors of oxide on with sponges. *Photo: Alphabet and Image.*

parts you want to remain uncolored with masking tape, wax, adhesive paper, liquid **latex,** or a stencil (14-19) and then painting over it with an oxide or slip.

SLIPS AND ENGOBES   A slip is basically a mixture of clay and water. With an added deflocculant, the slip mixture can become a medium for casting in plaster or bisque clay molds (Chapter 13). In this chapter, however, the term is used in relation to water-diluted clays that are used for decoration. Correctly, the term *slip* refers to this clay-and-water mixture used for decoration or for casting, whereas the term **engobe** should be applied only to any slip that covers the whole of a pot or sculpture. However, the two terms *slip* and *engobe* are frequently used interchangeably. White or cream engobes are often used to cover the reddish tone of earthenware clay in order to create a light background suitable for painted decoration. White slips are often made from white porcelain clay blended into a liquid state, and white slips can be colored with the basic oxides or with the wider range of colors available in commercial stains. (See Appendixes 1A and 1C for several slip recipes.)

You will find that slips and engobes do not melt and run in the same way that many glazes do, and the color does not blur. For this reason, a beginner often finds slips easier to use for decoration than glazes. In addition, because slips or engobes are also made of clay, they have a natural

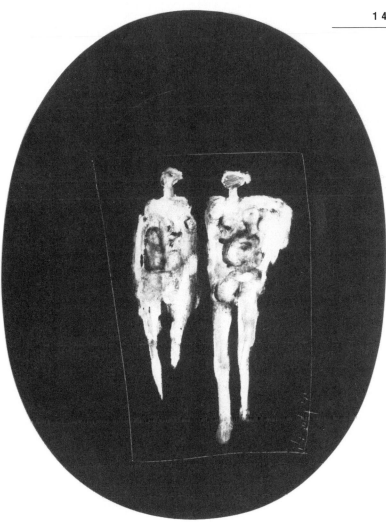

Figure 14-13
Agnese Udinotti, U.S.A., created her *Shadow Image* plates as an extension of her painted canvases. To create similar images on ceramic plates, she first covered the plate with black slip and then wiped away the surface with a wet sponge or her fingers dipped in water, using a subtractive technique in much the same way she works on her canvases. *Shadow Images,* she says, refer to . . . *those haunting memories which exist at the point of recollection/forgetfulness. Courtesy the artist. Photo: Bill McLemore.*

(a)

(b)

Figure 14-14
St. Crow Plate. **(a)** Michelle Gregor, U.S.A., decorates her dinnerware with slip drawings under a clear glaze. 1992. Diam. 13 in. (33 cm). **(b)** She uses drawings and the name of her dinnerware—PALM Ceramics—as decoration on the back of a bowl. 1992. Diam. 11 in. (28 cm). *M. Gregor, sole manufacturer and creator. Courtesy the artist.*

visual relationship to the clay body, and with a transparent (or salt) glaze over the whole, a slip or engobe decoration seems particularly appropriate. Slip decoration can have a painterly quality when manipulated with brush or fingers (14-13, 14-14, Color Plate 34).

FITTING THE ENGOBE OR SLIP It is usually a good idea to make (or buy) slip or engobe from the same clay body as that used for your pot or sculpture in order to ensure a good "fit" between the slip and the clay body. Since clays vary in their shrinkage rates, an engobe or slip made of a different clay may not have the same rate of shrinkage and therefore may peel off during drying or after firing. Early potters faced this problem when they made their white or cream engobes to cover the red earthenware body, and the pottery found in early sites frequently will show the results of this peeling, with very little of the original color left. If you use a slip of the same clay body as that used for the pot or sculpture, this will not be a problem, but one reason for using a slip or engobe is for color change.

To mix the light-colored engobes and slips, you can use light-colored clay materials such as kaolin, bentonite, and ball clays in varying proportions. Since each of these has a different rate of shrinkage, however, you may have to add flint to counteract shrinkage or borax or frit to help the slip adhere to the pot.

If you have difficulty with a slip or engobe peeling after applying it or during firing, then reformulate the slip, engobe, or clay body so that they fit each other better. You can also try adding a solution of **gum** to the slip. This may not solve your difficulty completely, but it will help to counteract the tendency to peel. Use a solution of 196 grams of CMC gum or gum tragacanth with 1 gallon (3.785 liter) of water. If the slip is to be stored for a long time, you *can* add an antispoilant solution to keep the gum from spoiling. Either Dowicide G or formaldehyde (¾ ounce per gallon [6 fluid drams]) will do this. Since both of these products are toxic, we suggest that, in line with our recommendations to avoid using toxic materials when possible, you mix only the amount of slip you need for immediate use so that you do not have to use an antispoilant. If you do use them, ask the dealer to provide you with an MSDS information sheet giving handling precautions, and follow them.

Running a series of tests of a slip or an engobe on test tiles made of the clay you want to cover is the only *sure* way to see that it will fit and adhere to that particular clay body. Appendixes 1A and 1C provide some slip recipes that you can alter and test on your clay bodies.

DECORATING WITH SLIP Early potters devised a number of ways in which to decorate with slips and engobes. Since both are opaque, if you apply several coats you can color the whole pot or sculpture with a uniform color. In the past, one especially popular method used was trailing the slip onto the damp clay, creating lines, marbling, or "feathered" effects (7-2). The slip was simply trailed on in patterns, rather as one would write "Happy Birthday" on a cake. Nowadays, potters use variations of the slip-trailing technique (14-15) to suggest traditional European designs or adapt it to designs based on African scarification (14-16). Robert Sperry, however, uses very

Figure 14-15
Trailing slip from a squeezable syringe is the modern way to decorate with slip — potters formerly used a ceramic slip cup with a goose quill inserted in a small opening. Load the slip trailer with a viscous underglaze, slip, stain, glaze, or engobe, then squeeze the bulb as you draw your design.

Figure 14-16
Plate: Scarification Series, by David R. MacDonald, U.S.A., approaches the traditional method of slip trailing in a free manner, using slip to create patterns inspired by the scarification patterns of Africa. Stoneware. Diam. 22 in. (56 cm).
Courtesy the Hanover Gallery and the artist. Photo: Clifford Oliver.

Figure 14-17
To print the surfaces of his *New Visions* series, Les Lawrence, U.S.A., uses a photo silk-screen monoprint technique to transfer his images from a plaster slab. He screens the image onto a plaster slab, using black porcelain slip, then alters the image with various instruments — brushes, strings, erasers, stencils, or wire. Next he pours specially formulated casting slip over the slab and peels it off when it is still soft, lifting the slip decoration with it. He then uses these decorated slabs to construct his *New Visions*. Porcelain, cone 10, stainless steel, steel wire, photo silk-screen monoprint. 20 × 20 × 4 in. (51 × 51 × 10 cm). *Photo: John Dixon. Courtesy the artist.*

direct methods to apply slip to his plates (12-2) or to his large murals (16-10), sometimes splashing the slip on directly from a bucket, while Les Lawrence developed a monotype method of decoration (14-17).

SGRAFFITO The early use of white slip over reddish clay led to the **sgraffito** technique. In this process, lines were scratched through the light slip to reveal the darker clay beneath. Contemporary potters now use variations of this method, brushing the slip on thickly and then drawing into it with a sharp-pointed tool (14-18).

Slips and engobes can also be brushed on over a resist material. One of these is a commercial wax-resist medium that is used to create **wax-resist** effects with glazes. To do this, you apply it to the areas in which you wish to retain the color of the clay body. Then, when you brush the slip over the piece, the slip will adhere only to the untreated areas of the pot. The resist material will burn off in the fire and leave the contrasting body color showing in the areas that have been covered. To get sharp-edged color decoration, use masking tape, adhesive paper, or a paper stencil instead of painted resist. Apply tape or stencil to the damp clay, paint over the stencil with slip, and then carefully pull it off. This method — known as the reserve method because you are *reserving* the color of the pot or sculpture itself — will result in an image that remains the color of the body with the contrasting slip surrounding it.

Patrick Siler works with a complex stencil process using two colors of slip to create his figurative images. He uses a black slip over the greenware, then applies a light ivory slip thickly over stencils made of blotting paper. After the slip has dried for a few minutes, he peels off the stencils, and the black underslip appears in the protected areas (14-19 to 14-21). Siler's slip recipes are in Appendix 1C.

If they are used alone, without a glaze coating or burnishing, slips and engobes fire with a dry, matt surface that can be extremely effective. On the other hand, the slip or engobe can be covered with a transparent glaze that, along with protecting the surface, gives it a glossy finish and enriches its color.

TERRA SIGILLATA Terra sigillata is nothing more than a slip, made of clays whose particles are extremely fine and that contain micalike minerals such as illite. The glossy red and black of the

(a)

Figure 14-18
(a) Jens Morrison, U.S.A., painted on thick, juicy brushfuls of slip, then drew through it to expose the darker surface beneath.
(b) *Tea Temple. Farmounian Reliquary.* Detail of the surface shows the incised drawing and the rich encrustment, made up of indigenous clays, underglaze, and glaze. *Courtesy the artist.*

(b)

Greek vases (2-17, 2-20), and the glowing red of the Roman ware (2-28) were produced by the use of this fine coating. On the Greek pottery, the black was obtained by reduction. Today, terra sigillata is used to give a much wider range of effects than in classic times. Like slip or engobe—which it basically is—terra sigillata appeals to those who wish to develop an intimate relationship between the surface of their work and its form, and who respond to the way in which the terra sigillata becomes an integral part of the clay body rather than coating the surface like a glaze. Such contemporary ceramists as Pierre Bayle (12-1, Color Plate 9) and Richard Hirsch (14-22, Color Plate 13) use terra sigillata for sculptural vessels whose rich surfaces are nevertheless subordinated to the strong forms of their work, while Marilyn Lysohir (14-23) finds that using terra sigillata on the bodies and clothing of her figurative sculpture gives them the warm surface she wants.

Terra sigillata is made by mixing a fine clay with water and water softener, then allowing it to settle—Marilyn Lysohir lets hers settle for at least two weeks. The particles fall to the bottom—first the coarsest, then the finer particles—

Figure 14-21
A group of stencils are attached to one of Siler's three-dimensional pieces in preparation for brushing the second coat of slip. On the left side, the thick, light slip has already been applied over the stencils, and after drying for about five or ten minutes, they have been peeled off. *I like to apply the overslip thick enough to be stucco-like and crack a little in drying. . . . When the piece is thoroughly dry, I will spray on a simple clear glaze and fire the piece up to cone 5.* Courtesy the artist.

Figure 14-19
Patrick Siler cuts out one of the blotting-paper stencils with which he created the series *Clay Works. I like the contrast between the thick slip impasto and the sharp, severe stencil edge. . . . Courtesy the artist.*

Figure 14-20
First, Siler coats the piece with a heavy covering of black slip; then he dips the stencils in water and attaches them to the stiffened clay with straight pins. *When I reach an arrangement I like, I will then dip the stencils in water and carefully pat them on the surface. Only when the edges of all the stencils are well pressed into the dark underslip will I begin to paint on the light colored overslips.* Courtesy the artist.

Figure 14-22

Vessel and Stand #2. Richard Hirsch, U.S.A., says of his smaller vessels, *Their presentation on a tripod stand pursues the feeling of ceremony and develops a monumentality beyond their true dimensions. . . . By purposely raising the pieces on this type of pedestal, I give visual praise to the vessel as an art form.* Despite the small scale of this sculptural vessel, its powerful forms and effective use of negative space give it an imposing character. Its rich surface, produced with a layering of terra sigillata, glazes, and a raku firing, adds to the sense of antiquity. Thrown and handbuilt; blue and green terra sigillata under cone 04 glaze; raku fired. Ht. 8 in. (20 cm). *Courtesy the artist.*

leaving a layer of water on top. This water is then siphoned off, and only the top layer of very fine slip is applied in thin coats to the dry, unfired clay. Once a pot or a sculpture is coated with the terra sigillata, it can be fired at around 1760°F/ 960°C.

APPLYING TERRA SIGILLATA Terra sigillata can be brushed or sprayed on. It can then be left unburnished, since a good terra sigillata slip will dry to an attractive sheen. It can, however, be made even more glossy by burnishing. Marilyn Lysohir applies three coats to dry clay; then, on the fourth coat, she starts to burnish the surface, rubbing just a small area at a time.

Richard Hirsch also applies his sigillata to bone-dry clay

in two or three coats brushed on, which I burnish slightly—not a high gloss. Then I air brush some on to create contrast on the surface—i.e., glossy versus matt—and to give some detail to the sigillata surface.

Figure 14-23
Bad Manners, an installation by Marilyn Lysohir, U.S.A. (Color Plate 26). Lysohir burnished four coats of colored terra sigillata to create the rich surface on the figures. She carved the patterning on the dress of the figure on the right before painting it (14-8). The foods on the laden table are colored with underglaze. Clay and wood; terra sigillata and underglaze; fired at cone 06. 4 ft × 10 ft 4 in. × 7 ft (1.2 m × 3 m × 2 m). *Courtesy Asher/Faure Gallery, Los Angeles and the artist. Collection: Mr. & Mrs. Louis Taubman. Photo: James Reinke.*

COLORING TERRA SIGILLATA Richard Hirsch gave up using the usual glaze techniques some years ago and has experimented with a number of other methods in order to develop a surface that does not interfere with the formal aspects of his work. He has found that the use of a white terra sigillata that can be colored with stains or combined with low-fire glazes formulated to bring out its color enhances and emphasizes the forms of his work. Recipes for Hirsch's white and his red terra sigillata are in Appendix 1C, along with percentages of other colorants that you can add to the basic white.

In the same way that the color of clay bodies can be altered using oxides and stains, terra sigillata can also be colored with these materials. A number of ceramic artists have found that colored terra sigillatas lend themselves especially well to the surfaces they wish to develop. Both Hirsch and Lysohir find that with "sigs" they can get effects they can obtain in no other way. Hirsch says,

Figure 14-24
David Miller, England, first sprays slip onto his dry pots. He then bisque-fires them and colors them with underglaze colors and slip stains to which he has added a small amount of frit to make them less refractory and to help them adhere to the pot. *Courtesy the artist.*

I mix my "sigs" to get particular colors not obtainable through the use of one stain itself, just like mixing paint.

He then bisque-fires the pieces to cone 06 or 05,

never higher than 04 because the color burns out and the sigs get too hard to raku-smoke, post-reduce.

To get the rich surface characteristic of his work, Hirsch also uses a semiopaque glaze to which he adds a variety of coloring materials. These glazes interface well with the terra sigillata beneath them. His base glaze recipe is in Appendix 1C along with the percentages of colorants he uses in terra sigillata.

UNDERGLAZES

Underglazes, as the word implies, are used under other glazes. Whether they are applied as oxides or as commercial underglazes, they provide the ceramist with a wide range of colors with which

to achieve decorative effects (Color Plates 26 and 27) from which to choose (14-24 to 14-32).

Oxides as Underglaze

Historically, oxides have played an extremely important role in the development of ceramic colors and glazes. First, as components of the natural slips and clays, then, once the coloring properties of oxides were better understood, the oxides themselves were isolated and were often used for decorative effects under glazes. In Chapter 3 we saw how potters first experimented with copper oxide to produce red underglaze decoration, then abandoned it when the red bled into the glaze. They then turned to cobalt oxide, finding its blue a more satisfactory underglaze color that did not bleed as much as the copper red. The Chinese created their blue and white ware with cobalt, inspiring European potters to try to reproduce it (Chapter 6).

One of the advantages of using oxides under a glaze is that after firing, the color seems to float,

Figure 14-25
Dan Gunderson, U.S.A., makes many sketches from which he chooses the images he uses on his underglaze-decorated cones. He draws the images on the bisque-fired cone with a hard pencil before starting the process of stenciling on the color with underglazes.

Figure 14-26
Next, he uses masking tape and adhesive paper to cover areas that he does not want colored when he sprays the underglaze. As he proceeds with building up the colors, he removes sections of the masking tape.

Figure 14-28
With the images completed, Gunderson sprays on a transparent glaze to cover the entire piece before firing it to cone 04. For one of Gunderson's pieces, see Color Plate 27. *Courtesy the artist. Photos: Stetson University, Office of Public Relations.*

Figure 14-27
Gunderson airbrushes water-thinned commercial underglazes over a stencil held in place on his piece *Teeter Totter*. Note the original sketch tacked on the spray-booth wall as a guide. A respirator is recommended for added protection while airbrushing.

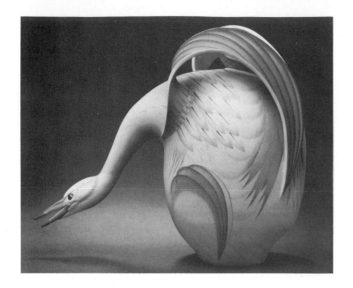

Figure 14-29
Great Egret Teapot, by Annette Corcoran, U.S.A. Corcoran used an air brush to spray underglaze stains onto the elegant bird, drew detail with a brush, then sprayed a light glaze to set the underglaze. In addition, she sprayed and brushed on china paint details and gave the piece multiple firings—sometimes she does as many as twenty firings, going lower and lower for each one. Although the teapot is made of porcelain, the top firing temperature was cone 04. Porcelain. 1988. Ht. 9½ in. (24.1 cm). *Courtesy the artist and Dorothy Weiss Gallery. Photo: Lee Hocker.*

Figure 14-31
Toilet Factory Toilet, by Ann Agee, U.S.A. While working in the arts/industry program at the Kohler Company, painter Agee used the bathroom fixtures produced there as painting grounds for underglaze decoration. She covered the fixtures with ornaments and views of the factory, along with portraits of the factory personnel, and then placed them in an installation titled *Lake Michigan Bathroom.* 1992. Kohler porcelain, underglaze, glaze. *Courtesy the collection of the John Michael Kohler Arts Center. Photo: Eric R. Johnson.*

Figure 14-30
James Caswell, U.S.A., slip-cast *The Arcade* in one piece using a five-part mold. He then painted it with underglazes—aqua greens, deep pinks, yellow, and purples—and fired it at cone 05. Slip-cast earthenware. Ht. 24 in. (61 cm). *Collection, Mr. and Mrs. Alexander Grass. Courtesy the artist.*

suspended in the glaze, giving the decoration a luminous quality. The Chinese cobalt-decorated porcelain was especially noted for this quality; the best of it, made in the imperial kilns (3-19), was so precious that it was kept for the emperor's sole use. Later, on the other side of the world, the American colonial potters used cobalt underglaze to decorate useful stoneware crocks and jugs for farmers, creating simple, direct images appropriate to the ware's use in rural homes (7-5). Oxides or slips can be applied with a variety of brushing techniques, with sponges, or with cords dipped in the oxide or slip and trailed across the object.

Prepared Underglaze Colors

Commercial opaque underglaze colors are prepared by calcining (heating to a high temperature) finely ground oxides, combining them with a flux and a refractory material, and mixing them with gum or some other binder to ensure adhesion. Generally, these prepared underglazes are formulated for low firing, because at higher temperatures the warmer colors such as red and orange will burn out. Although it is possible to make your own underglazes, it is difficult to formulate them so that they fit the clay body properly and adhere well. Most ceramists use commercially prepared underglazes for that reason. It is, however, possible to mix oxides and stains with a gum solution and to use these as transparent underglazes that you can apply using a watercolor technique. (See Appendix 1A.)

 Underglaze colors can be painted on with brushes as you would use watercolors, but you can also spray diluted underglaze on with an air brush—using a respirator and a spray booth—blending the colors much as you might on a canvas. Or you can apply underglazes over stencils or masking tape to create hard-edged images or patterns. By using these techniques in combination with other underglaze materials such as pencils and crayons, you can extend the range even further. David Miller, for example, decorates his vessels with a combination of techniques; first he sprays his teapots with slip and bisque-fires them; then he paints them with underglaze colors and slip stains. He adds a small amount of frit to the underglaze to make it less refractory and to help it fuse to the clay body during firing (14-24). Miller outlines areas with copper or cobalt oxide,

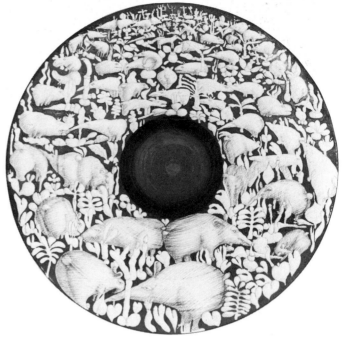

Figure 14-32
Decorated bowl, by Jack Sures, Canada, shows the detail one can achieve using underglaze pencils. Sures plays with the illusionary space he creates with strong perspective within the confines of the bowl form. Engobe, underglaze pencil. Diam. 5 in. (12.5 cm). *Courtesy Moose Jaw Art Museum and National Exhibition Centre and the artist.*

or sometimes a mixture of both, then gives his vessels a salt firing to coat them with a transparent glaze that will bring out the color.

One advantage of using underglaze is that as you paint, the colors appear closer to the way they will look after firing—a factor that makes the final appearance easier to visualize than when you use ceramic glazes, whose colors look dusty and pale until they are fired. Underglaze pencils and crayons that allow one to draw in detail and shading appeal to many artists, since this makes it possible to develop an image more easily (14-32).

Underglaze colors are especially popular today, when many artists are using ceramic materials in ways that were never dreamed of a few decades ago. Used in conjunction with glazes, underglazing allows a ceramic artist to achieve images with almost the same freedom as a painter working on paper or canvas. Such a technique is bound to be popular (14-24 to 14-32 and Color Plate 16).

Commercial underglazes come in a number of forms:

- *Liquid*—either opaque or translucent colors
- *Pan*—in pans as in a watercolor paint set, these will give translucent colors when applied as a wash and opaque colors when applied thickly
- *Tube*—as with watercolors
- *Crayon or chalk*—similar to colored chalks
- *Pencil*—used for drawing detail, especially on fine-grained clay such as porcelain or low-fire white earthenware

Application Methods

BRUSHING   The traditional method of applying underglaze was with a brush. You may use any type of brush that will give you the effect you wish.

SPONGING   Applying underglaze with a natural or synthetic sponge is another common method. With it you can achieve a stippled effect.

AIR BRUSH   You can also airbrush it on. To do this, you may need to add a little additional water and use a coarser tip in the air brush to allow it to go through. Use a spray booth and wear a respirator.

SILK SCREEN   If the ceramic object to be decorated is flat or nearly flat, you can easily use a **silk-screen** frame to apply underglaze colors directly onto it. If it is not flat enough to allow use of a framed screen, you can sometimes screen colors onto it by taping unframed silk-screen material to the curved surface.

DECALS   **Decals** can be printed on transfer paper with underglaze colors. Such decals are not available commercially, but they can be made to order. These decals are made with ceramic stains, a flux, and a vehicle. The image is silk-screened or photo-printed onto special transfer paper using underglaze colors and then is transferred onto the ceramic surface.

Once you have applied underglaze colors—by whatever method you choose—you might wish to cover the piece with a transparent glaze before firing it to enhance and protect the rather fragile underglaze colors (14-28). A transparent glaze is not essential as long as durability or solubility is not a problem, and the pastel matt colors that can be achieved by leaving off the glaze may suit your image better. As with every other ceramic technique, through experimentation you may discover a unique way of using underglaze that will be particularly appropriate to your individual style of working.

Precautions

Because certain colors used in underglazes do not pass the standards set up to monitor the use of toxic substances in glazes, you should take care when working with underglaze colors. In addition, because such colors could be soluble in certain food substances, if you mix your own underglazes and use them on any object that could be a container, you should send them to an independent laboratory for testing to find out if they are safe.

GLAZING YOUR WORK

You may be surprised the first time you see a glazed pot or sculpture ready for the kiln. Most people think that the potter has a palette of colors like a painter's and need only pick out a color from fired test tiles and paint it on for the pot to look as it will when it is fired. Instead, there sits a chalky, greyish-white pot, showing nothing of the brilliant color or rich gloss that the firing will reveal. Because of the difference between unfired and fired glaze, it is not always easy to visualize what the result will be, but once you become accustomed to the transformation that occurs in the kiln to change the powdery, unfired glaze coating on your ware, you will understand why glazes are so fascinating.

Glazes are not only functional, making the fired piece impervious to liquids and giving it a durable, watertight surface; they also add color and visual interest to pottery or sculpture (14-33 to 14-35; Color Plates 19, 21, and 30). Remember, however, that a beautiful glaze cannot transform your work if its forms are not well composed in the first place.

Thinking ahead to how you want to use glazes before applying them will help you arrive at more satisfactory final results. Rather than waiting until the bisqued form is ready to glaze, begin to think about the glaze as you are making the piece. Catherine Hiersoux (14-36) found that, as she be-

Figure 14-33
Edouard Chapallaz, Switzerland. Chapallaz's classic wheel-thrown forms display his perfectly fitted glazes in a pleasing integration of form and color. Stoneware, iron glaze, reduction firing. Ht. 12½ in. (32 cm). *Courtesy the artist. Photo: Rolf Zwillsperger.*

Figure 14-34
Susanne Ashmore, Canada, reformulates and tests glazes from various sources until she finds the one she likes. She used three glazes on this teapot—a high-fire volcanic ash glaze with tin and copper colorants, a soda feldspar transparent glaze with red iron oxide and rutile colorants, and an overlapping glaze with gold flecks and milky blue and purple accents. Fired to cone 6 in oxidation, with a 2–5 hour final soak. *Courtesy the artist.*

Figure 14-35
Snow Bowl. Les Manning, Canada, laminated stoneware and porcelain to create what he calls a sculptural clayscape. He then gave the porcelain a coating of Leach's clear glaze with 1 percent iron, which, he says *is very icelike and similar in color to the limestone silt-colored lakes in the Canadian Rocky Mountains.* For these landscape bowls, Manning says that he uses *heavily grogged stoneware for the immediate surroundings, medium stoneware for the distant horizon, and porcelain to depict the atmosphere.* Stoneware and porcelain; fired in reduction at cone 8. Ht. 6 in. (15 cm). *Courtesy the artist. Photo: Monte Greenshields.*

Figure 14-36

Two porcelain vases by Catherine Hiersoux, U.S.A., illustrate the visual effect of different glazes on similar shapes. On the glossy black vase (left), the profile becomes dominant as one's eye follows the swelling and narrowing contours, while on the copper-red-glazed vase (right), the eye lingers on the more complex surface before following its profile. Porcelain; reduction; copper red and black glazes. *Courtesy the artist. Photo: Richard Sargent.*

came more experienced and adopted this way of working, her glazes and decorations improved greatly. Many of the principles you may have learned in a painting or design class can be applied to glazing your work, and if you plan a design and color scheme with watercolors or chalks *before* you start to throw or to apply the glaze, you can choose the glazes from your test tiles with greater success.

Glazes can be glossy or matt, transparent or opaque, and the color range extends from subdued earth tones to brilliant reds and blues (Color Plates 2, 3, 22, 23, 25, and 28).

A glaze can be applied very thinly, allowing the texture of the clay to show through, or so thickly that it develops its own texture (Color Plate 23). The decorative effects possible with glazes are many, varying from those that neatly fit the shape (14-33), to those that run down the sides (14-34), to carefully controlled applications for special effects (14-35). (See also Color Plates 20, 21, 29, and 30).

Figure 14-37
Turning Together, Eileen Lewenstein, England. Lewenstein's vessels, like this one whose textured surface is coated with a dark turquoise high-fire glaze, frequently reflect the colors of the ocean beside which she lives and works. *These,* she says, *are part of a series of paired forms in which the two pieces are "identical" (well, almost), and differing arrangements can alter their relationships.* Coiled stoneware. Ht. 16 in. (41 cm). *Courtesy the artist.*

Choosing a Glaze

As you study the examples of **glazes** throughout the book, consider which type would be most appropriate to your work. For example, the delicate green of a celadon glaze can be successful as Harris Deller used it (Color Plate 19), but it would hardly suit a heavily grogged rough-textured piece. If the pot or sculpture to be glazed is heavily carved or modeled, a glossy glaze might destroy the impact of the carving by producing confusing reflections and highlights; on such a piece, a matt surface may be the solution. Deciding on what glaze to use, if any, is one of the important aesthetic and expressive decisions every potter and sculptor has to make (Color Plate 49). It usually takes a good deal of experience with glazes before your choices will always be successful (14-36, 14-37).

The first glazes you use may be school glazes made up in quantity from a formula that has been translated into a **batch** recipe. Or perhaps you will choose from the many prepared glazes available commercially. You can, for example, choose bright, low-fire glazes to bring animation to your work, or you may want to use a more subdued, high-fire glaze that will fire to a color similar to that on a sample tile you saw in the store. However, if you want to understand why glazes respond as they do to the fire, it is worthwhile to learn how to formulate your own, or at least how to make changes in the formulas given in Appendix 1A (Color Plates 51 and 52), or those that you find in magazines or get from other ceramists.

There are a number of advantages to mixing your own glazes. One is that you will know exactly what materials are used in them—for example, you can mix them with no toxic ceramic materials and no toxic antispoilants. Another advantage of mixing your own glazes is that, as when you mix clay, you will be able to make changes in the glaze composition, thereby often achieving qualities that are not available commercially. Learning more about the various chemicals that comprise glazes and the materials that provide those chemicals will help you to understand the unique qualities each component contributes to a glaze. For instance, some materials melt easily in the heat of the kiln, others add color, and still others can change the texture of a glaze. Depending on the ingredients used, some glazes may be pitted and lavalike (7-14) while others are glossy (14-36). As an example, Les Manning could not have combined stoneware and porcelain with a pale, glacier-green glaze on one piece without having a thorough knowledge of how clay and glaze act and interact in the kiln (14-35).

In the past, potters knew nothing about the chemistry of glazes, so they had to learn everything by trial and error. Modern chemistry, however, allows us to analyze the composition of a glaze and to learn exactly what materials are needed to change its composition in order to achieve certain effects (see Appendix 3B). As a result, glaze testing is simpler and faster now, because we can start out with a basic understanding of the chemistry of a glaze, and computer programs now available can make this process even easier. Nevertheless, it is still necessary to test, and by so doing you may find that your best glaze is the result of experimentation. Indeed, there is no reason why you cannot make excellent glazes by measuring out the basic ingredients within the generally known proportions, adding or subtracting materials, and then testing the glaze. Measuring cups and spoons and a creative approach can be successful for those who wish to avoid the chemistry, and there is no need to be put off by the "mystery" of glazes. Glaze making is not some form of alchemy performed by wizards in peaked hats.

What Makes a Glaze?

A glaze is basically a glassy, impervious coating that is fused to the surface of the clay by heat. As the kiln heat is raised and held at a certain temperature, the separate materials that you have mixed together begin to melt and fuse, eventually combining into a completely new material—the glaze. The oxides of silica, alumina, and others such as calcium, sodium, or zinc also play important roles in the formation of glazes.

Glazes are formulated from three categories of chemical compounds, each of which has a different function in the glaze. These are (A) the *fluxes* that help the glaze to melt in the heat; (B) the *refractories* that increase the viscosity and stability of the glaze in the fire, and (C) the *glass formers* that are what the word implies—the basic components of glaze (Table 1 in Appendix 3B). These compounds are obtained from a variety of materials. The type and percentage of these materials used in a glaze will vary in accordance with the temperatures at which the ceramist intends to fire the work (usually between 1500° and 2450°F/815.5° and 1343.3°C). Hundreds of glaze formulas that have already been formulated with the correct chemical balance needed to form a glaze are available to the ceramist (a few are given in Appendixes 1A and 1C). If, after reading this chapter, you want to go further into the subject of glaze calculation using chemistry, study the information on chemical analysis in Appendix 3B, "Calculating Glazes Using Chemical Analysis," where you will find out more about the role these three basic ingredients—flux, refractory, and glass former—play in making a glaze.

GLASS FORMER   The main glass-forming ingredient in glazes is silica, which is highly resistant to heat. A glaze could be made of silica alone, but since silica's melting point is so high (3115°F/ 1713°C), that would be impractical; few clay bodies could withstand such high heat, and few ordinary kilns could fire that high.

FLUX   The proportion of silica in a high-fire glaze can be greater than in a low-fire glaze, because at low temperatures too much silica would keep the glaze from melting. Generally, as much silica as possible is used in a glaze, because silica adds durability and helps the fired glaze resist the attack of acids and chemicals. Therefore, in order to lower the melting point of the silica, another ingredient must be added—a flux. The glaze melts as a result of the interaction of the oxides in the glaze materials when they are exposed to heat, and it is one of the basic facts of glaze making that glaze materials used in such a combination (**eutectic**) melt at lower temperatures than they would if they were used alone. The fusing temperature of a glaze may be lowered considerably depending on the *combination* of fluxing oxides and their proportions in the glaze in relation to the silica. (At this point, we are talking about oxides as glaze components, not as coloring agents. However, the oxides used to color a glaze, such as iron, can also bring extra fluxing action to the glaze, lowering its melting point even further.)

REFRACTORY The third ingredient necessary to most glazes is a refractory (high-melting) material, alumina. A common source of alumina is **china clay.** Alumina increases **viscosity,** helping to keep the glaze materials suspended as well as helping the glaze adhere to the ware. Alumina, even if used in very small amounts, also adds strength and durability to the glaze and helps prevent the glaze from running; without it, the glaze might run down and off the sides of the object during firing. Also, without alumina, glazes tend to crystallize during the cooling process and thus may become opaque. Sometimes the potter wants crystals to develop for decorative reasons; in that case the alumina content is reduced (Color Plate 30).

Each of the three basic glaze ingredients — *flux, refractory,* and *glass former* — may be introduced to the glaze by adding any of a variety of ceramic materials, and each of these materials in turn has individual properties and reacts in its own way with other materials. In order to understand what happens when you change the percentage of each, it is extremely important to become familiar with the glaze materials. For example, zinc oxide (ZnO) acts as a flux at temperatures above 2109°F/ 1154°C. It can also make a glaze matt and opaque if you add it in larger amounts. If used in small amounts, it can add smoothness to a glaze, but if too much is used alone as a flux, the zinc may make the glaze **crawl** on the pot or cause pinholes to develop. Zinc interacts well with copper to help produce bright turquoise, but if used with chrome, it sometimes produces brown rather than chrome green. You can see from this example that in order to make successful glazes you should understand the properties and behavior of each material as well as the effect it will have on the other ingredients in the glaze. Although ceramists today can rely on chemistry more than their predecessors, they must still test their glazes to see how they act on a particular clay or in a particular firing situation.

Frits

A **frit** is a combination of raw glass-forming materials that has been fired, fractured by immersion in water while still molten, and finally ground up in a **ball mill.** Fritting is done to make raw, soluble materials insoluble and to lower the fusion point of the individual materials by combining them. It is these qualities that make frits so useful to ceramists.

Frits are available commercially, and their chemical formulas are also available so that you can see exactly what materials they contain, allowing you to know the exact percentage of silica, alumina, and fluxes present in each frit. Produced primarily for the ceramics industry, frits offer the ceramist a wide range of glass-forming compounds, and because their chemical composition is known, it is easier for the user to control the uniformity of a glaze from batch to batch.

There is another reason for fritting. Many raw glaze materials, such as lead, barium, and cadmium, are poisonous, and some, such as borax, potash, and soda ash, are caustic **alkalies** that are soluble in water. Used raw, some of these materials would be toxic or injurious to the person using them. Others, when used in their un-fritted soluble state in a glaze, could be released from the glaze when the finished glazed object is used to hold foods that contain acids like vinegar, wine, coffee, whiskey, and lemon juice. Used in frit form, a number of these materials are safe, or at least less dangerous, so frits have become standard in the ceramics industry. There is still concern, however, about how safe some of the frits are, both for the person handling the glaze in the studio and the person eating or drinking from a glazed container. There is some controversy, for example, about the safety of handling lead even in frit form, and tests show that dangerous amounts of lead are released from even fritted lead glazes when the glazed object is exposed to acids. For that reason, we recommend that you do not use any lead, even in frits, for glazes on the interior of any container that could be used for foods or beverages. You must also consider whether you wish to expose yourself to *any* lead in *any* form. Appendix 1D lists some lead-free frits you may safely use. Have any glaze about which you are uncertain analyzed by a testing laboratory to be sure there is no danger in using it on food containers.

Another reason for using a frit instead of raw, soluble materials is that in some cases a raw material could be absorbed into the porous surface of the bisque-fired ware and thus change the chemical composition of the glaze. This would affect the texture, color, or other qualities of the glaze. In addition, dry, soluble materials are hard to store since they absorb water from the atmosphere and form lumps. It is clear, then, that by using frits you can reduce some of the problems caused by soluble materials and some of the hazards of using raw glaze materials.

Frits also lower the temperature at which the soluble materials can be used, and because of their fluxing qualities, frits are extremely useful in low-fire glazes. In addition, since the materials in a frit have already been melted once, no volatile materials are left to cause pinholes or pits as they burn out, which can happen with raw materials. However, frits in glazes fired above cone 6 may tend to bubble, especially when fired in a reduction atmosphere. Because of this tendency, and also because of the expense of frits, feldspars are generally used as the main flux in high-fire glazes where more flux is needed. (In a low-fire glaze where feldspar is used to introduce alumina, the feldspar acts as a refractory.) Feldspars are naturally formed frits, and using them is an economical way to introduce silica and alumina into a high-fire glaze. For example, comparing the composition of Frit 25 and Custer spar, we find that the frit contains 12.1% alumina while the Custer has 17.5%. When it comes to the silica, however, the difference is greater: The Frit 25 has 49.7%, but the Custer spar contains a much larger proportion of silica — 68.5%.

Fusion Testing

Fusion testing is a method of subjecting chemicals to different temperatures to determine their melting point and fusing ability. The value of fusion testing is that it will help you understand the physical changes a chemical undergoes when subjected to heat of varying temperatures. To make test tiles for this process, you can roll out a number of $3\frac{1}{2} \times 9\frac{1}{2} \times \frac{1}{2}$ inch ($9 \times 24 \times 1.25$ cm) slabs, using a cone 10 white stoneware or light buff clay. Then press ten to fourteen $1 \times \frac{5}{16}$ inch (25×8 mm) depressions into the slabs with your thumb. Identify each depression with the name of the chemicals you are going to test in that space, or mark each space with a code number for each chemical. Mark the tile with the cone at which you are going to fire it. Then bisque-fire the tiles to about cone 05. To test, place a small amount of any chemical in the depression. For example, if you take the feldspar nepheline syenite and place it in a testing tile made with thumb-sized depressions, then fire it to cone 05

($1915°F/1046°C$), you will notice that it looks like a white chalky powder. If you fire it to cone 5, you will see that it is beginning to flux and to develop a slight sheen. If you continue the fusion test and fire it to cone 10 ($2381°F/1305°C$), it will be apparent that the nepheline syenite has developed a glossy white sheen and has fused to the clay. Thus, you can see that by using this method of testing you have caused a physical transformation of the chemical nepheline syenite. It becomes clear that when it was subjected to a low temperature it did not mature or melt, but as the temperature was increased the feldspar began to become glassy and fused to the clay.

Some chemicals will change color and texture in addition to melting and fusing to the clay, whereas others, such as kaolin, will not fuse at all. If you test the kaolin used in the same formula and fire it at cone 05, 5 and 10, you will notice that it does not melt at cone 10. For it to melt at a lower temperature it would have to be blended with a flux. This phenomenon, in which two materials combine, results in lowering the melting temperature of the combined materials. The point at which this occurs is called the eutectic point. The atmosphere in which the tests are carried out also will affect the outcome of the test; if it is fired in a gas kiln under heavy reduction, the kaolin probably will take on a darker tone.

You can try fusion tests of the chemical components that make up the *Hands in Clay* glaze recipes cone 05 clear (G1), cone 5 clear (G9), and cone 10 matt (G17), and continue testing the glaze stains that color the glazes. Then proceed by trying every clay and glaze chemical in Appendix 1. After doing these tests, you will have a wealth of useful information recorded visibly about the physical properties of chemicals and how they react to heat.

Types of Glazes

Like clay bodies, glazes are classified into categories according to their firing ranges: low-fire glazes, medium-fire stoneware glazes, and high-fire stoneware and porcelain glazes. You can also choose from a variety of specific glaze types such as transparent or opaque, matt or glossy, ash glazes (Color Plate 11), slip glazes, crystalline glazes (Color Plate 30), salt glaze (15-19 to 15-27), and raku glazes (15-28 to 15-33; Color Plates 13, 32, and 33).

Low-Fire Glazes (Cones 015 to 1) Ever since the early potters in Egypt and the Middle East developed alkaline and then lead and tin glazes, potters have used low-fire glazes to make earthenware watertight or to add color to household vessels. Toby Buonagurio, for example, uses low-fire glazes, lusters, flocking, paint, and glitter (Color Plate 40). Today, these glazes are popular with potters and sculptors alike, because they provide bright, smooth colors with which to enliven their work (Color Plates 17 and 18).

As the name implies, low-fire glazes melt at low temperatures (1479°F/804°C to 2109°F/1154°C). Low-fire glazes have a much wider range of colors than high-fire glazes and will create surfaces that are transparent, matt, or opaque. Although most low-fire glazes begin to melt at cone 015 (1479°F/804°C) and mature at around cone 05 (1915°F/1046°C), they often can be fired as high as cone 5 (2185°F/1196°C). With the exception of the bright reds and oranges, most colors will fire at higher-than-expected temperatures with interesting results, although because the glazes tend to become more fluid with the higher heat, it may be necessary to apply less glaze to the surface. Thus, if you usually apply three coats by brushing, then two coats of low-fire glaze should be adequate if it is to be fired higher. Low-fire glaze colors tend to darken on stoneware clay bodies when fired to temperatures that are higher than those for which they were formulated.

It is possible to use low-fire glazes in consecutive firings. For instance, colors such as red and orange, which would burn out at stoneware temperatures, can be added using this technique. You could thus fire your ware with a high-fire glaze, leave some areas blank, and then, after the first glaze firing, apply low-fire glazes to those areas, then refire to create a high-fire look with low-fire accents.

Many ceramists layer slips, underglazes and glazes, firing them in successive firings. Sandra Taylor creates the images on her vessels with underglazes and multifiring (Color Plate 35). Richard Hirsch says he sometimes uses low-fire glazes over the bisqued-on terra sigillata, or he raku-fires the piece.

Finally sometimes I sand blast the glaze surface to reveal the colored terra sigillata underneath. I have now returned to the use of glaze because I think it is appropriate to the layering effect of age I am after. Also I like the hardness vs softness, tactile vs visual play.

Throughout history, two types of fluxes have traditionally been used to give low-fire glazes their low-melting characteristics. Alkaline glazes depend on an alkali, such as sodium or potassium, to melt them. These alkaline glazes, although they produce brilliant colors when coloring oxides are added to them, are rather soft and can easily be scratched, so use them for objects that will have little wear. For example, if you want to make glazed tiles for installation in your home, you could use colorful alkaline glazed tiles in a spot that receives relatively little wear and moisture; for heavy-use areas such as a floor you would instead use stoneware clay and high-fire stoneware glazes. Alkaline glazes are difficult to fit to the clay body. They tend to craze, developing small cracks over their entire surface, because they have a wide range of expansion and contraction in the kiln. This may be decorative, but it weakens the glaze, which may wear or weather off with use. Food containers should never be glazed inside with an alkaline glaze because of the possibility of food getting in the cracks. Use alkaline glazes only on nonfunctional pieces, where their brilliant colors will be decorative but not subjected to wear.

Historically, lead was extremely popular, because glazes made with it melt at a low temperature, fit the clay well, and take color well. Combined with tin, lead made possible the cream-colored glazes that early Italian potters used so successfully on their maiolica ware as background for bright-colored glazed decoration (6-5, 6-6, Color Plate 4). Unfortunately, lead is hazardous to work with, and we know from historical documentation that many workers, including women and children who worked in the decorating rooms of pottery factories, died as a result of lead poisoning. We will never know how many more people throughout history were made ill by eating or drinking from improperly fired lead glazes used on food containers.

Using lead in fritted form is an improvement over using it raw, but unfortunately even fritted lead can later be released from the glaze. Improper firing (not high or long enough), improper application (too thick), or the addition of even a small amount of copper to a fritted lead glaze can increase the danger that the lead will be released in contact with acids. Because the public generally does not know about this risk, some people recommend putting a hole in any lead-glazed convex form that might hold liquid to make it impossible for a child to drink from it. To be absolutely sure that what you make in the ceramic studio does not present a possible hazard to others, we recommend that you use only high-fire glazes for anything that could possibly be used for food or liquid consumption.

MEDIUM-FIRE GLAZES (CONES 2 TO 7) Medium-firing glazes were developed partly as a result of the energy crisis of the 1970s and partly because a good many electric kilns on the market do not heat above cone 6 or 8. Once ceramists started to fire within this range of cone 2 (2124°F/1162°C) to 7 (2264°F/1240°C), they found that the lower firing range often gave more brilliance to their glazes. Certain colors, such as the maroons and yellows, do not hold their color well in high temperatures and in a reduction atmosphere, but these colors, which could be lost in a cone 10 reduction firing, hold their color better in the medium firing range. For these reasons, many ceramists have continued to use the medium-range glazes.

HIGH-FIRE GLAZES (CONES 8 TO 13) High-fire glazes are formulated to be fired from cone 8 to 13 (2305°F/1263°C to 2455°F/1346°C) and are used on stoneware and porcelain clay bodies (14-33, 14-35, 14-36). Unlike the low-fire glazes, which always remain as a surface coating on the fired object, properly fired high-fire glazes actually interact and bond with the clay body, creating a buffer layer between the glaze and the body. The advantage of this close bond is that the glaze has a greater resistance to the stresses that cause crazing or peeling. Because of this interaction between clay and glaze, the glaze may pick up "impurities" from the clay body that will cause spots, such as iron spots, or splotches of color to appear in the fired glaze. Whether you consider these spots and splotches desirable or undesirable depends on your personal taste.

ASH GLAZES The ashes that were blown onto the shoulders of the pots from the wood fires in early Chinese and Japanese stoneware kilns often formed accidental glazes on the ware (3-10). Ob-

serving this, potters started to experiment, and gradually they developed deliberately applied ash glazes. It was from this experimentation that high-fire glazes developed in China and Japan.

Nowadays, potters continue to use ashes to make attractive and interesting glazes. Since the plant materials that are burned to make the ashes take up minerals from the earth while they are growing, their ashes are rich in glaze-forming ingredients such as potash, lime, alumina, and silica, as well as various oxides that provide color. You can obtain ashes for glazes by burning wood, berry canes, grasses, sawdust, corn cobs, rice hulls, and even fruit pits. If you wish to control the ingredients so that you will be able to replicate the glaze, then you should keep each type of ash separate and test them independently, because each one will have a different chemical composition. For example, the ashes of some plants, such as grass, wheat, and fast-growing weeds, contain more silica than those from slow-growing trees. Therefore, the ashes from grasses and weeds create more stable glazes, whereas ashes from trees will make runnier glazes. Even the locality where the tree or other material was cut may make a difference, because the minerals present in the soil vary from place to place.

You can experiment making a glaze using ashes alone, burning any organic material you can gather in sufficient quantity; potters have even gathered ashes from state park barbecue pits, and Ericka Clark Shaw has developed a low-fire glaze in which she uses ashes from charcoal briquettes (Appendix 1C). If you use the ash on a clay body that contains a considerable amount of silica, you may find that it makes an adequate and beautiful glaze without any additions. Or you may want to add feldspar, clay, and perhaps whiting as an additional flux. Generally, the proportions suggested are approximately 40% ash, 40% feldspar, and 20% clay, but the percentages can vary. Some ash glaze recipes are given in Appendix 1C.

To prepare ashes for making glazes, soak them first in water to leach out the soluble materials. The water drained off will contain lye and can burn your skin, so be careful and wear rubber gloves when you pour it off. Even if you mix ashes dry, it is wise to wear gloves. After the ashes have soaked, put them through a sieve and mix them with the other ingredients. Although you can add small percentages of ash to low-fire glazes, the best effects with ashes come with high-firing glazes, to which larger amounts can be added.

To give the effect of an accidental ash glaze, you can sprinkle dry ash directly on the ware before placing it in the kiln, duplicating to a certain extent what happens when ashes fly in a wood-fired climbing kiln. Many ceramists have also become interested in the effects that can be achieved with the accidental ash glazes that may form on pots in Japanese-style wood-firing kilns (15-15, 15-17, Color Plate 8). These kilns are discussed in Chapter 15.

SLIP GLAZES   Some clays or powdered rocks will make a glaze when they are used alone. For example, feldspars are natural frits that could form a glaze if fired at high enough temperature, such as those possible in industrial kilns. But feldspar's melting point is so high it would require additional flux in order to fuse in the average studio kiln. There are, however, natural clays that will form slip glazes in the brown range when fired at the lower temperatures because they contain iron and manganese. In these, the iron functions as both a flux and a colorant. Because a slip glaze contracts when it dries, it does not adhere well to a bisque-fired surface, so it is generally applied on damp clay or greenware. This will allow the two clays to shrink at similar rates. Even so, in order to fit well, a slip glaze should be carefully formulated to have the same shrinkage rate as the clay body. An example of a natural slip glaze was the terra sigillata that the Greeks and Romans used to create the glossy surface of their pottery. It was formed of fine-grained natural clays that contained micalike substances. The dark-brown-firing Albany slip used by the early stoneware potteries in New York (7-5) was, until it was recently mined out, also a popular natural slip glaze. Now that Sheffield slip is widely used as a substitute, potters have had to reformulate their glazes due to color difference.

Although some substitutes for Albany slip are being mined, slip glazes are now more likely to be specially mixed rather than used in their natural forms. They are formulated to provide special qualities—for example, a light hue so that the slip can be colored with stains.

MATT GLAZES   There may be times when, instead of a glossy surface, you would prefer to use a nonshiny, or matt, glaze. The characteristic satin surface of a high-fire matt glaze is hard and durable, but without strong gloss. The matt effect is produced by large numbers of tiny crystals in the glaze—too small to be seen by the naked eye—which break up the light. These satin-matt glazes, along with "buttery" or "fat" matt glazes, are often sought for certain types of pottery. Introducing a larger amount of clay, such as china clay, into the glaze will increase the alumina and make the glaze more refractory so that it will tend to be underfired. It is this underfired quality that gives it its matt appearance. Matt glazes can also be produced by incorporating zinc oxide into the glaze, by increasing the silica, calcium oxide, titanium dioxide, or magnesium, or by underfiring a gloss glaze. A matt glaze produced in this way is usually very porous, so it is used primarily for decorative purposes. Barium carbonate has long been the standard material used to create high-fire matt glazes, but since it is extremely poisonous, many people no longer use it. If you use it, take great care in handling it and do not use it on the inside of food containers.

To produce a matt glaze, it is also important that the cooling rate of the kiln be controlled and the kiln temperature be brought down slowly in order to allow the formation of the crystals responsible for the matt surface. You will find the percentage recipes for several matt glazes in Appendix 1C.

CRYSTALLINE GLAZES   Unlike the matt glazes, where the crystals are too small to be seen, in crystalline glazes the crystals are visible to the eye, creating unusual decorative effects on the surface of the pot and often giving a quality of depth to the glaze in which they lie suspended. Although these crystals will form in glazes used on both stoneware and porcelain, usually ceramists use them on porcelain because the crystals show to greater advantage against the white clay background. The crystals catch the light and reflect it, visually breaking up the glaze surface and often creating strong patterns. For this reason, crystalline glazes are best exhibited on simple forms.

The snowflake-like crystals that form in this type of glaze are actually grown, through the use of certain materials, by careful control of the rise and decline of kiln temperature, and by **soaking** the ware in the kiln. Crystalline glazes are produced by reducing the alumina content and using a variety of materials and chemicals such as zinc oxide, borax, sodium, potassium, rutile, or iron. In order to create crystals, these glazes must contain only a small amount of alumina, so they are very runny, and the glazed ware must be placed on special clay or porcelain supports dusted with alumina to prevent it from sticking to the kiln shelves as the glaze melts.

The creation of crystalline glazes requires a thorough knowledge of glaze materials and firing procedures, but even an expert such as Arnold Zahner (Color Plate 30), who has formulated crystalline glazes for a number of years, may open a kiln and find unexpected results. Speaking of the vase illustrated in the color plate, Zahner said,

> The glaze is a cone 8 glaze, containing 27% zinc oxide. Normally, it gives starlike or sunburst crystals of a darker green on a light ground. I fired this vessel in an electric kiln, and introduced propane gas into the kiln during the cooling period. For unknown reasons, the color and the shape of the crystals and their pattern came out quite differently; a typical example of the excitement and adventure of working with crystalline glazes. One has to be willing to experiment carefully, and use the best workmanship possible, but then be ready to accept whatever happens. Very often there are good or bad surprises. This is the rule of the game.

Zahner's glaze recipe is in Appendix 1C—try it and see what it does on your clay and in your kiln.

SALT GLAZE Potters in the Rhine Valley in Germany developed salt glazing in the Middle Ages and used it for centuries to create watertight, acid-resistant utilitarian ware. Later its use spread in both Europe and colonial America (Chapters 6 and 7). Produced when damp salt is introduced into the heated kiln (at a temperature of at least 1940°F/1060°C), the glaze is formed when the sodium is released in the presence of moisture, and as the salt volatizes its vapors fill the kiln. As the heat sends the vapors swirling around, they settle on the pots, the shelves, and the kiln walls. The sodium combines with the silica and alumina in the clay, forming a thin glaze on everything in the kiln. A salt glaze can be thin and smooth—an especially effective surface on pieces that have carving or incised decoration, as it does not fill the lines and obscure the design (15-27)—or it can have a mottled and pitted orange-peel texture caused by the glaze beading on the surface (15-25). Since a salt glaze does not usually penetrate and coat the interior of the pots, ceramists usually apply another high-fire glaze in the interior. Salt glaze is, however, no longer used for traditional forms alone; ceramists are now exploring its effect on sculptural creations as well (15-24, 15-27). (For more information on salt firing, see Chapter 15.)

Other Glaze Materials

Any mineral material has the possibility of providing additives that may create interesting glaze effects. A number of contemporary ceramists have explored the use of mineral materials that they find in their locality. These have included volcanic materials, crushed rocks and gravels, cement, and mine tailings. If you experiment with unusual materials, test them on small test tiles first.

Since glass is compatible with the glass-forming ingredients of glazes, it can also be used along with glazes. You can used smashed glass bottles (wear gloves and a face shield when breaking them), colored beads, or rods of glass. The glass melts and becomes fused with the glaze, creating small areas of contrasting color within it.

OVERGLAZES

After firing your pot or sculpture with either high-fire or low-fire glazes, you can carry the process of enriching the surface and color further by using overglazes, enamels, china paints, lusters, and metallic lusters on top of the glaze (14-38 to 14-40).

Overglaze Decoration

Sometimes called on-glaze painting, overglazing is a traditional method of decorating. It was used in Spain, Italy, and the rest of Europe for all low-fire color-decorated pottery until the European potters eventually learned how to imitate the Chinese blue and white underglaze decoration on porcelain (6-18). To prepare work for overglazing, you will generally apply a base coat of glaze—usually white or cream or light gray in color—to the surface to be glazed. Once this base glaze is dry, the piece can be sprayed with a solution of gum (128 grams gum to 1 gallon [3.785 liters] water) that will protect it from being disturbed when the overglaze is painted on it. Then you can brush on coloring oxides mixed into some of the

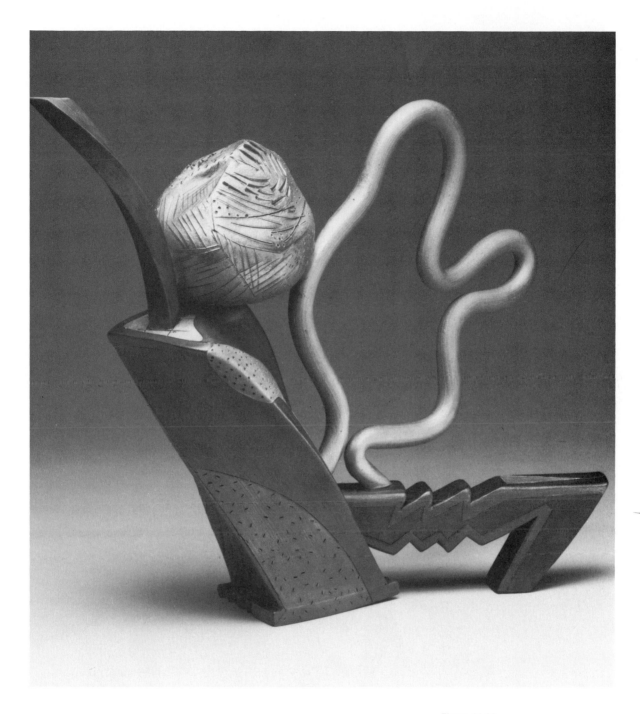

Figure 14-38
Zig-Zag. A nonfunctional teapot provides the "canvas" on which Mayer Shacter, U.S.A., creates a rich surface by painting layers of luster colors on unglazed porcelain, firing them after each layer. The satin surface and subtle color relationships integrate the assembled forms. Unglazed high-fired porcelain. Luster, multiple firing. 9 × 10 × 3 in. (23 × 25 × 8 cm). *Courtesy the artist. Photo: Charlie Frizzell.*

◀ **Figure 14-39**
For his earthenware wall plates, Patrick Loughran, U.S.A., uses a layering of surface techniques, employing slips, underglazes, glazes, lusters, sgraffito, and wax resist: The fresh and spontaneous-appearing surface is actually carefully controlled as he builds it up (Color Plate 25). Loughran considers his display plates to be in the tradition of maiolica (6-5), Bernard Palissy's work (6-17) and decorated giftware, and he also makes decorated functional ware (9-19). *Courtesy the artist.*

Figure 14-40
A Different Woman. Jindra Viková, Czech Republic, casts porcelain slabs from slip, forms them into her figurative sculptures, and then uses underglazes, overglaze painting, salt, metallic oxides, and transparent glazes to develop her rich surfaces (Color Plate 16). Fired at 2372°F/1300°C in an electric kiln. 43 × 24 in. (110 × 62 cm). *Courtesy the artist and Art Centrum, Prague. Photo: Pavel Banka.*

(a)

(b)

Figure 14-41
(a) Larry Murphy, U.S.A., painted cobalt oxide over a white glaze to test how the oxide would appear on it when fired; he found it too bland and discarded the glaze. **(b)** Murphy demonstrates using a banding wheel that makes it easier to paint decoration over the glaze.

original base glaze, or ceramic stains, or other glazes. Use quick strokes, disturbing the base glaze as little as possible (14-41). The same method may be used with **sulfates** or **nitrates** of different oxides.

China Paint and Enamels (Cones 020 to 016)

With the contemporary interest in complex colored surfaces on ceramic sculpture, overglazes have become popular, and china painting, which used to be associated with Victorian ladies painting flowers on teacups, has become quite a different process in the hands of contemporary ceramic artists (Color Plate 41).

China paints and **enamels** are basically very low-fire glazes (1175°F/635°C to 1323°F/717°C) that you can apply on top of an already fired glaze. They were used in the past to decorate household china, which is why they are often grouped together and called china paints. However, the word *enamel* correctly refers to overglaze colors that are opaque, whereas *china paint* is the correct name for the translucent overglaze.

There are a number of advantages to using china paint and enamels. Aside from the range of colors they produce, they are available in matt or gloss, translucent or opaque forms; they hold their position when they are applied; and they give excellent detail (Color Plate 25). Since china paints and enamels mature at low temperatures, they are generally used for the final firing, because if you apply a glaze that requires a higher temperature over the china paint, the china paint would be likely to change color in the higher heat. If you want to do multiple firing and have the color hold, you should fire the highest-firing glaze first, then follow it with a lower-firing glaze, and finally end with the china paint or luster on top of that. On the other hand, some artists have found that they like what happens with china paints or enamels when they are fired at higher temperatures: The china paint burns into the glaze, leaving residues that will be darker in hue and somewhat mottled.

Some overglaze paints are available that are like transparent watercolor paints and can be brushed on in thin washes of color. Others are opaque oil-base overglazes that can be mixed with a special paste to produce raised textures. Most colors (as long as they are mixed in the same medium) can be mixed with each other to create new shades. Some, such as reds, pinks, and purples, may not mix well, however, because the various oxides and chemicals that are combined to produce these particular colors of china paint have little tolerance for contamination.

The easiest way to use china paint colors and enamels is to buy them ready-to-use in tubes or pans. If, however, you want to prepare your own, you can buy the colors in powder form, add an oil- or water-base **china paint medium,** and mix the colors with a mortar and pestle or on a glass palette. Whichever type you use, the paint can be brushed on, sprayed on, or applied with a silk screen or as decals. Successive sprayed coats of china paint, usually requiring firing between coats, can create subtle gradations and depth of color. You will find information on firing china paints and enamels in Chapter 15.

For fine line decoration and outlining you can mix a blend of china paint powder thinned to a painting consistency with turpentine and French fat oil. The French fat oil can also be used as a thickener for oil-base, china-painting medium. To thin china-painting medium use oil of lavender or balsam of copaiba.

China paint is not very durable — witness your great-grandmother's teacups, whose carefully applied flowers have worn off — so it is generally used for sculpture, for decorative objects, or on the outer edges of dinner plates, where it will receive less wear.

Lusters and Metallics

Lusters and metallic lusters, like china paints, are usually applied on top of a fired glazed surface. Made from metallic salts, the earliest deliberately induced lusters were those used by Persian potters on top of opaque tin glazes (3-37). The technique they developed spread to Spain with the Moslem expansion and then on to Italy and the rest of Europe. The metallic salts in these early lusters were first painted on the fired tin glaze, then were refired in the heavy reducing atmosphere necessary to develop the luster of the metal. As is still the case, the base glaze on which they were painted had to be capable of becoming soft enough during firing at a low temperature to allow the metals to adhere, but it could not become too molten or the color would be ruined. The Persian methods were used until a new, easier luster technique was developed in France involving liquid gold. Some contemporary ceramists have replicated the ancient Persian and Spanish luster techniques, but nowadays most use commercially prepared lusters whose metals are dissolved in oils that provide a local reducing agent. Although traditionally lusters are used on top of a glaze, some contemporary ceramists use them on unglazed pieces.

TRANSLUCENT LUSTERS   These are known for their shimmering quality, with colors ranging from shades of blue, green, and orange to pinks, gray, purple, maroon, and pearl. Because they are translucent, the color of the glaze on which they are applied tends to show through, making it possible to create sumptuous effects.

METALLIC LUSTERS   These are opaque overglazes available in various shades of gold, platinum, and copper. Because of their opacity, metallics are not greatly affected by the color of the glaze on which they are applied. When the oil burns out in firing, the metal becomes fused to the surface of the glaze. Gold and platinum are also available in pens for writing or fine line decoration.

APPLYING LUSTERS   Apply luster with proper local ventilation to remove the fumes (10-6). Since lusters are easily contaminated, the surface on which you apply them should be clean, dust free, and dry, while the brushes you use for applying lusters and metallics should be clean. Either use a separate brush for each color or plan on cleaning your brush thoroughly between colors with a special nonacetone cleaner.

Mayer Shacter (14-38) uses only one brush, but he cleans the brush thoroughly between colors and finds that

I can use one brush for all the colors, except for yellow and orange. For those I use separate brushes because they are contaminated easily by the other colors.

A little luster goes a long way. Although Shacter uses it directly out of the bottle, most people pour small amounts into a paint-mixing pan or onto an impervious surface such as a glazed dish or the convex bottom of a glass jar. If any is left over when you finish working, you can cover it with plastic wrap to keep it for future use instead of pouring it back into the bottle. This will prevent possible contamination of the luster in the bottle.

If your luster paints need thinning, add gold or luster essence sparingly to make the solution brushable or sprayable. A combination of luster essence and oil of lavender can be added to thin luster paints that may have congealed. For special projects it is often better to buy fresh luster paints rather than try to recondition old ones because old paint may not fire well.

Nowadays, lusters are used not only for decorating pottery and china to give it the luxurious, gleaming look of precious metals, but also to give a distinctive surface to sculptures. Richard Notkin brushed two thick coats of silver-grey luster directly onto the surface of unglazed, vitrified stoneware to achieve a galvanized steel effect on his *Heart Teapot* (13-16), and Mayer Shacter has experimented with layering lusters, producing subtly glowing surfaces on his nonfunctional teapots.

> I started to experiment with lusters, using them in ways in which they normally are not used. Using them directly on my high-fired, unglazed porcelain body, I found that by a simple, though laborious, process of layering—often four or five layers—and a series of cone 018 firings after each layer, that I could get beautiful surfaces and effects that would not have been possible using the luster over a glaze. For example, a darker color like purple or carmine coated with mother of pearl becomes bleached out, creating a totally new shade that you couldn't get with the usual luster. If a color doesn't work as I want, I may paint a metallic luster over it, or I paint a color on top of a metallic. If I get a total disaster, which doesn't happen often, I can high-fire the piece to obliterate the luster completely. Sometimes I paint over the luster with china paint, perhaps applying a polka dot of bright red, or an orange accent. Or I may use a thinned down orange or other color to get a similar though nonlustrous effect.

Shacter's less-than-orthodox methods of using luster are just one more example of how ceramics techniques are developed and changed through experimentation and testing on the part of individual ceramists who approach their work with a spirit of "try it and see." For information on firing lusters, see Chapter 15.

Silk-Screening Overglazes

Using this transfer method of adding color, image, or detail to the surface of your work requires some background in silk screening. When this technique is used for ceramics, the image is screened directly onto a fired and glazed surface. A silk screen usually consists of a fine mesh of real silk or a synthetic held taut in a wooden or metal frame. A stencil is applied onto the screen (see a book on silk screening for the methods) and china paint is applied through the screen with a squeegee. Obviously, this method works only on flat surfaces. However, it is possible to tape unframed, stenciled silk-screen material directly onto curved or irregular ceramic surfaces and then apply the china paint through it. Photo silkscreening methods can also be used with underglaze materials.

Decals

Decals for ceramics are basically images printed with china paint that is held in suspension on a special paper between two layers of decalmania lacquer. To apply a decal to a glazed surface, cut out the chosen decal, soak it in water for 15 seconds, and then slip off the decal and transfer the image to the ceramic surface. Once you apply the decal, be sure to remove any excess water from between the decal and the glazed surface by gently blotting the decal with a paper towel, cloth, or squeegee, beginning at the center and working outward. This will get rid of bubbles caused by too much water or insufficient adhesion of the decal. Improper adhesion or bubbles may cause a **blistered** area when the ware is fired.

You can also make your own decals by silk-screening, painting, or photo-transferring an image with china paint onto special decal paper on which you have first silk-screened a layer of decalmania lacquer. When the china paint has dried, silk screen another layer of decalmania lacquer over the image; then let the decal dry thoroughly before transferring it to the ceramic surface.

Layering Glazes and Overglazes

The work of both Richard Hirsch and Mayer Shacter shows that it is possible to achieve extremely rich surfaces by using layering methods.

The point to remember in using any overglaze technique is that the glaze that fires at the highest temperature should be applied and fired first; then the lower-firing ones can be applied and fired in successively lower firings, one over the other. Working in this way, developing the surface of your work in a continuous process, you can produce a great variety of surface enhancements, as seen in the work of Patrick Loughran (14-39, Color Plate 25), Jindra Viková (14-40), and Benet Ferrer (Color Plate 21). However, before using these overglaze methods, it is a good idea to learn more about the base glazes on which you will use them. Testing is the best way to do that.

GLAZE TESTS

In the early days of ceramics, all glaze formulation was based on trial and error. Learning through their successes and failures, the Chinese potters developed their subtle celadon (Color Plate 1) and brilliant **flambé** glazes (Color Plate 2), the Persian potters created their bright blue-green glazes, and the Europeans perfected colored decoration on tin-glazed earthenware (Color Plate 4). Modern chemistry, however, has given the potter considerable information about the components of glaze materials, and many ceramists use the methods of chemical calculation to analyze their glazes.

Then why test glazes? Despite modern chemical analysis, the ultimate test of a glaze is how it fires, so the ceramist still depends on testing to find out how an individual glaze will respond to a particular clay body in a kiln fired at a certain temperature or in a given kiln atmosphere. Testing on small tiles allows you to change the proportion of a material in the glaze and quickly see what will happen to the glaze as a result (Color Plate 52). Since slight changes in the amount of one ingredient can change a glaze radically, by running tests you can see how these changes will alter the glaze and can gain an understanding of how the chemicals react under controlled conditions. Glaze tests also provide clues that can be useful in formulating special colors and textures or in producing such glaze qualities as viscous or fluid, matt or glossy. The clues to glaze-material behavior that you pick up while doing these tests on tiles in small test kilns will help you when you come to mixing a full batch of the glaze. Remember, however, that the same glaze applied to a larger work and fired in a different kiln may vary from the small tests. The length of firing time, thickness of the clay, position of the glazed work in the kiln, presence of any residues of oxides as dust in the kiln or absorbed into the kiln bricks from a previous firing, and even the fumes burning off from other glazed ware in the kiln can all affect the outcome of the final glaze firing. As you gain a greater understanding of glaze components and how they react under test conditions, you will be better able to predict how a tested glaze will fire on larger objects in a regular kiln in varying atmospheres. As you test, keep a notebook to record the formulas and the results of each test. Susanne Ashmore, one of whose teapots won a top prize in Japan, says,

> I do many glaze tests but I do not formulate my own glazes. I will find a base formula with certain characteristics and run a series of colour tests with different percentages and combinations.

(See Appendix 1C for two examples of glazes Ashmore has tested.)

Formulating Test Glazes

The glazes for tests are generally formulated in batches ranging from 100 grams to 500 grams of dry glaze materials.

To conduct a series of tests, first form test tiles out of the clay body to be glazed. One way to make test tiles is to cut a slab into a series of rectangles and then bend these into L-shaped tiles. You can also throw a low cylinder and slice it into sections. Either type of tile will stand up, allowing you to see how the glaze acts on a vertical surface, or you can fire flat tiles in a rack. Bisque-fire the test tiles after punching a hole in the top so that you can hang the tile for easy reference.

Test by changing an ingredient a small amount at a time — in increments of .5% to 5% — fire the tiles, and record the temperature, the placement in the kiln, and the kiln atmosphere in your notebook. It is also a good idea to write the proportions on the tile itself with an underglaze pencil or with oxide. In this way, you can go back over your records and compare test results.

Appendix 1A contains some cone 05, cone 5, and cone 10 glazes formulated for *Hands in Clay* for testing on the white clay body you already have tested. These are simple glazes, easy for a beginner to use, and they contain no toxic materials. If you follow through the process of testing and altering the clays and glazes given in Appendix 1A, you will develop a basic understanding of the composition of clays and glazes and their relationship to each other. The equipment chart in Figure 14-42 shows the equipment used in both testing and glaze mixing.

Mixing a Glaze for Tests

Wearing a respirator and following the precautions given at the beginning of this chapter, mix at least a 100-gram batch of your selected glaze. Avoid mixing smaller batches because the possibility of measuring errors increases in small batches. Through these small tests, you will gain clues to the behavior of the components. Then, when you have narrowed the formulas down to one or two from which you might want to make a glaze, you can test 500 gram batches in which you refine each glaze by changing the percentage of certain chemicals, by eliminating some chemicals, or by adding others.

If you use oxides such as cobalt, iron, chromium, copper, or nickel for color in the final batches of glaze, you may have to grind the oxides with a mortar and pestle or put them through a ball mill to reduce the particle size. This will eliminate the possibility that streaks of color may mar the fired glaze. Of course, you may like the streaky effect or specks of color, in which case you need not grind the oxides.

To mix the batch, weigh out the dry ingredients with a balance gram scale (14-43) and add the water, using the proportion given in the table in Appendix 1A. Put this mixture through a **sieve** with a number 50 to 80 mesh. For the small amount of glaze you are making for tests, mix the ingredients by shaking the glaze in a small covered container. Repeat this mixing each time you use the glaze so that you always keep the glaze materials in suspension. Brush some of the base glaze mixture on a tile (or dip it), fire the test tiles, and note the results.

Color Tests

To find out exactly what effect a certain oxide has on the color of a glaze, test it by making changes in its proportions in the glaze. Remember, however, that an oxide that produces a certain color alone may give a totally different color in combination with another oxide. A striking example is cobalt, which alone in certain glazes will yield a brilliant blue, but in combination with vanadium can give a mustardy yellow. Because oxides interact, we recommend that at first you test only one coloring oxide or stain at a time. In addition to causing color changes through interaction, one oxide may burn out in the kiln at a particular temperature while another may hold its color intensity. The kiln atmosphere—whether oxidizing or reducing—also has an important effect on the color, with each oxide reacting differently to varying kiln atmospheres. As an example of the various colors that just one oxide can produce, consider the range of iron. It can yield creams, yellows, red-browns, and also the gray-greens so popular in ancient China, and it can also produce the black and brown tenmoku glaze.

The glaze color that each oxide will produce will also vary depending on the color of the clay body under it, on how finely the oxide was ground, on how the glaze was applied, and on the temperature, duration, and kiln atmosphere of the firing.

You can see from these examples that there are so many factors involved in color formation, the only way you can be sure of how an oxide will perform is to test it in *your* glaze, on *your* clay, in *your* kiln, or even in one area of your kiln. Working in this way is a lengthy process, but it will add to your understanding and control of your glazes. By testing one oxide at a time, changing its proportions for each test, you will get a good idea of how certain colors develop in glazes. Later, when you have tested the single oxides given in Appendix 1A, you can test several oxides in combination. To test for black, for example, you would use cobalt, iron, and chromium according to the percentages given in the charts.

Not only do all the components making up a glaze affect the color, but the earth elements present in the oxides and clay can vary depending on where they were mined and the industrial processing they have undergone. An anecdote will highlight this situation. One ceramist found color tone differences in batches of glaze stain from a supplier, although they were all labeled with the same name and number. When he asked the salesman why the color varied so much, the man replied, "Oh, the wind could have been blowing hard that day, affecting the heat of the processing

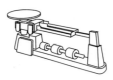

Triple beam scale

For precision weighing of oxides, stains, and chemicals, and for test batches. Capacity approximately 2,600 gm (5.72 lb).

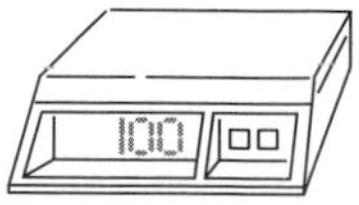

Digital scale

Fast and accurate scale for weighing small quantities of material with a total weight capacity of approximately 2,000 gm (4.40 lb). Electronic scale also operable by battery.

Spring scale

Portable scale for weighing bulk chemicals in the 1–100 lb (.45–45 kg) range.

Package scale

For weighing bulk materials in the 5–25 lb (2.27–11.35 kg) range.

Platform scale

Outfitted with wheels for easy maneuverability. Large platform for weighing bulk materials in the 50–100 lb (22.7–45.4 kg) range. Capacity 1,000 lb (454 kg).

Cup and spoon

For mixing small test batches of glaze.

Mixing bowls and containers

Bowls and containers (16 oz to 5 gal [.5 to 19 L]).

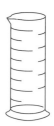

Graduated cylinder

Marked in ounces and milliliters for accurate measuring of water, sodium silicates, other electrolytes, and liquids.

Mortar and pestle

Grinds oxides, glaze stains, chemicals, and both wet and dry glaze test batches. For reducing and refining particle size of chemicals.

Ball mill

Mill has porcelain jar and high alumina pebbles or porcelain balls for grinding oxides, frits, chemicals, and both wet and dry glazes.

Kitchen blender

Efficiently mixes small glaze batches or tests in quantities from 4 to 24 oz (.12 to .7 L).

Drill mixer

Variable speed hand-held electric drill with mixer blades of various sizes for mixing from 4 oz to 5 gal (.12 to 19 L) batches of glaze or slip.

Rapid mixer

Fits over a 5 gal (19 L) bucket. Good for mixing 2 to 4 gal (8 to 15 L) glaze batches.

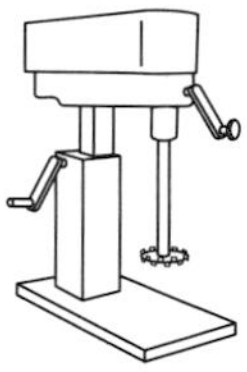

Dispersion blender

Professional high-speed blender for mixing glaze in volumes from 1 to 50 gal (4 to 190 L). Mixes glazes to homogeneous solution.

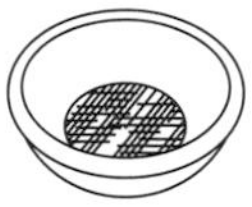

Sieve

Brass or stainless steel mesh sieve for screening dry materials, glazes, and slip (30–120 mesh).

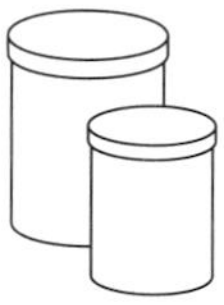

Jars

Plastic jars with lids 4 to 16 oz (.12 to .5 L) for water-base compounds when mixing small test batches. Glass jars with solvent-resistant lids for storing oil-base compounds.

Figure 14-42
Here is the equipment you will use as you prepare your own glazes. Some of the equipment is basic, whereas some is for more advanced use or for large-quantity preparation.

Figure 14-43
A balance scale is essential for proper measuring of glaze ingredients. Be sure to place it on a level surface. When handling dry glaze materials, you should have good local ventilation and wear a respirator. Wear rubber gloves when handling toxic materials.

furnace and that could have affected the color." Thus, to get color consistency in one's work over a period of time, you would need to purchase enough of a material to ensure that all components of your glaze remain the same for a reasonable period of time. This is especially important if you are going to construct a large mural or make a dinner set that requires a consistent color.

Running a Series of Color Tests

Taking as an example the *Hands in Clay* cone 05 base test glaze in Appendix 1A, start your color testing. Use tiles made of the cone 05 white clay body given in Appendix 1A. The recipe for the base glaze in percentage is:

Frit 3195 (3811)	88	88 grams
Kaolin (Georgia)	10	10 grams
Bentonite	2	2 grams
	100%	100 grams

Mix this according to the directions on page 330, adding water in the proportion given in the table in Appendix 1A. A batch mixed with 100 grams of glaze material and water will give you about 4 ounces (118 milliliters) of glaze, an adequate amount for this test. If you want to convert the percentage recipe to other amounts, such as ounces

or even pounds, you can use the table in Appendix 2B.

Mix the 100-gram batch; then dip or brush it on a test tile and mark it cone 05 base glaze. Set this tile aside to be fired. For the first colorant, add cobalt. Because cobalt is such a strong colorant, add it in extremely small increments of ½ gram. When you test the other colors you can add them in larger increments.

Next, to the base glaze mixture, add ½ gram cobalt. Dip or brush a tile and mark it .5% cobalt.

Repeat this three more times, adding cobalt in ½-gram increments and marking these tiles 1, 1.5, and 2% cobalt. Fire the tiles at cone 05 in oxidation and see how the changes in the cobalt content affect the glaze.

Continue the testing process with new tiles, adding the other coloring oxides in increments up to the percentage given in the table for the cone 05 test glaze in Appendix 1A. When you finish testing the cone 05 glaze, continue testing through the cone 5 and cone 10 glazes, firing them to the appropriate cones. You may want to fire both glazes in reduction to see what effect that has on the glaze. By the time you have worked through these tests, you will have a good understanding of glaze materials and you can move on to test some of the glazes from other ceramists in Appendix 1C.

Out of the many tests you do, you may get only one glaze that you like, but in the process you will learn a great deal about colorants that will help you analyze all your glazes when they come out of the fire. Eventually, you will build up a body of knowledge that one day will enable you to look at a glaze test and know just why it was successful or what you can do to refine it.

In these tests, you have changed the colorants. In Appendix 3A, you will find an example of changing and testing the flux in a high-fire glaze. After working through that, if you want to go into the subject of calculating glazes using chemical analysis, see the section on that in Appendix 3B.

Line Blend Testing

Line blend testing is another method of testing glazes. It is especially useful for developing shades of a color for low- to high-fire glazes. Testing is done by methodically blending the proportions of various materials in two glazes. For example, as one glaze is increased by 10%, the other is decreased by 10%. You can test any low- to high-fire

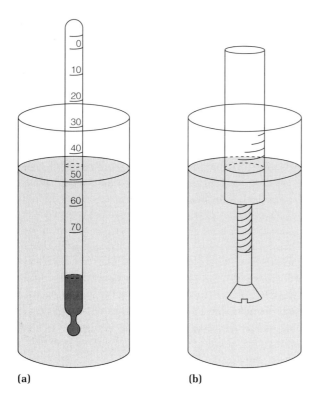

(a)   **(b)**

Figure 14-44
A hydrometer measures the specific gravity of liquids. Ceramists use it to calibrate and monitor the correct amount of water in a glaze or slip, which affects its suspension and viscosity. After mixing your glaze or slip properly for application, gently drop the hydrometer into the liquid **(a)** and note the number on the scale at the top of the liquid. This number is the specific gravity. Monitoring this number will allow you to calibrate and replace the correct amount of water as it evaporates from the glaze or slip. **(b)** When your glazes and slips are properly formulated for application, you can make a nonbreakable Jeff Johnson hydrometer that is calibrated to a specific container for each liquid. Simply cut a ½ in. (8 mm) diameter dowel to 4 in. (10 cm) in length. Insert a 2 in. (5 cm) long screw, ¼ in. (6 mm) deep at one end of the dowel. Now gently drop it screw side down into your glaze or slip, and draw or cut a line on the dowel at the flotation point. Label the Johnson hydrometer for each liquid, and use it for that glaze or slip only. It will tell how much water to add when it evaporates. If the line you marked is above the top of the liquid, that means evaporation has taken place and you need to add more water. If the line drops below the surface, then you added too much water.

glaze in this manner. By conducting line blend testing using the *Hands in Clay* glaze formulas in Appendix 1A, you will be able to achieve a wide range of colors and glazes with various firing ranges. A sample line blend test in that appendix takes you through the process.

MIXING GLAZES

Now that you have carried out some tests, have decided on a glaze, and are ready to glaze some pieces, you will need to mix your glaze in a batch big enough to coat them. The chart (14-42) shows the equipment for mixing glazes in small or large batches mentioned in the following paragraphs. Mixing is a relatively simple process, but be sure to read the precautions at the beginning of this chapter before you mix. Use a balance scale to measure the dry ingredients, making sure that you set it on a level surface. Weigh out the dry ingredients and add them to the water. (See Appendix 1A for suggested glaze–water ratio.) Put the mixture through a sieve with number 50 to 80 mesh; then if necessary add water until the glaze is the right consistency for dipping or brushing. Adding gum powder (.5 to 1%) to a brushing glaze will make it thicker, so you may have to add more water. When you dip a test tile or an object in a glaze and a lot of **pinholes** develop on it, the mixture may be too thick. In that case, you will need to add more water. Using a **hydrometer** (14-44) to measure the water content will make it easier to keep it constant so that the glaze will have the same consistency at all times.

Use a container large enough to allow you to mix comfortably. You can mix batches of less than a gallon with a stick, paddle, or kitchen wire whip; old kitchen blenders have also been used with excellent results for small batches. For batches of more than one gallon (3.785 liters) an electric paint mixer can be a help, but since thorough blending of glaze components often takes ten to twenty minutes, a mixer on a stand is easier to use than one you have to hold. Ball mills can mix glaze materials in the dry or wet state, with the added advantage that they will grind the particles to a very small size. If you do not use a ball mill, screen the mixture through a 50 to 80 mesh sieve in order to eliminate lumps and coarse particles. This is especially important if the glaze is going to be sprayed, as larger particles clog the spray-gun tip. A high-speed **dispersion**

blender with a special blade that creates a vortex effect refines the particles even further than an ordinary mixer does and prepares the glaze quickly and thoroughly, blending it rather than mixing it. A glaze blended with this type of mixer will stay in suspension better and melt more evenly in the kiln, because the particle size will be finer and more homogeneous throughout. Whatever method you use to mix the glaze, it is extremely important to see that the glaze ingredients stay in suspension rather than falling to the bottom.

Occasionally, however, the heavy material *will* settle on the bottom. If you have that problem, consider doing the following with your next batch. After weighing the proper amount of water, mix the most glutinous materials first—such as the suspending agents, macaloid, bentonite, or gum. (See Appendix 1B for percentages of these materials to add.) Using hot water may help too. Once these materials are well blended, add the clay—such as kaolin or ball clay—followed by feldspar, frits, opacifiers, oxides, and other components, in that order.

Glazes that contain either CMC or gum tragacanth as a binder for brushing may decompose over time, and as they do, the gum, which also acts as a suspending agent, will lose its effectiveness and cause the glaze to smell like rotting plants. The glaze may also turn dark. This will affect only the suspension and brushing qualities. Although it is possible to slow decomposition by adding formaldehyde or Dowicide G, since both of these substances can affect your health adversely, we recommend instead that you mix only the amount of glaze you will use in a reasonably short period of time. In that way, you will not have to use antispoilants.

APPLYING GLAZES

You probably will be applying the glaze to bisque-fired ware. Although it is perfectly possible to apply a glaze to greenware and give it just one firing, in general glazes fire more satisfactorily when they have been applied to bisque-fired ware, so it is best to put your work through a first firing before applying the glaze.

The bisque ware should be free of dust and grease. Handle it with clean hands to prevent leaving oily fingerprints that will resist the glaze. Wipe the ware off with a damp sponge or rinse it quickly under a tap to dampen it slightly, and clean off the dust. This will also keep it from absorbing too much glaze. Experienced potters can mix glazes to a consistency that does not require the pot to be damp, and they can often dip or pour expertly enough to dispense with damping, but for the less experienced it is usually better to dampen first.

In the kiln, the glaze can run off the bottom of a pot, actually fusing it to the kiln shelf with glaze, often making it impossible to remove the pot without breakage. To avoid this, either dip the bottom and a minimum of 3/16 inch (5 mm) up the sides of a pot in melted wax or a wax resist before glazing, or clean the glaze off this area with a sponge after applying the glaze. Alternatively, prior to glazing, Ross Spangler (15-8), dips the feet of his pots into an oil-based water sealer. After this dries, he dips the ware in the glaze.

Which method of applying glaze you will choose depends on personal preference, on the object you are glazing, on the type of glaze used, and on the effect you wish to create on the fired piece.

Dipping

Dipping a bisque-fired piece in a bucket of glaze is one way to apply the glaze (14-45). Each person will work out a glaze consistency and method of dipping that is most comfortable or efficient. Some dip only once, others mix the glaze thinner and double dip, a process that will cover any pinholes that may appear in the first coat. Wear rubber gloves, or use tongs (14-46) to dip the piece in the glaze. How long you immerse the piece in the glaze—usually only a few seconds—and how long you let it dry between dips if you double dip will also affect the way the glaze will turn out. Any marks remaining from holding the piece can be covered by touching up with a brush, but if you hold the piece carefully by the very bottom while dipping, this should not be necessary. After dipping, shake the piece to get rid of the excess.

Pouring

You can get interesting effects by pouring more than one glaze on the exterior of a piece or by pouring glaze on only part, allowing some of the clay body or another glaze to show through

Figure 14-45
Larry Murphy hand-dips a stoneware teapot into a bucket of glaze. The length of time a piece is held in the glaze and the amount of time allowed between double dips are individual choices, determined by experience. Although Murphy is not wearing gloves, we recommend that you wear them when dipping to protect your hands from glaze materials.

Figure 14-46
Dipping with tongs eliminates the need for rubber gloves and guarantees full immersion in the glaze. Ron Judd dips a wax-resist–treated plate in a third glaze. The small marks left by tongs can be touched up with a brush.

Figure 14-47
By pouring glazes you can cover your work with a single glaze, or achieve decorative effects by pouring one glaze over another.

(14-47). Pouring is also the most efficient way to coat the interior of tall, narrow vases (14-48), and it is also a good way to glaze the inside of a bowl with a glaze different from that on the outside.

Glazes for pouring are usually mixed for one- or two-coat application. If you use a glaze that has been mixed for brushing, you will need to thin it for pouring.

Brushing

When brushing on a glaze with a wide brush, you can control the thickness of the coat you apply, but it is sometimes difficult to get the coats even. On the other hand, you may be more comfortable using a brushing technique because it is similar to painting and allows you to vary the brush-strokes or their thickness, to alter textural qualities, or to paint accents on certain areas (14-49). Usually, brushing a glaze evenly requires at least two coats, each applied after the previous coat is dry—which normally takes only a few minutes.

You can also use brushing to add a second or third glaze and to apply decoration over the glaze. You can also trail a second glaze or an oxide over a glaze with a slip syringe (14-15).

(a)

(b)

Figure 14-48
Pouring allows glaze to penetrate into the interior of a narrow vase. **(a)** To lighten the interior color, Judd pours light matt glaze over one coat of Albany slip.
(b) The vase must be turned constantly to ensure even application as the glaze coats the interior then is poured out.

Figure 14-49
Reuben Kent, U.S.A., glazing one of his bisque-fired sculptures. *Some pieces,* he says, *will be glazed with up to five to seven glazes. Not all glaze combinations are compatible with each other. Some are not esthetically pleasing so that the result is pretty uncontrollable.* Raku and sculpture clay with fine sifted grog. (See also 15-30.) *Courtesy the artist.*

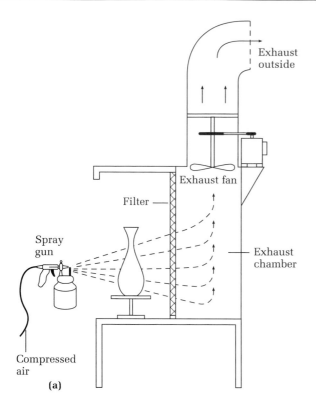

(a)

(b)

Figure 14-50

(a) A spray booth works on a simple principle of exhaust, with a filter to catch the glaze overspray. Even if you have access to a booth, wear adequate protection when you spray. **(b)** Spraying outdoors may be necessary if the piece is too big for your booth. Here, Jeff Johnson, U.S.A., sprays glaze outdoors with a siphon-feed spray gun operating with forty pounds of air pressure. Be sure the wind is blowing away from you, and wear a respirator, gloves, and goggles when spraying toxic or irritating materials.

Spraying

Before **air compressors** and **spray guns** were developed, potters sprayed glazes or areas of glaze onto their pottery by blowing them through a wooden or metal tube—exposing themselves to hazardous glaze materials. Now that we have spray guns, air brushes, and ventilated spray booths and respirators, we can protect ourselves more fully from the glaze materials. Preferably, do *all* spraying in a booth (14-50a) and wearing a mist-rated respirator (10-6). If the piece is too large, however, to fit in a booth, then glaze it outdoors with the wind blowing the spray *away* from you (14-50b). Wear a respirator and goggles so that if there is any back spray it doesn't get in your eyes; this is especially important for contact lens wearers. Before spraying, reread the precautions about using glaze materials.

Spray guns are useful for spraying glazes, engobes, and slips where a wide fanning spray is required to cover the piece and for fast coverage of a large area. Spraying allows you to develop gradations in color, but it takes practice to learn to spray the glaze on evenly, building up the coating gradually. Glazes for spraying should be well sieved or ball milled so that coarse particles will not clog up the spray-gun orifices. Usually, ten to forty pounds of air pressure will pull the glaze through the spray gun.

Use air brushes for spraying oxides, ceramic stains, underglazes, lusters, and china paints, and for detail work over small areas (14-25 to 14-28). As with spray guns, the material must be sieved, ground fine with a mortar and pestle or in a ball mill. When using oxides or stains in an air brush, you can add a small amount of gum solution to help them stay in suspension and adhere to the object's surface. The gum-solution recipe is in Appendix 1A.

Various orifice sizes are available for spray guns and air brushes. The coarser and more viscous the material the larger the orifice it will require. The type of glaze material and the tip size will also affect the amount of air pressure needed to pull it through the brush; ten to twenty pounds will usually suffice.

Resist Methods

You can achieve many decorative effects by covering sections of a piece with commercial wax-resist compounds, latex, or other resistant materials. The covered areas will repel the glaze when the piece is dipped or poured. You can mask off areas with paper or tape so that parts of the clay body will remain unglazed, or use stencils through which to spray a contrasting image or pattern onto an already glazed area (14-51 to 14-54). There are resist materials available that do not require heating; thus, they are safer to use. If you use an electric skillet to heat wax-resist material, keep the skillet set to the lowest possible temperature that will keep the wax melted.

Figure 14-51
Brushed-on and resist decoration on glazed ware by Eric Norstad, U.S.A. Norstad's high-fire domestic ware is made in his production pottery workshop where tableware is produced in series—somewhat standardized for control but keeping the quality of individually produced pottery. *Courtesy the artist.*

Figure 14-52
Jeff Irwin, U.S.A., treats his plates much as a painter would a canvas—as a ground for images that express his responses to various issues and environments, or that narrate stories. *Courtesy the artist.*

◄ **Figure 14-53**
In *Spontaneous Combustion,* 1989, Jeff Irwin used a number of materials and techniques—underglaze, vitreous engobes, wax resist, glazes, and acrylic sealer—in varying combinations to achieve the black and white wood-block-like images on his hump-molded plates. He now uses vitreous engobe instead of underglaze, because it gives a smoother, satin sheen on the surfaces. He also uses *. . . non-brush-like items such as string and sponges to apply the wax resist and develop different kinds of textures. To create the thin black lines that look like a pen mark I scrape away the wax with a sharp tool and then fill in the area with a vitreous slip.* Once-fired earthenware, underglaze, glaze. Diam. 22 in. (56 cm). *Courtesy the artist.*

Figure 14-54
Gary Holt, U.S.A., formed this platter from a slab, then decorated it with a latex-resist technique. Shino glaze, sprayed with various glazes over it. 1991. Stoneware. Diam. 19½ in. (50 cm). *Courtesy the artist. Photo: Richard Sargent.*

READY TO FIRE

Assuming that you have chosen one of the methods of applying glaze discussed in this section, you are now ready to fire your work. The next chapter discusses loading the kiln, firing temperatures, duration, and kiln atmospheres, all of which affect your glaze.

When you finally take your fired piece out of the kiln, you may be very happy with the glaze or you may see things in it you want to expand on or refine. This is the time to go back over your records, study your tests, and ask yourself some questions. It is only by understanding what happened in the kiln that you can build up a knowledge of glazes that will allow you to go further into this fascinating subject with understanding.

COMMON GLAZE PROBLEMS

If you have problems with a glaze, it is important to study and analyze your formula, and later your fired glazed pieces, to try to determine why a particular defect appeared when the glaze was fired. Since the way the glaze was formulated, the way it was applied, and the way it was fired may *all* contribute to the problem, it is often difficult to know just what went wrong. To figure out which factor or factors may have caused the problem, it helps to look back over each step in the process leading up to and including the firing. Asking yourself the questions in the following checklist may help you to find the answer:

- *Check the original formula.* Was the glaze correctly weighed and mixed?
- *Were there any chemical substitutions?* This is often the key to defects and is often overlooked.
- *Was the clay body changed since previous tests?* This could affect the color or the fluxing of the glaze.
- *Was the test glaze applied to a different clay body?* Perhaps you used a slightly different clay body than the one you used for your tests.
- *To which cone or temperature was the ware bisque-fired?* If it was bisqued too low (015 to 010), that could cause pinholes to form. Refire at a higher bisque temperature.
- *Were there changes in the glaze firing pattern?* Did you give it a longer or shorter firing?

- *What about the placement of the ware in the kiln?* Where was it placed? In a cooler or hotter area?
- *What was the kiln shelf pattern like?* Were the shelves tightly packed or loosely stacked? This can affect the heat rise and cooling of the kiln, which in turn will affect the glaze.
- *What type of fuel was used?* Was it changed or altered?
- *What was fired in the kiln previously?* Clays or glazes containing oxides such as copper can affect a glaze in the next firing because traces remain in the kiln.
- *Does the glaze look thin or washed out?* The glaze mixture may have been thinned to the point where the glaze materials settled. Thus, when you applied the glaze you did not apply all the components equally.

With all these factors in mind, look at the defects that may have appeared on your pieces and see if you can figure out what happened.

Glaze Defects

CRAZING Several factors can cause fine cracks to develop in a fired glaze. For example, **crazing** may be caused by incompatibility between the glaze and clay body owing to different rates of expansion and contraction. Altering the clay body may solve the problem. On the other hand, one person's defect may be another person's decorative effect; then the crazing is called crackle. Chinese potters appreciated the surface cracks and deliberately increased certain ingredients in order to produce them, learning to control the spacing of the cracks, and often rubbing color into them for emphasis. Crazing is characteristic of low-fire alkaline glazes.

CRAWLING This defect can occur when there are fingerprints, dust, oil, or grease on the bisque-fired ware, or when the unfired glaze shrinks as it dries. **Crawling,** where glazed areas alternate with areas of bare clay, can also be caused by starting to fire when the glaze is not completely dry or by adding too much of certain materials with high shrinkage rates, such as zinc oxide, to the glaze. The presence of certain ingredients, such as colemanite, that give off gases when they reach high temperatures in the kiln can also cause pinholes and craters, which in turn may cause the glaze to crawl. Opaque glazes that are more viscous than transparent ones are more prone to crawl. Crawling can also occur when a glaze is applied over areas painted with underglaze, especially if the underglaze has been applied thickly. A low-fire glaze applied to a high-fire porcelain bisque may peel after it is applied or crawl when it is fired owing to differing shrinkage rates. This can sometimes be remedied by adding a few drops of **electrolyte** (Darvan #7) to the glaze.

PINHOLES AND PITS Sometimes pinholes and pits are caused by applying glaze to a bisque that is too porous so that during firing, air or moisture escaping from the pores of the clay body may cause these holes to develop in the glaze as the vapor bursts through it. Also during firing, tiny gas bubbles form while the clay body and glaze components break down in the heat, sometimes causing pinholes and pits to come through the glaze and burst on the surface. Tiny pinholes sometimes also appear in glaze that has been intentionally underfired to achieve a matt effect. Too much zinc oxide or rutile can also cause pits in a glaze. Bisque-firing to a higher temperature, adding more flux, applying the glaze less thickly, increasing the heat, soaking the kiln, or lengthening the firing may all help to prevent pinholes.

BLISTERING In blistering, the surface looks like a magnified photo of the moon's surface with many little craters. It is usually caused by gases escaping from a glaze that was fired too rapidly; by applying the glaze too thickly; or, in some low-fire glazes containing frit, by firing them above cone 6.

Refiring Additional Glazes

An already glazed piece that is to be coated with a second or third coat of glaze in order to reglaze it can be warmed first in the kiln to ensure that the glaze will be dry. Adding a small amount of gum to the second glaze will also help the additional glaze to adhere. When reglazing and refiring high-fire pottery, it is often necessary to reglaze the inside of a pot, as well as the outside, with one thin coat. This helps to equalize the tensions created on the piece by the second glaze and thus to prevent cracking of the ware on refiring.

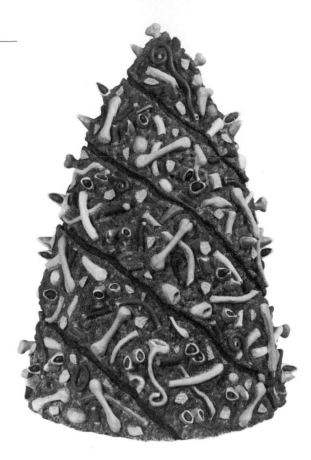

Figure 14-55
Shell, by Burton Isenstein, U.S.A. Isenstein studied biology before becoming a ceramist, and many of his works reflect his interest in nature. His sculpture is formed of porcelain, then painted after firing with alkyd oil paint in natural, although not necessarily realistic, colors. 1986. Porcelain. *Courtesy the artist. Photo: Tom Van Eynde.*

If you continue to study and analyze your glazes as you remove your ware from the kiln, you will find that your control over this important aspect of ceramics will increase, and as your knowledge expands so will your satisfaction. You will then be able to concentrate on the form or the image, using, if you wish, many of the techniques shown in this chapter.

POSTFIRING COLOR

If, after trying some glazes, you find that finishing your nonfunctional objects or sculpture with glaze is not for you, then there is no reason why you cannot do as many artists do — use paint. There is nothing new about using paint on fired clay. In fifteenth-century Italy, religious figures sculpted by Dell'Arca and other artists were coated with a thin coat of **gesso** and then painted very realistically, as were many of the terra-cotta portrait busts by such sculptors as Verrocchio in the sixteenth century. Acrylic paints, stains, oil paints, enamels—any coloring material you would use on wood or canvas—may give you just the surface you want on your sculpture or nonfunctional vessel. Louise McGinley, for example (8-17), never glazes her work but uses acrylic paint either watered down to a transparent stain or left thick for opaque areas. M. C. Richards is now painting on canvas, along with continuing to make pots. Her painting experience has led her to use acrylics in a painterly manner on her pots after they are fired (Color Plate 31). Burton Isenstein (14-55) and Beverly Mayeri (9-13) also paint their fired work with nonceramic colors. On the other hand, Clayton Bailey can thank the kiln for an appropriate addition to the surface of his face pot (14-58).

OTHER SURFACES

Some ceramists—Jamie Walker, Gertraud Möhwald, and Beth Thomas (14-56, 14-57), among others—apply ceramic shards or mosaics to their

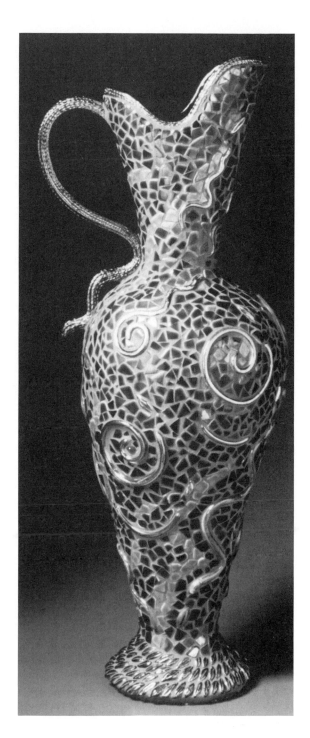

Figure 14-56
Gertraud Möhwald, Germany, develops a rich surface on her sculptures by applying shards of glazed pottery, contrasting their glossy colors with the roughly textured clay. 1986. Stoneware, porcelain, oxides, and glaze. Ht. 21¾ in. (55 cm). *Courtesy the artist and Galerie Schneider.*

Figure 14-57
The vessel *Athena's Bluer Ewer,* by Beth Thomas, U.S.A., is *dedicated to the goddess Athena for her wisdom in saving the ocean.* Thomas sees her mosaic-encrusted vessels as metaphorical medicine bottles for spiritual healing, protection, and survival. She says, *I am interested in surface as the place where inner and outer meet,* so after bisque, glaze, and luster firing, she coats her vessels with broken and sometimes lustered commercial and handmade ceramic mosaic tiles, using ceramic adhesives and colored grouts. 1991. Ht. 29 in. (74 cm). *Courtesy the artist.*

sculptures or constructions somewhat in the manner of the Spanish architects Antonio Gaudí and Josep Maria Jugol. Aurore Chabot (Color Plate 20) inlays leather-hard fragments on her forms and uses terra sigillata, underglazes, and glazes in multiple firings to create her intricate surfaces. Others sandblast their glazed pieces in order to change the surface of the glaze. If you do this, be sure to do it only in an isolated area with good ventilation and wearing a respirator.

Now that the definition of an appropriate ceramic finish has been expanded in these ways, you are free to explore and experiment with the surface of your work in any way you wish.

Figure 14-58
Face Jug, by Clayton Bailey, U.S.A. Inspired by the jugs made by African-American potters in the 1880s (7-4), Bailey created this jug and fired it, and when it came from the kiln he saw it winking at him — a kiln speck had landed in its eye: The kiln works its will. 1991. Pink stoneware and porcelain. 8 in. (20 cm). *Photo: the artist.*

15

Firing

Considering the destructive aspects of fire and its ability to transform clay and metal, it is not surprising that early humans believed that fire was a gift from the gods, or that in many early cultures metal workers and potters were considered to be magical or supernatural beings. From the ancient Greeks to contemporary Native Americans, many peoples have created myths in which gods or goddesses teach humanity how to shape metal and harden clay with fire. Even today in ceramics studios you will usually see a handformed kiln god or goddess seated atop the kiln — a symbol of fire's power, a protective spirit for the ware being fired (15-1).

Is it really true that the fire controls the outcome of your hours of work? Yes and no. It depends a great deal on the type of clay you use, the type of glaze, and the type of kiln, as well as on your approach to firing. There are those who believe in giving a considerable amount of control to the fire, enjoying the unexpected effects it can create on the contents of the kiln, and responding to the sense of adventure that type of firing gives them. Others are more concerned with retaining their original conceptions, so they try to regulate the firing as much as possible.

STARTING TO FIRE

If you carried out the clay-body and glaze tests recommended in Chapters 10 to 14, you have al-

Figure 15-1
Peter Coussoulis, U.S.A., adjusting the dampers on a kiln at the Walnut Creek Civic Arts Studio. Mary Law used this 30-cubic-foot (.85-cubic-meter) catenary arch updraft kiln for the salt/sodium bicarbonate vapor firing illustrated in Figures 15-19 to 15-21.
Courtesy the artist and the City of Walnut Creek, California, Civic Arts Education Program, Walnut Creek Civic Arts Center. Photo: David Hanney.

ready had some experience with a kiln. Firing clay tests, however, although interesting, hardly gives one the same satisfaction as firing one's own pot or sculpture. So, let's suppose that now, after many hours of work, you have a hollow piece of sculpture ready to fire or a glaze-coated pot waiting to be miraculously transformed from a chalky gray to rich, glossy color. You have been told that the fire makes its own demands and imposes its own limits, and that it will transform—or destroy—your carefully shaped creation. After investing so many hours of time and effort, you may be apprehensive about what the kiln will do to your pot or sculpture, and you may approach the

firing with some trepidation. If you are working in a school situation, you will often place your glazed piece on a shelf, go off to other classes, and come back a few days later to find the pot fired. But even if you get no nearer to the firing than this, it is important for you to know what happens in the kiln, because in ceramics everything works together—clay, glaze, and heat interact so that any change in one area of the kiln affects the others. It is important to recognize this, for it means that the aesthetics of ceramics continues through the firing process.

Firing Ranges of Clays

How your pot or sculpture will look when it leaves the kiln depends not only on the type of clay body with which you built it and the glaze with which you may have coated it. It also depends on the fuel that you used in the kiln and on how high a temperature your kiln can reach burning that fuel.

The type of clay used dictates to a considerable extent the temperature at which finished work is fired. Early earthenware pottery, for example, was usually fired only once to a low temperature, generally in an open fire or a rudimentary kiln (15-2). Depending on the heat and duration of the firing, the ware—pots or sculpture—was either heated barely beyond the sun-dried state or its low-fire clay was brought to maturity—for most earthenwares this would be about 920°F/510°C. Later, however, when it was discovered that certain clays became more dense and vitreous at higher temperatures, and high-firing glazes were developed, kilns and their firing became more complex (15-3 to 15-6, 15-10). Today, a bewildering number of firing choices are available to a ceramist. These range from single firing, in which dry greenware is placed in a kiln that is slowly brought up to the desired temperature, to multiple firings, in which a piece may be given a bisque firing, then a high firing, and possibly additional successive low firings to mature layers of overglaze.

Some examples of the temperature ranges of modern commercial clay bodies include low-fire clays that begin to get hard but not mature at cone 015 (1479°F/804°C) and mature from cone 06 (1830°F/999°C) to cone 1 (2109°F/1154°C); medium-range clays that fire between cone 2 (2124°F/1162°C) and 7 (2264°F/1240°C); high-fire

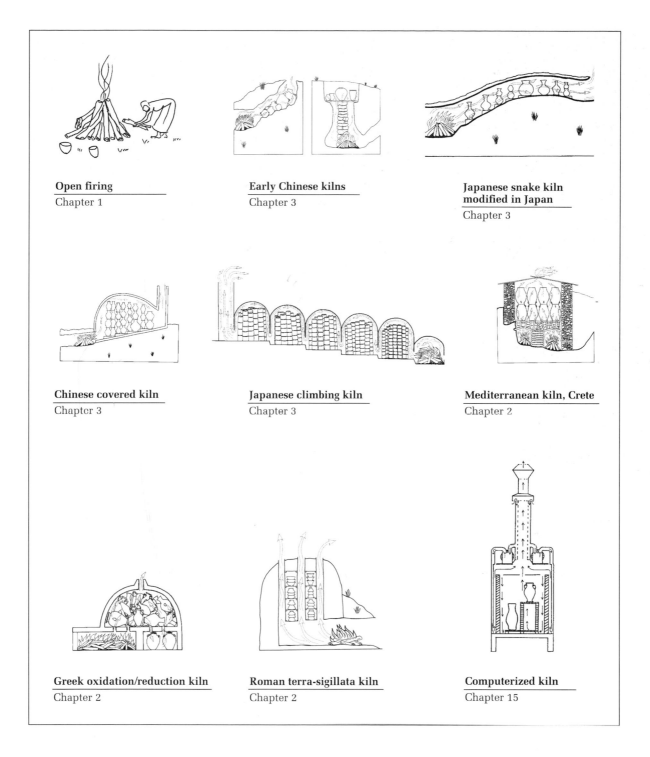

Open firing
Chapter 1

Early Chinese kilns
Chapter 3

Japanese snake kiln modified in Japan
Chapter 3

Chinese covered kiln
Chapter 3

Japanese climbing kiln
Chapter 3

Mediterranean kiln, Crete
Chapter 2

Greek oxidation/reduction kiln
Chapter 2

Roman terra-sigillata kiln
Chapter 2

Computerized kiln
Chapter 15

Figure 15-2
The chart shows some of the developments in firing technology throughout history from open firing through various forms of up, down, and multi-draft kilns, to today's electric and gas computerized kilns. More information is available in the chapters listed.

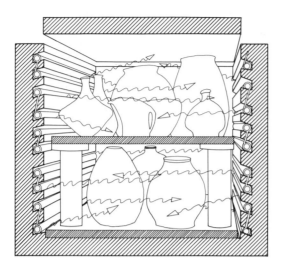

Figure 15-3
The heat in an electric kiln is radiated outward from the elements set in the walls. In the United States, electric kilns are generally used for bisque firings and oxidation firings. In other parts of the world, electric kilns are frequently the only type available to ceramists, so if a reduction atmosphere is needed, it must be produced through the introduction of reduction materials either in the kiln or in individual saggers. *Drawing: Danute Bruzas.*

Figure 15-5
In a modern updraft gas kiln, the heat from the burners goes up through the ware on the shelves and is vented out through the top of the kiln. The modern updraft uses the same principle of rising heat that led to the development of early kilns in the Orient and the Mediterranean (see Chapters 2 and 3). *Drawing: Danute Bruzas.*

Figure 15-4
Bisque firing is often done in an electric kiln even if the glaze firing will be done in a gas or wood kiln. For a bisque firing, a kiln can be loaded tightly with pieces touching each other or even nested.

Figure 15-6
A modern downdraft kiln is designed to send the heat from the burners first up- ward and then down through the ware to the flue at the bottom. Finally, the heat is vented out the stack at the back of the kiln. A bag wall may be built inside the outer walls to direct the flames and heat upward. *Drawing: Danute Bruzas.*

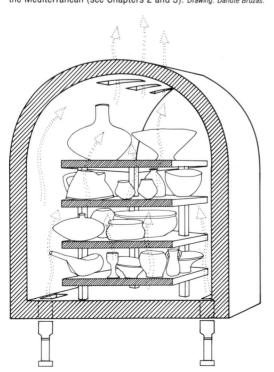

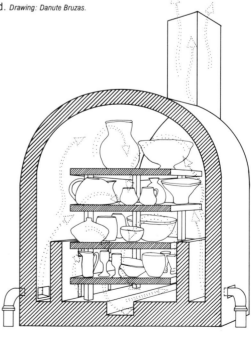

stonewares that mature at cone 8 (2305°F/1263°C) to 12 (2419°F/1326°C); and porcelains, whose range is from cone 10 (2381°F/1305°C) to 13 (2455°F/1346°C). The potential range of most clays, however, is considerably wider than labels or recipes may suggest, and you might well find that a particular clay can go to a higher temperature than you would expect. Be sure, however, to test before you try to fire your favorite pot beyond the recommended range.

Drying Before Firing

We cannot emphasize strongly enough the importance of drying. Thorough drying is crucial and, especially when a thick-walled piece is to be fired, the drying process cannot be hurried. To be sure that it is completely dry, you can give a thick-walled object extra drying with a space heater, place it near a kiln that is firing so that it dries as it waits to be loaded, or use the tent method described in Chapter 11.

You can also place it in the kiln with the door left open about 5 to 10 inches (13 to 26 cm) while the heat starts to rise. Once the piece is thoroughly heated and dry, you can then close the door and proceed with the firing.

Temperature and Duration

How do you know when the kiln has reached the point at which your clay or glaze has matured? It is important to recognize that clay and glaze need *time* in addition to heat to become fully mature. Thus, firing involves duration as well as temperature. The experienced ceramist can look into the kiln through a peephole and judge the temperature of the kiln by the color of the interior as the temperature rises — from dull red-orange through light orange to white. (See Appendix 2A for a table that shows temperatures and kiln colors.) If you peer into the kiln, always wear special goggles to protect your eyes from the infrared radiation, which has a cumulative effect on the eyes, possibly causing cataracts. The damage increases with frequency of exposure. The goggle shades that will protect your eyes from damage range from #3 for low temperatures to #5 for high firing. Number 5 will protect you through the entire range. A dull red kiln interior is associated with temperatures of around 1200°F/648.8°C, when

you would be firing luster and china paint; an orange color is seen during bisque or low firings; yellow appears at the usual temperatures for firing earthenware and medium-fired stoneware; and an intense white glow is seen when the kiln is firing high-fire glazes.

The experienced ceramist also knows how long to leave the kiln at the correct heat and how long it would take to bring it down to a temperature low enough for unloading. But until you have fired many kilns, to ensure successful firing it is best to use cones and/or a pyrometer or to set a computerized kiln to the appropriate firing program that will control the heat rise and decline over a specified period of time.

Pyrometers

A **pyrometer** is a gauge that measures the temperature inside the kiln. It shows the temperature readings as you raise or lower the heat in the kiln. A pyrometer is usually calibrated to show increments of 20°F/−6.6°C. Installed on kilns — gas or electric — a pyrometer allows you to check the temperature as it rises and falls in the kiln. When a pyrometer is installed in a gas kiln, a special porcelain tube can be placed over the thermocouple to protect its metal from accelerated deterioration. Since the pyrometer is usually installed on the inside wall of a kiln rather than in the middle of the chamber, the readings you get from it will not indicate the temperature throughout the entire kiln; but because the pyrometer shows any temperature change almost immediately, it will indicate if the kiln is heating or cooling too fast. In that case you can slow the rise or fall of the heat. A pyrometer is a useful aid, but since it can measure only the temperature in the kiln, not the effect of time plus temperature, ceramists usually use **pyrometric cones** as well.

Pyrometric Cones

A pyrometric cone will show you when both the time and the temperature have reached the point at which the clay or glaze has come to maturity. For this reason, these cones are made of ceramic materials that are formulated to fuse and bend when they have been exposed to a certain amount of saturation. In effect, cones are carefully calculated miniature tests (15-7).

(a)

(b)

Figure 15-7
(a) The cones in place show that the second shelf from the bottom of the kiln fired considerably hotter than the lowest shelf.
(b) The cones are reassembled in the order in which they were placed. From bottom to top they show the wide range of temperatures in the kiln.

American Orton cones and European Seger cones are formulated to bend according to the work done by the heat during a certain temperature rise per hour. The large Orton cones used in the United States cover temperatures from cone 022 (1112°F/605°C) to cone 13 (2455°F/1346°C), with their numbers representing a series of points at which they bend over. The cone numbers and temperatures used in the text are those for the large Orton cones with a temperature rise of 270°F/150°C per hour (see table in Appendix 2A). The same table shows equivalent Seger cones and temperatures. The most commonly used Orton cones run from the lowest number of cone 022 (1112°F/605°C) through cone 020 to 018, used for firing lusters and china paints, up to cone 13 (2455°F/1346°C), used for stonewares and porcelains. The cones below cone 1 are numbered so that the lower the cone temperature, the larger the number — that is, 022 is lower than 019 — a fact that sometimes confuses beginners. There are cones as high as 36, but they are used normally for industrial firings.

To use cones in a gas kiln, you would insert three consecutively numbered cones in a series, placing them at an eight-degree angle in a wad of clay or in soft fire bricks cut to support the cones at the correct angle (15-8). You can also use specially designed reusable, heat-resistant metal cone holders. You usually would use three cones known as the guide cone, the firing cone, and the guard cone. For example, you might use cones 06 (1830°F/999°C), 05 (1915°F/1046°C), and 04 (1940°F/1060°C), placed in a series. To use cones as guides, you must check on them periodically (wearing special shaded goggles) through the kiln peepholes. Once the first cone has bent, you should begin to check on the middle one every fifteen to forty-five minutes, because at this point the kiln is approaching the desired temperature. As soon as the middle cone bends, stop the heat rise. If the third cone starts to bend, you have overfired. Since there can be a wide difference in heat saturation in a large kiln — as much as several cones' difference — it is best to place several sets of cones at different shelf levels (15-7a).

Kiln Sitters and Electronic Controls

Since the heat of a kiln must be raised slowly to the correct point, firing requires the ceramist's careful attention. For electric kilns, **kiln sitters** eliminate the need to watch the kiln constantly. Kiln sitters allow you to place a small cone of the appropriate number in the sitter, set the mechanism, and leave it to the sitter to switch off the kiln mechanically at the point the clay cone bends and trips a switch that breaks the electric circuit. The cones used in sitters are called junior size, and their response is different from that of the large cones placed in the interior of gas kilns. One of the strong points of kiln sitters is that they help prevent the overfiring of a kiln. Nevertheless, it is recommended that a person firing with a kiln sitter, timer, or other automatic control check the kiln within an hour or two of the expected firing time, since equipment is not always 100 percent foolproof. If there is any question in your mind about what is happening inside the kiln, or if the equipment seems to be malfunctioning, turn off the kiln manually, let it cool, and check it thoroughly, or call a repair person.

(a)

Computer Controls

Computers that can be programmed to fire either an electric or gas kiln are now available, relieving the ceramist of a great deal of kiln watching (15-10a). Computers for electric kilns can be programmed to do everything you would normally do in a firing with the exception of lowering the lid, plugging spyholes, or closing the damper. Turning dials and setting cones or automatic kiln sitters can be eliminated with the use of a computer. Some computerized electric kilns can be outfitted with a downdraft venting system that

Figure 15-8
(a) Ross Spangler, U.S.A., places cones in his updraft kiln. A production potter, he says he prefers to use a kiln that is under 35 cubic feet (.99 cu m). *Firing frequently,* he says, *gives me flexibility in glazing and faster turnaround time for glaze testing.* The ware was bisque-fired before being loaded for the firing. **(b)** The glaze firing lasted eleven hours with a six-hour reduction to get good copper reds. After four hours the kiln reached cone 011 (1641°F/894°C), and Spangler started reduction, continuing it until the kiln reached cone 10 (2408°F/1320°C). Now the glaze firing is completed and the kiln is open, displaying a load of glazed bowls, plates, and vases ready for shipping. Stoneware, chun glaze.

(b)

draws fresh air in through the top of the kiln lid and lets it out through the floor of the kiln to be exhausted outdoors. With this type of system, you can fire the kiln with the lid and spyholes closed throughout the entire firing. It is recommended that the kiln operator return at the end of the firing to be certain the kiln has shut off at the desired cone or temperature. (See Chapter 17 for more details.)

KILN INSTALLATION

Gas Kilns

The installation of a gas kiln (15-5, 15-6) is a complicated business, not only from the point of view of safety but also to ensure that the kiln will achieve the proper firing temperature. Not only is it essential to follow the manufacturer's specifications for installing a commercial kiln or, if you are building your own, to refer to books on the subject, but it is also essential to check with your utility company and code officials about local conditions and requirements. (For further details see Chapter 17.)

Electric Kilns

Although an electric kiln (15-3, 15-4) does not use open flame, it can still present some installation problems. One does not simply buy an electric kiln and then plug it in. If you are considering purchasing one, first study where you will place it and how to vent it. Have a licensed electrician check any existing wiring against the manufacturer's or supplier's information on requirements. For example, is the existing voltage 110–120 volts, 208 volts, or 220 to 240 volts, or is it European wire at 230 volts? (For further details see Chapter 17.)

 ### Ventilation

It is essential that any indoor kiln—gas or electric—be well vented. This is done to draw away the gases that are released during firing from the organic materials in clay, the carbon monoxide produced during incomplete combustion (as in reduction firing), and the heavy metal fumes that

escape from the kiln during glaze firings. Venting can be done on a gas kiln by building a hood over the kiln, extending it beyond its edges, and installing a fan to pull the fumes and heat away and exhaust them outside. Ready-made venting systems for electric kilns are also available now that actively draw fresh air directly into the kiln, through the chamber, and then exhaust the fumes outside. (See Chapter 17 and the health and safety chart in Figure 10-6).

PRECAUTIONS

Remember that while working around a kiln, you are dealing with high heat and, in the case of a gas kiln, an open flame. Especially around a gas kiln, take the same precautions you would take around any gas appliance or open flame:

- Tie back long hair and loose clothing and keep them under control.
- Protect your eyes from flame and the infrared radiation that can damage your eyes. When looking into a kiln, wear either shaded goggles (#3 to #5) or a face shield with a #3 to #5 shade that will protect your entire face from infrared radiation and the flames that often escape through the spyholes during reduction.
- Use aramid fiber (non-asbestos), heat-resistant gloves (or leather welding gloves) whenever you have to touch the hot parts of a kiln.
- When the time comes to unload the kiln, remember that even if the exterior seems cool, the pots inside will be hot. Curb your desire to grab your glazed pot with your bare hands; it may be hotter than you think. If your gloves start to smoke, it's too hot!

Alternative Fuels and Energy Saving

It is beyond the scope of this book to go into kiln design, but you should be aware that experiments have been made with fuels other than natural gas, propane, or electricity. Some potters have fired successfully with used crankcase oil, recycling it, but perhaps polluting the air. Others have fired with methane gas from the sludge of a paper mill, and another has managed to fire very small pots in a solar-heated kiln. Some have saved energy by using extra insulation—from a mixture of vermiculite and clay applied to the outside walls of a kiln to a ceramic fiber wrap around the kiln. Such ceramic fiber insulation is most efficient when applied to the *inside* walls of a kiln, where it reflects the heat best, but it still helps hold in some heat if it is used on the outside.

THE FIRING PROCESS

Let's assume that you now want to preserve and then glaze your first pieces of ceramics. They have been completely dried to the touch and are ready for placing in the kiln as greenware—dried, unfired clay objects. You have a choice at this point between glazing the greenware and firing it in a single firing or firing it first unglazed in a bisque firing, then in a glaze firing. Since, in single firing, the ware is handled only once, this can save fuel and labor. Indeed, when the pot or sculpture to be fired is heavy, or when thick walls require a very slow firing, a single firing is preferred in order to eliminate the effort of a second loading. However, for glazing, many potters prefer to bisque-fire first, since greenware is fragile. In a school studio or a production pottery where a large number of objects must be fired, at least two kilns are a necessity—one for bisque firing and one for glaze or sculpture firing.

Bisque Firing

Greenware can easily break while you are handling it or when applying a glaze. Also, if the ware has not been bisqued, the chance is greater that it might blow up in the kiln, causing its glazed fragments to stick to the interior or to other ware. In addition, some glazes are affected by the release of gases from organic materials in the clay bodies that would have been eliminated during a bisque firing. As a result, glazes that have been applied to bisqued ware are generally less likely to be subjected to the bubbling that the escaping gases from these organic materials can cause. Ware that is bisque-fired before glazing also tends to have brighter, clearer colors after it is fired. For all these reasons, you probably will choose to bisque-fire your work to somewhere between 1661°F/905°C and 1900°F/1037°C before glazing. Bisque firing can be done in any type of kiln, but many prefer to use an electric kiln for the bisque firing, even if they use gas for the glaze firing.

A bisque firing at cone 010 (1661°F/905°C) not only saves fuel but also leaves the fired ware more porous. This can be a help in applying certain glazes that require an especially absorbent surface in order to build up the correct thickness. On the other hand, some glazes may develop defects such as excessive pinholes or craters when the clay body has been bisque-fired too low. If that happens, try a cone 05 (1915°F/1046°C) bisque.

Loading a Bisque Kiln

To stack an electric kiln with greenware, you would first set the kiln sitter or electronic control, then load the ware and turn on the kiln. In a gas kiln, you would first place the ware on the shelves and then insert the cones and set the controls.

It is easier to load a bisque kiln than a glaze kiln, because without any melting glaze to cause the ware to stick together, the pots or sculpture can be tightly stacked, even touching or nested inside each other (15-3, 15-4). A closely stacked bisque load, however, necessitates a slower firing than one more loosely stacked. It is wise to turn thick-bottomed pots or sculpture upside-down so that the moisture can escape more efficiently.

In a bisque firing, you would not want the clay to reach full maturity, because the objects to be glazed should remain absorbent enough for the glaze to adhere to them. Once the kiln has reached the desired temperature for the bisque, the kiln must be cooled very slowly, probably overnight, and you should resist the temptation to open the door too soon, or the ware may crack. When you do open it, you will see the clay pieces changed by the action of the fire to a new material—one that can never revert to its original chemical or physical state.

Raising the Temperature

Now that your work is in the kiln, the computer is set or the cones are in place (15-8), the controls are set, and the door is closed or bricked in, you can begin to raise the temperature. As you watch the kiln, you may wonder what is actually happening to your creations behind that closed door. They will go through many transformations before you open the door again.

Water Release

By the time the heat in the kiln has slowly increased to a temperature of about 660°F/348°C, most of the physical water that was still left in the clay has been driven out in the form of vapor. This is a tricky time in firing, because if the heat is raised too rapidly during this period, the object can explode as the steam escapes. The more temper there is in the clay, the more porous the clay will be. These spaces between the particles allow the steam and gases to escape. It is for this reason that thick-walled pots or sculpture should be made with a high percentage of grog or other temper — 20 to 40%.

Now the physical, or free, water has left the clay. As the temperature continues to rise slowly to between 1650°F/900°C and 2010°F/1100°C, the chemical water (H_2O) that has combined with the molecular structure of the clay particles is also driven out along with the gases formed by the decomposition of any organic materials remaining in the clay. These gases can cause problems as they escape, so the temperature should be raised slowly at this point. It is essential that the fumes and smoke that will be emitted from the kiln as these organic materials decompose are removed by a well-functioning ventilation system.

Quartz Inversion

As it is fired, clay undergoes various changes, some visible, some invisible. One invisible change that takes place as the kiln is heated and the silica crystals in the clay change in volume and form, is a phenomenon called **quartz inversion.** As it is heated, the silica contained in the flint, quartz, or sand in the clay first expands gradually; then, at the quartz inversion point — between about 440°F/227°C and 1070°F/577°C, a series of rapid changes and expansions in the silica take place. After the clay has been fired to maturity, if the temperature changes during these expansion and contraction periods have been too rapid, they can cause fracturing of the clay body. The same applies to glaze

firings during which these stresses can affect the fit of the glaze to the clay.

Vitrification

The term *maturity* refers to the point at which the clay has been fired as high as possible, before it starts to slump and melt. At maturity, certain clays become vitrified, rocklike and dense. Potters like to fire their high-fire ware to **vitrification** so that it becomes impermeable to moisture, and liquids will not seep through. However, even though low-fire clays are said to be vitreous when they are fired to maturity, they are generally not impervious to water. For this reason, to make low-fire ware watertight, the potter will often glaze it on the bottom as well as the inside.

GLAZE FIRING

Before you start to fire a kiln, you will need to know something about kilns and the atmosphere in the kiln because these factors will affect your ware. The school studio will frequently have a gas kiln as well as an electric one, and chances are you will be using the gas kiln to fire your glazed ware.

There are many types of gas kilns — updraft, downdraft, cross-draft, with natural or forced-air–type burners, and ones with multiple burners at angles that can create a swirling effect — but the most common types are variations within the two categories of updraft and downdraft kilns. These terms describe the flow of the heat as it enters from the burners or other fuel source and exits through a vent or chimney (15-5, 15-6). The kiln may also have a **muffle** or a **bag wall** in the chamber to protect the ware from the direct flame.

Kiln Atmospheres

There are two atmospheres that may develop in a kiln as it fires — oxidation and reduction. The effects these two atmospheres produce on clays and glazes vary enormously.

OXIDATION   Any burning requires some oxygen to continue, and if there is plenty of air entering a fire, it will produce an oxidizing atmosphere, in which the fire can burn bright and clear, with full combustion taking place. If you have ever helped a smoky fire to burn well by blowing on it or using a bellows, you were providing the oxygen necessary for full combustion to take place, thereby creating an oxidizing atmosphere, which, in a kiln, would give your glazed work a certain appearance (see "Firing Low-Fire Glazes," p. 355.)

REDUCTION If, however, you were to smother the open fire so that most of the air was shut off, then the incomplete combustion would produce smoke and carbon. This incomplete combustion is what creates a reducing atmosphere, and when such an atmosphere is produced in a kiln, the carbon and carbon monoxide formed in the oxygen-starved fire will draw oxygen from the clay body or from the oxides in a glaze. When this happens, some of the oxides in the clay or glaze will lose oxygen; they are then said to be reduced. Depending on how much oxygen is removed from the oxides, the color of clay or glaze can change color radically when they are reduced. A dramatic example of what reduction can do to the color of a glaze ingredient is the color change that takes place in copper oxide. Fired in an oxidizing atmosphere, copper oxide becomes green, but in a successful reduction atmosphere it becomes red. It is clear that the atmosphere of the kiln plays a vital role in creating glaze effects.

In preindustrial societies, potters and sculptors traditionally used any fuel available to them; in arid lands this might be the sparse vegetation or manure from their herds, whereas in lush tropical areas it might be palm fronds. Starting out with open pits and simple kilns, gradually, over the centuries, potters perfected their kilns to reach higher temperatures and fire more efficiently. Chinese and Japanese potters developed wood kilns that could fire to porcelain temperatures (Chapter 3), whereas the European potters used wood for low-firing maiolica. Then, when the Europeans learned to fire high-fire stoneware (Chapter 6), they fired it in kilns that were fueled with wood, or, later, coal. With these fuels, combustion was not as complete, so it was easier to achieve a reduction atmosphere than an oxidizing atmosphere. By the early 1900s some kilns burned oil; then, finally gas and electric kilns were developed and perfected, making it possible to maintain greater control over the firing process and the kiln atmosphere than with wood or coal.

During a reduction firing, there are visible evidences of the reduction process: In an updraft kiln, the flames may have a greenish tinge, and in an up- and downdraft kiln, black carbon forms around the spyholes or door jambs. As the reduction firing is nearing completion with all burners on, the gas pressure up, the air valves open, and the damper adjusted, a sense of excitement builds up. At this point, when the heat is high, a soft roar comes from the kiln, and the flames dance as they leave the chamber. The kiln deity is working its magic while the fire gives the clay a new life.

Depending on the kiln, or on the methods used, you can change the kiln atmosphere from oxidizing to reducing either by controlling the air flow into the kiln or by cutting down on the draft. Closing the damper of a gas kiln, for example, forces the air to back up and prevents new air from entering the kiln; thus, as the oxygen in the kiln is consumed, the fire is forced to draw oxygen from the oxides. Many stoneware and porcelain glazes require reduction to reach their best appearance, but the reduction must be controlled and not become too heavy, or the clay body can become brittle. One way to monitor the amount of reduction in a kiln is to use an **oxygen probe,** which will help you achieve a consistent reduction atmosphere inside the kiln during firing.

Each ceramist develops an individual reduction firing pattern. For example, some begin reducing at cone 05 and maintain that atmosphere all the way to the end of the firing, whereas others reduce two times—once around 1900°F/1038°C for one hour and again during the last hour of firing.

Reduction in Electric Kilns

You will always get an oxidizing atmosphere in an electric kiln unless you take special steps to change the atmosphere. Where stringent fire regulations prohibit gas kilns in built-up areas, ceramists who want to achieve glazes that require reduction have to reduce in their electric kilns by adding smoke-producing materials. This material may range from excelsior or straw to mustard seeds, seaweed, sawdust, pine needles, or paper—anything that will burn and create a local reducing atmosphere. You can place the materials directly in the kiln or place your ware in a sagger (a protective container) along with the reducing material. This way of using saggers contrasts sharply with the original use of saggers, which was to protect the delicate ware in the kiln from the effects of flame and carbon (3-17). You can also add reducing material to the clay body itself or add approximately 1% to the glaze mixture; **silicon carbide** 3F (carborundum) powder is sometimes added to glazes to create reduction. Some artists have experimented with reduction methods by introducing a small amount of propane gas into the kiln chamber.

These methods make it possible to reduce in an electric kiln, but constant reduction firings can wear out the electric elements and wiring connectors, and any reduction material that remains in the kiln after such a firing can spoil certain glazes that you might want to fire in it later. To cut down on wear on the elements and to clean the kiln, it helps to heat an empty electric kiln to high heat, or fire it under oxidizing conditions, after each reduction firing. Even heavy-duty electric elements, however, will have to be replaced eventually if they are subjected to frequent reduction atmospheres.

THE GLAZE KILN

Assuming that you have bisque-fired and have applied glaze to your work (Chapter 14) and that the glaze has dried, you are ready for the next firing—the glaze firing. Before loading the kiln, be sure that its interior is clean and that there are no loose fragments in the brick lining that can fall on the ware. The next step is to load the kiln, using kiln furniture.

Kiln Furniture

Kiln furniture consists of heat-resistant slabs, shelves, and posts that support the ware in the kiln during firing. Kiln shelves are commonly made of three materials—silicon carbide, high-alumina, and cordierite. Cordierite shelves, ½ inch (13 mm) to ⅝ inch (16 mm) thick, are commonly used in electric kilns up to cone 8, and 1 to 1½ inch (25 to 38 mm) thick to cone 10. These can withstand the rapid heat rise and decline of your firings without cracking. Silicon carbide and

high-alumina shelves are used in gas kilns, since they can withstand without excessive warping the high temperatures needed to fire stoneware and porcelain. Silicon carbide shelves range in thickness from ⅝ inch (16 mm) to 1¼ inch (32 mm); the higher the temperature and the heavier the load on each shelf, the thicker the shelf you should use.

There are now new lightweight and thin (approximately ⁵⁄₁₆ inch [14 mm]) thick silicon carbide kiln shelves available. These shelves are popular with potters because they cause less strain on their backs when loading and they take up less space inside the kiln.

Kiln Wash

Most potters and sculptors coat the top surfaces of new kiln shelves with two or three coats of **kiln wash.** This, like the flour in a cake pan, acts as a separator, so that if the glaze drips onto the shelves from the ware, the shelves can be easily cleaned. The wash is a mixture of one-half china clay (kaolin) and one-half flint, diluted with only enough water to make it possible to paint it on. Usually, after a dozen or more firings, glaze drippings will need to be scraped off and a new coating of kiln wash applied. Shelves that are heavily coated with glaze and kiln wash may need to be brushed and scraped or sandblasted to clean them thoroughly and then recoated with kiln wash by brushing or applying it with a paint roller.

Arranging the Shelves

It can take a good deal of ingenuity to arrange the shelves on the posts so that they provide the most space for the varied shapes of work you may want to fire. When you start to build up the shelves, use three rather than four posts for each shelf; three points make for a less wobbly support.

If a shelf does not sit evenly on three posts, you can take a small wad of clay, shape it into a wafer (called a shim), and dip it into alumina oxide or high-fire kiln wash powder. It is best to use high-fire clay—preferably a white stoneware type—for such shims. Place the soft wafer on the uneven post, then position the kiln shelf on the posts and lightly pound it with the palm of your hand until it seats itself. To shim a large kiln with many shelves, use a heavy rubber mallet to tap the shelves down onto the clay shims. When there are large gaps between shelves and posts, use a low-shrinkage mixture of coarse grog mixed with the smallest amount of fire clay necessary to bind it, blend it with water into a stiff, putty-like consistency, and use it to shim the posts.

Stilts

If you want to make low-fire ceramics watertight by glazing the bottom, then to keep the glaze from sticking to the shelves you will need to use **stilts** to keep the ware up off the shelves (15-9). Stilts are triangular supports on which the piece is balanced on the kiln shelf and which leave only small marks in the glaze when they are removed. Three types of stilts are available commercially. For low-fire ceramics, the stilts may be made of clay. Generally these are rated to stand heats from 05 (1915°F/1046°C) or lower up to cone 1 (2109°F/1154°C). Clay stilts with metal points inserted in the clay are also good for low firing and leave smaller marks on the foot when they are removed after firing. The sharp edges left after removal can be filed or ground down (wear goggles and a respirator), and the spots can then be touched up with paint, colored epoxy, or marking pens. The third type of stilts is all metal—special heat-resistant metal that can be fired to cone 1. Although these are rated to cone 1, some potters

Figure 15-9
Triangular ceramic stilts support ware and keep glazed bases and feet from sticking to the kiln shelves during firing. They are used primarily for low-fire applications at under cone 1 (2109°F/1154°C). **(a)** Stilt showing three points of contact. **(b)** Section through low-fire bowl that has been entirely glazed, including base and foot, resting on a reusable stilt which will keep the bowl from sticking to the kiln shelf.

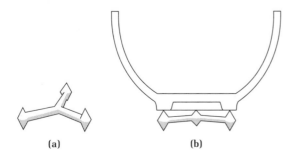

(a)   (b)

fire them to cone 5 or higher. These are reusable, so they may be well worth the extra cost. It is possible to make your own supports from nichrome wire for low firing and from Kanthal A1 or kiln-element wire for high firing—but don't use coat hanger metal—it will fatigue or disintegrate in high firings.

Because clays that fire above cone 10 (2381°F/1305°C)—porcelain and even some high-fire stonewares—soften as they reach the high temperatures at which they mature, anything made from them will slump and warp if it is placed on stilts. Therefore, objects made of these clays must be placed flat on the shelf; for that reason they must have unglazed feet. Early Chinese potters frequently fired their porcelain bowls upside-down to keep them from warping, leaving a band of unglazed clay around the rim to keep the piece from sticking to the shelf. They turned this glaze-free rim into a decorative feature by covering it with a band of metal. Ewen Henderson, of England, stilts his sculptures by placing them on oyster shells and fires them to stoneware temperatures.

Loading a Glaze Kiln

Any glazed ware, whether it is high or low fire, will stick together if the pieces touch each other during the firing. One of the challenges of loading a kiln is to find just the right spot for each piece where it will not touch any other (15-8a). You should leave at least ¼ inch (6 mm) between glazed pieces, because when the glaze goes through its maturing process, it bubbles up and objects that are closer together than that may actually touch, then stick as the kiln cools.

Each kiln—gas, electric, or other fuel—has its idiosyncrasies. For example, many kilns have hot spots where certain glazes would be overfired. Once you have become acquainted with a particular kiln, you will know which areas go to a higher heat and which areas get more reduction than others, so you will be able to load the kiln according to the heat and atmosphere each piece requires. When you have loaded everything properly into the kiln, place sets of cones in appropriate places, usually in the middle of the kiln and possibly also at the top and bottom. The number of sets you use will depend on the size of the kiln and its individual variations.

What Happens to Glaze in the Kiln

We have seen that the chemical composition of clay or glaze is affected by the heat of the kiln, as well as by the type of fuel used to fire it. It is also important to remember that glazes fired quickly in a small test kiln (for example, about 6 × 6 × 6 in. or 15 × 15 × 15 cm) will yield different results even though its atmosphere is similar to that in which they will be fired in the larger kiln. In general, glazes are brighter and richer in depth when fired in a full-size kiln.

 While the glaze kiln is firing, if you look through the peepholes at the right moment (wearing the correct goggles) you will see the glaze actually melting. In this active stage, the glaze bubbles and boils, and you may wonder if it will ever become the smooth, glossy surface you pictured for your pot. It usually does, and the bubbles generally smooth out as the melting process continues—assuming that there are no problems with formulation, fit, application, or firing!

Speed of Temperature Rise

The slower the temperature rise of the kiln, the better. No ware was ever damaged by raising the temperature too slowly, and the speed at which you raise the kiln temperature is especially critical in the initial stages of glaze firing. Even if the glazed bisque ware appears to be thoroughly dry, there may be some moisture in the clay, and if this is too quickly driven off as vapor through the glaze, it can damage the adhesion of the glaze to the clay surface, causing defects. The average kiln is raised at a rate of around 150°F/65.5°C to 210°F/100°C an hour as an average for the firing.

How long it will take to bring a kiln to the point at which a particular clay or a glaze will mature will vary from kiln to kiln, from clay to clay, from glaze to glaze, and depend on the amount of ware in the kiln. A tightly packed kiln will take longer to raise its temperature. The type of objects being fired in the kiln will also influence how quickly the temperature should be raised. For example, some potters will bring a kiln of thrown ware up to cone 10 reduction in ten hours. Sculptors, on the other hand, may preheat the kiln with the sculpture in it for two days before starting to fire it. Other factors may also influence the amount of time needed: A kiln that is outdoors may retain moisture in the porous

brick of the firing chamber and require a much slower start to dry it out. A good rule of thumb is to go slowly until the pyrometer gauge is at 1200°F/648.8°C, or the entire kiln becomes red-orange; then you can go faster. This is where cones are very helpful. Place the cones where they can be seen easily but as far as possible out of the direct flame or draft so that they will give more accurate readings. Then check them often for signs of bending. As the first one bends, monitor the kiln more carefully (every 25 to 45 minutes for an electric kiln, every 15 to 60 minutes for a gas kiln) to be sure that you leave enough time between the bending of the cones. Using such conservative timing, thirty students (who used and fired about nine to ten tons of clay in a semester) had 100% firing success, with no kiln disasters.

The chemical and structural changes that take place in different types of glazes as they are fired are beyond the scope of this book, but it is important to be aware that the speed at which the kiln is heated or cooled at certain points in the firing cycle affects the relationship between the glaze and the clay body and the ultimate fit of the glaze. Changes in the clay and glaze materials taking place under heat and on cooling can cause either desired glaze effects, such as crystalline glazes, or defects such as **dunting,** which is the term used for cracks that go through both the glaze and the clay body.

Soaking

Soaking simply means keeping the kiln at a specific heat, often for about thirty minutes to an hour. Glazes need time to smooth out, and to give them time to do so, the potter often gives the kiln a soaking period, holding the temperature steady while the glaze sits and smooths out. To soak in a gas kiln, once the appropriate firing cone has bent, turn half the burners down to low heat (or to about ⅛ to ½ inch [½ to 1 millibar] in gas pressure) for about an hour, with the damper open. After the soaking time, shut off the kiln, close the damper, and plug all spyholes while the kiln cools.

To soak in an electric kiln, when the cone has bent and the kiln has been shut off by the kiln sitter or electronic controls, turn the kiln back on and set one or all switches to low for about 30 minutes. At the end of the soaking period, shut the kiln off, plug all spyholes, and allow the kiln to cool. Some people never soak, or they use an alternative method, firing either an electric or a gas kiln to one or two cones higher than usual. You can also program a computer for a hold/soak pattern.

Cooling the Kiln

Careful control of the kiln during cooling is essential to prevent defects in your work or to produce certain effects such as matt and crystalline glazes. In general, the most critical period for glazes is during the first period of cooling, when slow, careful lowering of the temperature is essential. The number of hours it takes depends on the mass of ware in the kiln, how closely it is packed, and the mass of the kiln itself. The time involved depends on so many factors that you should treat each firing individually. To give an electric kiln plenty of cooling time, after the kiln shuts off, wait between nine and twelve hours, then open the peephole. When you feel that the heat coming from the kiln is well below searing hot, then open the lid an inch every 2 to 6 hours. With a large gas kiln, on the other hand, to be sure of giving it adequate cooling time, leave it with everything shut for a minimum of 12 hours, and then open the damper 1 inch every 3 to 6 hours. These are conservative cooling times, but by cooling this slowly it is possible to have a high success rate in firing. Once the kiln has cooled to about 150°F/65.5°C, the door can be opened to reveal the kiln of glazed ware ready to unload (15-8b).

If the glazed ware comes out of the kiln with bubbles hardened into them, this is often the result of too-rapid cooling, although it might also be the result of a too-low bisque firing which failed to burn all the volatile materials out of the clay body. They would then have escaped through the clay pores as gases and have bubbled up through the glaze.

Firing Low-Fire Glazes

Low-fire ware is made of clays that mature at low temperatures and is decorated with glazes that mature between cones 015 (1479°F/804°C) and cone 1 (2109°F/1154°C). The most common low-fire firings are to cone 07, 06, 05, and 04 (1784°F–1940°F/984°–1060°C). Low-fire glazes are frequently fired in an electric kiln, because in order to achieve the clear, bright glaze colors associated with them, they require the clean oxidizing atmosphere characteristic of that type of kiln. If overfired, the red and orange glazes will look splotchy black or clear. In electric kilns, you generally would fire these glazes in the coolest areas of the kiln—usually the very bottom or the very top. They need a well-ventilated kiln atmosphere, so you may even consider firing with most of the spyholes open. If you are firing reds and oranges, avoid firing other ware with copper or other metallic oxides that could affect the red or orange colors in the same kiln.

Firing Overglazes (China Paint)

Overglazes are either water- or oil-base enamels that melt at between cone 022 and 018 (1112°–1323°F/605°–717°C). Firing overglazes is a much faster process than bisque firing or glaze firing, because overglaze paint melts in a relatively short time at temperatures that need only be high enough to soften the base glaze somewhat so that the china paint or enamel will fuse with it. Because overglazes melt at such low temperatures, the firing process usually takes only about 2½ or 3 hours from beginning to end (not counting the cooling time).

The firing temperature depends on the color as well as the glazed surface on which it is painted. The cone to which the ware is fired is determined not only by the melting point of the overglaze, but also by the relation of the clay and the base glaze to the overglaze. For example, china paint over low-fire glazes can be fired at a lower temperature than china paint over high-fire glazes, because it takes less heat to make the base glaze tacky. Thus, china paint on a low-fire glaze can be fired at cone 020 to cone 017, whereas the same color may need a hotter firing (cone 016) on glazed porcelain ware. China paint is often fired in multiple firings, one color at a time, because many of these colors will be contaminated by touching another color. Too many layers could also cause peeling, so a number of coats of paint and multiple firings may be required to build up a particular color effect. These successive coats of china paint can create subtle gradations and depth of color.

(a)

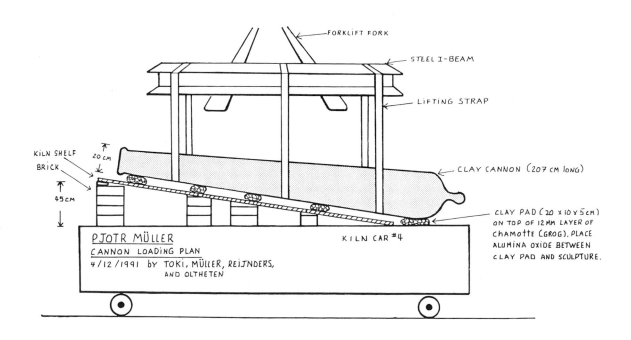

FORKLIFT FORK

STEEL I-BEAM

LIFTING STRAP

KILN SHELF

BRICK

20 CM

45 CM

CLAY CANNON (207 CM long)

CLAY PAD (20 x 10 x 5 CM)
ON TOP OF 12 MM LAYER OF
CHAMOTTE (GROG). PLACE
ALUMINA OXIDE BETWEEN
CLAY PAD AND SCULPTURE.

PJOTR MÜLLER
CANNON LOADING PLAN
4/12/1991 by TOKI, MÜLLER, REIJNDERS,
AND OLTHETEN

KILN CAR #4

A clean oxidation atmosphere is crucial to the brilliance of some overglaze colors. To achieve this in an electric kiln, keep all spyholes open through the *entire* firing. Then follow this procedure: Turn all switches to low and keep the lid propped open about 2 inches (5 cm) for 30 to 40 minutes. Turn switches to medium with the lid still propped open about 1 inch (2.5 cm) for another 30 to 45 minutes. Then close the lid, turn switches to high, and fire until the kiln sitter shuts off, the cone bends, or the fast-fire program is completed. This usually takes another 1½ hours. Cool for approximately 15 to 20 hours.

Firing Lusters

Although there are ceramists who have researched and duplicated the ancient lusters as they were fired in strong reduction in Persia, the lusters most people use today are commercial oil-base colors that contain their own reduction materials in the glaze medium. Lusters emit toxic fumes during firing that necessitate careful venting of the kiln to prevent anyone nearby inhaling them. All spyhole plugs should be left open during the entire luster firing. Often the kiln lid is also left cracked open about ⅛ to ¼ inch (3 to 6 mm) so that the kiln is not trapping the fumes and creating too heavy a reduction atmosphere. This could cause discoloration of the colors or might leave a murky film or residue on the surface. Today, lusters are usually fired in an electric kiln.

◄ **Figure 15-10**
(a) The kiln room with the computerized gas kiln in the European Ceramics Work Centre in Holland. Workshop supervisor Peter Oltheten and visiting technical advisor John Toki are loading two of the greenware cannons for Pjotr Müller's installation (9-10). The forklift, outfitted with polyester straps, lifted and lowered the cannons onto wet clay pads dusted with alumina oxide and sitting on coarse grog. The tilted kiln shelves relieved the pressure of the weight of the cannons by allowing them to slip down as they shrank, reducing danger of breakage in the firing. **(b)** This working drawing shows the method used to load the cannons for safe firing in the kiln. *(a) Courtesy the European Ceramics Work Centre, Holland. Photo: Els van den Boorn.*

SCULPTURE IN THE KILN

Although much of the firing information so far can also be applied to sculpture, some special factors must be taken into consideration when firing sculpture (15-10 to 15-12).

Firing Small Sculpture

The process of firing small pieces of sculpture is basically the same as that used when firing pottery, provided that it was built hollow or was hollowed out adequately and that it was well dried (see Chapter 11). Because the walls of handbuilt sculpture may be of uneven thickness, it is especially important that it be dried slowly and, to keep it from exploding, that the heat in the kiln be brought up extremely slowly.

Before starting to fire a kiln load of sculpture, be sure to preheat it with the kiln door open. This is critical. Follow the preheating by gradually increasing the temperature: In an electric kiln, turn one switch one notch every 1 or 2 hours until all switches are at the high position; in a gas kiln, adjust the gas pressure by ⅛ inch (½ millibar) every 6 to 12 hours until the kiln reaches 1200°F/537.7°C or is dull orange in color. After that temperature has been reached throughout the entire kiln from top to bottom, raise it by ¼ inch (1 millibar) gas pressure every 3 to 6 hours. The length of the complete firing will vary depending on the size and thickness of the sculpture, and how tightly it is loaded. Slip-cast sculpture generally takes less time, because the slip used in the casting process is homogenous. Now, with a computerized kiln, you can set the entire process to fire automatically to match the type of clay and glaze. If a small sculpture has been bisque-fired first, there is no chance it will blow up during a glaze firing. In an electric kiln, the glaze firing of a sculpture may take between 8 and 12 hours to bring it up to the desired cone, and in a gas kiln it may require 8 to 16 hours, depending on the amount of ware and kiln size.

Loading Large Sculpture

Loading a large sculpture can be a challenge. First, you have to get it into the kiln, then place it in the best spot for firing. Large sculptures are not normally bisque fired first, because this

Figure 15-11
Figuring out the best way to load unusual shapes of sculptures can present a challenge. Marilyn Lysohir, U.S.A., contemplates parts of her *Bad Manners* figures. While they await loading, the sections rest on foam pads, protecting their unfired finish. Lysohir fires her terra sigillata–coated pieces to cone 06 in a single firing in a downdraft gas kiln. *Courtesy the artist. Photo: Arthur Okazaki.*

Figure 15-12 ▶
Stephen De Staebler, U.S.A., unloading a section of one of his large sculptures from his car kiln. Although the kiln carriage (right) rolls easily in and out of the kiln on a track, it still takes careful maneuvering to load or unload the work, using a hoist and considerable pushing on grog-coated pallets. 1993.

would just double the effort and the time needed for the process. Since sculpture is therefore often loaded in the green state, and because a heavy sculpture must often be pushed or forklifted into a kiln or loaded with a hoist using nylon slings, it should be constructed carefully to accept the stresses that will be applied to it at that time. Generally, a large sculpture will be constructed in relatively small sections, partly for convenience during forming and partly so that the sections can be fitted into the kiln more easily. There may be instances, however, when a large sculpture cannot be made in sections and must be loaded in one piece. The key to loading large sculpture is careful planning, so before tackling the job, organize your loading equipment to give you as much help as possible and work out the placement of each piece before you load the kiln (15-11). John Toki, whose large, thick sculpture takes careful loading, says,

First, I bring everything that I plan to load in the kiln near to the kiln where I can study and measure them. I use a tape measure and make charts, measuring each piece, and deciding where it should go in the kiln; the three key issues are: position in the kiln relates to heat, which in turn affects color. I measure and mark the bricks inside the kiln where the shelf will be positioned, and to show me where each piece will go. I also chart which piece will go in first, second and third and so on, and calculate how many shelves and posts will be needed for each piece. It's only when I have all this worked out that I actually begin to load. If I am working alone, it can take as much as forty hours to load the 100 cubic foot kiln.

A level floor and level shelves are important when sliding large work into the kiln. This is where the newspapers you planned to take to the recycling center come in handy—heavy works slide easily on three to six layers of paper (the heavier the work, the more layers needed), especially on the glossy Sunday sections. To help you push large sculpture into a kiln, you can also attach braces to the floor, positioning them so that you can get leverage against them while you push. For extremely heavy pieces, however, no amount of manual work may be enough, and you may have to use a hydraulic hand cylinder with a hose and ram, a scissor-style automobile jack, or a forklift. If you use hydraulic aids to push the sculpture, it is extremely important to pad the surfaces against which the ram will push.

But even the hydraulic alternatives to muscle power and leverage frequently require a good deal of physical labor and ingenuity, and one of the most important qualities you must call on at this point is patience. Allow yourself plenty of time. To load one large section, allow anywhere from 2 to 5 hours, and for an entire large sculpture, the process of loading a 100-cubic-foot (2.83-cubic-meter) kiln can take one person as many as 40 hours. Remember, too, that unloading the sculpture from a large kiln after firing can take a good 12-hour day of effort as well.

One way to avoid the pushing and pulling required to load a large sculpture is to build the kiln up around the sculpture instead. Maria Kuczynska, who works in Poland and Australia, did this when she constructed one of her draped slab pieces on a larger scale than usual (15-13). Building a temporary kiln around a sculpture takes a knowledge of kiln construction and burner installation, so it is not a job for the inexperienced.

Figure 15-13
To fire *Icarus,* a larger-than-usual example of her slab sculpture, Maria Kuczynska used a kiln specially built up around the sculpture. Kuczynska's sculptures are built of slabs draped while still damp over an interior hollow clay support that has been allowed to stiffen enough to support the slabs. *Courtesy the artist.*

Firing Large Sculpture

It takes time to raise the heat of a kiln containing large sculpture that has not been given a preliminary bisque firing to the required firing temperature, then cooling it down slowly after firing. Firing large sculpture can be a lengthy process. Because a large sculpture is often constructed with varying thicknesses of clay walls, it is crucial to raise the temperature of the kiln gradually and to gauge the firing time correctly in relation to its thickest section. It is also important to preheat a thick piece of sculpture and then to increase the temperature of the kiln very gradually. For example, sections of sculpture 1 to 10 inches (2.5 to 25 cm) thick may take 3 to 5 days of firing: about 1½ to 2 days to preheat and about the same time to get up to full heat.

In an electric kiln, you can fire any size of sculpture that will fit in the kiln by turning up each switch one notch every 1 to 4 hours until all switches are in the high position. In a gas kiln, you can adjust the burner by changing the gas pressure by ⅛ inch (½ millibar) every 6 to 12 hours until about 1200°F/537.7°C is reached or the kiln interior is red-orange. The temperature could be raised faster with thinner-walled sculpture.

When firing a pre-programmed computerized kiln, use the slow-fire setting. For good results, it is generally best to use a temperature rise of between 40°–60° F/4.4°–15.5°C per hour. (Note: The thermocouple sensing the heat in a computerized kiln may not respond accurately to a temperature-rise setting lower than 40°F/4.4°C per hour, and the computer may show an error.) Although a slow rise in temperature is recommended throughout the entire firing, some ceramists using such a long firing period successfully increase the temperature-rise-per-hour once the kiln has passed through the critical quartz inversion point, or after the entire kiln chamber has risen beyond 1200°F/648.8°C. (See Temperature Rise per Hour chart under "Bisque and Single Firing" in Appendix 2A).

Since sculptures vary so much, each firing has to be planned individually depending on the number of pieces you have placed in the kiln and their thickness. The placement of the work in the kiln is also important, as the heat in different areas of a kiln may vary by several cones (15-7). The final temperature to which you fire the sculpture will, of course, depend on the clay from which it is built and the type of glaze, if any, or other colorants you have applied. And just as it

Figure 15-14
John Toki, U.S.A., removing shelves and bricks before unloading one of his wall sculptures. Note how the shelves have been doubled and built up with fire bricks to provide adequate support for heavy sections.

was essential to raise the heat slowly, it is equally important to give a kiln loaded with large sculpture a long, slow cooling period, which can extend from one to three days.

Unloading Large Sculpture

Unloading large fired sculpture is not as difficult as loading it into the kiln in the fragile green state, but it can still give you plenty of exercise. It is often impossible to get hydraulic equipment into the small space of the kiln to help you unload. If that is the case, tap wooden wedges under your large piece to lift it enough so that you can slide layers of newspaper or a series of three or four steel pipes or wood dowel rollers under it. Then you can slide or roll it out of the kiln chamber more easily (15-14). You can usually tilt sculpture that does not have a flat bottom enough to insert a thick plywood board under it. You can then lift the board on which the sculpture rests with a pry bar in order to insert rollers under it.

A hydraulic-lift hand truck is a valuable piece of equipment to have if you have to slide a large sculpture off a kiln shelf. The lift platform can be raised or lowered to the exact level of the shelf, thus making for safe removal of the sculpture. Some artists (15-12) use a chain hoist equipped with ropes or polyester lifting straps tied around their sculpture to help them lift it off the kiln floor. Engine hoists, forklifts, or cranes are also useful in unloading large sculpture, and are invaluable for people with limited strength or for those with back problems.

If a large sculpture was well constructed in the first place, if it is handled with care, and if it is

fired slowly with patience you can usually fire it without breakage—at least a percentage of the time. On the other hand, if the sculpture has developed cracks during the firing and could be further damaged by moving it out of the kiln, leave it in its firing position and glue any broken parts with an appropriate adhesive before moving it. Let the glue dry, and then unload the work. For further information on what adhesives to use, see Chapter 11 and Appendix 4C.

WOOD FIRING

In recent years, the ancient process of wood firing has regained popularity with Western ceramists. There is, of course, nothing new about using

Figure 15-15
Catherine Hiersoux, U.S.A., with ten helpers, built her modified *anagama* kiln of brick with cast refractory arches. For insulation, the kiln was coated with a 4 inch (10 cm) thick mix of cement, adobe, and straw. Access from the side of the kiln provides easier loading of the 90 cubic foot (2.5 cu m) kiln. A second chamber is sometimes used for salt firing. During firing, the kiln reaches cone 11 to 12. 1993. *Courtesy the artist.*

wood to fire a kiln full of pots. Through the centuries, especially in China and Japan, designs of wood-burning kilns showed a progression from the simple pit fire to highly sophisticated structures that maximized efficiency of combustion and heat retention. Today, wood-fired kilns are built to many differing designs, some of which still carry Japanese names. Although in the West the trend toward wood firing started with concern about the use of fossil fuel, it was also the result of an interest in Japanese ceramics that had led numerous British and American potters to study in Japan. As these ceramists discovered that with wood firing they could achieve effects impossible to get in any other way, they came to value the process for itself. Impressed with what they saw in Japan, some of them returned to build their own Japanese-style kilns (15-15). Many potters are building such kilns as more ceramists turn to wood firing to give their work a distinctive surface. Peter Voulkos (15-16), who likes the effects possible with wood firing, ships his bisque-fired pots across the country to be fired in Peter Callas's kiln (15-17).

In addition to the effect of the fire flashing on the pots, the minerals in the ash deposited on their surface may interact with the minerals in the clay, fuse, and form a glaze (15-18). These ashes will also affect any slips or glazes applied to the pots, as will the type of wood used for fuel, its degree of seasoning, and even the soil in which it grew and from which it drew minerals.

After spending a year in Japan, where he studied the history and methods of wood-burning kilns, Paul Chaleff (8-32, Color Plate 8) built a large wood-burning kiln designed for firing his own work. Speaking of the increasing popularity of wood firing Chaleff says,

> One of the reasons I believe that this technique has such allure for potters, beside the obvious excitement of the firing process, is that the finished work imparts a sense of history, a continuum of human emotion.

Chaleff prefers the terms *fire-glazed* or *kiln-glazed* for his pottery, and he is, like other Western artists, adapting the process so that his work reflects his own creativity and the society in which he lives rather than an ancient Oriental style.

Chaleff chooses clays that he feels will have good visual and tactile character when fired properly. They are often clays that are difficult to use

Figure 15-16
Peter Voulkos, U.S.A., still attacks his vessel forms with the same vigor with which he challenged ceramics tradition in the 1950s and 1960s. This greenware sculptural vessel awaits bisque firing. Many of Voulkos's vessels have been shipped across the country to New Jersey for firing in Peter Callas's wood kiln (15-17). *Courtesy Braunstein/Quay Gallery. Photo: Schopplein Studio, San Francisco.*

owing to their extreme shrinkage or the impurities and stones they contain. Workability, for Chaleff, is now secondary.

> Quiet strength is the overall effect I try to achieve. Form is the most important element of that effect. Surface quality and color serve to help define the form, interact with it, and of course enhance its character. . . .

Figure 15-17
Peter Callas, U.S.A., built his 300 cubic foot (8½ cu m) stacking space *anagama* kiln in 1987, using natural materials. The rocks along the side support the arch. He fires to approximately cone 12 using pine wood, and each firing lasts seven days. The round counterweight balances the door when firing. Callas uses iron-bearing and iron-free clay bodies in saggers and on open shelves, and he is now experimenting with glazes such as black shino.

Courtesy the artist. Photo: Bruce Riggs.

Figure 15-18
Jack Troy's wood-fired bottle received a natural glaze from the wood ash on its shoulders, recalling a jar made by a Chinese potter in about 200 B.C. (3-10). Because the heaviest ash particles settle near the port through which the wood is introduced and the kiln temperature may vary as much as eight cones, Troy's placement of his ware in the kiln affects how the glaze develops. (See also Color Plate 11.) Porcelain. Ht. 14 in. (35 cm).

Courtesy the artist and Helen Drutt Gallery. Photo: Schecter Lee.

Since wood firing of kilns is prohibited in some cities or areas because of the air pollution caused by the smoke, be sure to check your local ordinances before you build a wood-fired kiln.

SALT-VAPOR FIRING

Salt glazing has had a long tradition in Europe, England, and the United States (6-15, 7-5), where it proved to be ideally suited for use on containers for domestic use. This is due to the fact that the glaze that develops when the sodium in the salt combines with the silica in the clay is impermeable to both water and acids. In the days before refrigerators, when many foodstuffs were preserved in brine and vinegar, this was an important feature of salt-glazed ware. It is no wonder that when European and British potters came to the American colonies, they searched for a stoneware clay on which they could use their traditional glaze.

In order for a salt glaze to develop, the clay body must contain the right amount of silica, the silica must be softened enough by the heat of the kiln to be ready to fuse with the sodium, and the salt must be damp in order to form a vapor. When the damp salt is introduced into the kiln at about cone 7 (2264°F/1240°C), the sodium combines with the silica of the clay to produce a transparent glaze.

Since salt releases chloric and hydrochloric acid fumes when it vaporizes — fumes that are capable of seriously damaging the lungs and causing metal corrosion — you must take special precautions in placing the kiln and stack so that the gases will not be released too close to people or buildings (15-22, 15-23). In addition, insert the salt when there is no wind and avoid any fumes as you insert it. For added protection, wear a respirator rated for vapors, acid mists, and fumes.

Low-Salt Firing

Aware of the environmental impact of salt-vapor firing, potters have looked for ways to reduce the amount of chlorine gases emitted by their kilns. For example, Mick Casson in England (12-58) first cut down on the amount of salt and found that a smaller total amount put into the kiln more frequently in smaller batches worked well. He then switched to using sodium bicarbonate. Experiments showed that spraying a heated, saturated solution of sodium bicarbonate and water through several ports in about five-second bursts gave excellent results.

For salt-vapor firing in his catenary arch gas kiln (15-1), Peter Coussoulis uses a low-salt mixture combining 90% sodium bicarbonate and 10% fine-grain salt and adds a small amount of water to make a paste. He prepares twenty paper cups full of this blend, and beginning at cone 8 (2305°F/1263°C) he adjusts the dampers of the kiln to create a turbulent reducing atmosphere. When the kiln reaches about cone 10 (2381°F/1305°C), he begins to add the salt mixture, one cup in each kiln port every ten minutes.

After Coussoulis completes the firing, he turns the kiln off and closes all the burner ports and the damper. When the kiln has dropped to 1750°F/954°C, he fumes the pottery by introducing a mixture of 2.5 ounces (70 grams) of tin chloride and 1.06 ounces (30 grams) of bismuth subnitrate. He combines the chemicals into two packets and throws them through the burner ports into the kiln chamber, or he places them at the end of a long piece of angle iron that has been prewarmed and pushes this deep into the kiln. He then closes the kiln burner port tightly so that fuming occurs. These chemicals react with the glaze to develop mother-of-pearl and glimmering rainbow colors.

Janet Mansfield of Australia (12-9, 12-10) fires her work in a 10-cubic-foot (.28-cubic-meter) low-polluting salt kiln, designed by Max Murray. The kiln has a stainless steel "scrubber" chamber attached to the kiln flue. Inside the chamber is a pressurized water spray system that dissolves the hydrochloric acid fumes into a solution, which in turn is collected in a tank and drained into a neutralizing tower filled with limestone chips. This process neutralizes the acidic water, resulting in water safe enough to be discharged into a sewer.

If you choose not to use salt for vapor firing, you can use a more environmentally friendly mixture of dampened borax, pearl ash, soda ash, whiting, lithium carbonate, and bentonite. (See Appendix 1C for the formula and some slips to use with salt firing.)

Although it is possible to build a special kiln with a calcium alumina lining that can be used for both bisque and glaze firing as well as infrequent or lightly salted firings, usually a salt kiln is used only for salt firing. This is because the

Figure 15-19
Mary Law, U.S.A., opening the salt-vapor kiln at Walnut Creek Civic Arts Center (see also 15-1), in which her work had been fired to cone 11. She left the exteriors of some pots unglazed — their surface differences are due to placement in the kiln. 1993. Stoneware.

Figure 15-20
Shown partially unloaded, Law's salt-vapor firing displays her work's varied forms and the surfaces she achieved through the use of several clays, slips, and a few glazes. For environmental reasons, she used a vapor-producing mix of about 95% sodium bicarbonate, 4% salt, and 1% borax packed in paper cups, dampened with a weak saltwater solution. Every fifteen minutes she placed two cups in the burner ports over a period of two to three hours.

bricks lining the kiln become glazed at the same time the objects receive their glaze. If a salt kiln were to be used for bisque firing or ordinary glaze firing after salt-glaze firing, the salt glaze on the bricks would melt again and cause problems with the newly introduced ware. Electric kilns cannot be used for salt glazing, as the elements would be harmed by the buildup of glaze.

Many potters respond to the surface that salt glazing creates (15-1, 15-19 to 15-27). Janet Mansfield (12-10) says,

Salt firing offers me an aesthetic that suits my temperament. Both form and clay quality are enhanced by the glaze texture and every part of the technical processes demands creative attention.

In order to get a combination of smooth areas and the characteristic mottled and textured "orange-peel" glaze that salt can produce, Walter Keeler

Figure 15-21
Mary Law fired a number of mugs in the salt-vapor firing illustrated here and in Figure 15-20. The differences in surfaces are due to the kiln placement. 1993. Stoneware. *Courtesy the artist. Photo: Richard Sargent.*

(15-26) often coats part of a jug or pot with a colored engobe (see Appendix 1C). Where he sprays the engobe onto the clay, the surface will fire smooth, but when he leaves the clay uncoated, the orange-peel effect appears.

Eileen Murphy, on the other hand, does not want the details of her delicately incised and painted vessels to be obliterated by the orange-peel texture, so she fires her work very carefully, avoiding the "blast" that could destroy the delicacy of the image drawn on the pot (15-27). Of her salt firing Murphy says,

> *The firing is magic! Especially in the fall when the stars are clear and the air cold and it's dark and time to salt.*

Traditionally, salt ware was fired without added color, and the pots emerged predominately the color of the fired clay body—sometimes brownish, if there was iron in the clay, sometimes gray, if the fire was heavily reducing and the iron content low. The only added color was in the cobalt blue decoration (7-5). Contemporary ceramists, however, use oxides, slips, stains, and glazes to impart color to their salt-glazed objects. Robert Winokur, for example, uses slips and engobes along with ash glazes on his table-vessel constructions (15-22 to 15-24). This is another example of how contemporary ceramists have taken an historical process, experimented with it, expanded its traditional limits, and found ways to adapt it to their needs.

(a)

(b)

Figure 15-22
(a) Robert M. Winokur, U.S.A., measures out the salt compound, pouring it into an angle iron in preparation for introducing it into the kiln. (b) He inserts the angle iron "spoon" in order to drop the compound into the firebox. As the salt vaporizes, the sodium will combine with the silica in the clay, causing a glaze to form on the surface. The angle iron allows him to stand well away from any vapors that might escape as he inserts the salt. *Courtesy the artist.*

Figure 15-23
Winokur adjusts the damper on his salt-glaze kiln to create a reducing atmosphere during salting. Note the chlorine vapor escaping from the chimney — the reason salt kilns must be carefully placed so that the fumes are kept well away from people and houses. *Courtesy the artist.*

Figure 15-24
Ceramic table with grid inset by Robert M. Winokur, U.S.A. 1989. Salt-glazed stoneware, blue wood ash glaze, slips, and engobes. 30 × 10 × 14 in. (76 × 25 × 36 cm). *Courtesy the artist.*

Figure 15-25
The pitted and mottled surface of salt glaze was characteristic of the functional salt-glazed studio pottery Karen Karnes, U.S.A., made in the 1970s. Now Karnes fires in a large wood kiln (8-29). Stoneware. Ht. 16 in. (40.6 cm). *Courtesy of the artist.*

Figure 15-26
Walter Keeler, England, created a variation of a traditional metal jug form in salt-glazed clay. Keeler fires his stoneware to cone 10 (Orton), reduces from 1832°F/1000°C, and salts the kiln at cone 9 for an hour, finishing with a half-hour soak. He achieves the variation in texture by coating part of the ware with an engobe, which fires smooth, while the remaining part fires with an "orange-peel" salt texture. Stoneware, gray/gray-blue. Ht. 17 in. (43 cm). *Courtesy the artist.*

Figure 15-27
To create portrait vessels of the animals that live on her country acreage, Eileen Murphy, U.S.A., first sands her dry greenware (wearing a mask and goggles), then brushes on slips, and incises detail into the dry clay. For a glaze that will not fill the lines, Murphy depends on salt firing to coat, but not destroy, the complex colored surface. Stoneware, slips, stains, and sgraffito. *Courtesy Smith Gallery and the artist. Photo: Richard Walker.*

RAKU FIRING

Another process that has spread from one culture to another is **raku** technique, developed in sixteenth century Japan (Chapter 3), where raku-fired pots were used in the tea ceremony. Its popularity in the West began in the 1950s and 1960s, when an interest in Zen philosophy developed in the United States and Europe. Linked with a keen appreciation of nature and a recognition of beauty in nonperfection, raku also appealed because of its participatory aspects and the spontaneous and dramatic results it produced. Now, like many of the processes that have spread around the world, the raku process has been absorbed, changed, and adapted to each area (15-28 to 15-33). More significant than the use of new methods and equipment are the aesthetic changes that have taken place as contemporary ceramists around the world have adapted the raku tradition into their work, using what is applicable and discarding what is inappropriate to their work or their own ceramic traditions (11-64, 15-30 to 15-33).

Before a pot or a sculpture can be fired using the raku process, it should be built of a clay that can withstand the thermal shocks to which it will be subjected (see Appendix 1C). The pot should then be bisque-fired in any type of kiln and glazed with a low-fire glaze adapted for raku firing (see Appendix 1C). Although the traditional raku kiln was a small wood-burning kiln with an inner sagger in which the ware was fired, you can use any kiln that can be heated quickly to red-hot heat—between 015 (1479°F/804°C) and 08 (1751°F/955°C)—and that provides easy access to its firing chamber. It can be an electric or gas kiln (15-28 to 15-30) or a specially constructed insulated one (15-31), and it can be fired with whatever fuel is available. Since the process involves placing the preheated pot directly in the hot firing chamber and then withdrawing it, the interior should be accessible so that you can easily insert and withdraw the pots. Be sure you use tongs and protective gloves when you do this (15-30), and wear shaded goggles when you look into the fire. Depending on the design of the kiln, as the firing progresses, you may be able to look in and see the glaze actually maturing on the ware.

As soon as the glaze matures, remove the pot and leave it to cool rapidly or treat it in one of several ways. You can place it immediately in a heat-resistant container of sawdust, charcoal, newspapers, seaweed—anything that will burn and create a reducing atmosphere when the con-

Figure 15-28
An old electric kiln stripped of its control box and elements can be turned into a raku kiln. This one has a capacity of about 5 cubic feet (.14 cu m), and is fired by a propane gas burner inserted through a hole in the wall. Another hole in the lid serves as a vent with a damper plate. Here, Anita Liroff, with instructor Tom Heid, loads a pot. *Courtesy Richmond Art Center Ceramics Studio, Richmond, CA. Photo: Carl Duncan.*

Figure 15-29
The pot in the trash-can reduction chamber. To produce a crackle texture, the pot was removed from the kiln and placed on a shelf, where it was immediately fanned to increase the crackle; then it was quickly placed in the reduction can while still hot but not glowing. After the newspaper flamed up, the can was covered for twenty minutes. *Courtesy the Richmond Art Center Ceramic Studio, Richmond, CA. Photo: Carl Duncan.*

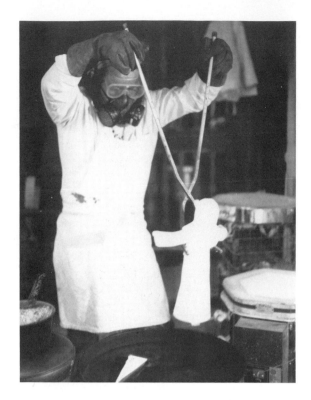

Figure 15-30
Reuben Kent, U.S.A., places a piece of his sculpture in the reduction chamber. Although he usually uses wood shavings, he says that for a nice flash he uses paper printed with color—*advertisement circulars are good. However,* he says, *a healthy artist is a happy artist,* and since this particular paper stock usually has lead in the ink it is advisable to use any and all safety precautions. *Courtesy the artist.*

(a)

(b)

(c)

Figure 15-31
Contemporary raku equipment can be a far cry from that used in sixteenth-century Japan. **(a)** Alan Widenhofer, U.S.A., fires a large glazed bowl by lowering a lightweight wire and ceramic fiber–insulated gas kiln around it. **(b)** The bowl is removed from the kiln while hot and placed on a bed of newspaper, which ignites from the heat. **(c)** The bowl was so large it required a specially built cover of wire and ceramic fiber. Once lowered, the ring was immediately covered with sheet metal to smother the fire and cause reduction. *Courtesy the artist.*

tainer is covered. Reduction will cause iridescent luster areas to appear, and fire marks that enrich the surface will often develop. Most raku develops crackles in the glaze, but if you want more crackle, you can plunge the piece into water while it is hot.

In the past, the glazes used for raku firing were lead glazes, because lead was a readily available flux that made it possible for the glaze to be melted at the low temperature the kilns achieved. Nowadays, however, for health reasons, lead is generally avoided, and in addition, the raku-fired pots with their pitted, cracked glazes are not considered hygienic for use as containers for food.

The experience of pulling a pot from the kiln and plunging it into sawdust, or seaweed and water, can be exhilarating for those new to clay. But raku-firing techniques, when developed by an artist to meet his or her individual artistic requirement, become an expressive tool, used not just for the excitement of the process but, more important, for the results that can be obtained with it (11-64, Color Plate 33, 15-32). One artist who uses raku in a highly expressive manner is Richard Hirsch (Color Plate 13).

Hirsch uses a combination of terra sigillata and low-fire glazes to surface his tripod vessel forms (see Chapter 14 and Appendix 1C for details). Of his raku firing method, Hirsch says,

the piece is removed while very hot (1400°F/ 760°C approx.) and sprayed with several metallic salts (i.e., copper, iron). I use a mask when spraying outdoors and never do this indoors because the fumes are toxic.

(Note: The respirator you use should be rated for toxic fumes.) Hirsch continues this process for several removals and sprayings to build up the surface. His final step is removing the piece from the hot kiln and placing it in straw for the postfiring reduction. Hirsch says this

further enhances the visual depth of the surface and changes the coloration of the salts and sigs. The results are a colored patination that expresses age and history which is an integral aspect of my work.

Raku firing, with its unexpected results, appeals to many people for its spontaneity. Nevertheless, there are health and safety precautions you should follow when working with flaming materials and red-hot objects. Keep a hose or bucket handy; don't go barefoot, and wear safety shoes to protect you against burning straw or a

Figure 15-32
Enviroman, by Stephen Braun, U.S.A., was raku-fired in sections. Braun created the surface with matt raku glazes and a semiglossy white glaze with various oxides under it. White raku clay with 30% grog. 1992. Ht. 94 in. (2.39 m), not counting the airplanes.
Courtesy the artist. Photo: Tony Novelozo.

dropped pot. Keep the area around the kiln free of combustibles, and if you reduce in a container also keep the area around it clear of loose straw or paper. Lift the lid of the reducing container carefully so that any flames will be directed away from yourself or other people. And, as Reuben Kent demonstrates, use all safety precautions (15-30).

Figure 15-33
In *Viaje Despues de la Vida* (*The Voyage to the Afterlife*), Jack Thompson, U.S.A., created a sculpture that combines the Japanese raku-firing technique with Egyptian and indigenous American images — symbolic of the many influences at work in ceramics today. Egyptian blue glaze on the figure of Anubis and the interior of the vessel-figure. 1992. 8 × 19 × 4 in. (20 × 48 × 10 cm). *Courtesy the artist.*

Figure 15-34
Hookers, by Paul Soldner, U.S.A. Soldner stenciled the figures on this wall piece, using a white slip with copper-green slip on top. The low-fired clay was salt fumed, with local reduction. Ht. 20 × 27 in. (51 × 68 cm). *Courtesy the artist. Photo: Charles Frizzell.*

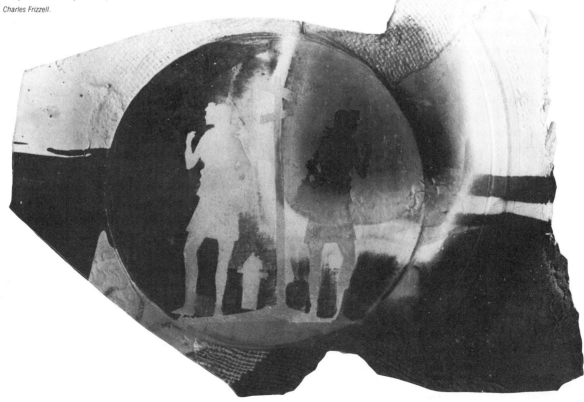

POSTFIRING SMOKING

A number of artists use postfiring smoking and fuming techniques to give a rich, smoky quality to their pots or sculptures without subjecting them to the stresses of the raku method. By using this process, they can also achieve interesting reduction effects without damaging the elements of their electric kilns. There are various ways to do this, but basically it is a matter of exposing the already fired piece to the effects of a reduction atmosphere. Glenys Barton, in England, smoked her poetic figurative wall plaques because she felt they would not stand the raku process, while Paul Soldner used a salt fuming and local reduction to give his wall piece its misty night-time quality (15-34). Do not fume or smoke your pieces by burning straw soaked in salts without wearing a respirator rated for protection against toxic fumes.

PIT FIRING

The earliest potters fired in open firings on the top of the ground or in shallow pits. This tradition has continued throughout history and to the present in nonindustrialized areas around the world—Africa (4-12), the American Southwest (5-18), Mexico (5-12), and Fiji (1-31), for example. This type of firing produces a porous type of earthenware that is not watertight. Contemporary potters, entranced with the fire marks and other effects that can be achieved with pit firing, have experimented with firings ranging from sawdust and peat in an open-top brick kiln to pit firing on a beach. Each person has a favorite way of conducting this type of firing, so it is impossible to generalize about the method. For example, some people use only earthenware clay for objects to be pit fired, feeling that it will survive the stress of the firing better than high-fire clays, but Carol Molly Prier (15-35 to 15-37) has fired every type of clay in pit fires—from low-fire to porcelain—and finds that no clay seems to crack more or less than another. Since her vessels are usually burnished, she chooses clay with no grog. At one group pit firing, held on a beach, the ware was partially buried in a layer of sawdust with seaweed and driftwood placed over it to provide salt and other minerals. The pots were then sprinkled with copper carbonate, covered with cow dung, and prepared for firing by piling wood on top of the cushioning of the dung. With everyone pitching in to dig the pit, to gather driftwood and

Figure 15-35
A group pit firing on a beach can be a rewarding experience, especially if the fire is good to your ware and creates the colored surface you desire. Here, Carol Molly Prier sprinkles copper carbonate on some of the pots that have been buried in sawdust at the bottom of the pit and then covered with seaweed.

seaweed, and to place their pots in a layer of sawdust, the sense of community effort gave this group of contemporary clay crafters a vivid sense of identification with early potters.

CHOOSING *YOUR* MEANS OF EXPRESSION

Never in the history of ceramics has the person working in clay had such a wide choice of techniques or such an extensive range of available materials. The alternatives open to you today demand that you make aesthetic choices as well as learn techniques for forming, coloring, and firing clay. Ceramics can be a seductive medium in which to work, offering processes that in themselves are fascinating. As a result, the craft or technique sometimes becomes an end in itself. Nobody would deny that craft is a vital part of ceramics, but craft without artistic sensibility will never form a beautiful pot or build an expressive piece of sculpture. Nurturing your creativity, fostering your imagination, developing your aesthetic awareness, and learning to trust them is as much a part of your development in ceramics as is mastering the process.

(a)

(b)

Figure 15-36
(a) After the pots have been covered with cow dung and wood, and after a ritual scattering of cornmeal over them, the fire begins to play its part. **(b)** The fire has burned down and the pots emerge surrounded by the ashes, which hold the shape of the dung until they are disturbed. The hardest part of pit firing is not digging the pit or lugging the wood and dung, but waiting until the ashes are cool enough so that you can remove and study your pots.

Figure 15-37
On a windy beach within sound of the surf, the fire, the clay, and human artistry unite to create an elegant vessel using a firing method as old as the art of ceramics. Pit-fired, burnished vessel by Carol Molly Prier, U.S.A. *Courtesy the artist. Photo: Charles Frizzell.*

16

Installations, Large-Scale and Architectural Works

One of the fascinating things about clay is the way the material adapts itself to so many different styles of working and to so wide a range of scales—from hand-sized fertility figures (1-2) and miniature teapots (9-8) to an installation in a pond (16-1) and decorative works that can bring warmth and color to an architectural space (16-14, Color Plates 6, 15, 41, 50, and cover).

Historically, ceramists have used their skills to bring color and texture to architecture since the days when sun-dried building bricks were covered with glazed tiles that protected them from the weather continuing to the present and including the works of late-nineteenth-century architect Louis Sullivan (7-9), who sheathed his metal-framed buildings with curtain walls of ceramics and enhanced them with rich ornament.

Even during the early and middle decades of the twentieth century when the anti-ornament philosophy of the International Style of architecture was dominant, some individual clients and architects continued to call on ceramists to create works for plazas, hospitals, universities, subway stations, and private homes. Today, when more architects show a reawakened interest in ornament, many new opportunities are open for the ceramic artist working in the architectural field. These can range in scale from a sculptural fireplace (16-19) to the enhancement of a city traffic circle (Color Plate 50).

Figure 16-1

Rise and Shine, Magical Fish, by Kate Malone, England, an installation placed in the disused filter beds which once purified water for East London (see also Color Plate 44). The brightly glazed heads and tails of the surfacing fish, contrasting with the power line, underline Malone's environmental message that reaches hundreds of children who observe at the Lea Valley Park Nature Reserve. Malone said, *I just wanted to have a bit of fun with the fish, but as well as that I think public art should have some kind of spirit to it — to cheer people up, basically. Courtesy the artist.*

Since large-scale installations and site-specific projects present problems in construction, firing, and installation, if you are a beginner in ceramics you are unlikely to start out by constructing a large arch (16-2), a tall sculpture for an entranceway (16-6), or a series of columns to brighten a waiting area in an airport (16-7). But because the use of ceramics in architecture is becoming increasingly popular, you should become aware of the possibilities it offers to the more experienced ceramist you may one day become.

INSTALLATIONS

Creating large-scale sculpture appeals to many experienced ceramists, however, and even when they have not received a commission to create a work for a specific site, they may create large-scale temporary installations for settings that range from temporary gallery exhibits (16-3), to the top of a French mountain (Color Plate 46). American artist John Toki (Color Plate 48) constructed his sculpture *'s-Hertogenbosch* in Holland and named it after the Dutch city in which he was working at the time. He says the sculpture was

> *inspired by elements in nature, such as water, sky, and mountains. I am attracted to pure abstractions and wish to convey a timelessness about my work. I pursue interaction between the fluidity of the clay during the building process and the frozen stillness of the work after it is fired.*

Such works may be temporary or permanent, personal in subject matter, or focused on more general public concerns. For instance, Kate Malone has expressed her concern with the environment in commissioned works (16-1). Her first interest in creating work for a public space was when she made a fountain for the drab hospital courtyard she had stared at for weeks from her hospital bed. She made it in the form of a giant jug that continuously pours water because she feels that jugs symbolize the warmth of gatherings of friends or family. She also has a number of other site-specific works to her credit, ranging from a mural for an HIV unit to one for a restaurant. On the other hand, Nobuko Tsutsumi addresses the mingling of Japanese and imported

Figure 16-2
Wabi Sabi Special, by Nobuko Tsutsumi, Japan. Tsutsumi's work combines Japanese folktale images and the traditional gate that leads into temple enclosures with Western images such as Botticelli's *Birth of Venus.* Tsutsumi poses the question of how Japanese culture will integrate these imported images with the concept of *wabi sabi* — the poetic philosophy surrounding the tea ceremony and its ceramics. Installation in Museum of Modern Arts, Hyogo, Japan. White stoneware, high- and low-fire glazes, china paint, and luster. *Courtesy the artist. Photo: Takashi Hatakeyama.*

images in a temporary gallery installation (16-2), while Ellen Driscoll's gallery installation (16-3) reflects a desire for personal expression. She feels that it

> *poses a kind of dichotomy between conflicted sides of a self or two sides to a psyche — an accumulative, material, "earthbound" self, and one which moves freely with few attachments.*

When American ceramist Dierdre Daw installed her *Underground Room* (Color Plate 45) in a San Francisco gallery, she planned it as a space in which viewers could walk on the tiled floor or sit on the bench, interacting intimately with the work. Daw sees her underground imagery as symbolic of the unconscious/intuitive, and the teapots and cups as the conscious/rational aspects of the human psyche.

Japanese sculptor Kimpei Nakamura has been creating ceramic murals and site-specific works for a number of years, constantly exploring new images and new techniques. Lately, he has turned to gallery and outdoor installations that include many elements. In an outdoor installation (Color Plate 53), he combined small sculptures with a massive steel cylinder covered with large high-fired tiles. The small sculptures are made up of diverse elements formed in molds which in turn are made from plumbing supplies, machine parts, and the rough rocks favored in Japanese landscaping. Nakamura often coats these cast rocks with gold luster, echoing the name of his native town, Kanazawa, whose name means *gold marsh.* The name originated with the discovery of gold in the area's marshlands, and the town is also famous for one of the most impressive gardens in Japan. Nakamura lived in Kanazawa until he was thirty-four and acknowledges its influence on his work. He also acknowledges the influence of downtown Tokyo, where he now lives: The tiles that cover the pillars in his installations are decorated with decals made from enlarged photos of crinkled paper, computer-generated images, and overglaze brushwork — images that are more suggestive of the cityscape than of Kanazawa's garden.

Approaching clay with a quite different philosophy, British sculptor Antony Gormley created a number of installations which he calls *Fields* — celebrations of humanity's shared expe-

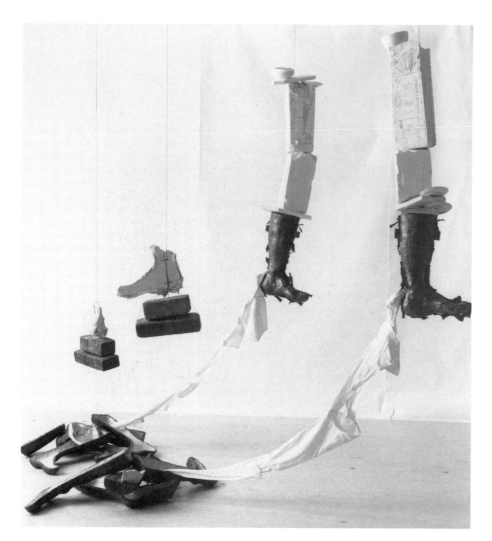

Figure 16-3
For her untitled installation, Ellen Driscoll, U.S.A., used pulleys, weights, and
counterbalancing to imply a notion of
causality. The clay feet, made in press
molds, are suspended about 3 feet
(91 cm) in the air but are connected to
the ground by trailing cloth and ceramic
shards carrying map images. The plaster
feet appear to ride more lightly in the air,
but in actuality they are equal in weight
to the visually heavier clay feet. 1991.
Clay, cloth, shards, plaster, and pulleys.
Courtesy the European Ceramics Work Centre, Holland,
and the artist.

Figure 16-4
Cannery Row Catch, by Andrée Singer
Thompson and Valerie Otani in collaboration with Elizabeth Stanek, was commissioned by the City of Monterey, California,
for Cannery Row, to commemorate the
once-active sardine canning industry
there. The mixed-media site-specific
work was fabricated from the rubble of
the burned-out San Carlos Cannery. The
fish are reflected in a stainless-steel mirror placed on the wall of the abandoned
holding tank. Kiln brick, red brick, concrete slabs, beach rocks, and stainless
steel. 1991. 40 × 10 × 10 ft (12 ×
3 × 3 m). *Courtesy the artists.*

rience throughout the millennia (Color Plates 42 and 43). The figures for these installations are made by men, women, and children in various parts of the world: The one illustrated, installed in a New York gallery, was created in Cholula, Mexico, with the Texca family. To make the hordes of 30-to-40,000 clay figures for his installations, Gormley suggests that the makers use their hands like molds, forming the figures no larger than they can hold. He asks them not to copy, but to let the forms just arise, and he says he has been amazed at the ancient images that appear. Gormley considers *Fields* to be about the recovery of memory and about the return to the body as an antidote to our contemporary electronic environment. The figures for this installation were formed of locally dug clay—about 30 tons of it—then were fired in a local brick factory.

Given a commission to create a permanent installation at an unusual site, a group of California ceramists placed their work in the ruins of a burned-out building, using part of the building itself as components (16-4).

CERAMICS AND ARCHITECTURE

Ceramist Rita Pagony of Hungary sees a link between architecture and sculptural vessels, and working with her architect husband, Miklós Olasz, Pagony proposed innovative schemes in which huge vessels made of bricks would be incorporated into buildings (16-5). These would function as fountains, with the water flowing down the building into brick-lined basins.

In the United States, a group of ceramists and architects in New York joined forces to explore ways to use ceramics in architecture. Among the proposals that emerged were site-specific projects for vacant lots or redeveloped neighborhoods in Manhattan, and studies for the facades of row houses shown in an exhibit and a catalogue titled *Firing the Imagination*.

(a)

A SYMBOL OF CERAMICS TRADITONS

(b)

Figure 16-5
(a) Rita Pagony, of Hungary, and her architect husband, Miklós Olasz, created a series of proposals inspired by Pagony's large vessels for the urban planning competition of the Faenza Concorso. **(b)** Using the vessel as an architectural form, they proposed a brick vessel over which water would run down into a fountain in a plaza. Proposal. Ht. 3 stories (9.1 m). *Courtesy the artist.*

Figure 16-6
Portal, created by architects Alexander
Brodsky and Ilya Utkin of Russia for the
entranceway of the new European Ceramics Work Centre, consists of a stainless steel portico that rises to the roofs
of the surrounding buildings, sur-
mounted by a steel pyramid-shaped
"roof" to which three hundred ceramic
elements are attached. Stoneware and
stainless steel. 1992. 46 × 23 × 23 ft
(14 × 7 × 7 m). *Courtesy the European Ceramics Work Centre, Holland. Photo: Peer van Kruis.*

An innovative use of ceramics in architecture
has been that of Nader Khalili, who has experimented with firing adobe houses to make safe,
affordable shelter—shelter that would not be subject to collapse due to heavy rain. Khalili has
actually fired entire buildings, truly integrating
architecture and ceramics (see Further Reading at
the end of the book).

Site-Specific Works

The kind of thinking an artist must use to design
and carry out a large commissioned work is different from that needed to create a personal, expressive work that is not planned for a specific
place. Thorough planning, from design through

installation, is the key factor in creating a work for a commission.

Most of the clay-forming techniques demonstrated in earlier chapters can be adapted to large-scale works; the main limitation is the difficulty or impossibility of building, firing, and transporting such work as a single piece. For this reason, a large work must usually be fabricated and fired in sections that will fit the kiln (16-6). These smaller clay units can be fired more successfully and transported to the site more easily than single large pieces and can be reassembled for either temporary or permanent installation. By using a variety of forming techniques — handforming and modeling, rolling out slabs, extruding forms, pressing clay into molds, or by working on the wheel — a ceramist can construct components to build at almost any scale, from small wall pieces to a tower (16-18).

Obviously, the planning and carrying out of such large projects is a lengthy, time-consuming, and exhausting process. In designing a work for architecture, the artist must give thought to many factors, among them, the scale of work that would be most appropriate for a particular building or outdoor environment. For example, an extremely heavy or large mural might dominate and overwhelm a small room, while the same mural could be highly appropriate for an extensive outdoor wall. An airport waiting area (16-7), a bench (16-8) or a hospital courtyard (16-9), a govern-

Figure 16-7
For her commissioned work in the Zürich airport, Elisabeth Langsch, Switzerland, decided that columns ending in organic forms would bring color and animation to the functional surroundings. In planning an architectural work, Langsch tries to anticipate the feelings of those who will use the space and to make their time there more pleasant. Handmodeled reliefs on columns, colored engobes. Ht. 14 ft (4.20 m). *Courtesy the artist.*

Figure 16-8
Karen Park, Denmark, known for her fountains and murals, has also created benches to enliven a city street, courtyard, or garden. This one displays a strong black and white spiral pattern reminiscent of designs on prehistoric pottery, yet contemporary. *Courtesy the artist.*

(a)

Figure 16-9
(a) Jan Snoeck, the Netherlands. These reclining figures will bring color and humor to a hospital courtyard. Sectioned and fired, they are ready for shipping; note small models that will aid the workers who assemble them on site. Dense, brightly colored glazes protect the surface from freezing and thawing.
(b) Snoeck and one of his seated figures in progress. Built solid, it will be cut into sections while still damp, hollowed out, and fired, creating components that will be assembled in a city plaza, park, or outside a public building. *(a) Courtesy the artist. (b) Courtesy Struktuur '68, The Hague.*

(b)

Figure 16-10
Untitled #645. Robert Sperry, U.S.A. (standing in front of the mural), won the Honors Program Award of the King County Arts Commission to create a wall for the County Administration Building, Seattle. Since he could not see the mural in its entirety until it was fired, Sperry made full-scale studies using acrylic paints, and he also developed some of the forms and their relationships in a series of etchings. To create the ceramic images, he applied the black and white slip freely, sometimes flinging it at the black-glazed modules, creating explosions of texture and atmosphere that he then stabilized with strong geometric shapes. Ht. 10½ ft × 30 ft (3 m × 9 m). *Courtesy the artist. Photo: Jim Ball.*

ment building wall (16-10), a hotel lounge (16-11), a conference or lecture room (16-12), a remodeled historic building (16-13)—all present unique situations in which the ambience of each site must be retained and the needs of those who will use the spaces respected.

Factors the artist must consider include the following: From what distance or what angle will the viewer see the work? How will the space in which the work is installed be used? Under what type of lighting will the work be seen?

The color of the work as it relates to its surroundings is also important. For example, the brilliantly colored glazes that might be appropriate in an informal restaurant probably would be out of place in a bank president's office. The scale of surface texture or the type of glaze treatment would also appropriately vary according to placement of the work. For instance, an extremely detailed surface would be lost on a work in a tall lobby where people do not linger, but would create interest in an intimate setting or a lounge area where people would have the leisure to study it. If any images are included in the work, these too would vary according to the use of the site.

Figure 16-11
Eduardo Andaluz, Spain, created a mural for the lounge of a beach hotel, using undulating organic forms. The reddish color of the terra-cotta clay, coated with engobes, is repeated in the leather of the chairs, while its natural surface contrasts with the smooth marble of the walls and floor. 1989–90. Length 43 ft (13 m). In the Gloria Palace Hotel, Grand Canary Island. *Courtesy the artist.*

▼ **Figure 16-12**
A relief by Carlo Zauli, Italy, brings a suggestion of the natural world — tide-pools? ploughed fields? a geological formation? — to a conference room at the headquarters of the organization known as Conosce Italia S. I. in Bologna. It is unglazed, colored yellow, orange, green, and brown, with red-brown clay. Stoneware, 2282°F/1250°C. Length 33 ft (10 m). *Courtesy the artist. Photo: Antonio Masotti.*

Other factors apply to three-dimensional sculpture. What about the space in which it will be placed? Will viewers merely look at the work, or will they walk around it or through it or even climb on it? When designing work for children's playgrounds, the artist should consult a playground consultant, who will explain the special safety considerations that must be taken into account. These include height limitations, planning the surface treatment so that children are protected from injury from sharp forms or edges, and the provision of soft material (sand, bark) into which they may jump or onto which they would land if they fell from the sculpture. If the work will be accessible to the public, then possible vandalism must also be anticipated; the same is true for the danger of injury to the public that might be caused by structural failure. If the work is intended for outdoor use, the artist must take climate into account; in a mild climate, a mural or sculpture intended for the outdoors will not encounter the same difficulties as it would if installed where winters are harsh. In cold climates, however, if water enters the pores of the fired clay and then alternately freezes and thaws, the work can develop cracks and eventually be destroyed.

Preplanning

There are many other aspects to be considered in making a large-scale work for a specific site; for example, the budget, as it relates to all aspects of construction, must be carefully worked out at the beginning, and installation must be planned from the start because the engineering requirements may necessitate changes in the design. Thus, the artist who works on architectural commissions must either develop some engineering skills or be able to work with an engineer to design the installation of the work. Artists may have to become familiar with the use of engineered steel supports that will keep columns from falling on passersby, with built-in arrangements for bolts, rods, or brackets with which to attach the heavy sections of a mural, or with the use of construction-grade adhesives to attach sections to a backing. (See Appendixes 4B and 4C for information on adhesives and installation.)

If an artist is called in to propose a sculpture or ceramic mural for a specific site after a building has been completed, he or she should first of all arrange to see the architect's drawings and

Figure 16-13
Birthplace, a sculpture by Stephen De Staebler, U.S.A., for the historic Old Post Office building in St. Louis. De Staebler, himself born in St. Louis, appropriately chose forms that evoke atavistic symbols of earth, water, and the human figure. The mural was mounted on a support of steel channels and brackets for which holes had been built into the clay sections. The piece was commissioned through the Architecture Program of the General Services Administration; a local committee chose three artists to be reviewed for final choice by the administration. Stoneware; fired in sections in six firings at cone 5. 129 × 83 × 20 in. (328 × 211 × 50 cm). *Courtesy the artist.*

construction details. For an interior site, these should include wall-construction details and the electrical plans; for an exterior site, the artist should contact the landscape architect to obtain irrigation plans, and plans showing the location of wiring and lighting outlets, as well as information on the amount of power available. These electrical specifications are especially important if the artist's work requires electrical power for lighting, pumps, or motors, or when digging is necessary to place the foundations for a sculpture in the vicinity of electric cables, gas lines, or water lines.

The lighting arrangement will greatly affect how the viewer will see a work once it is installed. Will the lighting be natural or artificial? Poor lighting has more than once obscured art works that have taken artists months to create, and more than one artist has been shocked to discover unexpected lamps hanging in front of his or her mural. The type of lighting — incandescent, fluorescent, low-voltage, spot lighting — and its placement, should be agreed on with the architect or client, and the amount of electric current needed to supply the fixtures should be analyzed and included in the plan from the start.

These are just some of the factors with which the artist who designs architectural works must deal.

THE COMMISSION PROCESS

How does the commission process work, and how do artists get commissions?

Many countries and a number of states in the U.S. now have what are known as "percent for art" laws that require them to set aside between .5 and 2% of the cost of any new public building to be spent on art. Commissions to create this type of work are usually awarded either by open competition or from the proposals presented by a group of selected artists, who may work in a variety of media. Elisabeth Langsch (16-7), for instance, frequently enters competitions as an invited artist, competing for a commission with painters, metal sculptors, or fiber artists.

Corporations and private clients are another source of commissions, or a request might come from the architect who is designing the building and who is familiar with a particular artist's work. Ideally, the ceramic artist would work with the architect from the very beginning to integrate ceramics into the building design. In reality, however, an architect generally does not call on an artist until a building is already planned.

If the commission is awarded before the building has been constructed, it is important for the architect and the artist to consult well before construction starts in order to agree on the structural changes that may be needed to accommodate the proposed art work. Placing a heavy ceramic work on a wall may mean that the wall will have to be reinforced with steel to support the load, or a free-standing work of sculpture may need a steel-reinforced concrete foundation poured as part of the floor, complete with in-place mounting bolts. The artist usually bears the expense of installation, and arranging for this engineering to be built in from the start will cost less than tearing down a wall or ripping up floors to install it later.

On the other hand, it often happens that once a building is finished, the owner will decide that a particular space will be enhanced by a work of art. In this case, the owner may approach an artist directly, through an art consultant whose job it is to find art for the client, or through an artists' representative or gallery that may have approached the owner as a possible purchaser of art.

Whatever method brings the commission and the artist together, carrying out a site-specific commission requires an ability on the part of the artist to work with others — architect, engineer, and client. It also requires a flexibility that an artist accustomed to working alone in a studio may find either satisfying or impossible, depending on his or her personality.

Creating a Commissioned Work

Once having decided to apply for a commission, the artist must present the proposed work as attractively and as graphically as possible so that the jurors can visualize it. In order to convince the competition jury, architect, or client that his or her particular design is the most appropriate one for the chosen site, the artist's presentation generally covers concept, design, material, budget, site specifications, time schedule, and installation details. This presentation also often includes a written description, plans, and elevation drawings showing the proposed placement, plus a three-dimensional model of the proposed work. Upon the artist's receipt of the commission, a signed contract between artist and client becomes the final binding document.

American artist Marylyn Dintenfass was invited to prepare a presentation for an art work to be placed in the Superior Court Complex in Enfield, Connecticut. In order to select artists for this and similar commissions, the Connecticut State Commission on the Arts maintains an Artist Bank registry, and for this particular assignment, the commission chose a number of artists from it to submit proposals and reviewed the finalists' entries to make the final choice. After this review, Dintenfass's proposal was chosen. The illustrations in Figures 16-14 to 16-17 show some of the steps through which Dintenfass proceeded as she designed the work, presented her proposal, constructed the components, and installed them.

Dintenfass says that she was helped in deciding on the concept of her work by the architect's design, which included references to classical architecture, although the building was, she says,

> constructed in contemporary fashion, modularly. The portico, the columns, the oculus and colonnade were all fabricated elsewhere and assembled on site. My response to this was to propose a frieze fragment, over-scaled so it might seem to have come from a monumental building, but built in the contemporary way, in units. This is also a requirement for fabricating large-scale ceramics work.

Her work, *Diagonal Frieze*, was conceived to present three distinct perspectives. *The observer approaching from the main entry will see a series of volumetric units; viewed from the left it appears to be two-dimensional bands of varying widths; and upon leaving the courthouse the volume disappears and becomes undulating vertical edges.*

In addition to the drawings and model, Dintenfass submitted a statement explaining her concept, a complete list of materials, and a description of her fabrication techniques. She also provided instructions for unpacking the piece, and once the work was installed, she provided suggestions for maintenance. Since the work was to be installed indoors, hung on a wall well off the floor, and in a secure environment, she was not concerned with the demands of a harsh climate, nor did she need to worry about vandalism.

In addition to large public (16-18, page 392) or corporate commissions, there are also possibilities for obtaining commissions for smaller works to be placed in private or public settings.

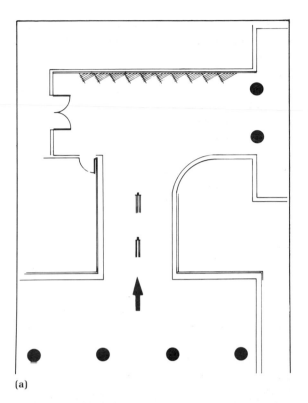

(a)

(b)

Figure 16-14
As an entrant in a nationwide search for an artist to create an art work for the Superior Court Complex at Enfield, Connecticut, Marylyn Dintenfass, U.S.A., studied the architect's plans and aesthetic concepts before submitting plans and drawings proposing her *Diagonal Frieze*. **(a)** Plan of the lobby, showing placement of the frieze on the wall facing the main door. **(b)** View of the entrance to the building and through to the interior wall on which the frieze was installed. *Courtesy the artist.*

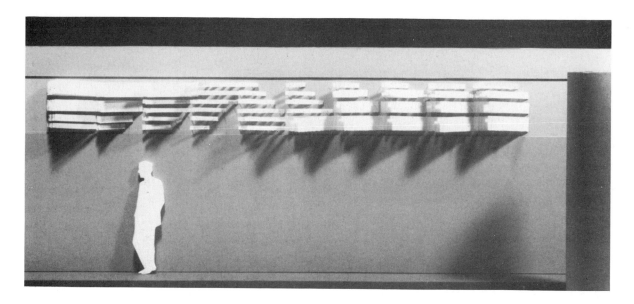

Figure 16-15
Dintenfass constructed a three-dimensional model to show the scale of the proposed work in relation to passersby and to the building. The model also made clear the dimensional quality of the frieze. *Courtesy the artist.*

(a)

(b)

Figure 16-16
(a) Dintenfass passing porcelain through a slab roller, rolling it to a thickness of ½ inch (12.5 mm). She then hand-rolled it to ¼ inch (6.25 mm) and ripped and cut the edges of the components, using templates. The curved units were draped over arched bisque forms to support them as they dried and were fired. After firing the sections in an electric kiln to 2150°F/1176.6°C, she strengthened them with cotton/polyester cloth laminated onto the back. (b) Dintenfass supervises the installation of *Diagonal Frieze.* The wall was specially designed and constructed to support the steel rods for the slabs, while a jig maintained the necessary 63-degree angle for the drilled insertion holes. Slabs were also secured to the wall with silicon adhesive. *Courtesy the artist.*

These can range from hand-thrown sinks to city benches, to fireplace surrounds (16-19, 16-20, page 393), to imaginative individual sculptures for public spaces.

Modules

The term *module* is most correctly applied to standardized components that can be used interchangeably, but it is also loosely used to describe any similar units that can be combined to create a larger work. As defined in this way, modules can extend the possibilities of architectural ceramics; they can be used as decoration in small

Figure 16-17
Diagonal Frieze. After months of thought and work, the frieze is finally in place and the appropriateness of Dintenfass's design becomes apparent. Responding to the classical references in the architecture, she comments that *the frieze, while recalling a classical frieze, is quite exaggerated in its scale, suggesting perhaps that it may have come from a monumental structure.* Porcelain slabs, ¼ inch (6.25 mm) thick, mounted on ⅜-inch (9.38-mm) threaded steel rods. Ht. 3 ft × 30 ft × 17 in. (91 cm × 9 m × 43 cm). Commissioned by the Department of Administrative Services and the Connecticut Commission on the Arts. *Courtesy the artist. Photo: Joann Sieburg-Baker.*

areas or can be extended to cover a whole wall (16-10, Color Plate 6). The units can be made by being pushed through the die of an extruder, by using press molds (13-8), or by slip casting in molds. Extruders come in all sizes; Gladding McBean, an architectural ceramic and pipe-manufacturing company in California, has one several stories high that pushes out huge sections of culvert pipe. The company also has smaller ones fitted with custom dies that will press out architectural moldings or components with any desired profile. Tile extruders, available for the ceramics studio, take the handwork out of making small modules, while other types of extruders can make tubes or solid components that can be combined to form larger works. The industrial extruders that make bricks provide another sort of modular unit. Beate Kuhn, in Germany, Ulla Viotti and Lillemor Petersson in Sweden, and Karen Park in Denmark have all worked at brick companies, where they took ordinary building

bricks as they came from the extruder, altered or glazed them, and then assembled them into one-of-a-kind reliefs that became part of walls.

Used throughout history, tiles (6-4, 7-9) have been handformed, shaped in press molds, cast in slip molds, or mechanically formed for use as wall decorations. Nowadays, tiles still bring color and texture to walls in the hands of accomplished ceramists. Beth Starbuck and Steven Goldner (13-8), for example, built up a business creating custom designs. Working with architects, designers, contractors, and homeowners, they design for specific sites or spaces and accommodate their work to particular requirements such as color, texture, thickness, and surface.

While some artists make their own tiles (16-21, page 394); others alter commercial greenware or glazed tiles by adding clay relief, by glazing or reglazing them, or by painting on them with under- or overglazes, transforming these mass-produced modules into the components of highly

individual works. James Melchert (Color Plate 41), for example, has been using glazed commercial tiles on which he paints with glazes and which, after firing, he assembles into individual wall pieces or wall-size murals. During her residency at the Kohler Company in their Arts/Industry Program, painter Ann Agee used factory-produced tiles for a 43 by 8 foot (13.1 by 2.4 m) mural. On them, she painted local scenes and views of the factory (16-22).

Marylyn Dintenfass, whose recent work is illustrated on the cover of this book, was one of twenty ceramic artists from eleven countries invited to work in factories in Israel. The factory she chose, Negev Ceramica, is outside the city of Beersheba, and the daily ride to the factory took her through the colorful desert. The desert landscape presented her with a new color palette, and she saw Bedouin families living in tents topped with television antennas. Dintenfass says that the sense of paradox this engendered

> was amplified once in the factory. The isolated setting gave no indication of the advanced technology housed within. Using local ingredients—clays found and dug in the Negev—with computer-run kilns, the factory was producing high-quality, high-fired floor tiles which passed through the kiln from raw clay to 1100°C in thirty-one minutes. This phenomenon, once absorbed, provided the most exciting and creative energy for the work and fostered an enormous amount of experimentation.

Another area in which ceramists can apply their skills is that of architectural preservation. The increasing interest in historic preservation

Figure 16-19
Sculptural fireplace surround by John Toki, U.S.A. This was a private commission, built for the home of Ray and Betty Ann Barnett. Designed to bring texture and mass into the living room, it was planned to reflect the forms of the hills surrounding the San Francisco Bay. Stoneware. 46 × 66 × 8 in. (1.2 m × 1.7 m × 23 cm). *Courtesy the artist. Photo: Scott McCue.*

Figure 16-20
John Toki drilling through a predrilled hole in a ceramic section into the thick plywood backing. For this top left section, he attached three 3½ inch (9 cm) wood screws through the sculpture and into the 1½ inch (3.8 cm) plywood to hold the section in place. The recessed screw was covered with a small ceramic plug to hide the screw head. In addition to using long wood screws to hold the sections in place, Toki installed a welded angle iron frame with 2 inch (5 cm) long lag bolts to help support the 70 pound (32 kilo) middle section.

Figure 16-21
Pastoral #1. Patrick Siler, U.S.A., uses units made from handformed slabs to create large ceramic walls, creating the images with his slip and stencil process (14-19 to 14-21). Fired at cone 5, oxidation. 7 ft × 13 ft × 10 in. (2 m × 4 m × 25 cm). *Courtesy the artist.*

has created a demand for the restoration of terra-cotta decoration on vintage buildings, and since there is now also greater interest on the part of some architects in using decorative detail on their buildings, there is a need for well-designed contemporary architectural components.

Considering these possibilities, it appears that ceramic artists will have increasing opportunities to apply their creativity and skill to architectural applications, continuing the tradition started thousands of years ago when glazed tiles were used to cover the sun-dried bricks of palaces and processional gates in the ancient Middle East.

Figure 16-22
Sheboygan County Mural (detail), by Ann Agee, U.S.A. While working as an artist in residence at the Kohler Factory, in Wisconsin, painter Agee created a tile mural featuring decorative medallions surrounding realistically painted scenes of local life. She also made an installation that included scenes of the factory and portraits of the people who worked there (14-31). 1992. White slip over porcelain with underglaze decoration. Cone 10. Detail. 72 × 84 × ½ in. (183 × 213 × 1.27 cm). *Courtesy the John Michael Kohler Arts Center. Photo: Eric R. Johnson.*

17

Setting Up Your Studio

Whether you are graduating from a school ceramics program or have decided to pursue ceramics as an avocation, you will want to consider setting up your own studio. Before you start, take some time to think about your needs, and design and plan your work space so that it and the equipment you buy will satisfy them.

It can take years to set up and organize your own ceramics studio properly. One way to organize your purchases is to draw up a plan of your dream studio. Prioritize your list with the most important items at the top and the least important at the bottom. Put a timeline next to the list using realistic target dates as to when you will purchase each item with the prices of the equipment so that you can develop a budget. Think in terms of your needs today and what it will take to achieve that goal, then project your needs for the near future and ask yourself if the equipment purchased today and your studio space will be adequate one year from now. Again, think in terms of what the essentials are, and be resourceful, patient, and realistic in your studio goals.

Your studio requirements are based on the type of work that you do. This is reflected by the scale of your work and the processes used, which in turn influence the equipment you will need. Geographic location and weather conditions can also have an effect on your studio location and work schedule. Take a look at some artists around the world who have adapted their work space to fit their special needs. For example, Kate Malone (16-1) got a bank loan to build a new studio in London to house her large electric kiln. She recoups some of the expense by renting space and the use of her **car kiln** to other artists. Marylyn Dintenfass's (16-14 to 16-17) New York studio, in an old building that she and a friend remodeled into artists' studios, is spacious, with large work tables planned specifically for her slab pieces. Kimpei Nakamura (Color Plate 53) creates his ceramics in a basement studio in downtown Tokyo, and calls the work produced there *Urban Ceramics*. For large-scale commissions he builds his sculptures at ceramics factories. The Potter's Shop in Massachusetts, where Steve Branfman and Carol Temkin (10-3) work, is adapted to be both a teaching studio and work space for pottery production.

Each of these artists, facing a unique situation, adapted existing space or built a new studio to fit their specific creative needs. With the customary inventiveness of artists, each achieved a space that is workable and comfortable.

Before setting up your own studio, take the time to visit schools, community ceramics centers, and professional pottery studios, and note their equipment and studio layout. Talk with the people who work there, and ask them what equipment they are using and what they recommend for you to get started. Ask what works best in their studio and what they would change to improve the conditions, and also what they are planning on improving. This information will give you a good idea of what is needed for a safe and functional studio. There are different approaches to setting up a studio based on each individual's special needs, but often the simplest approach is also the most economical in time and money. Rather than feel overwhelmed by everything you think you must have, think first in terms of what the essentials are. By being resourceful in terms of collecting tools and equipment and utilizing your available workspace, you can keep your expenses to a minimum.

Your work space can be an extra room in your house, a vacant garage, or a back porch. On the other hand, you may be in a position to set up a professional studio with adequate electrical service to accommodate electric kilns; clay mixers or other equipment; a gas meter and plumbing capable of handling a gas kiln; proper ventilation for kilns; a sink with sediment trap to catch clay, glaze, and plaster sludge; slop buckets for clay trimmings; a wedging table; and shelves or bins for storing raw materials, work in process, and completed work. In addition, a studio may contain heavy-duty tables; a spray booth and compressor to operate spray equipment; proper lighting; turntables for sculpture; or banding wheels for decorating. The list can go on and on.

Other major investments are potter's wheels, slab rollers, clay extruders, pug mills, slip mixers, glaze mixers, and a high-quality micro filter vacuum cleaner. Refer to Chapter 10 for additional information on equipment.

WHEELS

If you intend to throw, you will need to buy a potter's wheel. Electric wheels are popular because they are variable speed, powerful enough to handle up to 50 pounds (22.70 kilos) of clay or more, and easier than kick wheels to move around, which is important if portability is one of your concerns. Many potters who have developed back problems prefer electric wheels mounted on a table or on high legs so that the wheel head is close to waist level. By standing up while throwing, they alleviate the problem of having to bend over constantly. Individuals with serious health problems should contact their physicians before sculpting or throwing on the wheel. For persons confined to wheelchairs, there are fully adaptable electric wheels with extra space between the legs to accommodate wheelchairs. These are variable speed and available with or without hand or foot control. Wheels also come with a reversible wheel head for left-handed individuals.

Many potters like foot-powered traditional kick or treadle wheels, which are foot powered, because they are stable, quiet to use, and very responsive because of their manual nature; also, their speed can be easily monitored. Some potters just like the romantic notion of kick wheels. Used kick wheels are often available at reasonable prices and are excellent for a first wheel especially if funds are limited. Some kick wheels can be motorized to be made into an electric kick wheel, but if your aim is production, then a variable-speed electric wheel will greatly increase your output and is worth the cost.

KILNS

A kiln is one of the most essential pieces of equipment you will need to get started, unless you avoid the major expense of purchasing a kiln and begin by renting space from an established pottery. Many such potteries allow artists to fire their own work there, or fire it for them, charging by the weight or volume of the work. The advantages of having your own kiln are that you control the outcome of the work, save time in transportation, and move your work fewer times minimizing the possibility of damage.

Kilns come in many different styles, shapes, and sizes. They are usually fueled by electricity or gas, although now wood-burning kilns are popular with many artists. Gas and electric kilns can be accessed from the top or through a door in the front. Another type in which the entire kiln shell is lifted off the kiln floor and straight up is called a "top hat kiln." There is also the car kiln, or "shuttle kiln," which has a stationary shell and floor with wheels that roll into the kiln on a track. In addition, there is an envelope kiln, which has a stationary floor with burners and a shell that rolls on a track over the floor. These kilns make loading and unloading faster and easier.

Your decision on the best size of kiln to buy often comes down to output. Remember that the total volume will be reduced by approximately 10 to 20% once you have stacked the kiln posts and shelves inside. If you purchase a smaller kiln, then you can load it to capacity and fire more often. However, a larger kiln will hold more work, but the question you must ask yourself is: How long will it take to fill? A larger kiln is easier to load, and the firings are likely to be more even if there is additional space around each piece. With this information you will be able to make an informed judgment on purchasing a kiln.

Some kilns such as car kilns and shuttle kilns are better for individuals with special needs. Reaching deep into kilns to place heavy kiln shelves and ware can be a strain on your body. Therefore, if you expect to fire frequently, a car kiln or shuttle kiln would be a good investment. With this type of kiln the floor rolls out from the kiln shell on a track and is accessible from three or four sides. Remember that you must load unfired work carefully so that when the floor is rolled into the kiln the work will not fall over. Some production potters have two rolling floors so that while one load is firing, the other floor is being loaded.

If wheelchair access is necessary, some kiln manufacturers can modify the kiln by making it lower to the ground and by widening the space between the legs of the kiln stand to accommodate a wheelchair. It is advisable to have the control panel lowered into a position that is easily accessible to the person sitting in the wheelchair. In some instances, computer-controlled kilns will make programming and firing easier for the person in a wheelchair because with them it is not necessary to turn numerous dials or set cones into automatic kiln sitters.

Computerized Kilns

Computer software that can be used to control the firing of either an electric or gas kiln is now available, relieving the ceramist of a great deal of kiln watching. Setting pyrometric cones and kiln sitters as well as turning dials can be eliminated. For electric kilns, the computer can be programmed to do everything you would normally do in a firing except lowering the lid, plugging spy holes, and closing the damper. These kilns also have a digital readout screen on the computer that shows you the interior temperature (in Fahrenheit and centigrade) of the kiln at all times.

There are a number of advantages in firing with a computerized kiln. Fuel is economized because the kiln operates automatically; it increases in power/heat in the manner you have programmed it to climb, to hold, or to turn off. This eliminates monitoring the time to check when you need to turn up the kiln. You can program a kiln to start at midnight or early in the morning so that when you arrive at your studio it is already up to heat; the kiln can thus be programmed to turn off when you are present. However, although computerized kilns are a technical wonder, kiln manufacturers recommend that the kiln operator be present when the kiln is timed to turn off—no mechanical device is foolproof.

Some computerized electric kilns can be outfitted with an electric fan–driven downdraft venting system that draws fresh air in through the top of the kiln lid and lets excess moisture, heat, and fumes out through the floor of the kiln. The fan is not computerized, but by turning it on manually, you can fire the kiln with the lid and spy holes closed throughout the entire firing.

Many computerized controllers have preprogrammed settings for a slow, medium, and fast firing. These programs have been established for firing most pottery and sculpture. On the other hand, although these preprogrammed firing schedules are simple to operate, for firing thick sculptural work you may want to establish your own program for slower firing over three or four days, or longer. The entire firing can be preset for the critical stages in the firing cycle. For example, you can program the computer to control the kiln so that it will rise at a slow rate up to 212°F/ 100°C, then continue at a slightly faster rate through quartz inversion (1070°F/576°C), then continue again at a slightly faster rate up to your desired cone (see Appendix 2A). Many controllers will retain your last firing in memory, so if you want to use the same schedule for your next firing you will have it already programmed.

Computer-programmed controls are also ideal for firing glazes that are sensitive to heat rise and fall, such as crystalline glazes (Color Plate 30), which usually require carefully monitored firings to allow for the crystals to grow. Many new gas kilns, such as the ones used at the European Ceramic Work Centre in Holland (15-10), are totally computerized with software that programs the air-gas mix as well as the amount of reducing atmosphere, along with the temperature rise and fall.

Computers can be a great aid to firing, but even when using a computer, many kiln operators place cones inside the kiln from top to bottom to provide a way of accurately checking the overall firing conditions in relation to the digital read-out, which provides only an average temperature reading.

Electric Kilns

Many ceramists favor electric kilns because they fire relatively evenly from top to bottom and now are available with computerized controls, making operation simpler. Most are easily transported, and setup time is minimal. In a home studio, the simplest electric kiln to install is one that can be plugged into standard house current (120 volts). The sizes available for this type of kiln are generally limited to under 1 cubic foot (.028 cubic meter) with a maximum of cone 6 (2232°F/

1222°C). This type of kiln is excellent for firing small pots and sculptures. Smaller kilns, approximately .30 cubic foot (.01 cubic meter) in size, will fire to cone 10 (2381°F/1305°C) and are good for firing tests quickly or for firing small cups and bowls. Electric kilns larger than 1 cubic foot (.028 cubic meter) normally operate on 220/240 or 208 volts and require special wiring, but a licensed electrical contractor should be called in to run new wiring to match the electrical specifications for kilns operating on special voltage. There are also special electric kilns that operate on two 120-volt circuits. They are usually under 2 cubic feet (.057 cubic meter), have two plugs, and generally are limited to low temperatures.

BUYING USED ELECTRIC KILNS These can be purchased at reasonable prices, often less than half the current retail price for a new kiln. If you are interested in buying a used electric kiln, find out if it is a name brand and if the manufacturer is still in business; if so, this will assure you that replacement parts are available. Ask the seller at what temperature the kiln has been fired: If it was used for low firing, approximately cone 05 (1915°F/1046°C), then it is probably worth investigating. On the other hand, if the kiln was used for high firing, approximately cone 5 to 10 (2185°–2381°F/1196°–1305°C), the kiln elements might be worn, affecting the speed of firings, in which case the kiln may have difficulty reaching maximum temperature. In addition, if the kiln was used strictly for high firing over a number of years, then the kiln elements probably have been rewired at some point. You should ask the seller if that is the case and how many firings have taken place since that time. This can help you determine the life of the kiln.

The number of expected firings for 120-volt kilns when fired to their maximum temperature is about thirty. If they are used only for low firing, the total is approximately fifty. For 220-volt kilns, when fired to their maximum, the number of expected firings is nearer fifty. If used only for low firing, or for china paint firings (1261°F/683°C), the total can reach as high as 250 firings. Since individuals' firing schedules vary, use these totals only as a guide.

If kiln elements are broken, you will need to evaluate the time required to make the repair, not to mention the cost of parts. In addition, check to make sure the elements are not hanging out of their grooves or that the kiln brick under the elements is not heavily chipped, or chunks broken off leaving the elements vulnerable to excessive sagging. Elements in this condition can get worse over time and are difficult to push back into place without risk of permanently breaking them.

Kilns that have been installed outdoors with limited cover are susceptible to excessive corrosion on electrical parts, which can lead to insufficient heating of elements or other problems. If you buy such a kiln, check the electrical wiring. First, unplug the kiln, then open the electrical box and check all wiring connections for excessive rust or corrosion. If connections are rusted, carefully loosen them and clean all contact points with sandpaper or emery cloth. Kilns stored outside are also susceptible to bugs and spiders building webs or nests inside the control box, which, along with dust and dirt, can lead to poor electrical connections, causing electrical problems. In addition to cleaning all electrical contacts, it is important to vacuum out control boxes and to check the seal between the door jam or top rim of the kiln and the lid. Gaps over ⅛ inch (3 mm) could have a negative effect on heat rise. You can fill larger gaps with kiln cement, a castable refractory, or a ceramic fiber gasket.

Doing the electrical repairs yourself can save money, but it requires knowledge, tools, and experience to perform the electrical work involved in repairing a kiln because many of the parts are specially adapted to high-temperature applications. If you feel unqualified to do the repairs, then call your dealer for a repair estimate.

INSTALLING AN ELECTRIC KILN If you plan to install an electric kiln in a rented studio, find out what type of electrical service comes to the studio so that you can match the kiln to your power supply, or at least understand the necessary steps to bring in the correct power for your needs.

For maximum efficiency in powering electric kilns ranging in size from 1 to 20 cubic feet (.028 to .57 cubic meter), it is best to operate them on 240 volts (single-phase power). Homes usually have the capability of 220/240 volt service. Many schools and industrial buildings operate on 208 volts (single- or three-phase power), and some factories operate on 440 volts. In Europe, wiring for electric kilns is usually 230 volts. These types of electrical service require kilns with special wiring to match the input power, so it is best to contact the kiln manufacturer or your local dealer for specific information about the electrical re-

quirements for each kiln. Call in a licensed electrician to perform any wiring related to the installation of a kiln.

Gas Kilns

If you want to be able to do reduction firings, to fire between cone 5 and 10 (2185°–2381°F/1196°–1305°C) or above, or if you have limited electrical power, you probably will decide to buy a gas kiln. Front-opening gas kilns are available in **updraft** and **downdraft** styles; the downdraft type tends to fire more evenly. Among the many variables to consider when you decide to purchase and install a gas kiln is whether it will be updraft or downdraft. Also, will it be front- or top-loading? Front-loading kilns make loading easier for large sculptural or odd-shaped work that is often difficult to position into top-loading kilns, and for individuals in wheel chairs small front-loading kilns are the easiest to load.

GAS FUEL FOR YOUR KILN Will the kiln operate on natural gas or propane, and if operated on natural gas, is there a gas meter large enough to handle the BTU requirements for the kiln? You must also remember that in order to allow for the fire box the actual stacking space of gas kilns can be up to 30% less than the total volume.

One of the most important factors to remember when installing a gas kiln is that there must be adequate gas pressure and volume at the kiln—usually 7 to 8 pounds (1,010 millibar) of pressure. The size of pipe necessary to carry the needed volume of gas to the kiln is also critical to its operation because kilns that have been plumbed with undersized piping, or operated on an undersized gas meter, may never reach stoneware temperatures (cone 10, 2381°F/1305°C). The closer the kiln is to the gas meter the more likely there will be adequate gas pressure and volume, but as the distance of the kiln from the gas meter is increased, so the size of the piping must be increased. In addition, every bend in the pipe line also affects the gas flow and efficiency. You can find calculations for proper pipe sizes in books on kiln building. Gas kilns up to 20 cubic feet (.57 cubic meter) are operable on a standard house gas meter, but if you are looking for a kiln over 10 cubic feet (.28 cubic meter), the total BTU load should be carefully calculated to see if you will need a larger gas meter. Remember that before a utility company will install a larger gas meter on your site, the kiln must be physically in place. Your gas kiln dealer has the BTU requirements on all kilns it sells and can advise you on the steps necessary in a proper installation.

If the kiln is installed inside a room, there must be a way to draw off excess heat and fumes. An updraft kiln will need a hood, and a downdraft kiln will need a stack. Custom hoods can be fabricated by licensed sheet-metal contractors. Usually each city has building codes for installation of equipment operating on gas and will require permits from your local building department. It is also a good idea to contact your kiln manufacturer or dealer for information on the latest safety devices and controls for operating the kiln and also for the correct type of ventilation system necessary to draw off excess heat and fumes.

Portable Gas Kilns   There are a number of light-duty and reasonably priced portable top-loading gas kilns on the market that range in size from about 3 to 20 cubic feet (.08 to .57 cubic meter). Most come in sections that two people can move. These kilns are usually updraft in style and can work off a standard house gas meter. To monitor the evenness of a firing, some computers have thermocouples mounted at the bottom, middle, and top of the kiln so that a median temperature is achieved during a firing. With these, the operator must still adjust the damper for reduction and plug the spy holes manually.

Gas Kiln Fuels   Natural gas is commonly used for firing kilns—it is economical, readily available, and clean burning. You must have a gas meter carefully calculated to match the BTU capacity of your kiln, and the plumbing must be accurately calculated. In addition, the pipes must be properly installed so that you have the required volume of gas as well as pressure at the kiln.

Propane is a hotter-burning fuel than natural gas and is often used in rural locations where there is no natural-gas service. Propane is stored in tanks ranging in size from 5 to 500 gallons (19 to 1900 liters) or larger. Portable tanks come in sizes from 5 to 100 gallons (19 to 379 liters). The 5- and 10-gallon (19- and 38-liter) sizes are easily handled by one person. Although a 20-gallon (76-liter) tank is considered portable, keep in mind that it weighs about 150 pounds (68 kilos) including the tank, so you might need help.

Kilns under 7 cubic feet (.20 cubic meter) can be operated on portable 20- to 30-gallon (76- to 114-liter) tanks. It is a good idea to have two tanks, one as a main gas tank and the other as a backup in the event the first tank runs out of gas partway through the firing. On the other hand, if you are considering a kiln larger than 7 cubic feet (.20 cubic meter) and plan on firing often, it is worthwhile to investigate the cost of installing a 250- to 500-gallon (946- to 1893-liter) permanent tank. These tanks can be purchased or rented and are always installed outdoors. Large tanks are more convenient because they contain enough gas to fire a number of loads; and since the tanks are never totally filled for functional purposes, it is best to have a larger tank than you think you will need. Portable tanks are filled at propane-filling stations, larger tanks can be filled on-site.

Each propane tank has a manufactured date stamped into the cylinder, and for safety reasons all tanks must be requalified within twelve years of the manufactured date. Any tank over twelve years old will likely have another stamp showing that it was checked against damage, heavy rusting, or deficient valves or seals. Tanks can be requalified for continuous use or disqualified if deemed unsafe. This check is done by authorized personnel from propane-fuel companies.

Installing a Gas Kiln   Before selecting a gas kiln, draw up a plan showing the future kiln location, indicating the position of the existing gas meter, or where a new meter will be located, along with all the measurements to the kiln from the gas meter, property line, and all structures. Include notes on the type of building the kiln will be positioned next to—for example, a cinder block walled building or a wood structure—as this will affect the building code requirements. It is also important that the kiln be easily accessible for loading and unloading work and that there is enough room for easy access to kiln shelves, posts, and equipment, and elbow room for maneuvering as you load. If you will be rolling ware carts to the kiln, you will need a hard and relatively flat surface to move your work smoothly. Remember also that a tremendous amount of radiant heat can be dissipated from a kiln, especially from thin-walled (approximately 2.5 in./ 6.35 cm) types. This must be kept in mind when positioning a kiln in confined spaces or near combustible materials, and a detailed plan will assist your city building department in helping you position the kiln in accordance with safety codes. You must submit this plan, along with drawings of the site and all kiln specifications and installation requirements, to the city building department when applying for a permit. This information will also help the kiln dealer, contractor, plumber, and transport companies provide you with accurate cost estimates, and it will help you immeasurably at the time of installation.

Collecting accurate information prior to a gas-kiln installation can save you thousands of dollars. When the time comes to move a bulky and heavy gas kiln into your yard, the moving company will want to know the dimensions of the kiln, what type of materials the kiln is constructed of, its weight, the type of paving and width of access to the site before giving you an estimate. In some cases it is important to have the moving company come to your site to provide you with an estimate.

When it comes time to install a (nonportable) gas kiln, be sure to get professional help. Usually gas kilns require special equipment and handling by transport companies. Sometimes this is a two-step operation: An independent trucking firm drives the kiln to your site. Then a transport or crane service company unloads the kiln and moves it from the street to inside your property. In some instances this company will arrange for a forklift to be on site to pick up and move the heavy kiln into your studio. When you begin looking for a company to move your equipment, look in the phone book under crane, rigging, drayage, or forklift. Most companies have a three-hour minimum and an hourly fee thereafter. In the end, it is well worth the investment in hiring professionals to transport your kiln from the manufacturer or dealer and move it into your studio.

If you plan to do most of the installation work yourself, read books on kiln installation and talk with other potters and sculptors in your area who have already installed a gas or electric kiln. They can share their installation experiences with you and provide you with the names of individuals and reliable companies who can help you. Careful planning for the installation is crucial in having a safe kiln capable of successful firings.

Alternative-Fuel Kilns

Wood, oil, coal, and charcoal are generally used where unique reducing atmospheres are desired, as in high-fire wood firings, pit firings, and raku firings. Alternative-fuel kilns are usually more appropriate for rural areas, but there are local, state, or national air-quality rules or restrictions that may affect use of these types of fuels anywhere. For example, some areas require special permits to fire with wood, and others prohibit it entirely. To get some of the effects of wood firing, some ceramists begin by firing with gas and get the temperature up to approximately cone 08 (1751°F/955°C) or above, and then introduce wood through a special fire box or add charcoal briquettes through the spy holes in strategic places.

CLAY PROCESSING AND EQUIPMENT

Most ceramists begin by purchasing premixed clay because there are dozens of clays available on the market from which to choose, and when using small quantities it can be more economical in time and money to buy ready-mixed clays. However, you can recycle dry clay in small quantities by soaking down scraps in a garbage can until the material is totally saturated and becomes a thick slurry. Then you scoop out this slop and place it to dry on a plaster bat, wooden board, or concrete slab. Once the clay slurry has dried out enough to be workable, you can wedge it into reusable clay.

For those who buy premixed clay and need a machine to reprocess scraps, a pug mill is a valuable piece of equipment. If you intend to process clay for the wheel, a de-airing type of pug mill will homogenize the clay and eliminate or minimize wedging. If you plan to use white or porcelain clays, it is important to purchase a pug mill with stainless-steel blades and a nonrusting chamber to avoid clay contamination. However, if you are going into production or using large quantities of clay, you may want to consider mechanical mixing equipment.

Clay mixers are valuable for blending custom clay bodies or for processing large quantities of clay. They can also serve as a reclaimer of scraps. Scraps must be premoistened before being dumped into the hopper. Most small mixers require blending a minimum of 150 pounds (68 kilos) of clay.

If you plan to work at a large scale, want to make slabs quickly, or anticipate producing a large number of slab-built shapes, then you probably should buy a slab roller. Slab rollers can efficiently roll out clay slabs of uniform thickness and consistency, especially useful for ceramists making slab-built pottery, sculpture, jewelry, or tiles. The machines are available in sizes that will produce slabs from 12 to 40 inches (30–102 cm) wide by up to 48 inches (122 cm) long, by ⅛ to 1¾ inch (3–44 mm) thick. They are either powered by hand or motorized for the high-production artist.

Clay extruders efficiently produce solid or hollow extrusions or narrow slabs. Ceramists find them useful for producing handles for pottery, tubes that can become containers, or coils for handbuilt vessels. If you plan to work in white or porcelain clays, buy an extruder with a stainless steel or aluminum chamber and dies to avoid contaminating the clay from iron residue or rust that could be released from extruders with steel chambers. Extruders are available in sizes from hand-held, to caulking-gun size, to larger table or wall-mounted types. The small units can produce coils as fine as ¹⁄₁₆ inch (1.6 mm) up to 8 inches (20 cm) in diameter as coils or tubes. For large extrusions, expansion boxes can be attached to the smaller units to widen the opening so that it can accept larger dies. You can buy extruders that are operated either manually or mechanically with a hydraulic plunger driven by compressed air.

Slip-Casting Equipment

Slip casting generally requires a mixer for the slip and a special table for pouring and then draining the excess clay from the plaster molds. Fiber-glass casting and draining tables are commercially available, and the ultimate setup comes with a mixer and tank, a casting and drain table, and an electric pump for pouring slip into the molds, all in one unit. However, a casting setup can simply be a bucket or a bowl (13-14) with two wooden slats for mold draining. If you are going into production or are planning to do large-scale casting, then it is worthwhile to consider purchasing commercially available equipment for mixing the slip. Popular slip-mixer sizes for individuals are the 15- to 50-gallon (19- to 190-liter) types that come with mixer/motor, container, spigot, and stand. Mixing slip from dry powder requires a gram scale to measure chemicals and 30 to 45 minutes of mixing to blend all the components thoroughly (see Appendix 1C). For mixing small test batches of slip under 1 gallon (3.785 liter), you can set up a mixer blade on the end of a drill press and run it at the lowest speed to mix for 30 to 45 minutes. If, however, your production is limited to occasionally casting a few gallons (8 liters) of slip, then it usually is time saving to purchase premixed slip.

When you are shopping for clay processing and mixing equipment, seek out machinery that will enhance your output or the quality of your work. Machinery can be costly to purchase, install, and maintain, so before you buy it, ask yourself how it will improve your operation and, if acquired, how often you will use the equipment. The most valuable piece of equipment in the studio is one that works properly, is used on a consistent basis, and helps you be creative with clay.

GLAZES IN YOUR STUDIO

When it comes time to glaze your work, you can either purchase commercially prepared colors or mix your own. Some ceramists prefer to purchase glazes, slips, and other glaze compounds premixed. In fact, some companies will take your own glaze formula and custom-mix it into a liquid or dry form. This can save you purchasing numerous chemicals and mixing equipment, not to mention the dust created by mixing glazes and the storage problem caused by bags of chemicals. On the other hand, mixing and then firing your own glazes can be a satisfying experience. By doing so you will come to understand how glazes function in relation to your work, and by following specific formulas you will learn how to alter a glaze to achieve varying colors and textures.

If you decide to set up a glaze mixing and glazing area in your studio, there is some equipment you will need to acquire (14-42). You will need a gram scale for accurately weighing out test glaze batches, and a package or platform scale for weighing bulk items such as bags of clays, frits, and feldspars. You will also need a mixer blade attached to a drill for mixing glazes and an assortment of sieves to screen liquids and dry materials. For grinding small quantities of glaze materials a mortar and pestle is adequate, but for grinding large quantities of stains and oxides, such as cobalt and copper-based colorants, you may want to invest in a ball mill. If you expand your production of glazes, you may decide to buy a professional-style dispersion blender.

Some ceramists prefer to buy a small electric test kiln that allows them to glaze-fire a test immediately, rather than wait to fire their tests in a large kiln that may take weeks to fill and fire. A small test kiln can be fired in one day, and some very small test kilns can even be fired two or three times in one day. For convenience it is ideal to place your test kiln in the glaze room, and it is important to have venting over the kiln to draw off fumes. Most test kilns operate on 120 volts (European, 230 volts) and can be plugged into standard electrical outlets.

SPRAY BOOTH

If you want to spray your glaze on pottery or sculpture, you should consider installing a spray booth in your studio. It is important to draw off any glaze overspray. To help you know when to change the filter, invest in a **draft gauge,** which measures the air draft through the filter and lets you know if there is adequate draft to properly collect and filter the overspray.

When spraying your pottery, it helps to place a banding wheel or turntable inside the spray booth so that you can place your work on the turntable and turn it by hand as you spray to achieve an even glaze over the entire work. Some production potters set up an electric potter's wheel inside their spray booth and use an electronic foot pedal to activate the wheel head, thus freeing themselves from having to spin the top and spray at the same time, not to mention that their hands do not get covered with glaze.

Purchasing a Spray Booth

Spray booths are available in a variety of sizes and styles. They have fiber-glass, painted steel, or galvanized steel interiors, and they come in free-standing or table-mounted models. Most standard spray booths for ceramics are meant for spraying water-based liquids. However, if you are also planning to spray flammable liquids such as lusters, metallics, or oil-base paints, you will want to purchase a spray booth installed with a totally enclosed explosion-proof motor.

SPRAY-BOOTH WIRING   Most spray-booth motors operate on 120, 208, or 230 volts. For advice on wiring a spray booth, contact the spray-booth manufacturer or your local dealer. Most studio spray-booth fan motors operate on 120 volts (European, 230 volts) for a ¼ to ½ horsepower (.19–.37 kw) motor.

Spraying Equipment

SPRAY GUN   If you are going to spray underglazes, glazes, or stains over large broad surfaces, then you will need a spray gun. Two types of spray guns are popular among ceramists, and each usually holds about ½ to 1 quart (.473 to .946 liter) of glaze. One style is the siphon-feed type that is activated by air being blown through a horizontal tube intersecting a vertical siphon tube inside the glaze canister. You may, however, prefer using a gravity-feed spray gun, which usually holds about 8 ounces (.24 liter), because you can change spray material more quickly and frequently than with the siphon-feed gun. Spray guns are available with different orifice sizes. The larger the particle size of your glaze the larger the orifice it requires. If your glaze, underglaze, or stain is finely ground, then a smaller tip will deliver a finer-misting spray. It is important to sieve your glaze through a 50- to 80-mesh screen before spraying, but if the gun clogs up you may need to screen your glaze through a finer-mesh sieve.

AIR BRUSH   If you will be doing detail work over small surfaces using stains, underglazes, china paints, lusters, or metallics, then consider purchasing an air brush. These usually have a 1- to 3-ounce (30- to 90-milliliter) jar attached to the brush for spraying. A variety of replacement spray tips, from fine to coarse, are available to provide the type of spray you will need for your work. For most ceramic spraying, a medium or coarse tip is recommended.

AIR COMPRESSOR   Spray guns and air brushes need compressed air to function. Two common types of air compressors are the oil-less and the air tank–mounted styles. If you need clean (oil-free) air, then you should consider an oil-less compressor installed with a tank, but if portability and size are important concerns, consider purchasing an oil-less compressor without air tank, which operates on standard house current at 120 volts (European wire, 230 volts). Because the pump is not lubricated with oil, it puts out the clean air that is especially critical when spraying materials such as lusters, metallics, and china paint, which are sensitive to contamination. A ⅓ horsepower (.25 kw) oil-less compressor that delivers 50 pounds (170 bar) of pressure will operate both a spray gun and an air brush. A ¹⁄₁₀ horsepower (.075 kw) oil-less compressor delivering 30 pounds

(120 bar) of pressure will spray thinned-down glazes, underglazes, and stains.

A ¾ to 1 horsepower (.56–.76 kw) compressor with an oil-lubricated pump and an 11-gallon (42-liter) tank will be powerful enough to spray all of your water-based glazes and paints. Compressors with motors up to 1 horsepower (.76 kw) operate on 120 volts (European wire, 230 volts). If you are in production, operating more than one piece of spray equipment at the same time, or setting up a shop to accommodate other air tools, then you will want a heavy-duty compressor with a tank. A 5-horsepower (3.7 kw), 80-gallon (303-liter) compressor will handle almost all the requirements of a large studio setup; it will also have the power to sandblast.

AIR LINES   Most compressors have a flexible hose attachment to the spray gun or air brush. If you plan to operate more than one spray unit, you will want to consider installing a union tee, which will accommodate two air hoses. In addition, if you are going to operate more than two spray units, or are planning on using other air tools from one compressor, consider installing **quick couplers** on all of your air tools. This makes it convenient to remove them from your air line without the need of wrenches. If you are using oil-based paints sensitive to contamination from water moisture, you will want to install a **moisture trap** in your air line.

PLASTER IN YOUR STUDIO

If you are going to make plaster molds for slip casting or for press molding, or if you plan to turn plaster on a lath or carve plaster in your studio, then you should set up an area specifically for use of this material. This is because plaster chips can become a contaminant if they are wedged into the clay and a piece made of that clay is bisqued and then glaze-fired; what can happen is that moisture absorbed by the plaster that has been embedded in the fired clay may expand over a period of months or even years and pop pieces of clay or glaze off the surface. Keep plaster away from your clay! For example, always use separate mixing and cleaning buckets for the plaster; they should never be used for clay storage.

If you intend to integrate plaster into your studio, install a sink trap below your sink. This is a stainless steel, ceramic, or plastic container that receives water and material from the sink and traps the particles before the water enters the sewer line. Its primary function is to keep your drain pipes free of large particles of clay, plaster, or chemical contaminants. It usually has three traps set at equal distance from each other and at consecutively lower levels; the first trap collects the largest particles of debris, and the third trap collects the finest.

HEALTH AND SAFETY

A clean, well-lighted, and organized studio makes for a pleasant, safe, and productive work space. Planning your studio to include proper personal safety equipment is your best insurance against illness or accidents. It is also important to stay informed on the proper methods of handling ceramic chemicals and materials and operating machinery.

The very basic equipment needed to keep your studio clean is a large synthetic sponge and a bucket of water—to sponge off dusty or dirty tables—and a wet mop for damp-cleaning your floors. For greater cleanliness, install a ceiling-mounted electrically operated air purifier that filters out very fine clay and chemical particles; this is also a good investment in your health.

One of the most effective pieces of equipment for keeping your studio clean is a vacuum cleaner with an "absolute filter"—one that collects the finest clay and chemical powders and dusts from the floor, shelves, and table tops. You can also use it when sanding greenware or drilling dry clay: Place the vacuum nozzle in front of the area where you are sanding or drilling.

The European Work Centre, Holland, is an example of a large studio that was built from the ground up with the health and safety of its staff and artists-in-residence in mind. In addition to a complete venting system for clean air, floor drains and sinks lead to special underground tanks that collect all clay or glaze sludge, and when they become full the contents is tested for heavy metals and the materials are properly disposed of or recycled. Excess amounts of heavy metals or toxic materials are processed through a special sifter, and the residue may later be fritted in order to be reprocessed into other products. The kiln room also has gas-detection devices set in the ceiling to monitor any leaks from gas lines. Over each scale in the glaze room an overhead flexible vacuum tube with hood and light removes the dust generated from measuring and weighing chemicals, which then is drawn into a dust collector. When chemicals are being weighed, the vacuum is turned on and the hood lowered to just above the chemicals. The European Work Centre is a good example of complete health, safety, and ecological awareness. Although its systems may be beyond your budget, you can use it as an example of the ultimate in clean ceramics environments.

Every studio needs fire extinguishers positioned near combustible materials. Your local fire department can tell you how many and what size fire extinguishers you will need for your studio, as well as their correct location. They can also advise you on fire alarms and other fire safety equipment.

Personal Safety Equipment

You will also want to invest in some personal safety equipment. For example, a form-fitting dual cartridge respirator rated for dusts is essential when handling clay powders and chemicals. When handling toxic materials you should wear a pair of neoprene gloves or light-duty vinyl gloves (disposable after using); safety goggles or a face shield; and a respirator with filters rated for protection against the toxic materials you will be handling. Pants, long-sleeve shirt, and shoes are necessary to protect you against excessive exposure to toxic chemicals. For handling hot kiln shelves, pots, or sculpture, you will need a pair of heat-resistant gloves, or leather welding gloves. When looking through kiln spy holes to check pyrometric cones, you will need to wear shaded goggles or a welder's hand-held face shield with a number 3 lens to protect you against harmful ultraviolet rays and heat. When doing raku be sure to wear high-top leather shoes and leather welding pants or overalls, or a heavy sweat shirt and thick cotton pants that extend over the tops of your shoes. Do not wear any synthetic or flimsy material that would burn.

Recycling Your Ceramic Materials

With increased awareness of environmental issues related to human health and concern about how we interact with our earth, there is a heightened awareness of the need to recycle ceramic materials and toxic wastes. Some ceramists have come up with ingenious ideas about what to do with these wastes.

For example, Bill Roan and Clayton Bailey, of the California State University at Hayward, developed a "No Waste" system for reprocessing clay and clay sediment from the school studio. They begin by washing buckets of clay and glaze scraps in an industrial parts washer, with a recirculating water spray. The water from the parts washer can also be collected and used for mixing the clay, thus utilizing all materials in a recycling process. The damp residue is screened through a 30-mesh sieve and mixed with a flux, a refractory, and a colorant, and then used as a glaze. They also make up a clay body they call "Reprocessed Glaze Sediment," by taking the same residue and mixing it at a one-to-one ratio with scrap clay and floor sweepings screened through a 16-mesh sieve, or with sand or fire clay (see Appendix 1C). They then press out tiles, fire them to cone 10, and sell them for income for their school studio. This simple recycling method can be adapted for use by any small or large studio.

WORKING IN YOUR STUDIO

Once you have gathered and set up your studio with whatever equipment you can afford, organized the space to function efficiently, taken care of safety and health concerns, and stored your materials where they can be easily reached, you are ready to work. Although this setting-up process may take much of your energy at first, certainly the most important function of an organized work space and good equipment is to free you to use your skills creatively and to work with joy. Good luck!

APPENDIXES

CONTENTS

The information in these appendixes is designed to supplement the information in the main text. It includes a series of clay and glaze tests that you can follow in progression, using the accompanying charts. If you work through the clay and glaze tests in Appendix 1, you will develop a basic understanding of both the composition and the qualities of different clay bodies and glazes. Appendix 2 gives you information you will find useful when you fire your tests and ware. If you want to go deeper into testing and glaze calculation, Appendix 3 provides an example of changing the flux in a glaze, and follows a potter calculating, testing, and modifying a high-fire glaze. It also includes charts of chemical information you will need.

Clays and Glazes Formulated for Testing

The following clay body and glaze recipes were formulated for *Hands in Clay* to provide a guide for mixing and testing as a learning experience. The clay recipes will produce clay bodies with various qualities and firing temperatures, while the glaze recipes will give you practice in changing the color of a base glaze. Testing is only a means to extend your creativity in clay. What makes a successful ceramic technician and artist? He or she must maintain a bright spirit, solid determination, and hope for a dash of luck!

CLAY BODIES FOR TESTING

Although the clay body-tests were fired at cone 05, cone 5, and cone 10, allowing for a wide range of firing temperatures, the actual range of the cones and temperatures for these tests is less rigid than the charts imply. For example, the low-fire white clay can be fired as low as cone 010 and as high as cone 1, whereas the cone 5 porcelain develops a richer sheen when fired at cone 7 or even as high as cone 10. Changes in firing temperatures will affect the shrinkage and color of the clay, and changes in components will affect the workability of the body. While you are developing your own clay bodies through tests, it is wise to be flexible about material substitutes, temperatures, and kiln atmospheres. Each of these factors will subtly affect the outcome of your tests, adding to the excitement as you proceed. Do not be discouraged from mixing clays or glazes if the names of the materials listed in the following recipes are not the same as those in your area. For example, the names of fire clays, ball clays, and feldspars will vary depending on where you live. You will just have to test the substitutes thoroughly.

Components of Blended Clay Bodies

BALL CLAY Ball clay has highly plastic qualities, and for that reason it is used in both low-fire and high-fire clay bodies that require plasticity — for example, those to be thrown on the wheel. It is also used in low-fire slip for casting bodies.

FIRE CLAY Maturing at a high temperature and readily available and inexpensive, fire clay is used in stoneware bodies to provide silica and alumina, refractory materials, and to increase the heat-resistant quality of the clay. Fire clays are relatively plastic.

TALC Talc is a magnesium-bearing rock that sometimes contains impurities of iron and alumina as well as alkalis and lime. Because of its magnesium content, it acts as a flux for low-fire clays and casting slips.

FELDSPARS Feldspathic rocks are among the most common rocks in the earth's crust, and the feldspars used in ceramics come from those rocks as they are broken down by geologic forces. Feldspars contain alumina, silica, and, depending on the composition of the particular feldspar, varying amounts of sodium, potassium, or calcium. Feldspars are heat resistant and can be used as the principal flux in stoneware clays, because stoneware is heated to temperatures high enough to melt the feldspar (above 2192°F/1200°C). Since feldspars mined in different places vary in composition, it is important to know the chemical formula of the feldspar used.

Clay Bodies Formulated for Use in Color and Glaze Tests

The following clay bodies were mixed in 300-gram batches. The clays were first blended dry; then they were mixed with water into a slip. For the smooth clay bodies, the water content was about 20% of the batch, while the bodies with 20% grog required roughly 13–15% water content per batch. The slip was poured onto a plaster bat and left 5 or 10 minutes or until enough moisture had been absorbed to bring the clay to the right consistency for wedging. The base recipes for these clay bodies were formulated to total 100%. Coloring oxides and stains were added to the base clay in varying percentages. The letters and numbers in parentheses refer to the test tiles in Color Plates 51 and 52. Be sure that you follow the precautions given in Chapter 10 for handling dry clay when you mix these clay bodies.

Hands in Clay White Cone 05, 5, and 10 Clay Bodies   (CL1, CL2, CL3)

Components	Percent		
	Cone 05 (CL1)	Cone 5 (CL2)	Cone 10 (CL3, 4)
Kentucky ball clay (OM4)	50.0	21.0	20.0
Kaolin (Georgia)		27.0	28.0
Fire clay (Lincoln)			
Feldspar (Custer)			25.0
Feldspar (nepheline syenite)		25.0	
Silica 200 mesh (flint)		25.0	25.0
Talc	50.0		
Macaloid		2.0	2.0

Notes:
White base clay bodies in oxidation: (CL1 to CL3)
Cone 05 — smooth, warm-white body. (CL1)
Cone 5 — smooth, slightly off-white. (CL2)
Cone 10 — smooth, slightly off-white. (CL3)
White base clay bodies in reduction:
Cone 10 — smooth, light grey. (CL4)

Substitutions for the materials and chemicals listed in the recipes will cause changes in the color, texture, and firing range of the clays. If you substitute, you will need to carry out additional tests. Some possible substitutes:

- *Kaolin:* EPK or Grolleg or other kaolin may be substituted for Georgia.
- *Feldspar:* Locally available feldspars may be substituted for Custer, a potash feldspar.
- *Fire clay (Lincoln):* Other fire clays such as IMCO#400 or #800, Cedar Heights, Goldart, Pine Lake, or Missouri may be substituted for Lincoln.

- *Macaloid:* Assists in giving plasticity to some clays; it may be eliminated for test purposes, or Vee gum or bentonite can be substituted.
- *Any red earthenware,* such as Newman or Kreth Red earthenware or Cedar Heights Redart terracotta, can be substituted for the Red Horse clay.
- *Stains:* Other pink or yellow (praseodymium) glaze or body stains may be substituted, as can other color stains. Be aware of the maximum cone or temperature range of whatever stain you substitute because some colors fade at high temperatures (D320 pink and #6440 tin-vanadium yellow are both high-temperature stains).

Coloring Clay Bodies with Natural Clays (CL5 to CL8)

To make subtle changes in the color of a clay body, you may simply wedge two colors of clay together to create a lighter or darker shade. However, the following clays for testing were mixed dry, and then water was added to make a slip that was poured onto a plaster bat to absorb the water and stiffen the clay. (See the general instructions for mixing clay bodies in Chapter 10.)

Components	Percent		
	Cone 05 (CL5)	Cone 5 (CL6)	Cone 10 (CL7)
Kentucky ball clay (OM4)	30.0		35.0
Earthenware (Red Horse)*	50.0	50.0	
Fire clay (Lincoln)		50.0	65.0
Talc	20.0		

Notes:
Coloring white clay bodies with natural clays:
Cone 05 — warm light red, smooth (would burnish well). (CL5)

*For test purposes, Red Horse clay can be substituted with Kreth Red, Redart, or any red earthenware clay.

Cone 5 — rust-red, slightly grainy. (CL6)
Cone 10 oxidation — gray-buff, smooth. (CL7)
Cone 10 reduction — warm brown, smooth. (CL8)

Texturing Clay Bodies with Grog/Fillers/Tempers (CL9 to CL12)

To give differing textures to clay bodies, you can introduce various types of grog or filler in place of the buff grog (30–70 mesh) or the molochite. You can also blend the texturing materials in combinations, adding even greater tooth and openness to the clay body. For example, for a sculpture body use half sand, half grog, or a variety of mesh sizes of ione grain, or sand and grog and pearlite in combination.

Components	Percent			
	Cone 05 (CL9)	Cone 5 (CL10)	Cone 10A (CL11)	Cone 10B (CL12)
Kentucky ball clay (OM4)	40.0	50.0	28.0	28.0
Kaolin (Georgia)				
Fire clay (Lincoln)		30.0	52.0	52.0
Feldspar (Custer)				
Silica 200 mesh				
Talc	40.0			
Macaloid				
Grog (buff 30–70 mesh)	20.0	20.0	20.0	20.0
Molochite (porcelain grog)				

*Silica sand	(30–90 mesh)	5–10%
Ione grain	(30–150 mesh)	5–20%
Red grog	(9–30 mesh)	5–20%
Pearlite	(fine or coarse)	1–5%

*Sand in some clay bodies fired to around cone 10 may form a gritty surface.

Notes:
Texturing clay bodies with grog/tempers:
Cone 05 — white, slightly rough surface. (CL9)
Cone 5 — off-white, rough surface. (CL10)
Cone 10A oxidation — gray-buff, slightly rough surface. (CL11)
Cone 10B reduction — warm brown, lighter speckles, rough surface. (CL12)

White Cone 10 Stoneware Clay Body   (WS1 Oxidation, WS2 Reduction)
A textured stoneware body for general use.

Components	*Percent*
Kentucky ball clay (OM4)	25.0
Silica 200 mesh (flint)	20.0
Georgia China clay	20.0
Custer feldspar	20.0
Macaloid	2.0
Molochite	13.0

Shrinkage Test

If you are planning to make a large sculpture or even a series of thrown wine goblets, you will want to know how much the clay will shrink on drying and during firing. Since clay bodies have different rates of shrinkage, when you formulate a clay body it is important to test the amount of shrinkage. For example, the white 05 clay used in these tests shrank about 5% from wet to dry and about 6% from dry to fired state. One way to measure the amount of shrinkage of a clay is to cast a block of plaster, carve lines into it 1 inch apart, and number the lines from 1 to 10. To make a clay test tile, simply press a slab of clay onto the block to imprint the pattern of lines and numbers in the clay, then dry and fire the slab. You can then measure how much the clay shrinks after drying and firing by comparing its measurement before and after with the plaster ruler that you made or with a plastic **shrink ruler.**

CASTING SLIP

Hands in Clay Low-Fire (Cone 05) White Casting Slip (SL1)
Batch Formula: For 128 Fluid Ounces (1 Gallon) (3.875 Liters)

Components	Amount	Percent
Kentucky ball clay (OM4)	2,027.25 gr	50
Talc	2,027.25 gr	50
		100 total percent
Additives		
Soda ash	4.46 gr	.11
Sodium silicate (N)	18.65 gr (fluid wt)	.46
Water	1,900.60 gr (67 fluid oz)	46.69 gr (1.65 fluid oz) water 100-gram batch

Notes:
Weigh the deflocculants sodium silicate and soda ash on a gram scale and mix with water. Add talc and ball clay and mix for 30 minutes, then screen the slip through a 40- to 60-mesh sieve. Accurate sequence, measurement, and mixing time are crucial to suspension and fluidity, and screening is essential for smoothness. Be sure to follow the given sequence in mixing the components, the water, and the sodium silicate. Immediately before casting, slip should be mixed again for 1–2 minutes. See Chapter 13 for pouring directions.

Hands in Clay White Porcelain Cone 5–7 Casting Slip (Electric Kiln)   (SL2)
Batch Formula: For 128 Fluid Ounces (1 Gallon) (3.875 Liters)

Components	Amount	Percent
Kaolin (Georgia)	1,380.0 gr	25.0
Feldspar (Custer)	552.0 gr	10.0
Feldspar (nepheline syenite)	1,656.0 gr	30.0
Silica 325 mesh	552.0 gr	10.0
Kentucky ball clay (OM4)	1,380.0 gr	25.0
		100% total
Additives		
Soda ash	5.52 gr	.10
Sodium silicate (N)	22.08 gr (fluid wt)	.40
Darvan #7	13.80 gr (fluid wt)	.25
Water	1,564.92 gr (55.20 fluid oz)	55.60 gr (2.0 fluid oz) water per 100-gram batch

Notes:
Follow the same measuring and mixing directions as for the cone 05 slip. For casting an object with fine detail, it is a good idea to put the slip through a ball mill. You may also want to use up to an 80-mesh sieve to screen the slip. In that case, you probably will have to push the slip through with a flexible spatula. One way to check the amount of water needed in the casting slips is to measure out 1 pint (.48 liter) of slip and weigh it. If it weighs less than 26 to 28.5 ounces (735.8 to 806.6 grams) for low-fire slip, or less than 28.5 to 32 ounces (806.6 to 905.6 grams) for high-fire slip, your mixture has too much water. This could cause settling.

Hands in Clay White Porcelain Cone 10–11 Casting Slip (for Gas or Electric Kiln)   (SL3)
Batch formula: For 128 Fluid Ounces (1 Gallon) (3.875 Liters)

Components	Amount	Percent
Kaolin (Grolleg) (English china clay)	1,951.20 gr	40.0
Feldspar (Custer)	1,219.50 gr	25.0
Silica 325 mesh	975.60 gr	20.0
Kentucky ball clay (OM4)	731.70 gr	15.0
		100% total
Additives		
Soda ash	6.09 gr	.125
Sodium silicate (N)	19.51 gr (fluid wt)	.40
Darvan #7	19.51 gr (fluid wt)	.40
Water	1,936.0 gr (68.29 fluid oz)	39.62 gr (1.40 fluid oz) water per 100-gram batch

Notes:
Fired in oxidation, this is a white slip; in reduction it will be gray. Follow the same measuring and mixing directions as for the cone 05 slip. For casting an object with fine detail, it is a good idea to put the slip through a ball mill. You may also want to use up to an 80-mesh sieve to screen the slip. In that case, you probably will have to push the slip through with a flexible spatula.

EGYPTIAN PASTE

White Egyptian Paste (Cone 015)   (EP1-4)
The components of this clay body form an integral glaze on its surface as it is fired. (See Chapter 2 for historical information on Egyptian paste.)

Components	Percent
Nepheline syenite	25.0
Frit 3134	15.0
Silica 200 mesh	20.0
Silica sand 70 mesh	8.0
Kentucky ball clay (OM4)	24.0
Soda ash	3.0
Borax (powder)	3.0
Macaloid	2.0
	100% total

Notes:
Mix the dry components, then add enough water to form a stiff paste. Shape it into whatever small object you wish, then dry it slowly until soluble salts form on the surface. Fire it at cone 015. Although the Egyptian objects made of this type of clay were usually turquoise, nowadays, ceramists add other colorants to produce a wider range of colors. Once you mix the base white body, you can experiment with a variety of stains and oxides. The following percentages will give you a starting point for your testing.

Colorants:
Turquoise: Copper carbonate   2.50%(EP2)
Blue: Cobalt carbonate   .75%(EP3)
Soft lavender: D320 pink stain   3.00%(EP4)
                          Cobalt carbonate   .15%

Speckling
Granular ilmenite: forms tiny black specks
Silicon carbide (36 grit): forms prominent black specks

COLORING CLAY BODIES WITH OXIDES AND STAINS (CS1 TO CS6)

The dry stains can be mixed directly into the dry clay. In the following tests of cone 05, cone 5, and cone 10 clay in oxidation, the same percentages of stain were used, so only one chart is given below with notes on the colors achieved in each clay.

Stains and Oxides Added to All the White Clays

Colorants	Percent					
	Blue (CS1)	Medium Brown (CS2)	Green (CS3)	Pink (CS4)	Yellow (CS5)	Dark Brown (CS6)
Cobalt oxide	3.0					1.0
Iron oxide (red)		5.0				4.0
Chromium oxide			3.0			2.0
Manganese oxide						3.0
Pink stain (D320)				5.0		
#6440 Tin vanadium yellow					5.0	

Notes:

Coloring code 05 white clay body with oxides and stains (oxidation) (CS1 to CS6):

Blue — a light, rather watery blue. (CS1)

Red-brown — a light reddish brown, the color of flower pots. (S2)

Green — pale leaf green, no blue tones. (CS3)

Pink — very pale pink, almost off-white. (CS4)

Yellow — pale, beige-yellow. (CS5)

Brown — more gray than brown. (CS6) On this clay, the low-fire clear glaze (G1 formula on page 416) has a milky appearance.

If you like a matt finish, fire the test without a glaze; if you want to deepen and intensify the color and add a glossy finish, apply a clear glaze.

Coloring cone 5 white clay with stains and oxides (oxidation) (CS1 to CS6):

Blue — rich deep blue with very slight purple tinge. (CS1)

Medium brown — warm brown. (CS2)

Green — dark leaf green. (CS3)

Pink — light pink, flesh color. (CS4)

Yellow — earthtone yellow; not clear lemon yellow. (CS5)

Dark brown — rich chocolate brown. (CS6)

Applying the clear glaze over these clays does not intensify the color, but adds a glossy surface.

Coloring cone 10 white base clay body (oxidation) (CS1 to CS6):

Blue — very dark blue, slightly purplish tone. (CS1)

Medium brown — cold gray/brown. (CS2)

Green — yellow green. (CS3)

Pink — paler than cone 5 pink. (CS4)

Yellow — slightly yellower than cone 5 yellow. (CS5)

Dark brown — rich chocolate brown. (CS6)

GUM SOLUTION FOR TRANSPARENT UNDERGLAZE STAIN OR OXIDES USED ON WHITE CLAY BODY

If you would like to make your own transparent water-base underglazes, you can mix oxides and ceramic stains using a solution of CMC gum in water:

Basic Stain Solution

Water	CMC gum
1 gallon (3.875 liters)	130.66 grams
or	
1 pint (.48 liter)	16.33 grams

SURFACE COLORS/UNDERGLAZES, STAINS

Colorants (Stains and Oxides) for Use on White Clay Body

Colorant	Solution	Color: cone 05	Color: cone 5	Color: cone 10
Cobalt	5 grams 3 oz (91 milliliters)	Matt gray blue (S1)	Dark blue, slight gloss (S5)	Dark blue, slight gloss (S9)
Yellow stain	5 grams 3 oz (91 milliliters)	Bright yellow (S3)	Pale yellow (S7)	Pale yellow (S11)
Iron	8 grams 3 oz (91 milliliters)	Matt red-brown (S4)	Dark matt brown (S8)	Dark matt brown (S12)
Chromium	5 grams 3 oz (91 milliliters)	Matt leaf green (S2)	Dark leaf green (S6)	Dark leaf green (S10)

Apply thinly in one coat; otherwise, any glaze you use over the underglaze may crawl. You may brush, spray, or paint on the underglaze. The test underglazes applied with this solution were fired from cone 05 up to cone 10 in oxidation. The oxides and stains tested held their colors at these cones. You will need to make more tests to see which proportion of coloring agents will work best for you, depending on your clay and the temperature at which you fire the tests. If you plan to keep the solution for later use, you may add a few drops of formaldehyde, but rather than use formaldehyde we recommend that you mix only enough solution for immediate use. Formaldehyde can produce allergic reactions. With a coat of transparent glaze over the underglaze the colors are generally brighter (ST1 to ST2).

GLAZES FORMULATED FOR TESTING

The following glazes were tested on the base white clay body. Since a glaze consists of a combination of chemicals that fuse and adhere to a clay body under proper application and firing, both the clay body and the firing are equally important in developing successful glazes, and the two must work in a symbiotic relationship. The glazes in this section were formulated to be used on the clays that you have already tested. The cone 05 glaze fits that clay, the cone 5 glaze fits the cone 5 clay, and the cone 10 glaze fits the white cone 10 clay.

How you apply the glaze and the type of kiln and atmosphere in which you fire it will also affect the final result. Make notes as you test so that you can make changes based on what happened in your tests. Devise a system of displaying or storing your test tiles so that they are easily available for reference. Our notes following the clay and glaze recipes describe the appearance of the test tiles after firing in a test kiln. Your tests may differ from these descriptions, and the colors or textures as they appear on these small test tiles may also look quite different on a piece of sculpture or a pot.

Water Proportions for *Hands in Clay* Glazes

Glaze	Per 100 Grams Glaze Material	Per 100 Grams Glaze and Colorant
Hands in Clay Cone 05	2.5 oz (75.67 milliliters)	2.5 oz (75.67 milliliters)
Hands in Clay Cone 5	2.5 oz (75.67 milliliters)	3.0 oz (90.81 milliliters)
Cone 10	3.4 oz (102.91 milliliters)	4.0 oz (121.08 milliliters)

Water Ratio

You must control the amount of water you add to the glaze materials because it affects glaze-material suspension as well as application properties. The percentages in the following chart indicate the water-to-glaze ratio for the glaze test formulas in this Appendix. Use the chart only as a guide when formulating your own test glazes. In our testing, the glazes were applied with two to three brushed-on applications. For dipping or pouring, more water would be needed. The varying porosity of bisque ware affects the water ratio. For example, Murphy's cone 10 glaze needs 3.40 ounces (102.91 milliliters) of water per 100 grams of glaze for dipping. For brushing two coats will usually suffice; for dipping it takes one to two dips.

Once you have established the water content for a glaze through testing, if settling occurs, try reducing the amount of water, and refer to the glaze-suspension chart in Appendix 1B. Start by adding .5 to 2% of bentonite or macaloid. Purified bentonite was used for the tests in this appendix. The addition of gums, which will thicken a glaze, may necessitate increased amounts of water.

GLAZE RECIPES TO MIX AND TEST

ced *Hands in Clay* Cone 05 Glaze Recipe (For Testing Only)

Components	Percent							
	Clear Base (G1)	White (G2)	Blue (G3)	Brown (G4)	Green (G5)	Black (G6)	Pink (G7)	Yellow (G8)
Frit 3195 (3811)	88.0	88.0	88.0	88.0	88.0	88.0	88.0	88.0
Kaolin (Georgia)	10.0	10.0	10.0	10.0	10.0	10.0	10.0	10.0
Bentonite	2.0	2.0	2.0	2.0	2.0	2.0	2.0	2.0
Added Colorants								
	Clear Base (G1)	White (G2)	Blue (G3)	Brown (G4)	Green (G5)	Black (G6)	Pink (G7)	Yellow (G8)
Tin oxide		12.0						
Cobalt oxide			2.0			2.0		
Iron oxide (red)				6.0		4.0		
Chromium oxide					6.0	2.5		
D320 Pink stain							7.0	
#6440 Tin vanadium yellow								7.0

Note:
Cone 05 tests fired in a small test kiln in oxidation:
Clear—good clear glaze, no crackle; pencil shows. (G1)
White—glossy, almost opaque, but black underglaze pencil shows through slightly. (G2)
Blue—deep blue with attractive mottling; covers pencil. (G3)
Brown—rich, opaque dark brown with golden-brown areas; covers pencil. (G4)
Green—opaque shiny green, completely covers clay surface and underglaze pencil. (G5)
Black—brownish-black, slight pinholing; covers pencil. (G6)
Pink—pale pink, underglaze pencil runs, but shows clearly. (G7)
Yellow—glossy yellow, more opaque than the pink, underglaze pencil shows somewhat. (G8)

Hands in Clay Cone 5 Glaze Recipe and Colorant Percentages (For Testing Only)

Components	Percent								
	Clear Base (G9)	White (G10)	Blue (G11)	Brown (G12)	Green (G13)	Black (G14)	Pink #1 (G15A)	Pink #2 (G15B)	Yellow (G16)
Calcium carbonate (whiting)	3.0	3.0	3.0	3.0	3.0	3.0	3.0	3.0	3.0
Kaolin (Georgia)	13.0	13.0	13.0	13.0	13.0	13.0	13.0	13.0	13.0
Gerstley borate	27.0	27.0	27.0	27.0	27.0	27.0	27.0	27.0	27.0
Nepheline syenite	45.0	45.0	45.0	45.0	45.0	45.0	45.0	45.0	45.0
PV clay (plastic vitrox)	10.0	10.0	10.0	10.0	10.0	10.0	10.0	10.0	10.0
Bentonite (purified)	2.0	2.0	2.0	2.0	2.0	2.0	2.0	2.0	2.0

Added Colorants	Clear Base (G9)	White (G10)	Blue (G11)	Brown (G12)	Green (G13)	Black (G14)	Pink #1 (G15A)	Pink #2 (G15B)	Yellow (G16)
Tin oxide		12.0							
Cobalt oxide			2.0			2.0			
Iron oxide (red)				6.0		4.0			
Chromium oxide					6.0	2.5			
D320 Pink stain #1 test*							7.0		
F444 Pink stain #2 test*								7.0	
#6440 Tin vanadium yellow									7.0

*This test was run first with the Pink stain D320 in the same proportion as in the cone 05 glaze. Since no pink color showed, a new test was run with Pink stain F444 substituted, which produced a true pink at cone 5. This shows that a stain that gives true color at one cone may not hold color in another cone range. For this reason, it is important to run tests at a number of temperature ranges, using other colors of stains to see which colors hold true.

Notes:
Cone 5 glaze tests fired in a small test kiln (oxidation):
Clear—smooth, clear, with some crackling; pencil shows. (G9)
White—semiopaque white, pencil shows slightly. (G10)
Blue—rich, smooth, and glossy dark blue; pencil covered. (G11)
Light brown—translucent golden brown; some crackle; underglaze pencil shows. (G12)
Green—shiny green, slightly darker than in cone 05 firing; covers body and pencil completely. (G13)
Black—shiny; almost a true black with only slight brown tone; covers pencil. (G14)
Pink #1—no pink color using stain D320; milky white matt; pencil shows through, blurry. (G15A)
Pink #2—stain F444 gave a true pink at this cone. (G15B)
Yellow—runny and slightly more transparent than in cone 05; pencil blurred, but shows more. (G16)

**Larry Murphy's (*Hands in Clay*) Matt Cone 10 Glaze Recipe
(Very slightly changed from the proportions given for this glaze in Appendix 3.)   (G17 to G32)**

Components	*Percent*							
	Matt Base (G17)	*White (G18)*	*Blue (G19)*	*Brown (G20)*	*Green (G21)*	*Black (G22)*	*Pink (G23)*	*Yellow (G24)*
Kaolin (Georgia)	28.0	28.0	28.0	28.0	28.0	28.0	28.0	28.0
Silica (flint)	13.0	13.0	13.0	13.0	13.0	13.0	13.0	13.0
Feldspar (Custer)	35.0	35.0	35.0	35.0	35.0	35.0	35.0	35.0
Calcium carbonate (whiting)	24.0	24.0	24.0	24.0	24.0	24.0	24.0	24.0

Added Colorants								
	Matt Base (G17)	*White (G18)*	*Blue (G19)*	*Brown (G20)*	*Green (G21)*	*Black (G22)*	*Pink (G23)*	*Yellow (G24)*
Tin oxide		12.0*						
Cobalt oxide			2.0			2.0		
Iron oxide				6.0		4.0		
Chrome oxide					6.0	2.5		
D320 Pink							7	
#6440 Tin vanadium yellow								7

*Varying quantities of tin oxide may affect glaze smoothness and will affect opacity.

Notes:
Cone 10 glaze tests fired in small test kiln in *oxidation:*
Murphy formulated this to be a cone 10 matt. The surface is smooth and pleasantly matt, the colors more subtle as a result.
The glaze was applied on the *Hands in Clay* cone 10 white test clay (CL 3, 4) given on page 409 rather than on Murphy's stoneware clay because the white clay provided a better background for testing color.

Matt—semiopaque. (G17)
White—completely opaque. (G18)
Blue—handsome, matt blue, softer color than when shiny. (G19)
Brown—still golden brown tinge, but darker than at cone 5; slightly rough surface. (G20)
Green—deep green. (G21)
Black—truer black than either of the other glazes. (G22)
Pink—the brightest pink of all! Semiopaque with the underglaze pencil fuzzy but quite clear. (G23)
Yellow—soft, almost golden yellow; pencil shows. (G24)

Cone 10 glaze tests fired in gas kiln in *reduction:*
Matt base—semimatt white, underglaze pencil shows. (G25)
White—yellowish pale beige. (G26)
Blue—deep blue, matt, slightly mottled. (G27)
Brown—yellowish brown. (G28)
Green—semimatt green. (G29)
Black—semimatt black. (G30)
Pink—pale pink; underglaze pencil shows. (G31)
Yellow—turned gray with some white speckles, which came from the clay. (G32)

LINE BLEND TESTING

After testing any combination of *Hands in Clay* glazes from G1 to G24, you can continue developing glazes by line blend testing. If you take 90% (by volume) of the *Hands in Clay* cone 05 clear base glaze (G1) and blend it with 10% of (G3) blue, you will achieve a light-blue transparent glaze. If you continue the process and blend 80% of the clear with 20% blue, you will have a slightly darker blue transparent glaze and so on. By continuing in this manner and changing percentages of the glazes, you will end up with nine different shades of blue.

You can take this process a step further by blending one of these glazes with another glaze to develop yet another color. For example, to make a blue-green transparent glaze, blend one of your light-blue transparent glazes with a green glaze such as (G5).

Although used primarily for achieving color variations in glazes, line blend testing can also be used to test changes in ingredients in order to affect any glaze's maturing point. For example, to lower the maturing of a high-fire glaze such as *Hands in Clay* cone 10 matt glaze (G17), you could perform a line blend test by blending 90% of (G17) with 10% of *Hands in Clay* cone 5 clear base (G9). Then continue this process by blending 80% of the high-fire glaze (G17) with 20% of the cone 5 clear (G9). As you continue increasing the proportion of the cone 5 glaze to the high-fire glaze, you will gradually lower its maturing point. The surface color and texture of the glazes will also be affected: One glaze will be matt and the other a gloss glaze.

Using this method of testing, you will also be able to explore the wide ranges of glazes between cone 05 (1832°F/1000°C) and cone 10 (2381°F/1305°C). You can best understand this process by following through a line blend test. The test shown in the chart uses two *Hands in Clay* glazes, G1 Clear and G3 Blue.

Explanation of Line Blend Testing

First, the two dry base glazes (G1 and G3) were mixed in 200-gram batches and were scooped into 1 pint (.48 liter) plastic containers with 5 ounces (151.35 milliliters) of water, and shaken up until all the chemicals were blended. Then the glaze, G1 Clear, was painted on a test tile and identified as Test G1. G3 Blue was painted on a test tile and identified as Test G3. When fired, these test tiles showed what the base glazes looked like.

Now the line blend testing began: Nine jars, each 1 ounce (30.27 milliliters), were marked (Test 1, Test 2, Test 3, Test 4, Test 5, Test 6, Test 7, Test 8, Test 9). Test jar 1 was placed on a gram scale, and using a slip trailer to transfer the glaze from container G1 to the test jar, 9 grams (90%) of glaze was dripped into the jar. Then, 1 gram (10%) of G3 was dripped into the same jar. The two glazes were mixed and painted on a test tile. This process continued with Test 2, by taking 8 grams (80%) of G1 and blending it with 2 gram (20%) of G3; on through Test 9, incrementally changing the proportions as shown in the chart. These test tiles were then fired to cone 05.

If you see lumps of chemicals floating on top of the liquid glaze, that means it is not thoroughly mixed. For faster and more thorough mixing of the

Sample Line Blend Test

Base Glaze Clear G1	100%	Base Glaze Blue G3	100%
(Test 1)	90%		10%
(Test 2)	80%		20%
(Test 3)	70%		30%
(Test 4)	60%		40%
(Test 5)	50%		50%
(Test 6)	40%		60%
(Test 7)	30%		70%
(Test 8)	20%		80%
(Test 9)	10%		90%

Note:
If necessary, the percentage shown in the chart can be changed to grams, pounds, ounces, spoonfuls, tablespoons, cups, liters, quarts, gallons, or any other measure you wish to use. For example: 90% can equal 9 grams, 9 ounces, 9 spoonfuls, or 9 cups, and so on.

base glazes, you can use an electric kitchen blender. Hot water will also help to dissolve sticky clays and chemicals such as bentonite, macaloid, or gums that do not disperse easily when mixed. You can also screen the glazes through a 50- to 80-mesh sieve. Oxides or stains that are not thoroughly ground can show up on test tiles as spots. To avoid this, use a mortar and pestle to grind the glaze components.

FLUIDITY TEST

Mark your glaze tiles with a line lightly scored into the clay or with a black underglaze pencil, halfway or a third of the way down the test tile. (The lower section is useful for marking the cone number, glaze components, glaze number, or firing atmosphere; e.g., OX for oxidation, RE for reduction.) If the glaze when fired travels past the line, you can see how much it flowed. It is a good idea to fire your tiles set on end at about a 10-degree angle.

OPACITY TEST

To test the opacity of the glazes, make a mark on each tile with a dark-colored underglaze pencil prior to glazing and firing. In this way you can observe the opacity of the glaze when fired by noting how clearly the dark pencil mark shows through the glaze.

Glaze Additives in Relation to Suspension and Application

The quantity and type of glaze additive is related to the composition of the glaze. Testing is essential.

For Glaze Suspension

Components	Percent
Bentonite (Wyoming)	.5–3
Bentonite (ferro-purified)	.5–3
Macaloid	.5–2
Vee gum	.5–2
Calcium chloride	.5
Magnesium carbonate	1
Magnesium sulfate (Epsom salts)	.2
Setit A	.5–2
Dextrin	3

Notes:
Bentonite is a sticky clay; 2% is commonly used as a suspending agent to keep glaze components from settling. The purified bentonite has greater suspending properties than the Wyoming.

Macaloid and *Vee gum* have greater suspending properties than bentonite, so smaller quantities are needed.

For Glaze Fluidity

Components	Percent
Darvan #7	.1
Dispersal	.1
Sodium silicate N	.1

Note:
These act as deflocculants in glazes that tend to become thixotrophic (viscous). Useful for glazes that are to be sprayed.

Gums

Components	Percent
CMC gum (synthetic) Carboxymethyl-cellulose)	1–3
Gum tragacanth (natural gum)	1–3
Gum arabic	1–3

Notes:
1% gum is usually added to glazes to delay drying and to alleviate brush drag. Also helps to keep glazes, underglaze, engobes, and slips from dusting or crumbling; assists in suspension of glaze components and adhesion of glaze to ware. Hardens the glaze surface, and, in solution, can be sprayed over oxides or underglazes to keep them from smearing during handling prior to firing.

Gum tragacanth and *gum arabic* are natural gums, often used with stains or oxides sensitive to contamination, such as low-fire red and orange glazes with cadmium or selenium stains where CMC gum may cause discoloration.

Clay, Slip, and Glaze Recipes from Ceramists

The following recipes shared with us by a number of ceramists were included to offer you a wider range of clays, slips, and glazes to test. Some of the recipes came originally from other ceramists through personal sharing, books, or magazine articles—an example of how information now spreads throughout the clay community.

The recipes are given in percentages; in some cases, the recipe does not total 100% or exceeds 100%. These small percentage differences will only slightly affect the quantity of the batch by weight. In some cases, we changed the percentages slightly to bring them closer to 100%. We did not test any of these formulas. Remember to observe precautions when mixing glazes. See Chapter 14 for mixing directions.

Ann Roberts, Canada, offers a low-fire talc clay body for sculpture (*Ceramic Review,* vol. 133, 1992).

Components	Percent
Ball clay	45.90
Silica (flint)	20.20
Talc	12.20
Whiting	6.10
20-mesh gray grog	15.60
	100.00

The 45.9% ball clay allows the body to remain plastic even with the addition of 15.6% grog to prevent thermal shock during multiple firings.

Mary Parisi, California, offers her modification to Jerry Rothman's low-shrinkage clay for building thick, solid sculpture walls (up to or exceeding 10 inches [25.40 cm]). Like Rothman, she is able to fire steel in her sculpture without the piece cracking. She says that the different sizes of ione grain grog fill up more space in the clay body than particles of only one size, lessening the shrinkage as well as contributing to the openness of the body. *The clay dries better and fires easier. Bentonite is used to give plasticity, but since it increases shrinkage, it is used in a small amount. . . . The grog can be increased or decreased to reduce graininess or increase plasticity. Water should be carefully controlled; the wetter the clay, the greater amount of shrinkage.*

White Low-Shrinkage Cone 06 Clay

Components	Percent
C-1 Clay (Pfizer Co.)	14.0
Calcined kaolin	7.0
Talc	7.0
Nepheline syenite	21.0
Ione grain grog #400	14.0
Ione grain grog #412 or #414	14.0
Ione grain grog #420	14.0
Wollastonite	7.0
Bentonite	1.4
Chopped fiber glass (optional)	1.4
	100.8

William Daley, Pennsylvania, builds his vessel forms using the following clay body and fires them in oxidation.

Cone 6 Clay

Components	Percent
Valentine fire clay	20.0
Kentucky ball clay (OM4)	20.0
Missouri fire clay	20.0
Red Art Clay	40.0
	100.0

Additive

Medium grog 10%

Gary Holt, California, throws his stoneware clay on the wheel as well as using it to form slab plates. He says that this lightly grogged clay fires to a toasty brown in reduction and is very strong and durable. The white stoneware clay body contains no grog and fires to a gray-white. Holt says, *It throws easily. I use it for both my large slab platters and for functional pieces — casseroles, dinner plates, etc.*

Cone 10 Stoneware

Components	Percent
IMCO #800 clay	25.0
Kaiser Missouri fire clay	25.0
Kentucky ball clay (OM4)	25.0
Silica 200 mesh (flint)	9.0
Custer feldspar	7.0
Ione grain grog #420	7.0
Talc	2.0
Macaloid (200 mesh)	1.0
	101.0

Cone 10 White Stoneware

Components	Percent
6-Tile Kaolin	45.0
Custer feldspar	20.0
Silica 200 mesh (flint)	15.0
C-1 clay (Pfizer)	10.0
Kentucky ball clay (OM4)	10.0
Bentonite	1.5
Macaloid	.05
	101.55

Walter Keeler, England, throws his jugs using a clay body consisting of stoneware, ball clay, and sand. He then coats part of the jug with an engobe and salt-glazes the jugs.

Cone 10 Stoneware (For Salt Glazing)

Components	Percent
Dorset ball clay	60.72
Staffordshire stoneware clay	30.36
Sand (80 mesh)	9.20
	100.28

Melissa McRaney's Snow White Cone 10 Stoneware Clay Body   (WS1 Oxidation, **WS2** Reduction)
A textured stoneware body for general use

Components	Percent
Kentucky ball clay (OM4)	25.0
Silica 200 mesh (flint)	20.0
Georgia china clay	20.0
Custer feldspar	20.0
Macaloid	2.0
Molochite	13.0

Karen Massaro, California, contributes a clay along with a compatible glaze. These were shared with her when she was a graduate student at the University of Wisconsin, Madison, by Dennis Caffrey, who had studied with Fred Bauer in Seattle — a good example of how information is shared and spreads. Massaro says, *This is a beautiful porcelain surface. Some shrinkage, some crackling. A bit tricky, but interesting for throwing smaller pieces. Very responsive.*

Cone 9 Porcelain

Components	Percent
Kaolin (EPK)	40.0
Custer feldspar	30.0
Silica	20.0
Nepheline syenite	10.0
	100.0

Frank Boyden, Oregon, says this porcelain body for wood firing is translucent if thinly thrown. He suggests that for firing in an *anagama* kiln where the pieces will be stacked on each other, one should avoid brittle, thin shapes; cylinders do well, as do large, thick, flat plates.

Cone 13 to 14 Porcelain Clay

Components	Percent
Kaolin (EPK)	37.50
PV (plastic vitrox) clay	11.25
Custer feldspar	26.25
Silica 200 mesh (flint)	22.50
Pyrophyllite	2.25
Macaloid	.75
	100.50

SLIP RECIPES FROM CERAMISTS

Gary Holt, California, offers two slips. The white slip is to be used on damp ware, *not on bisque.* The other slip is, Holt says, *particularly well suited for use on a glassy glaze like my Amber glaze. Applied over the glaze, it melts in when fired, giving caramel orange/browns, tans, and occasionally bluish purple.* Since Albany slip is no longer available, you might try a slip mined in Washington called Seattle slip or Sheffield slip from Massachusetts, both offered as substitutes for Albany. This slip recipe came from Jack Troy through Leon Paulos.

Cone 8 to 10 White Slip (Damp Ware)

Components	Percent
Kaolin (EPK)	25.0
Kentucky ball clay (OM4)	25.0
Nepheline syenite	15.0
Talc	7.0
Silica (flint)	20.0
Zircopax	5.0
	97.0

Cone 8 to 10 Troy Slip

Components	Percent
Albany slip	75.0
Rutile	10.0
Red iron oxide	10.0
Custer feldspar	5.0
	100.0

Note:
Ball-mill for 1 or 2 hours for even consistency and better flowing characteristics.

Hands in Clay offers an engobe/slip for stoneware decoration.

Cone 6–10 Stoneware Engobe

Components	Percent
China clay	21.0
Kentucky ball clay (OM4)	21.0
Silica 200 mesh	29.0
Nepheline syenite	24.0
Borax (powder)	5.0
	100.0

Colorants/Additives	Percent
Red: iron	6.0
Blue: cobalt	2.0
Green: chrome	3.0

Patrick Siler, Washington, stencils black and white images on greenware using these slips. Then, before firing, he covers the slip with a sprayed-on clear glaze. Single-firing to cone 5.

Cone 5 Black Slip

Components	Percent
Lincoln fire clay	66.6
Kentucky ball clay (OM4)	33.3
	99.9

Colorants/Additives	Percent
Black stain	15.0
Red iron	15.0

Cone 5 Ivory Slip

Components	Percent
Lincoln clay	33.3
Kaolin	33.3
OM4 ball clay	33.3
	99.9

Walter Keeler, England, applies an engobe to the lower part of his salt-glazed jugs in order to achieve a contrast between the characteristic "orange peel" salt-glaze surface and the smooth engobe. He then sprays on color mixed with a little engobe to prevent it from brushing off the unfired pot when it is handled. He salt glazes, firing to 2336°F/1280°C (Orton cone 10), salts at 2280°F/1250°C (Orton cone 9), then soaks for half an hour.

Keeler Engobe for Salt Glaze

Components	Percent
Feldspar	60.0
China clay	40.0
	100.0

Colorants/Additives

Mixtures of oxides and/or stains — for example, chrome oxide and cobalt oxide

Black stain

Black stain and cobalt or manganese dioxide and iron

Ericka Clark Shaw, California, offers a crackle slip that, she says *is a lot like Bob Sperry's. It can be applied over green or bisque ware, either under or over a glaze.*

Crackle Slip

Components	Percent
Nepheline syenite	50.0
Magnesium carbonate	50.0
	100.0

Colorants/Additives

Gum for working consistency

Stains for color (except lilac)

Jim Gremel, California, forms his raku vessels in plaster molds cast from a special slip-casting body. Gremel says, *I switched from throwing to slip casting about four years ago. The cast pieces survive the raku process much better than their predecessors, and their color development seems to be better.*

Cone 07 Raku Slip-Casting Body

Components	Percent
Imco #400 fire clay	27.02
Tennessee ball clay	27.02
Custer feldspar	13.52
Ione grain #65 F grog (very fine powder)	16.22
Mullite 100 mesh	16.22
	100.00

Additives

45.95 pounds (20.86 kilos) of water and 351.36 grams of Darvan #7 deflocculant per 100-pound (45.40-kilo) batch. Additional water, Darvan #7, and sodium silicate N are added as needed to achieve a specific gravity reading of about 1.75. It is important to bisque-fire the clay to cone 06 before raku firing.

Richard Hirsch, New York, uses terra sigillata combined with low-fire glazes to develop the rich patina of his vessel forms. He colors his white terra sigillata with stains, then may intermix the terra sigillatas themselves. He says that the firing limit for good color is cone 04 and that the color values can be changed by varying the percentages of the stain in the white base. The frit helps in hardness and color.

White Terra Sigillata

Components	Percent
Kentucky (OM4) or Tenn. #5 ball clay	20.0
Frit 3110	.5
H_2O (water)	80.0
Calgon*	1.0
	101.5

Colorants/Additives	Percent
Medium blue: Medium blue stain	10.0
Medium green: Medium green stain	10.0
Orange: Saturn orange stain	10.0
Purple: Red and medium blue sigillatas mixed	

Red Terra Sigillata

Components	Percent
Kentucky ball clay (OM4)	50.0
Iron oxide	50.0
Calgon*	5.0
	105.0
Water (H_2O)	61.0 grams

*The active ingredient in Calgon is sodium carbonate.

GLAZE RECIPES FROM CERAMISTS

Low to Mid-Range Glazes

Richard Hirsch, New York, uses a low-fire cone 04 base glaze to which he adds a variety of colorants to create semiopaque glazes that interface well with the terra sigillata beneath, creating a patina and layering effect. The cone 04 limit ensures good color.

Base Glaze, for Use with Terra Sigillatas (Cone 04)

Components	Percent
Gerstley borate	31.54
Lithium carbonate*	8.30
Nepheline syenite	4.15
Kaolin (EPK)	4.15
Silica (flint)	34.86
Whiting	16.60
	99.60

Colorants/Additives	Percent
Blue-green: leave out lithium, add	
Copper carbonate	4.0
Yellow-blue-green	
Copper carbonate	4.0
Rutile	4.0
Red-rust	
Rutile	10.0
Golden ambrosia stain	3.0
Orange-rust	
Red iron oxide	6.0
Rutile	4.0
Saturn orange stain	2.0

The Richmond Art Center, California, uses a raku glaze that develops a coppery luster. Ceramic instructor Larry Henderson says, *After the glaze bubbles and then flattens out and turns glossy, I take the pots out and place them in a covered garbage can with sawdust for 10 minutes, then remove them from the can and spray them with water.*

Clear Raku Glaze (Cone 09–07)

Components	Percent
Colemanite (Gerstley borate)	79.0
Nepheline syenite	21.0
	100.0

Colorants/Additives for Black/Copper Luster	Percent
Iron oxide	4.0
Cobalt	2.5
Copper carbonate	3.0

The Richmond Art Center, California, also contributes a white crackle raku glaze. To achieve a green color, they brush on a copper carbonate solution over the glaze and fire in oxidation. When fired under reduction the same colorant turns into a copper luster.

White Crackle Raku Glaze

Components	Percent
Frit 3134	54.00
Kaolin (EPK)	20.68
Silica 325 mesh (flint)	20.68
Bentonite	2.58
Zircopax or tin oxide	2.06
	100.00

Roslyn Myers, California, contributes a low-fire texture glaze to which she added silicon carbide, molochite, steel and brass shavings, and so on, in order to produce unusual textures.

Low-Fire Texture Glaze

Components	Percent
Borax (powder)	30.0
Kaolin (Georgia)	10.0
Custer feldspar	20.0
Soda ash	18.0
Silica 325 mesh (flint)	20.0
Bentonite	2.0
	100.0

Colorants/Additives

For varying texture effects on white clay: use .5 to 1.5%, either sprinkled over the tile or mixed in the glaze.

> *Notes:*
> *Silicon carbide* (36–100 grit) — white background, widely spaced dark gray texture.
> *Silica sand* (30–60 mesh) — 30 mesh gives white texture, large granules.
> *Ilmenite* (granulated) — small brown granules catch the light and give golden sparkles.
> *Ione grain #420* — very rough gray texture.
> *Molochite* — similar to silica sand, but smaller white granules, overall texture.
> *Steel grindings* — very rough, shiny, black lava effect.
> *Stainless steel grindings* — particles did not melt and flow at cone 05, leaving sharp tooth, dark gray.
> *Brass* — mottled light and dark green, flowed, but clear spaces remain.

Hands in Clay offers two more cone 05 glazes. The clear glaze fires to a clear gloss over white clay, and clear glossy with a white granulated mottle when applied over red clay.

Hands in Clay Cone 05 Clear Glaze

Components	Percent
Gerstley borate	65.0
Kaolin (Georgia)	15.0
Silica 325 mesh (flint)	18.0
Bentonite	2.0
	100.0

> *Notes:*
> *On white clay body* — clear gloss.
> *On red clay body* — white granulated mottle.

For a clear 05 crackle glaze, eliminate the copper carbonate used as colorant in the green crackle glaze. For other colors, test it with glaze stains instead of the copper.

Hands in Clay Cone 05 Green Crackle Glaze

Components	Percent
Frit #25	80.96
Kaolin (Georgia)	12.38
Bentonite	1.90
Copper carbonate	4.76
	100.00

> *Notes:*
> *On cone 05 white clay body* — blue-green, medium crackle.
> *On cone 05 red body* — dark olive green, medium crackle.
> *On cone 5 clay body* — olive green, transparent with small crackles.
> *On porcelain at cone 5* — at this temperature, the glaze runs.

Medium-Range Glazes

Susanne Ashmore, Canada, offers a glaze from Emanuel Cooper's *The Potter's Book of Glaze Recipes.* She finds it an excellent base glaze for overlap experiments with other glazes, and fires it at a wide range of temperatures, from cone 05 to 8. Of the Zakin glaze, Ashmore says: *I found this in* Electric Kiln Ceramics *by Richard Zakin. I fire with an electric kiln so these two glazes have been tested only under those conditions. I do try to achieve long soaking periods at cone 6 to 7.*

Cooper's Clear Base Glaze (Cone 05 to 8)

Components	Percent
Soda feldspar (Kona F-4)	38.0
Whiting	14.0
Zinc oxide	12.0
Kentucky ball clay (OM4)	6.0
Silica (flint)	30.0
	100.0

Zakin Medium-Range Glaze

Components	Percent
Nepheline syenite	40.0
Dolomite	18.0
Silica (flint)	18.0
Kaolin	12.0
Bone ash	6.0
Lithium carbonate	2.0
Zinc oxide	4.0
	100.0

Colorant/Additive	Percent
Copper carbonate	2

Two Cone 5 Glazes

To add more medium-range glazes *Hands in Clay* tested some cone 5 and cone 6 glazes, one of which is an example of how radically a glaze may vary when fired in oxidation or in reduction. For this reason, the matt glaze is called "Night and Day."

Cone 5 "Night and Day" Matt Glaze

Components	Percent
Dolomite	18.0
Gerstley borate	10.0
Kona F4 feldspar	15.0
Nepheline syenite	23.0
Kentucky ball clay (OM4)	18.0
Silica (flint)	10.0
Titanium dioxide	6.0
	100.0

Notes:
Oxidation—pale warm yellow gloss glaze.
Reduction—handsome granite gray, dry matt.

Cone 5 Japanese Wood Ash Glaze

Components	Percent
Ash	16.0
Silica (flint)	33.0
Custer feldspar	21.0
Gerstley borate	4.0
Kentucky ball clay (OM4)	7.0
Dolomite	10.0
Iron oxide (Spanish red)	9.0
	100.0

Notes:
Oxidation—reddish brown, pebbly.
Reduction—rich, glossy brown/black.
At cone 10—matt, purplish.

Cone 6 Matt Glaze (Oxidation)

Components	Percent
Custer feldspar	33.0
Gerstley borate	5.0
Silica (flint)	25.0
Whiting	24.0
Kaolin (Georgia)	11.0
Bentonite	2.0
	100.0

Note:
A buttery, white, translucent matt glaze with no toxic ingredients that would be good for the inside of food containers.

High-Fire Glazes

Gary Holt, California, uses the following high-fire glaze mainly on stoneware. *On my stoneware, with a medium to heavy reduction it will fire to a honey brown color. Takes iron oxide decoration well. It will craze on white stoneware or porcelain.*

Cone 9 to 10 Amber Glaze

Components	Percent
Custer feldspar	52.00
Whiting	18.25
Silica (flint)	16.75
Kaolin (EPK)	10.00
Tin oxide	1.30
Rutile	1.70
	100.00

Frank Boyden, Oregon, applies this Shino-type glaze to porcelain, which he fires to high temperature in his wood-fired *anagama* kiln. Boyden says, *This is not my own glaze, but Tom Coleman's, I think. I use it along with many others. Most Shino glazes will fire extremely high.* He recommends avoiding delicate brushwork and strong stains containing cobalt, chrome, and copper.

Cone 13 to 14 Shino-Type Glaze

Components	Percent
Feldspar Kona F4	15.0
Spodumene	13.0
Soda ash	3.0
Nepheline syenite	50.0
Kentucky ball clay (OM4)	16.0
Kaolin (EPK)	3.0
	100.0

Colorant/Additive	Percent
Iron oxide	.125 to .25

Karen Massaro, California, sends a clear glaze that came originally from Fred Bauer. It is compatible with the clay-body recipe she gave earlier (see page 423), and she says it is good in oxidation or in reduction. *For celadon, you may add 1 to 3 percent iron oxide to yield a lovely blue-green color.* Of the barium matt glaze, Massaro says, *Colorants can be added singly or in combination. Results are interesting; the richer hues with varied undertones come when using two or more oxides. Single oxide gives flatter color.*

Cone 9 to 10 Clear Glaze

Components	Percent
Silica (flint)	14.56
Cornwall stone	66.37
Whiting	12.41
Colemanite	2.49
Zinc oxide	2.49
Magnesium carbonate (or 2% bentonite)	1.72
	100.04

Colorants/Additives	Percent
Red iron oxide	2–5
Copper carbonate	1–5
Nickel oxide	1–3
Manganese dioxide	2–8

Cone 10 Dry Barium* Matt Glaze (Not for food containers)

Components	Percent
Nepheline syenite	44.93
Kentucky ball clay (OM4)	6.69
Barium carbonate (*toxic*)	35.37
Rutile	8.60
Flint	2.61
Bentonite	1.91
	100.11

*Toxic material.

Cone 8 to 10 Matt Black Glaze

Components	Percent
Nepheline syenite	17.51
Dolomite	13.98
Cornwall stone	25.23
Whiting (calcium)	3.80
Talc	14.36
Kaolin	21.50
Silica (flint)	3.83
	100.21

Colorants/Additives Add All for Black	Percent
Iron chromate	4.00
Iron oxide	6.01
Cobalt oxide	2.00
Nickel oxide	2.00
Ilmenite (powder)	3.51
Bentonite	2.00

Ernst Haüsermann, Switzerland, glazed the bowl shown in the text (Figure 13-1) with the following simple ash glaze fired to 2462°F/1350°C. It fires on stoneware to a matt, clear gray. Haüsermann's feldspar comes from Norway and is similar to Custer feldspar. The ashes he uses in his glazes come from the wood he burns in his ceramic-tile heating stove.

Ash Glaze

Components	Percent
K-feldspar	30.0
Mixed ash	30.0
Kaolin	26.0
White stoneware clay	14.0
	100.0

Harris Deller, Illinois, says, *A heavy reduction beginning at cone 010 all the way to a hot cone 10 is very important for this cone 10 Chun celadon glaze,* adding, *I clear the kiln atmosphere at the end of the firing for five to ten minutes by oxidizing.*

Cone 10 Chun Celadon Glaze

Components	Percent
Feldspar* potash	42.1 to 37.1*
China clay	1.8
Silica* (flint)	27.2 to 32.2*
Whiting	2.6
Colemanite	8.8
Dolomite	8.8
Zinc oxide	1.7
Barium carbonate (*toxic*)	4.4
Iron oxide	2.6
(Total will vary)	100.0

Colorants/Additives	Percent
Green-blue: Spanish red iron oxide[†]	1.5
Green: Spanish red iron oxide	2–3
Red: Copper carbonate	.50

*Adjustments may be made in feldspar and/or flint to control crazing. (Custer feldspar is a potash spar.)

[†]Deller says, *I use Spanish red iron oxide because it's a finer mesh iron with a good consistency from batch to batch. Some red iron oxide, because of larger particle size, will cause the glaze to have freckles or iron spots. Since this glaze contains [toxic] barium, it should not be used on the interior of food containers, and you should protect yourself against exposure to barium when mixing it.*

William S. Holoway, California, offers a purple semimatt glaze, saying, *This glaze must be screened and mixed thoroughly to ensure a smooth consistency and must be applied relatively thick to ensure a good all-over violet to purple. Stable, will hardly drip or move in the kiln.*

Cone 8 Purple Semi-matt

Components	Percent
Nepheline syenite	22.5
Colemanite (Gerstley borate)	12.1
Wollastonite	6.8
Macaloid	6.4
Dolomite	5.4
Kentucky ball clay (OM4)	11.3
Silica (flint)	35.3
	99.8

Colorant/Additive	Percent
Cobalt	3.0

Arnold Zahner, Switzerland, sends a crystalline glaze. He says that to develop crystals the exact weight of the components is not so important; the control of temperature, cooling, and so on, is of decisive influence.

Cone 10 to 12 Crystalline Glaze

Components	Percent
K-feldspar	25.0
Kaolin	5.0
Silica (quartz)	20.0
Barium carbonate (*toxic*)	5.0
Lithium carbonate	5.0
Frit	13.0
Zinc oxide	27.0
	100.0

Colorant/Additive	Percent
Copper carbonate	4

VAPOR FIRING

Peter Coussoulis, California, offers a salt-free mixture as an alternative to salt-vapor firing. Because the gases emitted from a salt firing are poisonous, some ceramists are now using more ecologically safe substitutes for salt. To his 30-cubic-foot (.85-cubic-meter) kiln, Peter Coussoulis (15-1) adds about 38 pounds (17.25 kilos) of a carbonate vapor compound that contains the mixture listed in the table that follows. He inserts the mixture in the kiln in small cups. Coussoulis suggests the following proportions for this mixture:

Cone 8 to 10 Vapor Mixture

Components	Percent
Soda ash (sodium carbonate)	34.0
Pearl ash (potassium carbonate)	8.0
Lithium carbonate	4.0
Whiting (calcium carbonate)	50.0
Borax	2.7
Bentonite	1.3
	100.0

Coussoulis uses various slips and colorants for his low-salt firing.

Cone 10 Porcelain Slip

Components	Percent
Grolleg china clay	53.94
Custer feldspar	19.60
Silica (flint)	11.76
Pyrophyllite	12.74
Bentonite	1.96
	100.00

Colorants/Additives	Percent
Flesh: Cerium oxide	8.0
Rutile	1.5
Pink-gray: Rutile	8.0
Iron chromate	5.0
Bleeding blue: Cobalt carbonate	1.5
Copper carbonate	4.0

Cone 10 Blue Pearly Slip

Components	Percent
Ball clay	23.85
Fire clay	11.00
Custer feldspar	27.54
Silica (flint)	22.95
Rutile	13.75
Cobalt carbonate	.91
	100.00

Larry Henderson, California, uses this glaze with salt-glaze firing. It requires a strong dose of salt to make it shiny. Because salt vapor does not penetrate the inside of pots readily, to achieve full gloss, use glaze only on the outside of objects.

Cone 8 to 10 Salt Glaze

Components	Percent
Custer feldspar	53.41
Wollastonite	10.90
Gerstley borate	5.45
Silica (flint)	22.89
Kentucky ball clay (OM4)	5.45
Bentonite	2.18
	100.28

Colorants/Additives	Percent
Iron oxide (red)	4.36
Cobalt	.55

Bill Roan and Clayton Bailey, California, offer a formula for reprocessing glaze and clay sediment into a clay body. Fire it at your normal studio temperature depending on the firing range of your clay and glazes.

Roan–Bailey Recycled Clay Body

Components	Percent
Glaze or clay sediment	50.00
Floor sweepings, sand, or fire clay	50.00
	100.00

1D

Percentage Charts: Clays, Frits, Feldspars, and Opacifiers

Percentage Composition of Clays and Chemicals

Clays and Chemicals	Percent											
	SiO_2	Al_2O_3	Fe_2O_3	CaO	MgO	TiO_2	K_2O	Na_2O	P_2O_5 & F	SO_3	Alkaline	Ig Loss*
EPK kaolin	45.91	38.71	.42	.09	.12	.34	.22	.04				14.15
Grolleg kaolin	47.70	37.20	.60	.10	.25	.03	1.92	1.92				12.60
Georgia kaolin	44.90	38.90	.40	.10	.10	1.30	.20	.20				14.21
#6 Tile clay	46.90	38.20	.35	.43	.53	1.42		.04				13.90
PV clay	78.70	12.80	.09	.28	Trace		.28	.28				4.42
Talc	56.29	1.07	.43	9.26	28.31		.57	.69				3.49
Kentucky ball clay (OM4)	53.80	30.00	.90	.30	.30	1.70	1.10	.30				11.80
Tennessee ball clay	52.90	31.10	.80	.20	.20	1.60	1.20	.40				11.60
Sagger clay	59.40	27.20	.70	.60	.20	1.60	.70	.30				9.40
Pyrophyllite	73.00	20.40	.50			.50	.20					3.50
Spodumene	63.60	26.50	.64	.30			.50	.30	.43			.55
C-1 clay	75.60	15.80		.80		1.55						4.84
Lincoln fire clay	52.57	29.41	2.90									11.51
Missouri fire clay	53.41	30.41	1.61									11.22
Goldart	57.32	28.50	1.23	.08	.22	1.98	.88	.30	SO_2/.24			9.39
Pine Lake	70.40	24.80	1.35	.27	.29	2.03	.86	.86		.17		N/A
Red Horse clay	67.46	21.99	6.61	.45	.62		1.20	.30				1.18
Redart	64.27	16.41	7.04	.23	1.55		4.07	.40	.17			4.78
Jordan clay	67.19	20.23	1.73								2.23	6.89

*Ignition loss, or loss on ignition (LOI). This phrase indicates the loss of weight on ignition that results from the carbonates being burned off when the clay or mineral is heated to from 1832° to 2012°F/1000° to 1100°C. This change in the weight of the material is shown as a percentage of the dry weight in the "Ig Loss" column.

Percentage Composition of Leadless Frits

Leadless Frits	Percent														
	Na_2O	Na_2F_2	$NaKO$	K_2O	Li_2O	CaO	CaF_2	CdO	ZnO	B_2O_3	Al_2O_3	SiO_2	F	Sb_2O_3	MgO
P-25	14.70			5.40		.50			.70	16.90	12.10	49.70	1.80		
P-283	16.30					.30					5.90	76.50			.70
3124	5.60			.60		14.50				12.50	10.00	56.80			
3134	10.20					20.10				23.20		46.50			
3195	5.70					11.30				22.40	12.00	48.50			
2106		21.67				3.42		3.60		13.00	9.13	45.20		3.98	

Notes:

Leadless frits We included a small selection of leadless frits. Other frits are available that contain the chemicals for which no percentages are listed. The numbers of equivalent frits that can be substituted are listed below.

Frit equivalents The composition of these equivalent frits may vary slightly from those on the chart above: P-25 = 3269; 3124 = 90 = 311; 3195 = 3811; P-283 = 3293; 3134 = 14 = P54.

Percentage Composition of Feldspars

Feldspars	Percent								
	Na_2O	K_2O	Al_2O_3	SiO_2	Fe_2O_3	CaO	MgO	P_2O_3 & F	$Ig Loss*$
Custer	3.00	10.40	17.50	68.50	.08	.30	trace		.30
Kona F-4 (#56)	6.90	4.80	19.60	66.80	.04	1.70	trace		.20
G-200	3.20	10.36	19.28	65.76	.06	.98	trace		.20
Nepheline syenite	4.60	9.80	23.60	60.40	.08	.70	trace		.70
Cornwall stone	4.00	3.81	14.93	72.90	.13	2.06	.25	1.40	.61

*See note to chart of clays and chemicals on preceding page.

Percentage Composition of Opacifiers

Opacifier	Percent						
	ZrO_2	$ZrSiO_4$	SiO_2	TiO_2	Fe_2O_3	Al_2O_3	Other Components
Zircopax		96.00		0.25	0.10		
Ultrox	65.00		35.00				
Superpax		93.40		0.25	0.10		
Zircon G milled		98.60		0.20	0.04		
Calcium zirconium silicate	50.50		26.70				CaO 18.80
Magnesium zirconium silicate	53.60		27.50				MgO 17.40
Zinc zirconium silicate	46.40		24.20				ZnO 28.60

1E

Chemicals and Materials

This list includes the main oxides used in glaze forming and coloring as well as the materials that yield them. Colorants and opacifiers are listed separately.

 Use all of these materials with great care and proper protection. The precautions that should be taken when using all ceramics materials are discussed in Chapter 10. The bold letter in front of each material indicates its degree of toxicity. However, new findings may change these ratings, so it is important that you keep up to date on current information. See Appendix 5A for sources of information on health and safety.

H = highly toxic

M = moderately toxic

S = slightly toxic

N = nuisance

H Alumina (Aluminum) (Al_2O_3) A refractory material that increases the viscosity of glazes, making them less runny, and that helps to control the melting point of a glaze. The main sources of alumina are china clay and ball clay. Because of its high melting point, only a small amount of alumina is needed—the proportion can be higher in a high-fire glaze. The quantity of alumina is increased for a matt surface and decreased if a crystalline glaze is desired. Alumina also helps to make glazes more durable.

H Antimony oxide (Sb_2O_3) Infrequently used to produce light yellow.

H Barium carbonate $(BaCO_3)$ A source of barium oxide for glazes.

H Barium oxide (BaO) A refractory, but in high-fire glazes it acts as a flux. Helps produce a matt surface. Adds brilliance to certain colors.

Bentonite $(Al_2O_3 \cdot 4SiO_2 \cdot 9H_2O)$ A colloidal clay of volcanic origin that increases plasticity of other clays. Used in glazes to keep glaze particles in suspension. Formula varies according to source.

Bone ash $(Ca_3(PO_4)_2)$ **(Tricalcium phosphate)** Made from animal bones. Formulas vary. A source of calcium and phosphate. A plasticizer for clay bodies. Used in clay bodies such as bone china, it lowers maturing point, increases translucency. In glazes, gives texture and acts as opacifier.

M Borax $(Na_2O \cdot 2B_2O_3 \cdot 10H_2O)$ Generally used in fritted form, since it is soluble in water. A low-fire flux, but small amounts in high-fire glazes can help a glaze melt more smoothly. Source of sodium and boric oxides.

M Boric oxide (B_2O_3) A useful flux that operates at both high and low temperatures. Helps produce a smooth glaze and increases brilliance of colors. Although a glass-forming material, it is also a strong flux at high temperatures. With iron, it may produce opalescent blues.

Boron See **Boric oxide.**

H Cadmium sulfide (CdS) Used with selenium in stains and low-fire frits for overglazes to produce red and orange. *It can be released into food, so do not use on food containers.*

N Calcium oxide (CaO) A useful glaze ingredient. Glazes with calcium are durable and resistant to acids. Has a high melting point, but is a very active flux at high temperatures. For this reason, it is used especially in porcelain glazes. In low-fire glazes, it is usually combined with other fluxes. See **Whiting.**

China clay See **Kaolin.**

H Chromium oxide (Cr_2O_3) In glazes without zinc, it yields green; with zinc, browns and tans. With tin, under proper conditions, it may produce pink. Reduction darkens the green color.

H Clay (theoretical formula $Al_2O_3 \cdot 2SiO_2 \cdot 2H_2O$) Clay bodies are made up of various types of clays and range from low-fire to porcelain. In glazes, clay is generally used in the form of kaolin or ball clay to provide alumina and silica. Amounts will vary according to the particular clay used. In a glaze, it helps to keep the ingredients suspended and helps the glaze adhere to the ware.

M Cobalt oxide (CoO) and **cobalt carbonate** $(CoCO_3)$ Formulas vary. Strong blue colorants that do not burn out. Used for centuries for decoration, cobalt can be fired from low to high temperatures. Cobalt alone gives rather strong blues that can be softened by adding manganese, iron, rutile, or nickel. A combination of cobalt oxide, chrome oxide, manganese oxide and iron oxide produces a strong black.

M Colemanite ($2CaO \cdot 3B_2O_3 \cdot 5H_2O$) (Calcium borate) A source of boric oxide in insoluble form, it also yields calcium oxide. Acting as a flux in both high- and low-fire glazes, it is also popular for the effects it produces in glazes—with rutile, for example, it gives a mottled appearance and may also give a milky blue. (See **Gerstley borate.**)

M Copper oxide (CuO) and **copper carbonate** ($CuCO_3$) Copper gives greens, blues, or reds depending on the other ingredients in the glaze and the atmosphere in the kiln. In reduction it produces reds in certain glazes; in oxidation copper gives greens, and in alkaline glazes it gives turquoise. Copper was used in China to produce the famous red oxblood and peach-bloom glazes.

H Cornish stone (Cornwall stone) (theoretical formula $K_2O \cdot Al_2O_3 \cdot 8SiO_2$) Formula varies. An English feldspathic material that requires high temperatures to fuse. Shrinks less than kaolin and feldspar, so it is less subject to glaze defects. Helps form tough, hard glazes. Used as a source of silica, Cornish stone contains varying amounts of silica as well as potassium and sodium. In ancient China, a similar rock, called *petuntze,* made possible the development of porcelain.

Cryolite (Na_3AlF_6) A natural source of sodium. Can be used when both sodium and alumina are needed. Gives brilliant colors, but sometimes glazes containing it are subject to pits.

S Dolomite ($CaCO_3 \cdot MgCO_3$) A natural source of magnesium and calcium oxides. Used as a flux in stoneware glazes, it helps produce smooth matt surfaces and can help in crystal formation.

H Feldspar (also spelled **felspar**) Yields alumina and silica. Feldspars vary in composition and availability, with some containing potash, and others, soda. The formula of a commercial feldspar is usually available from the supplier, so you can see which oxides are present (see Appendix 1D). At high temperatures, some feldspars melt with no additional flux at 2280°F/1250°C. At lower temperatures, talc, dolomite, gerstley borate, or whiting is added to lower their melting point. Used in porcelain clay bodies.

Ferric oxide, ferrous oxide, and **ferro-ferric oxide** *See* **Iron.**

H Flint (SiO_2) Also called quartz, this is the main source of silica in glazes and combines with a variety of fluxes to fuse at lower temperatures. In glazes it increases viscosity and hardness. In clay bodies, use coarser mesh (around 200); for glazes, use finer grind (around 300 mesh).

H Fluorspar (CaF_2) (**Calcium fluoride**) Used in some glazes as a source of calcium, it fluxes at a lower temperature than most calcium compounds. Helps develop blue-greens of copper in oxidation firing. *Toxic fumes of fluorine gas are released in firing.*

Gerstley borate ($2CaO \cdot 3B_2O_3 \cdot 5H_2O$) A source of boric oxide. Used as a flux, it is more stable than colemanite, another source of boric oxide. (See **Colemanite.**)

Ilmenite ($FeO \cdot TiO_2$) An ore in granular or powder form, contains both iron and titanium. Added to glazes, the granular form gives specks of dark color. May also encourage crystals in glazes.

Iron Varying amounts of iron are responsible for the buff and reddish colors of natural earthenware clays, where its fluxing action lowers their firing temperatures. Iron is also used in glazes to give warm cream or yellowish tones, tans, redbrowns, and black; in reduction it gives grays, blue-greens, and black (see Appendix 1F). Most commonly used forms are:

N Ferric oxide (Fe_2O_3) Red iron oxide or hematite
   Ferrous oxide (FeO) Black iron oxide
   Ferro-ferric oxide (Fe_3O_4) Magnetite

H Iron chromate ($FeCrO_4$) Usually gives grays and browns. With copper, it yields black, with tin it may give pink or red-brown.

H Kaolin (theoretical formula $Al_2O_3 \cdot 2SiO_2 \cdot 2H_2O$) Also called china clay. The main source of alumina and silica in glazes. Since it contains only traces of iron, it is also used in white clay bodies. (For example, EPK kaolin contains .42% iron; English .60% iron, and Georgia .40% iron.)

H Lead oxide (PbO) A very active flux at low temperatures, used for this purpose for many centuries in the Near East, Europe, and the United States until its toxicity was understood. When fritted with silica, the danger of handling this poisonous material is lessened, but even fritted lead is suspect. *We do not recommend the use of lead,* but if you do use a commercial lead frit in a glaze, fire it properly to avoid releasing lead into food, and check the frit to make sure there is enough silica in proportion to the lead—at least in the proportion of ($PbO \cdot 2SiO_2$). If in doubt, get a laboratory to test. *Red lead and white lead are highly toxic raw materials.*

M Lepidolite ($LiF \cdot KF \cdot Al_2O_3 \cdot 3SiO_3$) Formula varies. Used in china bodies and as a flux in some high-fire glazes. It contains lithium and helps make most glazes brighter than soda or potash feldspars, but it can cause pitting.

Lime *See* **Calcium oxide** and **Whiting.**

M **Lithium carbonate** (Li_2CO_3) A source of lithium in glazes, at high temperatures it is an active flux, allowing the use of more alumina and silica in alkaline glazes to increase their hardness. It widens the firing range and brightens the colors, as well as having low expansion and contraction coefficients, helping the glaze fit.

Macaloid A suspending agent in glazes similar in effect to bentonite. Also a plasticizer in clay bodies.

Magnesium carbonate ($MgCO_3$) Provides magnesium oxide. Often introduced into glazes as a high-fire flux and matting agent.

Magnesium oxide (MgO) Acting as a flux at high temperatures, magnesium is a refractory in lower firings. Increases viscosity, improves the adhesion of glazes, and at high temperatures gives a smooth surface. At lower temperatures, helps produce matt, opaque surfaces.

Magnetite (Fe_3O_4) The mineral form of black iron oxide. Produces speckling in clays or glazes.

Manganese carbonate ($MnCO_3$) A strong flux. Produces light browns; in alkaline glazes gives a purplish color.

H **Manganese dioxide** (MnO_2) Gives purple when used with alkaline fluxes (sodium, potassium, and lithium), but usually brown in most glazes. Used with cobalt, depending on the other ingredients, purple or black may develop. A strong flux.

H **Nepheline syenite** ($K_2O \cdot 3Na_2O \cdot 4Al_2O_3 \cdot 9SiO_2$) A potash feldspar. Since it has more potassium and sodium, it melts at lower temperatures and is particularly useful in medium-range temperatures in both clays and glazes. Mutes the color of bright colorants in glazes. The formula varies depending on sources.

M **Nickel carbonate** ($NiCO_3$) Used as a colorant, it produces muted browns, blues, grays, greens, and yellows.

M **Nickel oxide** (NiO) Refractory. Will dull down other colors in a glaze. Produces muted colors such as browns, grays, and greens. Produces lime green when applied as a stain to bisque-fired porcelain and glaze fired to cone 5.

Opax One of several commercial opacifiers. *See* **Tin oxide.**

H **Pearl ash** See **Potassium carbonate.**

H **Petalite** ($Li_2O \cdot Al_2O_3 \cdot 8SiO_3$) A lithium feldspar used in clay bodies and glazes to reduce thermal expansion.

H **Potassium carbonate** (K_2CO_3) Used in frits as a source of potassium. *Soluble material that is highly toxic in the raw state.*

H **Potassium dichromate** ($K_2Cr_2O_7$) Acts as a green colorant with boric acid. In a frit, with tin in low-fire glazes, it develops red and orange. *Soluble and poisonous in raw state.*

H **Potassium oxide** (K_2O) An active flux that operates at all temperatures. It has a high coefficient of thermal expansion that can cause crazing if used in large amounts. A component of feldspars and commercial frits.

Pyrophyllite ($Al_2O_3 \cdot 4SiO_2 \cdot H_2O$) **(Aluminum silicate)** By decreasing thermal expansion, shrinkage, and cracking, it extends the firing range of clay bodies.

H **Quartz** *See* **Flint.**

N **Rutile** (TiO_2) **(Titanium dioxide)** An ore that contains titanium and some iron. When fired in oxidation, it gives tans and browns, often in streaks. In reduction, it can give blues and oranges. In glazes with copper, cobalt, chrome, or iron, it may produce subtle grayed colors. Promotes the growth of crystals.

Seattle slip A slip glaze mined in Washington. Offered as a substitute for Albany slip.

Sheffield slip A slip glaze mined in Massachusetts. Offered as a substitute for Albany slip.

H **Silica** (flint) (SiO_2) The essential glass-forming oxide. It is the high silica content in high-fire glazes that causes them to be more durable and have greater resistance to chemicals, so the more silica used in a glaze the harder it will be. Requires high temperatures to fuse. At lower temperatures it is necessary to bring down the melting point of silica with a flux. *Free silica is extremely damaging to the lungs.*

H **Silicon carbide** (SiC) A chief ingredient in heat-resistant kiln furniture. In powder form, used in glazes to produce local reduction with copper oxide. In granular form it adds specks to glazes.

H **Soda ash** See **Sodium carbonate.**

H **Sodium carbonate (Soda ash)** (Na_2CO_3) An active glaze flux, usually used only in frit form because it is soluble. Also a deflocculant and, when used in a clay body for slip casting, it reduces the amount of water needed.

Sodium oxide (Na_2O) Used widely in low-fire glazes as a flux. It can also be used in high-fire glazes; when introduced into a kiln at at least 1940°F/1060°C, it will combine with the silica in clay to form a glaze. Has a high expansion coefficient that can cause crazing. Glazes high in sodium are apt to weather and flake off. Most useful if used with other fluxes. *Fumes of sodium when released in salt glaze firing are caustic.*

M **Sodium silicate** ($Na_2 \cdot SiO_2$) Varies in formula. Used as a deflocculant in casting slips, where it helps to keep the particles in suspension, and increases fluidity reducing the amount of water needed to form the slip, thus reducing shrinkage. Also used in producing crystalline glazes.

M Spodumene ($Li_2O \cdot Al_2O_3 \cdot 4SiO_2$) A source of lithium in glazes. If used instead of feldspar, it lowers the fusing temperature and helps to eliminate crazing.

M Strontium Carbonate ($SrCO_3$) A glaze flux with a wide firing range, it is also used in glazes to lessen crazing and improve the hardness of the fired glaze.

Superpax ($ZrSiO_4$) An opacifier that contains zirconium and produces a semiopaque white. It also helps to control texture, crazing resistance, and color stability in glazes.

H Talc ($3MgO \cdot 4SiO_2 \cdot H_2O$) **(Magnesium silicate)** Formula varies. Used widely in low-fire clay bodies, it can also be used as an opacifier in glazes. As a source of magnesium, it acts as an effective high-fire glaze flux as well as lowering the melting temperatures of ball clays, feldspars, and kaolin in clay bodies. *Some contain asbestos, which is harmful to the lungs*; however, non-asbestos talc is now available.

S Tin oxide (SnO_2) Gives opaque and semi-opaque white. Has been used for centuries to create opaque glazes to cover the reddish tones of earthenware. Since it is relatively expensive, many ceramists now use commercial products such as **Zircopax, Superpax,** and **Opax** to take its place.

Titanium oxide (TiO_2) An opacifier that also helps create a somewhat matt surface. Gives white and cream opaque glazes. Used in frit form or combined with other chemicals. (Rutile is a source of titanium that also contains iron.)

H Vanadium pentoxide (VaO_5) Alone, it gives light yellow; with tin, it gives a bright yellow. Reduced, it can produce blue-gray.

Whiting ($CaCO_3$) **(Calcium carbonate)** The main source of calcium oxide in glazes and an important high-fire flux. Small amounts can be added to low-fire alkaline glazes to increase durability.

M Wollastonite ($Ca \cdot SiO_3$) **(Calcium silicate)** Used in clays and glazes as a source of calcium oxide. Reduces shrinkage and increases strength. Often introduced into clays and glazes for ware that may need to resist thermal shock, such as ovenware.

S Zinc oxide (ZnO) A high-fire flux that reduces thermal expansion. Increases strength of glazes and helps produce smooth surfaces. Often used as a substitute for lead. In small amounts it helps create matt glazes; too much, however, causes glazes to become dry, to pit, or to crawl.

S Zirconium oxide (ZrO_2) An opacifier, usually fritted with other oxides. Not as strong as tin, but cheaper.

Zircopax ($ZrSi_4$) A commercial zirconium opacifier. Generally used where semiopaque glaze is desired.

1F

Colorants and Opacifiers

 Many of these materials are toxic, and you must take cautions when using them. The relative toxicity is indicated by the following letters:

H = highly toxic   S = slightly toxic
M = moderately toxic   N = nuisance

In addition to these colorants, many glaze and clay body stains are available commercially. Check ceramic supply catalogues to see the range of colors.

Colorant	Colors Yielded	Percent
H Antimony oxide Sb_2O_3	Below cone 1 or 2, infrequently used for light yellows.	10–20
H Cadmium sulfide CdS	In low-fire overglazes, produces red. Disappears if fired over cone 010. Usually combined with selenium in stain.	10–20
M Chromium oxide Cr_2O_3	Greens; with tin, pinks; with zinc, browns. In reduction, may darken or blacken colors.	1–6
M Cobalt carbonate $CoCO_3$ M Cobalt oxide CoO	Blues; with magnesium, purple. Higher percent gives blue-black. Powerful colorant, frequently used with iron, rutile, manganese, or nickel to soften harsh color. Withstands high firing. Carbonate with manganese, iron, or ochre gives black tones.	.01–2
M Copper carbonate $CuCO_3$ M Copper oxide CuO	Blue and turquoise in alkaline glazes. In lead glazes, gives soft greens (copper facilitates release of toxic lead in contact with acidic foods). In some high-fire glazes, copper gives blues; in others, browns. In certain formulations and firing conditions, produces the red oxblood and peach-bloom glazes of ancient China.	1–5
Ilmenite $FeO \cdot TiO_2$	Gives brown specks and spots.	1–7
Iron Ferric oxide Fe_2O_3 (red) Ferrous oxide FeO Ferro-ferric oxide Fe_3O_4 H Iron chromate $FeCrO_4$	Iron can produce a wide range of colors in clay or glaze. In most glazes, from tans to reddish brown to black. With other oxides it modifies their brilliance. Under correct firing conditions, produces the Japanese tenmoku or the famous gray-green celadon of China.	1–10
H Manganese carbonate $MnCO_3$ H Manganese dioxide MnO_2	In alkaline glazes, gives purples; with cobalt, produces violets. In high-fire reduction, brown; with cobalt, yields violets.	2–10
N Nickel oxide NiO	Browns and grays. Used mostly to modify other oxides. In some reduction glazes with zinc, it may yield yellows or blues, but results are uncertain.	1–3

Colorant	Colors Yielded	Percent
H **Potassium dichromate** (bichromate) $K_2Cr_2O_7$	Soluble, used in frit form. In low-fire glazes with boric oxide, gives greens, with tin, gives reds and oranges.	1–10
N **Rutile** TiO_2	Tans and browns. With cobalt, and sometimes with iron, gives blues and oranges. Produces streaks and mottled effects.	2–10
S **Tin oxide** SnO_2	In low-fire glazes, gives soft, opaque whites. Used as opacifier in early Persian, Spanish, and Italian tin glazes. Higher percent gives opaque glaze; lower percent yields semiopaque glaze.	5–12
Titanium dioxide TiO_2	Whites and creams.	5–15
H **Vanadium oxide** (pentoxide) V_2O_5	Generally used in frit, with tin. Gives opaque yellows.	5–10

Opacifiers	Percent
Tin oxide	5.0–12.0
Titanium dioxide	5.0–15.0
Zircopax	5.0–15.0
Superpax	5.0–15.0
Ultrox	5.0–15.0

Notes:

Tin oxide provides white when introduced into glazes in oxidation firing, or off-white in reduction firing. It also possesses strong opacifying properties, and therefore usually a smaller percentage is necessary when formulating a glaze. Since tin is substantially more expensive than the other opacifiers listed, Superpax and Zircopax are commonly used instead, or along with a smaller percentage of tin oxide. Titanium dioxide generally yields soft cream whites and may be combined with the other opacifiers to develop a range of white glazes.

2A

Bisque and Single Firing;
Orton and Seger Cones;
Centigrade and Fahrenheit

BISQUE AND SINGLE FIRING

Kiln Temperature Rise per Hour Based on Cone 05 (1915°F/1046°C)

Use the following chart only as a guide in establishing firing patterns for ware. Differing clay types — such as a smooth-body porcelain or a heavily grogged stoneware — will have varying firing patterns, even though the objects have the same thickness of walls. Coarse clays can generally be fired faster, and kiln size and fuel difference will also affect temperature rise. In addition, different types of kiln brick, or a ceramic fiber interior, will affect the heat saturation of ware per hour of temperature rise. Variations in moisture content of the ware when it is placed in the kiln will also affect the temperature-rise-per-hour pattern. This chart is based on establishing a firing pattern in relation to the thickest portion of a work. The temperature ranges are *averages* based on the total number of hours required to fire the ware to cone 05.

Temperature Rise per Hour	*Type and Thickness of Object to Be Fired*
25°–40°F/ − 6.4°–4.4°C	¾–6 in. (19–152 mm) Massive sculpture or handbuilt
40°–60°F/4.4°–15.5°C	⅜–¾ in. (10–19 mm) Handbuilt, wheel thrown
60°–100°F/15.5°–37.7°C	³⁄₁₆–⅜ in. (5–10 mm) Small handbuilt, wheel thrown
100°–210°F/37.7°–98.8°C	⅛–³⁄₁₆ in. (3–5 mm) Slip-cast ware, thin wheel thrown, thin handbuilt

ORTON AND SEGER CONES

Comparative Temperatures, Centigrade and Fahrenheit; Orton and Seger Cones (Large Cones, Rise of 270°F/ 132.2°C per Hour); Kiln Interior Colors; Maturing Points of Clays and Glazes

Kiln Interior	Seger Cone	Degrees C	Degrees F	Orton Cone	Clays	Glazes
Black		400	752			
		605	1112	022	Clay	Lusters
		615	1137	021	dehydrates	China paint
Dull red-orange		635	1175	020		(020–016)
		683	1261	019		
	019	685	1265			
	018	705	1301			
		717	1323	018		
	017	730	1346			
		747	1377	017		
	016	755	1391			
	015a	780	1436			
		792	1458	016		
		804	1479	015		
Red-orange		838	1540	014		Raku glazes
		852	1566	013		(014–05)
		884	1623	012		
		894	1641	011		
		905	1661	010	Bisque ware	
		923	1693	09	(010–05)	
	09a	935	1715			
Orange	08a	955	1751	08		Low-fire glazes
	07a	970	1778			(015–1)
		984	1784	07		
Orange	06a	990	1803			
		999	1830	06	Low-fire	
	05a	1000	1832		(015–1)	
	04a	1025	1847			
		1046	1915	05		
	03a	1055	1931			
		1060	1940	04		
	02a	1085	1955			
		1101	2014	03		
	01a	1105	2021			

Kiln Interior	Seger Cone	Degrees C	Degrees F	Orton Cone	Clays	Glazes
Yellow		1120	2048	02		
	1a	1125	2057			
		1137	2079	01		
	2a	1150	2102			
		1154	2109	1	Stoneware	
		1162	2124	2	mid-range	Stoneware glazes
		1168	2134	3	(2–7)	(mid-range)
	3a	1170	2138			(2–7)
		1186	2167	4		
	4a	1195	2183			
		1196	2185	5		
	5a	1215	2219			
		1222	2232	6		Salt glaze
	6a	1240	2264	7		(8–11)
	7	1260	2300			
		1263	2305	8	Stoneware	Stoneware glazes
	8	1280	2336	9	(8–12)	(8–12)
	9	1300	2372			
		1305	2381	10	Porcelain	Porcelain-glazes
White		1315	2399	11	(9–13)	(9–13)
	10	1320	2408			
		1326	2419	12		
	11	1340	2444			
		1346	2455	13		

Converting Fahrenheit to Centigrade and Centigrade to Fahrenheit

To convert Fahrenheit to centigrade (Celsius), subtract 32 degrees, multiply by 5, divide by 9.

To convert centigrade (Celsius) to Fahrenheit, multiply by 9, divide by 5, add 32 degrees.

2B

Useful Measurements and Equivalents in U.S.A. and Metric Systems

U.S.A.	Equivalent	Metric
Liquids		
1 fluid ounce		29.573 milliliters
1 fluid pint	16 fluid ounces	.473 liter
1 quart	2 fluid pints	.946
1 gallon	4 fluid quarts	3.785 liters
4.302 quarts	1 imperial gallon	4.546 liters
2.1134 pints		1 liter
1.0567 quarts		1 liter
0.26418 gallon		1 liter
Length		
1 inch		2.54 centimeters
.3937 inch		1 centimeter
1 mil	.001 inch	.0254 mm
1 foot	12 inches	0.3048 meter
1 yard	36 inches	.9144 meter
39.37 inches		1 meter
Weight		
1 dram		1.772 grams
8 fluid drams	1 fluid ounce	29.573 milliliters
1 ounce		28.350 grams
1 pound	16 ounces	453.592 grams
2.2046 pounds		1000 grams = 1 kilogram
35.274 ounces		1000 grams = 1 kilogram
Volume		
1 cubic inch		16.38716 cubic centimeters
.0616234 cubic inch		1 cubic centimeter
1 cubic foot	1728 cubic inches	.028317 cubic meter
1 cubic yard	27 cubic feet	.76456 cubic meter
1.30794 cubic yards		1 cubic meter

3A

Changing the Flux in a Glaze

In the tests that you did earlier, you changed only the colorants in some glazes. Colorants are not, of course, the only glaze components that can be changed and tested. Changing the amount of flux in a glaze, then running a series of tests on it, will prepare you for the testing you will do if you work through the example of calculating glazes using chemical analysis in Appendix 3B.

The following series of tests alters the type and amount of flux in a cone 10 glaze, while the accompanying table shows a similar glaze formulated for low, medium, and high firings, allowing you to test those as well. (They are given for test purposes only.) If you test all three firing ranges, you will then have a good idea of how fluxes work in a wide range of temperatures, and also a good cross reference between cone 05, cone 5, and cone 10 glazes. Although the cone 10 glaze is a reduction glaze, for test purposes you can use an electric kiln in oxidation — the results will just be different.

Components	Percent		
	Cone 05	Cone 5	Cone 10
Potash feldspar			35.0
Nepheline syenite		45.0	
Whiting		3.0	24.0
Frit 3195 (or 3811)	88.0		
Kaolin (Georgia)	10.0	13.0	28.0
Bentonite	2.0	2.0	
Silica 325 mesh (flint)			13.0
Gerstley borate		27.0	
PV clay		10.0	

In this example, the formula is expressed in percentages, giving the option of mixing the batch in any amount. This means that the 35 parts of feldspar could be 35 grams, pounds, or tons, but the relationship remains the same. To get 500 grams, you would multiply each number by 5, although actually you are multiplying each percentage by 500 to get the following:

Potash feldspar	35% (.35)		175 grams
Whiting	24% (.24)	× 500	120 grams
Kaolin (Georgia)	28% (.28)		140 grams
Silica 325 mesh (flint)	13% (.13)		65 grams
	100%		500 grams

First mix the cone 10 glaze. Then add coloring materials in the following proportions. (If you wish to use another colorant, find the correct percentage in the chart in Appendix 1F):

Rutile	8% (.08)		40 grams
Tin	1% (.01)	× 500	5 grams

Dip a tile and mark it; then add to the mixture:

Talc	25 grams

In this instance, talc is used as a high-fire flux. It can also be an opacifier. Dip a tile in this mixture and mark it. Add 25 more grams of talc, dip and mark another tile, and repeat the additions for 2 or 3 more tiles. Fire the test tiles at cone 10.

Repeat the same type of tests for the cone 5 and cone 05 glazes, adjusting their main fluxes by increasing or decreasing their percentages in the glazes. You can do this by altering the main flux (Frit 3195 or 3811) in the cone 05 glaze and the Gerstley borate in the cone 5 glaze. Increasing the fluxes will make your glazes more fluid in the kiln and glossier when fired, whereas decreasing the fluxes will make them less runny during firing and less shiny when fired to maturity.

Calculating Glazes Using Chemical Analysis

For generations, potters made glazes using an experimental approach. Based on the knowledge handed down from earlier potters, they tried out various combinations of materials much as you followed the progression of clay and glaze tests in Appendix 1. By working in this way, a ceramist can develop a clear sense of what each material does in combination with others without necessarily knowing the exact chemical composition of each material in the glaze—as potters did for centuries before the development of modern chemistry. You may wish to continue working in this way, trying and testing. But if you want to go into the chemistry of glazes in greater depth, in this appendix you can follow a potter who works with high-fire stoneware glazes as he goes about analyzing, calculating, and testing a glaze. The method is the same whether the glaze is high-fire or low-fire, matt or glossy, transparent or opaque. By working through this step-by-step process, you will learn how to apply the basics of glaze calculation to any glaze.

Modern chemistry enables one to break down glaze materials into their chemical components and to work out formulas that represent the chemical, rather than the physical, proportions of its components. Using such chemical formulas, it is possible to analyze and compare glazes in a more detailed manner. The chemical structure as well as the behavior of ceramic materials in the kiln has now been analyzed, tested, observed, and recorded, and rules have been established to express their chemical relationships, making it easier for the ceramist to supply the needed chemical components of a glaze from the available ceramic materials. This method of calculation involves some understanding of chemistry and of the basic atomic and molecular composition of glaze materials. A calculator is also helpful, and computer software is now available that makes glaze calculation easier.

ELEMENTS AND COMPOUNDS

Before going further with the calculations, it is important to understand something about the chemical composition of the minerals used in glaze making.

The earth's crust, from which these materials come, is made up of elements and compounds. An element is a substance that cannot be separated into substances different from itself by ordinary chemical means; it contains only one kind of atom. The atoms of the 108 known elements have been assigned weights in relation to the lightest element—hydrogen—which was given the weight of 1. In order to calculate glazes, you must use the atomic weights of the elements.

The elements, however, rarely exist in pure form, but rather exist in compounds. Made up of combinations of different elements in a definite proportion, these compounds have been formed by natural forces and may exist as gases, liquids, or solids. The compounds with which the potter is mainly concerned are oxides produced when various elements become chemically combined with the oxygen that is so plentiful in our environment.

ATOMS AND MOLECULES

Molecules are the smallest particles of a compound that retain chemical identity with a substance in mass. The weight of a molecule consists of the total combined weights of all the atoms in that molecule. For example, water, which is made up of two atoms of hydrogen to one atom of oxygen, is written as H_2O. Since the atomic weight of one atom of hydrogen is 1, the weight of two atoms is 2. Add that 2 to the atomic weight of one atom of oxygen, which is 16, and you have a total molecular weight of 18. It is this concept of molecular weight that you will be concerned with in glaze calculation.

It helps to remember that the gram weight is the actual physical weight of the materials you will use when mixing a glaze, whereas the molecular weight is the chemical weight based on the atomic structure of the molecules. When making changes in a glaze, which is made up of different compounds, it is necessary to convert all calculations to molecular weights, since the weight of a compound in molecular terms differs markedly from its physical weight. If you simply mixed by gram weight, you would not achieve the desired result. Here we are concerned with the chemical reactions determined by the *pro-*

portion of molecules of the various substances, rather than with the gross amounts of the substances.

EXAMPLE OF GLAZE CALCULATION

Now let's follow a potter through a calculation*:

I need to calculate a cone 10 glaze for the interior of casseroles and cups. I want a glaze that is glossy and either colorless or a very light gray or off-white. Most glazes that don't have glaze-coloring oxides (such as cobalt, iron, or copper oxide) added to them turn out to be clear or light gray. I will test a glaze without coloring oxides, fire it, and see what it looks like. Later I can add a colorant or an opacifier if I wish and test again. Experience has given me some basic knowledge as a starting point. I know, for instance, that most cone 10 glazes have ingredients, by weight, in the following very general proportions:

Feldspar (either soda or potash)	35–50%
Clay (china clay or ball clay)	5–20%
Additional flux for texture (whiting, colemanite, talc, dolomite, etc.)	15–30%
Silica 325 mesh (flint or quartz)	5–25%

Each of these ingredients functions in one or more ways in a glaze:

Feldspar 35–50% This extremely useful and important material is present in most glazes. In high-fire glazes it is usually the main flux because feldspars have a relatively low melting point (around 2264°F/1240°C). Feldspar lowers the point at which the silica fuses and will also bring some additional silica and alumina to the glaze. Used with another flux, the fusing point can be lowered even more.

Clay (china clay, or ball clay) 5–20% This is the main source of the refractory, alumina, in a glaze. China clay is white, so for my particular glaze I would use china clay rather than ball clay, which fires to a gray or cream. The clay, along with the feldspar, will generally supply all the alumina needed in a glaze. The sticky physical property of clay when added to a glaze helps to keep the glaze on the ware.

Additional flux 15–30% One of several high-fire fluxing materials can be used, such as talc,

whiting, dolomite, or colemanite (gerstley borate). The additional flux may lower the melting point of the glaze by a cone or two, or even more if large quantities are added, and will also bring other oxides to the glaze. Talc, for instance, contains magnesia and silica, while colemanite yields calcium and boric oxide. When you use feldspar alone as a flux, the fired glaze surface is usually "glassy." If additional fluxes are used, the surface of the fired glaze changes. Potters use terms like *buttery, satin,* or *soft matt* to describe these glaze surfaces.

Silica (flint) 5–25% Flint (or quartz) is the main source of silica, the glass-forming oxide. It is best to use as much silica as possible in order to give a glaze the desired qualities of durability, hardness, and resistance to acids.

Using these proportions as a rough guide, I'll select the ingredients I'll use from those available to me, mix a glaze by gram weight, and test it.

These are the proportions I choose:

Custer feldspar Because it is the principal and most efficient flux material, used to lower the melting point of silica.	45%	(.45)
China clay Because it is the source of the refractory and it is whiter than ball clay.	15%	(.15)
Talc Because in combination with the feldspar it acts as a stoneware flux that promotes highly glossy textures at cone 9 or 10, as well as being an opacifier.	15%	(.15)
Silica Flint is the source of silica, the glass former.	25%	(.25)
	100%	

Since I want to have enough glaze to dip the tiles, I'll mix a batch of 500 grams. To do this, I'll multiply the preceding proportions by 500, to get the following amounts in grams:

Feldspar	225 grams
China clay	75 grams
Talc	75 grams
Silica (flint) 325 mesh	125 grams
	500 grams

Now I measure out these ingredients on my balance scale and add 17 ounces (503 milliliters) of water to form a soupy mixture (Chapter 14). This mixture is the basic glaze. After mixing these ingredients, I dip some test tiles in the glaze and put

---

*In this edition the glaze has been recalculated to use Custer feldspar rather than the original Kingman feldspar, which is no longer available.

them in the kiln with pottery I am ready to fire to cone 10.

After I have fired the kiln and looked at the test tiles, I can see that the glaze has some characteristics that I want to change. I'm unhappy with its rather bland, glassy, and uninteresting texture. I feel it lacks the smooth, rich quality I like in a stoneware glaze, so I decide to make some alterations in the glaze ingredients.

Since the proportions of feldspar, china clay, and silica are constants in most stoneware glazes, I decide not to change them. This means I'll have to make my alterations in the additional flux, which in this case is talc. But in order to decide how much to change the proportions of the talc, I have to get involved in some chemistry. I'll have to examine the molecular makeup of the glaze, as well as take into consideration certain known limits of amounts of materials, altering the formula of the glaze accordingly. Before I do that, I'll explain some basic procedures that apply to glaze calculation.

EMPIRICAL FORMULA

For the purposes of glaze calculation, the materials used in a glaze are divided into three categories, according to their function in glazes. In Table 1, these categories are arranged in columns. The fluxes (both high- and low-fire) are listed under the heading RO/R_2O (also called bases); the refractory materials are listed under the heading R_2O_3 (also called neutrals); and the main glass former is listed under the heading RO_2 (also called acid). In this method of

listing the ingredients, the R symbol represents the element and the O represents oxygen.

Notice that the oxides in the flux column (RO/R_2O) are all made up of one or two atoms of the element for each atom of oxygen (for example, MgO, PbO, Na_2O). Some of these fluxes, like lead, are only effective in low-fire glazes. The second column (R_2O_3) contains the oxides that make up the refractory ingredients. Notice that these oxides are all formed in a ratio of two atoms of the element to three atoms of the oxygen. The third column, which contains the glass-forming agent (silica), is called the RO_2 column because the oxide in it consists of the element combined with two atoms of oxygen.

This arrangement of glaze materials in three columns is called the empirical method, and glaze formulas that list ingredients in the same three-column arrangement are called empirical formulas. Later, when we discuss the unity formula and limit formulas, we will see that the three-column (empirical) method of writing formulas provides a convenient format for checking the proper proportions of glaze ingredients.

ATOMIC AND MOLECULAR WEIGHT

As we have seen, because ceramic materials vary so widely in weight, in order to calculate the chemical composition of a glaze, you cannot merely take so many grams of that material or so many grams of this. If you did, you might get many more molecules of the heavier material than you wanted. Unless you know the weight of the molecules in each of the

Table 1   Glaze Oxides

A Flux	B Refractory	C Glass Former
RO/R_2O (Bases)	R_2O_3 (Neutrals)	RO_2 (Acid)
Oxides of:		
Lead, $PbO^{\dagger}$	Alumina, Al_2O_3	Silica, SiO_2
Sodium, Na_2O	Boric oxide, B_2O_3*	
Potassium, $K_2O^{\dagger}$		
Zinc, ZnO		
Calcium, CaO		
Magnesium, MgO		
Barium, $BaO^{\dagger}$		
Lithium, Li_2O		
Strontium, SrO		

*This is a neutral that can function as an acid or a base. It is an effective flux in both low- and high-fire glazes.
†Highly toxic (see Appendix 1E for toxicity of ceramic materials).

materials, you cannot select 1 or 20 or 500 or 10,000 molecules.

Each of the 108 known elements has been assigned an atomic weight in relation to hydrogen (see Appendix 3C). Since the atomic weight of hydrogen is 1 and oxygen 16, calcium 40, and silica 28, this means that the atomic weight of oxygen is 16 times the weight of hydrogen, while calcium is 40 times the weight of hydrogen, and silica is 28 times the weight of hydrogen. Unfortunately, ceramic materials are not conveniently made up of pure elements, but rather combinations of elements. In order to find the molecular weight of each material, I must first refer to its chemical symbol in Appendix 3D, to see the kind and number of atoms that compose the material. For example, the symbol for silica (or flint) is SiO_2, and that, I know, means silica consists of 1 atom of silicon (Si) and 2 atoms of oxygen (O_2). By looking at Appendix 3C, I can see that the atomic weight of silicon is 28 and the atomic weight of oxygen is 16. Doing some arithmetic, I can figure out the molecular weight of flint. To do this, I first multiply the atomic weight of silicon by 1 atom:

$$Silicon: 28 \times 1 = 28$$

Then I multiply the atomic weight of oxygen by 2 atoms:

$$Oxygen: 16 \times 2 = 32$$

Added together these come to 60, which gives me the weight of one molecule of silica (that is, the molecular weight of SiO_2). However, I don't have to go through this arithmetic each time, for the molecular weights are listed in Appendix 3D.

EQUIVALENT WEIGHTS

You will notice that there is also a column of equivalent weights in Appendix 3D and that, for some of the materials, the equivalent weight is not the same as the molecular weight. The reason for this is that some materials are structured in such a way that they would yield more or less than one molecule of the desired oxide. In these cases, an altered, or equivalent, weight has been assigned to the material in order to introduce one molecule of the desired oxide into the glaze formula (and other oxides in proportion). In these cases, the equivalent weight should be used because it will yield precise quantities for the purposes of glaze calculation.

THE UNITY FORMULA

Before I do the necessary calculations to change my glaze, I must explain one more procedure. You have

seen the reason for the empirical formula and the three-column arrangement, and also how to express the materials in molecular weights. However, in a formula based on the relationship between three groups of materials, there must always be one constant for the purpose of comparison. Remember, it is the *relative* amount of the materials that is important in formulating a glaze. So, arbitrarily, it has been decided that the RO/R_2O column will always represent 1—or *unity*. By accepting this, and by comparing this column to the other two columns, you will always understand the relationships of the materials in a glaze. Remember my glossy white glaze? Its original recipe was as follows:

Custer feldspar	45%
China clay	15%
Talc	15%
Silica (flint)	25%
	100%

In order to be able to work with molecules, I will divide these percentages of the materials by their molecular weights (or their equivalent weights). By consulting Appendixes 3D and 3E, I see that the molecular weight of Custer feldspar is 694, that of China clay is 258, that of talc is 379, and that of silica is 60.

Now, taking each material in turn, I do the necessary arithmetic to find out the existing proportional amounts of the glaze ingredients:

Components	*Molecular Proportions*
Custer feldspar	45 ÷ 694 = .065
China clay	15 ÷ 258 = .058
Talc	15 ÷ 379 = .039
Silica (flint)	25 ÷ 60 = .417

Now I can consult Appendixes 3D and 3E for the formula of each of my ingredients. I know which materials I am using and the molecular proportion of each one in this particular glaze. The formula for talc, for example, is $3MgO \cdot 4SiO_2 \cdot H_2O$, and I have already worked out that its molecular proportion in this glaze is .039. With this information, I can now construct a chart of my own glaze, which will give me a clear picture of its contents and the relationship of the parts to each other. I do this by multiplying the molecular proportion of each raw material by the quantity of each oxide in its formula. For example, in the case of talc, which has 3 parts of magnesium, I multiply 3 by .039. This shows me that the talc will contribute .117 part of magnesium oxide to this glaze ($3 \times .039 = .117$).

There is one complication. Feldspars are composed of many oxides, so I must be sure to have the

Table 2

Material	Molecular Proportions	Oxides					
		K₂O	CaO	Na₂O	Al₂O₃	MgO	SiO₂
Custer feldspar	.065	.044	.002	.020	.068		.45
China clay	.058				.058		.116
Talc	.039					.117	.156
Silica (flint)	.417						.417
Totals		.044	.002	.020	.126	.117	1.139

correct formula for the type of feldspar I use. Ceramic material suppliers usually provide the necessary information about the composition of various feldspars, but these formulas may vary somewhat depending on where the feldspar is mined. Also, feldspars usually have to be brought to unity. I have worked out the empirical formula for Custer feldspar:

RO/R₂O	R₂O₃	RO₂
Na₂O .300	Al₂O₃, 1.04	SiO₂, 6.94
K₂O .670		
CaO .030		
FeO₂ trace*		

*Small amounts can be ignored.

This means that there is .300 part of sodium oxide, .670 part of potassium oxide, and .030 part of calcium in the Custer feldspar formula, as well as 1.04 parts of alumina and 6.94 parts of silica.

Now I draw up a table in which I arrange the ingredients down the left side, next to the molecular proportions for my particular glaze (see Table 2). Across the top I list the oxides that my materials will yield. This table makes it possible for me to see very clearly the quantity of each oxide that is present in my white glaze. Since water and gases burn away or change in the firing, they are not included in the calculations, nor are the small amounts of other elements in the feldspar.

Now, again using the three columns, I arrange my oxides according to the empirical formula:

RO/R₂O		R₂O₃		RO₂	
K₂O	.044	Al₂O₃	.126	SiO₂	1.139
Na₂O	.020				
CaO	.002				
MgO	.117				
Totals	.183		.126		1.139

As I said before, I want to make a unity formula by expressing the RO/R₂O column as a unit of 1. Now it adds up to .183. How do I fix this? By dividing everything in the preceding formula by .183, I get a true unity formula, as follows:

RO/R₂O		R₂O₃		RO₂	
K₂O	.241	Al₂O₃	.688	SiO₂	6.224
Na₂O	.109/.108				
MgO	.639				
CaO	.011				
Totals	1.00		.688		6.224

LIMIT FORMULAS

Now I can see my glaze expressed in a unity formula that can easily be analyzed and compared to other glazes. The amount of each oxide in the glaze can also be checked easily against the limits suggested on page 451. These limit formulas have been worked out as guides to show the amount of each oxide that occurs in a particular type of glaze maturing at a particular temperature range. Remember, however, that although limit formulas are generally accurate, there are many glazes that exceed either the upper or lower limits but which can still be successful glazes. These limits should be taken only as broad guidelines and should not keep you from experimenting. However, in order to solve my problems with this particular glaze, it will help me to look at the proportions of the materials in the unity formula of my glaze and compare them to the limits suggested in the limit formula for stoneware or porcelain glazes in the cone 8 to 12 range.

Cone 8 to 12 Stoneware Limit Formula

KNaO	.2–.40	Al_2O_3	.3–.5	SiO_2	3.0–5.0
CaO	.4–.70	B_2O_3	.1–3		
MgO	0–.35				
ZnO	0–.30				
BaO*	0–.30				

*Highly toxic

When I look at the two sets of numbers and compare the formula of my glaze with the limit formula, several facts become apparent:

1. My sodium and potassium are within limits. I combine these two ingredients by addition to get the total of the KNaO:

K_2O	.241
Na_2O	.109/.108
CaO	.011

.361 versus a limit of .2–.40

2. My magnesium is very high: .639 versus a limit of .35.
3. My alumina is high: .688 versus a limit of .5.
4. My silica is high: 6.224 versus a limit of 5.0.

So now I can figure out that the combination of high silica and high flux made a very shiny, glassy glaze, but it did not run off the test tile because the alumina was also high.

ANALYZING THE GLAZE

I now examine the glaze ingredients closely in view of their functions. This will give me some information about how to change the glaze so that it may suit my purposes better. After firing, I saw that the glaze was glossy. This means that despite the silica being high, the actual proportion of glass (silica) to glass melters (feldspar and talc) was all right. If there had been too much silica and not enough flux, the final product would have been underfired, rough, and granular. On the other hand, if there had been too much flux, the glaze would have run down off the wall of the test tile into a pool at the base of the tile. Also, I see that the glaze is not brittle, nor is it crazing, crackling, or shivering off the clay body. This means that the proportion of the refractory (alumina) must be all right. Too little alumina would cause the glaze to be brittle and probably shiver, whereas if there is too much alumina, the glaze surface will be matt and dull.

The only thing I find wrong with this glaze for my purposes is that I don't care for the texture. I know that texture is controlled largely by the oxides in the optional fluxes (such as calcium, magnesium, zinc, or barium). So, considering the high proportion of magnesium (.611 versus a limit of .35), I decide to reduce the magnesium to bring it within the usual limits. I'll then substitute another flux for the quantity of magnesium I remove. (Remember that I am still testing, and all experimentation at this point can be modified according to the results that show after the tiles have been fired in the kiln.)

I decide to reduce the magnesium by .30 to a total of .311 and to substitute .339 molecule of calcium. I choose calcium for several reasons: It is easily available in whiting, a staple in most pottery studios; it is known to provide a smooth, matt surface in some glazes; and it is a proven trouble-free stoneware flux. Also, when calcium is added in the form of whiting, it will promote a light color in the glaze, suiting my purpose.

After I have made the substitution, my formula looks like this:

K_2O	.241	Al_2O_3	.688	SiO_2	6.224
Na_2O	.109				
MgO	.311				
CaO	.339				

CONVERTING FROM EMPIRICAL FORMULA TO BATCH RECIPE

Now that I have decided how to alter my empirical formula to achieve the desired results, I must find a way to supply the ingredients from the dry materials. I do this by constructing another table with the ceramic materials and their formulas on the left and the oxides of my empirical formula running across the top (Table 3). Starting with the oxides that come from single-oxide materials, I continue with the materials that have two or more oxides, putting the silica last. Under each oxide I enter the desired proportional amount needed as I determined them for my altered formula. Table 3 (page 452) includes remarks to clarify the process for the reader.

To determine the required amounts of each material, I must fill in the table using the amounts I found in my empirical formula and which I have listed across the top of the table. Starting with the oxides that come from the materials that have only one

Table 3   From Empirical Formula to Batch Recipe

Materials	Proportional Requirement	Remarks	CaO .311	MgO .339	Na₂O .108/.109	K₂O .241	Al₂O₃ .688	SiO₂ 6.224
Whiting, $CaCO_3$	.311	I need .3 part of CaO. Whiting has 1 part CaO, so I divide .3 by 1 to get my proportional requirement.	Satisfied by $1 \times .3 = .3$ (still need .011)					
Talc, $3\ MgO \cdot 4\ SiO_2$	.113	I need .339 MgO. Talc has 3 MgO. The materials proportion is thus $.339 \div 3 = .113$. I multiply each part in talc by this figure. Magnesium is satisfied, but we need more silica.		Satisfied by $3 \times .113 = .339$				$4 \times .113 = .452$ (Still need 5.772)
Custer feldspar, $.30\ Na_2O \cdot$ $.67\ K_2O \cdot$ $.03\ CaO$ $1.04\ Al_2O_3 \cdot$ $6.94\ SiO_2$	.361	I need .108/.109 Na_2O. There is .30 Na_2O available in the feldspar. I divide .108 by .30 to get .361. Then I multiply each part in the feldspar formula by this figure. I find I still need more Al_2O_3 and SiO_2.	Satisfied by $.03 \times .361 = .011$		Satisfied by $.30 \times .361 = .108$	Satisfied by $.67 \times .361 = .241$	$1.04 \times .361 = .375$ (Still need .313)	$6.94 \times .361 = 2.505$ (Still need 3.267)
China clay, $Al_2O_3 \cdot 2\ SiO_2$	.313	.313 Al_2O_3 is needed. There is one part Al_2O_3 available in china clay. $.313 \div 1 = .313$, which is the materials proportion still needed of alumina. China clay satisfies .626 silica. I still need 2.641 silica.					Satisfied by $1 \times .313 = .313$	$2 \times .305 = .610$ (Still need 2.355)
Silica (flint), SiO_2	2.641	Remaining silica needed satisfied by 2.641 of flint.						Satisfied by $1 \times 2.641 = 2.641$

oxide in them, I determine the required amounts by using the following equation:

$$\text{Proportional requirements of materials} = \frac{\text{Amount wanted in formula}}{\text{Amount present in material}}$$

For example, I want .3 CaO. Whiting has one part CaO, so I divide .3 by 1, which of course gives me .3. (If there were any other elements in whiting, I would have to multiply each of them by .3, since that is how much I will use of the entire material.) As you can see, my needs for CaO are thus satisfied entirely by the whiting. I can now go on to calculate the proportional figures for the remaining materials.

I need .339 MgO and I find that talc has 3 MgO in its formula. Therefore, I divide .339 by 3 to arrive at the proportional figure of .113 for talc. I then multiply each oxide in the talc formula by .113, which gives me .339 of MgO (satisfying my needs) and .452 of SiO_2. I subtract that amount of SiO_2 from my needed amount of 6.224 and put the remaining needed amount (5.772) in parentheses.

The next material listed in my empirical formula at the top of the chart is Na_2O and I need .108/.109 part of it. In the Custer feldspar formula I see that there is .30 available. To get my proportional figure, I divide .108/.109 by .30 and get .361. I then multiply each part in the feldspar formula by .361 to get the equivalent amount of each part contained in my empirical formula. So I get .109 Na_2O (satisfying the amount needed), .241 K_2O (also satisfying that amount needed), .375 Al_2O_3, which I subtract from the needed amount of .688, and I put the remaining amount needed (.313) in parentheses. Finally I get 2.505 SiO_2 and subtract that from the needed amount of 5.772 and put the remainder (3.267) in parentheses.

Now I have satisfied all my needs except for the remaining amounts of Al_2O_3 and SiO_2. I can complete my alumina needs with china clay by using .313 of it, since it contains one part of Al_2O_3. However, there are two parts of SiO_2 in china clay, and when I multiply by .313, I get .626. I subtract this amount from the needed 3.267, leaving me with

2.641 parts of silica still needed. I complete my remaining requirements by adding the needed amount (2.641) with flint, which is a nearly pure form of silica.

Now that I have determined the proportions required of each material, I simply multiply this amount by the molecular (or equivalent) weights for each ingredient. The molecular or equivalent weights of the most common materials are listed in Appendix 3D. Thus, I have what is shown in Table 4. A batch recipe is what I started with, and now I have another batch recipe of the altered glaze ready to mix, test, and fire.

Once again I will mix a batch of 500 grams of the glaze, dip some test tiles in the batch, and fire them to cone 10. It is a good idea to dip several tiles and place them in different locations in the kiln. In this way you will see if small variations in kiln atmosphere will affect the glaze.

The fired result of the test is a glaze that has changed somewhat. Its glossy finish has a softer texture that suits my purpose as a liner glaze. If I decide to alter it later, I could add a little Zircopax (2 to 10%) to try to introduce some opacity and whiteness to the glaze, or I could add some other colorants.

What I have followed here is the basic method for testing glazes using chemical analysis, using most of the procedures required in order to go from batch recipe to molecular formula and back to batch again. If you have followed this example through these procedures, you now have seen the basic process of calculating and analyzing glazes.

As you proceed to work with more complex materials and to formulate more sophisticated and elaborate glazes, the calculations can become more complex. However, no amount of knowledge of chemistry can substitute for patient testing and retesting of trial formulas in your own kiln, with your own clay body, and with the available materials. The use of chemistry answers many technical questions and gives you a method of formulating a glaze, but experience, patience, hard work, and aesthetic sensitivity are what really create beautiful glazes.

Table 4

Ingredient	Material (Proportional Amount)	×	Molecular Weight (or Equivalent Weight)	=	Batch Amount (Grams)	Percent
Whiting	0.311	×	100	=	31.1	6
Talc	0.113	×	378	=	42.7	8
Feldspar	0.361	×	694	=	250.5	44
China clay	0.313	×	258	=	80.8	14
Silica (flint)	2.641	×	60	=	158.5	28
					563.6	

3C

Atomic Weights of Elements Used in Ceramics

Element	Symbol	Atomic Weight	Element	Symbol	Atomic Weight
Aluminum	Al	26.98	Manganese	Ma	54.93
Antimony	Sb	121.75	Nickel	Ni	58.71
Barium	Ba	137.34	Nitrogen	N	14.00
Bismuth	Bi	208.98	Oxygen	O	15.99
Boron	B	10.81	Phosphorus	P	30.97
Cadmium	Cd	112.40	Platinum	Pt	195.09
Calcium	Ca	40.08	Potassium	K	39.10
Carbon	C	12.01	Selenium	Se	78.96
Chlorine	Cl	35.45	Silicon	Si	28.08
Chromium	Cr	51.99	Silver	Ag	107.86
Cobalt	Co	58.93	Sodium	Na	22.98
Copper	Cu	63.54	Strontium	Sr	87.62
Fluorine	F	18.99	Sulphur	S	32.06
Gold	Au	196.96	Tin	Sn	118.69
Hydrogen	H	1.00	Titanium	Ti	47.90
Iridium	Ir	192.22	Uranium	U	238.02
Iron	Fe	55.84	Vanadium	V	50.94
Lead	Pb	207.20	Zinc	Zn	65.37
Lithium	Li	6.94	Zirconium	Zr	91.22
Magnesium	Mg	24.30			

3D

Molecular and Equivalent Weights

Material	Formula	Molecular Weight	Equivalent Weight
Alumina	Al_2O_3	101.9	101.9
Antimony oxide	Sb_2O_3	291.5	291.5
Barium carbonate	$BaCO_3$	197.4	197.4
Barium oxide	BaO	153.4	153.4
Bone ash	$Ca_3(PO_4)_2$	310.3	103.0
Borax	$Na_2O \cdot 2B_2O_3 \cdot 10H_2O$	381.4	381.4
Boric acid (Boron)	$B_2O_3 \cdot 3H_2O$	123.7	123.7
Boric oxide	B_2O_3	69.6	69.6
Calcium borate (colemanite)	$2CaO \cdot 3B_2O_3 \cdot 5H_2O$	412.0	206.0
Calcium carbonate (whiting)	$CaCO_3$	100.09	100.1
China clay (Kaolin)	$Al_2O_3 \cdot 2SiO_2 \cdot 2H_2O$	258.1	258.1
Chromium oxide	Cr_2O_3	152.0	152.0
Cobalt carbonate	$CoCO_3$	118.9	118.9
Cobalt oxide	CoO	74.9	74.9
Copper carbonate	$CuCO_3$	187.0	187.0
Copper oxide (cupric)	CuO	79.57	79.57
Copper oxide (cuprous)	Cu_2O	143.0	80.0
Cornish stone	$\left.\begin{array}{l} CaO \cdot 304 \\ Na_2O \cdot 340 \\ K_2O \cdot 356 \end{array}\right\} \begin{array}{c} Al_2O_3 \\ 1.075 \end{array} \left.\right\} \begin{array}{c} SiO_2 \\ 8.10 \end{array}$	667.0	667.0
Cryolite (soda)	Na_3AlF_6	210.0	420.0
Dolomite	$CaCO_3 \cdot MgCO_3$	184.4	184.4
*Feldspar (potash)	$K_2O \cdot Al_2O_3 \cdot 6SiO_2$	556.8	556.8
*Feldspar (soda)	$Na_2O \cdot Al_2O_3 \cdot 6SiO_2$	524.5	524.5
*Feldspar (lime)	$CaO \cdot Al_2O_3 \cdot 2SiO_2$	278.6	
Flint	SiO_2	60.06	60.06
Ilmenite	$FeO \cdot TiO_2$	151.74	151.74
Iron chromate (ferrous-ferric)	$FeCrO_4$	172.0	172.0
Iron oxide, black (ferrous)	FeO	71.8	71.8
Iron oxide, red (ferric)	Fe_2O_3	159.7	159.7
Kaolin (calcined)	$Al_2O_3 \cdot 2SiO_2$	222.0	222.0

*Feldspar formulas vary. See Appendix 3E.

Material	Formula	Molecular Weight	Equivalent Weight
Lead carbonate (white lead)	$2PbCO_3 \cdot Pb(OH)_2$	775.6	223.0
Lead oxide	PbO	223.2	223.2
Lead oxide (red)	Pb_3O_4	685.6	228.0
Lithium carbonate	Li_2CO_3	73.9	73.9
Magnesium carbonate	$MgCO_3$	84.3	84.3
Magnesium oxide	MgO	40.3	40.3
Manganese carbonate	$MnCO_3$	114.9	114.9
Manganese dioxide	MnO_2	86.9	86.9
Nepheline syenite	$\left\{ \begin{array}{l} K_2O \cdot 25 \\ Na_2O \cdot 75 \end{array} \right\} \begin{array}{l} Al_2O_3 \\ 1 \cdot 11 \end{array} \right\} \begin{array}{l} SiO_2 \\ 4 \cdot 65 \end{array}$	462.0	462.0
Nickel oxide	NiO	74.7	74.7
Potassium carbonate (pearl ash)	K_2CO_3	138.2	138.2
Quartz (silica)	SiO_2	60.0	60.0
Rutile	TiO_2	79.1	79.1
Silica (flint)	SiO_2	60.1	60.1
Sodium carbonate (soda ash)	Na_2CO_3	106.0	106.0
Sodium silicate	$Na_2 \cdot SiO_3$	122.1	122.1
Spodumene	$Li_2O \cdot Al_2O_3 \cdot 4SiO_2$	372.2	372.2
Talc (magnesium silicate)	$3MgO \cdot 4SiO_2 \cdot H_2O$	378.96	378.96
Tin oxide	SnO_2	150.7	150.7
Titanium oxide	TiO_2	80.1	80.1
Vanadium pentoxide	V_2O_5	181.9	181.9
Whiting	$CaCO_3$	100.1	100.1
Wollastonite	$Ca \cdot SiO_3$	116.0	116.0
Zinc oxide	ZnO	81.4	81.4
Zirconium oxide	ZrO_2	123.2	123.2
Zirconium silicate (Zircopax)	$ZrO_2 \cdot SiO_2$	182.9	182.9

3E

Formulas of Some Feldspars

The formulas and molecular weights may vary slightly depending on area mined and other factors.

Feldspar	Formula	Molecular Weight
Cornwall stone	$.356\ K_2O \cdot 1.075\ Al_2O_3 \cdot 8.10\ SiO_2$ $.340\ Na_2O$ $.304\ CaO$	667
Custer	$.67\ K_2O \cdot 1.04\ Al_2O_3 \cdot 6.94\ SiO_2$ $.30\ Na_2O$ $.03\ CaO$	694
Kona F-4 (56)	$.58\ NaO \cdot 1.00\ Al_2O_3 \cdot 5.79\ SiO_2$ $.26\ K_2O$ $.16\ CaO$	518
Lepidolite	$.39\ K_2O \cdot 1.00\ Al_2O_3 \cdot 3.74\ SiO_2$ $.06\ Na_2O$ $.55\ Li_2O$	383
Nepheline syenite	$.75\ Na_2O \cdot 1.11\ Al_2O_3 \cdot 4.65\ SiO_2$ $.25\ K_2O$	462
Oxford	$.58\ K_2O \cdot 11.07\ Al_2O_3 \cdot 1.07\ SiO_2$ $.42\ Na_2O$	556
Petalite	$1.00\ Li_2O \cdot 1.00\ Al_2O_3 \cdot 8.00\ SiO_2$	612
Plastic vitrox	$.61\ K_2O \cdot 1.33\ Al_2O_3 \cdot 14.00\ SiO_2$ $.34\ Na_2$ $.05\ CaO$	1051
Spodumene	$1.00\ Li_2O \cdot 1.00\ Al_2O_3 \cdot 4.00\ SiO_2$	372
Volcanic ash	$.47\ KNaO \cdot 1.09\ Al_2O_3 \cdot 9.52\ SiO_2$ $.17\ CaO$ $.25\ MgO$ $.11\ FeO$	720

4A

Types of Plasters and Their Uses

Plaster Type	Parts Water per 100 lb (45.4 kgs) Plaster	Setting Time	Density	Uses	Notes
Casting	67–80	20–25 min[†]	soft	a, b, c, d, h, k	All-purpose; harder, somewhat coarser than Pottery Plaster #1.
Pottery Plaster #1	67–70	20–25 min[†]	softer	a, b, c, g	Slip casting; excellent detail, produces high-quality casting molds.[‡]
Hydrocal (white) TM*	38–42	20–30 min[†]	hard	d, e	Sculpture and carving.
Hydrocal A-11 TM*	42–44	16–20 min[†]	hard	h, j	Original model making.
Hydrostone TM*	28–32	17–20 min[†]	hardest	d, e, h, i	One of the hardest gypsum cements; used for molds, casting, finished art works.
Ultracal 30 TM*	35–38	25–30 min[†]	hard	f, h, j	Super strength gypsum cement; often used for original model making, block and case, and mother molds.

Letter Codes in Uses column:
a. Plaster bats, wedging table tops
b. Press molds
c. Slip-casting molds
d. Sculpting and carving
e. Casting art works
f. Model making, block and case, and mother molds
g. Molds for jiggering
h. Cases for supporting flexible molds
i. Ram press dies
j. Template models
k. Waste molds

*Trademarks owned by United States Gypsum Company.

[†]Time varies according to age of material, temperature of water and atmospheric conditions, ratio of water to material, quantity of batch, and mixing methods.

[‡]Density will be affected by water to material ratio and mixing methods.
Soft = Can be easily sanded, chiseled, carved, and drilled.
Hard = Can be filed, drilled, chiseled, and sanded.
Hardest = Can be filed, chiseled, and drilled.

4B

Preplanning for Installation

LIGHT TO MEDIUM INTERIOR WORKS For interior installations, interior or exterior plywood is adequate for panels on which to assemble the work before attaching it to the wall. For outdoor installation, water must not penetrate the wood; use high-grade exterior or marine-grade plywood. For light pieces, sanded wood backing is adequate for surface bonding. For bonding heavier sections, score the wood and the ceramic sections to increase the gripping power of the adhesive. Inserting screws, nails, or bolts through clay sections and wood will ensure a safe bond.

LARGE WORKS Preplanning before or while the work is in the damp stage is helpful and avoids tiresome reworking and grinding later. Score damp surfaces that are to be glued after firing. Drill holes for screws or bolts in the leather-hard clay or greenware. Drill holes approximately 15 to 20% larger than final bolt size to allow for shrinkage in the kiln. Countersink holes so that after firing and assembling they can be plugged with colored epoxy, grout, adhesive, or mortar to hide the hardware. Sections may be mounted directly on the wall or attached to plywood panels then mounted on the wall. Be sure that the plywood is dry and free of oil, grease, or other chemicals that could affect the adhesive, and that the wall construction will handle the weight.

CONNECTORS/NUTS AND BOLTS Mild steel or plated steel is adequate for interior installation, but for outdoor installation use stainless steel, galvanized metal, brass, bronze, or other rust-resistant materials. Consult a structural engineer for information on which of these materials is appropriate for your application.

4C

Repair, Adhesives, and Colorants

Unfired Work

1. If a large section (more than ¼ inch [6.3 mm] thick) breaks off of an unfired piece, you can often repair it by wrapping the two pieces in saturated cotton rags, thus gradually dampening them, and then scoring and rebonding them with water or slip.
2. For smaller pieces, if you dampen the two areas with water, water and vinegar, or plain vinegar, you may be able to rescore and bond them again before firing.

Bisque Repair   There are commercial products that are advertised for repair of greenware and bisque ware before refiring. Ericka Clark Shaw shares her formula for what she calls "bisque glue":

White glue	50%
Sodium silicate	50%

She says, "Add EPK (kaolin) and water until it becomes the consistency of mayonnaise" and apply. Can be fired to cone 10.

Acrylic Adhesives and Mastics   Single-part adhesives for fired ware. For interior or exterior use. Use these adhesives to glue ceramics where dampness is present: showers, kitchen floors, and walls; to glue ceramic to ceramic; to bond ceramic sections with relatively flat surfaces with gluing gaps under ¼ inch (6.3 mm). Useful for gluing sculpture or light wall pieces, such as thin slabs installed indoors. Follow manufacturer's instructions.

Epoxy Tile-Setting Adhesives   These consist of two-part epoxy resin and hardener that is blended with a cement/sand filler. Usually gray or white. White can be tinted with glaze stains to match sculpture colors for repair and postfiring construction. Especially good where resistance to physical abuse or salts, dilute acids, and/or cleaning agents is necessary. Bonds ceramic to ceramic, ceramic to wood (interior only unless protected from weather and with properly prepared understructure), ceramic to concrete, terrazo, vinyl, steel, stone, or gypsum board (interior only). Epoxy should only be used with **gloves and adequate ventilation to draw its fumes away from the worker, and with a respirator rated by the National Institute for Occupational Safety and Health (NIOSH) for toxic fumes.** Follow manufacturer's instructions.

For works to be installed in public places, consult a structural engineer before starting to build.

Gluing Glazed Surfaces   For glazed areas glued to glazed areas, silicon or epoxy will work for non-structural, lightweight areas. For larger works, outdoor work, or work coming in contact with moisture or water, before gluing it is essential to prepare the glaze by grinding until the clay is visible. It is also strongly recommended that you make a physical bond using metal bolts or wooden dowels in conjunction with adhesive between parts.

A general-purpose polyurethane adhesive is adequate for gluing works to be placed in all extremes of temperature, moisture, and alternate freezing and thawing. These adhesives range in viscosity from thick paste to pourable liquid and have varying coefficients of expansion, which is important to consider in selecting an adhesive to be used for gluing works placed in outdoor settings. This is especially important under harsh weather conditions. Contact the glue manufacturer for technical information when using polyurethane adhesives in areas with adverse weather conditions or when safety in mounting a glued work is an issue.

Proper Surface Preparation   This is essential when gluing ceramic to ceramic or to other surfaces for installation of ceramic works. Clean each surface thoroughly. Both should be dry, dust free, and free of scale or loose parts. Painted surfaces should be sanded or wire brushed until raw material is visible; metal surfaces such as steel, galvanized metal, aluminum, sheet brass, or bronze should be cleaned, sanded, or ground until shiny. Mild steel is adequate for interior installation. For outside installation it must be painted, or use stainless steel, galvanized metal, aluminum, brass, bronze, or other rust-resistant materials.

COLOR ADDITIVES FOR EPOXY

The following coloring materials can be mixed with epoxy to color repaired areas or to glue sections. Because these colors are not fired, almost any powdered color, such as tempera or oil-base paint, will work. Universal oil-base tinting colors can also be used, and many intermediate colors can be mixed. The numbered stains are those available in the U.S.A. Most stains available elsewhere will work as well, but have not been tested for color results. Since many of the ceramic stains and oxides contain materials that are **toxic,** they should be used with **proper precautions.** When using epoxy, **wear neoprene gloves,** have **adequate ventilation** to draw its fumes away, and wear a **respirator** NIOSH rated for toxic fumes.

Color Desired	*Additive*
Clear	Epoxy
Red brown	Red iron oxide, concrete colors, Kreth red clay, Neuman red clay
Browns	Brown ceramic stain, concrete colors, burnt umber, raw umber, ball clay, Jordan clay, manganese dioxide, Barnard clay
Light browns/tans	EPK Kaolin, fire clay (Lincoln), cement, rutile
Light tans	Talc, white cement, dolomite
Black	Black ceramic stain (K470), lamp black, black iron oxide, cobalt oxide, concrete colors, black ink concentrate
Blue-greens	Blue ceramic stain (#100), turquoise blue stain (C490)
Blues	Dark blue ceramic stain (#1166), blue resin dye
Yellows	Yellow ceramic stain (F222A or #6433), cadmium yellow, yellow ochre, tin vanadium
Oranges	Universal oil-base tint (yellow-orange), universal tint (raw sienna), orange enamel paint
White	Tin oxide
Off-white	Talc, dolomite, Zircopax, Ultrox
Green	Victorian green ceramic stain (B211), chrome oxide
Pink	Pink ceramic stain (D-320)
Red	Apple red ceramic stain (#6006), cadmium red (highly toxic), red enamel paint
Purple	Ceramic stains; mix pink and blue
Silver	Aluminum paint
Gold	Gold paint

5A

Sources of Health and Safety Information

Art Hazards Project
Center for Occupational Hazards Inc.
5 Beekman St.
New York, NY 10038
(212) 227-6220

This center is not only a source of pamphlets and bibliographies on the subject of art hazards but also will provide lecturers to conduct workshops at art schools and professional organizations of artists and teachers. Its Art Hazards Information Center answers telephoned or written inquiries and publishes the *Art Hazards News Letter*. In addition, the Center runs a Consultation Program that will conduct health hazard surveys in schools and arts centers, and provides consultation services to institutions that are building or renovating studio space.

The Art and Craft Materials Institute, Inc.
100 Boylston St., Suite 1050
Boston, MA 02116

The Institute provides toxicological evaluation of art materials, and compiles brand-name lists of art materials that are judged by the Institute to be nontoxic. They also publish a newsletter, *Institute Items*.

Ceramic Manufacturers Association
1100-H Brandywine Blvd.
P.O. Box 2188
Zanesville, OH 43702-2188

This program evaluates ceramic art materials in accordance with the American Society of Testing and Materials (ASTM).

ASTM Committee on Standards, American Society for Testing and Materials (ASTM)
1916 Race St.
Philadelphia, PA 19103

This organization sets standards for hazard labeling in art materials that are revised automatically every five years and more often if needed. Write for a copy of the standards.

The American Lung Association issues pamphlets explaining how to protect yourself against health hazards in the arts and crafts, with particular emphasis on dusts, fumes, and gases. Contact your local chapter.

The National Institute for Occupational Safety and Health (NIOSH) is primarily concerned with safety in the workplace, but many of its standards also apply to ceramic studios. Local and state health departments, labor unions, and industrial relations organizations are sources of health and safety information, as are occupational health clinics, poison-control centers, and toxic-information centers at local hospitals.

Occupational Safety and Health Administrations (OSHA) run by the states are primarily concerned with safety in the workplace but are sources of information for studio standards.

The Cancer Information Service of the **National Cancer Institute** provides information on related subjects, while the **American Heart Association** is also concerned with occupational hazards that may affect people with heart disease. They will give information on this aspect of art hazards. Contact your local chapters.

In your local telephone directory, you will find local and national safety equipment companies, many of which issue catalogues describing safety and health-protection equipment. These catalogues are often a source of information on respirators, gloves, dust collectors, supplied air systems, and other protective equipment. In addition, many of the catalogues of the ceramic equipment and supply companies listed in Appendix 5B include information on protective measures and equipment.

In countries outside the U.S.A., contact the appropriate agency for information on Health and Safety rulings for your area. In the United States, state clean air agencies may enforce ordinances that govern kiln emissions. In other countries, such as the United Kingdom whose Inspectorate of Pollution requires registration for certain types of firing, you should contact the appropriate government office or local craft or ceramics organization for information.

Safety Equipment Companies (U.S.A.)

Direct Safety Company
7815 South 46th St.
Phoenix, AZ 85044

E. D. Bullard Co.
P.O. Box 187
White Oak Pike, Cynthiana, KY 41031-0187
(800) 227-0423

Testing Laboratories (U.S.A.)

The following laboratories will test the glazes on your ware for the release of toxic material.

Bio-Technics Laboratories, Inc.
1133 Crenshaw Blvd.
Los Angeles, CA 90019

Coors Spectro-Chemical Laboratory
P.O. Box 500
Golden, CO 80401

Pittsburg Testing Laboratory
850 Poplar St.
Pittsburg, PA 15220

Twining Laboratories, Inc.
P.O. Box 1472
Fresno, CA 93716

5B

Sources of Equipment and Materials

U.S.A.

The following are some of the largest suppliers. For local sources, check your local telephone directory under Ceramic Equipment and Supplies as well as advertisements in ceramics magazines.

AIM Kiln Manufacturing Company, 2471 Montecito Rd., Ramona, CA 92065

AIM Kiln Manufacturing Company, 350 S.W. Wake Robin, Corvallis, OR 97333

Al Johnsen, Scott Creek Pottery, 9106 Peacock Hill Ave., Gig Harbor, WA 98332

Alaska Clay Supply, Inc., P.O. Box 111155, Anchorage, AK 99511

American Art Clay Co., Inc., 4717 West 16th St., Indianapolis, IN 46222

A.R.T., 1555 Louis Ave., Elk Grove Village, IL 60007

Axner Pottery Supply, P.O. Box 1484, Oviedo, FL 32765

Bailey Ceramic Supply, CPO 1577, Kingston, NY 12401

Bennett's Pottery and Ceramic Supplies, 431 Enterprise St., Ococee, FL 34761

Bluebird Mfg. Co., Inc., P.O. Box 2307, Ft. Collins, CO 80522

Brent Equipment, 4717 West 16th St., Indianapolis, IN 46222

Ceramic Corner, Inc., P.O. Box 1206, Grants Pass, OR 97526

Ceramic Fiber Fabrication, Inc., 56828 Skyline Ranch Rd., Yucca Valley, CA 92284

Columbus Clay Co., 1049 W. Fifth Ave., Columbus, OH 43212

Contemporary Kiln Inc., 26 "O" Commercial Blvd., Novato, CA 94949

Creative Industries, 5366 Jackson Dr., La Mesa, CA 91942

Cutter Ceramics, Box 151, Waltham, MA 02154

Del Val Potter's Supply Company, 7600 Queen St., Wyndmoor, PA 19118

Geil Kiln Company, 1601 West Rosecrans Ave., Gardena, CA 90249

Giffin Tec, Inc., Box 4057, Boulder, CO 80306

Hammill & Gillespie, Inc., P.O. Box 104, Livingston, NJ 07039

Jack D. Wolfe Co., 2130 Bergen St., Brooklyn, NY 11233

Kemper Tools, P.O. Box 696, Chino, CA 91710

Kickwheel Pottery Supply, 6477 Peachtree Industrial Blvd., Atlanta, GA 30360

Laguna Clay Company, 14400 Lomitas Ave., City of Industry, CA 91746

Leslie Ceramic Company, 1212 San Pablo, Berkeley, CA 94706

Marjon Ceramics, Inc., 3434 W. Earll Dr., Phoenix, AZ 85017

Miami Clay Co., 270 N.E. 183rd St., Miami, FL 33179

Mile Hi Ceramics, Inc., 77 Lipan, Denver, CO 80223-1580

Minnesota Clay, 8001 Grand Ave. South, Bloomington, MN 55420

Ohio Ceramic Supply, P.O. Box 630, Kent, OH 44240

Priority Supply Co., 2127 Lake Lansing Rd., Lansing, MI 48912

Randall Pottery, P.O. Box 774, Alfred, NY 14802

Seattle Pottery Supply, Inc., 35 South Hanford, Seattle, WA 98134

Shimpo West, 3500 Devon Ave., Lincolnwood, IL 60659

Skutt Ceramic Products, 2618 S.E. Steele St., Portland, OR 97202

Soldner Pottery Equipment, P.O. Box 90, Aspen, CO 81612

Standard Ceramic Supply Co., P.O. Box 4435, Pittsburgh, PA 15205

Trinity Ceramic Supply, Inc., 9016 Diplomacy Row, Dallas, TX 75247

Venco Products, 15 La Patera, Camarillo, CA 93010

West Coast Ceramic Supply, 756 N.E. Lombard, Portland, OR 97211

Australia

BPQ Controls, Beachmere Pottery Qld., 14 Margaret St., Beachmere, Qld 4510

Hilldav Industries Pty. Ltd., 108 Oakes Rd., Old Toongabbie 2146 NSW

Port-O-Kiln, 63 Dandenong St., Dandenong, Victoria 3175

Potters Equipment Pty Ltd., 13/42 New St., Ringwood, Victoria 3134

The Puggoon Kaolin Company and Ceramic Supplies, P.O. Box 89, Gulgong, NSW 2852

Venco Products, 29 Owen Rd., Kelmscott, WA 6111

CANADA

Culpepper Pottery, #18, 700 58th Ave., S.E., Calgary, Alberta T2H 2E2, Canada

Tucker Pottery Supplies, 15 West Pearce St., Richmond Hill, Ontario L4B 1H6, Canada

FRANCE

Peter Lavem, 5 Rue de Picardie, 94100 Saint Naur, France

Ceradel Socor, 19 Rue Pierre Curie, 87025 Limoges Cedex, France

Les Terres de Puisaye, 58310 Saint Armand en Puisaye, Les Perchers, France

GERMANY

Klück Keramik, Hafenwey 26, 4400 Münster, Germany

Kahlen-Keramik, Neuhausstr. 2–10, Aachen, Germany

CREATON, Bahnofstrasze 4, 56427 Siershahn, Germany

HOLLAND

Silex, De Meerheuvel 5, 5221 HA, 's-Hertogenbosch, Holland

Keramikos, Prinses Beatrixplein 24, 2033 WH, Haarlem, Holland

UNITED KINGDOM

Fulham Pottery Ltd., 8-10 Ingate Place, London SW8 3NS

Potterycrafts Ltd., Campbell Road, Shelton, Stoke-on-Trent, Staffordshire ST4 4ET

FASTENERS (USA)

ThunderBolt and Nut Co., Inc., 2700 Rydin Road (unit G), Richmond, CA 94804

SOFTWARE

There are now a number of glaze-calculation programs available. Some of these are commercially available, others are free except for the cost of the disk and mailing. They vary in approach, in what they cover, and in the ease of use. For reviews and up-to-date information on available programs it is best to turn to ceramics magazines.

Annapolis Potter's Guild, P.O. Box 152, Arnold, MD 21012, USA

David Hewitt, 7 Fairfield Rd., Caerleon, Newport, Gwent NP6 1DQ, England

INSIGHT ceramic chemistry software: IMC 134 Upland Dr., Medicine Hat, Alberta T1A 3N7, Canada

The Generator, Innovations and Frivolities, P.O. Box 431, Lancaster, NY 14086, USA

Glasure, Ulrik Krabbe, Ndr Strandvej 50, DK 3000 Helsingoer, Denmark

UNIQUALC, J. B. May, 19 Church Rd., Boldmere, Sutton Coldfield, West Midlands B73 5RX, England

Glossary

For a complete list of chemicals and materials, see Appendix 1E.

Acids In glaze calculation, the term refers to glaze chemicals that combine with **bases** and **neutrals** under heat, interacting in the formation of glazes. Silica is the most important acid. Acids are represented by the symbol RO_2. (See Appendix 3B.)

Air brush An atomizer that uses compressed air to spray a liquid. In ceramics, used for spraying oxides, underglazes, glaze stains, china paint, and lusters.

Air compressor A device that compresses air to below atmospheric pressure. In the studio, used to activate spray guns and air brushes.

Albany slip A natural slip glaze made of clay that was mined near Albany, New York. It was used for glazing stoneware in the United States until recently, when it became unobtainable.

Alkalies Mainly sodium and potassium, but also lime, lithium, and magnesia. They act as fluxes in certain glazes.

Alkaline glazes Glazes in which the fluxes are alkalies (mainly sodium and potassium). The earliest glazes developed in the Near East were alkaline.

Alumina One of the refractory (high-melting) materials in glazes. (See Appendixes 1E and 3B; Chapter 14.)

Amphora An ancient Greek vase form used there for transporting liquids and for prize presentations to Olympic games winners.

Antefix An ornament placed to cover the ends of tiles on the roofs of Greek and Etruscan temples. (See Chapter 2.)

Armature A framework of any rigid material used as a support while building clay sculpture. Most armatures must be removed before firing.

Ashes In ceramics, ashes from trees, plants, or animal bones may provide fluxes for use in glazes. Ashes contain varying amounts of silica and alumina, as well as potash, iron, magnesia, phosphorus, and lime. Oriental glazes such as the tenmoku (tienmu) frequently used rice straw ash, naturally high in silica. Tree and plant ashes are still popular glaze ingredients, while bone ash is used in making china.

Aventurine glaze A glaze which, when cooled slowly, crystallizes and produces small spangles that catch the light. Generally high in iron.

Bag wall A wall built inside a **downdraft kiln** to separate the firing chamber from the fire. It directs the flames upward, producing even circulation, and also protects the ware from direct contact with the flame.

Ball clay A plastic fine-grained, secondary clay. Often containing some organic material, it is used in clay bodies to increase plasticity, and in glazes to add alumina. Ball clay fires to a grayish or buff color.

Ball mill A rotating porcelain jar filled approximately half full with flint pebbles or porcelain balls that revolve and grind dry or wet glaze materials or pigments into powder or refined liquid state.

Banding wheel A turntable that can be revolved with one hand to turn a piece of pottery or sculpture while the other hand decorates it.

Basalt ware A black, unglazed stoneware first developed by Josiah Wedgewood in eighteenth-century England. (See Chapter 6).

Bases Glaze oxides that combine under heat with the **acids,** acting as fluxes. Represented in glaze calculation by the symbol RO. (See Appendix 3B.)

Bas-relief Three-dimensional modeling that is raised only slightly above a flat background.

Bat A plaster disk or square slab usually ¾ to 1½ inches (6.35 to 38.1 mm) thick on which a pot is thrown or is placed to dry when removed from the wheel. Also used when handbuilding.

Batch A mixture of glaze materials or ingredients that have been weighed in certain proportions to obtain a particular glaze or clay body.

Bisque (bisquit) Unglazed ceramic ware that has been fired at a low temperature to remove all moisture from the clay body and to make handling easier during glazing.

Bisque firing The process of firing ware at a low temperature, usually from cone 010 to 05, to produce bisque ware.

Bizen ware Produced in Japan in wood-fired kilns in which the pots are stacked along with straw that is high in silica content. Its combustion causes fire markings, and ashes from the fire may also create glazed areas. Traditionally used in Japan to create ware for tea ceremony, modifications of the technique are now popular with potters elsewhere.

Black figure A term applied to early Greek pottery on which the decoration was black. To achieve this, the vessel was painted with a specially formulated slip, then fired in a sequence of reducing and oxidizing firings that turned the decoration black but left the background the natural reddish color of the clay. (See Chapter 2.)

Blistering A pitted, craterlike surface of a glaze caused by gases bursting through the glaze as it is fired, often caused by too-rapid firing or overfiring.

Blunger A machine with revolving paddles used to mix slips or glazes.

Body (clay body) Any blend of clays and nonplastic ceramic materials that is workable and that has certain firing properties. Clay bodies are formulated to serve particular purposes and to achieve maturity at various firing temperatures. See **earthenware, stoneware,** and **porcelain.**

Bone ash Calcium phosphate ash made from animal bones. Used in a clay body for making **bone china.**

Bone china Ware made of clay to which bone ash has been added to lower its maturing point. Produced mainly in England, it matures at lower temperatures—usually around 2270°F/1240°C—than true porcelain.

Burner (gas, propane, oil) The system through which fuel, combined with air (usually controlled by a butterfly valve or air shutter), is fed into the kiln, creating the necessary mixture for combustion.

Burnishing Rubbing leather-hard or dry clay with any smooth tool to polish it, tighten the clay surface, and compress the clay particles.

Calcine (calcining) To heat a substance to a high temperature, but below its melting point, causing loss of moisture.

Caliper An instrument used to measure the inside and outside diameter of an object. (See Chapter 12.)

Car kiln (shuttle kiln) A kiln that is loaded by moving a stacked car on rails into the kiln. Used widely for production pottery and also for firing large sculpture. (See Chapter 15.)

Casting The process of forming pottery or sculpture by pouring liquid clay (slip) into absorbent plaster or, historically, into terra-cotta molds.

Celadon The Western name for a type of glaze first used in China on stoneware and porcelain in an attempt to imitate the color and texture of jade. Its colors, ranging from shades of green to graygreen tones, depend on the percentage of iron it contains. Historically, celadon has been fired in a reducing atmosphere, but celadon colors may now be attained in an electric kiln. (Color Plate 1.)

Centering The act of forcing a lump of clay by hand into a symmetrical form at the center of a spinning potter's wheel in preparation for throwing pottery.

Centrifugal force The force that tends to impel an object or material outward from the center of rotation. It acts on the clay while it rotates on a potter's wheel, and the action of the potter's hands in conjunction with this force causes the walls to rise.

Ceramic-fiber materials Refractory materials developed for the space exploration program. When exposed to the heat range for which each one is designed, they reflect heat and are resistant to thermal shock, are light in weight, and are excellent insulating materials. Used for kiln insulation.

Ceramic-fiber rigidizer A liquid that can be applied to ceramic fiber to harden the surface, make it more rigid, and help eliminate the dust it releases when handled. There is also a form of ceramic-fiber cement that will stiffen the material even more when applied to the surface.

Ceramics Objects made from earthy materials with the aid of heat, or the process of making these objects.

Chambered kiln A type of kiln developed in China, built on a hillside with several separate firing chambers opening into each other. Sometimes called a climbing kiln.

Chamotte A term generally used in Europe for **grog.** (See Chapter 10.)

China A term usually applied to any white ware fired at a low porcelain temperature. It was developed in Europe to compete with the expensive imported Chinese porcelain.

China clay Primary clay, or kaolin, that is white, **refractory,** and not very plastic.

China paint An opaque overglaze paint that is fired onto already-fired glazed ware at various lowrange temperatures. Because of the low temperatures used, colors like red or orange do not burn out. Sometimes called **overglaze enamel.**

China paint medium A substance in which china paint pigment is ground so that it can be applied like paint. China paint may have either an oil or water base.

Chinoiserie Decoration used in eighteenth-century Europe inspired by the newly imported Chinese crafts. The motifs were used on furniture, china, and other objects.

Chuck An open container used to hold work in place while trimming on the wheel. (See Chapter 12.)

Clay A variety of earthy materials formed by the decomposition of granite. In the process, these may have been combined with a variety of other materials, forming clay bodies with differing maturing points. See also **primary clay** and **secondary clay.**

Clay body See **body.**

Coiling A method of forming pottery or sculpture from rolls of clay melded together to create the walls. (See Chapter 11.)

CMC A synthetic **gum** used as a binder for pigments and glazes.

Compressed air See **air compressor.**

Cone See **pyrometric cone.**

Cornish stone (Cornwall stone) A feldspathic material found in England, containing silica and various fluxes. Similar to the Chinese *petuntze* used in the first porcelains.

Crackle glaze A glaze with deliberate crazing that forms a decorative surface. Color may be rubbed into the cracks to emphasize them or the ware may be soaked in tea or coffee.

Crawling Crawling is characterized by bare, unglazed areas on fired ceramic ware alternating with thickened glazed areas. Usually caused by surface tension in the molten glaze pulling it away from areas of grease or dust on the surface of the bisque ware. Also may occur in glaze applied over underglazed areas, or low-fire glaze containing gum applied to high-fire porcelain bisque, or through use of a glaze solution containing too much gum.

Crazing Unintentional cracks that occur over the entire glaze surface because the glaze expands and contracts more than the clay body to which it is applied. Caused by improper "fit" of glaze to clay.

Crystalline glazes Glazes in which crystals are formed, causing the light to reflect. Large crystals may be caused to grow, creating a deliberately sought decorative effect. Slow cooling helps to produce crystals in glazes that are low in alumina. (Color Plate 30.)

Cuenca An Hispano-Moresque technique in which designs for tiles or pottery were impressed into damp clay, forming ridges that acted as barriers between glaze colors, keeping them from running into each other. (See Chapter 6.)

Cuerda seca A technique used by Hispano-Moresque potters in which they drew lines around the designs on tiles or pottery, using a mixture of manganese and grease. This barrier kept the multicolored glazes from melding together and provided a dark outline to the areas. (See Chapter 6.)

De-airing Any method of removing air from clay, making it less likely to cause bloating of fine grain clay in firing. Wedging de-airs clay to a certain degree, but a **pug mill** equipped with a de-airing vacuum chamber does a more complete job.

Decal An image or a design printed with ceramic material on a special paper so that it can be transferred to bisque ware or glazed surface and fired to permanency. (See Chapter 14.)

Deflocculant Material such as sodium carbonate or sodium silicate, used in slip for casting to aid in maintaining the fluidity of the slip. Less water is needed to produce a slip containing deflocculant; thus less shrinkage will occur in drying the cast object. (See Appendix 1A.)

Die A pattern made of steel, acrylic, or wood for cutting or stamping clay, or pressing it through an **extruder** in order to produce the desired form.

Dipping Applying glaze or slip to the body by immersing the piece and shaking off excess glaze.

Dispersion blender A type of high-speed (vortex) blender useful in mixing glazes. Reduces glaze particle size and blends glaze more thoroughly and efficiently than traditional propeller blades.

Downdraft kiln A kiln designed so that the heat moves up through the firing chamber, down through the ware, then is vented into a stack (chimney) opening at the bottom of the kiln. (See Chapter 15.)

Draft gauge A gauge in a glaze spray booth that measures the strength of the air current passing through the filter. This lets the person spraying know if there is adequate air circulation to collect and filter the glaze overspray properly. (See Chapter 14.)

Drape mold A support (such as a stretched cloth, a wooden frame, or rope network) in or over which a clay slab is draped to shape as it stiffens. The term is also sometimes used for a **hump mold** over which slabs of clay are stiffened.

Draw In ceramics, to take fired ware from the kiln.

Drill For drilling holes in ceramics, a carbide tip drill bit will penetrate soft bisque. For high-fired ceramics, use a diamond core drill bit lubricated and cooled with water.

Dunting The cracking of pots during cooling, caused by too-rapid cooling of the kiln, by drafts reaching the ware as it cools in the kiln, or by removing the ware from the kiln before it is cool enough.

Earthenware Pottery that has been fired at low temperature (below cone 2) and is porous and relatively soft. Usually red or brown in color. Used worldwide for domestic ware, glazed or unglazed.

Egyptian paste A self-glazing low-fire clay body that contains glass-forming materials. Used by the Egyptians for small sculpture and ceremonial vessels. Now available commercially in a number of colors. (Color Plate 51; see Chapter 2 and Appendix 1A.)

Electrolyte A substance, usually alkaline, that changes the electrical charges in clay particles so that they repel rather than attract each other, thus maintaining them in suspension in water. See **deflocculant** and Appendix 1B.

Enamels Low-temperature opaque or translucent glazes that are usually painted over higher-fired glazed surfaces. More commonly called **china paints.**

Engobe Originally, the term referred to slip that is applied over the entire surface of a piece of pottery or sculpture to change the color and/or texture of the clay body. The term now often refers to slip used for decoration.

Epoxy An adhesive made from a thermosetting resin. Often used in ceramic repair. May be colored with a variety of coloring additives. Ultraviolet light may affect the color over an extended period of time. (See Appendix 4C.)

Eutectic A combination of two or more ceramic materials whose melting point when combined is always lower than that of any one of the materials used alone.

Extruder A mechanical aid for forming moist clay by pressing it through a **die.** This causes the clay to take the shape of the die. Extruders can form clay quickly into many forms, from tubes to tiles to sewer pipes. (See Chapter 11).

Faience From the French name for the Italian town Faenza, where much tin-glazed earthenware (maiolica ware) was made. Frequently, a general term for any pottery made with a colored, low-fire clay body covered with opaque base glaze and decorated with colored glazes. (See Chapter 6).

Feathering A method of making a decorative feather pattern with slip or glaze.

Feldspar Any of a group of common rock-forming minerals containing silicates of aluminum, along with potassium, sodium, calcium, and occasionally barium. Used extensively in stoneware and porcelain bodies and in glazes as a flux. Feldspars melt at a range of temperatures between 2192°F/1200°C and 2372°F/1300°C depending on their composition. (See Appendix 1D.)

Ferric oxide and **ferrous oxide** The red and black iron oxides that produce reddish and brown colors in clay bodies and glazes, as well as acting as fluxes. They also produce the greens of celadon glazes when fired in a reducing atmosphere. (See Appendix 1E.)

Fettle The thin extrusion of clay left on a slip-cast form at the line where the mold sections were joined. (See Chapter 10.)

Fettling knife A long, tapered knife used for trimming clay, and removing the **fettle** from a cast.

Fiber glass A material consisting of glass fibers in resin. Sometimes called spun glass, it is used as an additive to clay bodies to strengthen them, or as a reinforcing material in a matrix of epoxy or resin applied to sculpture after firing.

Firebox The part of the kiln into which fuel is introduced and where combustion takes place.

Fire clays (refractory clays) Clays that withstand high temperatures. Used in kiln bricks and also as ingredients in stoneware bodies or in clay bodies for handbuilding or sculpture.

Firing Heating pottery or sculpture in a kiln or open fire to bring the clay or glaze to **maturity.** The temperature needed to mature a specific clay or glaze varies.

Fit The adjustment of the glaze composition to the composition of a clay body so that it will adhere to the surface of the ware.

Flambé glaze A high-fire red and purple-red glaze produced by firing copper in a reducing atmosphere. (Color Plate 2.)

Flocculant A material, such as calcium chloride or hydrated magnesium sulfate (Epsom salts), that aids in keeping clay particles together. Used in suspension of glazes or for thinning slip. (See Appendix 1B.)

Flues The passageways in a kiln designed to carry the heat from the chamber to the chimney or vent.

Flux A substance that lowers the melting point of another substance. Oxides such as those of iron, sodium, potassium, calcium, zinc, lead, boric oxide, and others that combine with the silica and other heat-resistant materials in a glaze, helping them to fuse.

Foot The base of a piece of pottery. Usually left unglazed in high-fired ware; occasionally glazed in low-fire, in which case the ware must be put on stilts to keep it from sticking to the shelf.

Frit (Fritt) A glaze material that is formed when any of several soluble materials are melted together with insoluble materials, cooled rapidly, and splintered in cold water, then ground into a powder. This renders them less soluble and less likely to release toxic materials. Feldspar is a natural frit.

Fusion testing A method of subjecting ceramic chemicals to various temperatures in order to determine their melting points and fusability.

Galena Lead sulfide, formerly used in Europe to glaze earthenware. No longer used because of its toxicity.

Gesso A mixture of plaster and gum used as a base for painting.

Glass former An essential component of any glaze. The main glass former is silica. (See Appendixes 1E and 3B; Chapter 14.)

Glaze Any vitreous coating that has been melted onto a clay surface by the use of heat. Made of fine-ground minerals that, when fired to a certain temperature, fuse into a glassy coating. Glazes may be matt or glossy, depending on their components.

Glaze firing (also called **glost firing**) The firing during which glaze materials melt and form a vitreous coating on the clay body surface.

Glaze stain Commercial blends formulated with various coloring oxides that produce a wide range of colors when used in glazes or clay bodies.

Glost Ware that has been glazed. *Glost firing* is another term for glaze firing.

Greenware Unfired pottery or sculpture.

Grog (chamotte) Crushed or ground particles of fired clay graded in various sizes of particles. Added to the clay body to help in drying, to add texture, and to reduce shrinkage and warpage.

Gum A viscous material, such as gum tragacanth, that is exuded from certain trees, or a chemically formulated substance; used as a binder for pigments. (See Appendix 1B.)

Hard paste True porcelain made of a clay body containing kaolin, traditionally fired between 2370° and 2640°F/1300° and 1450°C. It is white, vitrified, and translucent. See **porcelain.**

Hematite Iron oxide (Fe_2O_3) used as coloring on much early pottery.

High-fire Describes clays or glazes that are fired from cone 2 up to cone 10 or 13. Ware fired at cone 2 and up is usually considered to be **stoneware.**

Hispano-Moresque Term used to describe tin-lead glazed earthenware produced in Spain in the Middle Ages. Frequently decorated with luster, its style exhibited influences from both Islam and Christian Europe. (See Chapter 6.)

Hump mold A mold of plaster or terra cotta, or a found object such as a rounded rock, an up-ended bowl or a bag of sand, foam padding or crumpled newspaper over which a slab of clay can be laid to shape as it stiffens. (See Chapter 13.)

Hydrometer An instrument that determines specific gravity. In ceramics, used to monitor the proportion of water in a slip or a glaze. (See Chapter 14.)

In-glaze decoration Decoration applied on top of a glaze before firing. The colors sink into the glaze during firing.

Ione grain Hard, fired kaolin clay that has been crushed to various mesh sizes. White to grayish, its sharp particle shape adds tooth to clay bodies. Used for handbuilding and wheel clay bodies. Increases workability and strength, and reduces shrinkage in proportion to the amount added.

Jiggering A method of forming multiples rapidly. Soft clay is placed in a mold, pressed into or onto the mold walls either mechanically or by hand, then trimmed to size by hand or with a **jolley.** The Greeks and Romans used hand-jiggering methods to make utilitarian ware, and potters today use modifications of this method. Mechanical jiggering is used in ceramics factories. In industry, kerosene is used as a lubricant instead of water while jiggering.

Jolley The mechanical arm and template used to shape clay as it turns on a jigger machine or on a potter's wheel.

Kaolin (also called **china clay**) A white-firing natural clay that withstands high temperatures. An essential ingredient in porcelain, its presence in large quantities in China allowed the potters there to develop their fine white porcelain.

Kaowool Trademark of an insulating material for kilns. See **ceramic-fiber materials.**

Keramos A Greek word meaning "earthenware," from which our term *ceramics* is derived.

Kick wheel The traditional potter's wheel which is powered by kicking a lower wheel or by pushing a treadle back and forth with the feet. (See Chapter 12.)

Kiln A furnace or an oven built of heat-resistant materials for firing pottery or sculpture, sometimes referred to as a *kil.*

Kiln flue A shaft, pipe, or tube for the passage of hot air and fumes from the kiln chamber. Flues are usually constructed from brick, insulated steel pipe, or triple-wall stainless steel pipe. (See Chapter 15.)

Kiln furniture Heat-resistant shelves, posts, and slabs that support the ware in the kiln during firing. Kiln shelves may warp in firing if they are not well supported. (See Chapter 15.)

Kiln hood The metal hood containing a venting system permanently built over a kiln or lowered over a kiln during firing to exhaust the heat and gases that are released from clays and glazes during firing. It is extremely important that all kilns be vented properly and to building codes. (See Chapter 17.)

Kiln sitter A control that uses small pyrometric cones that slump when the desired temperature is reached and turn off power to an electric kiln by tripping a switch or to a gas kiln by shutting off the gas solenoid valve. (See Chapter 15.)

Kiln wash A coating of refractory materials (half flint and half kaolin) painted onto the kiln floor and the top side of shelves to keep the melting glaze from fusing the ware onto the shelves.

Latex An emulsion of rubber or plastic material with water. Used in ceramics as a resist material in applying glazes; also a material for making flexible molds for plaster, wax, or concrete casting.

Lead Until recently lead was used extensively in a variety of forms as a flux for low- or medium-temperature glazes. Although the dangers of handling toxic lead were known quite early, its solubility in acid foods and liquids was not understood until comparatively recently. Lead glazes should not be used on food containers. (See Appendix 1E.)

Leather hard The condition of a clay body when much of the moisture has evaporated and shrinkage has just ended, but the clay is not totally dry. Carving, burnishing, or joining slabs are often done at this stage.

Line blend testing A system of testing glazes through changing the proportions of two or more different glazes to develop a range of color shades. (See Appendix 1A.)

Low-fire The range of firing of clays and glazes in which the kiln temperature reached is usually in the cone 015 to cone 1 range.

Luster (lustre) A thin film of metallic salts usually, although not always, applied to a glazed surface, then refired at a low temperature in reduction. Modern luster mediums include a reducing material, so no further reduction is necessary, but the early lusters developed in Persia and brought to Europe by the Moors required a reducing atmosphere in the kiln to develop their characteristic sheen. (See Chapters 3 and 14.)

Luster resist A special water-base resist material used like **wax resist** for luster resist decoration.

Luting The method of joining two parts of a still-damp clay object. Used for constructing both pottery and sculpture, especially large objects that cannot be made in one piece.

Maiolica (Majolica) The Italian name for tin-glaze ware that was sent from Spain to Italy via the island of Majorca. Later, local styles of decoration were developed in Italian pottery towns such as Faenza and Deruta. Now a general term for any earthenware covered with a tin-lead glaze. (See Chapter 6.)

Matt glaze A glaze that has a dull, nonglossy finish due to its deliberate composition. Barium carbonate (toxic) or alumina added to the glaze, along with a slow cooling, assists the formation of matt glazes.

Maturing point (maturity) Refers to the temperature and time in firing at which a clay or glaze reaches the desired condition of hardness and density. Both clays and glazes have differing maturing points, depending on their composition.

Model The original form in clay, plaster, wood, plastic, metal, or other material from which a mold is made.

Moisture trap Used in the air lines of spray guns and air brushes intended for spraying oil-base paint such as luster and china paint. It traps any water vapor or moisture that might contaminate the oil-base paint. (See Chapter 17.)

Mold Any form that can be used to shape fluid or plastic substances. In ceramics, usually the negative form from which pottery or sculpture can be cast by pouring or pressing methods using either liquid slip or damp clay. Molds can be made in one piece or in multiple sections. See also **hump mold.** (See Chapter 13.)

Molochite Crushed, fired white porcelain. Added to clay bodies, it assists in reducing shrinkage, cracking, and warping.

Muffle A kiln, or section of a kiln, in which ceramics can be fired without direct contact with the flame.

Mullite An additive material available in raw or **calcined** form. Acting as a heavy-duty refractory, it aids in producing strong clay bodies with high resistance to thermal shock, cracking, warping, or other deformations.

Mullite crystals Crystals of aluminum silicate that start to form in clay as it is fired between 1850° and 2200°F/1010° and 1204°C. These crystals strengthen stoneware and porcelain when fully developed at high temperatures and also help in the interaction that unites high-fire glazes and high-fire clay bodies.

Neutral atmosphere The point at which the atmosphere in a kiln is balanced between oxidation and reduction.

Neutrals Materials that are neutral and can react as either an acid or a base. Also called *amphoteric,* they are represented in glaze calculation by the symbol R_2O_3. (See Appendix 3B.)

Nylon fiber Synthetic fiber added to a clay body for strength.

Opacifier A material that causes a glaze to become opaque by producing minute crystals. Tin, zirconium, and titanium oxides are used as opacifiers in combination with various oxides. (See Appendix 1F.)

Open firing Firing that is not done in an enclosed kiln. (See Chapter 15.)

Orifice (gas burner) The opening through which the gas fuel comes from the gas line and is mixed with air as it enters the burner. (See Chapter 15.)

Overfire To fire a clay body or glaze above its maturing point.

Overglaze A low-temperature ceramic enamel painted on a previously glazed and fired surface, then fired for a second time at a lower temperature, usually as the final firing process. Bright colors like red and orange that would burn out at high temperatures will be maintained in the lower firing (around 1300°F/705°C). Often called **enamel** or **china paint.** (See Chapter 14.)

Oxidation (oxidizing firing) The firing of a kiln or open fire with complete combustion so that the firing atmosphere contains enough oxygen to allow the metals in clays and glazes to produce their oxide colors. Electric kilns always produce oxidizing firings unless reducing materials are added. Bright and clear low-fire colors are often associated with glazes and clays fired in an oxidation atmosphere.

Oxide A combination of an element with oxygen. In ceramics, oxides are used in formulating glazes and for coloring glazes and clays. They are also used for decorating ware.

Oxygen probe (CO_2 analyzer) Inserted in your kiln while firing, this probe will monitor the **reduction** atmosphere inside the kiln so that you can keep your firings consistent time after time. Especially useful for a production potter.

Parallel-flue kiln A rectangular kiln used by Roman and later potters in which parallel flues were placed under the perforated floor.

Peephole A hole in the door or wall of a kiln through which the ceramist can watch the pyrometric cones, the color of heat in the kiln, and the process of the firing. (Always wear goggles of the proper shade [#3 to #5] when peering into a kiln through a peephole.)

Petuntze A type of feldspar rock in China from which, with kaolin, the Chinese formed their porcelains. In Europe and the United States it is called Cornish stone, Cornwall stone, or china stone.

Piece mold A mold for casting that is made in sections so that it can be removed easily from the cast object without distortion. Generally used to cast an object that has undercuts and that therefore cannot be removed from a one-piece mold.

Pinholes Small holes in a glaze caused by the bursting of blisters formed by gases as they escape through the glaze during firing.

Pithos (plural, **pithoi**) A Greek term for a large storage jar made of earthenware. (See Chapter 2.)

Plastic clay See **plasticity**.

Plasticity The ability of a damp clay body to yield under pressure without cracking and to retain the formed shape after the pressure is released.

Platelets (clay) The basic particles of clay.

Porcelain A translucent, nonabsorbent body fired at high temperature. White and hard, it was first developed in China. Traditionally fired in the 2370°–2640°F/1300°–1450°C range, some porcelain bodies have been developed that mature in the 2230–2340°F/1220°–1280°C range.

Potshard (potsherd) See **shard.**

Pottery Originally a term for earthenware, now loosely used to refer to any type of ceramic ware, as well as to the workshop where it is made.

Press mold Any mold made from plaster, fired clay, wood, or a found object into which damp clay can be pressed to reproduce the shape of the mold. (See Chapter 13.)

Primary clay Clay found in nature that was formed in place rather than transported by the action of water. Also called residual clay. Kaolin is a primary clay.

Proto-porcelain (proto-porcelaneous) Refers to an early high-fire ware developed in China as kilns became more efficient and capable of reaching higher temperatures. It preceded true porcelain.

Pug mill A machine used to blend clay into a moist, workable consistency. Also used to recycle clay scraps and, when equipped with a vacuum pump system, to **de-air** clay. (See Chapter 10).

Pyrometer A device for measuring and recording the exact interior temperature of a kiln throughout the firing and cooling process. (See Chapter 15.)

Pyrometric cones Small pyramids of ceramic materials formulated to bend over and melt at designated temperatures. Orton cones in the United States and Seger cones in England and Europe have different ranges. In addition to the brown and white Orton cones that range from cone 022 to cone 42 (for industrial use), there are now cones that contain color coding to avoid confusion. (See Appendix 2A and Chapter 15.)

Quartz inversion point The point at which the silica crystals in clay change in structure and volume during the rise and fall of the temperature in the kiln. This development influences the fit of glaze to clay body.

Quick coupler A coupling device that joins an air tool to an air line, allowing quick release without a wrench. This makes it easy to use the air line for several different air tools. (See Chapter 17.)

Raku Originally a name used by a Japanese family that has made tea ceremony ware since the seventeenth century. Now refers to both the process of raku firing and to ware glazed in such a firing. Soft and porous, traditional raku ware was lead-glazed, placed in a red-hot kiln, and quickly withdrawn when the glaze melted. In the West, lead is now rarely used in raku glazes. Leadless frits and Gerstley borate are now commonly used fluxes in place of lead. Raku ware is often reduced after firing by burying it in straw, sawdust, paper, or other combustible material, then covering it with an airtight lid to create a reducing atmosphere that aids in producing luster or opalescent colors. (Color Plates 32 and 33; see Chapter 15.)

Raw glaze Glaze that does not contain fritted material.

Reduction (reducing firing, reduction atmosphere) A firing in which insufficient air is supplied to the kiln for complete combustion. Under these conditions, the carbon monoxide in the kiln combines with the oxygen in the oxides of the clay body and glaze, causing the oxides to change color. Commonly associated with high-fire stoneware, porcelain, raku, and lusters.

Refractory Resistance to heat and melting. Refractory materials are used in porcelain and stoneware. Also used for building kilns and kiln furniture, and in combination with other materials, as kiln insulation.

Reserve A technique of painting *around* an area, reserving it so that it remains the color of the clay body or glaze while the painted area around it fires a different color. Used on Greek red-figure ware, and still in use today, as when using a stencil to mask areas. (See Chapter 2.)

Resist A method of applying a covering material such as wax, latex, or special luster resist to bisque or glazed ware, then coating the piece with a glaze or a second glaze. The resist material will not accept the glaze so that on firing, the color of the covered area will remain intact.

Rib A curved tool made of wood, metal, or plastic, used for shaping, scraping, or smoothing clay objects. (See Chapter 10.)

Roulette A carved or textured wheel that imprints repeated motifs or texture when run over a damp clay surface.

Saggar A refractory container in which glazed ware is placed during firing to protect it from the kiln fire. Saggers are also used to introduce local reducing material by placing leaves, seaweed, cow dung, or other organic material in the sagger with the ware.

Salt glaze A glaze formed by introducing salt into a hot kiln. The vaporized salt combines with the silica in the clay body, forming a sodium silicate glaze on the surface. It also combines with the silica in the kiln bricks, coating them with a glaze that will be transferred to any ware fired in the kiln later. Salt glazing releases noxious and toxic fumes, so many potters now use alternatives for **vapor firing**. (Color Plate 36; see Chapter 15.)

Sandblasting A method of etching the surface of a fired object or kiln shelves by directing a blast of air carrying fine sand onto the surface at high velocity. Since sand is largely silica and is extremely harmful to the lungs, use a sandblasting booth or wear a supplied air respirator that covers your head.

Sang de boeuf The French name for the oxblood red glazes of China. (Color Plate 3.)

Sealers Used to protect unglazed fired work from dust, fingerprints, and moisture as well as to heighten color use. Shellac, varnish, water-base acrylic paints, concrete sealers, linseed oil, or oil-base marble floor sealers can be used to seal ceramic. They are recommended for sealing objects for decorative purposes only, and not for food containers.

Secondary clay Natural clay that has been moved by water or wind from its source and settled elsewhere in deposits.

Setting Placing the ware in the kiln in preparation for firing.

Sgraffito Decoration of pottery made by scratching through a layer of colored slip to the differently colored clay body underneath.

Shard (sherd) A broken piece of pottery. From these fragments, archaeologists can learn much about ancient cultures.

Shivering The flaking off of slivers of glaze due to poor glaze fit, frequently due to greater shrinkage of the clay body than the glaze.

Short Clay that is not plastic. Cracks will form on handling after brief manipulation.

Shrink ruler A scale ruler used to calculate the percent of shrinkage of clay during firing.

Sieve A utensil of wire mesh (usually brass to resist rust) used to strain liquids or powdered materials.

Silica Oxide of silicon, SiO_2. Found in nature as quartz or flint sand, it is the most common of all ceramic materials. See Appendix 1E.

Silicate of soda A solution of sodium silicate that is used as a **deflocculant** to help in the suspension of clay materials in slip.

Silicon carbide Used in a glaze (as 3-F powder) to produce local reduction in an electric kiln. Also used in making kiln furniture for high-fire ware.

Silk-screening The process of transferring an image to a surface by forcing paint through a fine screening material, such as silk or polyester, on which a stencil of the image has been applied. In ceramics, it is generally used for applying china paint. (See Chapter 14.)

Sintering The stage in glaze firing during which the heat converts a powder into a cohesive mass before melting it into a glassy material.

Slab roller A mechanical device for rolling out slabs to a set, consistent thickness.

Slaking The process of chemically combining a material, such as plaster, with water.

Slip A suspension of clay in water used for casting pottery or sculpture in molds. Slip (sometimes called **engobe**) can also be used for painted decoration or for the **sgraffito** technique. Often contains sodium silicate "N" and soda ash, or Darvan #7, to help keep the particles in suspension and for fluidity.

Slip casting Forming objects by pouring slip into a plaster mold. The mold absorbs the water in the slip so that solid clay walls are formed to create a positive of the original. (See Chapter 13.)

Slip glaze A glaze that contains a large proportion of clay. Generally one that contains enough flux to form a glaze with few or no additives. Albany slip was widely used as slip glaze in traditional American potteries. Substitutes now offered to replace it are Sheffield (Massachusetts) and Seattle slip clays.

Slip reservoir In slip casting, a space left in a mold to be filled with additional slip. (See Chapter 13.)

Slip trailer A rubber syringe used to apply decorations of slip on ware.

Soaking Maintaining a certain temperature in the kiln for a period of time to achieve heat saturation.

Sodate retarder A material that can be added to plaster (in proportions of ¼ to 2 teaspoons to 100 pounds of plaster) to slow its setting time by ten minutes to an hour.

Soft paste A porcelain body that fires at a lower temperature than true porcelain.

Soluble Capable of being dissolved in a fluid.

Soluble salts Mineral salts such as silver nitrate, bismuth subnitrate, and copper and iron sulfate. When used in ceramics, they are applied to bisque ware or to glazes, then fired to create interesting color effects. (See Chapter 14.)

Spray booth A ventilated booth that removes chemicals and fumes from the air so that the worker does not inhale them while spraying glazes, underglazes, or overglazes. (See Chapter 14.)

Spray gun A gun-like device through which compressed air passes, forcing the substance into a fine mist for application. Used for spraying glazes.

Sprigging The process of attaching low-relief decorations of damp clay onto already formed **greenware.**

Stains Commercially processed and refined raw chemicals yielding ceramic stains offer a wide range of shades for coloring clays and glazes. They are generally more color stable than oxides. (See Chapter 14.)

Stilts Triangular supports with either clay (for low-fire) or heat-resistant metal points (for low- or high-fire), used to support pieces of glazed pottery during glaze firing. They support the ware above the shelves to keep the glaze from sticking the ware to the shelf. Small stilt marks can be filed, sanded, or ground smooth. (See Chapter 15.)

Stoneware A type of clay body fired to a temperature at which the body becomes vitrified, dense, and nonabsorptive, but not translucent. Natural stoneware clay is usually brownish in color because of the presence of iron, but there are formulated white stoneware bodies. Usually matures at temperatures above 2192°F/1200°C.

Temper Any material, such as sand, mica, or crushed fired pottery fragments (**grog**), added to a clay body to make it more porous and less likely to shrink and warp.

Template A wooden, metal, or plastic pattern used as a guide for shaping clay. A template can be used on the inside or outside of a pot as it turns on the wheel, in a process called **jiggering.**

Tenmoku (temmoku, tienmu) High-fired, saturated iron glaze; black, brown, and yellowish. Used by the Chinese and Japanese, especially on tea ware. Still a popular glaze. (See Chapter 3.)

Terra-cotta A low-fire, porous, reddish clay body, frequently containing grog or other temper. Used throughout history for common, utilitarian ware; also used for sculpture.

Terra sigillata A fine slip glaze used by the Greeks, Etruscans, and Romans to coat their pottery. It fired black or red according to the kiln atmosphere. Now used in a wide variety of colors by many potters and sculptors to surface their ware or sculpture. (See Chapters 2 and 14.)

Test tiles Small tiles made of clay used to test clay bodies in the kiln or to test glazes on a specific clay body. (Color Plates 51 and 52; see Chapter 14.)

Thermal shock The stress to which ceramic material is subjected when sudden changes occur in the heat during firing or cooling.

Throwing Forming objects on the potter's wheel using a clay body with plastic qualities (see **plasticity**).

Tin enamel A low-fire overglaze containing tin.

Tin glaze (tin-lead glaze) A low-fire, opaque glaze containing tin oxide.

Trailing A method of decorating in which a slip or glaze is squeezed out of a syringe. Historically, decoration trailed from a quill inserted in a narrow-necked clay cup.

Undercut A negative space in a solid form, creating an overhang. Casting a form with undercutting requires a multipart mold in order to release the mold from the cast.

Underfire To fire clay or glaze—accidentally or deliberately—to a point below its maturing point. Underfiring can turn a normally glossy glaze into a matt surface.

Underglaze Any coloring material used under a glaze. The color can be provided by oxides or by commercially prepared glaze and clay body **stains.** (See Chapter 14.)

Updraft kiln A kiln in which the heat goes up through the chamber and is vented through the top of the kiln. (See Chapter 15.)

Vapor firing (low-sodium firing) An alternative to the traditional use of heavy sodium doses in order to avoid or minimize the pollution of salt firing. (See Appendix 1C for an alternative recipe.)

Viscosity The ability to resist running or flow. A glaze must have enough viscosity to avoid flowing off the ware when it is melted under heat. China clay in a glaze assists in stabilizing it.

Vitreous Pertaining to or having the nature of glass. In ceramics, a vitreous glaze or clay body has been fired to a dense, hard, and nonabsorbent condition. High-fire glazes vitrify and combine with the glassy particles that form in the high-fire clay body as it approaches vitrification. This results in a glaze that is united with the clay body as compared to a low-fire glaze that merely coats the surface of the fired clay.

Vitrification The state of being vitrified, or glassy.

Ware A general term applied to any ceramic — earthenware, stoneware, or porcelain — in the green, bisqued, or fired state.

Warping Changes in the form of a clay body. Warping of ware can occur during drying or firing if the walls are built unevenly or if drying or firing is uneven or ware is improperly supported during firing.

Waster (kiln waster) A piece of pottery discarded due to slumping, warping, or breaking in the kiln. Many wasters have been found during excavations at ceramic sites such as Faenza, Italy, or early New England potteries, helping archaeologists date styles and types of ware.

Wax resist A method of decoration in which melted wax or oil emulsion is painted onto the clay body or onto a glazed piece. See **resist**. (See Chapter 14.)

Wedging Any one of various methods of kneading a mass of clay to expel the air, get rid of lumps, and prepare a homogeneous material. (See Chapter 10.)

Wedging table A table of plaster, wood, or concrete, often covered with canvas, on which clay can be wedged. A stretched wire attached to the table allows one to cut the clay to check for air bubbles, lumps, or lack of homogeneity. (See Chapter 10.)

Further Reading

PERIODICALS

General

American Ceramics. 15 West 44th St., New York, N.Y. 10036.

Ceramica. Apartado 70008, Acacias 9, Madrid, Spain.

Ceramic Review. 21 Carnaby St., London, W1V 1PH, England.

Ceramics: Art and Perception. 35 Williams St., Paddington, Sydney, NSW, 2021, Australia.

Ceramics Monthly. 1609 Northwest Blvd., Columbus, Ohio 43212.

Crafts. Crafts Council, London. Subscriptions: 44a Pentonville Rd., Islington, London, N19BY, England.

La Revue de la Céramique. 61 Rue Marconi, 62880 Vendin-le-Vieil, France.

L'Atelier des Métiers d'Art. 18 Rue Wurtz, 75013 Paris, France.

New Zealand Potter. Box 12-162, Wellington, New Zealand.

Pottery in Australia. 48 Burton St., Darlinghurst, 2010, NSW, Australia.

Studio Potter. Box 70, Goffstown, N.H. 03045.

Health and Safety

Art Hazard News. Center for Occupational Hazards, 5 Beckman St., New York, N.Y. 10038.

BOOKS: SHAPING THE PAST

General

Charleston, Robert J. *World Ceramics.* New York: McGraw-Hill, 1968.

Cooper, Emanuel. *A History of World Pottery.* 2d ed. New York: Larousse, 1981/England: Batsford.

Kingery, David W., and Vandiver, Pamela. *Ceramic Masterpieces: Art, Structure and Technology.* New York: Free Press, 1986.

Rice, Prudence M. *Pots and Potters: Current Approaches in Ceramic Archaeology.* Los Angeles: University of California Press Institute of Archaeology, 1984.

The Mediterranean World

NEAR EAST

Hodges, Henry. *Technology in the Ancient World.* New York: Knopf, 1970.

Kingery, W. D., ed. *Ceramics and Civilization: Technology and Style.* Columbus: American Ceramic Society, 1985.

Mellaart, James. *Earliest Civilizations of the Near East.* New York: McGraw-Hill, 1966.

GREECE, ROME, ETRURIA

Bendel, Otto J. *Etruscan Art.* Harmondsworth, England, and New York: Penguin, 1978.

Bibke, Joseph V. *The Techniques of Painted Attic Pottery.* New York: Watson-Guptill, 1965.

Boardman, John. *Athenian Black-Figure Vases.* London, New York, Toronto: Oxford University Press, 1975.

Herbert, S. *The Red Figure Pottery.* Athens: American School of Classical Studies, 1977.

Noble, Joseph V. *The Techniques of Painted Attic Pottery.* New York: Thames and Hudson, 1988.

Peacock, D. P. S. *Pottery in the Roman World.* New York: Longman, 1982.

Europe and England

Barton, K. J. *Pottery in England from 3500* B.C.–A.D. *1730.* South Brunswick/New York: Barnes, 1975.

Brears, Peter C. D. *The English Country Pottery. Its History and Techniques.* Rutland, Vt.: Tuttle.

Carnegy, Daphne. *Tin-glazed Earthenware: From Maiolica, Faience and Delftware to the Contemporary.* London: A & C Black (Publishers) Ltd. 1993. Radnor, Pa.: Chilton Book Co. 1993.

Lewis, Griselda. *A Collector's History of English Pottery.* New York: Viking, 1970.

Liverani, Guiseppe. *Five Centuries of Italian Majolica.* New York: McGraw-Hill, 1960.

Neuwirth, Waltraud. *Wiener Werkstatte Keramik: Original Ceramics, 1920–31.* Cincinnati: Seven Hills, 1981.

Ramié, Georges. *Ceramics of Picasso.* Poughkeepsie, N.Y.: Apollo.

Asia

Koyana, Fujio, and Figges, John. *Two Thousand Years of Oriental Ceramics*. New York: Abrams, 1961.

CHINA

Hetherington, A., and Hobson, R. L. *The Art of the Chinese Potter*. Magnolia, Mass.: Peter Smith, 1983.

Medley, Margaret. *The Chinese Potter*. Ithaca, N.Y.: Cornell University Press, 1982.

————. *Yuan Porcelain and Stoneware*. London: Faber & Faber, 1974.

KOREA

Adams, Edward B. *Korea's Pottery*. Rutland, Vt.: Tuttle, 1986.

d'Argencé, Réne-Yvon Lefebvre, ed. *5000 Years of Korean Art*. Asian Art Museum of San Francisco, 1979.

Asia Society. *The Art of the Korean Potter: Silla, Koryo, Yi* New York: Asia Society, 1968.

JAPAN

Cardozo, Sidney B., and Hitano, Masaaki. *The Art of Rosanjin*. Tokyo: Kodansha, 1987.

Cort, Louise. *Shigaraki Potter's Valley*. New York: Kodansha, 1980.

Jenyns, Soame. *Japanese Pottery*. London: Faber & Faber, 1960; New York: Praeger, 1971.

Leach, Bernard. *Hamada, Potter*. New York: Kodansha, 1975.

————. *A Potter in Japan*. London: Faber & Faber, 1960.

Munsterberg, Hugo. *The Ceramic Art of Japan*. Rutland, Vt.: Tuttle, 1964.

Peterson, Susan. *Shoji Hamada: A Potter's Way and Work*. New York: Kodansha, 1984.

Rhodes, Daniel. *Tamba Potter: The Timeless Art of a Japanese Village*. New York: Kodansha, 1982.

Saint-Giles, Amaury. *Earth 'n' Fire: A Survey Guide to Contemporary Japanese Ceramics*. Tokyo: Shufunotomo, 1981.

Sanders, Herbert H., and Tomimoto, Kenkichi. *The World of Japanese Ceramics*. Tokyo: Kodansha, 1983.

Wilson, Richard. *Kenzan: Meeting of Ceramics and Design*. New York: Weatherhill, 1991.

Islam

Atil, Esin. *Ceramics from the World of Islam*. Washington, D.C.: Freer Gallery of Art, 1973.

Caiger-Smith, Alan. *Lustre Pottery: Technique, Tradition and Innovation in Islam and the Western World*. London: Faber & Faber, 1985.

Mitsukuni, Yoshida. *In Search of Persian Pottery*. New York: Weatherhill, 1972.

Öney, Gönül. *Ceramic Tiles in Islamic Architecture*. Istanbul: Ada Press, 1988.

Wilkinson, Charles K. *Iranian Ceramics*. New York: Asia House, 1963.

————, ed. *Nishapur, Pottery of the Early Islamic Period*. New York: Metropolitan Museum of Art, 1974.

India

Philadelphia Museum of Art. *Unknown India. Ritual Art in Tribe and Village*. Philadelphia, Pa.: Philadelphia Museum of Art, 1968.

Singh, Gurcharan. *Pottery in India*. New York: Advent, 1979.

Africa

Cardew, Michael. *Pioneer Pottery*. New York: St. Martin's, 1976.

Clark, C., and Wagner, L. *Potters of Southern Africa*. New York: Hacker, 1974.

d'Azevedo, Warren L., ed. *The Traditional Artist in African Societies*. Bloomington: University of Indiana Press, 1973.

Fagg, William, and Picton, John. *The Potter's Art in Africa*. London: The British Museum, 1970.

Gardi, Rene. *African Crafts and Craftsmen*. New York: Van Nostrand Reinhold, 1969.

Gebauer, Paul. *Art of Cameroon*. Portland, Oreg., and New York: Portland Art Museum and Metropolitan Museum of Art, 1979.

Wahlman, Maude. *Contemporary African Arts*. Chicago: Field Museum of Natural History, 1974.

Indigenous America

MESOAMERICA AND SOUTH AMERICA

Banks, George. *Peruvian Pottery*. Aylesbury, England: Shire Publications, 1989.

Bushnell, Geoffrey H. *Ancient Arts of the Americas*. New York: Praeger, 1965.

Coe, Michael D. *The Maya*. New York, London: Thames and Hudson, 1987.

Lackey, Luana M. *The Pottery of Acatlan: A Changing Mexican Tradition*. Tucson: University of Arizona Press, 1982.

Litto, Gertrude. *South American Folk Pottery*. New York: Watson-Guptill, 1976.

Monti, Franco. *Precolumbian Terracottas*. New York: Hamlyn, 1969.

Schele, Linda, and Miller, Mary Ellen. *The Blood of Kings: Dynasty and Ritual in Maya Art*. New York: George Braziller, 1986.

North America

Brody, J.; Scott, Catherine J.; and Le Blanc, Steven A. *Mimbres Pottery: Ancient Art of the American Southwest.* New York: Hudson Hills, 1983.

Harlow, Francis H., and Frank, Larry. *Historic Pueblo Indian Pottery.* Santa Fe: Museum of New Mexico, 1967.

Lister, Robert H., and Lister, Florence C. *Anasazi Pottery.* Albuquerque: University of New Mexico Press, 1978.

Peterson, Susan. *The Living Tradition of Maria Martinez.* New York: Kodansha, 1981.

Trimble, Stephen. *Talking with the Clay: The Art of Pueblo Pottery.* Santa Fe, N.M.: School of American Research, 1987.

The United States

Barber, Edwin Atlee. *Tulip Ware of the Pennsylvania German Potters.* New York: Dover Publications, 1970.

Barret, Richard Carter. *Bennington Pottery and Porcelain.* New York: Crown, 1958.

Blasberg, Robert W., and Carpenter, J. W. *George Ohr and His Biloxi Art Pottery.* Port Jarvis, N.Y.: J. W. Carpenter, 1973.

Burrison, John. *Brothers in Clay: The Story of Georgia Folk Pottery.* Athens: University of Georgia Press, 1983.

Clark, Garth. *American Potters: The Work of Twenty Modern Masters.* New York: Watson-Guptill, 1981.

———. *The Mad Potter of Biloxi: The Art and Life of George E. Ohr.* New York: Abbeville Press, 1989.

Clark, Garth, and Hughto, Margie. *A Century of Ceramics in the United States 1878–1978.* New York: Dutton and Everson Museum of Art, 1981.

Ferriday, Virginia Guest. *Last of the Handmade Buildings: Glazed Terra Cotta in Downtown Portland.* Portland, Oreg.: Mark Publishing, 1984.

Ferris, William. *Afro-American Folk Arts and Crafts.* Boston: Hall, 1983.

Greer, Georgeanna H. *American Stoneware: The Art and Craft of Utilitarian Potters.* West Chester, Pa.: Schiffer, 1981.

Henzke, Lucile. *Art Pottery of America.* West Chester, Pa.: Schiffer, 1982.

Kurutz, Gary. *The Architectural Terra Cotta of Gladding McBean.* Sausalito, Calif.: Windgate Press, 1989.

Levin, Elaine. *The History of American Ceramics.* New York: Abrams, 1988.

Poor, Henry Varnum. *A Book of Pottery: From Mud into Immortality.* Englewood Cliffs, N.J.: Prentice-Hall, 1958.

Rosenthal, Lee. *Catalina Tile of the Magic Isle.* Sausalito, Calif.: Windgate Press, 1992.

Sweesy, Nancy. *Raised in Clay.* Washington, D.C.: Smithsonian Institution Press, 1984.

Vlach, John. *The Afro-American Tradition in Decorative Arts.* Cleveland, Ohio: Cleveland Museum of Art, 1978.

Watkins, Lura Woodsie. *New England Potters and Their Wares.* Cambridge, Mass.: Harvard University Press, 1968.

Webster, Donald Blake. *Decorated Stoneware Pottery of North America.* Rutland, Vt.: Tuttle, 1970.

Zug, Charles G., III. *Turners and Burners: The Folk Potters of North Carolina.* Chapel Hill: University of North Carolina Press, 1986.

BOOKS: SHAPING THE PRESENT

General and Aesthetics

Anderson, Bruce, and Hoare, John. *Clay Statements: Contemporary Australian Pottery.* Darling Downs Institute Press, Australia, 1985.

Axel, Jan, and McCreary, Karen. *Porcelain: Traditions and New Visions.* New York: Watson-Guptill, 1981.

Berensohn, Paulus. *Finding One's Way With Clay.* New York: Simon & Schuster, 1972.

Birks-Hay, Tony. *Art of the Modern Potter.* New York: Van Nostrand Reinhold, 1977; London: Hamlyn, 1976.

———. *Hans Coper.* New York and Sherborne, England: Harper & Row/Alphabooks, 1983.

———. *Lucie Rie.* Sherborne, England: Alphabooks, 1988.

Casson, Michael. *The Craft of the Potter.* England: Barron, 1979.

Dormer, Peter. *The New Ceramics: Trends and Traditions.* New York: Thames & Hudson, 1986.

Europaische Keramik der Gegenwart. Keramion— Museum für zietgenossische keramische Kunst, Frechen. 1986.

Grubbs, Daisy. *Modeling a Likeness in Clay.* New York: Watson-Guptill, 1982.

Hopper, Robin. *The Ceramic Spectrum.* Radnor, Pa.: Chilton, 1983.

———. *Functional Pottery: Form and Aesthetic in Pots of Purpose.* Radnor, Pa.: Chilton, 1986.

Khalili, Nader. *Racing Alone.* New York: Harper & Row, 1983.

Lane, Peter. *Ceramic Form.* New York: Rizzoli, 1987.

Lucchesi, Bruno, and Malmstrom, Margit. *Modeling the Head in Clay.* New York: Watson-Guptill, 1979.

Nachmanovitch, Stephen. *Free Play: The Power of Improvisation in Life and the Arts.* New York: G. P. Putnam's Sons. 1990.

Needleman, Carla. *The Work of Craft.* New York: Avon, 1979.

Nigrosh, Leon. *Claywork: Form and Idea in Ceramic Design.* 2d ed. Worcester, Mass.: Davis, 1986.

Nordness, Lee. *The Genesis and Triumphant Survival of an Ohio Artist.* Racine, Wis.: Perimeter, 1985.

Rawson, Philip. *Ceramics.* Philadelphia: University of Pennsylvania Press, 1984.

Richards, M. C. *Centering in Pottery, Poetry and the Person.* Middletown, Conn.: Wesleyan University Press, 1964.

Speight, Charlotte F. *Images in Clay Sculpture. Historical and Contemporary Techniques.* New York: Harper & Row, 1983.

Wildenhain, Marguerite. *The Invisible Core: A Potter's Life and Thoughts.* Palo Alto, Calif.: Pacific, 1973.

Wood, Beatrice. *I Shock Myself.* Ojai, Calif.: Dillingham.

Technical

GENERAL

Branfman, Steve. *Raku: A Practical Approach.* Radnor, Pa.: Chilton, 1991.

Cowley, David. *Molded and Slip Cast Pottery and Ceramics.* New York: Scribner's, 1973.

Coyne, John., ed. *The Penland School of Craft Book of Pottery.* New York: Rutledge, 1975.

Fournier, Robert, ed. *Illustrated Dictionary of Practical Pottery.* New York: Van Nostrand Reinhold, 1976.

Gregory, Ian. *Sculptural Ceramics.* London: A & C Black (Publishers) Ltd. 1992. Radnor, Pa.: Chilton Book Co. 1992.

Hamer, Frank, and Hamer, Janet. *The Potter's Dictionary of Materials and Techniques.* New York: Watson-Guptill, 1986.

Hamilton, David. *Thames & Hudson Manual of Architectural Ceramics.* New York: Thames & Hudson, 1978.

———. *Thames & Hudson Manual of Pottery and Ceramics.* New York: Thames & Hudson, 1982.

———. *Thames & Hudson Manual of Stoneware and Porcelain.* New York: Thames & Hudson, 1982.

Holden, A. *The Self-Reliant Potter.* Black, 1986.

Nelson, Glenn C. *Ceramics, A Potter's Handbook.* New York: Holt, Rinehart, & Winston, 1984.

Peterson, Susan. *The Craft and Art of Clay.* Englewood Cliffs, N.J.: Prentice-Hall, 1992.

Rogers, Mary. *Mary Rogers on Pottery and Porcelain: A Handbuilder's Approach.* New York and Sherborne, England: Watson-Guptill/Alphabooks, 1979.

Zakin, Richard. *Ceramics: Mastering the Craft.* Radnor, Pa.: Chilton Book Company. 1990.

CLAYS, GLAZES, AND FIRING

Brodie, Regis C. *The Energy-Efficient Potter.* New York: Watson-Guptill, 1982.

Chappell, James. *The Potter's Complete Book of Clay and Glazes.* New York and London: Watson-Guptill: Pitman, 1977.

Conrad, J. W. *Contemporary Ceramic Formulas.* New York: Macmillan, 1981.

Cooper, Emanuel, and Royle, Derek. *Glazes for the Studio Potter.* Batsford, England: David & Charles, 1986.

Dickerson, John. *Raku Handbook: A Practical Approach to Ceramic Art.* New York: Van Nostrand Reinhold, 1972.

Fournier, Robert. *Illustrated Dictionary of Practical Pottery.* New York: Van Nostrand Reinhold, 1973.

Fraser, Harry. *Glazes for the Craft Potter.* London: Pitman; New York: Watson-Guptill, 1974.

Hamer, Frank. *The Potter's Dictionary of Materials and Techniques.* New York and London: Watson-Guptill/Pitman, 1975.

Lane, Peter. *Studio Porcelain.* Radnor, Pa.: Chilton, 1980.

Mansfield, Janet. *Salt Glaze Ceramics: An International Perspective.* Roseville East NSW, Craftsman House. London: A & C Black (Publishers) Ltd. Radnor, Pa.: Chilton Book Co. 1992.

Mason, Ralph. *Native Clays and Glazes for the North American Potter.* Portland, Oreg.: Timber, 1981.

McKee, Charles. *Ceramics Handbook: A Guide to Glaze Calculation, Material and Processes.* Belmont, Calif.: Star, 1973.

Memmott, Harry. *An Artist's Guide to the Use of Ceramic Oxides.* Burwood, Australia: Victoria College Press, 1988.

Nigrosh, Leon. *Low Fire: Other Ways to Work in Clay.* Worcester, Mass.: Davis, 1980.

Olsen, Frederik L. *The Kiln Book.* Radnor, Pa.: Chilton Book Co. London: A & C Black (Publishers) Ltd. 1983.

Parks, Dennis. *A Potter's Guide to Raw Glazing and Oil Firing.* New York: Scribner's, 1980.

Parmelee, Cullen W. *Ceramic Glazes.* 3d ed. Chicago: Industrial Publications, 1973.

Piepenburg, Robert. *Raku Pottery.* Rev. ed. Ann Arbor, Mich.: Pebble Press, 1991.

Reigger, Hal. *Primitive Pottery.* New York: Van Nostrand Reinhold, 1972.

———. *Raku: Art and Techniques.* New York: Van Nostrand Reinhold, 1972.

Rhodes, Daniel. *Clay and Glazes for the Potter.* Radnor, Pa.: Chilton, 1973.

———. *Stoneware and Porcelain.* Radnor, Pa.: Chilton, 1973.

Rogers, Phil. *Ash Glazes.* London: A. & C. Black, 1991. Radnor, Pa.: Chilton, 1991.

Sanders, Herbert. *Glazes for Special Effects.* New York: Watson-Guptill, 1974.

Sutherland, Brian. *Glazes from Natural Sources: A Working Handbook for Potters.* London: Batsford, 1987.

Tichane, Robert. *Ching-Te-Chen.* Painted Post, N.Y.: New York Glaze Institute, 1983.

———. *Reds, Reds, Copper Red.* Painted Post, N.Y.: New York Glaze Institute, 1985.

———. *Those Celadon Blues.* Painted Post, N.Y.: New York Glaze Institute, 1983.

Troy, Jack. *Salt Glazed Ceramics.* New York: Watson-Guptill, 1972.

Tyler, Christopher, and Hirsch, Richard. *Raku: Techniques for Contemporary Potters.* New York: Watson-Guptill, 1975; London: Pitman.

Wittig, Irene. *The Clay Canvas: Creative Painting on Functional Ceramics.* Radnor, Pa.: Chilton Book Co. London: A & C Black (Publishers) Limited. 1994.

Zakin, Richard. *Electric Kiln Ceramics: A Potter's Guide to Clay and Glazes.* 2d ed. London: A & C Black. Radnor, Pa.: Chilton, 1994.

KILNS

Colson, Frank A. *Kiln Building with Space-Age Materials.* New York: Van Nostrand Reinhold, 1975.

Olsen, Frederick. *The Kiln Book.* Bassett, Calif.: Keramos Books, 1973.

Rhodes, Daniel. *Kilns.* Radnor, Pa.: Chilton, 1974.

SPECIALIZED TECHNIQUES

Cowley, David. *Molded and Slip Cast Pottery and Ceramics.* New York: Scribner's, 1973.

Frith, Donald E. *Mold Making for Ceramics.* Radnor, Pa.: Chilton, 1985.

Khalili, Nader. *Ceramic Houses: How to Build Your Own.* New York: Harper & Row, 1986.

Kosloff, Albert. *Photographic Screen Printing.* Cincinnati: The Signs of the Times, 1972.

———. *Ceramic Screen Printing.* 2d ed. Cincinnati: The Signs of the Times, 1984.

Whitford, Philip, and Wong, Gordon. *Handmade Potter's Tools.* New York: Kodansha, 1986.

Health and Safety

Arena, J. M., M.D., *Child Safety Is No Accident,* Rev. Ed. New York: Berkeley Press, 1987.

Barazani, Gail Coningsby. *Ceramics Health Hazards.* rev. ed. Occupational Safety and Health for Artists and Craftsmen, 1984.

Center for Occupational Hazards. (5 Beekman St., New York, NY). *Ventilation Handbook for the Arts.* New York: Center for Occupational Hazards, 1984.

Ceramic Guidelines. Appendix to ASTM C1023, American Society for Testing and Materials, 1916 Race St., Philadelphia, PA 19103.

Cutter, Thomas, and McGrane, Jean-Ann. *Ventilation: A Practical Guide.* New York: Center for Occupational Hazards.

Data Sheets from the Art Hazards Project, Center for Occupational Hazards: *Ceramics, Respirators, Silica Hazards.*

McCann, Michael. *Artist Beware! The Hazards and Precautions in Working with Art and Craft Materials.* New York: Watson-Guptill, 1979.

———. *Health Hazards Manual for Artists.* New York: Nock Lyons Books, 1985.

Occupational Health Guidelines for Chemical Hazards. Cincinnati: NIOSH, 1981.

Perry, Rosemary. *Potter's Beware.* This is a booklet available from Rosemary Perry, 865 Cashmere Rd., Christchurch 3, New Zealand.

Rosso, Monona. *Ceramics and Health.* Articles compiled from Ceramic Scope. New York: Center for Occupational Hazards, 1984.

Safe Practices in the Arts and Crafts. A Studio Guide. New York: College Art Association of America, no date.

Seeger, Nancy. *A Ceramists's Guide to the Safe Use of Materials.* Chicago: School of the Art Institute of Chicago, 1984.

Qualley, Charles. *Safety in the Artroom.* Worcester, Ma.: Davis Publications, 1986.

Note: This list includes only a few of the books and pamphlets that are available on the subject of Health and Safety. New material appears frequently. Up-to-date information lists are available through the Art Hazards Project of The Center for Occupational Hazards, 5 Beekman St., New York, NY 10038, as well as local chapters of The American Lung Association.

Videos

Most ceramic supply distributors now carry videos in their catalogues, and ceramics magazines review them. Check these for current availability.

Kalkspatz e V, a German potters' association (a member of the Studio Potter Network) has published an international catalog of over eight hundred films and videos in the ceramics field. Kalkspatz e V, Waldstr. 11, 0-2721 Lenzen, Germany.

Art on Video carries videos on all phases of the arts and crafts. For a catalog, write to: Art on Video, 12 Havemayer Pl., Department NY5, Greenwich, CT 06830, (203) 869-4694.

A large selection of books and videos is available from The Potter's Shop, 31 Thorpe Rd., Needham Heights, MA 02194, (617) 449-POTS.

Index

The index lists only the most important individual ceramics materials. A complete listing of these materials appears in Appendixes 1E and 1F.

Page numbers of illustrations and color plate (pl.) numbers appear in bold type.